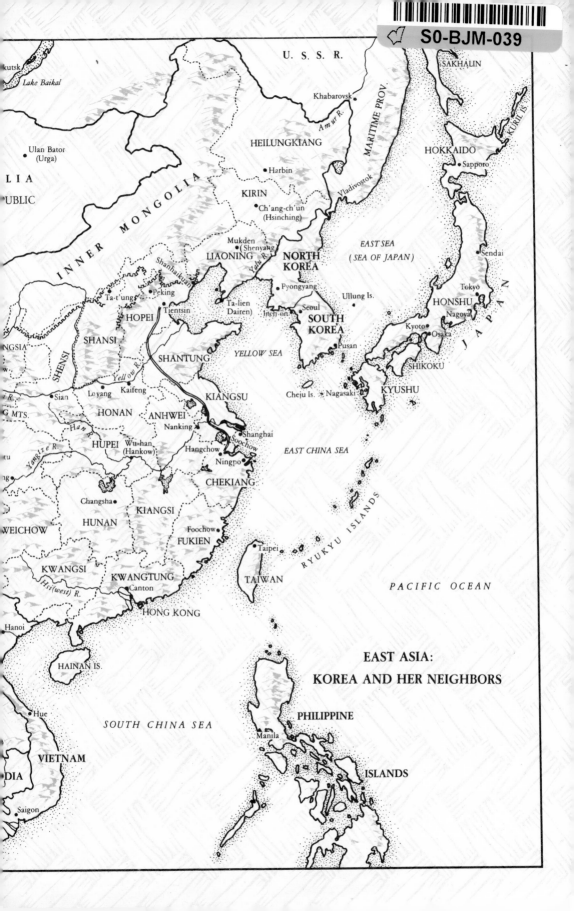

EAST ASIA:

KOREA AND HER NEIGHBORS

Korea

Tradition & Transformation

A HISTORY OF THE KOREAN PEOPLE

Korea

Tradition & Transformation

A HISTORY OF THE KOREAN PEOPLE

Andrew C. Nahm

Western Michigan University

HOLLYM

First published in June 1988
Second printing, October 1988
Third printing, 1989
by Hollym International Corp.
18 Donald Place
Elizabeth, New Jersey 07208 U.S.A.

Published simultaneously in Korea
by Hollym Corporation; Publishers
14-5 Kwanchol-dong, Chongno-gu
Seoul, 110-111 Korea
Phone: (02)735-7554   FAX: (02)730-5149

ISBN: 0-930878-56-6
Library of Congress Catalog Card Number: 86-81681

Printed in Korea

To My Parents, Their Ancestors,
and Those of Other Koreans

Contents

Development / Education and Culture / The Society and People /
Unification Strategy and Hostile Actions / The Founding of the Kim
Dynasty

Maps and Charts

Preface

Korea, known in the Western world as "The Land of Morning Calm," is one of the oldest nations in the world. Her history began three millennia before the birth of Christ when the early settlers formed tribal societies in the Korean peninsula and in South Manchuria, and nurtured a unique culture, creating what became Korea's heritage. As a land bridge between the Asian mainland and Japan, Korea always possessed great strategic geopolitical significance. For centuries Korea played the role of a middleman of cultural transfusion to Japan from China while she herself was transformed in a variety of ways under the Chinese influence.

During the long period of her history, Korea was frequently invaded by, or under the domination of some foreign power. But despite the rise and fall of native dynasties and foreign suzerains, the Korean people maintained a remarkable homogeneity as well as their national characteristics and independence for more than twelve hundred years after the unification of Korea in 668.

In the modern age, Korea turned into an arena of politics of imperialism as the powers immediately surrounding her, as well as those of distant places, became engaged in the struggle to establish control over her. The efforts made by the Koreans to modernize their country and preserve the independence of their nation fell short of their goals. Consequently, Korea became a victim of Japanese imperialism, and suffered in many ways under Japan's colonial rule which lasted nearly a half century.

The unity of the Korean people was broken when the country was partitioned into two zones of the Allied occupation at the end of World War II, making Korea an ideological battle ground of the Cold War between the East and the West, as well as between the north and the south. A bloody war was fought there not too long ago, and tens of thousands of lives were sacrificed in order to prevent the spread of Communist aggression.

Korea has become a focal point of world politics, one of the most sensitive spots in the scheme of balance of power. Yet, she is a little known country, and a vast majority of Western people have little or no knowledge about Korea, her people, history, and culture. Worse yet, some are not even able to locate Korea on the world map. An American scholar once lamented that most American college graduates knew more about the moon than they knew about Korea.

Recently, many more Americans and other Western people have visited Korea, more American and European institutions of higher education have become involved in Korean studies, and diplomatic and commercial ties between Korea and the nations of the world have increased, thus many erroneous

11

notions about Korea and her people have been corrected. Meanwhile, the appreciation of the Western people for the remarkable economic and other achievements of the Korean people in recent decades has also increased. However, understanding of the Korean people and a knowledge about their history and culture are still pitifully lacking in the West as a whole.

The true understanding of Korea requires more than doing away with old notions and clichés and having more objective and balanced views. It requires some basic knowledge of Korean history, as well as the internal and external forces which shaped and colored Korean society and effected the psychological and social development of the Korean people.

Several versions of Korean history in English have been published either at the end of the nineteenth or in the early twentieth century, and more books on Korea have been published since then. Be that as it may, a comprehensive, up-to-date single-volume Korean history, which includes coverage of both north and south Korea, has long been wanted. This book was prepared as an attempt to meet this need.

In the limited space, efforts were made to present a maximum amount of historical information, interpretation, and explanation, highlighting the major historical processes in political, economic, cultural, and social aspects of the Korean people. Because of space limitation, some facts may have been omitted and inadequate amount of explanation may have been offered in this book. Due to lack of historical sources, the history of the early period is dealt with briefly. As a result, this is not a complete history of Korea. Be that as it may, it is my earnest hope that this short history of the Korean people will help the reader to acquire a greater knowledge and a deeper understanding of the tradition and the transformation of Korea.

To attempt to thank all those who have given me valuable suggestions and guidance, or the many scholars on whose work I have drawn, would be well-nigh impossible. While grateful to all of them, I wish to express my special appreciation for the invaluable advice and guidance which the late Dr. Yi Sōn-gūn, a distinguished Korean historian, has given to me. I am indebted to Ann Brunhumer and Jozette Benson for their editorial assistance, Opal Ellis for typing the manuscript, and to my wife, Monica, for her moral support and literary suggestions.

Kalamazoo, Michigan

The Pronunciation of Korean, Chinese and Japanese

The pronunciation guide for Romanized Korean, Chinese and Japanese words is given below in order to help those who do not speak these languages to pronounce Romanized words more accurately. The Romanization systems used in the book are those of the Ministry of Education, which is a modified form of the McCune-Reischauer system, for Korean, Wade-Giles for Chinese, and Hepburn for Japanese, which are widely used in the English-speaking world.

All Korean words are Romanized according to the McCune-Reischauer system with the following exceptions. Standard Romanization is given in parenthesis:

> Personal names: Syngman Rhee (Yi Sŭng-man), Park Chung-hee (Pak Chŏng-hŭi), Chun Doo-hwan (Chŏn Tu-hwan), and Kim Il-sung (Kim Il-sŏng).
>
> Place names: Seoul (Sŏul) and Pyongyang (P'yŏngyang).
>
> Names of commercial firms: Hyundai (Hyŏndae), Daewoo (Taeu), and Samsung (Samsŏng).
>
> Names of Universities: Yonsei (Yŏnse), Ewha (Ihwa), Sookmyung (Sungmyŏng), and Kyunghee (Kyŏnghŭi)

All Korean words are Romanized as they are pronounced. Thus, *kungmin* in stead of *kukmin*, and *kabo* in stead of *kap-o*. Although such Korean surnames as 林 and 任 are Romanized as Yim, in this book 林 is Romanized as Lim in order to differentiate it from 任. The Korean surname Romanized as Yi in this book appears as Lee, Li, or Rhee in other books. In fact, Lee or Li represents a more accurate sound of the character 李.

Because the consonant *s* in Korean words, including surnames, is often pronounced as the *sh* in English, all Korean words beginning with the consonant *s* followed by vowel *i* are Romanized in this book as *sh*, thus Silla as Shilla.

The basic Korean, Chinese and Japanese vowels *a, e, i, o* and *u* are pronounced as follows:

> a as the *a* in father   e as the *e* in egg
>
> i as the *i* in India   o as the *o* in Ohio
>
> u as the *u* in rule

In Korean, ŏ should be pronounced as *u* in but, and ŭ should be pronounced similar to the *e* in taken or spoken. Certain double vowels (diphthongs) in Korean words are pronounced as a single word. For example:

> ae like the *a* in apple   oe like the *ö* in German

Each vowel in certain double-voweled Korean words should be pronounced separately. For example:

ai like the *ie* in tie

ŭi has no English equivalent: pronounce *ŭ* first like the *e* in token or spoken, and then pronounce i as the *i* in India.

Certain double consonants in Korean are easy to pronounce in English. For example:

tt like the *d* in dam   pp like the *b* in bang

kk like the *g* in god

Nearly all consonants in Korean and Chinese are generally pronounced as they are in English with the following exceptions:

ch like j   k like g   p like b or v   t like d

The aspirated consonants (consonants with diacritical mark ') in Korean and Chinese sound more like the corresponding English consonants as follows:

ch' like the *ch* in chance   k' like the *k* in king

p' like the *p* in pepper   t' like the *t* in toy

Certain Korean words, which end with consonants, *k, p, t* and ch(j), and followed by consonant *h*, are Romanized as follows:

kuk'wa in stead of *kukhwa*

hyŏp'oe in stead of *hyŏphoe*

tach'ida in stead of *tathida*

When there is a possibility of confusion in pronunciation, or a need for segmentation, a hyphen is used, e.g.

Tan-gun   Taewŏn-gun   *han-gŭl*

hong-ik   Yong-in   *yŏng-ŏ*

Chongno-e   *mulka-e*

In Chinese, *j* is pronounced as *r* and *e* often sounds like the *u* in up. Thus, a Chinese word, *jen* is pronounced as run. *Hs* in Chinese sounds like the *ss* in Mississippi.

A – mark over two vowels (o and u) in Japanese means that they are long vowels. Prolong the sound of each vowel with a – mark over when read. This distinction between long and short vowels is important in Japanese. Often the vowel *u* used as a final vowel in a Japanese word is not pronounced, or is barely audible, e.g., *desu* is pronounced as *des*.

PART I

THE SHAPING OF KOREAN TRADITION

1. Land, Climate, and People

Korea, known in the West as "The Land of the Morning Calm" and the home of homogeneous people with strong individualistic traits, was a country of key importance in East Asian history. As a land bridge between the Asian mainland and Japan, Korea always possessed great strategic geopolitical significance. Conquerors from the north invaded Korea to attack Japan, and the Japanese themselves invaded Korea to conquer the Asian mainland. For centuries, Korea played the role of a middleman in the transfusion of culture from China to Japan, and was itself transformed as it absorbed many Chinese cultural, political, and social patterns.

A peninsula jutting southward from the Asian mainland, Korea is faced by vast and teeming China to the west, is bordered by Manchuria and the Soviet Union to the north, and only 120 miles across the Korean Strait to the east lies Honshū, the main island of Japan. Because of its location, Korea has been called the "heart of East Asia."

The Land.   Korea, a land mass of 86,360 square miles (220,911 sq. km.) is equal in area to Michigan and Indiana combined. It is 600 miles long and from 120 to 150 miles wide, covered mostly with massive, rugged mountains. Early Catholic missionaries described Korea's terrain as "a sea in a heavy gale." There are five major mountain ranges: the Changbaek (Long White) in the north, where Mt. Paektu (White Head) towers 8,400 feet above sea level; the Nangnim, which branches southward from the Changbaek range into the north central region; the Myohyang in the northwest, which is a limb of the Changbaek; the T'aebaek (Greater White), which runs along the

17

east coast in the topographical backbone of the peninsula; and the Sobaek (Lesser White) in the southwestern region. In addition, there are several minor ranges which are of special importance in forming the political, military, and economic geography of Korea. Mt. Paektu, the source of the Yalu (Amnok) and the Tumen (Tuman) rivers, and Mt. Halla on the island of Cheju are the two dormant volcanoes. Among the most beautiful mountains are Mt. Myohyang and Mt. Kŭmgang (Diamond Mountain) in the north and Mt. Sŏrak, Mt. Songni, and Mt. Chiri in the south.

Throughout history, these mountains have served as a bulwark against invasions and conquests, thus enabling Korea to escape at times the full consequences of its vulnerable geopolitical position. Likewise, they have been conducive to the maintenance of local customs while not preventing the establishment of overall cultural unity. On the other hand, the mountainous terrain has been a severe handicap to national economic development. Not only is less than 25 per cent of Korea's land arable, but most of it had been infertile, having been exhausted by nearly 2,000 years of intensive cultivation. Consequently, until recent times the vast majority of Koreans have been peasant farmers scratching out a meager subsistence. The flat land in the western part of the peninsula, where rugged mountain ranges are absent, provided the invasion routes for foreign invaders.

The staple crop of Korea is rice, but millet, wheat, and barley have also been grown. Rice is grown primarily in the western half of the peninsula, which is flatter, more fertile, and receives greater rainfall than the eastern side. Other important crops are soya beans, potatoes, sorghum, and corn. Dry cereal grains are produced in the highlands, the lowlands being largely reserved for growing rice. Due to the shortage of farmland, even mountain slopes have been cleared and terraced into *hwajŏn* or "fire fields." In order to supplement their diet, the Koreans have always turned to the sea: offshore fishing, concentrated along the northwestern, western, and southern coasts, is highly important to the national economy. Until recently, there was comparatively little in the way of livestock, and there was no dairy industry.

There are seven major rivers in Korea, five of which flow westward into the Yellow Sea: the Yalu (Amnok in Korean) River which marks the boundaries between Korea and Manchuria; the Taedong River in the northwest, the Imjin and Han rivers in the west central region, and the Kŭm River in the southwest. The Changjin River, a tributary of the Yalu, flows northward along the Nangnim Range, and the Naktong River in the southeast flows southward along the Sobaek Range into the Korea Strait. The Tumen (Tuman in Korean) River, which originates at Mt. Paektu, flows eastward, marking the boundaries of Korea with Manchuria and the Maritime Province of the Soviet Union.

Most of Korea's major cities are located either on or at the mouth of these rivers: Shinŭiju on the Yalu, Pyongyang and Chinnamp'o (now Namp'o) on the Taedong, Seoul on the Han, and Kunsan on the Kŭm rivers. Other major cities are located on the coast: Inch'ŏn and Mokp'o along the Yellow Sea (West Sea to the Koreans): Yŏsu, Chinhae, and Pusan along the southern coast; Unggi, Najin, Ch'ŏngjin, Sŏngjin, Hŭngnam, and Wŏnsan in the north along the Sea of Japan (East Sea to the Koreans); and Kangnŭng, Samch'ŏk, and P'ohang on the southeastern coast. The major cities which are situated inland are Hamhŭng near Hŭngnam in the north and Taejŏn, Chŏnju, Taegu, and Kwangju in the south.

Although there are no great plains in Korea, there are many fertile lowlands and river basins which are worth mentioning. They are the Pyongyang Plain in South P'yŏng-an Province, the Yŏnan and Shinch'ŏn plains in North and South Hwanghae provinces, the Pup'yŏng Plain along the lowest Han River, the Honam Plain along the Kŭm River, and the flat lands of North and South Kyŏngsang provinces along the Naktong River which have been the major food producing areas.

Originally, Korea's mountains were densely wooded with fir, spruce, pine, cedar, and oak trees. However, centuries of indiscriminate timbering for building materials and fuel have badly deforested the land. Furthermore, the Korean War destroyed millions of acres of forest lands, leaving mountains, valleys and lowlands almost treeless. The process of increasing production of foodstuffs also contributed to the deforestation of the land. Nevertheless, much natural wealth remains, inspiring the people of Korea to sing in praise of their land. As a stanza of the South Korean national anthem reads: Korea is *mugunghwa samch'ŏlli hwaryŏ kangsan*, meaning "three thousand *li* of the land of the Rose of Sharon, the splendid garden of mountains and rivers."

Mainland Korea has 6,000 miles of coastline. While the eastern coast is realtively smooth, the western and southern coastlines contain innumerable natural harbors and bays and there are thousands of scattered offshore islands. The main islands are Kanghwa, off Inch'ŏn; Chindo and Wando in the south-western corner; Namhae, off Yŏsu; Kŏje, near Masan and Chinhae; and Cheju (Quelpart to Westerners) and Ullŭng in the Sea of Japan. The tidal flats of the west coast provide excellent salt manufacturing facilities. The eastern shores are washed by the northern current of the Mamiya while the western shores are influenced by the southern current from the South China Sea as well as the western Pacific.

Climate. The climate of Korea is continental rather than oceanic, being largely determined by the winds which sweep southward from Siberia and eastward from China across the Yellow Sea. Although there is a monsoon or rainy period, there are four distinct seasons. Spring is long and warm, beginning in the middle of March when the wind, known in Korea as the "defreezing wind," blows from the southwest, announcing the arrival of the season.

This season of cherry blossoms, peony, azalea, broom, and hundreds of other flowers is followed by a hot and humid summer, with heavy rainfall during the months of June and July, the period which is called the "season of long rain." The summer temperature averages 75 ° F. (24 °C), but it may go as high as 104 °F. (40 °C). The average annual precipitation ranges between 20 inches in the north and 60 inches in the south. During the rainy season, storms are often severe and typhoons and floods periodically rampage across the land, causing considerable damage to land, crops, and buildings, and sometimes resulting in heavy loss of life.

The fall, a long, golden season known as the "season of high sky and fat horses," begins in September, signalling the advent of the farmer's busiest season. Frost normally occurs in the middle of November although an early freeze frequently takes the farmers by surprise. The nights grow colder and the first light snow soon follows. Winter is windy and brisk, and temperatures drop. The northern half of the peninsula suffers a great deal more than the south, due to cold air masses moving into Korea from the high pressure area near Lake Baikhal. The average winter temperature is 33 °F (1 °C). Sharp seasonal contrasts are characteristic, as shown by extremes around Seoul, where the high is over 100 °F. (37 °C) in the summer and the low is 10 degrees F. (–12 °C.) in winter.

Although in recent years Korea's winter weather has been irregular, its winter weather pattern traditionally has had distinctive characteristics. This pattern is known in Korea as *samhan saon*, meaning "three cold and four warm" days alternating in a cycle. One can be reasonably certain that after three cold days, a temperate climate will prevail during the next four days. Snowfall, however, is light in the southern regions, where less than an inch of snow falls per year. Winter is bitterly cold and snowfall is heavy in the northern and eastern regions north of the 38th parallel line, particularly in the highlands and plateau area in the north central region. The winter temperature has a great bearing on agriculture. Where the cold is not overly severe, two crops, usually rice and barley, may be grown.

The People.   Although the identity of the first settlers in the Korean peninsula has not been ascertained, it is believed that the palaeolithic people migrated into the peninsula some time around 30000 B.C. as evidenced by the skulls and other items unearthed at Sŏkchang-ri in the southwestern region of Korea. They are often called the Tungusic people who migrated from central Asia via the Mongolian-Manchurian plains. Subsequently tribal units of the Puyŏ, the Ye, the Maek, and the others arrived in Korea some time after 3500 B.C. As the political situation changed radically in China with the fall of the Shang (Yin) dynasty around 1200 B.C. the people whom the Chinese called Tung-i (Tong-i in Korean) who had inhabited the southern Manchurian and the eastern coastal region of China north of the Yangtze River emigrated into the peninsula. These people had Alpine features and dark, slanted eyes, high cheekbones, straight, brown hair, and little or no

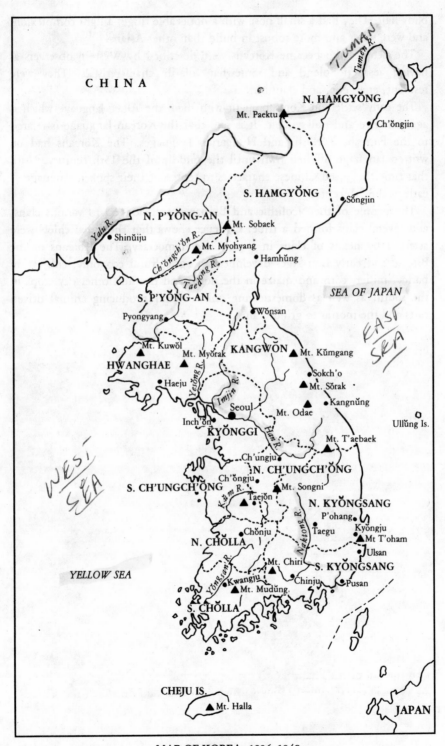

MAP OF KOREA, 1896–1948

body hair. They had a small nose with a noticeable ridge, a light complexion, and were taller and more robust in build than other Asians.

The people who became Koreans were described by Western observers as having aesthetic blend and somewhat volatile characteristics. They were resilient, energetic, and clannish.

The early settlers in Korea brought with them the Altaic language which is agglutinative and polysyllabic. It is said that the Korean language is related to the Finnish, Turkish, and Hungarian languages. The Koreans had no written language of their own until the middle of the 15th century. Until that time they used Chinese characters to represent their spoken language as early as the 7th century.

The people of the Neolithic and Bronze ages belonged to various clans, and several clans formed a tribe. Evidence shows that the tribal chiefs were selected by heads of clans in a primitive democracy. The Koreans of the Bronze and early Iron Ages developed an agricultural economy, cultivating barley, millet, corn and maize in the north and rice and other dry crops in the south, as well as domesticating animals, and producing animal driven carts and the mortar to grind grains.

2.   Early Historical and Cultural Development

Prehistoric Cultures

Recently, archaeologists have discovered both Palaeolithic and Neolithic culture sites in Korea. The Palaeolithic sites are believed to have been established around 30000 B.C., and the artifacts which were unearthed in 1964 at the Sokchang-ri site, in South Ch'ungch'ŏng Province in the south central region, have been radiocarbon dated 20825 B.C. No definitive Mesolithic culture sites have been found to date and it is believed that such sites may have submerged below the water level of the Yellow Sea.

The Neolithic period began about 4000 B.C. Many Neolithic artifacts such as stone knives, stone axes, and other stone tools have been found in various parts of Korea. Among the many prehistoric remains discovered in Korea are bone tools and shell mounds, which indicate that the people were engaged in hunting and fishing. The shell mounds were discovered near the coastline and major rivers. Evidence shows that the Stone Age Koreans lived in caves along the river banks or semi-subterranean pit dwellings.

The Neolithic period was followed by the Bronze Age around 1200 B.C. when the megalithic culture represented by dolmens and menhirs developed. At the same time, the black pottery culture, similar to that of the Lungshan pottery culture of northwestern China, emerged in the Korean Peninsula. Among pottery pieces unearthed in Korea were those with comb marking as well as those without surface design. Pieces of painted (red) pottery were also unearthed in the northeastern region.

Bronze mirrors, knives and other ceremonial utensils, along with bronze

23

bells which have been discovered in Korea, strongly suggest that the influence of Chinese culture had already been felt in Korea before the 5th century B.C. The Iron Age began in Korea around 300 B.C., and many iron tools, including weapons manufactured in the southern region played a significant role in trade with China and Japan, in agricultural development, and in the pattern of change in military affairs.

The prehistoric Koreans developed a belief in the existence of a supreme, universal authority in heaven which they called *hanulnim*, or the "Lord of Heaven". Although they did not develop any theology regarding *hanulnim*, Koreans entertained the notion that such a supreme force reigns over all the creatures of the world and demonstrated their reverence to it. They also worshipped the Sun as a benevolent deity while fearing spirits (ghosts) of the dark world, and held religious reverence for sacred animals such as bears, tigers, and a mythical animal they called dragon. There is evidence that they believed in life after death and the indestructibility of soul.

The animistic religion which they cultivated was shamanism. It was brought to the Korean Peninsula by the people who migrated eastward from central Asia. Its belief was that all natural objects had spirits which were indestructible. It revered all kinds of gods—the gods of the earth (ground), the mountain, the river, the tree, the rock, village, house, and household goods. It manifested the belief that all human miseries, misfortunes, and sicknesses were caused by unhappy and displeased spirits. The development of Korean geomancy had much to do with Shamanism.

Shamans (*mudang* or *musok*) were the medium between humans and the spirits, and they were the peacemakers, healers, and fortunetellers, who sought the peaceful relationship between the spirits and humans. Most shamans were women, and the male shamans were called *paksu mudang*. Shaman rituals (*kut*) were performed in order to restore the peaceful and harmoneous relationship between the dead and the living. The music and dance of the shamans had a powerful impact upon the development of Korean folk culture. The *ch'ilsŏng*, or the "Seven Stars" (the Big Dipper) was regarded as the god of life.

The ancient Koreans nurtured a rich folklore and created many legends, believing in the physical union between deities and humans, as well as the direct intervention of supernatural forces in human affairs. For example, Tangun who is considered the founder of the first Korean "kingdom" of Chosŏn in 2333 B.C. was, according to the Tan-gun myth, the son of a bear who turned into a woman and united with the divine being. According to the myth, a bear and tiger prayed to Hwanung, a descendant of the celestial lord, that they might become human. Thereupon, Hwanung gave each of them a bundle of mugwort and twenty pieces of garlic, and told them to eat them and avoid the sunlight for one hundred days in a cave. Both mugwort and garlic have been, and are still regarded as having magical (medicinal) and purifying (bleaching) as well as cleansing effects.

The bear followed the instruction faithfully and became a woman, but the impatient tiger could not endure and failed to fulfill its wish. Hwanung eventually married the woman and had a son named Wanggŏm who became known as Tan-gun. A credible assumption might be that the rivalry between the tribe whose totem was a bear, or the people who belonged to the Bear Tribe, and the tribe whose totem was tiger, or the people who belonged to the Tiger Tribe, resulted in the victory of the former in 2333 B.C. and the establishment of the domination of the Bear Tribe over others.

Chumong, who was born from a large egg and became the first king of Koguryŏ, is said to have been conceived by his mother when a ray of the sun passed over her. It is said that he was protected by the birds and animals. Pak Hyŏkkŏse, the first king of Shilla, is said to have been born from a golden egg which had been protected by a mythical horse. His queen is said to have been a child which a dragon dropped as it flew away from a well. Sŏk T'ar-hae, who became the 4th king of Shilla, is also said to have been born from a large egg laid by the queen of the "Kingdom of Women."

The clan unit of the ancient Korean tribes was based on blood ties, and all members of the tribal unit had a common ancestor. Several clan units formed a tribal "nation" much like the American Indian nations. Each tribal and clan unit had a name. With social developments, however, clan units became more important. It is evident that the ancient Korean societies were patriarchal.

The ancient Koreans also nurtured knowledge of astrology and geomancy, as well as fortunetelling. Tan-gun is said to have established a heaven worshipping religion and taught the harmonious way of life among the people, as well as the harmonious relationship between heaven, earth and man.

Recently discovered ruins have shown that the ancient settlers of the post-Neolithic Age built houses with heated floors. With the development of a sedentary life, fishing and hunting became less important as an agriculture economy grew. Animals were domesticated, particularly after rich river basins and valleys were utilized for livelihood.

The Emergence of the Tribal States

Like the histories of all ancient peoples, Korea's early history is shrouded in clouds of mythology and ambiguity. The scarcity of source materials makes the study of the early history of Korea difficult and the writing of factual history impossible. Be that as it may, with the migration of the people the Chinese called Tung-i from the east coast of China and other nomadic people from Manchuria into the Korean Peninsula, political and social evolutions took place as more organized tribal nations emerged.

Early Northern Kingdoms. According to *Samguk yusa* (*Historical Annec-*

dotes of the Three Kingdoms) by Iryŏn of the late thirteenth century, the first Korean kingdom (later named Old Chosŏn) was founded by Tan-gun Wang-gŏm in 2333 B.C. somewhere in present-day Laioning Province in Manchuria. Later its capital was re-located at Asadal where Tan-gun built his palace called Wanggŏmsŏng. Many believe that Asadal was present-day P'yŏngyang in north Korea. On October 3 each year, the Koreans celebrate the founding of the Korean nation by Tan-gun. Tan-gun ruled over his nation as a ''king'' and high priest, and his dynasty is said to have lasted some one thousand years. At the end of the Tan-gun period, a new ruler named Kija (Ch'i-tsu in Chinese) established a new dynasty, replacing the Tan-gun dynasty, around 1120 B.C. Kija Chosŏn with its center of power near present-day Pyŏngyang is said to have included the northeastern regions of China and southwestern Manchuria and to have lasted a thousand years. A poem by Kwŏn Kŭn, who was a contemporary of Chaucer, said:

'Tis said that when the earth was waste and void Tan-gun came down and stood beneath the trees. His world was in the region of the East; His times were those of Yao and Shun.* How many tribes had come and gone I know not. Thousands of years had passed; till in the end Great Kija came, and called our state Chosŏn.

*Yao and Shun were legendary kings of ancient China before the Hsia dynasty (2205?–1176? B.C.).

According to the *Historical Record* (*Shih-chi*) of Ssu-ma Ch'ien, a historian of the Han dynasty of China, Kija was a scion of the Chinese royal house of the Shang (Yin) dynasty, which was overthrown by the Chou king around 1122 B.C. Ssu-ma related that Kija migrated to the eastern region with some 5,000 followers rather than submitting to the Chou ruler. Korean historians have disputed Ssu-ma's notion, and insisted that Kija was a member of the Han tribe of the Tong-i people who migrated to Korea. Whether Kija was a Chinese or a Korean, it is said that he and forty-two ''kings'' who succeeded him ruled the Kingdom of Chosŏn for nearly 1,000 years.

During the fourth and third centuries B.C., there emerged other tribal federations of the Tungusic people in Manchuria and the Korean peninsula. These were: Imdun in the northeastern region and Chinbŏn in the west central region of the northern part of Korea, and numerous federations of the Han tribes in the southern half, Puyŏ in northern Manchuria and Yemaek in southern Manchuria along the Yalu River. The southward movement of the Tungusic people in Manchuria became accelerated during the third century B.C. as they sought better climate and living conditions. In the second century B.C. the Yemaek tribal federation which became known as Koguryŏ challenged Han China and other tribal federations.

In about 195 B.C., according to Ssu-ma Ch'ien, Wiman, a refugee from the state of Yen, fled to Korea, and the king of Kija Chosŏn made him commander of a military unit deployed along the Yalu River. Wiman eventually rebelled against his king and overthrew Kija Choson, forcing Chun, the last ruler of Kija Chosŏn, to flee to the south. Korean historians have challenged the identity of Wiman. It is their contention that he was a native of Korea. Be that as it may, Wiman made Wanggŏmsŏng his capital, subjugated other tribes, and expanded the territory of his kingdom which is said to have included the northwestern part of Korea and southwestern Manchuria. The population of Wiman Choson is estimated to have been 2.7 million. With a strong army with cavalry, it challenged the security of Han China. Wiman Chosŏn lasted briefly, however. The ambitious Emperor Wu of the Han dynasty of China, seeking economic benefits and wishing to strengthen the security of his empire, invaded Korea in 109 B.C. with some 13,000 troops and destroyed Wiman Chosŏn in 108 B.C. Emperor Wu then established three commanderies (colonies) in the former territory of Wiman Choson and a commandery in the east central region along the Sea of Japan where the Okchŏ and Ye (Tongye) states had existed from about the fourth century B.C. The people of the Okchŏ and Ye states had been engaged in agriculture and fishing and had developed astronomy and a well functioning social system. During the period when the Chinese were exploiting Korea's natural resources, Chinese political, social, and cultural influence grew, bringing Korea into the Chinese cultural orbit. Regardless, the Chinese commanderies were overthrown, one by one, by Koguryŏ, a newly emerged kingdom in south Manchuria, and the Chinese commandery in Korea, Lolang (Nangnang in Korean) was overthrown by Koguryŏ in 313 A.D. and Koguryŏ unified northwestern Korea. With the fall of the Chinese control in Korea, the states of Okchŏ and Ye reemerged.

Three Han Federations in the South.   While the northern half of the peninsula was thus experiencing political changes, the Chin state of 78 tribal units of the Tong-i people which had existed in central Korea was pushed southward, and eventually separated into the three tribal federations of Mahan with 54 clans, Chinhan and Pyŏnhan with 12 clans each. It is generally agreed that Mahan's territory covered the western half of Korea below the Han River, Chinhan was located in the southeastern part, east of the Naktong River, and Pyŏnhan was located between Mahan and Chinhan, i.e., the present South Kyŏngsang Province west of the Naktong River with its center of power near present Kimhae. In the extreme southern region of Pyŏnhan was located a small tribal federation called Kaya (also known as Karak). The people of Kaya had developed lucrative trade relations with the people in northern Kyūshū, Japan, as well as Ye, Chinese colonies to the north, and China herself.

The strongest clan of Mahan was the Paekche clan, which was located in the fertile river basin of the Han River near present Seoul, and the most powerful clan of Chinhan was Saro (or Sŏra), which had its basis in the fertile plain

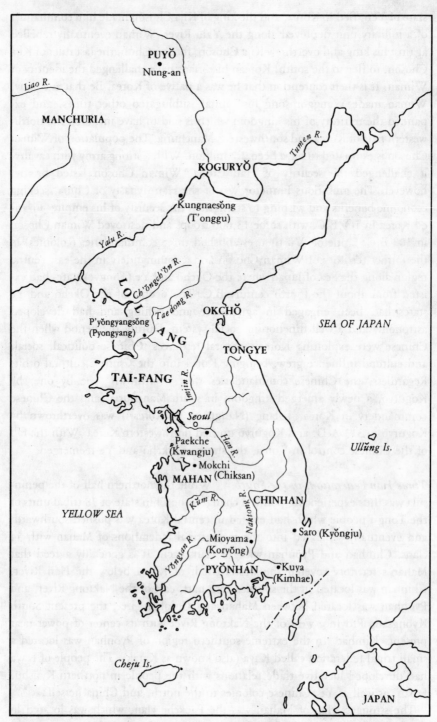

KOGURYŎ AND THE THREE HAN FEDERATIONS
(ca. 1st–3rd Centuries A.D.)

of present Kyŏngju.

The scarcity of source materials on the three Han federations resulted in a lack of precise informtion about their political, economic, and social systems and conditions. However, it is generally believed that each federation was governed by a council of tribal chieftains and that people belonged to one of the tribal units which included a number of clans. The tribal council of Chin-han was known as *hwabaek*. Marriage among clan members was forbidden. Each federation developed an agricultural economy and fostered the manufacture of clothes, tools, iron and ceramics. The peoples of the three Han federations practiced Shamanism, observing seasonal rituals as well. Evidence shows that a tumuli culture flourished in the three Han federations as well as in the north.

The Rise of the Three Kingdoms

Political Change.   During the first century B.C., further political evolution occurred in the Korean peninsula as well as in south Manchuria. Shortly before Julius Caesar emerged in Rome, the Pak clan of the Saro tribe established its supremacy in 57 B.C., with Hyŏkkōse as the first "king" of the Saro tribe of six clans. With this, the system of hereditary rule of a clan was established in what became known as the Kingdom of Shilla.

Meanwhile, around 37 B.C. Chumong, (58–19 B.C.), of the Ko clan and the leader of the five tribes of Koguryŏ in south Manchuria consolidated power and established the Kingdom of Koguryŏ with its center in the middle region of the Yalu River. Chumong became King Tongmyŏng, and the capital of Koguryŏ was established at Kungnaesŏng (T'onggu) on the Yalu. In about 18 B.C., Onjo, a son of Chumong who became the head of the Paekche tribe of Ma-han, followed suit and established a new state of Paekche with its center of power in central Korea.

Only Pyŏnhan did not become a unified state, this region shrank as Paekche to the north and west and Shilla to the east robbed its territories. However, in 42 A.D., its twelve tribal units were consolidated into six states, each assuming the name of Kaya (Karak). Two Kaya states, one in Kimhae and another in the Koryŏng area, maintained a balance of power in the former Pyŏnhan area. Evidently, some non-Han people had migrated into the Kaya region either from south China or from northern Kyūshū in Japan during the subsequent centuries and Chinese sources indicate that some people in that area had tattoos on their bodies and practiced a twice-burial system.

Although a dynastic rule of a powerful clan in each of the unified states in the former territories of Mahan and Chinhan as well as in Koguryŏ was thus established, it was perhaps not until the times of Naemul (reigned 356–401) of Shilla, Sosurim (reigned 371–384) of Koguryŏ, and Paekche's King Koi (reigned 234–286), who had been honored as founder-king, or Kŭnch'ogo (reigned 346–375), that a bona fide nationhood was established in each area with a solid dynastic rule with a viable bureaucracy. Whereas Koguryŏ and Paekche rulers were known as kings in the third century, Shilla rulers were not called king until the beginning of the sixth century when the Saro state consolidated all the tribal units of Chinhan into the Kingdom of Shilla. Until that time, Shilla rulers were called by such titles as *kŏsŏgan*, *isagŭm*, or *maripkan*.

The newly emerged kingdoms in Korea and Koguryŏ soon found themselves in a state of constant warfare, and territorial shifts began. Koguryŏ, with its cavalry forces and a highly mobile population, was most aggressive, constantly engaged in warfare with Chinese states, as well as with the newly emerged Khitans to the west and the Jurcheds (Jurchins: Yŏjin in Korean) to the east. It penetrated into the Korean peninsula, and following the overthrow of the Okchŏ and Ye states in Korea in the second half of the first century, Koguryŏ threatened the Paekche and Shilla kingdom to the south.

Following the overthrow of a Chinese commandery named Lolang in the north western region by Koguryŏ in 313, and another Chinese commandery named Taebang (Taifang in Chinese) to the south of Lolang in 314, Koguryŏ moved its capital in 427 from Kungnaesŏng (T'onggu) to Wanggŏmsŏng. Thus, Koguryŏ became a greater threat to the kingdoms of Paekche and Shilla. During the periods of two Koguryŏ kings, Kwanggaet'o (reigned 391–412) and Changsu (reigned 413–491) the power of Koguryŏ reached its zenith. In 494, Koguryŏ annexed the state of Puyŏ in northern Manchuria, uniting the Yemaek and Puyŏ peoples.

The growing power of Koguryŏ and its territorial expansion into central Korea forced Paekche to move its capital first from Hansŏng to Ungjin (now Kongju) in 475 and then to Sabi (now Puyŏ) in 538. Facing the threats from the north, Shilla and Paekche formed an alliance against Koguryŏ in the middle of the sixth century. However, Shilla promoted aggressive designs not only against Koguryŏ, but also against Paekche and Kaya. Thus, the alliance between Shilla and Paekche was broken, marking the beginning of a long period of war between the two former allies, as well as between Shilla and Koguryŏ.

With a vastly increased military strength, Shilla destroyed units of the Kaya state one by one between 532 and 562, and its western frontiers reached into the territory of Koguryŏ, occupying most of the former Paekche, Okchŏ, and Ye territories during the sixth century. Shilla built numerous massive stone walls in the frontier regions and established a large number of military outposts. With the conquests of the fertile Han River basin and the rich farm lands of the Naktong River region, the wealth of Shilla grew enormously.

Facing the aggressiveness of Shilla, Koguryŏ and Paekche formed an alliance in the late sixth century against Shilla. It was at that time that Paekche and the Yamato state in Japan became allies. Meanwhile, Koguryo took over the Liao River area in 598, fought against the invading forces of Sui China, and in 612 General Ulchi Mundok demolished the forces of Yang Ti of Sui.

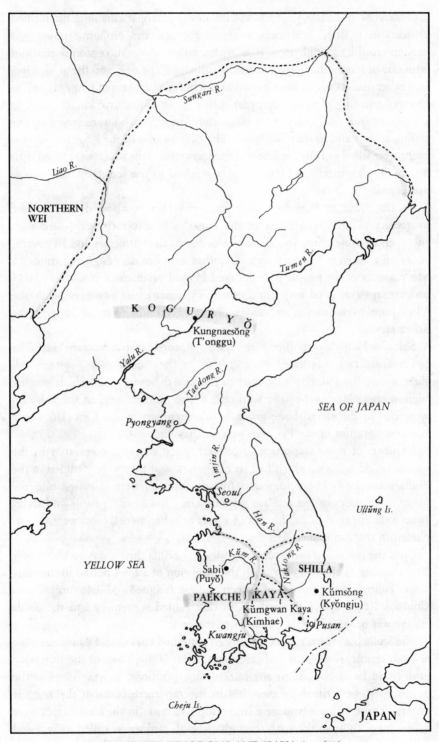

THE THREE KINGDOMS AND KAYA (ca. 600)

Government and Society.   Each of the newly emerged kingdoms established aristocratic, political and social systems. Political and economic power was monopolized by a single royal clan, with a father-to-son succession system and with one or more other clans in marriage alliance. The size, and the gold, silver and other objects which were buried in the burial chambers of kings, as well as the wall-painting of the tombs, particularly those of Koguryŏ kings, testify to the power and glory enjoyed by kings and aristocrats who were served by the toiling masses and slaves of all kinds. The twelve ranks of the Koguryŏ government were filled only by members of four powerful clans which were allied with an absolute monarchy. Chinese sources referred to the society of Koguryŏ as aristocratic.

Various clans of Paekche under the royal clan constituted the Paekche aristocracy. The sixteen ranks of the Paekche bureaucracy were filled with members of those clans, and all who belonged to the aristocracy and all government officials wore a certain style of clothes with certain designated colors. A vast majority of the people were engaged in food production. Buddhist monks and artisans associated with Buddhism enjoyed particular privileges, while the "low born" (*ch'ŏnmin*) and slaves produced various goods to support the aristocracy.

Shilla had a highly stratified social system, headed by an aristocratic class. The Shilla aristocracy was based on *kolp'um*, or the "bone rank" system. All members of the Pak clan belonged to the sacred bone group, which was the highest class. Members of the Kim clan whose mothers were of the Pak clan were also in the sacred bone group, while members of the Kim clan whose mothers were not of the Pak clan were in the true bone (*chin-gol*) group.

Members of other important clans were given the top three ranks in the system called *tup'um*, which had six categories, and they were included in the Shilla aristocracy. The commoners (mostly farmers) were classified into the lower three ranks in the *tup'um* system. The "low born" people and slaves (who were engaged in production of goods or other menial jobs) were not included in the commoner class.

Until the middle of the seventh century, the Shilla throne was occupied only by a member of the Pak clan, with the exception of a brief period in the early stage. Following the periods of Queen Sŏndŏk (reigned 632–646) and Queen Chindŏk (reigned 647–653), the Kim clan gained supremacy and the Shilla throne was occupied by its members to the end.

The Shilla bureaucracy, which had been patterned after that of China since the seventh century, had a total of seventeen ranks. While those of the true bone rank could be appointed to any bureaucratic positions, top positions in the government were filled by members in the top three ranks in the *tup'um* system. Those officials who were in the top five ranks in the bureaucracy were called *yŏng*, those in the sixth through eleventh ranks were called *kyŏng*, and others below the eleventh rank were called *taesa*, *saji*, and *sa*, respectively.

There is no evidence that Shilla imported the Chinese civil service examination system.

In order to maintain the aristocratic order, various rules and codes governing the size and style of residence, riding carts, and clothes were issued and enforced. With the growth of monarchical power in Shilla, the old system of *hwabaek*, a tribal council which had made collective decisions, all but disappeared. All military commanders and top-ranking military officers were members of the true bone groups. The commoners were recruited into the military.

The young aristocrats of the true bone and top *tup'um* ranks constituted the main core of the military. They were collectively called *hwarang* (the "Flowery Princes"), and they are said to have excelled in moral and physical strength, military skill, comradeship, music and dance, and the art of living. Their absolute loyalty to the king and their bravery and military skills contributed much to the rise of the military power of Shilla. They practiced what is known as *hwarangdo* (the "way of *hwarang*"), and it is said that the *bushidō* (the "way of *bushi* or *samurai*") of Japan had its origin in the *hwarangdo* of Shilla.

The Emergence of Clan Names.   The Chinese who migrated to Korea transplanted such Chinese clan names as Cho, Hwang, O, Ryu and Yi in Korea, influencing the ruling Korean families to adopt Chinese-style surnames. The early Koreans had been identified by their tribal names. In Koguryŏ, which had contacts with China earlier than others, such clan names as Ko and Myŏngnim had already existed, and in Paekche, which came in contact with the Chinese culture later, such clan names as Chin, Hyŏp, Kuk, Paek, Sa and Yŏn of aristocratic families emerged. With the exception of a few, most of the new clan names which the Koreans adopted had a single Chinese character.

With the establishment of new kingdoms in the second half of the first century B.C., clan names increased in number. As has been discussed earlier, the founders of the three kingdoms and certain early kings of Shilla were known by their new clan names originated in mythology. Among them were such names of royal clans of Shilla as Pak, Sŏk, and Kim, and that of the founder of Koguryŏ which was Ko.

Following the adoption of clan names by the royal clans of Shilla, in 33 A.D., King Yuri gave new clan names for six tribes of Saro (Shilla), and such clan names of Koreans as Yi, Ch'oe, Son, Chŏng, Pae, and Sŏl appeared, replacing their former tribal names. After that, the kings gave certain meritorious individuals new surnames, giving birth to new clan names such as An, Ch'a, Han, Hong, Kim, Kwŏn, Nam, Ō, and Wang. A similar process took place in Koguryŏ and Paekche. Meanwhile, more Chinese with different clan names immigrated to Korea, establishing clans. As a result, such clan names as Kang, Yŏ, Ro, Ŏm, Sŏ, Chu, and Myŏng were added after 580.

Some Korean clans split into branches, and together with Chinese clan names which were brought to Korea by the Chinese immigrants led to the increase of clan names some of which were identical. Therefore, the Koreans with an identical clan name did not necessarily belong to the same blood (patriarchal) line.

The identification of a clan was usually associated with the locality in which the clan name was originated (pon-gwan). Hence, the Kim of Kyŏngju, the Kim of Kimhae, or the Kim of Kwangsan; the Yi of Kyŏngju, the Yi of Yŏnan, or the Yi of Chŏnju; the Pak of Miryang, or the Pak of Shimyang; the Nam of Ŭiryŏng, the Nam of Yŏngyang, or the Nam of Kosŏng. All upper-class families and some commoners kept their genealogy called chokpo, and the marriage between man and woman who had the same clan name and pon-gwan was prohibited by law, no matter how distantly they were related by blood.

The Pattern of Economic Development

With the steady growth of a sedentary life style, hunting and fishing gave way to agricultural life. The transformation of economy was particularly rapid in the southern part of the peninsula which was more suitable for agricultural economy, and during the Three Han Federations period, rice, maize, millet, and three varieties of beans (red, green, and soya) were cultivated and animals were domesticated for food and transportation.

Wild ginseng was harvested, and the production of silk, as well as leather goods had already begun. Iron production began in the fourth century B.C., and simple farm tools were produced. Cash economy did not develop, but apparently shell-money was used as ''cash'' as a medium of exchange. Meanwhile, the institution of slavery emerged as criminals and certain foreigners were enslaved and forced to work on the land or cut timber. Communal ownership of land was a common pattern.

Agricultural activity increased during the Three Kingdoms period, but with the rise of nation-states, the pattern of land ownership changed as land grants were made to those individuals who rendered meritorious services to the founding of new dynasties, creating private ownership of land by ruling clans and local magistrates who received large domains called either shigŭp or nogŭp. The former was a large area entrusted to regional aristocrats or high officials as their source of income, and the latter was salary land entrusted to other government officials. Buddhist temples in Paekche and Shilla received large land grants.

Each tribe or clan had its own communal land, but the individual peasant owned no land. Major agricultural products were the same as those of the Three Han Federations period, but the cultivation of sesame seed plants, ginseng, and hemp became increasingly important. Lands owned by the royal clans, aristocrats, and high officials, as well as Buddhist temples were cultivated by slaves and semi-slaves who lived in specially designated areas collectively called pugok. Slaves were also engaged in the production of leather goods and tools. Prisoners of war and children of slaves became slaves along with criminals. The irrigation system that developed in Paekche was a significant aspect of agriculture. Animal husbandry became increasingly important during the Three Kingdoms periods.

The manufacturing of gold, silver, and iron increased, and more iron tools for farming and household goods, as well as iron weapons were produced as the production of silk and hemp cloth and leather goods, such as hats, saddles, and shoes, increased. An enormous number of gold decorative items, such as belt, rings, earrings, and bracelets, as well as Buddha's statues were produced. Some large iron statues of Buddha were produced.

Ceramic workers, most of whom were slaves, produced roof tiles and ceramic wares in greyish color. The use of the potter's wheel became widespread. As large palaces and Buddhist temples and pagodas were built, the number of stone masons, lumberjacks, roof-tile makers and dye makers grew vastly.

The governments of the three kingdoms collected land, head, and household taxes which were paid in goods and grains. In addition, they collected corvée tax which was paid in labor services. The collection of tributes from the commoners after the unification of Korea by Shilla added to the tax burden of the peasantry.

A market economy developed, and markets were established both in the capitals and local areas. However, trading was done in a barter system, although gold, shells and iron were used as money. Chinese coins circulated in Korea, particularly in the metropolitan markets where foreign traders (mostly Chinese and some Japanese) went. There is no evidence that coins were minted in Korea during this period.

Foreign trade between Korea and China flourished after the unification of Korea, and trade with the Japanese in the northern part of Kyūshū was carried out on a limited scale. A Korean merchant, Chang Po-go (d. 847), built a commercial empire with his main base at Ch'ŏnghaejin (an island off the south coast, now known as Wando), and dominated Korea's foreign trade in the 830's. He provided transportation to governemnt officials of Shilla who went to the T'ang court, as well as others from Korea and Japan to China, and with his trading communities established in the southern coast of the Shantung Peninsula and the lower region of the Huai River, he was known as "Commissioner" of trade of Korea.

With his commercial power, Chang helped Kim U-jing take the throne as King Shinmu in 839. Shinmu reigned only three months, but his son, King Munsŏng, rewarded Chang with a domain (*shigǔp*) with 2,000 households, and put him in charge of security of the southwest coast of the kingdom. He was assassinated when his political ambition grew too strong, and his commercial empire collapsed. With this, foreign trade with Korea declined rapidly.

As society and economy changed, transportation was improved, and more ships navigated inland waterways as well as along the seacoasts. A growing number of ox-driven carts were used to transport tax goods. A record showed that in 652 two thousand carts were used to transport several tens of thousands of bushels of grain to the capital of Shilla from local regions. In order to facilitate rapid communication between the capital and local regions, courier (pony) stations were constructed, beginning in the fifth century.

Shilla's Unification of Korea

Facing the Paekche-Koguryŏ alliance, Shilla sought the assistance of T'ang China, which emerged in 618, and the T'ang dynasty, which was interested in reestablishing Chinese colonies in Korea, came to Shilla's aid by dispatching troops to Korea. The combined forces of Shilla and China finally brought about the fall of Paekche in 660. Prince P'ung, who returned from Japan, fought three more years with Japanese military help to preserve Paekche, but their forces were demolished at the Battle of the Paekch'on River in 663. After this, the combined forces of Shilla and T'ang turned against Koguryŏ. Koguryŏ had fought successfully against the forces of Sui China in 612, 613 and 614 but it encountered numerous internal problems as its strength was drained by wars against the T'ang forces between 645 and 668. The struggle for power among aristocrats and the death of an able general Yŏn Kaesomun in 666, sealed Koguryŏ's fate, and in 668 it was overthrown by the combined forces of Shilla and China.

When Koguryŏ fell, a Koguryŏ general, Tae Cho-yŏng, and his followers fled to Manchuria and established in 698 the state of Chin (renamed Parhae in 712), thus bringing the period of the northern and southern dynasties. Its territory covered Manchuria east of the Liao River and the northeastern part of Korea. One of its four sub-capitals was located in Korea. A prosperous state though it was, it fell to the Khitans in 926.

Shilla achieved the unification of the three kingdoms with the military assistance of China. However, following the conquest of Koguryŏ, Shilla became engaged in a series of military actions until 676 against the forces of T'ang China, which attempted to establish Chinese control in the northwestern region of Korea. In 735, Shilla successfully compelled the Chinese to give up their territorial ambitions of Korea, and maintained the unity of Korea below the Taedong River in the west and present-day Wŏnsan in the east. However, Koguryŏ's territories in Manchuria were lost forever to the Chinese and others. Since the fall of Koguryŏ, even the northern parts of Korea were controlled by the Chinese and the Jurcheds for some time.

Shilla established an amicable relationship with China, sending no less than forty-five missions in the thirty-six-year period between 703 and 738. These missions included scholars, as well as courtiers. Meanwhile, a large number of Buddhist monks of Shilla, including Hyech'o, made journeys to China, and many of them stayed in China for many years. Some Koreans who went to Ch'ang-an studied Chinese subjects, passed the civil service examinations, and served in the Chinese government. Some Koreans were officials in the Chinese

Dolmen on Kanghwa Island, circa 20th century B.C.

Pottery with comb markings. Neolithic Age.

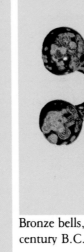

Bronze bells, probably a harness ornament, 8th–7th century B.C.

37

Bronze buckles in the form of horse and tiger, Early Iron Age, 2nd–1st century B.C.

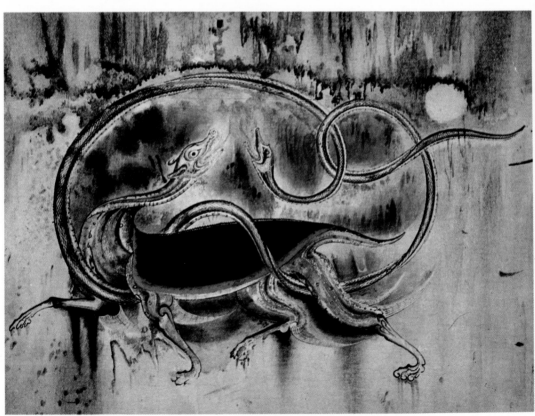

Tortoise-Serpent in the mural painting in a Koguryŏ tomb (500–650 A.D.).

Mural paintings on the walls of a Koguryŏ tomb, Interior designs of a Koguryŏ tomb.
357 A.D.

Gilt-bronze Maitreya of the Three Kingdoms period.

A gilt-bronze trinity produced in Paekche period.

Interior of the tomb of King Muryŏng of Paekche, located at near Kongju.

Tile with landscape in relief of the Paekche period.

A pair of earrings of Queen Muryŏng found inside the monarch's tomb, Paekche period.

A golden girdle with pendents, of Shilla origin, circa 5th–6th centuries.

A Shilla gold crown.

Gold bracelet of Ancient Shilla origin.

"Heavenly Horse" painted on a birch bark mudguard, Shilla period.

41

Mirŭk Temple Pagoda of Paekche period, 7th century.

Ch'ŏmsŏngdae, astronomical observation tower built in 647 in Kyŏngju.

Emille bell of the Shilla period.

Gold sarira casket, Shilla period, 8th century.

The Pulguk Temple built in the 8th century.

Turtle tablet, dedicated to King Muyŏl, Shilla period.

The Tabo Pagoda on the ground of the
Pulguk Temple.

43

The *Sŏkkuram*, a grotto temple in the hill behind the Pulguk Temple (8th century).

11-headed Kwanŭm (Kuanyin) made of granite in *Sŏkkuram* grotto.

Stone lamp in the form of a pair of lions, Pŏp-chu Temple, Shilla period.

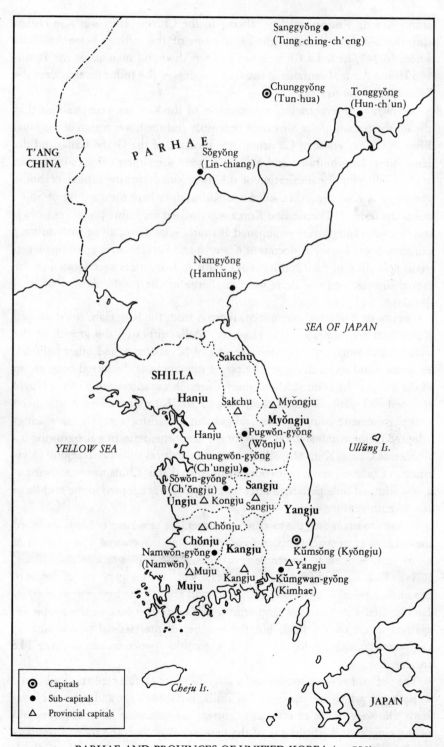

Sanggyŏng ●
(Tung-ching-ch'eng)

Chunggyŏng ◎
(Tun-hua)

Tonggyŏng
(Hun-ch'un)
●

T'ANG
CHINA

P A R H A E

Sŏgyŏng
(Lin-chiang)

Namgyŏng
(Hamhŭng)
●

SEA OF JAPAN

Sakchu

SHILLA

Hanju

Sakchu △ △ Myŏngju
Myŏngju

Hanju △
△ Pugwŏn-gyŏng
● (Wŏnju)

YELLOW SEA

Chungwŏn-gyŏng
(Ch'ungju) ●

Sŏwŏn-gyŏng
(Ch'ŏngju) ● **Sangju**

Ungju △ △ Kongju
Sangju △

△ Chŏnju

Chŏnju

Namwŏn-gyŏng ● **Kangju**
(Namwŏn)

△ Muju Kangju △

Muju Kangju △

Ullŭng Is. △

Yangju

Kŭmsŏng (Kyŏngju) ◎

△ Yangju

Kŭmgwan-gyŏng
(Kimhae) ●

◎	Capitals
●	Sub-capitals
△	Provincial capitals

Cheju Is.

JAPAN

PARHAE AND PROVINCES OF UNIFIED KOREA (ca. 750)

army. Among Korean military officials in the Chinese army was Kao Hsien-chih (Ko Sŏn-ji in Korean) who became one of the military heroes of China when, in 747, he led a Chinese army of ten thousand men across the Pamirs and Hindu Kush Mountains to the upper waters of the Indus River against the Tibetans and the Arabs.

Meanwhile, several trading communities of the Koreans were established in the southern coast of the Shantung peninsula and the lower region of the Huai River in China. Those at Ch'uchou, the juncture of the Grand Canal and the Huai River, Lienshuihsien and Mt. Ch'ih were the largest colonies of Korean traders.Following the unification of the three kingdoms, the capital of Shilla remained at Kyŏngju (then known as Kŭmsŏng) where the majority of Shilla aristocrats resided. The unified Korea was divided into nine provinces (*chu*), and five sub-capitals were established at strategic locations, along with military garrisons. Some former aristocrats of Koguryŏ and Paekche were given privileged status according to their former ranks. Nine military units were located in the capital district, and ten units were in charge of the public security of local districts.

Twenty-six kings and one queen, mostly, from the Kim clan, ruled unified Korea between 668 and 935. However, Shilla witnessed the growth of the monarchical autocracy, the strengthening of bureaucracy, and other political, economic, and social changes. The power monopoly of the sacred bone group of the Pak clan had ended when Queen Chindŏk was succeeded by King Muyŏl (reigned 654–660). With it, the power of the Kim clan and the true bone group increased, bringing the realignment of aristocracy. The new kings adopted Chinese monarchical titles for the first time, reflecting the growing influence of China. King Muyŏl's Chinese monarchical title was T'aejong (T'ai-tsung in Chinese), and a state council similar to that of China was established as a new criminal code patterned after that of China was adopted in the middle of the seventh century.

In order to strengthen the monarchical power, the new kings of Shilla abolished the old land-grant system applied to aristocrats, and inaugurated a new system of salary land applied to government officials. Certain meritorious individuals, such as Kim Yu-shin (595–673), a general who made a great contribution to the unification of Korea, received special land grants. The new system of salary land created a new type of landlordism in Korea. The bulk of the people remained toilers on the land, but the number of professional people such as carpenters, potters, gold, silver, and ironsmiths, paper makers and the like increased.

The old and new aristocrats and a large number of absentee landlords lived in Kyŏngju, which was the capital of Shilla, but some large and powerful landlords who were either ex-officials or current officials arose in different regions of the kingdom. With the rise of the new landlord class, the style of architecture of private houses and the way of life of the upper class changed rapidly. It is said that Kyŏngju had a population of over one million and all its houses had tiled roofs.

The kingdom was divided into provinces, counties and districts, and below districts were towns, villages and hamlets. There were nine provinces, three in the original Shilla region, and three each in the former Paekche and Koguryŏ territories. There were five sub-capitals. Nine military units were located near the capital and ten military commanderies were established at key places throughout the kingdom. In order to meet military and labor needs, the common people were classified into nine household categories according to the size of the family, and were classified into six categories according to their age and sex. Conquered people and criminals were classified as slaves or were placed in the semi-slave category of the "low-born" who lived in hamlets.

The Cultural Development of the Three Kingdoms and the Unified Periods

Profound changes occurred in Korea during the Three Kingdoms period as societies became more organized and economic conditions improved. Confucianism, Taoism, Buddhism and other cultural influences from abroad found fertile soil and flourished in Korea. While Confucianism, and to a certain degree Taoism, found adherents in the ruling class, Buddhism made headway not only among the common people, but also among the aristocrats, becoming the religion of the majority.

The Arrival of Buddhism. The proximity of Koguryŏ to China caused it to be influenced by Chinese culture first. Although Mahayana Buddhism was officially introduced to Koguryŏ in 372, evidence shows that it did not make any significant impact in that kingdom although a few outstanding Buddhist monks and scholars emerged and some temples were built.

Buddhism, which migrated southward, became a strong religion in Paekche following the arrival of a Chinese monk in 384. The first Buddhist temple in Paekche was built in 385, and Buddhism became the national faith of Paekche. Buddhism arrived in Shilla sometime in the 5th century, but it did not receive official sanction until after the martyrdom of Ich'adon in 527. With the arrival of such Koguryŏ monks as Kyerang in Shilla in 551, Buddhism became the religion of the kings and queens, and the renowned Hwangnyong Temple was constructed in 553. Many Shilla kings and queens were devout Buddhists and their reigning titles reflected their religious aspirations.

With the arrival of Buddhism in Paekche and Shilla, new forms and styles of music and musical instruments, painting, and architecture developed as countless elegant and graceful Buddha statues were produced by the artisans. The golden statues of Maitreya and others produced by the artisans of Paekche witnessed the rise, not only of religious zeal, but also of artistic tastes and metallurgical and other skills.

As intellectual activities and religious studies grew rapidly, many eminent monks emerged in Shilla. Among them were Anhong who studied Buddhism in China and returned to Shilla in 576, Wŏn-gwang who returned from China in 600 after his study there, Wŏnhyo (622–686) who wrote many Buddhist books, and Ŭisang who studied in China and returned in 670. Much like Christianity in the sixth century Europe, Buddhism in Korea not only became the dominant religion, but also a force which unified the people.

The Absorption of Chinese Culture.   Confucianism entered Koguryŏ, and a government school for Confucian learning was established in 372. However, Koguryŏ refused to be Sinicized, and like that of Buddhism, the impact of Confucianism in Koguryŏ was minimal, judging from available evidence. Both Paekche and Shilla had a Confucianized bureaucracy, but Koguryŏ did not. Evidently, many refugees from Lolang and Taifang migrated to Paekche and contributed to the growth of Chinese culture in that kingdom.

Having no written language of their own, the Koreans borrowed the Chinese writing system and produced books and documents in the Chinese language. The use of written Chinese increased during the 4th century as state papers sent by Shilla to China in 337 and those between Shilla and Paekche in 373, as well as memorial stone monuments of the period show.

With the dissemination of Chinese culture in Korea, the number of Confucian scholars and their intellectual activities grew as more books of both Buddhism and Confucianism were brought into Korea. Although Koguryŏ did not become Confucianized, Confucian influence was reflected in the production of historical records of Koguryŏ such as *Yugi* (100 volumes) and *Shinjip* (5 volumes). *Sŏgi* (Historical Records) of Paekche by Ko Hŭng was produced in the 4th century and historical writing appeared in Shilla in the 6th century.

It is not clear whether or not Paekche established Confucian schools, but Shilla established a Confucian school in 682 and there was an office of government in charge of education in Shilla. Confucian studies grew rapidly in Shilla with the establishment of the National Learning (*kukhak*) in 682, and many outstanding Confucian scholars arose. Among them were a master calligrapher Kim Saeng (b. 711), a historian named Kim Tae-mun, who wrote a *Collection of Life Stories of the Hwarang, Biographies of High Priests*, and *Local History of Hansan* (now Seoul), and Ch'oe Ch'i-wŏn (857–?) who was the Superintendent of Learning. Many students of Shilla went to Ch'ang-an, China, to study, and many of them passed T'ang civil service examinations. A Chinese type of civil service examination system was said to have been established in Shilla, but its effects were undetectable.

One of the most important results of Buddhist and Confucian studies in Korea was the rise of foreign language studies. Korean Buddhist monks and scholars became engaged in the study of Sanskrit as well as the Chinese languages.

All books written by Korean monks and scholars were in Chinese. Confucian classics became standard textbooks in a new learning that grew in Korea while studies in foreign languages and medicine developed steadily.

Another significant cultural development in the early 7th century was the adoption of the *idu* system, which enabled the transliteration of Korean words using Chinese characters. The *idu* system became more sophisticated when the *hyangch'al* method was adopted later. This method brought about the replacement of Korean nouns with Chinese nouns, while verb stems and inflections, and other parts of speech lacking in Chinese were written in Chinese characters having the same or similar sounds. With the use of the *idu* system the writing of Korean songs (*hyangga*) flourished. A scholar named Sŏl Ch'ong, a son of Monk Wŏnhyo, deviced the *kugyŏl* system which enabled the reading of Chinese classics in Korean. Confucian classics became standard textbooks in a new learning that grew in Korea while studies in foreign languages and medicine developed steadily.

Native Songs and Poetry.   Ancient Chinese sources described the Koreans as "a people who enjoy singing and dancing," referring to religious festivals of the ancient Koreans. Songs and dances were involved in spring and autumn communal religious affairs. The Koreans honored heaven and thanked the earth with their songs and dances.

The Korean native songs called *hyangga,* and ancient songs and dances of the Koreans were by and large religious and magical in character, and they were the means of communion with the deities and spirits. The early Koreans believed that magical powers of words would please the gods, help avoid natural calamities, bring rain and stop the winds, and cure diseases. Some songs were secular, composed by men and women of all walks of life. Many of them praised the superior quality of young warriors (*hwarang*), who were regarded as the pillars of the state and the paragon of youth. The *hwarang* themselves contributed much to the development of *hyangga* and a variety of forms of dance.

With the introduction of the *idu* system, native songs which had been transmitted in oral tradition were written down. *Samdaemok*, a collection of *hyangga*, was produced during the reign of Queen Chinsŏng in the late 9th century. Unfortunately, most books written during the Three Kingdom and the unified Korean periods, including the collection of *hyangga*, were destroyed during the Mongol wars of the 13th century. A few examples of *hyangga* of Shilla are given below. Princess Sŏnhwa of Shilla met a young man named Madung accidentally and became his wife eventually, and the young man became King Mu (600–641) of Paekche. A poem about this episode says:

> *Princess Sŏnhwa*
> *Hoping for a secret marriage*
> *Went away at night,*

With Madung in her arm.

An unidentified poet wrote the following piece entitled *Ode to Yangji* around 635:

> *We have come, have come,*
> *Woe, woe to us—*
> *We have come*
> *To cultivate wisdom*

On one occasion, a princess of Shilla wished that someone would pick the flower on a cliff. When no one came forward, an old man of the humble state, (a member of the *ch'ōnmin* class) who tended cattle, volunteered. A poem entitled *Dedication* by "an old man" of the early 8th century says:

> *If you would let me leave*
> *The cattle tethered to the brown rock,*
> *And feel no shame for me,*
> *I would pluck and dedicate the flower!*

A poet named Shinch'ung of the mid-eighth century wrote in a poem entitled *Regret* as follows:

> *You said you would no more forget me*
> *Than oaks would wither before the fall.*
> *O that familiar face is there still,*
> *The face I used to see and admire.*

> *The moon in the ancient lake, it seems,*
> *Complains of the transient tide, ebb and flow.*
> *Your face I see no more, no more,*
> *O the vain world, it hates and harasses me.*

A monk named Kwangdōk (ca. 661–681) in a poem of repentance entitled *Prayer to Amitabha* wrote:

> *O Moon,*
> *Go to the West, and*
> *Pray to Amitabha*
> *And tell.*

> *That there is one who*
> *Adores the judicial throne, and*
> *Longs for the Pure Land,*
> *Praying before Him with folded hands.*

Can the forty-eight vows be met
If this flesh remains unannihilated?

Following the arrival of Buddhism, many songs and dances associated with Buddhist rituals developed. The *hyangga* by Kwangdŏk cited above is a good example. Buddhist chants and dances became an integral part of Korean culture. Confucianism also fostered part of Korean culture, particularly the new music and dance associated with Confucian rituals. Many Chinese musical forms and instruments, along with dance forms, were appropriated by the Koreans, enriching their cultural life. Meanwhile, Koreans created new musical instruments, or modified Chinese instruments. Among the new musical instruments were *hyŏnhakkŭm*, (also called *kŏmun-go*) a seven-string zither of Koguryŏ, and *kayagŭm*, a twelve-string zither of Kaya. Despite the growing influence of Buddhism and Confucianism, native religious beliefs continued to be practiced by the people. Seasonal communal rites were performed, songs were sung in praise of native gods and spirits, and sacrifices were offered in thanksgiving. One of the dances, which was performed around the pagoda on the temple ground, symbolized the life of the moon (waxing and waning) and expressed the human desire to have an everlasting life, and has been a poetic expression of the Korean sentiment. The shaman ritual known as *kut*, the religious ceremony performed to appease the spirits, was widely performed. There is much evidence that the people of Shilla practiced phallic culture.

A pottery culture developed in Shilla along with the skills to produce bronze and iron objects which amply demonstrate the creativity, imaginativeness, and sophisticated taste and quality of the artists. A Korean scholar observed that Koguryŏ arts were "marked by a forceful and passionate form of expression," while Paekche "developed a highly refined and elegant style of art." It was said that Shilla maintained "primitive simplicity in its arts for a long time," but later it too developed "sophisticated balance and solemnity."

The arrival of Chinese culture and the Buddhist religion along with music and dance, stimulated the cultural development of the Koreans in the three kingdoms as the quantity of both religious and secular music and dance increased. Such a new cultural growth resulted in the establishment of a new form of art called *kamugiak*, or "song, dance and musical skills." A fresco on the walls of the Muyongch'ong (Tomb of the Dancers) at T'onggu and the mural paintings of the Koguryŏ tombs in the northern regions of Korea sufficiently revealed the existence of such art.

Meanwhile, many Korean Confucian scholars, Buddhist monks, and artisans and musicians were sent to Japan in the 5th, 6th, and 7th centuries. Paekche, which developed more cordial relations with Japan than Shilla, sent numerous educated and skilled people to Japan and helped the Japanese to cultivate a new culture called the *Asuka bunka* in the 7th century. Many tombs which were discovered in the Kinki region of Japan showed a resemblance to those of Paekche and Shilla. The renowned Hōryūji temple near Nara and other architectural masterpieces in and around the ten capitals of Japan abundantly demonstrate the contribution which the Koreans made toward the development of a high culture in Japan. Korea's *kamugiak*, which was introduced to the Japanese, became the *kabuki* of Japan. Among many Paekche people who civilized the Japanese was a scholar named Ajikki, who went to Japan in the early fifth century, introducing Chinese studies. He became a court historian. Some time later, another Paekche scholar named Wang In (Wani in Japanese) went to Japan, and promoted Chinese learning. The descendants of these and other scholars and monks from Korea served as teachers in the Japanese imperial household and court historians.

Art and Architecture.   There are no remains of paintings other than a few cave paintings in the primitive style and the mural paintings of the tombs of the Three Kingdoms period. However, the depiction of dragons, tigers, fairies, peacocks and human figures in the murals of the Koguryŏ tombs along with other decorative designs in various colors, the painting of the "Heavenly Horse" on the mudguard of a horse unearthed from a tomb of a king of Shilla, and the mural of a Paekche king's tomb near Kongju, indicate that the painters of that period were highly sophisticated and skillful, and their style was graceful yet powerful. Many Korean artists who went to Japan left behind fine examples such as the portrait of a Japanese prince named Shōtoku and mural paintings on the walls of Hōryūji near Nara.

All secular wooden buildings of the Three Kingdoms, as well as many Buddhist temples and pagodas of Paekche and Shilla, were destroyed. As a result, it is difficult, if not impossible to know what the architectural style of the Three Kingdoms period was. However, tombs of Koguryŏ in the Kangsŏ-Yonggang region in South P'yŏng-an Province and other places amply demonstrate the artistic quality and architectural engineering skills of Koguryŏ. The tombs of Paekche and Shilla rulers likewise evidence the highly developed form of architectural engineering of the time. Such remains as defensive walls, foundation stones of Buddhist edifices and pavilions of P'osŏkchŏng and Imhaejŏn in Kyŏngju are examples of the high culture which developed in Shilla. Ch'ŏmsŏngdae (Tower of Star Observation), a stone tower in Kyŏngju built in 647, evidences the architectural engineering technology which existed in Shilla. Ch'ŏmsŏngdae is said to be the oldest known astronomical observatory in Asia. The artisans of Paekche and Shilla produced countless exquisitely designed golden crowns, golden earrings, golden buckles and belts, golden bracelets and other decorative objects for the kings, queens and aristocrats. They also produced many graceful Buddhist statues made of gold, iron, and other materials. Solgŏ, who painted the mural paintings of the Hwangnyong Temple in 553, was the most renowned painter of the Three Kingdoms period.

A massive stone statue of Maitreya in a standing position on the ground of the Mirŭk Temple in Iksan, near Puyŏ and a five-story stone pagoda in Puyŏ, were the cultural treasures which the Kingdom of Paekche left behind. The Hwangnyong Temple, in addition to Ch'ŏmsŏngdae and tombs of the kings were architectural masterpieces of the Kingdom of Shilla.

The ceramic art that flourished during the Three Kingdoms period was evidenced in the Shilla earthenwares of red and grey colors, as well as roof tiles with floral designs and demon faces. Some earthenwares of red clay baked in the kilns of Shilla were as hard as iron and they sounded like ironware when struck.

The Golden Age of Buddhism.   The golden age of Buddhism followed the unification of Korea by Shilla as three new sects emerged and joined the two sects which had been established toward the end of the Three Kingdoms period. Of these five Buddhist sects, the two which exerted more influence were the *Pŏpsŏng* (also known as the *Haedong*) sect founded by Monk Wŏnhyo with the Punhwang Temple in Kyŏngju as its home base and the *Hwaŏm* sect founded by Monk Ŭisang with the Pusŏk Temple as its home base. These five sects were supported mostly by aristocrats and members of the royal clans.

The commoners subscribed to the doctrine of the *Chŏngt'o*, or Pure Land (*Jōdo* in Japanese) sect which stressed the importance of chanting the name of Amitabha and Buddhist texts as a means of securing salvation (entry into the Pure Land in the West). Non-intellectual and rather superstitious in nature, the doctrine of the *Chŏngt'o* was easily understood by unsophisticated masses who manifested certain anti-establishment sentiments. Wonhyo who became an apostate popularized the doctrine of *Chŏngt'o* as a "wandering monk" and converted the majority of the population to Buddhism.

Meanwhile, the doctrine of the *Sŏn* (*Zen* in Japanese) which was introduced from China began to exert its influence among intellectuals. Among outstanding monks of the golden age of Buddhism was Monk Hyech'o, who made a pilgrimage to China and India and wrote a diary of his journey in the early eighth century when the printing of Buddhist texts began.

The construction of such architectural masterpieces as the Pongdŏk Temple and the Punhwang Temple clearly reflected the strength of Buddhism and the devotion of the people to that religion. A Buddhist temple built in the mid-sixth century was reconstructed in 751 and renamed the Pulguk-sa, "Temple of the Land of Buddha" with the elegant *Tabo* ("Many Treasures") and *Sŏkka* ("Sakyamuni") pagodas on its grounds. The grotto temple of *Sŏkkuram* in the hills behind Kyŏngju was constructed in the middle of the eighth century when large bronze bells with graceful and exquisite surface designs were produced.

The End of the Shilla Kingdom

The Delcine of Shilla.   Shilla began to show signs of maladies and deterioration from the middle of the 8th century, leading toward the disintegration of the kingdom. Corruption and jealousies among the members of the ruling class, conflict between the monarchy and aristocracy, the power struggle between the Pak and Kim clans, conflict between the upper and lower aristocrats, disunity between the civil and religious leaders, and a decline of morality and ethics among the members of the ruling class, as well as the decline of the spirit of *hwarangdo*, and the growing discontentment of the toiling masses, constituted the major causes for the downfall of Shilla. The long military conflict with the Chinese in the 7th century, the Japanese invasion of 731, and the rebellions of 822 and 839 also had severely damaging effects on Shilla.

Luxury, extravagance, lack of incentives, and mismanagement of government affairs wrecked the foundation of the kingdom. By the beginning of the 10th century, a profound decadence prevailed in Shilla. In order to support the luxurious and extravagant life of aristocrats living in the capital of over one million population where "there never was a moment without the sound of merrymaking," the peasants were forced to overwork or were overly taxed.

With the strengthening of the monarchy, the power struggle between the monarchy and aristocracy grew intense, particularly during the reign of King Kyŏngdŏk (reigned 742–765) who strengthened the Confucian bureaucracy. His successor, King Hyegong (reigned 765–780), encountered determined opposition by aristocrats who were joined by other clan chiefs and this created a chaotic situation. King Hyegong was assassinated in 780, and the Kim clan, which had established its political supremacy, lost control of the throne to the Pak clan. In 822, another rebellion of a member of the Kim clan hastened the decline of the Shilla kingdom. The succession disputes within the royal family also added serious political problems: in 838 and 839 two kings were assassinated, and during the 150 years after 780 some nineteen kings and a queen came and went. Meanwhile, lower-ranking aristocrats who had been unhappy with the dominance of upper aristocrats created numerous problems when they challenged the basic premise of the political order. Among lower aristocrats were many Confucian intellectuals who embraced the newly arrived Sŏn Buddhism which was antagonistic toward other Buddhist sects that flourished under the patronage of a royal clan and upper aristocrats. In alliance with local magnates and certain commanders of the military they challenged the power of upper aristocrats, disuniting the ruling class. Among the new intellectuals of the lower aristocracy was a scholar named Ch'oe Ch'i-wŏn. Seeing the chaotic situation arising, the peasants, who were heavily burdened with taxes and exploited by landlords, revolted under certain bandit leaders. The kingdom was doomed.

The Fall of Shilla.   Taking advantage of the prevailing conditions and restlessness among the toiling people during the reign (887–897) of Queen Chinsŏng more bandits rose, and in 889 Shilla witnessed the eruption of rebellions and uprisings led by several rebel leaders such as Yanggil and Kyŏnhwŏn. The Shilla court was unable to deal with the situation and before the end of the reign of Queen Chinsŏng, the Kingdom of Later Paekche, founded by Kyŏnhwŏn, emerged in 892 in the southwestern region. Meanwhile, Kungye, an illegitimate son of King Hŏn-gang (reigned 875–886), who had narrowly escaped death in a court feud and became a Buddhist monk, joined the bandit group of Yanggil. Kungye took over the leadership from Yanggil, and in 901 with the help of Wang Kŏn he established the Kingdom of Later Koguryŏ with its capital at Ch'ŏrwŏn in the central part of the peninsula. Thus, the Later Three Kingdoms period ensued. Kungye changed the name of his kingdom to T'aebong, applied the bone rank system, and became a tyrannical ruler. However, Wang Kŏn, a leading subordinate of Kungye, overthrew the rule of his master in 918, and succeeded to the throne and changed the name of the kingdom to Koryŏ with his capital at Song-ak (now Kaesŏng). Warfare among Shilla, Later Paekche, and Koryŏ ensued. In 927, Kyŏnhwŏn invaded Kyŏngju and killed a Shilla king as his troops sacked the city. The invasion of Shilla by the troops of Later Paekche led King Kyŏngsun, the last monarch of Shilla, to seek the help of Koryŏ. In 935, Wang Kŏn attacked Later Paekche which was embroiled in a rebellion led by a son of Kyŏnhwŏn. In the same year, King Kyŏngsun of Shilla surrendered to Koryŏ, and in 936 Wang Kŏn overthrew Later Paekche, thus uniting Korea, this time without foreign military assistance.

PART II

THE TRANSFORMATION OF KOREA

3. The Kingdom of Koryŏ: Internal Development and External Pressures

The Kingdom of Koryŏ and the new dynasty which Wang Kŏn established lasted 475 years, and Koryŏ came to be known in the West as Corée or Corea. During this long period, the Korean kingdom was ruled by thirty-four kings of the Wang clan, (two of whom were on the throne twice), and the Korean people witnessed numerous internal changes while encountering an increasing amount of external influence and military threats.

The process of the Sinification of Korea was to be completed in later years, but during the Koryŏ period the political system and culture changed in many respects, reflecting the growing influence of China. In the political field, Chinese influence was clearly reflected in the new political structure and the adoption of the Chinese civil service examination system, as well as in the choice of titles given to the Koryŏ kings, posthumously. All Koryŏ kings until 1274, except the founder of the dynasty, were known by their posthumous title of *chong* (宗, or "ancestor," *tsung* in Chinese). After 1274, and under the Mongol pressure, the Koryŏ kings were not given the posthumous title of *chong*, and they were called such-and-such *wang* (王, or "king"), signifying their inferior status vis-à-vis the rulers of the Yuan dynasty of the Mongols in China.

Political and Administrative Reform

The Founder.   Wang Kŏn (reigned 918–943) is known in Korean history by his posthumous title as T'aejo ("Great Progenitor") of the Koryŏ dynasty. He laid the firm foundation for the new dynasty, renamed Song-ak as Kaegyŏng

59

(also known as Songdo, now Kaesŏng), and initiated the construction of a magnificent capital with numerous majestic palaces, splendid government buildings, beautiful pavilions and Buddhist temples. In the beginning, only the royal palace was surrounded by walls, but in 1029 the construction of the outer walls, with a total of twenty-five gates which surrounded the entire capital city, was completed. With the completion of the outer walls, the capital was divided into five wards, thirty-five sections, and 343 districts. It was a magnificent city with numerous architectural masterpieces, well designed boulevards, and carefully arranged districts with a population of 130,000 in the early twelfth century, and even an official from Sung China who visited the capital in 1123 was impressed by its beauty.

Unfortunately, the capital city of Kaegyŏng was sacked first by the Khitans in the eleventh century, the Mongols in the thirteenth century, the Japanese in the late sixteenth century, and then by the Manchus in the early seventeenth century, leaving only foundation stones of palaces, pavilions, temples and government buildings. The ruins of the Full Moon Terrace (*Manwŏltae*), which was the palace ground of the Koryŏ dynasty, give evidence of the grandeur which once was the pride of the kingdom.

Besides being an able warrior, T'aejo proved to be a great innovator and a diplomat. He won the allegiance of the people of Shilla by giving the highest rank of chief minister (*chŏngsŭng*) to the last Shilla king who surrendered to him, making him governor of the Shilla capital after renaming it as Kyŏngju. T'aejo made a large land grant to the former king of Shilla, and also appointed many former "lords of the castle (*sŏngju*)" and heads of powerful regional clans of Shilla and Later Paekche as local magistrates, giving them land grants and much autonomy. He married daughters from many ruling clans of Shilla and Later Paekche, in order to bond them with the royal clan. He had six queens and twenty-three other consorts, one queen being a princess of the royal clan of Shilla. He made heritable land grants to those who contributed toward the founding of his dynasty and the reunification of Korea. He reconstructed the old capital of Koguryŏ, and designated it as Sŏgyŏng (the "Western Capital"), and established an educational institution there. He not only reduced the tax burden of farmers, but also gave them a three-year tax exemption; he emancipated over one thousand slaves, thereby winning their support for the new dynasty.

Claiming that Koryŏ was the successor to Koguryŏ, T'aejo, after overthrowing Later Paekche and uniting his kingdom with Shilla, carried out military campaigns to recover former Koguryŏ territories, particularly those in the Korean peninsula, and built numerous fortresses in the frontier regions after extending the northern boundaries of his kingdom toward the Yalu River. He brought Cheju Island, then known as T'amna, into the kingdom in 938.

Although he was an ardent Buddhist, T'aejo encouraged the rise of Confucian learning; his religious policy encouraged the harmonious growth of the native religion and Buddhism; his administrative reform increased the efficiency of the central bureaucracy; his public works projects and land and tax reforms improved both economic and social conditions; and his defense projects enhanced the security of the kingdom against the Jurcheds in the northeastern region of the Korean peninsula and the Khitans in south Manchuria.

Toward the end of his reign, T'aejo issued the "Ten Injunctions" for his posterity. In them, he pointed out that the new dynasty was established under the blessing and protection of the Buddhas, and he warned against careless selection of sites for new Buddhist temples, or conversion of private dwellings into temples. He instructed faithful observation of Buddhist festivals, but he warned against over frequency of such festivals. Although he supported the inheritance right of the first son, he permitted the succession of rights and power of the father to the second or the third son when the first son proved incapable or unsuitable. He warned against the adoption of the "barbarous" customs of the Khitans and the Jurcheds; he emphasized the need to reduce the people's tax burden, and he stressed the importance of applying equal justice to all. Although some of his instructions were superstitious in nature (Taoistic), his hope was to lead his successors to be good rulers, shunning mean and unenlightened people while cultivating cordial relations with men of wisdom and virtue.

Government Organs and Administrative Districts.   After rejecting the bone-rank system of Shilla, T'aejo and his immediate successors adopted the bureaucratic system of T'ang China. However, the establishment of a Confucian bureaucracy took many years, a process which was not completed until the reign of the eleventh king, Munjong who reigned from 1046 until 1083.

The early kings of Koryŏ had considerable difficulty in establishing the absolute power of the monarchy; they encountered serious power struggles and succession disputes within the Wang clan and between it and those of the queens, as well as the resistance of former aristocratic families. The second and the third kings were assumed to have been assassinated. The fourth king, Kwangjong (reigned 949–975), carried out bloody actions, eliminating a large number of his own relatives and others whom he regarded as his opponents. The sixth king, Sŏngjong (reigned 981–997) finally consolidated monarchical power and established a central bureaucracy with the help of a Confucian scholar, Ch'oe Sŭng-no (925–985), but it was Munjong who actually completed the construction of the Chinese-style bureaucracy and monarchical power.

The central government of Koryŏ after the reign of King Munjong consisted of four primary offices. The first three were collectively called *samsŏng*. They were: the Royal Secretariat (*Naeri*, later *Chungsŏsŏng*), which drafted the king's orders and decrees; the Royal Chancellery (*Munhasŏng*), which reviewed the king's orders and decrees and put them into final form; and the State Council (*Sangsŏsŏng*), which was the executive branch of the government consisting of six boards (*cho*) : Personnel, War (Defense), Revenue, Rites. (Ceremonies and Diplomatic Affairs), Punishment (Justice) and Public Works. The fourth highest organ was the Privy Council (*Chungch'uwŏn*), which was a deliberative council for policy matters. In addition, there were two censoring institutions of Ŏsadae and Ḳanwŏn, which were directly responsible to the king and had an encompassing investigative and supervisory power over all government branches and agencies. Nine government agencies (*kushi*) managed the general and miscellaneous functions of the court and the royal estates. The joint conference of the heads of the four highest organs where national security matters were discussed was called *Tobyŏngmasa* (later *Top'yŏng-ŭisasa*).

The adoption in 958 of the Chinese civil examination system (*kwagŏ* in Korean) ended the practice of appointing government officials through family connections. With this, more and more well-educated individuals who passed civil examinations became government officials, and bureaucrats of the new nobility emerged. Be that as it may, some individuals, such as the relatives of the five highest bureaucratic ranks under the privilege called *ŭnsŏ* could obtain direct appointment to office without taking examinations, and the sons of civil officials of the central bureaucracy enjoyed favors and certain preferential treatment. The bureaucrats were classified into nine ranks (*p'um*), each rank classified into senior (*chŏng*) and junior (*chong*), thus making a total of eighteen ranks, and each rank had its own official costume of distinctive style and color.

In the beginning, the kingdom of Koryŏ was divided into one royal district (*kinae*) and twelve administrative districts (*mok*), but the twelve districts were soon replaced by ten provinces (*to*). Each province was divided into districts (*chu*), counties (*kun*), and prefectures (*hyŏn*). Villages (*ch'on*), hamlets (*hyang*), and wards (*pugok*) were sub-units of a prefecture. When provinces replaced the previous administrative units, Kyŏngju was designated as Tonggyŏng (the "Eastern Capital"), and Hanyang (now Seoul) was designated as Namgyŏng (the "Southern Capital"). Thus, there were three sub-capitals of Tonggyŏng, Sŏgyŏng, and Namgyŏng. Kaegyŏng was commonly called Chunggyŏng (the "Central Capital") and was located within the royal district. In the early eleventh century, the nation was redivided into one royal district, five provinces, and two frontier districts (*kye*).

All provincial governors and heads of districts, counties, and prefectures were appointed by the central government, and administrative functions and tax collection in the areas below the prefectural level were handled by the unranked "country-district clerks" called *hyangni*, who were selected from the local population. In order to make *hyangni* loyal to the central government, their sons were held at the capital as hostages and they were called *kiin*, or "their men." All government officials with or without bureaucratic ranks who were appointed by the central government received land grants as their source of income (stipends), as well as a fixed amount of grains (rice, barley, and millet)

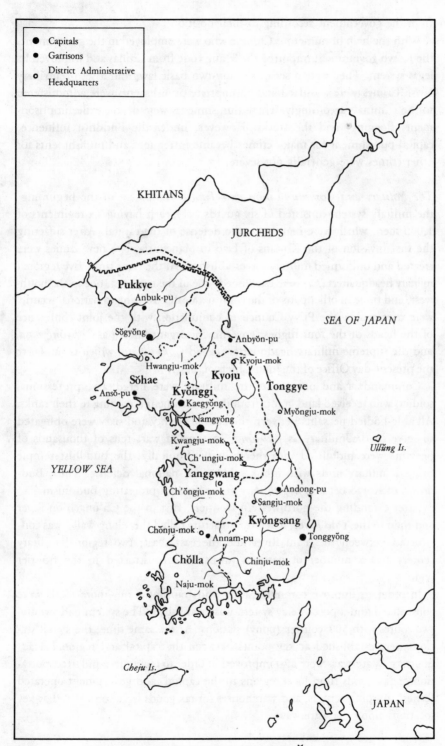

- ● Capitals
- ● Garrisons
- ○ District Administrative Headquarters

KHITANS

JURCHEDS

Pukkye
Anbuk-pu

SEA OF JAPAN

Sŏgyŏng
Anbyŏn-pu
Kyoju-mok
Hwangju-mok
Kyoju
Sŏhae
Ansŏ-pu
Kyŏnggi
Kaegyŏng
Tonggye
Myŏngju-mok
Namgyŏng
Kwangju-mok
Ullŭng Is.
Ch'ungju-mok
YELLOW SEA
Yanggwang
Ch'ŏngju-mok
Andong-pu
Sangju-mok
Kyŏngsang
Chŏnju-mok
Annam-pu
Tonggyŏng
Chŏlla
Chinju-mok
Naju-mok

Cheju Is.

JAPAN

ADMINISTRATIVE DISTRICTS OF KORYŎ (1009–1392)

from the government according to their position.

With the help of numerous Chinese who were employed in the government, the Koryŏ government imported the T'ang code from China, and improved its legal system. They were a set of seventy-two basic laws and a set of auxiliary laws. Crimes were classified and appropriate punishments were administered to the criminals accordingly. These punishments were death, exile, imprisonment, flogging, and the stocks. However, under the Buddhist influence, capital punishment for major crimes became infrequent and punishments for other crimes were generally not severe.

The Military and Communication and Transportation.   In the beginning, the military system consisted of six guards (*wi*), each having six regiments of 1,000 men, which were mainly for the defense of the capital. After suffering the first invasion of the Khitans of Liao in Manchuria, two new armies were created and uniformed military was established. At the same time, five regional military headquarters (*pu*) were established: one in the northeast, one in the northwest, and three in other parts of the country. Matters relating to national security were overseen by the Privy Council in conjunction with the joint conference of the heads of the four highest government organs known as *Tobyŏngmasa*, and the supreme military headquarters called *Chungbang*, which is similar to the present-day Office of the Joint Chiefs of Staff.

Commanders and officers of the military were hereditary, professional soldiers who received land grants from the government according to their ranks. All able-bodied peasants between the ages of twenty and sixty were obligated to serve in the military as *pubyŏng*. In time of war, tens of thousands of peasants were mobilized into the military. Ironically, the Buddhist temple formed military units with monk soldiers for national defense. Thus, Buddhism of Koryŏ became *hoguk Pulgyo*, or "nation-protecting Buddhism."

After extending the northwestern frontiers, first to the Ch'ŏngch'ŏn River and then to the Yalu River, a defense structure called the "long wall" was constructed between the Yalu River and the east coast; two regional military centers and a number of garrison towns were constructed in the frontier regions.

In order to improve communication and transportation, more roads were constructed and a postal relay system was established. The system had twenty-two routes with 500 courier (pony) stations. At the same time, fire signal stations were established at key points between the capital and regional headquarters. Waterways were also improved in order to facilitate rapid transportation of tax goods from local regions to the capital, and government operated ferries, shipping centers, and warehouses for tax goods were constructed at key locations along the waterways.

Social Structure and Economic Life

Social Structure. Although Korea's social structure and habits were not completely Confucianized, the establishment of the new dynasty, the rejection of the bone-rank system of Shilla, the adoption of the Chinese civil service examination system induced the emergence of the new élite and brought about a new social structure. However, the concept of social distinction by birth remained strong. The rise of a new feudalistic ruling class (landed gentry)called *sadaebu* and the establishment of clear class lines according to profession, constituted a significant aspect of social evolution in Korean history.

There were four classes of people: upper, middle, lower, and inferior. The upper class included the royal clan and its collateral branches, which constituted the top rank of the new nobility, the bureaucrats in civil and military branches of the government with official ranks (*p'um*), and a certain number of regional élites. The families of ranking bureaucrats and regional élites were also members of the nobility which was the ruling class. These were the ones who were well educated, enjoyed special privileges, and generally were holders of large amounts of land.

The middle group included palace functionaries (who were called *namban*) and civil and military officials in the lower positions without ranks (*p'um*). The families of these officials were also included in the middle group. Being educated and having professional training in law, medicine, mathematics, and other fields, the members of the middle group were also landholders and they enjoyed some special privileges. Thus, the officialdom of Koryŏ consisted of nobility and the privileged, absentee landlords.

The low class included those who were collectively called *yangmin*, or the "good people" who were free men. This group consisted of soldiers, farmers, artisans, merchants and fishermen who supported the livelihood of the upper and the middle class people with their labor, taxes, and other services.

The fourth class included the people who were collectively called *ch'ŏnmin*, or "the inferior people" who were unfree. Those who worked at the ferries and courier stations, as well as hunters, butchers, public entertainers, and public and private slaves belonged to this class and lived at designated localities such as hamlets (*hyang*), wards (*pugok*) and places (*so*) where government manufactories were located. As much as peasants were bound to the soil, slaves (mostly public slaves) who produced a variety of goods at government manufactories were bound to their work places. A large number of slaves worked on the estates belonging to the royal clan and the upper class. All miners were slaves.

Slaves were bought and sold. In the early period only the children of female slaves became slaves. Male domestic slaves were called *kano*, female domestic slaves were called *kabi*, and boy slaves were called *kadong*. Many conquered people, criminals, and some foreigners became slaves, and on some occasions, those members of the upper and middle classes who committed serious crimes became slaves.

During the Koryŏ period, a large number of Chinese immigrated to Korea and were naturalized, adding at least twenty more clan names to the Korean society. Among the Chinese clan names which become Koreanized were Chang, Chin, Pyŏn and Yŏ.

Although the population of Korea in the early eleventh century was reported to have been 2.1 million, this may not have been an accurate total. One source suggests that the total population could have been no less than 5 or 6 million. The adult population (ages between 15 and 60) of Kaegyŏng was reported to have been little over 300,000 of which some 8,500 were artisans.

Economic Life.   Although handicraft industries and foreign trade existed, Koryŏ was mainly an agrarian nation. The main agricultural products were rice, barley, millet, spices, ginseng, beans (soya, red and mung beans), and fruits. There were virtually no commercial establishments except in the capital city where an area of shops was established called *kyŏngshi*. Periodic markets called *hyangshi* were held throughout the country where goods were traded (bartered). Both in the capitals and other places, traveling peddlers played an important role in commercial transactions. Wealth was concentrated in the capital where the aristocratic bureaucrats and their families, along with the petty civil and military officials and their families, lived.

The most significant economic change was the establishment of state owner-ship of land, and the adoption of the Chinese system of land distribution called *kwajŏnpŏp*. Land grants made to the "merit subjects (*kongshin*)" and ranked civil and military officials, created absentee landlordism. Hereditary land grants were made to the "merit subjects," and land grants made to govern-ment officials according to their ranks were only for the duration of their tenure in office, and when they left the services or died, the land was returned to the state.

In 976, during the reign of King Kyŏngjong, and shortly thereafter, the system of land grant was modified, establishing a new system called *chŏn-shikwa*, or "grain-and-fuel land grant." It included the following categories: the hereditary land grants made to the meritorious subjects (*kong-ŭm chŏn-shikwa*); the grain-and-fuel land grants (*chŏnshikwa*) made to ranked govern-ment officials currently in office; *konghae chŏnshikwa* which were land grants made to government institutions and agencies, as well as local government units in order to defray expense with the income from the land; the salary land grants (*nokkwa chŏnshikwa*) made to minor officials; *sawŏn chŏnshikwa*, land grants made to Buddhist temples; and *kubunjŏn* which were given to retired officials, childless widows, and widows of civil and military officials.

During the reign of Munjong (reigned 1046–1083), eighteen categories of land grants were established, using the system of *kyŏl* as the official measure, *Kyŏl* refers to the quantity of grain produced on a parcel of land, not to the size of the parcel. The size of land grants for the highest ranking officials was set at 100 *kyŏl* of grain land and 70 *kyŏl* of fuel land, and the lowest ranks were given 21 *kyŏl* and 10 *kyŏl*, respectively. Miscellaneous officials received 15 *kyŏl* of grain land, and peasant-soldiers (*pubyŏng*) received a small amount of land at the age of twenty, and when they left the military at the age of sixty the land was returned to the government as was the case of land granted to other government officials. The landholders were absentee landlords, and their land was cultivated by peasants as tenant farmers who were supposed to pay one-tenth of the harvest as rent to the landlord, but who actually paid one-fourth.

With the rise of the nobility and the deterioration of government management, the number of large estates (*changwŏn*) grew, bringing the concentration of landholding into the hands of a smaller number of powerful families of *sadaebu*. Thus, despite the fact that private ownership of land was illegal, privately owned land increased in acreage, and land was bought, sold, and traded freely. There were some 360 large estates in the early twelfth century, and thousands of free peasants became serfs, bound to soil. All efforts made by the government to curtail the power of the nobility failed. The primogenitor entail system was to develop after 1392 following the establishment of the Yi dynasty. During the Koryŏ period property was divided among the children, including female children, more or less equally. Widows had rights of inheritance.

Manufacturing was largely in the hands of the government which established manufactories called *so* (places) throughout the country. These manufactories were engaged in the production of raw materials and gold, silver, iron, thread, silks, paper, ornaments, charcoal, salt, inkstone, oil, and ceramics. Public slaves contributed the bulk of workers at these manufactories; they had no freedom of movement and lived in designated places such as wards (*pugok*) and places (*so*).

Iron coins were minted in 996 during the reign of King Sŏngjong who encouraged the development of agriculture and improved land and water transportation. In 1097 brass-copper coins were minted, in 1101 silver money called *ŭnbyŏng* (silver urn in the shape of the Korean peninsula) was produced, and in 1102 new coins called *Haedong t'ongbo* were produced. Later, gold and silver coins and paper money were introduced and other kinds of coins were minted. But a cash economy as such did not develop although the circulation of coins increased.

The government collected several kinds of taxes. A land tax was imposed on all land except the land owned by the merit subjects, public land, temple land, and land granted to military families or widows. The land was classified into three grades according to its productive capacity, and one-tenth of the harvest was collected as land tax. A head tax was collected according to the number of taxable adults in the household. A corvée tax was paid by male adults of the lower class between the ages of sixteen and fifty-nine in various forms of service. A salt tax, a business tax, and tax on ships was also collected. All taxes, except the corvée tax, were primarily paid in goods. Various levies and special tribute were collected occasionally, and they were paid in goods produced locally.

The tax burden of the people steadily increased as the exploitation of peasants by landlords grew, and social unrest increased. In order to promote economic and social stability, King Sŏngjong of the late tenth century established two systems of government granary—the Charitable Storage (*Ŭich'ang*) and the Stabilizer Storage (*Sangp'yŏngch'ang*). The Charitable Storage was established to relieve the poor in times of severe food shortage and make grain loans to the peasants, and the stabilizer storage was established to stabilize the price of grains. This system, however, did not function as intended, and the poverty-stricken peasants suffered much as their tax burden became heavier and social unrest grew.

When cotton was introduced from China in 1363, cotton cultivation and the manufacturing of cotton cloth began. However, the production of linen (flax products) and silk remained the major textile industry carried out by the peasantry. Gunpowder which was introduced to Korea around 1370, led to the production of firearms, but it did not make any contribution to economic growth as such.

With the death in 847 of Chang Po-go of Shilla, who had established trading communities of the Koreans on the Shantung peninsula in China and built a commercial empire which dominated overseas trade, Korea's foreign trade declined sharply. However, trade between the Chinese merchants of the Sung and the Yuan periods continued, and the river ports of the Yesŏng River played an important role. Guest houses were built in the capital as well as in other places for diplomats and merchants from China. Meanwhile, trade increased with Liao in Manchuria. Korea's main export items were gold and silver utensils, raw copper, ginseng, hemp cloth, paper, inkstone, felt, and some goods traded with the Japanese, such as folding fans and swords. Korea imported tea, lacquerware, books, dye stuffs, and medicines. Be that as it may, foreign trade played an insignificant part in the Korean economy.

As economic activity and society simultaneously developed, the number of various guilds called *po* and public inns increased. A *po* was similar to a financial association, and some of them were money lending institutions. Even the Buddhist temples established such *po*. Some of them were commercial guilds, some of them were charitable *po*, and some *po* were established for the promotion of education.

Cultural Development

The complete Confucianization of Korea was achieved later, but the growing contact between Korea and China, Korea's adoption of Chinese political concepts and system, as well as the educational and civil service examination system

Printing blocks of the *Tripitaka Koreana* produced in the mid-13th century.

Nine-tiered, octagonal pagoda, Wŏl-chŏng Temple, Mt.Odae, Koryŏ period.

Gilt-bronze dragon-headed finial, Koryŏ period.

A celadon-glazed, porcelain incense burner, 12th century. Bronze ewer inlaid with silver, 12th century.

The *Muryangsu* Hall of the Pusŏk Temple. One of the oldest wooden building of Korea.

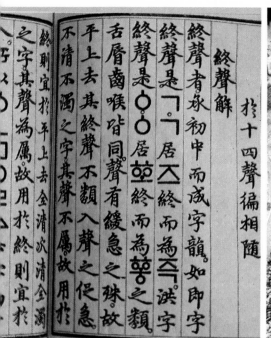

Hunmin chŏng-ŭm promulgated by King Sejong.

Water clock invented during the reign of King Sejong.

Kŭnjŏngjŏn (The Hall of Diligent Administration) of Kyŏngbok Palace.

White porcelain jar with a bamboo design of underglaze iron, 16th century.

Four-storied wooden cabinet with ox horn design

A weaponry displayed at Kanghwa Island, the target of naval assaults by the French in 1866 and again by the Americans in 1871.

The ironclad Turtle Ship constructed by Admiral Yi Sun-shin.

U.S. Marines from the *Colorado* after capturing Ch'ojijin Fortress on Kanghwa Island.

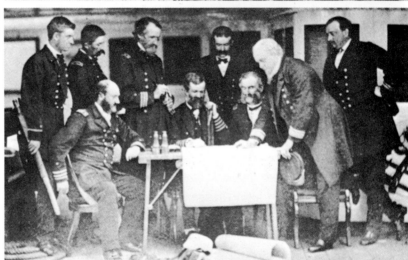

Admiral John Rodgers (seated, 2nd from left) at a war council.

Yi Ha-ŭng (Hŭngsŏn Taewŏn-gun, 1801-98).

A stone tablet warning against foreigners.

King Kojong

73

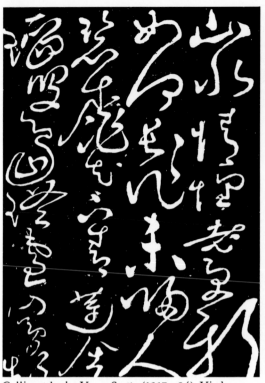

Calligraphy by Yang Sa-ŏn (1517–84), Yi dynasty.

"Goblin Playing with a Toad" by Shim Sa-jŏng (Hyŏnjae, 1707–69).

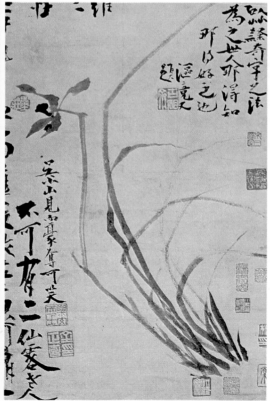

"A Sage at Rest on a Rock" by Kang Hŭi-an (Injae, 1419–64).

Painting of orchid by Kim Chŏng-hŭi (Ch'usa, 1786–1856).

"Village School *Sŏdang*" by Kim Hong-do (Tan-wŏn, 1760-?).

"The Diamond Mountains" by Chŏng Sŏn (Kyŏmjae, 1676-1759).

"Men and Female Entertainers Enjoying at the Pond" by Shin Yun-bok (Hyewŏn, 1758-?).   75

The first Korean goodwill mission of Korea sent to the United States in 1883.

First streetcar in Seoul, 1898.

The Independence Arch built in 1896.

A copy of *The Independent* and Philip Jaisohn.

brought about an inevitable evolution of Korean culture during the Koryŏ period. Meanwhile, Buddhism, which flourished in Paekche and Shilla, continued to grow strong in Korea as a state religion under government sponsorship. Shamanism continued to persist, but the mixture of Buddhistic, Taoistic, and Shamanistic concepts produced religious attitudes peculiar to the Koreans.

Buddhism of Koryŏ.   T'aejo made Buddhism the state religion of Korea, and many members of the royal clan themselves became prominent Buddhist monks. As *hoguk Pulgyo,* or "Buddhism for the Protection of the Nation," the influence of the Buddhist temple grew, and its monasteries and monks exerted enormous influence on politics, economy, and cultural and social development. In times of peace Buddhism played an important role in promoting the people's spiritual life and the welfare of the state, and in times of war, monk soldiers fought in defense of the nation. The Buddhist Lantern Festival (*Yŏndŭnghoe*) which was celebrated in the early spring, along with the Harvest Festival called *P'algwanhoe,* which honored the gods of heaven, the earth, the wind, and the rain in late fall, became the two most important national events.

Buddhism underwent a significant change, thanks to efforts made by Monk Ŭich'ŏn (1055–1101), who was the fourth son of King Munjong and brother of King Sŏngjong. He traveled to Sung China in 1085 where he studied not only various Buddhist thoughts, but also Confucianism and Taoism. After returning to Korea in early 1087, he first propagated the teachings of the *Ch'ŏnt'ae* (*T'ient'ai* in Chinese) sect, and then established a new sect named *Chogyejong,* uniting intellectualism of the *Sŏn* (*Zen* in Japanese) sect and popular Buddhism. It became and remained the dominant Buddhist sect in Korea. National Master Monk Ŭich'ŏn established an office in charge of compilation of Buddhist texts, and took charge of the newly constructed Hwaŏm monastery of Hŭngwang Temple of Kaegyŏng whose construction began during the reign of King Munjong.

In addition to Hŭngwang Temple, many other Buddhist temples and monasteries were constructed in Kaegyŏng as well as throughout the country. One of them was Kukch'ŏng Temple, built in 1097. A Chinese visitor described Kaegyŏng as the capital of Buddhism where more than seventy temples existed. The construction of enormous and magnificent Buddhist temples and monasteries promoted architectural skills as well as Buddhist painting. A hierarchy of Buddhist monks was established, and renowned monks were given the title of *kuksa* or *wangsa* ("national master" or "royal master"). Many members of the royal clan and families of the nobility, as well as sons of poor families became monks. In 1059, a law was promulgated to curtail the number of sons of poor families becoming monks.

Buddhist temples became large landholders and centers for Buddhist learning. The temple land was cultivated by peasants who were tenant farmers, as well as slaves owned by Buddhist temples and monasteries. A large amount of liquor was produced at the monasteries.

To be sure, the printing of Buddhist texts began in the eighth century, but it was the Buddhist temple of the Koryŏ period which produced an enormous number of printing blocks for the publication of Buddhist scriptures. The carving of the first set of Buddhist canon, *Tripitaka (Taejanggyŏng)* was undertaken as an act of faith in order to receive the protection of the Buddha when the Khitans invaded Korea in the eleventh century. Unfortunately, these wooden blocks were destroyed during the Mongol invasion of 1232. The second set of *Tripitaka Koreana* of 81,137 wooden blocks was completed in 1251 while the Koryŏ court was in exile on Kanghwa Island. These wooden blocks are today preserved in the monastery of Haein Temple on Mt. Kaya, near Taegu.

Educational and Intellectual Development.   Ch'oe Sŭng-no, a Confucian scholar who was associated with the establishment of a central bureaucracy patterned after the Confucian system of China, stated that Buddhism was for cultivation of the self for the future world while Confucianism was for regulating the state affairs of the present. T'aejo had already established a school in Kaegyŏng and another one in Sŏgyŏng to educate the sons of the nobility, and as the Chinese influence increased, Korean educational and scholarly activities grew rapidly.

The adoption of the Chinese civil service examination system in 958 by King Kwangjong marked a significant point in the development of Korean education. In 992, in order to produce more educated élites for the government, the government established a national academy called Kukchagam in Kaegyŏng. The academy had six divisions: three related to Confucian studies, and the others related to law, administration (office management), and mathematics. The sons of officials of the highest three ranks went to the first division called *kukcha,* those of the fourth and fifth ranks attended the second division which was called *T'aehak,* and those of the sixth and seventh ranks were enrolled in the third division called *Samunhak.* The sons of all ranks of unranked low grade officials were able to attend other divisions which trained petty government functionaries. Meanwhile, during the reign of King Sŏngjong in the late tenth century, a Confucian master and a master in medicine were dispatched to each district (*mok*) in order to promote education in local regions. A royal library called *Pisŏsŏng* (later *sasŏsŏng*) was established in Kaegyŏng along with the Susŏwŏn, which published books in Sŏgyŏng. Many books were imported from China.

The civil service examinations were given in three categories: the *chinsa* division in poetry and belles-lettres; the *myŏnggyŏng* division in the Confucian classics; and the miscellaneous division in medicine, astrology, mathematics, and geomancy. At the end of the tenth century, the metropolitan examination system (often called the royal examination) was established for advanced scholars (those who had earned the first degrees). After 958, civil examinations were administered 252 times, and 6,718 candidates passed various examinations.

While the government promoted education, individual scholars (both current or retired government officials) established private academies and promoted Confucian learning. Among them was Ch'oe Ch'ung (984–1068), who was known as the "Korean Confucius" (*Haedong Kongja*). He was previously a high ranking government official who established a private academy in Kaegyŏng which had nine divisions of studies. Eleven other private academies existed in Kaegyŏng, and they all enjoyed higher prestige than that of the national academy, producing more candidates who passed the civil service examination.

The rise of the number and the prestige of private academies led the government to reorganize its educational system at the end of the eleventh and in the early twelfth centuries, hoping to expand and elevate the educational standards of government schools in the capital (*kyŏnghak*) as well as those in local regions (*hyanghak*). It was at this time that the seventh division (military studies) was added to the curriculum of the national academy along with a new school for medical studies. For better or for worse, the military division was abolished during the reign of King Injong (reigned 1122–1146), who established a scholarship foundation named the "Treasury for Nourishing Wisdom" (*Yanghyŏn-go*).

The rise of public and private educational institutions and the growth of the number of students, coupled with the publication of Buddhist texts, brought about the publication of many books thereby promoting scholarship. The compilation of the dynastic history of Koryŏ began in 1013 during the reign (1009–1031) of Hyŏnjong, and a 36-volume history was published. However, it was destroyed by the Khitans who invaded Korea in the early eleventh century.

Among the historical works published were Kim Pu-shik's *Samguk sagi* (*Historical Records of the Three Kingdoms*), published in 1145, and Monk Iryŏn's *Samguk yusa* (*Historical Anecdotes of the Three Kingdoms*), published in 1285. These two works became the two most important historical sources for the study of the Three Kingdoms period.

During the period when the Koryŏ court was in exile on Kanghwa Island, the Koreans produced the world's first movable metal type printing press and published, in 1234, a 50-volume *Detailed Text for Rites of the Past and Present* authored by Ch'oe Yun-ŭi (1102–1162).

Architecture.   Most buildings and temples which were built during the early Koryŏ period were destroyed by the invaders. However, the three remaining wooden structures which were constructed in the fourteenth century show the taste and skills of the time; there are two Buddhist halls at the Pusŏk Temple and one at the Sudŏk Temple. The Hŭngwang Temple in Kaegyŏng, which was destroyed along with many palace buildings, was said to have been a splendid architectural work with the gold and silver pagodas. The marble pagoda of

the Kyŏngch'ŏn monastery which was built in 1348 is, along with the
buildings of the Pusŏk and Sudŏk temples, an excellent example of Koryŏ architecture.

Arts.   The paintings and sculptures of Koryŏ, like those of late Shilla, were
associated with Buddhism. While the artisans produced numerous statues of
Buddhas and Bodhisattvas, along with elegant pagodas, the carvers produced
many title plaques of the Buddhist sutras with ivory, bone, and wood on which
exquisite figures of Buddhas and Bodhisattvas were carved. The painters of the
period left such murals as those on the walls of the Sudŏk and Pusŏk temples.
Meanwhile, the art of Chinese-style landscape painting developed.

Koryŏ Celadon.   Perhaps the greatest cultural achievement of Koryŏ was its
ceramic art. The potters of Koryŏ improved the technology of pottery making,
and produced the artistic and elegant Koryŏ celadon, *ch'ŏngja* or "green
celadon" ware. The Chinese influence was always present, but Korean artists
were able to demonstrate their creativity and innovativeness. The Koryŏ
celadon ware provides indisputable evidences of that fact. The "restless inven-
tiveness" of the potters of Koryŏ at such kilns as Puan and Kangjin brought
about a remarkably high degree of achievement in ceramic art represented by
masterpieces of *sanggam* green celadon ware of exquisite color and quality, as
well as bronze wares inlaid with silver, with willow tree, lotus and floral, and
other designs. Celadon wares in the shape of a melon, bamboo shoot, and egg-
plant were uniquely Korean accomplishments. The halcyon glaze of Koryŏ
wares was described by Korean poets as having "the radiance of jade. . . the
crystal clarity of water. . . as if the artists had borrowed the secret from
heaven." A Korean poet glorified the beauty, elegance, and quality of Korean
celadon, as well as the soul of the Koreans embodied in Koryŏ celadon wares in
his poem entitled *Koryŏ Celadon*, which said in part:

> *Bluish green with subtle lines,*
> *O supple smooth curving,*
> *Like a Bodhisattva's shoulders.*
> *Grace and elegance combined.*
>
> *   *   *
>
> *Depth of color, softly shaded;*
> *Iridescent kingfisher;*
> *Blue sky glimpsed through autumn clouds*
> *As the rain squall passes on;*
> *on a white cloud, fresh with dew*
> *Winds its way on high.*
>
> *Pressed designs of clouds and waves,*
> *Inlaid gems and Seven Treasures,*

White cranes standing among flowers,
Buddhist figures, lines of verse;
Work of craftsman and of painter,
Art of sculptor in crude clay.
But awake!—for this is Koryŏ celadon,
This was ours for a thousand years.

The potters of Koryŏ also produced brown wares of elegant quality and style as if they were competing with the potters of the bygone days of Shilla, and they also produced a large quantity of unglazed ware, as well as white and black ware. However, the Mongol invasion in the middle of the thirteenth century destroyed the Koryŏ ceramic art almost completely as many kilns were destroyed and potters were either killed or taken captive to China. Thus the secrets of Koryŏ celadon jealously guarded by certain families of potters were totally lost.

Music and Dance.   During the Koryŏ period, the cultural tradition of Paekche and Shilla was further developed. Buddhism had lost its creative qualities and the lucidity of the Shilla period, but the adoption of Buddhism as a state religion, together with an increasing amount of cultural borrowing from the Chinese brought about the growth of religious music and dance as well as court music and dance known as the *Tang-ak* or *aak*. The establishment of the Lantern Festival (*Yŏndŭnghoe*), and the restoration of the Harvest Festival (*P'algwanhoe*) of Shilla as national events brought about the rapid development of the art of music and dance. In addition, the rise of the *kisaeng* (*geisha* in Japanese) culture also contributed to the development of certain forms of music and dance. *Kisaeng* were young women of beauty with skills in music, dance, and poetry who were employed as entertainers on various occasions. These developments brought about a further flourishing of the art of music and dance known as *kamugiak* (*kabuki* in Japanese) which grew during the Three Kingdoms period.

The Lantern Festival was held in the early spring to celebrate the birth of Buddha, and the Harvest Festival, a mixture of Buddhist and earlier religious (Shamanistic) traditions, was held in autumn. A dance known as the Ch'ŏyong Dance was performed at the Harvest Festival accompanied by singing of a shaman song of Shilla named *The Song of Ch'ŏyong*. In the Grand Festival of One Hundred Seats, some 30,000 Buddhist monks and 4,000 musicians participated. Meanwhile, mask dances such as the Lion Dance (*Sajamu*, or *Sajach'um*), became popular.

Poetry.   As Chinese cultural influence grew, the study of Chinese poetry and the writing of Chinese-style poems developed in Korea, and Chinese poets such as Li Po (Yi T'ae-baek in Korean) and Tu fu (Tu Po in Korean) became popular among the educated writers of Chinese-style poems known in Korea as the *Hanshi*.

A significant aspect in the development of Korean culture during the latter part of the Koryŏ period was the rise of new forms of poetry called *shijo*, or "occasional verses" and *changga*, or "long songs." Love themes which were frankly expressed in songs and poems constituted a marked difference between the poetry of Koryŏ and that of Shilla. Some representative ones are introduced below.

The *shijo*, which developed toward the end of the thirteenth century, became the major mode of expression of the Korean soul. A *shijo* consists of three lines, and the total number of syllables cannot exceed forty-five. Generally, the syllables in each line are arranged as follows:

> First line: 3 4 3 and 4
> Second line: 3 4 3 and 4
> Third line: 3 5 4 and 3

An unidentified *kisaeng* wrote a poem entitled "The Turkish Bakery" in the late thirteenth century or early fourteenth century, saying:

> *I go to the Turkish shop, buy a bun.*
> *An old Turk grasps me by the hand.*
> *If this story is spread abroad,*
> *You alone are to blame, little doll on the shelf.*
> *I will go, yes, go to his bower;*
> *A narrow place, sultry and dark.*
>
> *I go to the Samjang Temple, light the lantern.*
> *A chief priest grasps me by the hand.*
> *If this story is spread abroad,*
> *You alone are to blame, little altar boy;*
> *I will go, yes, go to his bower;*
> *A narrow place, sultry and dark.*
>
> *I go to the tavern, buy the wine.*
> *An innkeeper grasps me by the hand.*
> *If this story is spread abroad,*
> *You alone are to blame, O wine jug.*
> *I will go, yes, go to his bower;*
> *A narrow place, sultry and dark.*

U T'ak (1262–1342), a scholar who promoted the *shijo* form of Korean poetry, wrote the following piece:

> *East winds that melt the mountain snow*
> *Come and go, without words.*

Blow over my head, young breeze,
Even for a moment, blow.
Would that you could blow away the gray hairs
That grow so fast around my ears!

*   *   *

Sticks in one hand,
Branches in another:
I try to block old age with bushes,
And frosty hair with sticks:
But white hair came by a short cut,
Having seen through my devices.

Chŏng Mong-ju, a highly respected scholar-official, who was assassinated when he refused to serve the ruler who established a new dynasty in 1392, wrote the following *shijo:*

Whether I do die a hundred times over,
And all my bones turn into dust,
And my soul departs from my body,
Yet my loyalty for my Lord
Shall not perish.

The Appearance of Tales.   When the influence of military officials grew many intellectuals left government services. Among them were Yi Il-lo (1152–1220) and Lim Ch'un who were two of the outstanding literary figures known as the "Seven Sages of Bamboo Grove." It was this group of literary men who, in the twelfth century, promoted *p'aegwan* literature. *P'aegwan* were literary men who were appointed by the king to collect popular stories which reflected the people's conditions. These and other literary men also wrote popular tales in prose form, promoting *p'aegwan* literature which continued to develop in the succeeding centuries. Stories collected in Yi Il-lo's *P'ahanjip*, the *Paegun sosŏl* by Yi Kyu-bo (1168–1241), and tales produced in the thirteenth century by Yi Che-hyŏn (1287–1367) and collected in the *Yŏgong p'aesŏl* were typical examples of *p'aegwan* literature.

Meanwhile, allegorical stories personifying material objects, such as paper, money, wine, as well as turtles and tadpoles, became popular. Among these stories was the *Table of Master Yeast*, written by Lim Ch'un in which wine is personified.

Other Cultural Changes.   The Mongol domination and the marriage between the Koryŏ kings and the members of the royal clan and the Mongol women brought about a variety of cultural changes, as well as changes in social customs. First of all, the study of the Mongolian language grew among the official class members. Mongol words were Koreanized, and many upper class people adopted Mongolian-style names. Official costumes and hair style became Mongolianized, and music and dance of the Mongols were introduced. Islam was introduced by some Mongolian officials, but it did not grow.

A significant change in Korean social customs was the growth of child marriage. The parents of young girls married off their daughters in early age as a means of preventing their daughters from being taken to China as part of the annual tribute in which thousands of young Korean girls were taken away from towns and villages, and they became concubines of the Mongols.

Political Maladies and Social Upheavals

The Growth of Disunity.   Despite her brilliant cultural achievements, Korea's internal equilibrium was upset when political and economic conditions failed to improve. The "cyclic phenomenon," similar to that of China, seemed to be occurring in Korean history. Economic and social problems were destined to develop owing to an unbalanced distribution of wealth, the usurpation of power by the nobility, and the rigidly enforced class system. Although the Confucian civil service examination system (*kwagŏ*) was theoretically open to all, as in China, it tended to become a channel almost exclusively for those who already possessed power and privilege.

The growth of power of the nobility brought about the disintegration of the official land grant system when an increasing number of salary lands became privately owned by the nobility and as the number of manors (*changwŏn*) tilled by slaves and peasants grew rapidly. Many Buddhist temples became large landowners. With this trend, nearly all of the farming population became landless peasants and the number of agricultural slaves grew. All efforts made by the kings to curtail the power of the nobility failed.

Widespread poverty, plus mismanagement of the government and usurpation of privileges by the nobility, led the poverty-stricken and mistreated people finally to riot and then to rebel against both the government and the nobility. As the leadership of the Wang clan deteriorated, conflict increased between the civil and military officials, as did the power struggle among high ranking officials. Bloody coups in the capital were matched in intensity by local riots and uprisings.

Serious domestic, economic, and social, as well as foreign problems were compounding, but the political leaders were by and large either indifferent or insensitive to those issues. They were mainly concerned with gaining power and wealth, pursuing their selfish interests while paying scant attention to national issues. As noted earlier, the Koryŏ kings of the early period experienced difficulties in establishing the firm monarchical power, and numerous bloody incidents had already occurred in the tenth century.

Early in the eleventh century, the queen dowager, in collusion with her paramour Kim Ch'i-yang, attempted to depose King Mokchong (reigned

997-1009) and enthrone her son. Kim Ch'i-yang already had a considerable amount of power. When the king became aware of the plot, he solicited the aid of a military leader, Kang Cho, in Sŏgyŏng. Kang mobilized his troops, attacked the capital, and after killing Kim and sending the queen dowager into exile, he deposed the king and enthroned a new king, Hyŏnjong (reigned 1009-1031). Soon thereafter, King Mokchong was assassinated by Kang's men.

Political conditions continued to deteriorate and social unrest grew. Meanwhile, Kang Cho, who took an army of 300,000 troops against the Khitans, was badly defeated at the Battle of T'ongju (now Sŏnch'ŏn); he was captured and beheaded. Outer walls were constructed surrounding the capital and improving the defense of the city, but the internal conflict between the civil officials and the military officials brought about more bloody events which worsened the political situation. Following the rebellion of Yi Cha-gyŏm in 1126, there was not a single year between 1160 and 1389 which did not witness serious political or social disturbances.

The Yi Cha-gyŏm's Coup d'État. Like the Kim clan of Ansan which in the late eleventh century enjoyed power and wealth for fifty years by installing its female members as king's consorts, the influence of the Yi clan of Kyŏngwŏn grew strong in the early twelfth century and dominated the Koryŏ court for eight years, thanks to efforts made by Yi Cha-gyŏm and his father. Yi Cha-gyŏm's second daughter was King Yejong's queen, and his third and fourth daughters were queens of King Injong (reigned 1122-1146). After putting Injong on the throne, Yi occupied several key government posts concurrently, and many of his clan members became important officials in the central government. The king was their puppet.

The king, resentful of Yi Cha-gyŏm's usurpation of power, attempted to eliminate Yi's power in cooperation with those who were hostile to Yi. Detecting the plot to overthrow his power, Yi himself carried out a palace coup in 1126, burning down many palace buildings, including the royal library, and killing most of his enemies. Yi Cha-gyŏm could have overthrown the Koryŏ dynasty, but he was content with his power over the government, perhaps because of the threat of the Chin state which arose in north China. New challengers, most of whom came from the northwestern region, emerged against Yi, and he was overthrown in 1127 and died in exile.

The fall of the Yi clan's dominance fostered neither the unity within the government, nor social harmony in the kingdom. Those who overthrew Yi themselves were ousted in 1128.

The Rebellion of Myoch'ŏng. A Buddhist monk, Myoch'ŏng, who had a considerable amount of influence in the Sŏgyŏng region, told King Injong to move his capital from Kaegyŏng to Sŏgyŏng, saying that the site of Kaegyŏng lost its beneficent forces, and if Sŏgyŏng was made the new capital the dynasty would prosper and the nation's security would be improved. He also urged the king to declare himself emperor and attack Chin. Myoch'ŏng may have believed in geomancy, but he might have had ulterior motives also.

When the king refused to follow his suggestions, and when the officials in Kaegyŏng, including Kim Pu-shik, regarded Myoch'ŏng punishable for his treason, Myoch'ŏng raised an army and rebelled in the northwestern region against the government in 1135. With this, he proclaimed a new kingdom called Taewi. The Koryŏ court ordered Kim Pu-shik to subjugate the rebels, and after beheading many collaborators of Myoch'ŏng in Kaegyŏng, Kim Pu-shik marched on to Sŏgyŏng. Myoch'ŏng was assassinated by his own military commanders who betrayed him with the hope of gaining pardon. Sŏgyŏng fell to the loyalists, Myoch'ŏng's commanders were killed, and the rebellion ended in the spring of 1136.

Conflict Between the Civil and Military Officials.   One of the most serious problems of Koryŏ was the conflict between civil and military officials. There had already been a military rebellion in the early eleventh century during the reign of King Hyŏnjong. This conflict reached a critical point as military officials were treated with disrespect and contempt by civil officials. In the end, a rebellion of military officials came in 1170 under General Chŏng Chung-bu. King Ŭijong (reigned 1146–1170) led a luxurious and licentious life and during his reign eunuchs and diviners gained his favor and exercised political influence and the decline of the prestige of the military officials reached a climax.

Chŏng Chung-bu deposed and banished King Ŭijong to Kŏje Island, and the crown prince was banished to Chindo Island, and a new king, Myŏngjong (reigned 1170–1197), was installed. The rebels confiscated the property of the court and the civil officials, as well as that of the monasteries, and divided it among themselves. After putting military officials in key government positions, Chŏng and his collaborators exercised arbitrary and oppressive power.

In 1173, a military official from the northeastern region raised an army against Chŏng Chung-bu in support of the banished king. However, his efforts failed, and many more officials and the exiled king himself were killed. Another revolt against Chŏng's group came in 1174, but it was crushed immediately. Chŏng Chung-bu appointed himself chief minister, and his son eliminated several military officials who were potential challengers to power. In 1179, a general killed Chŏng and overthrew his clique. However, this did not restore peace and political stability.

Uprisings of the Peasants and Slaves.   Exploited and suffering peasants and slaves rebelled frequently here and there, seeking relief. In the early spring of 1176, a large-scale uprising of the *ch'ŏnmin* erupted at a government manufactory near Kongju in Yanggwang Province (present South Ch'ungch'ŏng Province). Several hundred government slaves attacked and took over the cities of

Kongju and Yesan.

Government troops were dispatched to subjugate the rebels, and an offer was made to raise the level of *so* to a regular prefecture, thereby improving the social status of the inhabitants. But the rebels did not accept the government offer, and sought better treatment. Meanwhile, the rebellion spread into other areas in the province, as well as into the neighboring province. The rebellion of the slaves was crushed when its leader was killed, but the social unrest of the suffering people continued to grow.

A peasant uprising in the Sŏgye which began in 1177 was crushed two years later, but a rebellion of soldiers and slaves at a shipyard at Chŏnju erupted in 1182 and caused much property damage and the loss of life. In 1198, the plot of the slaves in Kaegyŏng to kill government officials and burn the government slave records was discovered, and the conspirators were put to death. However, it, like other rebellions, clearly reflected the discontentment of the slaves and peasants throughout the country. Then, in 1199, the peasant uprising erupted in the Kangnŭng area in Tonggye (now Kangwŏn Province), and in other uprisings of the 1194–1199 period, more than 30,000 peasants in Kyŏngju and other parts of Kyŏngsang Province actively rebelled. In 1200, slave uprisings at various government manufactories brought about the death of thousands of petty local officials. The slave uprising of the Miryang area inflicted the most severe damage to government manufactories and caused the death of many petty officials and others.

The Military Dictatorship of the Ch'oe Clan.   In 1196, a military commander, Ch'oe Ch'ung-hŏn (d. 1218), carried out a palace coup, killed Chŏng Chung-bu, deposed the king (Myŏngjong), banished all Buddhist monks from the palace, and eliminated many of his opponents, including his own brother. After that, he established a military dictatorship, and the reign of terror of the Ch'oe clan lasted some sixty years until 1258. He was power hungry and ambitious, but he was not bold enough to take further steps to overthrow the Koryŏ dynasty and establish a new one of the Ch'oe clan.

After seizing power, Ch'oe Ch'ung-hŏn installed the new king (Shinjong, reigned 1197–1204), and in 1209 he established the Supreme Directorate called *Kyojŏng togam* (commonly called *chŏngbang*) and a military council named *chungbang*. His residence became the seat of the power. During his reign of terror, he deposed three kings and installed four on the throne. He was succeeded by his son, Ch'oe U, and the dictatorship continued. The Ch'oes could have established a military government similar to the Shogunate (*Bakufu*) in Japan which emerged in 1185. Perhaps, the invasions of the Mongols in 1231 prevented the rise of a full-fledged Shogunate-type military regime in Korea.

The second dictator returned land and slaves confiscated by his father to their former owners in an attempt to forestall plots and rebellions, and he employed some Confucian scholars and civil officials in the private government of the

Ch'oe clan. The kings had no authority to rule the kingdom and his ministers had nothing to do. The military arm of the Ch'oe dictatorship put the kingdom under its control, and it subjugated uprisings of the slaves and peasants of the late twelfth and early thirteenth centuries.

When the Mongols invaded Korea in 1231, the Ch'oe dictatorship organized the defense, but Ch'oe U could not resist the invaders and sued for peace. Then, in the summer of 1232, the court, the government, the Ch'oe's councils, and a large number of the population of Kaegyŏng fled to Kanghwa Island in defiance of the Mongols. The war with the Mongols continued.

Meanwhile, King Kojong (reigned 1213–1259) gained the support of more loyalists, and in 1258, they managed to assassinate Ch'oe Ŭi, the last dictator of the Ch'oe dictatorship, bringing sixty years of Ch'oe rule to an end. Following this, the Koryŏ government made peace with the Mongols and sent the crown prince to the Mongol court as hostage.

When King Kojong died, his son took the throne as King Wŏnjong (reigned 1259–1274). But he encountered another military coup which deposed the King. King Wŏnjong was restored to the throne with the help of the Mongols, and in 1270 the court returned to Kaegyŏng as the influence of military officials declined sharply.

The Koryŏ court which returned to Kaegyŏng was completely dominated by the Mongols. All crown princes were sent to the Mongol court as hostages, Koryŏ kings married Mongol princesses, and politics were manipulated by the court ladies and eunuchs. Meanwhile, the Mongol emperor established a state of the Koreans in southwestern Manchuria, where several thousands of Korean families resided, and installed members of the royal clan of Koryŏ as kings.

The Rebellion of Sambyŏlch'o.   When the Koryŏ king capitulated to the Mongols and moved back to Kaegyŏng, the leaders of the three special military units which had guarded Kanghwa Island refused to obey the royal order to disband their units, and under the leadership of Pae Chung-son they brought about what is known as the Rebellion of *Sambyŏlch'o* against the government and the Mongols. In order to strengthen their political position, the rebels moved to the island of Chindo, off the southwest coast of Chŏlla Province, and set up a rebel government there. In 1271, a combined force of Koryŏ and Mongol troops forced the rebels to flee to Cheju Island where they constructed a fortification. However, the Mongols invaded the island, and in 1273 they crushed the rebels, ending Korea's resistance to the Mongols.

External Problems and Wars

Korea and the Khitans.   The Koryŏ dynasty encountered the challenge of the Khitans from the beginning. The chieftain of the Khitans in southwest Manchuria, named Yehlu Apaochi, declared himself emperor of the Khitans in 916 and invaded Korea, and in 927 conquered the state of Parhae in the north-eastern region of the Korean Peninsula. With this, a state of Eastern Khitan was set up in that region, and the Khitans threatened the security of Korea itself. The Koryŏ government strengthened its national defense by raising an army of 300,000 men. Meanwhile, the Khitans established the state of Liao in Manchuria and north China in 947.

In 983 and 985, the Khitans overran the Jurcheds in south Manchuria along the Yalu River, and as the Sung dynasty extended in territory northward to Peking, the Khitans sought an alliance with Korea. When the Korean government ignored their request while increasing its own contacts with the Sung court, the Khitans in October 993, launched an attack against Korea with some 800,000 troops. The Khitans who advanced as far as the Ch'ŏngch'ŏn River area demanded that Korea surrender the former Parhae territory which she had taken over from the Khitans, cease relations with Sung China, and accept tributary status.

When the Korean court rejected these demands, the Khitans renewed their military actions against Korea. However, a long period of negotiation conducted by a Korean commander and a Khitan commander, combined with the Khitans feeling the growing pressure from the south, led in 994 to the Khitans abandoning their demands and establishing amicable relations between Korea and Liao. With this, the Koryŏ court temporarily suspended its contacts with the Sung government, and drove out the Jurcheds from the northwestern region.

In the early eleventh century, the Koryŏ court was embroiled in a power struggle and political turmoil. King Mokchong was assassinated in 1009. Taking advantage of the situation in the Korean capital, in 1010, the king of Liao himself arrived with 400,000 troops at the Korean border "in order to punish" the murderers of the king. The Korean army commanded by Kang Cho won the first battle at T'onggu (now Sŏnch'ŏn), but the Korean troops were defeated badly by the Khitans and Kang Cho was captured and executed. The Khitans besieged Sŏgyŏng, and the Korean court fled in panic to Naju in the south. The Khitans sacked the capital city of Kaegyŏng, and demanded, among other things, that Korea accept vassalage to Liao.

In order to pressure the Korean court to accept their demands, the Khitans initiated another military invasion in 1018, but they were badly defeated by the Korean troops under the command of an able general, Kang Kam-ch'an, in the Battle of Kwiju. The demolished Laio troops withdrew from Korea.

Korea and the Jurcheds.   The Jurcheds who arose in Manchuria occupied the northeastern region of the Korean peninsula, and in the early eleventh century they began to threaten Korean territories as their pirates plundered coastal towns in the eastern part of Korea. In 1104, the Koryŏ court dispatched two generals, Lim Kan and Yun Kwan, to subjugate the Jurcheds, but they were unable to do so. Yun said, excusing his defeat, that the "enemy rade horses and we walked. We were no match for them."

After raising a new army with cavalry units in 1107, the Koryŏ court sent Yun Kwan and another general with 170,000 troops against the Jurcheds, and the Korean troops defeated the Jurcheds and took over the area which is now known as South Hamgyŏng Province. With this, nine garrison towns, such as Hamju (now Hamhŭng), Yŏngju, Ungju, Kilchu, and Pokchu were established in the early conquered territory. However, the subsequent negotiations carried out between the Koryŏ court and the Jurcheds, when political instability developed in Kaegyŏng, led to the return of the conquered territory to the Jurcheds in 1109. Meanwhile, the Jurcheds in Manchuria established the state of Chin in 1115, and Chin in cooperation with Sung destroyed the Khitans' state of Liao in 1122.

The Mongol Invasions and Their Effect.   Korea's contact with the Mongols began when the Korean and Mongol forces attacked the Khitans in the early thirteenth century. Jinghiz Khan, who became the master over north China and Manchuria, sent an envoy to Korea demanding that Koryŏ send an enormous amount of tribute goods to the Mongols. The Korean government was not willing to accept the Mongol demand, and the Mongol envoy was killed near the Yalu River on his way back home. Ogadai, who succeeded Jinghiz Khan in 1227, sent an army in the autumn of 1231 against Korea, marking the beginning of the twenty-eight-year period during which wars were fought off and on between the Koreans and the Mongols. After taking northern cities, the Mongol force pushed southward, taking Kaegyŏng and the area south of the Kyŏnggi Province.

After forcing the Ch'oe dictatorship to sue for peace and after Korea's acceptance of a vassal status, the Mongols demanded that Korea provide 10,000 otter skins, 20,000 horses, 10,000 bolts of silk, and a vast amount of clothing for the Mongol soldiers. To see that their demands were carried out and that Korea would not renew the war against them, over seventy Mongol officials were stationed in the principal cities of Korea. Korea met these demands, but in the summer of 1232 the royal court and the government, the Ch'oe's councils, and a large number of the population of Kaegyŏng fled to Kanghwa Island in defiance of the Mongols.

In the winter of 1232, the Mongols re-invaded Korea, and occupied the area north of the Han River. When the commander of the Mongol army was killed by a Korean archer, the Mongol troops withdrew from Korea, only to return in 1235, and inflict devastation, including the destruction of numerous historic architectural masterpieces such as the Hwangnyong Temple's nine-story pagoda in Kyŏngju. A truce was concluded between Korea and the Mongols, which lasted until 1247. In 1254 a new war began, and another truce was signed in 1259. Korea became a vassal to the Mongols, the Korean crown prince was sent to the Mongol court as hostage, and in 1270 the Koryŏ court returned to Kae-gyŏng. After the capitulation of Korea to the Mongols, no posthumous reign-ing title of *chong* was given to the Korean kings following the death of King Wŏnjong in 1274. From that time, the title of the Korean ruler was degraded to *wang* (王, "king"), symbolizing the lower status of Korean rulers in relation to the Mongol rulers whose titles were either *tsung* or *ti* (emperor). The marriage of the Korean crown prince (later Ch'ungnyŏl Wang, reigned 1274–1308) to a Mongol princess, strengthened the ties between Korea and China of the Yuan dynasty, which the Mongols established in 1271. Many members of the Korean royal clan married Mongol princesses, and many Korean women became con-sorts of the Mongol rulers and others.

The effects of the Mongol invasions were disastrous. In one invasion in 1254 alone, the Mongols carried away over 200,000 captives from Korea after killing twice that number. Korea sent an enormous amount of tribute goods annually to the Mongol court. These tribute goods included gold, silver, grains, a large number of women and falcons. As a result, the economic and social conditions of Korea worsened. When the Mongol soldiers occupied the southern part of Korea, they inflicted severe and irreparable damages to the Koreans' cultural treasures. Printing blocks, palace buildings, Buddhist temples and pagodas, and many historical documents, along with many kilns where the renowned Koryŏ celadon wares were manufactured, were destroyed.

The Mongols further weakened Korea when they forced the Koreans to pro-vide, in addition to food and other supplies, 900 war vessels, 30,000 soldiers, marines, carpenters and other laborers for their disastrous attempts to conquer Japan in 1274 and 1281. Several thousand Korean soldiers died in the Mongols' vain attempts to conquer Japan.

The Japanese Piracy.   Korea's east coast and Ullŭng Island had been raided by the Jurchen pirates in the eleventh century, and her southern coast and islands were raided by Chinese and Korean pirates in the twelfth century. However, the damage done by the Japanese pirates, commonly called the *wakō*, in the thirteenth century had far reaching economic effects.

The piracy of the Japanese in the Korean waters began in 1223, and several teams of pirates (some of them Chinese and Koreans) scourged the Korean coasts, plundering coastal towns as well as inland villages. Hundreds of Koreans were taken captive, and many villages were burned down. In 1366, the Japanese pirates raided the area near Kaegyŏng. Between the period of 1375 and 1388, the Japanese piracy reached the peak when 378 raids were made against Korea.

In order to deal with the Japanese pirates, a military official Ch'oe Mu-sŏn had the government establish a Bureau of Armament in 1377, authorizing the manufacturing of a variety of firearms, including cannons, and building ships equipped with cannons to fight the Japanese pirates. Ships built by Ch'oe Mu-sŏn were said to have sunk or damaged some 500 Japanese pitate ships in a battle near the mouth of the Kŭm River in the southeast. In 1389, some 100 Korean armed ships attacked the base of the Japanese pirates at Tsushima, and sank some 300 ships. But the problem of Japanese piracy was not eliminated.

The Demise of the Koryŏ Dynasty

New civil officials such as Chŏng Mong-ju, Yi Saek, and Yi Sung-in who were highly respected scholars, and new military leaders such as Yi Sŏng-gye, Ch'oe Yŏng, and Ch'oe Mu-sŏn emerged in the middle of the fourteenth century. But the decline of the ruling dynasty and the kingdom was beyond repair. As the twilight of the Koryŏ dynasty approached rapidly, a total of eleven kings (two of them were on the throne twice) came and went between 1308 and 1392, creating a greater political instability. Meanwhile, Korea faced serious external problems.

External Problems.   1359 and 1361, Korea was invaded by the Chinese rebels known as the Red Banner bandits from north China. They sacked and burned the capital, forcing the Koryŏ court again to flee to Kanghwa Island. Although the Red Banner bandits were repelled in 1362, signs of the time clearly indicated that the end of the Koryŏ kingdom was at hand.

After the Chinese overthrew the Yuan dynasty of the Mongols in China in 1368, the Korean king adopted anti-Mongol (pro-Ming) policy and attempted to regain his power and the territory which had been lost. The Koryŏ army under General Chi Yong-su fought against the Mongols and regained some territory which Koguryŏ once had possessed, but Korea was unable to retain the Liao region in Manchuria when the Ming force arrived. Meanwhile, General Yi Sŏng-gye conquered the northeastern region which had been controlled by the Jurcheds.

King Kongmin (reigned 1351–1374) was in despair following the death of his Mongol queen, and led a licentious life paying no attention to the affairs of the state; during this time he empowered a Buddhist monk named Shin Ton to manage the government affairs. Shin Ton was a monk of humble origin who was made National Master by King Kongmin, and he attempted to continue the reform measures, including the emancipation of slaves, which the king had inaugurated. However, his tactics backfired, and his opponents brought about his fall. He was exiled and later killed, while the king himself was assassinated by a eunuch.

When a boy king U (reigned 1374–1388), was enthroned, Yi In-im usurped power, adopting anti-Ming policy. The Koryŏ court was split into pro- and anti-Ming factions, and such outstanding Confucian scholar-officials as Chŏng Mong-ju (1337–1392), who opposed pro-Mongol policy were ousted. A new relationship between the Koryŏ court and the Mongols was established, and the

Chinese emissary to Korea was murdered on his way back to China by a Korean who was presumed to have been employed by Yi In-im.

In order to appease the Ming court, the Koryǒ court sent a goodwill mission to China, but they were given discourteous treatment. In the end, the Koryǒ court dispatched Chǒng Mong-ju to China in 1384, and he was able to restore friendly relations between Korea and China.

Political conditions in Korea did not improve as the power struggle, as well as policy disputes became intense. Yi In-im and his supporters were eliminated by Generals Ch'oe Yǒng and Yi Sǒng-gye, but conflict between the old and new leadership groups, as well as between conservatives (mostly pro-Mongol elements) and those who advocated reform measures (mostly pro-Ming elements) only became more bitter. Meanwhile, King U led a corrupt and licentious life as economic and social conditions deteriorated further.

General Yi Sǒng-gye's Coup d'État.   The territorial dispute that developed between Korea and China over a large amount of land in the northern and northeastern regions of Korea led the Koryǒ court to dispatch, in 1388, two large armies against the Ming forces in the Liaotung region in Manchuria. The Ming Court had claimed that since China took over former territories of Koguryǒ, the land which had been Koguryǒ's territory should belong to China. The two Korean armies were under commanders Yi Sǒng-gye and Cho Min-su.

General Yi's troops arrived at an island named Wihwa in the Yalu River in late spring of 1388. However, he believed that the fall of the Mongols was inevitable, and the war against Ming China was not justifiable. Thereby, he petitioned the court to withdraw the troops, and pointed out that it was the wrong season of the year to fight a war and that the Japanese might take advantage of the situation. When the Koryǒ court rejected his petition, Generals Yi and Cho ordered their troops back to Kaegyǒng, and after seizing the capital they carried out a palace coup.

The succession question broke the coalition of General Yi and General Cho, and Cho, with the support of a few, put a nine-year-old boy (King Ch'ang) on the throne, despite the objections raised by General Yi and his supporters. However, General Cho lost his control, and was ousted.

After removing General Cho from power, General Yi carefully eliminated his opponents one by one, and after installing a new king (Kongyang, reigned 1389–1392), he took drastic measures to revamp the political and economic affairs of the kingdom. Among important measures which he took was land reform which was aimed at the curtailment of the power of the owners of large amounts of private land, particularly that of the owners of large estates. In 1392, he usurped the throne, bringing the end of the Koryǒ dynasty. In the process of establishing a new dynasty of the Yi clan, many prominent scholar-officials, including Chǒng Mong-ju, as well as military leaders such as General Ch'oe Yǒng were killed.

4. The Yi Dynasty and a Confucianized Korea

The new kingdom called Chosŏn which Yi Sŏng-gye (1335–1408) established lasted for 519 years. A total of twenty-seven kings of the Yi dynasty ruled the kingdom, and at no time was the throne occupied by a queen.

Two most significant aspects of Korean history of the early Yi period were the establishment of China's suzerain lordship over Korea and Confucianization of the country. Immediately after Yi Sŏng-gye established his dynasty, he sought the approval of the Ming court of China for actions which he had taken, seeking the legitimacy of his own dynasty. But it was one of his sons, T'aejong (reigned 1400–1418), who was the third monarch, who received the recognition of the Ming court for the new kingdom and its ruling dynasty. With this, Ming China assumed suzerainty over Korea and the Yi dynasty pledged its loyalty to China as her vassal, establishing the Sino-Korean relations based on the principle of *sadae* ("subservience to big power"), which lasted until 1894. From this time until 1894, all Korean government documents were dated according to the reigning year of the Chinese emperor. The seals of Korean kings contained only Chinese characters until the 1620s and after that they also contained Manchu script, but no Korean script.

Korean kings were granted permission to use Chinese monarchical titles such as *cho* (*tsu* in Chinese) or *chong* (*tsung* in Chinese). Thus, Yi Sŏng-gye was given the posthumous title of T'aejo ("Great Progenitor"), and all monarchs of the Yi dynasty, with the exception of two who were regarded by official historians an "unworthy" kings, were known by Chinese monarchical titles, such as T'aejong or Sejo.

Sinification of certain systems and aspects of Korean culture began during the previous periods, and had increased during the Koryŏ period. With the establishment of the lord-vassal relationship with China and the adoption of Neo-Confucianism as its state creed, the Yi dynasty brought about a thorough Confucianization of Korea's politics and political structure, social thoughts and institutions, as well as its economic, intellectual, and cultural patterns. In the end, Korea became more Confucian than Confucian China as its influence permeated every aspect of the life of the nation.

The Kingdom of Chosŏn

The Government Structure   The government of the Yi dynasty was based upon Confucian precepts: the monarch was to be a benevolent ruler, the bureaucracy was to be his agent, manned by virtuous and wise officials, and the monarch was to rule the kingdom with the advice and consent of Confucian literati. It took several years for the founder and his successors to complete the construction of a Confucian political structure. The chief organ of the government was the Council of State (*Ŭijŏngbu*), consisting of a Chief Minister (*Yŏngŭijŏng*), the Minister of the Right (*Uŭijŏng*), and the Minister of the Left (*Chwaŭijŏng*). It was a policy deliberation council. The executive branch consisted of six ministries or boards (*cho*) of Personnel, Revenue, Rites, War, Justice, and Public Works. The Royal Secretariat (*Sŭngjŏngwŏn*), consisted of six officials, transmitted king's instructions, and Ŭigŭmbu functioned as the highest judicial organ. Three other government organs which played vital roles were the Board of Censors (*Saganwŏn*), the Board of Inspectors (*Sahŏnbu*), and the Office of the Royal Lecturers(*Hongmun-gwan*). These three organs were commonly called *samsa*. An office in charge of the publication of Confucian texts also performed an important role in the politics of the Yi dynasty.

The government officials were divided into the "Eastern Branch" (*Tongban*) of civil officials and the "Western Branch" (*Sŏban*) of military officials: hence the emergence of the *yangban* ("two branches") class of the scholar-officials in Korea. The Yi dynasty maintained the supremacy of civil over military officials at all times. Although only 820 of some 4,820 government posts were held in 1410 by civil officials, the supremacy of the civil branch was unchallenged. The ruling bureaucrats were collectively called *sadaebu*. There were nine ranks (*p'um*) of bureaucrats, and each rank was divided into senior (*chŏng*) and junior (*chong*) groups, making up a total of eighteen grades.

The New Capital.   T'aejo decided to move the government from Kaegyŏng to Hanyang (also known as Hansŏng) in order to free politics from the old nobility and the influence of the Buddhist church. Although its name had been changed several times, it had been a key town during the Three Kingdoms period. It became a strategic place of Koguryŏ after 313. Shilla took it from Koguryŏ in 569, and the Koryŏ dynasty built summer palaces there and made it the southern capital. T'aejo's plan for a new capital reflected his grand design for a new kingdom and his ambition to construct a strong nation worthy of the new dynasty of the Yi clan, which he hoped would last forever.

The selection of the site for the new capital involved geomancy. The new capital, which has been commonly called Seoul, which means "capital" in Korean, faced the south across the Han River and it was protected by the Samgak, Pibong, Inwang and other northern mountains which surrounded the basin. Seoul was a replica of the ancient Chinese capital, Ch'ang-an (Sian). It was roughly square shaped with the outer wall following the natural irregularities of the high terrain. The heart of the city was surrounded by the inner wall, and there were four main gates, namely the East (the Hŭng-in), the West (the Tonŭi), the South (the Sungnye), and the North (the Sukchŏng), and four smaller gates and a water gate as parts of the inner wall. The distance between the East and West gates was approximately three miles and Kwanghwa Gate, the main gate of the Kyŏngbok Palace where the government was located, was about one and a half miles from the city's South Gate. Thus, the heart of Seoul was within these gates and formed a rectangular area that was substantially

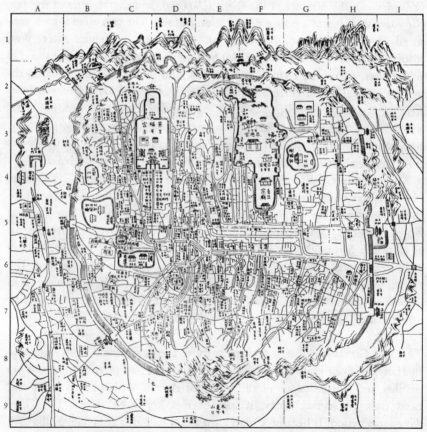

MAP OF SEOUL IN THE NINETEENTH CENTURY

smaller than the total area of the city. The mountain fortresses of Namhan and Puk'an were constructed in 1626 and 1711, respectively, to protect the capital.

The city was divided into five wards (*pu*), each ward was divided into sections (*pan*), and each section was divided into units (*pang*). The two main boulevards were the Street of Great Peace, which linked the palace in the north at the foot of the Inwang Mountain with the South Gate, and the Unjong Road (now Chongno, or the Bell Street), which linked the center of the city at the street of Great Peace with the East Gate. Minor streets were laid out in a checkerboard fashion.

Many magnificent palaces such as the Ch'anggyŏng, the Kyŏngbok, the Ch'angdŏk, and later the Kyŏng-un (now Tŏksu) were constructed along with such other architectural masterpieces as the Secret Garden, a pavilion named Kyŏnghoeru, and the Lotus Pavilion, all demonstrating the grandeur, mood, and taste of the Yi dynasty. The Kyŏng-un Palace in the heart of the city was the residence of the last monarch of the Yi dynasty. All government offices were located in or in front of the Kyŏngbok Palace, The Hall of Diligent Administration (*Kŭnjŏngjŏn*) was the main government building in the Kyŏngbok Palace and the Kwanghwa Gate was the main palace entrance.

The capital had special residential districts within its walls: the northern and southern sections for the *yangban* families, the eastern section for minor military officers, the western section for low-ranking government officials called *ajŏn*, and the central section reserved for the officials belonging to the middle ranks (*chung-in*). Merchants were allowed to establish stores and market places at certain designated areas in the center of the city such as along the Unjong Road.

New Territories and Administrative Districts.   Mindful of the threats of the Jurcheds in the northeastern part of the peninsula, the Korean government undertook military expeditions against the northern nomads. A series of successful military campaigns brought about the conquest of that region, extending the Korean territory to the Yalu River to the north and the Tumen River in the northeast.

Following the subjugation of the northeastern region in 1434, several garrison towns, such as Pukch'ŏng were established. Each garrison town was surrounded by massive defensive walls with gates and watchtowers. Government offices and military units were stationed within the walls as were the residence of the officials and shops of merchants and artisans. The peasants and the "low born" people lived outside the walls. Such towns as Kyŏngsŏng, Kyŏnghŭng, and Hoeryŏng in the northeast and Chasŏng, Much'ang and Ŭiju in the northern end of Korea were founded in the early 15th century.

In 1413, the country was divided into eight provinces (*to*), and each province in turn was divided into prefectures (*mok*), counties (*kun*), districts (*hyŏn*), and towns and villages. All officials, except those in the villages, were ap-

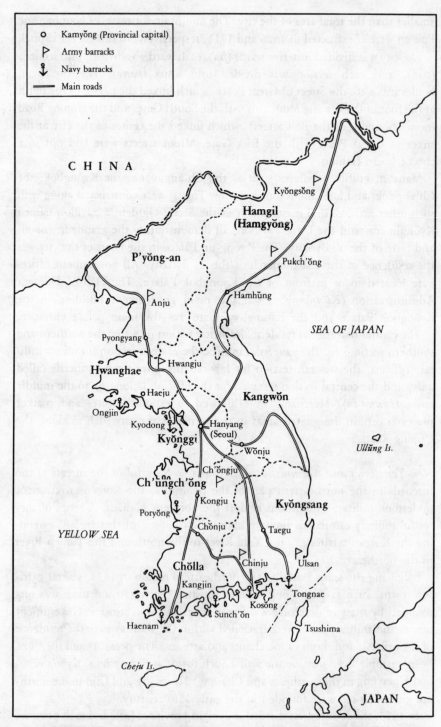

CHINA

Kyŏngsŏng

Hamgil
(Hamgyŏng)

P'yŏng-an

Pukch'ŏng

Anju

Hamhŭng

Pyongyang

SEA OF JAPAN

Hwangju

Hwanghae

Haeju

Kangwŏn

Ongjin

Kyodong

Hanyang
(Seoul)

Kyŏnggi

Wŏnju

Ullŭng Is.

Ch'ŏngju

Ch'ungch'ŏng

Kongju

Kyŏngsang

Poryŏng

Chŏnju

Taegu

YELLOW SEA

Chinju

Ulsan

Chŏlla

Kangjin

Tongnae

Kosŏng

Sunch'ŏn

Tsushima

Haenam

Cheju Is.

JAPAN

○ Kamyŏng (Provincial capital)
Ρ Army barracks
⚓ Navy barracks
— Main roads

EIGHT ADMINISTRATIVE DISTRICTS (PROVINCES), PROVINCIAL
CAPITALS, AND KEY MILITARY BASES (1392–1896)

pointed by the central government. There were four special cities (*pu*) of Kyŏngju, Chŏnju, Yŏnghŭng, and Pyongyang, 20 prefectures, 82 counties, and 175 districts.

Each province was governed by an official whose title was *kwanch'alsa*. While the officials of the central government were appointed for a period of three years, provincial governors were appointed by the central government for a period of one year. The superintendents of prefectures, counties, and districts were appointed for an indefinite period. No provincial governor or magistrates were to serve in the regions where they were born. All clerical positions of the central government as well as local governmental units were filled by the officials called *ajŏn*. The *ajŏn* of the local units were permanent residents of the area, and the *ajŏn* group constituted a particular socio-political class of petty government functionaries. Towns and villages were governed by local officials called *hyangni* who were selected from the local populace, and they carried out political and economic duties under the supervision of a local council called *hyangch'ŏng* or *hyangso*. The *hyangch'ŏng* was a self-governing socio-political village council, which operated under a locally selected "official" whose duties and obligations were prescribed in a set of Confucian precepts or moral principles called *hyangyak*, or "village compact" for the guidance of the peasants. The village council often acted as a censoring office, reporting the misconduct of officials while regulating the customs and practices of the people so as to conform to the orthodox Confucian standard. Generally, a local *yangban* headed the village council. An increasing number of village compacts were written in the early sixteenth century. One of the most well-known *hyangyak* was written by a Confucian scholar named Yi I (Yulgok, 1536–1584), for the village of Hae-ju, Hwanghae Province.

Military System. In the beginning, the Three Righteous Armies (*Ŭihŭng samgunbu*) were responsible for the defense of the capital district as a central army, and four regional military headquarters (*Sadae tohobu*) were established at four strategic places, namely, Andong, Anbyŏn, Kangnŭng, and Yŏng-byŏn. A compulsory military conscription system was adopted and all able-bodied males between the ages of fifteen and sixty were obligated to serve in the military as regular soldiers called *pubyŏng*.

In 1451, the five guards (*wi*) replaced the three armies, each guard having five regiments. The Privy Council (*Chungch'uwŏn*), and the Supreme Headquarters for the Five Guards (*Owi toch'ongbu*), along with the Military Training Institute (*Hullyŏnwŏn*) were established in order to strengthen national security. The local constabulary (*hyanggun*) performed both military and police duties. Later, in 1555, *Pibyŏnsa,* or the "Office in Charge of Frontier Security" replaced the Privy Council as the top military organ.

Each province had an army and a navy headquarters. Three strategic provinces—Hamgil, Kyŏngsang, and Chŏlla—each had two naval bases in order to guard the nation against the Japanese to the south and the Manchus to the north. All top military officers came from *yangban* families.

Social Structure and Institutions.   According to Confucian tradition, the people were divided into five classes, assuring the supremacy of the ruling class. Whereas the Shilla and Koryŏ societies were dominated by the aristocracy or nobility, Korean society in the Yi period was dominated by the scholar-gentry class called *yangban,* whose members controlled politics, sustained social morality and ethics, and nurtured what became known as *yangban* culture. It seemed as though the entire society existed to support this class, which was barred from engaging in farming, manufacture and commerce, as well as other professions. With the rise of the *yangban* class, regionalism grew as certain *yangban* clans such as Kim, Kwŏn, Yi, Yun, Cho and Min of Kyŏnggi, Kyŏngsang, and Ch'ungch'ŏng provinces became predominant in politics. Each stratum and substratum was bound by minute restrictions which not only gave undisputed power and privileges to the upper class, but even enumerated the particulars of language, clothing, and residence.

Yangban means literally ''two branches''—the civil and military branches of the bureaucracy. The term *yangban* implied the entire group of certain clans which produced office holders for the government and who owned lands. The political and economic power of the *yangban* families was, in most cases, perpetuated by educational opportunities for the civil service examinations which were limited almost exclusively to this class. Many *yangban* families were the descendants of meritorious subjects who helped the rise of the Yi dynasty. Not all were rich or powerful, but rich or poor, they enjoyed privileges denied to others. Many once powerful *yangban* families declined and new ones arose as time passed and conditions changed, but the *yangban* class as such remained intact.

While a large number of the *yangban* families known as the ''Seoul *yangban''* resided in the capital, the majority known as the ''local *yangban''* were located in Ch'ungch'ŏng and Kyŏngsang provinces. There were almost no *yangban* families in the northern and eastern parts of Korea, although there were a number of former *yangban* who were banished or demoted to these regions. P'yŏng-an, Hamgyŏng, and Kangwŏn provinces, along with the island of Cheju, were therefore often called the ''land of the exiles.'' Consequently, most of the high offices of the Yi government were in the hands of the southern *yangban,* particularly those from Kyŏngsang and Ch'ungch'ŏng provinces.

Beneath the stratum of the *yangban* was a group of petty central and local functionaries called the *chung-in* (the ''middle people''), which also included such professional people as medical, scientific, and foreign language specialists. Like the *yangban* class, which comprised perhaps less than 10 per cent of the total population, the *chung-in* class was relatively small in size, consisting primarily of less educated men. Although the *chung-in* enjoyed certain privileges such as educational opportunities and political and social prestige, this class nevertheless was subservient to the *yangban*.

Farmers, craftsmen, fishermen and merchants were lumped together into a commoner class known as the *yangmin* ("good people") or *sang-in* ("commoners"), who constituted some 80 per cent of the population. Theoretically, farmers were regarded as important people, and the nobility, according to Confucian tradition, gave them constant lip service as being the "foundation of the nation." However, the vast majority of farmers were landless peasants bound to the soil and they could not move their residence without government permission. Craftsmen were treated by the upper class with some degree of respect, but merchants were regarded as being "inferior," greedy, and dishonest. The lot of Korean merchants, with the exception of a few who handled certain government financial affairs, was one of degradation and deprivation. They were even denied, by an act of the government, the right to use the language of the upper class.

Below the *sang-in* class was another group called the *ch'onmin*, or the "low-born" or "inferior people." Members of this stratum engaged in such degraded professions as butchery, gravedigging, tanning and leather-work, carrier business, funeral business, basket making, bark peeling, sorcery (Shaman practice), and public entertainment. Both public and private slaves and hereditary domestic servants were also included in this category. Slavery of all types was an old social institution of Korea, and in spite of early laws against holding the grandson of a slave, the slavery of adult males persisted. The government itself held a large number of slaves who worked at state-owned manufactories. In 1650, all common prostitutes were converted into government slaves. There were some 400,000 slaves in the early period, but the number of slaves decreased to 190,000 by 1655. Although government slavery was abolished in 1800, the *yangban* families had domestic slaves until the end of the 19th century.

For the maintenance of political control and for the purpose of tax collection, the Yi dynasty instituted a Chinese type of social organization called *ogat'ong*, with five families constituting a unit called *t'ong* which was headed by a semi-official called *t'ongju*. Five *t'ong* were grouped into a *ri*, headed by a *rijang*, and a few *ri* made up a *myŏn*, a district. A *t'ong* was a semi-autonomous organization for purposes of mutual security and taxation. After 1520, the *hyangyak*, or the "village compact," was put into effect and improved local administration. The *hyangyak* also dealt with the promotion of industriousness, thrift, and social reforms at the lowest level of the government administration.

Widespread throughout Korea were mutual-aid groups called *kye* and *ture*. The *ture* was a social-economic club of professional people which provided a useful index of the stability of local and national economy. The *kye* had been a socio-economic group, frequently organized by patrilineal relations, and it functioned as a religious group; it was used to assist other mutual-aid projects within the extended family as well as to finance periodic clan reunions, and it worked as a cooperative means of pooling resources of money, food, and labor. Later the *kye* became a secret organization of those who conspired against the government. Both agricultural and commercial types of *kye* were organized by non-clan members in the cities and villages. The *ture* system became less important than the *kye* system as time passed but remained an important social organization of the peddlers.

The class structure of the Yi dynasty indicated the pattern not only of the distribution of political power, but also of the distribution of wealth. The *yangban* class, owned the bulk of the kingdom's wealth and was concentrated in the capital, enjoying tax exemptions and other privileges. The tax burden fell heavily on the commoners. The discontented and hopelessly poverty-stricken peasants and the "inferior people," who were subjected to ruthless exploitation by the landlords and tax collectors, constantly sought an opportunity to escape from the shackles of degradation, but they had no legal means to do so. The only way to free themselves from the yoke was to resort to violence, and such violence frequently threatened the life of the dynasty.

During the Koryŏ and Yi periods, more new clan names appeared, and a document compiled during the reign of King Sejong of the early fifteenth century indicated that there were 298 surnames in twenty categories. The nomenclature of "all the people" was *paeksŏng*, or "a hundred clan names." As it was in the case of the earlier periods, the Yi government did not permit slaves to adopt surnames. However, those who already had them and became domestic slaves were allowed to keep their surnames.

Economic Structure and Activity.   Although there was a handicraft industry, commerce, and business relating to transportation, Korea was by and large an agrarian society with agriculture as "the foundation of the nation." Food production was carried out by the landless peasants as tenants who supplemented their income with the cottage industry in silk, hemp and cotton cloth production. Because of the economic conservatism of Confucian scholars who were against commercialism, the growth of commerce and a cash economy was discouraged.

The first land survey conducted in 1389 in all provinces, excluding Hamgil and P'yŏng-an provinces, established the total size of farm and forest lands. When the second land survey was conducted in 1404, the increase of 125,000 *kyŏl* over the previous survey was recorded, bringing the total acreage to 923,000 *kyŏl*. The total production capacity of farmlands grew to 1,655,234 *kyŏl* during the reign of King Sejong (reigned 1418–1450). The improvement of survey techniques and reclamation of wild land brought about the increase of the amount of *kyŏl*.

In 1390, T'aejo confiscated all the estates belonging to the members of the Koryŏ nobility and the Buddhist temple, and with the burning of the land registers the state ownership of the land was restored. However, the new land distribution system called *kwajŏn*, or "rank-field" legally recognized the private ownership of land which was taxable and bought and sold, bringing about a modern landlordism.

Under the "rank-field" system, lands in the metropolitan district (Kyŏnggi Province) were used to reward those who had rendered meritorious services to the establishment of the dynasty and to the throne, as well as to provide the land for land grants to the high-ranking government officials. Lands in other provinces were used mostly to support the military. Those individuals who rendered exceptional meritorious services were called "Merit Subjects (*kongshin*)" and they received large land grants and slaves, and a large number of "Minor Merit Subjects (*wŏnjong kongshin*)" received lesser amounts of land. Land grants made to them were taxable hereditary private property which might be confiscated only as punishment for serious crimes. Those ranked officials who were appointed by the central government received a certain amount of land as a source of income for the tenure of office. Officials of the first (top) grade received 150 *kyŏl*, and those in the lowest (18th) grade received only 10 *kyŏl*. Thus, a source indicated that already in 1426 "over half of the farms and slaves" in the southern provinces "belonged to court officials."

Lands were also allocated to the government agencies and public institutions, including Confucian shrines and educational institutions, and the income from these lands was used to operate these institutions. Similarly, military land (*kunjŏn* or *tunjŏn*) was used to raise funds to meet military expenses of local military units. Retired high-ranking officials also received land grants from military land. In 1466, the government inaugurated a new system called *chikchŏn* or "job land," whereby the officials were paid from land tax collected from *chikchŏn*, as well as with grains. However, an increasing amount of farmland granted to government officials for their tenure of office became the private property of high officials of powerful *yangban* families, and by the early sixteenth century no land was available for distribution.

Under the new law of 1600, many peasants reclaimed wild land and restored farmlands which had been destroyed and abandoned during the "Seven-Year War" with the Japanese at the end of the sixteenth century, and they became small landowners themselves. In 1662, the government established an office of irrigation as well as land reclamation projects in order to increase food production.

The public land, including military lands, and the land owned by *yangban* families of merit subjects and officials were cultivated by the peasants as tenant farmers who paid rent. Many slaves worked on public and military lands, and the peasants who were mobilized into the military also worked on military land. The rent collected from public lands was called *cho*, and land tax collected from private lands was called *se*. The peasants who cultivated land paid as high as two-thirds of the harvest to their landlords, although one-third was regarded as a norm.

Major agricultural products were rice, millet, barley, buckwheat, a variety of beans, ginseng, cotton, and potatoes. Irish potatoes were imported from China sometime in the eighteenth century, and sweet potatoes were brought to Korea from Japan in 1763. Ginseng, which was an important export item, was cultivated mostly in the southern part of the peninsula, but wild ginseng (*sansam*) was harvested in most parts of the country.

A small number of carpenter, blacksmith, and hat shops were owned and operated by free artisans who produced furniture, simple farm tools (such as hoes and sickles), and traditional horsetail hats in black color, which they marketed through their shops or through peddlers. A large amount of silk, hemp, and cotton cloth was produced by the peasants who maintained their cottage industry. However, the production of manufactured goods was by and large done by state-owned manufactories.

Similar to the Koryŏ period, slaves and semi-slaves at state-operated manufactories produced most of what may be called "industrial goods." In the early Yi period, there were 129 such manufactories with 2,841 workers in the metropolitan districts, and there were 27 manufactories with 3,656 workers in local regions. They produced such items as ceramic ware, bows, arrows, and other weapons, reed mats, roof tiles, farm tools, paper, lacquer and varnish, leather and leather goods, metal goods, silk, and furniture.

Free carpenters produced fine furniture for the upper class while the potters produced a new ceramic ware called *paekcha,* or "white celadon" for the upper class and brown ceramic ware for others. The white porcelain ware which replaced the green celadon ware of the Koryŏ period was simple in form and had under-glazed designs of flowers, bamboos, fish and others in cobalt blue. Some potters used iron powder to create brown under-glazed designs. The most valued white porcelain ware was the *punch'ŏng* (powder green) ware.

An increased amount of brass and nickel was produced, and brassware such as rice and soup bowls and spoons and chopsticks became widely used. Both brass and nickel sheets were used as hinges and decorative pieces on furniture, including storage boxes. With the increase of production activities, the craftsmen's guilds (*kye*) and the "putting-out" system developed.

The mining of gold was first discouraged in order to avoid the shipment of gold and golden goods to China as tribute goods. However, gradually the mining of gold, silver, and iron ore was developed both by the government and private groups. The government mines were operated by slave workers. A large amount of gold dust (*sagŭm,* or "sand gold") was refined.

Commercial development was not encouraged, but with the increase of the population, commerce grew. The marketing of tax and tribute goods together with the upper class increasing its consumption of goods, brought about a steady rise of commercial activity. The following table shows the trend of population growth.

Year	Number of Households	Population
1657	658,771	2,290,083
1669	1,313,453	5,018,614
1675	1,234,512	4,703,505
1717	1,557,708	6,846,639
1768	1,679,865	7,006,248
1807	1,764,504	7,561,403
1834	1,578,823	8,755,280

The population of Seoul grew from 103,328 who lived inside the walls and 6,404 who lived outside the walls in 1528 to a total of 194,030 in 1669. Following the Japanese aggressions and the Manchu invasions, the population of Seoul dropped in 1657 to 80,572. In 1717, it increased to 185,872. In 1786, there were 42,786 households in Seoul comprising 199,227 persons. After that the population of Seoul did not grow in any significant way.

In order to control the commercial development, and for service to the government, the government set aside the Unjong Road (now Chongno) as a commercial district, and it designated six commercial firms as government purchasing agents in Seoul. These agents and thirty-one other specialty stores which developed monopoly enterprises under government protection operated the "capital market (*kyŏngshi*)."

There were 1,064 local periodic markets (*hyangshi*) throughout the country, normally held every five days in a staggered schedule, to which peddlers (*pobusang*) and the pack-horse merchants brought goods. Although the circulation of cash grew somewhat, the exchange of goods was done mostly by barter. The peddlers organized guilds, and allied with the government which provided protection through its local officials (*ajŏn*), while the peddler's guilds made handsome donations to both the government and the *ajŏn*, and often played a certain political role on the side of the government.

In addition to local periodic markets, semi-annual fairs were held at such places as Taegu, Chŏnju, and Kongju, specializing in the trade of medical herbs. The semi-annual fairs at Hoeryŏng and Kyŏnghŭng in Hamgil (later Hamgyŏng) Province specialized in the trade of animals and farm tools. Meanwhile, groups of merchants in Kaesŏng made that city the commercial capital of Korea. These Kaesŏng merchants were collectively known as *Songsang* and along with those merchants in Seoul who were collectively called *Kangsang*, who promoted trade along the Han River, in the metropolitan district, and in the southern provinces and those merchants at Ŭiju, P'yŏng-an Province, who were known as *Mansang*, they played a significant role both in domestic commerce and in foreign trade. As a result of the rise of markets, the number of inns increased, and many innkeepers (*kaekchu*) and shop owners engaged in wholesale brokerage and money lending.

Trade with China continued along the border region towns such as Chung-gang and Ŭiju in the northwest, and Hoeryŏng and Kyŏnghŭng in the north-east. Major export items were ginseng, animal skins, salt, cows, and farm tools. Books and medical herbs were import items. Trade with the Japanese was suspended following the Japanese invasions, but it was revived on a limited basis by the residents of Tsushima in the Korea Strait. Gradually, the Japanese arrived in Korea and established trading centers in the ports of Kyŏngsang Province. Those at Ulsan, Tongnae, and Ch'oryang, (there are now in Pusan) and Waegwan were the more important colonies of Japanese merchants in Korea. Korea exported to Japan such items as ginseng, cotton cloth, and leather while importing copper and spices.

The government collected a variety of taxes, mostly from the commoners. The land tax was the main source of state income. During the latter part of the reign of King Sejong, farmlands were classified into six tax categories, accord-ing to the quality of the land, and the land tax rate (normally 1/10 of the harvest) fluctuated according to the yearly harvest. In 1653, a uniform rate of land tax was established, and all taxable landowners paid 1/30 of the annual harvest as tax.

The peasants were heavily burdened with taxes. Although most of them did not own land, they were forced by their landlords to pay land tax to the state in-stead of the landlords themselves paying it as landowners. In addition, the pea-sants were obligated to pay corvée tax, providing free labor to the state in a variety of projects. They also paid military tax to support the military.

In addition, the government collected tributes from the peasants and other free people, payable in such items as cloth, paper, fish, lumber, gold, silver, ginseng, salt, animal skins, and sometimes cash. Merchants and artisans paid business taxes. Frequently, local officials collected additional tributes from the people to enrich themselves. Needless to say, the *yangban* class as a whole en-joyed tax exemption, or avoided the payment of land tax.

The circulation of money that began during the Koryŏ period did not in-crease in any significant way. In 1625, a new coin named *Chosŏn t'ongbo* was minted, but its use was suspended. In 1633, a new coin named *Sangp'yŏng t'ongbo* was minted and the circulation of coins steadily increased, particularly after 1678 when the government authorized both civil and military offices to produce coins. Meanwhile, Chinese coins were used on a limited basis. However, a cash economy as such did not develop. The Korean coins (circular in shape with a square hole in the center) were minted with the alloy of copper and brass, and they were commonly called *yŏpchŏn*, "leaf money."

Transportation and Communication.   In order to facilitate rapid transport of tax goods, river transportation was improved and more ferries and warehouses were constructed along major rivers and seaports. There were dozens of warehouses along the waterways in the middle of the sixteenth century. Some

41 land routes with approximately 500 courier (pony) stations (*yŏk*) were established, and 1,220 inns (*wŏn*) were built along these routes.

The mobility of the people, with the exception of peddlers and pack-horse merchants, was extremely low since the peasants and slaves who constituted the majority of the population were bound either to the soil or to their work places. Few members of the *yangban* class traveled, but when they did, men like high government officials rode horses while ladies were carried in enclosed sedan chairs (*kama*, or palanquin). Many male *yangban* traveled on palanquins as well.

The means for conveying goods remained simple. Although carts and wagons driven by cows and ponies were used to transport goods, horse-driven carriages did not appear. The peasants used an A-frame contraption called *chige* and carried goods on their backs. Women carried things on their heads. Ships on the rivers were small with one or no mast. No large ships for extended travel on the seas were constructed.

Some 623 fire-smoke signal stations were established at the top of high hills throughout the country, creating a communication network with the South Mountain in the capital as the central station. In time of war or local disturbances, fire-smoke signals were sent to the capital from local stations, conveying certain messages by the number of signals and the color of the fire.

Early Domestic Problems. The process of new nation building was not without problems. Succession disputes resulted in bloodshed and rebellions created an unstable political atmosphere.

The first bloody event took place in 1398 when T'aejo designated his eighth son (second son born of T'aejo's second queen) as his successor. Chŏng To-jŏn, a prominent official, who sided with the newly designated successor, attempted, in August 1398, to eliminate all six sons of T'aejo, who were born of the first queen. However, Chŏng's plot was uncovered and he and his co-conspirators were killed. In the wake of this event, T'aejo selected his second son to be his successor, but both sons born of his second queen were murdered. This unhappy event was followed by a rebellion of T'aejo's fourth son in January 1400, and after subjugating his brother's rebellion, Chŏngjong (reigned 1399–1400) abdicated the throne in favor of his younger brother (fifth son of T'aejo) who became T'aejong (reigned 1400–1416). The sixth monarch, Tanjong, a boy king, was forced to abdicate by his uncle who became Sejo (reigned 1455–1468), causing much bloodshed.

As these events took place in Seoul, in 1453 a rebellion erupted in the northeast which had recently been conquered. It was brought about by Yi Ching-ok, former military commander in Hamgil region, whose aim was to establish a new kingdom in that region in cooperation with the Jurcheds. Meanwhile, the Jurcheds in south Manchuria invaded Korea, but their invasions were crushed by Generals Shin Suk-chu in 1460 and Nam I in 1467, respectively.

In 1467, another rebellion erupted in the northeast, when Yi Shi-ae, a wealthy native of that region who had been a magistrate of Hoeryŏng, Hamgil, took up arms against Sejo who applied a discriminatory policy against the natives of that region. Not too long after this, in the spring of 1510, Japanese traders in three ports in Kyŏngsang Province brought about an uprising, supported by several hundred warriors from Japan. In order to strengthen the defense against barbarian invasions, a new Office of Frontier Security (*Pibyŏnsa*) was created in 1555, but the Japanese pirates on the southern coasts and the Jurcheds in south Manchuria remained constantly troublesome to the government in Seoul.

Confucianization and Cultural and Social Change of the Early Period

The rapid development of Confucianism brought about cultural and social changes. First of all, the new dynasty's anti-Buddhist policy removed the power and influence of the Buddhist monks in the government. Buddhist properties were confiscated, Buddhist monks were expelled from the capital, the number of monks and nuns at each remaining monastery and the amount of land owned by each monastery were regulated, and the construction of new temples in the capital and other places was strictly forbidden. But Buddhism still remained strong under personal patronage of certain kings such as Sejong and Sejo. King Sejong unified Buddhist sects into two branches of *Sŏn* (*Zen* in Japanese) as a school of meditation and *Kyo* for instructional functions. However, the three kings of the late fifteenth and early sixteenth centuries imposed restrictions, tore down Buddhist temples in the capital, abolished the examination system for the monks, and brought about a complete separation of religion and politics. Be that as it may, Buddhism maintained its strength as a religion of the common people, particularly that of women.

The growth of Confucianism not only increased the study of Confucianism itself, but also the study of Chinese culture in general. As a result, Chinese cultural influence grew strong, leading to the development of the upper-class culture of the Koreans. At the same time, a social structure and behaviorism patterned after Confucian principles developed, transforming Korean society to be much like that of China.

Confucianism of the Yi Dynasty.   The disciples of the orthodox Confucian School of Rites (*Yehak*) greatly emphasized the importance of the formal aspect of the Confucian way of life called *ye*, or rituals or rites. They insisted that ritualism and the proper observance of Confucian codes of conduct by individuals and the government, both in public affairs and in private life, were vital factors in maintaining law and order in society. Therefore, they prescribed in minute detail the court procedures, ceremonies, customs, language, music and the principle governing human relations, and the slightest deviations from the established patterns were severely criticized, making the life style rigid and intellectualism inflexible.

The School of *I* or *Sŏngnihak* (Moral and Natural Law) of a Neo-Confucian Chu Hsi (Chuja in Korean) became the dominant branch of Confucianism during the Yi period. It was this school which controlled the politics of the Yi dynasty and maintained the doctrine that behind the Universe stood the Supreme Ultimate which controlled the operation of two universal elements of *yin* and *yang* which manifest their "will" through the five elements of fire, water, wood, metal and earth.

According to Neo-Confucianism, which was more concerned with human nature and behavioral patterns, the Supreme Ultimate created the law of nature and rules over the real world and such phenomena as seasonal changes, life and death, fortunes and misfortunes, and the destiny of man. The proponents of the moral and natural law argued that the principles of nature (universe) and the nature of man must be understood and the ability to control oneself through intuitive knowledge and submission to the moral law must be cultivated. For this reason, they emphasized the development of such qualities of superior man as benevolence, righteousness, propriety, wisdom and trustworthiness, and they attempted to bring about moral and ethical reforms in order to promote political stability and social order.

Heavily influenced by the Neo-Confucian thought of the Sung dynasty of China, this school attempted to suppress any interpretation other than that of Chu Hsi regarding the nature and the behavioral patterns of government, society, and the people. Among the major proponents of this doctrine were Yi Hwang (T'oegye, 1501–1570) and Yi I (Yulgok, 1536–1584) who nurtured the growth of monism and dualism in Korea. However, they disagreed on one key point. Yi Hwang emphasized the importance of *ri* (*li* in Chinese) or the governing principle or reason, over the human energy or emotion called *ki* (*ch'i* in Chinese) which he regarded as the two basic elements in human nature. Therefore, he advocated the cultivation of *ri* (governing principle) through education. Yi I, on the other hand, gave primacy to *ki* (the inert matter) and argued that *ri* was merely a dependent principle. Therefore, he advocated the cultivation of practical ethics rather than metaphysical theory. The factionalism of Confucian scholars originated in such difference of opinion.

The School of Legalism emphasized the importance of law and order, advocating political, social, and education reforms in order to strengthen the central authority. At the same time, this school regarded philosophical and theoretical arguments on the nature of man as not only futile but harmful. Needless to say, the Legalists believed that human behavior must be controlled by law and a system of punishments. Among major proponents of this doctrine were Cho Kwang-jo (1482–1519) and Kim Chŏng-guk (1485–1541), who played important parts in numerous judicial reforms, changes in rituals of the government, and contractual systems in civil and commercial affairs.

Education, the Civil Service Examination System and Scholarship. The strengthening of the Confucian studies and the civil service examination system brought about a rapid intellectual development and an increasing number of government and private schools. The highest government institution of Confucian learning was Sŏnggyun-gwan in Seoul. Below it were four government schools (*sahak*) in Seoul and local schools called *hyanggyo*. These government educational institutions trained most of government officials who earned various degrees. A growing number of private schools (*sŏwŏn* and *sŏdang*) appeared in local areas, promoting education. Whereas *sŏwŏn* was a private upper level school of a reputable scholar, *sŏdang* was a primary school where Chinese characters as well as some Confucian classics were taught. *Sarim,* a collective noun for groups of scholars who were usually critical of government, was destined to play crucial roles not only in the intellectual field, but also in politics later.

The students at government schools beyond the primary level studied not only Confucian classics and history, but also foreign languages, medicine, astronomy and geomancy, law, and military science, according to their specialization.

The government officials were recruited through the examination system (*kwagŏ*), which consisted of three categories—civil, military, and miscellaneous. Whereas the military and miscellaneous divisions emphasized appropriate knowledge and skills, the civil division (both *sama* and *munkwa*) emphasized a high degree of achievement in poetry, belles-lettres, history, Confucian classics, and ability in the composition of documents. Theoretically the examinations were open to commoners, but only sons of the *yangban* families were able to take them.

The first (qualifying) examination in the *Sama* Division had two categories, namely *saengwŏn* and *chinsa*, and those who were qualified in the Confucian classics received the degree of *saengwŏn*, and those successful candidates in the literary division received the degree of *chinsa*, or "presented scholar." A total of 200 were selected in Seoul, and 400 were selected from the provinces, and the second examination given at the Board of Rites in Seoul selected 100 candidates and gave to them certificates written on white paper.

Those who specialized in the Literary and Classics Division (*Munkwa*) took the first (local) examination, and the second and the third examinations in Seoul. A total of 250 among several hundred candidates were selected in the first examination, and the second examination given at the Board of Rites in Seoul selected 100 from those who passed the first examination, and they were given a certificate written on red paper. Those who passed the second examination were graded in the third examination given at the court in the presence of the king into three categories: 3 in first place, 7 in second place, and 23 in third place. Generally, those who earned degrees in the *Sama* Division were given lower positions in the government, and those who passed the examinations in the Literary and Classics Division were given higher government positions.

Three categories of examinations were given in the Military Division (*Mukwa*). In the first (local) examination, 180 were selected, and in the second examination given at the Board of War in Seoul 28 were selected. They were graded in the third examination given at the court in the presence of the king into three ranks: 3 in first place, 5 in second place, and 20 in third place. Needless to say, those who passed the second examination, particularly those who ranked in the top two grades, became high military officials.

Usually, Seoul and Kyŏnggi, Ch'ungch'ŏng, Kyŏngsang, and Chŏlla provinces were allocated larger quota of degrees, and Kangwŏn, Hwanghae, Hamgyŏng, and P'yŏng-an provinces received small quotas, thereby assuring the preservation of the political domination of the *yangban* in those places. The population distribution may have had some relationship to the allocation of quota of degrees, but the desire of the officials in Seoul and the central and southern provinces to maintain political control had much to do with the allocation of a small number of degrees to other provinces.

In the Miscellaneous Division (*Chapkwa*), sons of minor officials took the first and second examination in foreign languages (Chinese, Mongolian, Japanese, and Jurchen), medicine, the Yin-Yang division which included astrology and geomancy, and law.

These examinations were normally given every three years, and special examinations were given irregularly on particular occasions. As in the Koryŏ period, Buddhist monks were given examinations until the middle of the fifteenth century. Separate examinations were given to the monks of the *Sŏn* sect and the *Kyo* branch, and each examination selected 30 from each group, and classified the monks into four categories.

Such monarchs as Sejong (1397–1450) who reigned between 1418 and 1450 and Sejo (reigned 1455–1468) contributed much to cultural development. During their period, scholarship grew, producing more literary works and historical studies, and developing arts and sciences. Since 1403, movable metal printing type had been in use, and during this time book printing accelerated. The *History of the Royal Dynasty* (*Wangjo shillok*) and the *Record of T'aejo* (*T'aejo shillok*) were published in 1413. The intellectual and cultural pattern which was established brought about many remarkable cultural achievements later.

King Sejong became known in Korean history as Sejong the Great because of his enlightened rule and his contribution to cultural and technical development. He established a new research institution called the Academy of Scholars (*Chip'yŏnjŏn*) to promote scholarship. Under the leadership of outstanding members of the Academy such as Sŏng Sam-mun and Chŏng In-ji, much was accomplished in classical studies, literature and legal and historical studies.

A total listing of the accomplishments of Korean scholars of this period would be too long, but some of the more important published works include: *History of Koryŏ* (*Koryŏsa*) of 1424, the *Guide to Agriculture* (*Nongsa chiksŏl*) of 1430, the *Essentials of Koryŏ History* (*Koryŏsa chŏryo*) of 1452, and an epic poem entitled *Songs of the Dragons Flying to Heaven* (*Yongbi ŏch'ŏn-ga*), and a political handbook called *Ch'ip'yŏng yoram,* which was published in 1445.

During the period of Sejo the *Mirror of Benevolent Rule* (*Kukcho pogam*), which included royal edicts, instructions and sayings of previous monarchs of the Yi dynasty, was published in 1458. A legal compendium called *Kyŏngguk tae-jŏn* was published in 1471, *Five Rites of State* (*Kukcho oryeŭi*) in 1474, and a *General History of Korea* (*Tongguk t'onggam*) in 1485. Meanwhile, interest in geographic studies and map making increased, resulting in the publication of the *Geography of Eight Provinces* (*P'alto chiriji*) during the reign of Sejong, and an official map of Korea during the reign of Sejo. The *Augmented Survey of the Geography of Korea* (*Tongguk yŏji sŭngnam*) was published in 1480 and a revised edition (*Shinjŭng Tongguk yŏji sŭngnam*) was published in 1530.

Confucian Ritual, Music and Dance. The rise of Confucianism and the impor- tation of Chinese music and musical instruments brought about the devel- opment of the *Tang-ak* (the music of T'ang China), the *aak* ("graceful music"), and the *chŏng-ak* ("authentic music"), and these became the cultural property of the upper class. The *Tang-ak* and the *aak* were associated with Confucian rituals and court ceremonies, and the *chŏng-ak* was non-ritual music of the upper class. Both Confucian rituals and court ceremonies were ac- companied by musical performance and ritual dance.

The *Tang-ak* and the *aak* were performed on various occasions by a group of professional court musicians and dancers in colorful costumes. Among the court dances (*Pŏmmu* or *Chŏngjae*) were "The Ball Throwing Dance," and "A Nightingale Singing in Springtime" which were created in the early 19th cen- tury. The ritual dances, which were collectively known as the *Ilmu*, consisted of the Civil Dance and the Military Dance. The *Ilmu* which was performed at Confucian shrines and at the Royal Ancestors Shrine in Seoul is a simple and slow ritualistic dance accompanied by music played by the court musicians for the purpose of ceremony and the offering of sacrifices. All court dances were highly stylized and were performed in slow rhythm by female dancers accom- panied by an orchestra. All ritual dances were performed by Confucian men. The court orchestra consisted of various wind and string instruments, a few drums such as a round drum called *puk* and an hour-glass shaped drum called *changgo*, and bells, stone and other percussion instruments.

Influenced by the *Tang-ak,* the old form of music and dance of the Shilla and Koryŏ known as the *hyang-ak,* or the "native music" grew further. The *hyang-ak,* which was promoted by the *hwarang* of Shilla and incorporated both Shamanistic and Buddhistic beliefs, included such dances as "The Dance of Four Fairies" which was performed at the *P'algwanhoe* festival, "The Com- ing of the Phoenix Dance," and "The Boating Dance." In 1426, a musical text, entitled the *Standard of Musicology* was published.

The Rise of a Confucian Social Behaviorism.   Confucian moral and ethical principles and the Confucian concepts regarding human relations transformed the Korean society. The *Book of Self-Cultivation* (*Sushinsŏ*) published in Chinese in 1431, and its Korean version of 1481, stressed the importance of the Confucian virtues of loyalty, filial piety, self-cultivation and self-control, affecting the patterns of behavior of the upper class as well as others. In 1413, T'aejong had said that Korean civilization was to follow that of Chinese except in marriage ceremonies.

The Confucian code of conduct that was stressed in Korea was related to the observation of three cardinal principles (*samgang*) and five ethical norms (*oryun*). The three cardinal principles were loyalty to the ruler (*ch'ung*), filial piety to parents (*hyo*), and *yŏl*—including such qualities in females as chastity, obedience, faithfulness and filial piety—which governed the conduct of women. Loyal subjects (ministers) were called *ch'ungshin*, filial sons and daughters were called *hyoja*, and *hyonyŏ*, respectively, and women who sacrificed their lives (and happiness) for their parents and husbands were called *yŏlnyŏ*. Those who showed no such qualities were regarded as *ssangnom*, or inferior (uncivilized) persons without principles and self-cultivation.

The five ethical norms dealt with certain responsibilities and obligations governing the relations between individuals, namely, the principle of righteousness and justice (*ŭi*) between the ruler and his ministers (subjects), cordiality or closeness (*ch'in*) between parents and sons (children), distinction (*pyŏl*) between husbands and wives, order (*sŏ*) between elders and juniors, and trust (*shin*) between friends.

These principles of *samgang* and *oryun* were regarded as those qualities possessed only by superior and civilized individuals, keeping them separated from inferior men. Regardless of whether they had high social status or not, all people were more or less expected to behave according to these prescribed principles. Without them one was regarded as a degenerate and worthless individual. As a result, formalities in speech and patterns of behavior prescribed in accordance with these principles grew, restricting the freedom of thought, expression, and action, and preventing any chance for progress beyond the limits of the Confucian standard. At the same time, these principles were conveniently employed by the *yangban* class to keep the commoners in their place. The violation of established Confucian conventions and customs was regarded as "crime," lack of decorum, and impropriety as the Confucian way of life became increasingly more concerned with the external formalities than with inner, spiritual and moral qualities.

The aristocratic class structure reenforced by the principles of a Confucian social order and behaviorism resulted in the development of a certain pattern of language (speech). That is to say, certain forms of addressing persons in the upper class or persons below one's class, as well as a certain pattern of sentence endings developed. To persons in the higher class, those in the lower class were required (by customs and social convention) to use an honorific form (*chondaeǒ* in Korean) of address, and to the lower class the higher class persons used a blunt form (*panmal* in Korean). In between these two was a familiar form. Such sentence endings as *naida, nida,* and *shipshio* were used to address persons of the upper class whereas such endings as *ta, ra,* and *ǒ* were used by upper class persons to those in the lower class. According to the tone of voice, these could be also the familiar form of sentence ending.

Those in the *yangban* class almost never used the honorific form to address their wives, children, or servants, while wives and children always addressed their husbands or fathers in this form. Younger persons always used the polite or honorific form when addressing their elders or older brothers or sisters.

"You" in English had several counterparts in Korean, and "I" also had several forms according to one's class status. The usage of the second person singular pronoun "you" was avoided as much as possible when a person was addressing those in the upper social order. "You" in familiar form was *nǒ*, and in blunt form was usually *ya*, or "hey, you" in English.

This pattern of speech and writing has been maintained until today, but certain changes in the pattern of speech have led to the growth of social democracy at least in this respect.

The status of women declined with the establishment of Confucian social order. Under strict moral code, marriage between individuals of different social classes, as well as between members of the same clan (*tongsǒng tongbon* in Korean) and among blood relations, and remarriage of widows were prohibited by law of 1485. The so-called *samjong* principle was practiced. Under it, a woman was to follow (to be subservient to) her parents before marriage, then her husband, and after her husband's death her first son.

Although divorce was not widely practiced, a man could divorce his wife under the principles of *ch'ilgǒjiak,* or "seven evils" which legitimized the grounds for divorce. They were: disobedience to parents-in-law, failure to bear a son, adultery, jealousy, hereditary disease, garrulousness, and larceny. On the other hand, women had no right to divorce their husbands. Whereas men of means were free to have concubines and practiced adultery, women's behavior was strictly controlled and regulated. Women, including wives, were not to be seen in public or heard, and when they went out in public they covered their head and face with a large scarf. With the exception of peddlers, peasants, and the like, most women were confined to domestic activities in what was called *anpang*, or the "inner quarter."

During the Koryǒ period, both male and female offspring and wives were entitled to inherit property and a joint ownership of property of the married couple was recognized. However, with the Sinification of Korea, particularly after the middle of the 17th century, only the first son who was responsible for performing ancestor-worship rituals (*chesa*) had inheritance rights, thereby establishing the primogenitor entail system.

Arts. Masters of brush painting promoted Chinese-style painting. Among them were Prince Anp'yŏng (son of Sejong), Kang Hŭi-an (1419–1464, penname: Injae), who painted a masterpiece entitled "A Sage at Rest on a Rock," and An Kyŏn (penname: Hyŏndongja), who painted "Visiting the Peace Garden in a Dream." These artists promoted an elegant and graceful style of landscape painting (*sansuhwa*) in the Chinese style. Prince Anp'yŏng was known for his style of painting pine trees and snow scenes (*songsŏlch'e*). Other masters contributed to the development of the style of painting "Four Gracious Plants" (*sagunja*)—plum, orchid, chrysanthemum, and bamboo—as well as the style of painting flowers and birds (*hwajo*). Since all the painters were scholars, their painting was collectively called *muninhwa*, or the painting of learned persons.

The Sinification of the Korean Language. One of the most significant results of the Sinification of Korea was the disappearance of old Korean nouns and pronouns. Korean nouns were replaced by Chinese words, and many original nouns completely disappeared and were forgotten. Meanwhile, the pronunciation of ancient words changed radically, and unfortunately there is no way of knowing how ancient words were pronounced. However, Korean scholars generally agree that the present-day pronunciation is vastly different from that of ancient times. For example, the present-day pronunciation of "mother" in Korea is *ŏmŏni*, but it is said that the old pronunciation was *emille*. Some still call mothers *emi*.

Among the Chinese nouns which became Koreanized, or a substitution of Korean word, are the following:

hwach'o for *kkot* (flowers)   *kaok* for *chip* (houses)
an for *nun* (eyes)   *kyo* for *tari* (bridges)
kak for *tari* (legs)   *ch'ŏn* for *hanŭl* (heaven or skies)
p'ung for param (wind)   *toro* for *kil* (roads)
mach'a for *sure* or *talguji* (waggon or cart)

Such words as *chŏngbu* (government), *chŏngch'i* (politics), *sahoe* (society), *sŏwŏn* or *sŏdang* (schools), and *yesul* (arts) were new Korean words borrowed from the Chinese. The names of all government organs as well as place and personal names were Chinese.

Many Chinese adjectives became Koreanized in combination with Korean post-positions. For example, among Korean adjectives *ttasŭhan* (warm) is expressed in Chinese as *onhwahan, nappŭn* (bad) is expressed in Chinese as *ak'an,* and *choŭn* (good) is expressed as *sŏllyanghan.*

Power Struggle and the Rise of Factionalism

Power Politics and the Purges.   The concentration of power in the central government, the attempts made by the kings to strengthen their control over the bureaucracy, and the contest for power among bureaucrats created a series of political crises which were often accompanied by bloodshed.

The first serious conflict between the monarch and the bureaucrats occurred when the third king, T'aejong, reorganized the government in order to strengthen the power of monarchy, reducing *Ŭijŏngbu*, which had been a policy making council, to a consultative council. The fourth king, Sejong (reigned 1419–1450), also created a serious conflict between the monarchy and the bureaucracy by attempting to strengthen the monarchical control over the government while his patronage for Buddhism antagonized Confucian scholars.

King Sejong was not only ambitious to strengthen the power of the monarchy, but he was also interested in elevating the status of the Korean monarchy vis-à-vis that of China. He had a scholar write an essay which stated that the Korean kings also had received the Mandate of Heaven. He himself performed rites at the Temple of Heaven and glorified the founder of the Yi dynasty despite the opposition of the Confucian officials. It was Sejong who commissioned an outstanding scholar, Chŏng In-ji, to compose a song dedicated to his ancestor Yi Sŏng-gye and his successors. It was entitled *Yongbi ŏch'ŏn-ga*, or "Songs of the Dragons Flying to Heaven," and was the first time that Korean kings were called dragons. "The Six Dragons of Haedong (Korea) fly: all their works have the favor of Heaven: their auspices are the same as those of worthies of old," says the opening canto. The last canto says: "His (Yi Sŏng-gye's) character suited Heaven. . . the oracle shows the dynasty to be without end, and Your Divine Majesty has succeeded to the throne. . . by respecting Heaven and laboring for the people You consolidated Your position. . . . ."

The way in which Sejo took over the throne from his nephew, a boy king Tanjong, in 1455, and his attempts to strengthen his power, caused a bitter controversy. The bureaucrats stubbornly resisted, but Sejo proceeded and closed down the Academy of Scholars which had been established by Sejong, abolished some posts in the Office of Censors, and crippled the Office of Royal Lecturers. Moreover, he instituted the practice of the king's private audience with individual officials without the presence of historians and censorate officials as was traditionally required.

The growing strength of Confucianism and of the Confucian bureaucracy was bound to cause more serious conflict with the monarchy, involving not only policy matters, but also the manner in which the government functioned as well as the personal conduct of the king, the queen, and the officials. The officialdom was split into factions by opposing interpretation of Confucian concepts as the power struggle between the monarchy and the bureaucracy continued. Two bloody purges of literati carried out by Yŏnsan-gun (reigned

1494-1506) and others which followed soon thereafter, caused considerable internal difficulties which weakened the foundation of the kingdom. These purges of literati which culminated in bloody political events are known in Korean history as *sahwa,* or "the disaster for scholars."

The first major purge occurred in 1498 during the reign of Yŏnsan-gun whose target was a group of Puritanic scholars known as the "Mountain and Forest" school. It was headed by a Confucian named Kim Chong-jik, who was critical of the way in which Sejo took over the throne from his nephew, Tanjong, as well as the tyrannical and morally corrupt Yŏnsan-gun himself. Hundreds of scholars were either executed or banished in 1498. Again in 1504, Yŏnsan-gun carried out a purge against those whom he regarded as responsible for the fall of his mother who was forced to commit suicide.

The Confucian bureaucrats were able to force Yŏnsan-gun to abdicate and to enthrone Chungjong (reigned 1506-1544), but in 1519 the new king carried out a purge against the reform-minded Cho Kwang-jo and his supporters. Cho criticized the land grants made by Chungjong to those who raised him to the throne, and he proposed that land granted to them be confiscated because the action taken by the king was not in accordance with Confucian principles. The last *sahwa* occurred in 1545, immediately after the accession of Myŏngjong (reigned 1545-1567), involving the legitimacy of the succession as well as the power struggle between two branches of the Yun clan which was that of the queen.

The Rise of Factionalism.   The factionalism of scholars and officials involved groups of Confucianists collectively known either as *sarim* or *yurim.* The first such factional struggle which caused an extremely unstable political situation took place in 1574 as a result of the power struggle and the personal rivalries between the queen's brother, Shim Ŭi-gyŏm and an official named Kim Hyo-wŏn as well as followers of these two individuals. Whereas Shim advocated the teaching of a Confucian master named Yi I, Kim and his supporters were the disciples of another Confucian master named Yi Hwang. Shim's group was known as the Western Men (*Sŏin*) because of his residence which was located in the western section of Seoul, and Kim's followers were called the Eastern Men (*Tong-in*) because Kim's residence was in the eastern quarter of the city.

An open warfare within the bureaucracy revealed the fundamental weakness of Confucian idealism and administrative institutions in Korea. Factionalism among Confucian scholars was an inevitable result of the gap between the ideal pattern of personal and institutional conduct prescribed by Confucian masters and the realities of the pattern of behavior of both the monarch and scholar-officials. Moreover, contradictory interpretations of the ideals and concepts of Confucianism, such as those of orthodox Confucianism vs. the Neo-Confucianism of Chu Hsi, provided a wide range of latitude in which a group of scholar-officials could easily find legitimate, however trivial, reasons to criticize and attack their opponents and even the king himself. The vanity and political ambitions of certain officials contributed much to the factional struggle, causing a progressive deterioration of political and economic conditions and the decline of creative spirits and energy.

The Western Men group was further split, first into the *Hunsŏ* and *Ch'ŏngsŏ* factions, and then into the Old Doctrine (*Noron*) and the Young Doctrine (*Soron*) branches during the latter half of the 17th century. The Eastern Men group was divided into the Northern Men (*Pugin*) and the Southern Men (*Namin*) factions at the end of the 16th century, and the Northern Men faction became further divided into the Greater Northern Men and the Lesser Northern Men factions during the 17th century. The Southern Men faction saw the rise of two branches, but it maintained more cohesiveness and unity than other groups. The Old Doctrine, the Young Doctrine, the Northern Men, and the Southern Men groups were collectively known as *Sasaek*, or the "Four Colors."

FACTIONAL GROUPS OF SCHOLARS

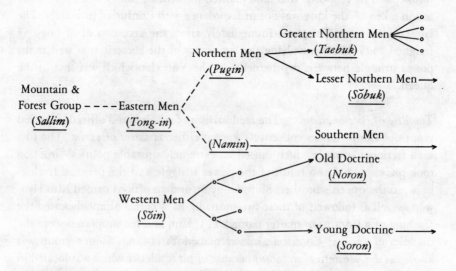

Although certain ideological factors were involved, the primary ones which promoted the ferocious factional struggles were: (1) the contest between the monarchy and bureaucracy, (2) the rivalry for high government positions among powerful families, (3) the competition among the literati for the control of such important government organs as the Board of Censors and the Board of Inspectors, and (4) the senior and junior personal animosities and hatred. By and large, the contenders ignored such issues as economic improvement and the welfare of the people. Deadly struggles were waged to gain power on vague and abstract principles, and whenever one faction succeeded in gaining control over key offices in the government, it used whatever means available to wipe out its opponents by applying moralistic principles and techniques of violence regardless of the consequences. The champions of factionalism knew nothing about the political technique of compromise. In Confucian tradition, especially that of Korean Confucianism, there was no room for political reconciliation or compromise in dealing with differences of opinion concerning policy, court rituals, and ethical and moral issues. Compromise would have meant dishonesty, disloyalty, and depravity.

The Development of National Culture

As Chinese culture grew steadily, transforming the Korean society, a certain national consciousness developed among the Koreans, resulting in the rise of an indigenous Korean culture during the early period of the Yi dynasty. Among the achievements of this culture were the creation of the Korean writing system, the growth of Korean poetry known as *shijo,* and scientific and technical innovations.

The Creation of the Korean Writing System.   The Koreans had no writing system of their own, and they used Chinese characters to express their thoughts in the *idu* system which was instituted during the Shilla period. Needless to say, the Confucian scholars wrote their works in pure Chinese as all government documents were compiled in the Chinese language.

King Sejong, who earlier had displayed his national consciousness glorifying the founder of the Yi dynasty in an epic poem, concluded that the Koreans ought to have their own script, and he commissioned such scholars as Sŏng Sam-mun and Chŏng In-ji of the Academy of Scholars to create a writing system for the Korean language, and in 1443 they presented to him a phonetic writing system. The king officially adopted it, and promulgated it with a royal edict in 1446, despite the opposition of many conservative Confucian scholars.

The new system was called *Hunmin chŏng-ŭm*, or "Authentic Sound for the Instruction of the People." Those who regarded Chinese culture as superior called it *ŏnmun*, meaning "vernacular writing." The Korean script is commonly called *han-gŭl*.

The simple but scientific system of writing consisted of eleven (now ten) vowels, fourteen consonants, eleven diphthongs (double vowels) and thirteen double consonants.

The six basic vowels are:

a ŏ o u ŭ and i
아 어 오 우 으   이

Four companion vowels are:

ya yŏ yo and yu
야 여 요   유

Double vowels (diphthongs) are:

ae yae e ye oe wi ŭi wa wŏ and wae
애 얘 에 예 외 위 의 와 워   왜

Single consonants are:

g/k n d/t r/l m b/p/v
ㄱ ㄴ ㄷ ㄹ ㅁ ㅂ

s ng j/ch ch' k' t' p' and h
ㅅ ㅇ ㅈ ㅊ ㅋ ㅌ ㅍ   ㅎ

Double consonats are:

kk ks nj nh tt lg lm lb lt lh pp ps ss tch
ㄲ ㄳ ㄵ ㄶ ㄸ ㄺ ㄻ ㄼ ㄽ ㅀ ㅃ ㅄ ㅆ ㅉ

The consonant ㅇ has a neutral sound as an initial consonant, but it has the *ng* sound as a final consonant. Thus, 앙 is pronounced as *ang*. The consonant ㅅ produces a *t* sound as a final consonant, but if followed by a vowel combined with the consonant ㅇ, its *s* sound is carried to the following word. Thus, 옷 is read as *ot*, but 옷이 is read as *oshi*.

The Koreans adopted the Chinese style of writing, that is to say, their writing begins from the upper right-hand corner and is read down vertically. The use of punctuation is a recent practice. One vowel and consonant each, or one double vowel and consonant or a double consonant each make up a word unit. For example, 다 is *ta*, 밤 is *pam*, and 닭 is *tak*. As shown above, a final consonant or a final double consonant is placed below the combination of an initial consonant and a vowel. The sound of the last consonant of a double consonant is linked with the sound of the vowel with the consonant ㅇ that follows it. Thus 닭이 (*talgi*) is read as if written as 달기 as in the case of 옷이 (*oshi*).

The new writing system enabled the Koreans to transcribe their spoken words into writing. However, with a few exceptions, Confucian scholars generally refused to write in Korean script. This was a result of the Sinification of Koreans and the development of what became known as *mohwa sasang* (admiration for things Chinese) and *sadaejuŭi* (subservience to big power). Consequently, almost all works of Korean scholars as well as all government publications were written in the Chinese language.

However, the *han-gŭl* became increasingly important as a medium of communication for the commoners as well as for the writers of *shijo*, folk tales and popular stories. Regardless of their status, both scholars and commoners wrote *shijo* in Korean to express their inner feelings. The moon, the rocks, the water, the trees, and other things in nature became subject matter for the expression of the feelings of lovers, the broken-hearted, the lamentation of old age, the vanity of life, and life's sadness as well as joy.

Kasa and Shijo Literature.   While many scholars composed Chinese-style poems known in Korea as *Hanshi,* an increasing number of people, including

Confucian scholars, wrote *kasa* (two four-syllable semantic units of Korean lyric verse) and *shijo*, a distinctive Korean poetic form which developed toward the end of the Koryo period. Among the *kasa* writers was Chŏng Ch'ŏl (1536–1593) who composed such song as *Kwandong pyŏlgok* (Song of the Eastern Scenes). All Chinese-style poems were written in Chinese characters, but all *shijo* were written in Korean after the promulgation of the *han-gŭl*.

The *shijo* or "occasional verses" became increasingly popular as a medium for expressing the sentiments of the people. The *shijo* was composed mostly by the *yangban* people, including many women, who were educated, but some popular *shijo* were written by the members of the "low-born" class known as *kisaeng* (female entertainers, or *geisha* in Japan).

Numerous outstanding scholar-poets of the middle and late periods of the Yi dynasty left behind masterpieces of *shijo*. Shin Hum (1566–1628), who was a state minister but was forced to retire to a remote area on the Soyang River near Ch'unch'ŏn, Kangwŏn Province, in order to escape from the tyrannical ruler, Kwanghaegun, wrote the following *shijo* around 1613:

> *Do not laugh, foolish people*
> *Whether my roof beams are long or short or*
> *The pillars are crooked.*
> *The snail shell, my grass hut,*
> *The vines that cover it, the encircling hills*
> *And the bright moon above,*
> *Are mine, and mine alone.*

An outstanding scholar named Sŏng Sam-mun (1418–1456) wrote the following immortal *shijo*:

> *Were you to ask me what I'd wish to become*
> *In the world beyond this world,*
> *I would answer:*
> *I would be a pine tree, tall and hardy*
> *On the highest ridge of Mt. Pongnae*
> *And I shall be green, alone green*
> *When snowflakes fly.*

Yun Sŏn-do (1589–1617), who is regarded as the greatest poet in the *shijo* form, wrote many *shijo* while creating a new (long) form of *shijo*. He wrote a lengthy poem entitled "The Angler's Four Seasons," but the following short *shijo* which he composed is more popular in Korea:

> *How many friends have I?*
> *Water and rock, pine and bamboo.*
> *The rising moon on the East Mountain,*

How glad am I to welcome you.
What else do I need?
I have five friends.

A literary critic has said that Yun was the first Korean poet who "exposed the beauty of the Korean language in exquisite felicities and graceful and delicately varied yet forceful rhythm."

Among many outstanding writers of *shijo* in the Yi period was a *kisaeng* named Hwang Chin-i (1516–1559), who wrote the following romantic *shijo*.

I would cut the waist of
The long November night,
And roll up one half
And keep it under my coverlet
Of the spring breeze.
And when my love returns to me
I would unroll it inch by inch.

Another *kisaeng* left behind the following *shijo*:

I send you branches of the willow.
Plant them, my Lord, to be admired,
Outside your bedroom window.
Perhaps the night rain will make them bud:
Think, then, that it is I
Who have come to be with you.

Science, Handicraft, and Technology.   Under the encouragement of Sejong, inventors and scientists, during the mid-fifteenth century, were as active as were the scholars and literary leaders, and such instruments as the water clock, the pendulum clock, the metal rain gauge, machine-gun-like weapons, flying machines, and various astronomical and navigational instruments were produced.

Korean master craftsmen in the field of furniture making produced exquisite and highly artistic decorative furniture such as bookcases, chests, desks, and brush holders. Lacquer-ware makers, silversmiths, and other metalworkers also produced artistic, high quality goods, including candle stands and dining utensils.

The secret formula of Koryŏ green celadon ware was lost when makers of this precious ware were killed and their kilns destroyed during the Mongol wars, but potters of the Yi period continued to produce the black-glazed as well as the white-glazed porcelain wares of the Koryŏ period. Influenced by the Ming porcelain art, the Korean potters produced high quality *paekcha*, or "white porclain ware" with blue, copper, or iron under-glaze, discarding certain feminine qualities of Koryŏ porcelain wares. They demonstrated their imaginativeness and artistic talent with new styles and new designs.

With the decline of Buddhism and the rise of Confucianism, the forms of porcelain ware, which had been popularized by a Buddhist-oriented élite of Koryŏ, were replaced by new forms, in response to a growing demand of the court and the *yangban* class. Among them were water droppers, brush holders and trays, and vases. More widely used porcelain ware was a heavy, unpretentious *punch'ŏng,* or "powder green" ware, such as variously shaped and sized bottles and jars with either over-glaze or under-glaze decorations, which became an important item in trade with Japan. Increasing amounts of brown-glazed ware of all sizes were produced as the potter's wheel was widely used.

Various ways developed by Koreans of the Three Kingdoms period to polish or grind grains continued to exist. Meanwhile, water mills (*mulbang-a*) became widespread. A typical water mill looked like a seesaw with a tank attached to one end of a long wooden shaft. When water filled the tank located outside the miller's hut, the other end of the shaft where a wooden pestle was pegged in went up, and as the tank tipped, losing water, the pestle end of the shaft came down, grinding the grain in the mortar. A seesaw type mill operated by the weight of one or two persons was also used. The grinding of grains was done also in the wooden mortar (*chŏlgu*) by a human-operated pestle, by an animal-operated millstone, or on a pair of round grinding stones with a wooden handle.

The Decline of the Yi Dynasty

The Yi dynasty displayed various symptoms of decay, revealing its weaknesses. A prolonged power struggle between the monarchy and the bureaucracy, as well as the factional power struggle among scholar-officials had created an unstable political situation and the prestige of the dynasty declined. The rebellions and foreign invasions of the late 16th and early 17th centuries further weakened the foundation of the nation.

Rebellions. The rebellion of Lim Kŏ-jŏng which erupted in 1562 in Hwanghae Province was the first peasant rebellion of the Yi period. When Lim, a man without a clear identity, formed a bandit group in the name of justice, hundreds of disgruntled and unhappy peasants who had been exploited by absentee landlords joined him and rampaged in the region, causing political havoc and much property damage. Many towns and villages were burned down and hundreds of people were killed.

Although the plot of Chŏng Yŏ-rip of Chŏnju, Chŏlla Province, was discovered in 1589 and Chŏng and his supporters were arrested and executed, a precarious political situation developed in Seoul as a result of Chŏng's attempt. Chŏng was a well-educated individual who was a member of the Eastern Men faction. He had served in the central government, but was forced to retire during the reign of Sonjo (reigned 1567–1608). Following this unsuccessful plot, the government in Seoul regarded Chŏlla Province as "the land of the rebels and untrustworthy people,'' and refused to employ men of that region and thereby caused a regional antagonism of Chŏlla Province against Seoul and men of Kyŏngsang and other regions who controlled the government. The derogatory attitude which grew toward the people of that region lasted throughout the Yi period and even longer.

Yi Kwal's rebellion of 1624, which erupted in P'yŏng-an Province, was the most serious rebellion of a military commander. Yi, who felt that he was not properly rewarded for his service in connection with the ousting of Kwanghaegun (reigned 1608–1623) and the accession of King Injo (reigned 1623–1649), raised a military rebellion. When his rebel forces invaded Seoul, Injo fled to Kongju in the southcentral region. It was the first time that a rebel force had ever invaded Seoul and forced the king to flee.

The Japanese Invasions.   Toyotomi Hideyoshi, who established his hegemony in Japan in the latter part of the 16th century, had hoped but failed to receive cooperation from the Ming dynasty in his attempt to make himself a new *Shōgun* (Japanese military dictator). He decided to attack China and then force the Chinese to recognize him as the new master over Japan. As the first step he launched a war against Korea, a vassal to China which had refused an alliance with Japan and denied the passage of Japanese troops through its country.

Some 160,000 Japanese invaded Korea twice, first in 1592 and again in 1597, in the "Seven-Year War," bringing the already deteriorated political, economic, and social order to a state of complete collapse. Korean troops who had no modern weapons were unable to check the Japanese who had rifles. The king and his court fled to Ŭiju, and Japanese troops occupied many key towns in the southern part of Korea. At one point, they advanced as far north as Pyongyang. It was at this juncture that Hideyoshi proposed to China the division of Korea—the north as a self-governing Chinese satellite, and the south to remain in Japanese hands.

With military assistance given by China, combined with the heroic efforts made by the Koreans themselves, and Korean naval victories won by General Yi Sun-shin (1545–98), together with Hideyoshi's death in 1598, the Japanese abandoned their grand design and withdrew from Korea. But the "Seven-Year War" between Korea and Japan left deep scars in Korea. The farmlands were devastated, irrigation dikes were destroyed, villages and towns were burned down, the population was first plundered and then dispersed, and tens of thousands of skilled workers (celadon ware makers) were either killed during the war or taken to Japan as captives. The long war reduced the productive capacity of farmlands from 1,708,000 *kyŏl* to 541,000 *kyŏl*. A Korean poet, Pak Il-lo, described the results of the Japanese aggression in his poem, *Song of Great Peace*, as follows:

> *Higher than mountains*
> *The bones pile up in the fields.*
> *Vast cities and great towns*
> *Became the burrows of wolves and foxes.*

Pillage by Chinese troops who went to Korea to oppose the Japanese only added to the unmitigated tragedy of a war from which the peninsula kingdom never fully recovered.

The ruling class of Korea, failing to read the writing on the wall, made no attempts to institute reforms so as to revitalize the economy and restore unity. No sooner had the Japanese withdrawn from Korea than factional disputes flared up again, wasting more human resources.

Following the Japanese wars, relations between Korea and Japan had been completely suspended. After the death of Toyotomi Hideyoshi, however, negotiations between the Korean court and the Tokugawa Shogunate were carried out via the Japanese lord on Tsushima Island in the Korea Strait. In 1604, Tokugawa Ieyasu, wishing to restore commercial relations with Korea because Japan needed Korean food grains, met Korea's demands and released some 3,000 Koreans who had been taken captive to Japan during the Hideyoshi's wars and allowed them to return to Korea. As a result, in 1607, a Korean mission visited Edo, and diplomatic and trade relations were restored on a limited basis.

The Manchu Invasion.   Korea, which served the Ming dynasty as its vassal, was considered by the Manchu leaders as an obstacle to achieving their ambition of overthrowing the Ming. Thus, in order to secure their flank, the Manchus overran northwestern Korea in 1627 and forced the Yi government to declare a state of neutrality. This declaration the Korean court never honored. Consequently, the Manchus invaded Korea again in late 1636 and forced it to accept vassalage to the Manchu Empire. Subsequently, a tremendous amount of gold, silver, grain and other products of Korea, as well as a large number of skilled workers, were sent to the Manchu court. Needless to say, the war with the Manchus and the tribute goods sent to them caused tremendous economic strain and hardship for the Korean people. Kim Sang-hŏn, who was taken hostage by the Manchus, wrote the following poem, expressing his sorrows:

> *Fare thee well, Mt. Samgak.*
> *We shall meet again, Han River.*
> *I leave the mountains and rivers of my homeland.*
> *In these uncertain times,*
> *Who could tell that I might return?*

Following the conquest of China by the Manchus and their establishment of the Ch'ing dynasty in 1644, Korea remained a vassal to China until 1894. When, in 1654 and 1658, the Manchus clashed with Russians in the Amur (Black Dragon) River region, the Korean government sent over one hundred riflemen to assist the Manchus. In 1712, negotiations carried out between Korea and China led to the establishment of new boundaries between Korea and Manchuria, and the stone monument marking the boundaries was erected at the foot of Mt. Paektu. With this, Korea lost her territorial claims in southeastern Manchuria.

The Westerners in Korea.   The first European who is known to have visited Korea was a Catholic priest who accompanied General Konishi Yukinaga, a "Christian *daimyō*" who invaded Korea in 1592. Not much about the Catholic priest is known, but evidently Konishi brought him to Korea to perform religious rites for him and his troops who were Catholics.

The first group of Westerners who arrived in Korea was of Dutch origin. A Dutch ship was wrecked near Cheju Island in 1628, and Jan Janse Weltevree and two other Dutchmen who were rescued by the Koreans were forced to work at government manufactories as slaves, helping the Koreans in weapon making and military training. During the war with the Manchus in 1636, two of

THE ROYAL SEAL OF KING INJO (reigned 1622–49) IN
CHINESE CHARACTERS AND MANCHU SCRIPT

Weltevree's countrymen died in military action, and Weltevree himself died in Korea under the Korean name of Pak Yŏn.

Another Dutch ship, the *Sparrow Hawk*, was wrecked near Cheju Island in August 1653. Like the earlier Dutch group, some thirty of the Dutch crew including Hendrick Hamel, who were rescued, were kept in Korea as workers at government arms manufactories. In September 1666, eight surviving Dutchmen, including Hamel who had met Weltevree, escaped from Korea to Japan. After returning to Holland, Hamel published a book in 1668, and introduced Korea to the West.

As in Japan, Western Learning could have developed in Korea in the seventeenth century and benefited the Koreans. However, the Korean government failed to take advantage of the opportunity to establish trade relations with the Dutch and bring about a new cultural development by importing knowledge and technology from the West.

Self-Awakening and the Reform Movement

Facing many problems following the Japanese invasions, Sŏnjo (reigned 1567–1608) carried out reforms in order to revitalize the national economy and restore social order. As a result, a new tax administration called Sŏnhyech'ŏng was established and a new system of tax collection called *Taedongpŏp* was instituted in 1608, requiring the payment of land tax in rice. But later the payment of land tax in cloth or coins as well as grains was allowed. The new tax payment system enabled the peasants to have more food and it stimulated the growth of the handicraft industry, especially cloth production, which in turn induced the growth of commercial activity as more merchants became involved in handling government collected tax goods. The number of "government merchants" and wholesale firms grew, fostering a capitalistic economy. Such large merchant firms as the *Kangsang* in Seoul and the *Songsang* in Kaesŏng arose and dominated commercial activities in the central and southern regions of the country. Meanwhile, the *Mansang* in Ŭiju played an important role in trade with China.

Sŏnjo's successor, Kwanghaegun, further reduced the factional struggle and strengthened national defense by improving military training programs as well as weapons. However, his deeds were nullified by the Manchu invasions.

No sooner had a new relationship between the Yi court and the Ch'ing dynasty in China been established than the factionalism revived. The reign of Sukchong (reigned 1674–1720) witnessed fierce and malicious factional struggles in 1680, 1689, and 1694, which resulted in the death of many outstanding scholars such as Song Shi-yŏl, leader of the Old Doctrine faction. The minimal economic recovery which was made during this period was negated by the steady increase of population from about 2.3 million in 1657, to 5 million in 1668, and 6.8 million in 1717. Food shortages became progressively worse, and in 1671 over 300,000 people died of famine.

With the accession of Yŏngjo (reigned 1724–1776), the Old Doctrine faction regained power, but it brought about in 1728 in Ch'ungch'ŏng Province the rebellion of Yi In-jwa of Young Doctrine faction. Following the subjugation of Yi's rebellion, the Old Doctrine faction maintained a relatively stable political situation under the enlightened rule of King Yŏngjo.

The Rise of Reformists of the Shirhak School.   The scholars of the *Shirhak* (Practical Learning) might be called the men of "New Economics and Statecraft," displaying more original and innovative ideas, as well as a more progressive and modernistic world outlook than other Confucianists. They advocated political, economic, social, and educational reforms which Korea desperately needed, particularly following the tragic events of the Japanese and Manchu invasions. Their awareness of Korea's weaknesses, contrasted with her rich cultural heritage, induced them to be rebellious toward the purely theoretical Neo-Confucianism and other schools of Confucianism as well as the inept and indifferent government. At the same time, perceiving the decline of political morality and the vastly worsened economic conditions of the people, they attempted to inaugurate a "New Deal" policy in order to bring about desired changes for the well-being of the nation and its people.

The ideals of the *Shirhak* scholars were aimed at the realization of the "Spirit of the Kingly Way" of the ancient sage kings of China, and at influencing the government to take positive and pragmatic actions to ameliorate the conditions of the people. The former would establish an enlightened and benevolent rule and political justice, while the latter would implement financial, educational, and social reform programs. The *Shirhak* scholars proposed the following criteria as prerequisite to the restoration of national power: (1) the critical examination of political and social conditions, (2) the reestablishment of morality and ethics in politics, (3) reconstruction of the economy, (4) adoption of a more liberal policy toward economic activities of the people, and (5) revitalization of the intellectual atmosphere and the promotion of education.

The *Shirhak* thoughts were germinated by such scholars as Kim Yuk (Chamgok, 1580–1658), Yi Su-gwang (1563–1628), and Yun Chŭng (1629–1714), some of whom had traveled to China and come into contact with the Jesuit priests there. The *Shirhak* movement, one of the most important intellectual movements of Korea, became most active during the 18th and early 19th centuries with the appearance of such scholars as Yu Hyŏng-wŏn (Pan-gye, 1622–1673), Yi Ik (Songho, 1681–1763), Pak Chi-wŏn (Yŏnam, 1737–1805), Pak Che-ga (Ch'ojŏng, 1750–?), and Chŏng Yag-yong (Tasan, 1762–1836).

The *Shirhak* scholars believed that all ideas and practices should be judged on their utilitarian merits, and their main concern was the promotion of the welfare of the nation and people. Yun Chŭng, for example, advocated a break with tradition and the discovery of new ways for the government to deal effectively with national problems. It was his belief that the king could not exist without the people, but the people could exist without the king.

Yu Hyŏng-wŏn in his *Essay on Social Reform* which is included in *Pan-gye surok* (*Collection of Essays by Pan-gye*) proposed, among other reforms, the establishment of a new land system under which equitable benefits could be had by all men, abolition of the civil service examination system and adoption of a new recruitment system in order to innovate the government, abolition of the existing social structure and the establishment of equality for all people, and the promotion of new learning. Echoing Yu, Pak Chi-wŏn in his article, "Petition on Mutual Discourse," criticized discrimination against illegitimate male descendants and petitioned the king to abolish this system. Another scholar named Yu Su-wŏn advocated the breakdown of class barriers, equality of opportunity in government and education, as well as the development of commerce. As they advocated new studies other than those of Confucian classics and subjects related to Confucianism, they emphasized the need to educate and enlighten the people and to promote scientific and foreign language studies. At the same time, they pointed out the need to import advanced civilization and knowledge and technology from abroad, promote trade and develop commerce, establish a banking system, as well as mining industry, fisheries, fruit cultivation, and stock breeding. Their advocacy of the breakdown of class barriers was revolutionary.

The new learning movement which was promoted by the *Shirhak* scholars brought about studies and the publication of books on military matters, finance, agriculture, as well as history and geography of Korea. The growth of interest in the study of Korean history and geography was a significant intellectual development which nurtured the national consciousness of the Korean people. Hong Man-jong produced a hand written book, *Tongguk yŏktae* (*History of the Eastern Country*), which included a map of Korea, between 1674 and 1704. Historical works published in the 18th century were books such as *Outline of the History of Korea* (*Tongsa kangmok*) by An Chŏng-bok (1712–1791), *Unofficial History of the Yi Dynasty* by Yi Kŭng-ik (1736–1806), and *History of Ancient Korea* (*Haedong yŏksa*) by Han Ch'i-yun (1765–1814). *Encyclopedia Koreana* published in 1770, as well as a book on geography entitled *Geographical Description of the Eight Provinces* by Yi Chung-hwan (1690–1760?), not only increased the knowledge about Korea, but also raised the national consciousness of the Korean people. Shin Kyŏng-jun's books on geography and language, and epigraphical works by Kim Chŏng-hŭi (Wandang/Ch'usa, 1786–1856) also contributed to the promotion of knowledge about Korea and Korean culture. A Korean language dictionary entitled *On the Names of Things* by Yu Hŭi, reflected the growing national consciousness among Korean scholars. Numerous maps of Korea were produced in the early 19th century.

Chŏng Yag-yong, a *Shirhak* scholar who became a devout Catholic and a

Western Learning scholar, authored many books on geography, education, agriculture, medicine, economic matters and politics. Among his works were a political handbook entitled *Mongmin shimsŏ,* an economic essay entitled *Kyŏngse yup'yo,* a pharmacological work entitled *On Vaccination for Smallpox,* and a jurisprudential work entitled *Hŭmhŭm shinsŏ.* His work on vaccination for smallpox heralded the rise of a new medical interest in Korea.

Those *Shirhak* scholars who paid special attention to the development of commerce and manufacturing, as well as urban development, were known as men of Northern Learning (*Puk'ak*) who imported knowledge about the West from China. Many of them traveled to China, and they endeavored to bring about housing innovations by using bricks, and they advocated general improvements of the living conditions and environment of the people in urban as well as in rural areas. This group of scholars included Pak Chi-wŏn, Hong Tae-yong (1731–1783), and Pak Che-ga. Like Pak Che-ga, Pak Chi-wŏn traveled to China in the 18th century, and in 1780 wrote a book entitled *Yŏrha ilgi (Jehol Diary),* a travelogue, which contained his reform concepts related to commercial development, foreign trade, and agriculture, and which emphasized the need to improve farming methods, including the irrigation system, as well as the development of land and sea transportation.

The *Shirhak* scholars made an enormous contribution to intellectual development and scholarship. At the same time, they stimulated the development of academic and scholarly activities of other Confucian scholars while influencing the kings to adopt reform measures.

Reforms of Yŏngjo and Chŏngjo.   The two enlightened monarchs, Yŏngjo and Chŏngjo who reigned during the period between 1724 and 1800, made various efforts to stabilize the political situation and reduced factional disputes by taking personal initiatives in state affairs. They adopted a policy of "equal opportunity" and employed men of all ideological persuasion, or factional colors, in the government. They revised the tax system making it more rational, revised laws and adopted supplementary codes of law, published textbooks on military strategy, history, and other subjects. Both Yŏngjo and Chŏngjo carried out the reform in hair style of women, acting against the traditional large wigs worn by women. They encouraged women to have simple hair styles and wear small hats called *chokturi.*

The reform work of King Yŏngjo was interrupted by the Rebellion of Yi In-jwa in 1728. Yi and his supporters in Seoul and P'yŏng-an Province, who were members of the Young Doctrine faction, rebelled against the government controlled by the Old Doctrine faction, causing a serious political crisis as well as social instability. To make matters worse, in 1748 famine and epidemics struck the nation, causing the death of over 500,000 people.

In order to ameliorate the conditions of the people, King Yŏngjo instituted the Equal Duty Law (*Kyunyŏkpŏp*) in 1750, and reduced the amount of tax paid in cloth by half while taxes on fish, salt, and fishing boats as well as a value-added tax on farmland, payable in rice or in cash, were added. Those male adults who were not in military service (there were some 500,000 in the military around 1750) were required to pay the military tax in cloth. However, the Equal Duty Law did not reduce the hardships of the peasants in any significant way.

In order to check the abuses of power of governors and other local magistrates, the government instituted a secret inspectorate, and the king frequently appointed *amhaeng ŏsa* (king's secret inspectors), granting them an ultimate authority equal to his own, and sent them out to various localities to check the immoral, unjust, and corrupt practices and behavior of the officials in order to reduce the grievances of the people.

During his reign, Chŏngjo (reigned 1776–1800), banished Shamans from the court, banned their entrance into the capital, and instituted a benevolent relief program for the poor. However, it was not possible for the Yi dynasty to revitalize the national economy as flood, famine, and epidemics worsened the situation. The cultivation of sweet potatoes after 1763 reduced the food shortage somewhat, but the steady population growth from 6.8 million in 1717 to 7.5 million in 1800 did not allow the economic improvement of the poor.

King Chŏngjo established the Royal Library (*Kyujanggak*), encouraging scholarly activities, and brought about further improvement of printing techniques. During his reign, *Supplement to Encyclopedia Koreana*, and *Collection of Grand State Codes*, and *Diplomatic Archives* were published. Yi Myŏng-yang, who visited Peking as King Sunjo's envoy's attendant in 1806, wrote a travelogue entitled *Puwa yŏllok*, and provided more information regarding the recent developments in China.

Growing Internal Problems. Two young kings, Sunjo (reigned 1801–34) and Hŏnjong (reigned 1834–49), succeeded to the throne at the ages of eleven and eight, respectively. During their reigns what little had been accomplished by Yŏngjo and Chŏngjo was almost completely undone as the influence of the queens and their relatives grew, power was usurped by the officials, and the tax burden on the people increased. In addition, the factional struggle of scholar-officials revived and the government became embroiled in palace intrigues and bitter power struggle first between the Kim and the Hong clans, and then between the Kim and the Cho clans. As a result of the rise of power and influence of queens' families, there developed what became known as *sedo chŏngch'i*, or "power politics" practiced by the bureaucrats of powerful clans, particularly those of the Kim clan of Andong in Kyŏngsang Province.

Usurpation of power by the officials and irregularities among them were rampant. The people's confidence diminished sharply as the economic situation worsened, and the restlessness of the unhappy people was expressed through anti-government agitators who appeared on the scene everywhere. In

1812, Hong Kyŏng-nae, a native of Yonggang, P'yŏng-an Province, who had been critical of the discriminatory policy of the government against the men of his province, brought about a large-scale rebellion.

Meanwhile, a plot of some officials to dethrone Sunjo was discovered, and a member of the royal house and several officials were executed. In 1813, a rebellion on Cheju Island erupted, and it was followed by an uprising of a group of bandits in 1816 under a misguided Buddhist monk named Haksang. Great floods of 1810 and 1818 in the southern provinces, and the 1820 floods which struck the whole country were followed by those of 1822, 1823, 1824, 1829, and 1832. To make matters worse, a cholera epidemic in 1812 ravaged the whole country for several years. These events reduced the population from 7.5 million in 1807 to 6.7 million. As the government was bankrupt and had no relief measures, the discontent and restlessness of the people reached a dangerous point. In the spring of 1862, a disgruntled ex-official brought about an uprising in Chinju, Kyŏngsang Province, and an uprising on Cheju Island and that in Iksan, Chŏlla Province followed soon after that, plunging the country into unmanageable chaos.

A Confucian scholar, Pak Hyo-sŏng, in an urgent petition to the throne advocating drastic and immediate reform, described the state of the kingdom as follows:

> The ministers spend all their time reading books; nepotism and bribery are the rule rather than the exception; the judges sit and wait for bribes; the examiners of the civil service examinations receive money in advance, and merit can make no headway against cupidity; the censors have been dumb; the prefects do nothing but extort money from the people; luxury saps the strength and wealth of the land; grain storage warehouses are empty and the government welfare programs are without means; and the whole commonwealth is diseased and rotten to the core.

King Ch'ŏlchong (reigned 1849–1863) did what he could to bring about stability, but his reign was cut short by his untimely death, leaving behind the kingdom in a state of hopelessness.

New Cultural Trends

Despite international and external problems, cultural vitality and the dynamism of Koreans was manifested in a variety of ways during the middle period of the Yi dynasty, bringing the development of new concepts, arts, and folk culture.

New Writers.   Although the *Shirhak* scholars did not establish such academic discipline as *Kuk'ak* ("National Learning") as such in a way similar to the Japanese Shintō scholars' promotion of *Kokugaku* in Japan, they did sow the seed of national consciousness as has been discussed earlier. They promoted studies about Korea, her geography, history, and language, as well as internal conditions.

Significantly, an increasing number of scholars wrote their works in Korean script, reflecting the growing national consciousness of the people. For example, Hong Tae-yong (Tamhŏn, 1731–1783), a *Shirhak* scholar of the Northern Learning branch, published his *Tamhŏn yŏn-gi*, a record of his journey to Peking, in 1765 in Korean. Hong, like Pak Che-ga and other reform advocates, emphasized the need to promote scientific studies and technology, importation of Western science and technology, as well as the improvement of the transportation system.

Another scholar whose identity is yet to be established (he used the pseudonym Limha Hosaeng) wrote a biography entitled *Chukch'ŏn ilgi* (*Diary of Chukch'ŏn*) in Korean script sometime in the mid-seventeenth century, and gave a detailed account of the life of a scholar-official named Yi Tŏk-hyŏng (Chukch'ŏn, 1566–1645), and of the accession of Injo to the throne in 1623. Many reform-minded Confucian scholars wrote popular literature as it will be discussed shortly hereafter.

A number of outstanding *shijo* writers emerged and produced masterpieces, popularizing *han-gŭl*. Among them was a Chief State Counselor named Nam Ku-man (1629–1711), who wrote the following *shijo*:

> *Does dawn light the east window?*
> *Already larks sing in the sky.*
> *Where is the boy that tends the ox*
> *Has he not yet roused himself?*
> *When will he get his plowing done*
> *In the long field over the hill?*

A *shijo* writer named Yi T'aek (1651–1719) expressed his notion of human equality in the following poem:

> *O rock, do not ridicule*
> *The smallness of black birds:*
> *You and they both fly*
> *In the ninety thousand-li-long sky.*
> *Both you and they are birds in flight;*
> *Who can distinguish you from them?*

Another poet, Yi Ch'ae (1725–1776) wrote the following *shijo*, lamenting the troublesome situation of his time as follows:

> *The morning star has set,*
> *The larks are in the sky..*
> *As I take my hoe and leave my cottage,*
> *Heavy dew soaks my hempen clothes.*

Lad, if these were peaceful times,
Who'd be fretting about his wet clothes?

The first anthology of the *shijo*, entitled *Eternal Words of the Green Hills*, compiled by a poet named Kim Ch'ŏn-t'aek, was published in 1728.

New Arts.   Many disillusioned Confucian scholars turned to the arts, fleeing from turbulent political controversies. Among them was Kim Chŏng-hŭi (1786–1836), whose many pen names included Wandang and Ch'usa. He was not only a master calligrapher, but also the author of the first book on Korean epigraphy and an outstanding essayist. It was he who established a new Korean calligraphic form, independent of Chinese models, known as the Ch'usa style.

The conservative, traditional, and unimaginative painters produced traditional Chinese style landscapes and other paintings. However, new painters emerged who produced nontraditional paintings in the 18th century. Chŏng Sŏn (Kyŏmjae, 1676–1759), was perhaps the first Korean to create a Korean style of landscape painting. He traveled widely in Korea, and his paintings depicted the beauty of his native land in a unique style.

An individualistic style of painting has been promoted by such painters as Kang Hŭi-an in the 15th century. Meanwhile, a group of Korean painters who were influenced by a new style of Chinese painting established a new school called *Chŏlp'a* in Korea. It developed in the Chiechiang region in China in the middle of the sixteenth century and emphasized men in action. Among many outstanding Korean painters who promoted the *Chŏlp'a* style were Kim Shi (Yangsongdang), Ham Yundŏk, and Kim Myŏng-guk (Yŏndam, 1623–1649).

During the seventeenth century, many painters produced unique paintings which departed from earlier emphasis on landscapes. Kim Myŏng-guk painted such masterpieces as "Dharma," "Moon Viewing by the River," and "Homeward Bound in the Snow." Han Shi-gak (Sŏlt'an, b. 1621) painted "Podae," a spirit of good omen, and others, enriching the field of art in Korea. Yi Myŏng-uk of the late seventeenth-early eighteenth century painted delightful pictures such as "Chat Between a Fisherman and a Woodcutter," while Shim Sa-jŏng (Hyŏnjae, 1707–1769), painted "Goblin Playing with a Toad," "Cat" and other masterpieces, promoting a new style of painting. Their bold strokes, simplicity, spontaneity, liveliness, and economy of line, and their humorous capture of the fleeting momentary scene of men in action were outstanding characteristics of this new modernistic style of painting.

The Rise of Genre Painters.   The loosening of the intellectual climate and the changing social environment, coupled with the growing interest in nativism and the search for realities, encouraged Korean artists to create new (non-Chinese) literature and arts. As a result, Yun Tu-sŏ (b. 1668) and Cho Yŏng-u (Kwanajae, 1686–1761) nurtured an entirely new Korean genre painting (*p'ungsok'wa*) whose style was further developed by such masters as Kim Hong-do (Tanwŏn, b. 1745), Shin Yun-bok (Hyewŏn, b. 1758) and Kim Tūk-shin (Kūngjae, 1754–1822). Tanwŏn Kim Hong-do, who was already an accomplished landscape painter in the Chinese style, produced many masterpieces of genre paintings using more colors and humorously depicting the manners and customs of the *yangban* gentlemen (*sŏnbi*), as well as portraying others such as farmers, travelers, housewives, teachers and pupils at a village school, shopkeepers and workers. His paintings of wrestlers, house-builders, and a boy dancer won him fame. The combining of the landscape with men in action became his trademark.

Hyewŏn Shin Yun-bok depicted the manners of the *yangban* at various social events, such as boating parties, officials visiting local inns, and gentlemen playing chess matches. His paintings of women in action, such as a *kisaeng* viewing the lotus, women washing their hair on *Tano* (the 5th day of the 5th moon) by a mountain creek, a rendezvous scene of a gentleman and a lady, and many others delighted the viewers. Kim Tūk-shin's "P'ajŏk" ("Breaking of the Calm") is one of the most delightful and humorous genre paintings of the time. These genre painters displayed exceptional creative and artistic qualities in their work, establishing a Korean style. Their nativism and their reproduction of the realities of life in their paintings contributed much to the development of Korean folk culture.

The Development of Folk Culture. The antagonism of the common people toward the *yangban* culture which was dominated by Chinese concepts and modes led to the rise of a new and significant Korean culture. The disenchantment of certain members of the *yangban* class with their established cultural world, the desire of some to preserve the native tradition and re-estabilish Korean culture identity, and a certain undeniable hunger of the common people for cultural outlets to express their emotions and relieve their anxieties, may have contributed to the rise of a new folk culture (*sŏmin munhwa*), which included literature, painting, and music and dance. The snobbish people, who "worshipped" things Chinese, looked down upon the new culture promoted by the common folk, but *sŏmin munhwa* flourished in competition with the *yangban* culture as the culture of the majority.

Contrary to a common notion that this movement was promoted entirely by the common people, with the exception of certain fields such as music and dance, as well as popular entertainment, the folk culture was nurtured by many members of the *yangban* class who had formal education in Chinese studies. They sought in disguise the nature of the universe, the true meaning of life, and the naked realities of human nature and desires, while they expressed their opposition to the established norms. Their desire to escape from inflexible conventions and to express their individuality, as well as their desire to flee from their dreary life, may have led them to engage in cultural revolt.

Folk Literature.   Several "unorthodox" works, such as strange tales, as well as short stories which dealt with the realities of life, appeared in the early Yi period, paving the way for the development of folk literature. These stories had Shamanistic, Taoistic, or Buddhistic overtones. The first of these to appear was *Kŭmo shinhwa* (*New Tales from the Golden Turtle*), which were written by Kim Shi-sŭp (Maewŏltang, 1435–93), a Confucian scholar known as "Mad Monk" at Kŭmo mountain retreat in Kyŏngju. He was the first writer who pointed out the need for the emancipation of women, expressing his idea that love was an acceptable reason for marriage.

New writers who made a radical departure from the established Confucian codes and conventions reflected vastly changed social realities in their works. A Confucian scholar named Hŏ Kyun (Kyosan, 1569–1619) wrote an immortal Korean fiction, *Hong Kil-tong chŏn* (*The Tale of Hong Kil-tong*), in Korean, in which he criticized political and social evils of his time. Kim Man-jung (Sŏp'o, 1637–92) wrote *Kuun mong* (*Dream of the Cloud Nine*), a novel with strong Taoistic and Buddhistic notions. He also wrote a domestic novel entitled *Sassi namjŏng ki* (*Lady Sa Travels to the South*), glorifying a chaste woman. Like Hŏ, Kim wrote his works in pure Korean. These writers, along with the authors of *Ongnu mong* (*Dream of the Jade Pavilion*) and *Kogŭm soch'ong* (*Humorous Stories, Ancient and Present*), as well as other stories, contributed much to the rise of folk literature in Korea.

In the 18th century, a *Shirhak* scholar, Pak Chi-wŏn, wrote satirical novels, *Yangban chŏn* (*The Tale of a Yangban*) and *Hŏsaeng chŏn* (*The Tale of Master Hŏ*), as well as others which became popular. In *Yangban chŏn*, Pak Chi-wŏn portrayed the plight of a *yangban* who was even willing to sell his title to a peasant. He praised the moral and ethical qualities and goodness of the common people. In *Hŏsaeng chŏn*, Pak not only ridiculed the way of life of the *yangban*, but also criticized the government's lack of concern for the common people.

Although the authorship of many masterpieces of Korean novels is not known, perhaps because they were written by Confucian scholars who did not wish to reveal their identities, love stories and critical tales against corrupt officials such as *Ch'unhyang chŏn* (*The Tale of Ch'unhyang*). *Unyŏng chŏn* (*The Tale of Unyŏng*), *Suk'yang chŏn* (*The Tale of Suk'yang*), and *Sugyŏng nangja chŏn* (*The Tale of Maiden Sugyŏng*), all of which had a heroine as a main character and dealt with social injustices of the time, were devoured by the common people as well as others. *The Tale of Ch'unhyang* became a classic in Korean literature.

Novels dealing with the domestic situation, which were usually critical of the social system and practices, also appeared. Among them were *Changhwa Hongnyŏn chŏn* (*The Tale of Rose Flower and Pink Lotus*) and *K'ongjwi P'atchwi* (*The Tale of K'ongjwi and P'atchwi*). Like Changhwa and Hongnyŏn, who were sisters by different mothers, K'ongjwi and P'atchwi were stepsisters. The evil nature of stepmothers and the triumph of goodness were described in these novels. Novels which praised filial piety and included moral instructions also appeared. Among them were *Shim Ch'ŏng chŏn* (*The Tale of Shim Ch'ŏng*) and *Hŭngbu chŏn* (*The Tale of Hŭngbu*). Shim Ch'ŏng was a young daughter of a blind man who sacrificed her life to make Buddha open the eyes of her father, and Hŭngbu was an industrious, honest, and good but poor farmer who received many blessing from mysterious sources and became prosperous. These moralistic novels were widely read then as they are today.

Meanwhile, historical novels, such as *Imjin rok* (*Record of the Year 1592*), which dealt with the Japanese invasion, and *The Tale of Yu Ch'ungnyŏl* and *The Tale of Cho Ung* appeared. Another historical novel, *Lim Kyŏng-ŏp chŏn* (*The Tale of Lim Kyŏng-ŏp*), was a story of General Lim who repulsed the Man-chu invaders in the early 17th century.

Lim Che's novels, such as *Hwasa* (*The Story of Flowers*) satirized party strifes at court while his *Susŏng chi* (*The Story of Grievance Castle*) protested against political corruption and injustice. Novels such as *Yŏjanggun chŏn* (*The Tale of a Woman General*) and *Pakssi chŏn* (*The Tale of Lady Pak*) glorified patriotism and heroism of Korean women shown during the foreign invasions of the late 16th and early 17th centuries. These and other tales and novels enriched the lives of the people as they increased their social consciousness. At the same time, many animal stories appeared. In these animal stories, rabbits, cows, tigers, and other familiar birds and animals talked, creating fantasies in the minds of the readers young and old.

Folk Painting.   The development of folk painting (*minhwa*) is another significant aspect of the ever growing folk culture in the middle and late Yi period. Folk painting was regarded by conservative Confucian artists of the period as the work of "uncultured and unsophisticated common folk" and of their "crude and uncouth" and simple mentality because its style, subject mat-ter and colors did not conform to the standards of conventional (orthodox) Chinese art form and content.

Although some members of the literati produced folk paintings, the majority of folk painters were of a lower strata of society whose works were regarded as ar-tistically inferior and outside the mainstream of art. New "commercial artists" capitalized on the increasing popularity of folk paintings. A trademark of this art form was the absence of the name and seal of the painter and date of painting. Whereas conventional (orthodox) painters used only hair brushes and painted in black ink or light colors on silk or special paper, and always wrote their names (or pen names) and affixed their seals, folk painters used hair brushes, as well as leather brushes, willow branches, twigs, red-hot iron and even their own fingers, and painted with more colors on a variety of materials—paper, hemp and cotton cloth.

The folk painting encompassed a broad range of subjects depicting the life and beliefs of the common people. The themes ranged from the serious to the frivolous, from real objects to imaginary ones. Some of the painting had Buddhist, Taoist, and Shamanist overtones, while others depicted the agony of the masses. In style, some incorporated unnatural shapes or forms and others distorted or exaggerated forms. The subject matter included particular birds and animals, which the people believed to have direct relations with their lives, flowers, plants, landscapes, and still life objects such as books, bookcases, desks, brush holders and the like. These paintings show a rather simplistic, unsophisticated, and carefree style, outside the restraints applied to formal painting of the *yangban* class.

A common trait of the folk painting, regardless of the motif, was an identity with the daily lives of ordinary people. A key characteristic of this painting is its coloring, which traces back to the "Five Elements of Thought" of Shamanism, which viewed the world in terms of the harmony and juxtaposition of five colors—blue, red, black, white and yellow. Many folk paintings reflected folk beliefs which were expressed in folklore and folk tales, and the paintings were often used to attract good spirits or fend off evil ones. They were pasted on pillars, gates, door panels, folding screens, walls, and other strategic places in and around the house. Ten symbols of longevity—the sun, clouds, water, rocks, pine trees, bamboo, tortoises, cranes, deer, and the "herb of eternal youth"—and "four gracious princes"—plum, orchid, chrysanthemum and bamboo—, and certain animals, including dragons and birds, were popular subjects.

In their paintings, Korean folk artists amply demonstrated sensitivity, popular beliefs, honesty and truthfulness in their perceptions, and certain "Korean tastes" of the unspoiled natural man, as well as their own creativity. The folk beliefs, sense of humor and satire, simplicity, the search for the realities and the meaning of being, and the relationship between nature and the animal world, as well as between one creature and another, are clearly reflected in systematic ways and in remarkably effective economized details. The efforts which the artists made to harmonize, or create a balance of colors and lines are clearly shown in the paintings. Bold strokes and colors, naturalized styles, and highly decorative qualities became unique aspects of folk painting which is a treasurable cultural heritage of the Koreans.

Folk Music, Dance and Plays.   The folk culture of the Koreans inherited many aspects of the earlier cultures, including those of the Three Kingdoms and Koryŏ periods, and the common people not only preserved folk tradition of the past, but also enriched them further.

The folk music that flourished during the Yi period included songs and farmer's music. Folk songs were called *t'aryŏng* among which were such as *Yukcha paegi* and several versions of *Arirang*. Most of them described an unhappy state of mind or the sad conditions of life. Some of them were songs of an erotic nature which contained metaphors and indirect references to sexual nature.

Another type of folk music that became popular included *p'ansori* and *ch'ang* or *ch'anggŭk* which were sung by a singer who narrated a long epic story accompanied usually by an instrument such as a round drum (*puk*) or an hour-glass shaped drum (*changgo*). It may be regarded as native opera of Korea. Such novels as *Ch'unhyang chŏn* and *Shim Ch'ŏng chŏn* became operatic pieces and were performed by professional *p'ansori* singers.

Nong-ak, or the farmers' music, was (and still is) performed by groups of amateur musicians dressed in colorful uniforms who danced as they played various musical instruments, such as *changgo*, small hand drums, and wind instruments made of reed, bamboo, or copper. The farmers' music was associated with agricultural activities, such as preparing the fields, planting rice seedlings, weeding, and harvesting. Some farmers' dances were highly acrobatic and each village had (and still has) a *nong-ak* team. Evidently, the farmers' music took on a military aspect during the Three Kingdoms period as the peasants were organized into military corps.

Buddhism, which was rejected by the Yi dynasty after 1450, became the religion of the common people, and the Buddhist ritual music and dance became rich properties of the folk culture of Korea. Among the Buddhist ritual dances were the "Butterfly Dance" (*Nabi ch'um*), the "Drum Dance" (*Pŏpko ch'um*), the "Cymbal Dance" (*Para ch'um*), and the *T'aju*, which was performed prior to eating food. The Lantern Festival of Buddhism became more important with the abolition of the P'algwanhoe Festival by the Yi dynasty. *Sŭngmu*, or the "Monk Dance," and the "Nine Drum Dance," which have been performed by both court dancers and folk dancers, originated in Buddhism.

Whereas the court and ritual music and dances were highly stylized and performed in a slow rhythm, the folk dances were highly rhythmic, free in spirit and had spontaneity, creating a certain mood called *mŏt* or *hŭng* which means "irrepressible joy. . . almost reaching the point of giddiness. . . a joy pouring forth from within. . . from a deep sense of beauty. . . a state of everlasting exhilaration" as a writer described. The folk music and dances were highly entertaining and they were less concerned with demonstration of techniques or refined styles, but were aimed at arousing ecstatic feelings. A Korean Confucian scholar named Nam Hyo-on of the 15th century described the Korean folk dancing as follows:

We Koreans have learned the dances. . . in which we bob our heads, and roll our eyes, hump our backs and work our bodies, legs, arms, and finger tips. We shut them up and shoot them out, round after round like a twanging bow. Then, bouncing forth like dogs, we run. Upright, bear-like, we stand and then like birds with outstretched wings, we swoop. From the highest lords of state down to the lowest music-girl, all have learned these dances and take delight therein.

Various forms of the mask dance (*t'alch'um*), which emerged during the Three Kingdoms period, flourished during the Yi period. *T'al* means mask or cover, and the *t'alch'um* was performed by highly acrobatic dancers. Many mask dances were humorous in nature, and a variety of masks were used by the dancers depending on occasions; some were faces of sacred beings, some were those of the spirits, and others were those of certain persons. Some of them were used to ward off evil spirits, some were those of hunters and rainmakers, and some were those of *yangban* people who were ridiculed in the mask plays. The performers not only danced, but they also spoke words. The music which accompanied the mask dance was that of percussion and wind instruments.

There were many regional mask dances. Among them were the Lion Dance (*Saja ch'um*) of Pukch'ŏng, Hamgil (Hamgyŏng) Province, the Pongsan *t'alch'um* and the Ŭnyul *t'alch'um* of Hwanghae Province. Actors, acrobats, and circus people who were collectively called *kwangdae* or *Namsadang* and performed mask dances were male. Among the most popular mask dances was the one called *sandae nori*.

Kut or *muak* (Shaman music) is the ceremony which was presided over by Shamans. Shaman ceremonies are classified according to their functions: they can be for the benefit of a dead person's soul, the healing of a living person, the promotion of good fortune, the cleansing of a complete village, or prevention of disasters. The one thing that they all have in common is their perceived effect which is to neutralize a spirit's power of influence so that it cannot harm a particular person or people.

Shaman rituals included certain mask dances such as the *Hahoe pyŏlshin kut* of the village of Hahoe in Kyŏngsang Province, and the *Yangju pyŏlsandae nori* of Yangju in Kyŏnggi Province. One of the most spectacular shaman dances was called the *salp'uri*, or the "dance to exorcise the evil spirit." It was performed by a female (sorceress) taking the form of a spirit and playing a small hand drum with a scarf in her hand, chanting strange shamanist syllables. The Sword Dance (*kŏmmu*) and the Dance of the Descending Spirit, associated with the the *Ch'ilsŏng gut* (the Ceremony of the Seven Stars—the Big Dipper) are those of Shamanism. The Sword Dance was performed with ceremonial swords by a female shaman in bright, colorful dress and a hat.

Puppet plays also flourished as a form of public entertainment for the common folk. There were two forms of puppet plays—one where the puppet was manipulated by a puppeteer, and the other played by actors wearing masks and acting like puppets. Nearly all puppet plays were humorous, rather earthy and vulgar, and satirical in nature. Like the mask dances, all puppet plays were performed by male actors and accompanied by music, and played outdoors. One of the most popular puppet plays was *Kkoktuk kakshi*, or "Lady Kkoktuk."

While suffering from social and economic deprivation, the common people of Korea found solace and relief from spiritual and material hardships in various forms of folk culture such as music, dance, and puppet plays. Without their patronage this unique folk culture of Korea could not have survived.

Catholicism and Western Learning.   With the importation of books written by such Catholic missionaries in China as Matteo Ricci. Adam von Schall, and others by Korean envoys to Peking in the early 17th century, the *Sŏhak,* or "Western Learning," developed including studies on Catholicism, as well as astronomy, calendar, mathematics, geography, weaponry, and science and technology. As Catholicism grew in Korea, a growing number of Confucian scholars of the *Shirhak* school became attracted to Western thought, science and technology, and a variety of other aspects of the West. Yi Sŭng-hun (1756–1801), a *Shirhak* scholar, who was converted to Catholicism in Peking, established in 1784 the first Catholic church in Korea at Myŏng-dong in Seoul. Kwŏn Ch'ŏl-shin and his brothers established the Matteo Ricci Study Society in 1800. One of the *Shirhak* scholars who became a devout Catholic and engaged in Western Learning was Tasan Chŏng Yag-yong.

Despite King Chŏngjo's anti-Catholic edict of 1785 and punishment of a few Catholics in 1791, enthusiasm for Catholicism continued to rise, thanks to efforts made by the Koreans themselves. Encouraged by such development, a Portuguese priest, Jean Dos Remedios, of Macao, made an unsuccessful attempt to enter Korea in 1791. A young Chinese Catholic priest, Chou Wen-mu, however, succeeded in entering the forbidden land in 1795, fortified with religious zeal and a pious sense of mission, at which time there were already some 4,000 Korean converts to Catholicism.

Anti-Catholic feelings and reaction to Western Learning were bound to develop. Then, in 1800, when Sunjo succeeded the late king, the Old Doctrine (*Noron*) faction, which was both strongly anti-Catholic and an ally of Queen Dowager Kim, took over power from the Southern Men (*Namin*) faction, which had been somewhat lenient toward Catholicism and Western Learning. As a matter of fact, many of the Southern Men faction members were Catholics themselves.

The Old Doctrine faction initiated in 1800 a bloody persecution against Catholics as a retaliation against the Southern Men faction, and young Catholics, such as Yi Sŭng-hun, Kwŏn Ch'ŏl-shin, and a brother of Tasan Chŏng Yag-yong, Chŏng Yak-chong, all of whom were members of the Southern Men faction, were put to death. The Chinese priest, Chou Wen-mu, who surrendered to the authorities, was also executed. Tasan Chŏng Yag-yong and another brother of his were sent into exile. Some three hundred Catholics were killed or died in prison.

In response to this situation, a Korean Catholic, Hwang Sa-yong, drafted a secret petition addressed to the French Catholic bishop in Peking. In it he requested that the bishop beg the Pope to persuade the Chinese emperor to force the Korean king to grant religious freedom to Catholics. This petition was intercepted in October 1801 by the government, and Hwang together with more

Catholics were put to death.

In spite of the anti-Catholic edict and persecution of 1801, enthusiasm for Catholicism grew in Korea. In 1836, Korea became a diocese and three French missionaries—Jacques Honoré Chastan, Pierre F. Maubant, and L.M. Joseph Imbert—arrived in Korea from China. In 1839, another anti-Catholic action was taken, and the three French priests and some thirty Korean converts were put to death. The Catholics were undeterred.

In 1845, Kim Tae-gŏn (André Kim, 1822–1846), a young Korean who was ordained as a priest in Peking, went to Korea from Shanghai, accompanying Bishop Jean Ferréol and Father Henri Daveluy. Father Kim was arrested in 1846 and was executed at the age of twenty-five, but several more French priests such as Siméon F. Berneux went to Korea from China. Despite the fact, Catholicism in Korea grew steadily, and the number of Catholics increased to 11,000 by 1850, and 23,000 by 1865. Catholicism nurtured the growth of the Western Learning in Korea, but its scope was limited and it created no impact comparable to that of the Western Learning in Japan. However, it contributed to the growth of new religious thinking, the increase of interest in scientific knowledge, and the sense of a need for economic and social reform.

The Rise of Tonghak.   Conditions in Korea in the 19th century were ripe for social upheavals and the rise of protest. Ch'oe Che-u (1824–1864) was such a voice of protest in the wilderness and the founder of a new religious sect called the *Tonghak* ("Eastern Learning"). While preaching the teachings of *Ch'ŏndo,* or the "Heavenly Way," he launched a protest movement against corrupt politics, social injustice, and economic exploitation of the poor by the rich. Ch'oe, who claimed that he received a vision in which he was commissioned by Heaven to spread the doctrine of the Heavenly Way, popularized the concept of the unity of God and man. The *Tonghak* movement was a protest against Sinification, and it was also opposed to Catholicism and Western Learning. He criticized Catholicism because he believed that it had no truth, no logical sequence in its doctrine and no decorum in its worship. He stated that the Catholics "pray for selfish benefits. They have no proper spirit to inspire the spiritual or physical life of the people, and there is no teaching concerning the true God. . . They do not have our Sacred Formula."

With his Sacred Formula and other associated principles, Ch'oe preached justice and honesty in politics, order and justice in social affairs, and faith and respect for life. Unlike the later *Tonghak* movement, the early teachings of Ch'oe made no radical proposal for political action against the corrupt government and its officials. However, contrary to his original intentions, he was forced to react to the corrupt local government officials whose methods of raising money through illegal means infuriated him. When Ch'oe launched a protest movement, he was arrested and imprisoned for his heretical religious teachings which "poisoned the minds of the people," according to the government charges. The specific charges were that he preached the existence of an ultimate being superior to the king and that his doctrine was in reality identical with that of Catholicism because of his use of terms such as *ch'ŏnju* ("heavenly lord") and *sangje* ("the superior ruler in heaven"), which the Catholics were referring to as their God. Ch'oe was executed in April 1864.

Despite Ch'oe's death, his teaching of the doctrine of the Heavenly Way continued to spread and grow, producing such aggressive leaders as Ch'oe Shi-hyŏng (1827–1898) and Chŏn Pong-jun (1854–1894). Chŏn, in spite of Ch'oe Shi-hyŏng's reluctance, reshaped the Teachings of the Heavenly Way into an anti-foreign force, and changed the *Tonghak* ideology into a political, if not a revolutionary, doctrine fomenting social unrest.

The Teachings of the Heavenly Way became increasingly popular among the people, who were mistreated by corrupt officials and tax collectors, and who suffered economic deprivation and exploitation, and social injustices, particularly in the south where many large landholders lived.

5. The End of Isolation, Modernization, and the Growing National Insecurity

The Yi dynasty which had endured many serious domestic and foreign problems was utterly ill-prepared to cope with the new forces of the modern age. When the winds of change and colonialism of the West arose, Korea was forced to end her isolation, to bring about certain inevitable changes, and witness helplessly the rapidly growing politics of imperialism in the country. Korea became a nation on the anvil.

King Kojong and the Regency of the Taewŏn-gun

On January 22, 1864, a twelve-year-old nephew of the late king became King Kojong (Yi Myŏng-bok, 1852–1919) with his father as regent. His father was Yi Ha-ŭng (1820–1898), whose full title was Hŭngsŏn Taewŏn-gun, or Grand Prince Hŭngsŏn. He was commonly known as the Taewŏn-gun. The young king inherited a kingdom in disarray. It was an economically bankrupt and a socially backward "hermit kingdom" with a population of ten million, isolated from the rest of the world except China and Japan.

The Taewŏn-gun's Rule and Reform.   The decade of 1864–1873 is known in Korean history as the era of the Taewŏn-gun, who was a strong-willed and ambitious individual. His objectives were to strengthen the dynastic rule and the royal house, make his son's reign illustrious, and promote national strength. In order to achieve his objectives, he restored the authority of the Council of State (*Ŭijŏngbu*) in 1864, reducing the role of the Office of Frontier Security (*Pibyŏnsa*), which had been the most powerful organ of the state for some time. In 1865, he abolished the Office of Frontier Security altogether whereby the Council of State became the supreme organ of the state. The Office of Three Military Guards (*Samgunbu*) was restored in 1868 as the supreme military headquarters.

In order to stabilize politics, the Taewŏn-gun reduced the power of the Kim clan of Andong, and employed men of talent regardless of their affiliations with various factional scholars. One of the most significant steps taken by him was the anti-corruption campaign, dealing with government officials, particularly provincial and local officials who had fermented anti-government sentiments among the people in the past. In 1864 alone, some one hundred and fifty corrupt officials were removed from office and severely punished. The anti-corruption campaign was followed by measures aimed at the reduction of malpractices in local governments. Many powerful local landlords were punished for either appropriating public lands or evading tax payments.

The Taewŏn-gun also carried out reform measures to increase government revenues. He dealt sternly with the illegal appropriation of land, even by Confucian academies, public or private. This resulted in a large amount of tax-free land owned by private academies being either confiscated or taxed. Many private academies were abolished and the land holdings of members of the royal house were reduced. All tax exemption for privately owned land was made illegal.

Reform implemented to meet the Taewŏn-gun's objectives had many negative impacts. For example, he carried out ambitious plans for palace reconstruction despite the poor financial condition of the country. In order to finance the reconstruction of the Kyŏngbok Palace, which had lain in ruins ever since the Japanese War of the late 1590's, he minted *tangbaekchŏn*, a larger and heavier money whose value was equal to one hundred copper coins. Other new coins were minted, and the exchange rate between the old and new coins was two to one. In 1867, he instituted a gate (transport) tax on goods, and in 1870 a military tax which each household was compelled to pay, and in 1871 he added a surtax on land, as well as taxes on the fishing and salt-manufacturing industries. In addition, he collected "voluntary" donation money and mobilized a large number of skilled workers to complete the project. Many magnificent palace buildings, pavilions, and gates were either restored or newly built, but the tax burden of the people vastly increased.

The Growing Western Pressure on Korea.   Mercantilism of the West that grew in the 19th century increased the number of Western ships that appeared in Korean waters. As early as 1831, a British merchant ship arrived in Korea and asked for trade. In 1845, several British ships appeared along the west and south coasts and after making marine surveys they asked for commercial relations with the Koreans. In the following year a French ship arrived in Korea for the same purpose. Meanwhile, in March 1866, a German, Ernest Oppert, who was a naturalized American citizen residing in Shanghai, went to the "forbidden land" of Korea on a British ship, the *Rona,* hoping to establish trade with the Koreans. He made the second voyage to Korea in August, but failed to achieve his objectives.

The eastward expansion of the Russian Empire brought about contracts between the Koreans and the Russians. Russian Vice Admiral Evfimi V. Putiatin arrived at Kŏmun Island off the southwestern coast of Korea in late March 1854 and sent a letter to the Korean government asking the opening of Korea to the Russians. In May, after visiting the Wŏnsan area which he named Port Lazarev, he sent another letter calling for Korea to open her doors. With the Russian acquisition of the Maritime Province from China in 1860 and construction of the port of Vladivostok as a naval base, contacts between the Koreans and the Russians became frequent as many Koreans moved into the new Russian territory. In March 1864, the Russians went across the Tumen River, and after arriving at Kyŏnghŭng they asked for the opening of the city for Russian merchants. During the months of October and November 1865, several groups of Russians arrived at Kyŏnghŭng and demanded that commercial ties between Russia and Korea be established without delay. The local Korean magistrate had no choice but to promise to give them an answer within a given time. Faced with Russian threats he urgently requested the government in Seoul to adopt a policy toward Russia.

American interests in establishing commercial ties with Korea grew. Shortly after concluding a treaty with China (the Cushing treaty) in 1844, H. Z. Pratt, Congressman from New York, introduced on February 15, 1845, a resolution in the House calling for immediate measures to effect commercial arrangements with Korea and Japan. The force of the American's "Manifest Destiny" was bound to create problems for Korea sooner or later. In late spring of 1866, an American merchant ship, the *Surprise,* which violated Korean waters, wrecked off the coast of P'yŏng-an Province. The crew were kindly treated by the Koreans and they were handed over to Chinese officials at Ŭiju.

The opening of Japan to the West in 1854, and the opening of northern ports of China following the conclusion of treaties between China and the Western powers in 1858, made it impossible for Korea to maintain her isolation. However, the Korean government was reluctant, if not unwilling to open the country to "evil influence of the barbarians" as it manifested its negative views of China and Japan which had succumbed to Western pressure.

The Taewŏn-gun did not pursue an anti-foreign policy as such, but he was not in favor of opening the country to the West; he was a nationalist at heart, and he was not fond of the Chinese and the Japanese who opened their doors to the Western powers. His ambition was to change the nature of Sino-Korean relations and to strengthen the authority of the Korean monarchy.

The Opium War of 1840–1842 and the Arrow War of 1856–1858 in China, as well as the ways in which the Western powers dealt with China, had a considerably negative impact on the Korean government's regard for the West. The frequent appearance of Western ships along the Korean coasts, the growing pressure from the Russians for trade relations, and the occupations of Peking by British and French troops in 1860 all increased the Korean court's concern for national security. The Korean leaders even feared that the Arrow War in China, begun by the British and the French against China, might spill over to Korea. The bloody persecution against the Catholics that was carried out by the Taewŏn-gun and the destruction of an American ship in 1866, must be understood against such an international climate in the Far East.

Two events that took place in Korea brought about direct confrontations with the French and the Americans. The first was persecution against the Catholics, including the killing of several French priests, and the second was the destruction of an American merchant ship and the killing of its crew.

The Massacre of the Catholics and the French Invasion. The Taewŏn-gun knew that Catholicism had grown and that many members of the *yangban* class had become converts to Catholicism. King Kojong's wet nurse, Martha Pak, was a Catholic, and Lady Min, the wife of Taewŏn-gun, herself was favorably inclined toward Catholicism.

When the Korean government was faced with Russian demands for trade in the northeastern region of Korea, some Catholics, such as Nam Chong-sam (Jean Nam) and Hong Pong-ju (Thomas Hong), suggested to the Taewŏn-gun that French aid might be sought against the Russians. It was the aim of these Catholics to secure French aid for Korea and bring about the legalization of Catholicism in the country. The Taewŏn-gun, who encountered a serious problem related to Russian demands, seemed to have authorized the Korean Catholics to seek French aid in cooperation with French priests such as Marie-Antoine N. Daveluy and Siméon-François Berneux. They failed, however, to secure the assistance of the French government against the Russians.

The growing criticism of conservative Confucian scholars against the Taewŏn-gun's reform measures, his apparent tolerance of Catholicism, and the failure of the Catholics to give him French assistance against the Russians, led to his bloody persecution of the Catholics in February 1866. While his edict forced many Koreans to give up the new religion, some 8,000 people who remained faithful to Catholicism were put to death, and nine French priests, including Berneux and Daveluy, were executed. Three French priests went into hiding, and until 1871, the hunting and killing of the Catholics continued.

When Father Felix Clair Ridel, who had managed to escape to China in

July 1866, informed the French minister in China about the deaths of French priests in Korea, the French minister proposed to the American minister in China that a joint military expedition be sent to Korea. The American government declined and in late September 1866, the French government dispatched a fleet to Korea under the command of Admiral Pierre Gustave Roze. The French troops carried out military actions in October on Kanghwa Island and along the Han River.

The French aggression, lasting two months, inflicted severe damage not only to military installations in that region, but also to the properties and lives of the inhabitants. However, the French failed to advance toward Seoul, and in mid-November they withdrew from Korea. Soon after this, the Korean government strengthened coastal defenses in and near Chemulp'o (now Inch'ŏn) and on Kanghwa Island, which are located a short distance away from Seoul.

The General Sherman Affair and the American Invasion.   In the summer of 1866, a heavily armed American merchant ship, the *General Sherman*, consigned to a British firm, made a voyage to Korea to establish trade relations with the "hermit kingdom." It departed from a Chinese port heading toward Chemulp'o, but the wind and high tide pushed it in a northerly direction. After arriving in the middle of August at an inlet in the Taedong River, near Pyongyang, it ran into a sandbank and was immobilized when the high tide receded. The Magistrate of Pyongyang, Pak Kyu-su, informed the shipowner, W. B. Preston, and Captain Page, that he had no authority to negotiate with foreigners. The ship's 24-man crew seized a local official and allowed Robert T. Thomas, a Scottish Protestant missionary to go on shore, distribute religious materials, and attempt to convert local inhabitants. They stole food and water from local inhabitants and also kidnapped women to the ship. As a result, on September 2, 1866, the local people, angry at "the crafty and beast-like foreigners," attacked the ship, burned it and killed all of its crew, including two Americans and a British citizen.

Frederick F. Low, the American minister to China, learned about the fate of the *General Sherman* and made attempts to secure Korean apologies as well as compensation for the lives and properties of Americans destroyed by the Koreans. When the Korean government refused to meet American demands, an American expeditionary force was sent to Korea and in May 1871, waged a "Little War with the Heathen." Several hundred U.S. Marines under the Asiatic Fleet Commander, Admiral John Rodgers, fought fierce battles for a few weeks with Korean troops on and near the Island of Kanghwa in June.

The Korean soldiers—the "Tiger Hunters"—in and around Ch'ojijin and Kwangsŏngjin (two of the forts on Kanghwa Island) under the command of Ŏ Chae-yŏn fought the desperate battles against the invaders, but they were unable to overcome the superior military strength of American troops. All the defenders fought with fanatical courage until killed or badly wounded; not one surrendered voluntarily. In a number of instances weaponless Koreans even scooped up gravel and threw it into the faces of the Americans. In the end about a hundred surviving "Tiger Hunters" fled down the hill to the river, where they drowned themselves or cut their own throats; among the latter was the commanding general. In all about 350 Korean soldiers died in the fighting, and only twenty, all of whom were wounded, were taken prisoner. Only three American soldiers were killed and ten wounded.

After silencing the guns at Ch'ojijin and Kwangsŏngjin, the Americans attempted to sail up the Han River toward Seoul, but they encountered unexpectedly strong resistance from the Korean troops on the mainland. Admiral Rodgers' fleet remained three weeks at the mouth of the Han River, vaguely hoping that the Koreans might even yet agree to negotiations. Finally, on July 3, the fleet raised anchor and set sail for China.

The Taewŏn-gun, who mistakingly believed any foreign threats or war could be dealt with successfully and that Korea could maintain her own security, was exultant when American troops withdrew. He, nevertheless, issued a proclamation warning the people of dangers from abroad. In it he

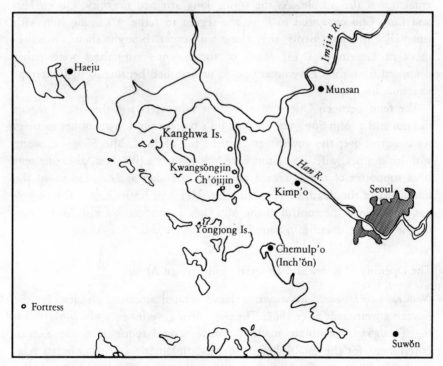

KANGHWA ISLAND AND ITS VICINITY

said: "Not to fight back when invaded by the Western barbarians is to invite further attacks; selling out the country in peace negotiations is the greatest danger to be guarded against." These words were inscribed on stone tablets which were erected in Seoul and throughout the kingdom, and in 1871 a policy of isolation was officially proclaimed.

Korea's anti-Western sentiments were fostered not only by the two military invasions by the French and the Americans, but also by the persistently arrogant attitudes of Western countries, including Russia. Moreover, Koreans were enraged by Ernest Oppert's April 1868 tomb-robbing expedition. Oppert and his collaborators went to Korea to steal treasures buried in the royal tombs; one of the tombs which they violated was that of the Taewŏn-gun's own father—a tomb located in Ch'ungch'ŏng Province. When the diggers were discovered, the tomb-robbing adventure failed, and after making an attempt to land on an island near Chemulp'o they fled back to China.

The End of the Regency of the Taewŏn-gun.   The Taewŏn-gun's relationship with Queen Min (1851–1895), wife of Kojong, as well as with Queen Dowager Cho, deteriorated considerably. Meanwhile, many Confucian scholars, antagonized by his reform measures, clamoured for the regent's removal. His palace restoration and construction projects had depleted the treasury, and his monetary reform and collection of compulsory donations antagonized the people. As the young king attained majority, Queen Min and Lady Cho conspired to force the regent to retire. Charging him with financial mismanagements, they along with others brought about his retirement in December 1873. Many of the regent's supporters were either dismissed from their government posts, or banished because of their attempt to restore him.

The feud between Queen Min and her supporters and the retired regent did not end as Min Sŭng-ho, Queen Min's brother, and many of her relatives took control over the government. In the fall of 1874, Min Sŭng-ho, along with his mother, wife, and a son were killed when a silk chest, allegedly sent by a supporter of the ex-regent as a gift, exploded and burned down the house. After the death of Min Sŭng-ho, Min Kyu-ho took over the power, and maintained the control of the Min clan in cooperation with Min Yŏng-ik, the adopted son of Min Sŭng-ho.

The Opening of Korea and Domestic and Foreign Affairs

New Korean-Japanese Relations.   Japan created a serious problem for the Korean government after 1867. The new Meiji government, which overthrew the Tokugawa Shōgunate in 1867, made several requests to the Korean government for the establishment of new diplomatic and commercial relations. The Korean refusal to accept the wishes of Japan, coupled with the disrespectful treatment of Japanese envoys by Korean local officials at Tong-naebu, near Pusan, led to the rise of so-called *Seikan-ron,* or "Conquer Korea Agitation" which was promoted by Saigō Takamori and others who were in favor of employing military means in achieving Japan's foreign policy objectives. Although such Japanese leaders as Iwakura Tomomi and Kido Kōin did not agree with Saigō and his supporters that Japan should go to war against Korea at that time, they were fully aware of the fact that the Korean question must be settled one way or another. The opportunity presented itself when in 1875 the *Unyō-kan* Incident took place.

Japanese warships, *Unyō* and others, had been involved in secret marine survey projects in Chinese and Korean waters for some time. On September 20, 1875, the *Unyō*, on its way back to Japan from a secret mission in Chinese territorial waters, arrived at a small island which was located at a strategic place between Kanghwa and Yŏngjong islands. Upon arriving at this point, the captain and a dozen sailors disembarked in a small craft, and under the pretext of searching for a source of water, they commenced a marine survey. At this juncture, the Korean soldiers at Ch'ojijin, which had been destroyed by the Americans but quickly rebuilt, fired at the ship, thinking that the intruders were the Westerners.

Instead of departing from Korean waters by taking the shots fired by the Koreans as a warning against their violation of Korean territorial waters, the Japanese prepared for combat, and on the morning of September 21 they bombarded Ch'ojijin, and the next day Japanese troops landed on Kanghwa Island and attacked the Ch'ojijin, killing 33 and wounding 16 Korean soldiers. After this, the Japanese departed from the island and arrived at Tongnae, near Pusan, where a contingent of Japanese troops landed and caused more armed clashes with Korean troops.

When the *Unyō-kan* returned to Nagasaki, its captain reported to his superiors in Tokyo that his ship was fired at by the Koreans. Taking advantage of this incident, the Japanese government resolved to settle the Korean question, and dispatched General Kuroda Kiyotaka and Inoue Kaoru to Korea in late January 1876 with six naval vessels and eight hundred marines.

Arriving at Kanghwa Island on February 10, they met Korean government representatives, Shin Hŏn and Yun Cha-sŭng, demanding an apology for the "unprovoked attack" on the *Unyō-kan* as well as a treaty establishing new diplomatic and commercial relations between Korea and Japan. They intimidated the Koreans, making it clear that they would not return to Japan without a treaty. Japanese gunboat diplomacy was at work.

Despite the vociferous and vehement opposition of the Taewŏn-gun and other conservative Confucian scholars such as Ch'oe Ik-hyŏn (1833–1906), King Kojong was persuaded by Minister of the Right, Pak Kyu-su, and O Kyŏng-sŏk, who was a government interpreter for the Chinese language, to pursue a peaceful solution for the Japanese problem. Both Pak and O were well informed of the world situation and they believed that the ending of Korea's seclusion would be beneficial to the kingdom. As a result, Korea and Japan signed the Kanghwa Treaty on February 26, 1876, in which Japan recognized that Korea was an independent nation enjoying the same sovereign rights as Japan. With this, Japan established her legation in Seoul and trading firms in Pusan. The Supplementary Treaty and the Trade Regulations were concluded between Korea and Japan on August 24, 1876. Through other agreements in mid-1883, Korea opened Wŏnsan and Inch'ŏn to the Japanese. Under these treaties Japan gained many special privileges similar to those gained by Western powers in China and Japan—demonstrating the speed with which the Japanese were learning the imperialistic tactics of the Western nations.

A Korean mission headed by Kim Ki-su was sent to Japan immediately after the conclusion of the Kanghwa Treaty to gather information on Japan. In 1880, another mission headed by Kim Hong-jip (1842–1896) visited Japan with the purpose of detecting Japanese intentions toward Korea. Kim Hong-jip returned to Korea with a booklet entitled *Chao-hsien ts'e-lueh*, or *"Korean Strategy'*„ written by a Chinese Councillor Huang Tsun-hsein, at the Chinese legation in Tokyo. In it Huang advised the Koreans that Korea should maintain a pro-Chinese policy, but should cultivate friendly relations with Japan, open her doors to the West, and import advanced culture and technology. He even advised the Koreans to conclude an alliance with China and Japan. Kim Hong-jip presented Huang's book to King Kojong. Kojong who was impressed with Huang's ideas asked his minister to read it. Copies of Huang's book were printed and distributed to Confucian scholars and officials. Some who read the book agreed with Huang in many ways, but a majority of Confucian scholars were antagonized. Kim Hong-jip was labeled by those who disagreed with Huang as a traitor for presenting Huang's book to the king, and a scholar named Yi Man-son demanded outright punishment of Kim Hong-jip as he accused the government of discarding the time-honored policy of "rejecting heretical thought and repelling the barbarians from abroad."

Initial Reforms and Reaction of the Conservatives.   The conclusion of treaties with Japan under threats, and the growing sense of danger associated with Russian expansionism, brought about the rise of reform advocates such as Pak Kyu-su, O Kyŏng-sŏk, and a Buddhist monk, Yi Tong-in. Yi Tong-in was the first one who openly advocated "opening the country and changing the spirit of time." These and others advocated the opening of the country to the West and modernization, thereby initiating Korea's self-strengthening movement. Kojong, who was influenced by such reform-minded officials as Kim Hong-jip, Ŏ Yun-jung (1848–1896), and Kim Yun-shik (1835–1922) proceeded to make changes despite the opposition of the conservative.

Korea's self-strengthening began with the establishment in January 1881 of a new government branch called *T'ongni Kimu Amun* (Office for the Management of State Affairs). It consisted of twelve departments, including those of Military Matters, Military Ordinance, Foreign Trade, and Language Study. It was accorded the same status as the Council of State. Many members of Queen Min's clan became key officials of the new branch of the government, which was given a mandate to implement various reform measures. With this, the old Five Armies were replaced by two large military units.

In February 1881, King Kojong dispatched another fact-finding mission to Japan. This mission, charged with the duties of conducting a detailed and careful investigation of Japan, consisted of sixteen scholars, including such reform advocates as Pak Chŏng-yang, Hong Yŏng-shik, and Ŏ Yun-jung. Staying in Japan until August, they talked with Japanese government officials and others, and studied conditions in Japan, including her economic and military strength and foreign policy. Meanwhile, the king secretly sent Yi Tong-in to Japan to negotiate with the Americans, and authorized Kim Ok-kyun (1851–1894), a reform advocate, to travel to Japan.

When in 1881 the Chinese emperor placed Li Hung-chang in charge of Korean affairs, King Kojong presented him with a request that negotiations be conducted for, among other things, the termination of the Korean tributary mission to China, and the establishment of a permanent Korean mission in Peking. The Chinese court rejected Kojong's proposal.

Meanwhile, changes made by the king in domestic and foreign affairs aroused a strong reaction on the part of the reactionary and conservative Confucian scholars. Hong Chae-hak and others presented a petition to the king, imploring him "to defend the right learning and to reject heterodoxy," and they agitated at the same time for the abolition of the Office for the Management of State Affairs and the restoration of the Five Armies.

In June 1881, in order to appease their conservative Confucian scholars, the government circulated a pamphlet entitled "Royal Message Concerning the Rejection of Heterodoxy." But it did not pacify the conservatives, who maintained that evil influence from abroad had spread all over the country. They condemned Kim Hong-jip, Hong Yŏng-shik and others who advocated reform measures. The government took stern actions; Yi Man-son was banished, and Hong Chae-hak was tried and beheaded in September 1881 because of his disrespect for the throne. A plot of the reactionaries to depose the king and the queen and remove those officials who opened the country to foreign influence was discovered in December. Those conspirators were punished, and Yi Chae-sŏn, an illegitimate son of the Taewŏn-gun, who was one of the conspirators, committed suicide.

In January 1882, Kim Yun-shik took a group of 69 students, artisans, officials, and others to China to receive technical training. The project was abandoned in November because of insufficient funds, lack of interest among the students, and the language barrier, and therefore it made no contribution toward the modernization and self-strengthening of Korea.

The Opening of Korea to the West.   The United States, having failed to settle the Korean issue in 1871, made various fruitless efforts to establish diplomatic and commercial relations with Korea. In May 1880, Commodore Robert W. Shufeldt sailed into Pusan harbor on the *U.S.S. Ticonderoga*, but he failed to open negotiations with the Korean ·officials. He then went to Nagasaki, Japan, and asked the Japanese for help in obtaining a treaty from Korea. The efforts made by the Japanese were also unsuccessful.

Commodore Shufeldt went to Tientsin in March 1882 at Li Hung-chang's invitation. Li was a leading Chinese statesman who enjoyed the confidence of the Empress Dowager Ts'u-hsi. It was Li's intention to induce the United States to recognize China's suzerainty over Korea in the treaty and thereby set one barbarian against another, but he failed to achieve his objectives. Through Li's mediation, however, Commodore Shufeldt concluded the Treaty of Amity and Commerce between the United States and Korea (commonly known as the Chemulp'o or Shufeldt treaty) on May 22, 1882, and thus opened Korea to the West and set the pattern of unequal treaty relationship between Korea and the Western powers. Under the treaty, the United States gained many special privileges from Korea, including low tariffs and extraterritoriality. Lucius H. Foote arrived in Seoul in May 1883 as the first American minister to Korea.

The American-Korean treaty was followed by ones with other Western powers. On November 26, 1883, Korea signed the Treaty of Amity and Commerce with England and Germany; the treaty between Korea and Italy was signed on June 26, 1884; and that between Korea and Russia was concluded on July 7. France was the last major power to sign the Treaty of Amity and Commerce, on June 4, 1886, with Korea.

With the increasing number of diplomats, merchants and others from foreign lands, new views, new interests, and new culture developed—Korea was at the threshold of a new age. Although some outspoken critics deeply rooted in conservatism were silenced, opposition from conservative Confucian literati and others against the modernization of the country did not diminish. The power struggle between the group headed by Queen Min and those who advocated more extensive and faster changes created a critical political atmosphere in Seoul. In the end, the Koreans witnessed two bloody events generated by this conflict; first in 1882 and then in 1884.

The Imo Incident of 1882 and Its Aftermath.   Preferential treatment given to the troops of the Special Skill Force which was established in 1881, and the modernization of the military created resentment among the members of the old military units. Simultaneously, the new foreign policy provoked the strong antagonism of the ex-regent.

In July 1882, the soldiers of the old military units, who had not been paid for nearly thirteen months, carried out a riot in Seoul, bringing about a military insurrection known in Korean history as *Imo Kullan* or the "Military Incident of the Year of Imo." The ex-regent, the Taewŏn-gun, took advantage of the situation to re-establish his control, and he changed the character of the insurrection into a palace coup. Many supporters of Queen Min were killed, but the queen escaped from a certain death by fleeing from the palace in disguise. She went to a rural area near Seoul. In this chaotic situation, King Kojong asked his father to take charge of the government. Meanwhile, anti-Japanese riots erupted in Seoul, and several Japanese, including Lt. Horimoto Reizō, were killed. After setting fire to the legation building, Japanese Minister Hanabusa Yoshitada and other officials fled to Japan via Inch'ŏn.

Discovering what had happened in Seoul, the Chinese government quickly decided to send troops to Korea and establish firm control over that country. Consequently, Chinese troops under Ma Chien-chung, T'ing Ju-ch'ang, Wu Chang-ch'ing, and Yuan Shih-k'ai arrived in Korea and crushed the insurgents. The ex-regent was taken captive by the Chinese to China. Queen Min returned to Seoul from her hiding place, and the pro-Chinese group re-established its control over the government. Meanwhile, the Japanese government sent its minister back to Korea with troops, and forced the Korean government in August 1882 to sign the Treaty of Chemulp'o, in which Korea agreed to pay 550,000 *yen* indemnity for lives and properties of the Japanese lost during the insurrection.

King Kojong issued an edict on August 31 to soldiers and citizens granting a general amnesty, and in September the king spoke to the people, blaming himself for the unhappy situation in the country. He promised to abrogate all government measures that had been harmful to the people, and initiate the movement for a "new beginning." Meanwhile, the sense of urgency to strengthen the nation by importing Western technology grew even among conservative Confucian scholars.

Following the Chinese military intervention, Li Hung-chang sent Ch'en Shu-t'ang to Korea in October as the "Chief Commissioner of Diplomatic and Commercial Affairs." The new Regulations for Maritime and Overland Trade between Korea and China, granting China special privileges that other foreigners did not enjoy, was concluded on October 4, 1882. After this, Li Hung-chang recommended two individuals to the Korean government to serve as its advisers; Ma Chien-chung and a German named Paul Georg von Möllendorff were dispatched to Korea in November in order to strengthen Chinese control over Korea. Concurrently, in October, the Korean government dispatched a goodwill mission to Japan headed by Pak Yŏng-hyo (1861–1939).

In December 1882, the *T'ongni Kimu Amun* (Office for the Management of State Affairs) was renamed the *T'ongni Amun* for the namesake of Chinese *Tsungli Yamen* (Foreign Office). In January of 1883 it was reorganized into the *T'ongni Kyosŏp T'ongsang Samu Amun* (Office for the Management of Diplomatic and Commercial Affairs), commonly called the Foreign Office by the Westerners. At the same time, the *T'ongni Naemu Amun* (Office for the Management of Internal Affairs) was created under the Council of State in December 1882. A month later, it was renamed the *T'ongni Kun-guk Samu Amun* (Office for the Management of Military and National Affairs).

Chinese control over Korea through their Chinese and foreign agents was greatly strengthened in 1882 and 1883. Von Möllendorff became vice-president of the Department of Revenue and Port Administration of the Foreign Office in January 1883. In February, both Ma and von Möllendorff became vice-president of the Foreign Office, while Ma served as adviser to the Council of State as well, and von Möllendorff oversaw the affairs of the newly established Korean Maritime Customs Service. Meanwhile, Yuan Shih-k'ai took complete control over the Korean Army.

King Kojong showed much enthusiasm for strengthening ties with the United States. In July 1883, he sent a special mission to the United States, headed by Min Yŏng-ik (1860–1914), which included such reform-minded scholars as Hong Yŏng-shik (1855–1884), Sŏ Kwang-bŏm (1859–1897), Yu Kil-chun (1856–1914), and Pyŏn Su (1861–1891). The mission arrived at San Francisco carrying the newly created Korean national flag, visited many places, met with the American president, and studied about the United States. At the end of September the mission left the country. Upon returning to Korea, Min Yŏng-ik was reported to have said "I was born in the dark. I went out into the light, and now I have returned into the dark again. . ." Yu Kil-chun stayed behind and studied briefly at a college in New England, returning to Korea in early 1885. In October 1883, and again in April 1884, King Kojong requested the American minister to secure services of an American adviser on foreign affairs and an American military instructor for the Korean Army.

The Kapshin Incident of 1884 and Its Aftermath.   When Korea encountered many serious problems, a group of young reform advocates, among whom were government officials, emerged in the 1870s, and the members of the group were influenced by the writings of the *Shirhak* scholars, such as Pak Kyu-su, a former high government official, and O Kyŏng-sŏk, a minor government official, who advocated modern reforms. The group included sons of *yangban* families such as Kim Ok-kyun, Pak Yŏng-gyo and his younger brother Pak Yŏng-hyo (1861–1939), and Sŏ Kwang-bŏm, as well as such commoners as Pyŏn Su. Pak Yŏng-hyo was the son-in-law of the late

King Ch'ŏlchong. Although the group had no formal organization, these Progressives came to be known collectively as *Tongniptang* (the "Independence Party") or *Kaehwadang* (the "Progressive Party").

The way in which the Japanese demonstrated their military strength against Korea and forced her to sign the treaty in 1876, along with increasing Chinese control, stimulated the rise of nationalistic sentiment among young progressive scholars and officials. Feeling a certain urgency for Korea's regeneration, Kim Ok-kyun, Pak Yŏng-hyo, Yi Tong-in, Sŏ Kwang-bŏm, and Pyŏn Su launched a reform removement in 1879. Others who preached nationalism and progressivism also joined the group, and among them were Sŏ Chae-p'il (1866–1952) and Yu Kil-chun who were sons of high *yangban* families.

Displaying his inclination toward reform, King Kojong first sent to Japan a monk named Yi Tong-in, who had been advocating the opening of Korea to the West. Then he authorized Kim Ok-kyun to visit Japan in 1881. When he sent a goodwill mission to Japan in October 1882, following the settlement of the case involving the deaths of Japanese and the destruction of their property during the riots of the summer of 1882 in connection with the Imo military insurrection, the king appointed Pak Yŏng-hyo, a key member of the group of Progressives, as head of the mission which included many Progressives. It was this mission which secured a 170,000 *yen* loan from a Japanese bank to finance various reform projects.

While in Japan, Kim Ok-kyun established ties with reform advocates there such as Fukuzawa Yukichi and Gotō Shōjirō. The members of the Pak's mission did likewise. Kim Ok-kyun visited Japan again in 1882 and 1883 accompanying several Progressives who, after visiting Japan, realized how backward Korea was. Those young Progressives who visited Japan developed strong desires to make their country both a modern and an independent nation. Needless to say, they were impressed with the progress made by the new Japanese leaders who brought about the Meiji Restoration in Japan. After returning from Japan in 1882, both Kim and Pak strengthened their determination to achieve their objectives, and recruited more like-minded individuals as they received favorable treatment from the king.

Hong Yŏng-shik and Sŏ Kwang-bŏm who visited the United States in 1883 as members of the first Korean diplomatic mission were impressed by the economic and military strength of the United States, and they along with other progressive officials became more eager to implement many reform measures in order to transform Korea into a modern state and establish Korea's independence from China. Hong Yŏng-shik, son of a former minister of the state, who said that he "saw the light" in the United States, joined the group of Progressives and became its key leader.

Hong Yŏng-shik and Sŏ Kwang-bŏm who returned to Korea with new ideas and knowledge about agriculture, commerce, and industry, as well as modern culture and military affairs, in cooperation with Pak Yŏng-hyo and Kim Ok-kyun, urged King Kojong to implement more modern reform measures, preaching progressivism and nationalism. Insisting upon the establishment of complete independence of Korea from China, they also advocated political, educational, and social reforms, including the equality of the sexes as well as of all men. At the same time, they submitted petitions to the king regarding agricultural modernization, industrialization, and the establishment of a modern transportation system.

The Progressives encountered many problems. The harder they pushed their reform programs, the stronger the opposition of the conservatives and reactionaries grew, causing the political struggle between the Progressives and their opponents who were collectively called *Sadaedang,* or the "party subservient to the big power," namely China. The *Sadaedang* was headed by Queen Min, and it included many members of the Min clan as well as others who were pro-China. Queen Min's nephew, Min Yŏng-ik, who had seen "the light" in the United States and then returned "into the dark..." did not join the Progressives. Instead, for his family interests and under Queen Min's pressure, he became a key member of the opposition *Sadaedang,* collaborating closely with the Chinese officials in Korea.

In 1884, the conflict between the Progressives and their opponents increased its intensity, and the Progressives were losing their influence over the king while many of them were removed from government positions by the conservatives. Some moderates such as Kim Hong-jip and Ŏ Yun-jung, attempted to mediate between the two opposing parties and accomplish national objectives. Even the American legation officials, particularly Naval Attaché George C. Foulk, made efforts to bring the two groups together for the sake of a peaceful transformation of Korea into a modern nation. However, the gap between the two groups was so wide and their opinions and desires were so different that no peaceful solution was found by those who attempted to mediate between them.

In the meantime, the Progressives felt the growing danger to their own personal safety when they discovered that their opponents were about to take drastic measures to eliminate (either exile or kill) them. In desperation, the Progressives sought American and Japanese assistance, but neither government was willing to provide the badly needed help to them. The Progressives did, however, manage to gain the personal support to Takezoe Shin'ichirō, the Japanese minister to Korea.

In an attempt to establish a new reform government under King Kojong and to institute various measures similar to those of Japan, and to overthrow Chinese domination over Korea and to establish complete independence of their country from China, they staged a bloody palace coup on December 4, 1884, with the support of Japanese legation guards. This event is known in Korean history as *Kapshin Chŏngbyŏn,* or the "Political Incident of the Year of Kapshin.'' A reform government was established on December 5 under the king, and the Progressives took over key government positions vacated by those conservatives who were either assassinated or went into hiding.

The new administration issued various edicts in the king's name, and they were eager to implement political, economic, social and cultural reforms. Then, only two days after they were able to form a new administration, they suffered a disastrous fate. The Chinese troops under Yuan Shih-k'ai's command, in collaboration with some misguided Korean soldiers, attacked the palace, and crushed the new government, killing many Progressives, including Hong Yŏng-shik. Yuan took custody of the king, and put him under his control. Once again, Queen Min and her clique rose to power. The majority of the Progressives were killed during the fighting, but a handful of the leaders such as Kim Ok-kyun, Pak Yŏng-hyo, and Sŏ Chae-p'il managed to flee to Japan with the Japanese minister and troops who took part in the *coup d'état*. The revival of the control of the Min clique over the government under Chinese protection sealed the fate of Korea.

On January 3, 1885, Japanese Foreign Minister, Inoue Kaoru, accompanying an American adviser named Durham White Stevens, went to Korea with two infantry battalions. A week later, he forced the Korean government to sign the Hansŏng treaty in which Korea offered an apology and agreed to pay a large sum of indemnity for damages inflicted on Japanese lives and property during the fighting, pay for the rebuilding of the Japanese legation building which was destroyed, and punish those who were responsible for the death of a Japanese captain.

China and Japan concluded on April 18, 1885, an agreement (the Li-Ito Agreement) in Tientsin, China. In it, they agreed (1) to withdraw troops from Korea within four months, (2) should either party find it necessary to send troops to Korea it would do so only to protect lives and properties of their nationals in times of upheaval, and each would inform the other before doing so, and (3) advise the Korean king to train troops and maintain internal order, and both Japan and China would not send military instructors to Korea. This agreement gave Japan the right to send troops to Korea under certain conditions, and it deprived China of its right to send troops to interfere in Korea's internal affairs. The Japanese withdrew troops from Korea, leaving a small number of legation guards, but the Chinese kept over 2,000 troops disguised as policemen or merchants. Meanwhile, Sŏ Chae-p'il, Pak Yŏng-hyo, and Sŏ Kwang-bŏm who had fled to Japan, went to the United States in May 1885. In 1886, Kim Ok-kyun submitted a petition to King Kojong, imploring him to implement more reform programs, and after returning to Japan from the United States, Pak Yŏng-hyo submitted a lengthy petition to King Kojong in early 1888, urging the king to implement many reforms for the modernization of Korea and strengthening of her national independence.

Whereas Pak Yŏng-hyo and Sŏ Kwang-bŏm returned to Japan, Sŏ Chae-p'il studied at American colleges, and in 1893 he earned a Doctor of Medicine degree from Columbia Medical College (now Medical College of George Washington University). Meanwhile, Pyŏn Su, who had fled to Japan with Kim, Pak, and Sŏ in 1884, went to the United States in early 1886, and after studying English at a private school, he enrolled at the University of Maryland, earning a Bachelor of Science degree in agricultural science in 1891. He was the first Korean to receive an academic degree from an American college. After graduating from the University of Maryland, he secured a part-time job at the U.S. Department of Agriculture, but was killed by a train in October 1891.

The Beginning of Modernization

The modernization of Confucian Korea was a monumental task which the Koreans were to bring about. The obstacles were insurmountable, but the process of modernization began soon after the signing of the Kanghwa treaty with Japan in February 1876. Following the visits to Japan in July 1876 by Kim Ki-su and in March 1881 by Kim Hong-jip, King Kojong issued a proclamation in July 1881 in which he stated his new policy for enlightenment and progress, signaling the beginning of the transformation of the "hermit kingdom" of Korea. The treaty signed between Korea and the United States in May 1882 accelerated the modernization process.

In addition to the structural reform of the government which had been discussed earlier, Korea witnessed the establishment of modern education, the development of Christianity, the emergence of modern commercial firms and journalism, the transition toward a modern military with an up-dated training program, as well as the appearance of a new culture. The modern postal system, established on April 22, 1884, was gradually extended throughout the country. Whether the Koreans liked it or not, the newly arrived forces of the modern age transformed their feudalistic, agrarian nation.

Educational Development.   Educational modernization began with the establishment of a small school named Tongmunhak in 1883 under the supervision of the Foreign Office. It was created under the advisement of von Möllendorff, who emphasized the need to train official interpreters for the Chinese and English languages. Some 40 students were recruited into the school, and instruction began with foreign instructors such as Thomas E. Halifax from England.

The plan to establish a palace school in early 1885 was frustrated by the December 4th incident of 1884, but a palace school named Yugyŏng Kong-wŏn was established and sons of the nobility were recruited as students. The creation of this school was strongly supported by such Progressives as Hong

Yŏng-shik as early as 1883. Dr. Homer B. Hulbert, an American missionary who had arrived in Korea in April 1885, along with two other Americans, were employed as instructors when the school opened in September of 1886. The school had two departments—liberal education and military education. Courses were taught in English using English-language textbooks. One of the school's graduates was Yi Wan-yong who later became prime minister.

The Protestant missionaries contributed much toward the development of modern education in Korea. Reverend Henry G. Appenzeller of the North American Methodist Church, who arrived in Korea in June 1885, established Paejae Haktang. This was the first school opened to the sons of commoners, and it was also attended by many government students. In the same year, Dr. Horace G. Underwood of the Northern Presbyterian Church of the United States began another school for boys called Kyŏngshin Haktang.

O Kyŏng-sŏk had preached the need to educate women, but the first school for girls was actually founded in 1886 by a foreign missionary. Mrs. Mary F. Scranton, the mother of Dr. William B. Scranton, a medical missionary of the Methodist Church, established a school which for the first time in history gave educational opportunities to Korean girls. This was a significant educational development and a major social change. The school which opened in May 1886 was renamed in 1877 by Queen Min who called it Ewha Haktang. It developed into one of the finest educational institutions in Korea. Another school for girls named Yŏndong Haktang began in 1887. It was established in Seoul by an American nurse named Annie Ellers of the Northern Presbyterian Mission, and in 1909, it was renamed Chŏngshin Girls' School. Both of these eventually became secondary schools (Ewha added a college division later), and trained many Korean women leaders among whom were Kim Maria and Kim Hwal-lan.

The establishment of these schools for girls was followed by the emergence of a secondary school for boys named Kwangsŏng in Pyongyang and a secondary school for girls called Sungdŏk in Yŏngbyŏn, P'yŏng-an Province established by the Methodist Mission in 1894. These two were the first modern schools in the northern part of Korea.

The Rise of Modern Journalism.   The publication of a newspaper named the *Chōsen Shimpō* in December 1881 by a Japanese in Pusan marked the beginnings of modern journalism in Korea. The paper was published in both the Korean and the Japanese language. It included news items, commentaries and various instructional articles. Its publication lasted only briefly, but it left its mark on the modern Korean news media.

The first "newspaper" published by the Koreans was the *Hansŏng Sunbo*, a thrice-monthly official government gazette published in Chinese characters by the *Pangmun-guk*, an agency of the Foreign Office. The first issue was published on October 30, 1883, with the assistance provided by a Japanese,

Inoue Kakugorō, sent to Korea by Fukuzawa Yikichi who was a prominent intellectual leader in Japan and also a supporter of the Korean Progressives. While disseminating information concerning government affairs, it also included essays and articles written by the Progressives concerning national development and modernization. Its existence was cut short in 1885 following the December 4th incident of 1884.

In January 1886, *Pangmun-guk* published a new newspaper named the *Hansŏng Chubo* (*The Seoul Weekly*). It was printed in Korean mixed with Chinese characters, and was under the supervision of Kim Yun-shik with editorial assistance from a Japanese, Inoue Kakugorō. The publication of a Korean-language newspaper was a significant development, and the paper itself played an important role as a communications media until it was abolished in 1888 by the government which was then controlled by the Chinese.

There were no Korean-language newspapers again until 1896. However, five Japanese-language newspapers were published by the Japanese in Korea, as of 1893. In 1894, another paper named the *Kanjō Shimpō*, (*The Seoul News*), which had both Korean and Japanese language sections, appeared.

Christianity and Modernization.   The arrival in Korea in September 1884 of Dr. Horace N. Allen, a medical missionary of the Northern Presbyterian Church of the United States, marked the beginnings of the Korean Protestant movement. Although proselytization was not legally permitted, through his connection with the Yi court (he had saved the life of the queen's nephew, Min Yŏng-ik, who was severely wounded by a would-be assassin on the eve of December 4, 1884), he was able to arrange for the appointment of other missionaries as government employees and thereby opened the way for the Protestant movement. He also introduced modern medicine in Korea by establishing a royal medical clinic named Kwanghyewŏn, in February 1885.

In April 1885, Dr. and Mrs. Horace G. Underwood of the Northern Presbyterian Church arrived; they were followed by the arrival of other missionaries: Dr. and Mrs. William B. Scranton, and Dr. Scranton's mother, Mary Scranton in May 1885, Dr. John W. Heron and Reverend and Mrs. Henry G. Appenzeller of the Methodist Church of the United States in June 1885, and an American nurse named Annie Ellers in 1886. Soon after the influx of Protestants in Korea, Catholic missionaries arrived reviving Catholicism which had suffered from the disasters of 1866 and the following years.

While winning many converts, Christianity made significant contributions toward the modernization of the country. The new concepts of equality, human rights and freedom, and the participation of both men and women in religious activities, the launching of group activities, and the establishment of modern schools all led to modernization. The Protestant missions introduced

Christian hymns and other Western songs which created a strong impetus to modernize Korean ideas about music. The religious tracts published by Christian missions, together with their educational programs significantly reduced illiteracy.

The Christian hymnal (*Ch'ansongga*) was published in 1893, and the New Testament in Korean was published in 1900. Although the New Testament, translated into Korean by Reverend John Ross of the Scottish Presbyterian mission in Manchuria, was available earlier, improvements were made and a new version was published. Reverend Ross and his brother-in-law, Reverend John McIntyre, won many Koreans in southwestern Manchuria to Protestantism beginning in 1882, but it was only in 1887 that Reverend Ross actually visited Korea. The entire Bible, once translated into Korean and published in 1910, became an important tool in reducing illiteracy.

Meanwhile, the Koreans learned how to sing Western songs introduced by Western missionaries. Many Scottish songs, such as *Auld Lang Syne,* and *Comin' Thru the Rye* became popular along with an Irish song, *Londonderry Air* often known as *O Danny Boy.* As a matter of fact, the tune of *Auld Lang Syne* later became the melody of the *Patriotic Song* written by Yun Ch'i-ho. The introduction of the organ and other Western musical instruments brought about a rapid development of modern music.

Military Modernization.   The replacement in March 1882 of the old Five Garrison System with two new battalions initiated military modernization. It was in May that the Special Skill Force (*Pyŏlgigun*) was formed and a Japanese army officer, Lieutenant Horimoto Reizō, was engaged to train the troops of the Special Skill Force. The Bureau of Military Study and Training (*Hullyŏnwŏn*) was created, and 14 Korean students were sent to Japan in 1883 to study military subjects at a Japanese military academy in Tokyo.

Modern weapons were imported from Japan and the United States in 1883; the first military related factories were established, and a new military uniform was adopted. However, King Kojong's hope for a rapid·military modernization was not fulfilled. The request he made in October 1883, to American Minister Lucius Foote for American military advisers and instructors, was "misplaced" in the Department of State for over a year. It was only in April 1888, that General William McEntyre Dye and two other military instructors arrived from the United States, followed in May by the fourth instructor. They helped the Koreans to modernize the military although they were, with the exception of General Dye, inadequately prepared to bring about rapid military development.

A new military school named Yŏnmu Kongwŏn was established, and an officers training program began, but no modern navy was created. As a result, Korea's military strength remained too weak to preserve her sovereignty and independence. To make matters worse, two of the American military instructors left Korea in September 1899, followed by a third in December 1899, and General Dye himself resigned in 1899.

Economic Change.   Following the opening of Korean ports to the Japanese and Western merchants, contact and involvement with them increased and foreign trade developed in the treaty ports such as Pusan, Inch'ŏn, and Wŏnsan. In 1883, the Maritime Customs Service was established with the help of the Chinese, and under the supervision of Sir Robert Hart of England. The Maritime Customs Service administered the business related to foreign trade and collection of tariff. In that year, the Korean government reduced trade barriers by abolishing the rights of the trade monopoly of certain Korean merchants called *togo.*

By 1883, modern Korean commercial firms such as the Taedong and the Ch'angdong companies emerged, and in 1883 the newly established Bureau of Mint produced a new coin called *tang-ojŏn* as coined monies increased in importance.

A German, A.H. Maeterns, was engaged in 1884 to promote modern agriculture, and with the assistance given by the Department of Agriculture of the American government, an experimental farm called the "American farm" was established on the land donated by the king. Farm implements, seeds and milk cows were imported from the United States, but the plan to establish a modern agricultural school did not materialize. In June 1883, the Bureau of Machines was established and steam engines were imported. However, modern manufacturing facilities did not emerge due to lack of funds and technology and, as a result, Korea remained basically an agricultural nation and economically backward.

Be that as it may, telegraph lines between Korea, China, and Japan were laid between 1883 and 1885, facilitating communication. Gas lamps were installed in Seoul, but a modern transportation system was yet to be developed.

The Growth of International Rivalries and Korean Reaction

During the decade between 1885 and 1894, the Koreans witnessed ever-increasing international rivalries in their country at a time when the imperialistic ambitions of powerful nations were growing. The weak and confused Korean government was powerless to check the growth of a power struggle between foreign nations within Korea.

The most serious conflict of interest was that between China and Japan, which culminated in the Sino-Japanese War (1894-1895). After the Japanese victory over China, the rivalry between Japan and Russia grew in Korea. Many efforts made by the Koreans to strengthen their country in order to protect their national interests and independence failed, and when Japan emerged victorious in the Russo-Japanese War (1904–1905), Korea became a Japanese protectorate.

The Rise of Russian Interests in Korea.   Paul G. von Möllendorff viewed that both China and Japan were already too influential in Korea, and that Korea should free herself from detrimental influences of these two countries in order to protect her own sovereignty and independence. It was his belief that China had no ability to protect Korea whereas Japan was too ambitious. Although he was sent to Korea by the Chinese government to protect and promote Chinese interest, he became increasingly concerned with the security of Korea.

In the wake of the *Kapshin Incident,* von Möllendorff thought about establishing a joint guarantee of Russia, China, and Japan for Korea's neutrality and integrity, and he discussed the possibility of a neutralization of Korea by the powers with William G. Aston, the British Consul General in Seoul. In his opinion, the best way to protect Korea was to neutralize Korea under a joint guarantee of the powers. But both China and Japan were unwilling to do so, while Western powers showed no such interest. On one occasion he considered possible German assistance for Korea, but he abandoned his idea. In the end, he sought Russian military assistance for Korea in return for certain privileges in Korea. He had already helped Karl I. Waeber in securing the Russo-Korean Treaty of Amity and Commerce in July 1884.

When the *Kapshin Incident* occurred in Korea, Alexis de Speyer, first secretary of the Russian legation in Tokyo, was dispatched to Korea by the Russian minister to Japan under his government's instructions. De Speyer's mission was to investigate the situation in Korea. Taking advantage of the presence of de Speyer in Seoul, von Möllendorff made a request for a Russian protectorate, offering Russia an ice-free bay or a port in Korea as a lease territory. De Speyer became immediately interested in von Möllendorff's proposition, and although he had no credentials to negotiate such matters, he expressed Russia's interest in helping Korea to von Möllendorff, as well as to the Korean king when he had an audience with him. He returned to Japan in January 1885, carrying a note from von Möllendorff to the Russian minister in Tokyo which included a suggestion for Russian aid to Korea.

In February 1885, King Kojong dispatched a secret mission consisting of several Koreans to Vladivostok to seek Russian help without the knowledge of his ministers, including the foreign minister. The Koreans met the Governor General of the Amur Region, who was in favor of extending Russian interests in Korea and sending Russian troops to the peninsula. Although no agreement was signed between the Korean mission and the Russian governor general, it was evident that the Koreans returned to Seoul with encouraging words from the Russians.

Meanwhile, von Möllendorff himself went to Japan with a Korean mission, and he was warmly received by the Russian minister. Early in March, he presented a note to the Russian minister in which he solicited Russian aid and suggested that Russia should occupy a group of three Korean islands collectively known as Kŏmundo, 18 miles off the south coast of Chŏlla Province. Von Möllendorff was aware of the fact that in 1857 Russian Admiral Putiatin attempted to establish a coaling depot on the island.

The Russian government did not respond positively to suggestions made by von Möllendorff, but it did instruct its minister to Japan to study the situation in Korea in the interest of sending Russian military instructors there if the Koreans made an official request. Meanwhile, in May, Karl I. Waeber, a Russian diplomat in China (who was designated to go to Korea as chargé d'affaires and consul general) was instructed to investigate the internal situation in Korea in promoting Korean trust in the Russian government. However, the Russian government made no aggressive move in Korea until the British occupation of Kŏmun Island.

The secret mission which the king sent to Vladivostok and secret diplomatic negotiations which von Möllendorff carried out with the Russians both in Korea and in Japan antagonized the Korean ministers, particularly Foreign Minister Kim Yun-shik, who was a pro-Chinese, if not a puppet of the Chinese. Under pressure from his ministers, the king abandoned his scheme, but rumors about the impending Korean-Russian alliance persisted. Meanwhile, the relationship between von Möllendorff and the Korean ministers deteriorated as Chinese distrust for von Möllendorff increased.

The Anglo-Russian Rivalry and the British Occupation of Kŏmun Island. As early as 1845 the British conducted marine surveys along the south coast of Korea, and in honor of the British Admiral, Lord George Hamilton, the British surveyor named a group of three small islands collectively known as Kŏmun Island, Port Hamilton. At this juncture, Cheju Island became known by the Westerners as Quelpart Island.

In the early part of the nineteenth century, Great Britain had been opposed to Russian expansionism in the Middle East and Central Asia, and it successfully blocked Russian advancement into the Mediterranean Sea by defeating the Russians in the Crimean War of 1854–1856. However, Russian occupation of the Amur region in 1858 and the Maritime Province in 1860, coupled with the construction of a naval base at Vladivostok, aroused British suspicion. In 1875 and 1876, the British displayed an interest in occupying Kŏmun Island which was strategically located in the Russian's navigational route to Vladivostok from the South China Sea, and in 1882 the British showed an interest in leasing the Korean island for naval purposes. Russian penetration into Afghanistan brought about a direct conflict between England and Russia, and when the November 1884 negotiations between the British and the Russians failed to settle the disputes, an Anglo-Russian war became imminent.

In view of the Anglo-Russian crisis, the British government authorized its naval units in the Far East to occupy a key point in the Russian's navigational route. As a result, on April 15, 1885, without giving any prior notification to Korea, or receiving the consent of the Korean government, the British warship, *Flying Fish*, and several other naval vessels, occupied Kŏmun Island. After this, the British hoisted their national flag on the island, and constructed military barracks. The British were well aware of the fact that, in 1857, Russian Admiral Putiatin had attempted to establish a coaling depot on the island, and that now the Korean king and von Möllendorff were seeking Russian protection. It was clear that the British would not allow the Russians to gain an upper hand, or to establish domination in Korea, and the British called their action a "preventive occupation."

The Korean government protested against the British, and made vain attempts to solicit American and Japanese assistance in order to bring about the British withdrawal and to prevent an open clash between the British and the Russians in or around Korea. Meanwhile, von Möllendorff, after visiting the occupied island via a Chinese gunboat, went to Nagasaki, and on May 18, protested to British Admiral Sir William Dowell concerning the British occupation of the Korean territory. Taking advantage of von Möllendorff's presence in Japan, the Russian minister sent a message indicating Russia's willingness to send military instructors to Korea. After returning to Korea, von Möllendorff threatened to sever Korea's treaty relations with Great Britain if the British did not evacuate Kŏmun Island. In contrast, the Japanese welcomed the British occupation of the Korean island, alleging that Russia was plotting to annex Korea.

A Russian diplomat in Japan, Alexis de Speyer, rushed to Korea and met von Möllendorff who presented him with a plan for an alliance between Korea and Russia. Von Möllendorff even suggested Korea's willingness to cede part of her territory in the north to Russia and to open her ports to Russian naval vessels. However, Foreign Minister Kim Yun-shik bitterly criticized the actions that von Möllendorff had taken when he met de Speyer, stating that Korea had already asked the United States for military instructors, and once made, such a request could not be withdrawn.

The Russian said that the United States was a distant country and could not help Korea, but that Russia was Korea's neighbor and was willing to assist her. The Korean foreign minister refused to give in to the threats de Speyer posted. De Speyer was able to have an audience with the Korean king on June 22, but Kojong evaded the issue of Russian assistance and politely asked the Russian to negotiate with his foreign minister. Frustrated and angry, de Speyer returned to Japan at the end of July.

Li Hung-chang took advantage of this situation to increase China's control in Korea, and to strengthen her claims over Korea as a suzerain lord. The Russian government protested against the British occupation of Korean territory and threatened to occupy some Korean territories, possibly Wŏnsan and other northeastern ports, if the British did not leave Kŏmun Island. However, Li secured the Russian's promise not to occupy Korean territory, and then he approached the British; it was only after the Russian gave assurance, that the British agreed to withdraw from the island. With the departure of the British from the island on February 27, 1887 the threat of an open conflict between England and Russia was finally removed.

Proposals for the Neutralization of Korea.   When Sino-Japanese and Anglo-Russian rivalries over Korea grew, several proposals for the neutralization of Korea were made. In early 1885, the German Vice Consul Herman Budler, in China, submitted a proposal to the Korean government for the joint protection of Korea by the great powers, and the same proposal was forwarded to Li Hung-chang. Both the Korean government and Li rejected the proposal.

In May 1885, shortly after the conclusion of the Tientsin Agreement (Sino-Japanese agreement) between Li Hung-chang and Itō Hirobumi, the Japanese Minister to China, Admiral Enomoto Takeaki, made a proposal to his government for joint Sino-Japanese protection for Korea, only to meet rejection. Enomoto had proposed in 1882 to American Minister Russell Young in Peking that an international conference of the United States, Great Britain, Russia, Germany, France, and Japan be held to deal with the possibility for the neutralization of Korea. Enomoto's proposal also was rejected by the Americans.

When the British naval forces occupied Kŏmun Island, Yu Kil-chun (who studied briefly at an American academy in Salem, Massachusetts in 1883 and 1884, and returned to Korea in early 1885) proposed Korea's permanent neutrality. He maintained that "the only way to protect our country" was to establish a perpetual neutrality with the international guarantee of England, France, Japan, and Russia under the leadership of China. He argued that Korea's neutrality would be beneficial not only to Korea, but also to other nations. The Korean government ignored his proposal although moderate officials such as Ŏ Yun-jung and Kim Hong-jip were in favor of Yu's ideas.

Several other proposals for Korea were suggested. The Chinese minister to Russia recommended to Li Hung-chang that China should either incorporate Korea into China or "put Korea under the joint protection of Great Britain, the United States, and Russia." K'ang Yu-wei, a prominent Chinese reform advocate, also proposed a joint protection of Korea by the powers. In July 1885, George Foulk of the American legation in Seoul suggested that there should be an international guarantee of the neutrality of Korea.

In July 1885, Japanese Foreign Minister Inoue Kaoru attempted to establish a joint Sino-Japanese protectorate in Korea. In his "Eight Points of Opinion" dated July 2, 1885, and sent to Li Hung-chang, Inoue suggested that von

Möllendorff should be replaced by an American adviser, that Chinese Commissioner Ch'en Shu-t'ang should also be replaced by a more capable Chinese official; and that Korea's diplomatic affairs should be carried out under Li's instructions. However, Inoue insisted that Li should confer in advance with the Japanese foreign minister before dispatching any instructions to the Korean government. Li sent a polite rejection to Inoue.

The Strengthening of Chinese Domination.   Between 1885 and 1894, the Chinese increased their domination in Korea, as the intensified rivalry between China and Japan culminated in the Sino-Japanese War in 1894.

In July 1885, Li Hung-chang had the Korean government dismiss von Möllendorff as vice president of the Korean Foreign Office, and in September the German lost his position in the Korean Maritime Customs Service as well. Li recalled him to China. Li replaced von Möllendorff with Judge Owen N. Denny, an ex-American consul-general in China, as foreign adviser, and Li sent Henry F. Merrill, another American as supervisor of the Korean Maritime Customs Service, replacing Sir Robert Hart. They had been working for the Chinese government for some time, and Li was distrustful of Sir Robert Hart.

In October 1885, Li sent Yuan Shih-k'ai back to Korea to establish total Chinese control over the Korean government. At the same time, Li released the Taewŏn-gun, who had been a captive in Paoting, China, and allowed him to return to Korea, hoping to gain his support against Queen Min and her pro-Russian allies. In April 1890, another American, General Charles W. LeGendre, replaced Denny when Denny showed more concern for Korea than for China.

Whereas Li Hung-chang said that he was "king of Korea, and I do as I please," Yuan who returned to Korea in November, claimed that he was "His Imperial Chinese Minister Resident," in chargé of diplomatic and commercial affairs of Korea, and as the American chargé d'affaires Foulk said, he "did pretty much as he liked" in Korea. In June 1886, Yuan, under his government's instructions, made attempts to dethrone King Kojong as well as to remove Queen Min and the crown prince claiming that they had plotted to remove Chinese control in Korea in cooperation with von Möllendorff and the Russians. The Chinese plan was either to put the Taewŏn-gun or his grandson, Yi Chun-yong, on the throne. Had Kojong's plan to solicit Russian aid materialized, or had it been proven that his written request for Russian help was actually sent to St. Petersburg, the Chinese would have sent some 7,500 Chinese troops to Korea from the Liaotung area, as Yuan had requested, to depose the king and queen of Korea. The various conspiratorial schemes of Yuan failed, but he was able to force King Kojong to either punish the pro-Russian officials or dismiss them from the government.

Li Hung-chang, on the other hand, did not wish to invite an open conflict with Russia. He was not convinced that King Kojong actually concluded a secret agreement with Russia or directly sought Russian help against China. The efforts Li Hung-chang made in the fall of 1886 to secure Russian consent to China's suzerainty over Korea failed when Russia insisted on maintaining the status quo in Korea. Meanwhile, Russia displayed no interest in becoming involved in Korean affairs or in taking over Korea, despite his suspicion regarding the non-existing secret understanding between China and Japan against Russia, or Japanese concessions to China for greater control over Korea.

Yuan failed to carry out his sinister plans in Korea, but he managed to antagonize the Korean and Japanese as well as other foreign representatives in Seoul. The Japanese leaders regarded as intolerable the reassertion of China's direct control over, or their interference in Korea's domestic and foreign affairs, for they were fearful that Chinese domination would eventually lead to the domination of Korea by a Western power such as Russia.

Karl I. Waeber, arrived in Korea in October 1884 as the Russian charge d'affaires, and carried out quiet diplomacy and promoted amicable relations with the Koreans. When Yuan Shih-k'ai became an annoyance, a Korean court official secretly asked Waeber to dispatch Russian warships to Korea to bolster the position of the king against Yuan. Waeber chose to avoid any friction with the Chinese because his government concluded that the annexation of Korea would not bring Russia any benefits. However, on August 30, 1888, after lengthy negotiations, he concluded the overland trade agreement with Foreign Minister Cho Pyŏng-shik.

The Chinese domination over Korea continued to grow. Whereas, Yuan was certain that Japan was striving to make Korea her colony, in June 1891, Li Hung-chang made it clear to the American minister, Augustine Heard, that China could not tolerate the independence of Korea, and he asked him to prevail upon Kojong and the Korean ministers to drop any thought of independence and to submit willingly to China. Meanwhile, Yuan reported to foreign representatives that the vassalage of Korea had been clearly stated in the letter from the Korean government to the Chinese government appended to the Korean-American treaty.

The United States and Korea.   As other powers increased their influence in Korea, Minister Foote and other Americans also wished to see the establishment of a strong and permanent American influence there. The American government, however, displayed indifference, if not a lack of interest by refusing to take any steps to implement what Foote and others had proposed. George McCune and John A. Harrison wrote: "American statesmanship was neither ready nor able to effect a Far Eastern policy of moment. The American State Department in the post-Civil War period was at one of its low ebbs in ability and vision." The only concern of the American government was to protect American rights and commercial interests as Secretary of State Frederick T. Frelinghuysen stated in his letter to Foote of March 17, 1883.

Had American economic interests grown in Korea and had Korea's economic importance to the United States increased, the American government might have adopted a positive Korean policy. But Korea's economic importance to the United States remained negligible, and the United States lost interest in Korea. Within a year after Minister Foote arrived in Seoul in May 1883, the State Department reduced his rank from that of Envoy Extraordinary and Minister Plenipotentiary to that of Minister Resident and Consul General, indicating the degrading of Korea's diplomatic status vis-à-vis the United States. The United States in October 1883 failed to take action on an urgent request made by the Korean king to employ Admiral Robert Shufeldt as a military adviser. In disgust, Foote took a leave of absence in February 1885, never to return to Korea. When the British in April 1885 occupied Kōmun Island, the American government did nothing to help the Korean government. Like Foote, Naval Attaché George C. Foulk (acting chargé d'affaires when Foote left Korea) championed the cause for Korean independence and modernization, but his government showed no such interest.

The new American minister, William H. Parker, arrived in Korea in June 1884, but he was recalled in September because he was habitually drunk and therefore ineffective. When Parker was recalled, Foulk became acting chargé and continued to antagonize the Chinese. In the end, Yuan Shih-k'ai pressured the subservient Korean Foreign Minister Kim Yun-shik to complain to the American government that Foulk "grossly calumniates Korea," and that his dispatch on the *Kapshin Incident* of 1884 contained disrespectful remarks concerning a member of the royal family. The State Department, which had not been supportive of Foulk, sent William W. Rockhill as new chargé d'affaires, replacing Foulk in December. However, Foulk remained as Naval attaché.

Yuan, who was determined to remove anti-Chinese Foulk from Korea, had the Korean foreign minister request the American government to remove Foulk from Korea. Kim did so on December 31, 1886, and the State Department recalled Foulk, cancelling his appointment as Naval attaché in June 1887. The Korean king's wish to keep Foulk in Korea as a government adviser was denied by the State Department lest his presence in Korea might damage Sino-American relations. After the departure of Foulk, the little American influence that there was in Korea declined, and as McCune and Harrison pointed out, "the United States had fumbled an opportunity that would not again be offered."

Korean Reaction to Chinese Domination.   When the Chinese reduced Korea to a protectorate, the Korean resentment against Peking grew and periodically the Korean government acted with defiance. The Peking government did not approve of the establishment of Korean legations abroad, insisting that the Chinese legations should handle Korea's foreign affairs in Japan and in European countries. However, in 1887, the Korean government sent Min Yŏng-jun as Korea's minister to Japan without notifying the *Tsungli Yamen* (Chinese Foreign Office) in Peking. When Pak Chŏng-yang was to go to the United States as the Korean minister, the Korean government asked Peking's permission, as had been demanded by the Chinese following the dispatch of Min to Japan. However, when Pak actually arrived in Washington and had a meeting with the United States secretary of state, he met the American in the absence of the Chinese minister, ignoring the instructions of the Chinese government. Despite Chinese protest, the Korean government sent another mission, headed by Yi Wan-yong (1858–1926), to the United States in the spring of 1889. It was at this time that two Korean women, wives of diplo-mats, also visited the United States for the first time. Soon after Yi's visit, Korean students arrived in the United States, and in 1896 six Koreans, including a woman named Kim Haransa, were enrolled at Howard College in Washington, D.C.

Although Korea's attempt to oust Yuan Shih-k'ai in 1888 and 1889 failed, during these years anti-Chinese riots did take place in Seoul, and Chinese shops were looted and burned down. After these events, Yuan ordered all Chinese merchants to reside in segregated areas in Seoul. The more the Koreans tried to shake off Chinese control, the stronger Chinese efforts were to keep Korea as their protectorate.

Japanese Reaction to the Growing Chinese Domination in Korea.   The majority opinion of the Japanese government leaders was that Korea's safe existence was the guarantee for Japan's security. One of them even remarked that Korea was "a dagger pointed at the heart of Japan" if an unfriendly power held it. Conse-quently, Japanese antagonism toward China and their fear of Russian domina-tion over Korea was reinforced.

The commercial activities of the Japanese steadily weakened as Chinese domination increased. In 1883, Japan secured fishing rights on the south and eastern coasts; in 1885 a new agreement between Korea and Japan enabled Japanese fishermen to purchase the fishing rights within three miles of the Korean coast; and in 1888 the Japanese secured the right to fish along the coast of Kyŏnggi Province, thereby competing with Chinese fishermen. Of 716 foreign merchant ships arriving in Korea in 1887, 673 were those of the Japanese, and the Japanese population in Seoul and other treaty ports steadily grew. In fact, whereas only a handful of Chinese merchants lived in Wŏnsan in 1891, there were some 600 Japanese in the city.

However, the Japanese became disturbed when the Chinese demonstrated their determination to re-establish China's suzerainty in Korea. Ōishi Masami, who arrived in Korea as a new Japanese minister in January 1893, realized how strong Chinese domination had grown. "Korea has already fallen," he said, "she exists only because other Powers have not taken [her]. . . She is like a house without walls or a warehouse without locked doors."

What disturbed the Japanese, in addition to the ways in which Yuan dominated the Korean government and handled foreign representatives, was the increase of Chinese exports to Korea. China's share in Korean imports increased from 18.5 per cent in 1885 to 45 per cent by 1892 while those from Japan decreased from 81.5 to 55 per cent during the same period. The dollar value of goods imported from Japan in 1885 was $1,480,000, and it grew to $2,556,000 by 1892, but the dollar value of Korean imports from China jumped from $313,000 in 1885 to $2,055,000 during that period. As China's exports to Korea grew, the Chinese established a branch of the Chinese Merchant Marine Company in Inch'ŏn breaking the Japanese shipping monopoly.

While Japanese apprehension regarding growing Chinese domination increased, the governor of Hamgyŏng Province provoked a dispute between Korea and Japan when, in 1889, he issued an embargo against grain (soybean) exports to Japan. Fearful of a grain shortage in his province, due to a drought in the southern provinces, which caused shortages of grain in the whole country, the governor in effect violated the grain export agreement between Japan and Korea. This action brought about the decline of Japanese business in Wŏnsan, as well as causing what became known as the "Bean Controversy."

The Japanese government protested the embargo, and demanded a 147,000 *yen* indemnity; although the damage done to Japanese grain exporters by the embargo was only estimated to have been between 47,000 and 69,000 *yen*. Upon arriving as the new Japanese minister, Ōishi Masami delivered Japan's ultimatum, and Korea, under the advice given by the Chinese, settled the issue on January 19, 1893, by agreeing to pay the Japanese a 110,000 *yen* indemnity and end the embargo. During the period when negotiations were carried out to settle the Bean Controversy, the Japanese in September 1891 also secured for themselves the right to mine gold at Yongdam in Kyŏngsang Province.

The *Tonghak* Movement, the Sino-Japanese War and the Growth of Japanese Domination

In the spring of 1894, the believers of the *Tonghak* took up arms and brought about the *Tonghak* uprising. Chinese troops arrived, upon the request of the Korean government, to quell the uprising, and Japanese troops arrived soon thereafter, uninvited, in order to counter the Chinese, causing the Sino-Japanese War which in turn resulted in the rise of Japan's domination of Korea.

The Tonghak Movement.   While the increasing commercial activities of Chinese and Japanese merchants, both in Seoul and elsewhere, caused the decline of Korean merchants, the government incurred heavy foreign debts, including indemnities owed to Japan estimated at $90,000. By 1889, Korea's indebtedness to foreign powers grew to between 1.3 and 1.5 million *yen* (about

$900,000). In 1892, the Korean government borrowed 200,000 *taels* from China in addition to a 210,000 *tael* loan in 1885.

The heavy tax burden and the intolerance of corruption of government officials had already caused many uprisings by impoverished peasants. The severe grain shortage that developed following the drought of 1889 only increased their plight, and their restlessness grew. Banditry became rampant and an increasing number of peasants joined armed bandit groups. Local uprisings of peasants, miners, and fishermen, as well as other socially mistreated people erupted frequently, sometimes under the leadership of former government officials and government slaves. The situation of discontent in Ch'ungch'ŏng and Chŏlla provinces was the worst.

The country was in a hopeless state. The Japanese minister, Ōishi Masami, observed in 1893, that "there was not a single Korean statesman capable of regenerating his own country." Meanwhile, the relationship between Queen Min and her allies on one hand, and her father-in-law, the ex-regent Taewŏn-gun, who returned to Korea from China in 1885, on the other, deteriorated to such an extent that she twice in July 1892 had her agents bomb his residence.

The *Tonghak* followers had been anti-government since the founder of the sect was executed in 1864. The suppression of the *Tonghak*, together with the worsening economic conditions and the practices of corrupt officials, made them more hostile to the government and the ruling class. They demanded tolerance for their religion and posthumous exoneration for Ch'oe Che-u, the founder of the sect who had been executed as a criminal. This suppression of the sect and confiscation of the *Tonghak* people's property by the governor of Poŭn, Ch'ungch'ŏng Province precipitated an uprising in 1892.

Being loyal to the king, however, the leaders of the sect went to Seoul in April 1893, where they waited for three days on their knees to present their petition to the king. Their requests were denied, and they were ordered to go back home. In May, some 20,000 people held a rally in Poŭn, Ch'ungch'ŏng Province, and demanded reform at home, expulsion of the Westerners and the Japanese, the suppression of Christianity, and the cancellation of all treaties with foreign powers.

The Tonghak Uprising.   The *Tonghak* movement has been characterized by some historians as either a "rebellion," a "peasants' war," or a "peasants' revolution." It began as a protest movement, but became an uprising when the government forces attempted to crush it. When the Sino-Japanese War began and the government forces under Japanese direction launched actions against *Tonghak* insurgents, the movement became both a rebellion against the government and a war against the Japanese.

Many of the leaders were members of the *yangban* class, ruined by past factional struggles, or were the illegitimate sons of *yangban* families. Needless to say, most of the insurgents were believers in the teachings of Ch'oe Che-u and peasants who had been exploited by landlords and corrupt officials.

The newly appointed magistrate of Kobu, Chŏlla Province, increased the people's antagonism by his misconduct, including the extortion of money and the misappropriation of wages of farmers who had worked on irrigation projects. When the appeals made by the *Tonghak* people to the provincial governor were turned down, Chŏn Pong-jun (1854–1895), the leader of the southern branch of the *Tonghak* sect, realizing that the only recourse was violence, led a thousand angry farmers in a revolt in February 1894. The government retaliated, arresting the *Tonghak* rebels and destroying their homes, thereby precipitating a full-scale uprising.

Chŏn Pong-jun circulated propaganda materials, in which he expressed loyalty to the king and explained that the purpose of the uprising was first the destruction of the *yangban* class, which was the source of official corruption, and secondly, the re-establishment of peace for the country and promotion of safety for the people. The rebel leaders indicated that it was their goal to abolish the aristocratic social structure and the economic system which had been harmful to the peasant. At the same time, demonstrating their revolutionary aspirations, they advocated the inauguration of political and legal reforms to end social injustice.

The victorious rebel forces took over Chŏnju, the capital of Chŏlla Province, on May 31. Meanwhile, the violence spread into Ch'ungch'ŏng and Kyŏngsang provinces. At this juncture, contrary to the advice of many officials, the king decided to request China's military assistance against the rebels.

Realizing his inability to defeat the rebels, the commander of the government forces in Chŏlla Province offered a truce to Chŏn, presumably on orders from the king. It included the following terms:

1. There will be no popular discrimination against *Tonghak* members. Anyone found guilty of such discrimination will be punished.
2. All debts and mortgages of *Tonghak* members will be cancelled.
3. *Tonghak* members will be permitted unrestricted travel and protection from violence.

Meanwhile, on June 4, the Korean government formally applied for Chinese aid and two days later Chinese naval and land units were ordered by the *Tsungli Yamen* to go to Korea.

Although the sincerity of the government was doubtful, Chŏn accepted the truce terms offered in the name of the king, and withdrew his troops from Chŏnju on June 14. The government established Correction Offices in Chŏlla Province, and *Tonghak* members served in an advisory capacity. Riding the favorable tide, the *Tonghak* leaders issued a manifesto which included twelve reform demands. It proclaimed, among other things, that the antagonism existing between *Tonghak* members and the government should be wiped out, and mutual cooperation should be sought; that the oppression by officials and rich *yangban* would no longer be tolerated; that the slave records should be burned and the old system of status abolished; that widows should be allowed to remarry; that farmland should be redistributed on an equitable basis; that corrupt officials should be punished; that unprincipled Confucian scholars and *yangban* should be punished and reformed; that no taxes other than the statutory ones should be levied; that government officials should be recruited on merit and competence, rather than by family background; and that all debt involving farmers should be cancelled. The government, however, did not, or was unable to, honor its agreements and meet the demands presented by the *Tonghak* leaders.

The Sino-Japanese War and Japanese Aggression in Korea.   The increasing Chinese domination over Korea aroused strong Japanese antagonism, and the opinion of the Japanese leaders reflected their belief that the war with China was unavoidable ''for the sake of Japan's own security.'' It was at this juncture that Kim Ok-kyun, who had suffered hardships and humiliating treatment at the hands of the Japanese government as an exile in Japan since 1884, went to Shanghai for unrealistic reasons, and was assassinated at the end of March 1894 by a Korean, Hong Chong-u, who was an agent of the Korean government. The Japanese friends of Kim Ok-kyun and those who had been advocating that the Japanese government should take positive steps to help the Progressives in Korea were angered by the death of Kim, and they urged their government to take strong actions against the Chinese.

The arrival of 1,500 Chinese troops in Korea on June 4 to help the Korean government to subjugate the *Tonghak* rebels, led the Japanese government to resolve to encounter the Chinese on positive terms. In accordance with the Tientsin Agreement of 1885, the Chinese Foreign Office informed the Japanese government regarding the dispatch of Chinese troops to Korea. In its note, however, the Chinese stated that China was dispatching troops to Korea ''in conformity with China's ancient custom of sending troops to protect vassal states.''

Needless to say, the Japanese government rejected the Chinese notion that Korea was a vassal to China, and in the note given to the Chinese the Japanese government stated that Japan had never recognized Korea as a vassal state of China. The Japanese government decided at this juncture to send troops to Korea under a new Japanese minister, Ōtori Keisuke. Ōtori arrived at Inch'ŏn with eight Japanese warships on June 9, and proceeded to Seoul the following day with some 400 marines.

A mixed brigade of 3,000 Japanese troops, under General Ōshima Yoshimasa, landed at Inch'ŏn, and on June 13 they marched to Seoul. The Chinese requested the Japanese to withdraw their troops from Korea, but the Japanese ignored the Chinese request. Meanwhile, the negotiations carried out in Tokyo between the Japanese Foreign Minister, Mutsu Munemitsu, and the Chinese minister to Japan brought about no satisfactory results. At this juncture, Ōtori suggested to his government that the Japanese reform plan "should be carried out by force" if the Korean government did not comply with the Japanese request.

China appealed to Russia for help in settling the disputes with the Japanese. Whereas, on June 20 the Korean government, after requesting the withdrawal of Japanese troops, solicited first the intercession of the United States, and then the intervention of the European powers, Great Britain proposed a five-power intervention, but the United States, France, and Germany were unwilling to become involved in the Korean situation. The Russians, who suspected the motives of the British, made no effort to prevent the war in Korea except to advise the Chinese to further negotiate with the Japanese.

The Chinese refused the Japanese proposal for joint actions in Korea to bring about reforms, restore peace, and improve the international relations of the Korean government. Thereupon, on July 3, Ōtori presented the Korean government with a reform plan that included the following five items: (1) reform of various systems and employment of talented people in the government, (2) financial and tax reform, (3) judicial reform, (4) improvement of the military and police and maintenance of domestic tranquility, and (5) educational reform and training of people. A council of elder statesmen studied the Japanese proposals and advised the Korean government to adopt them, but the government controlled by the pro-Chinese officials rejected the council's suggestion.

When the Korean government hesitated to accept the Japanese plan, Ōtori presented a demand on July 13, giving the Koreans three days within which to accept his reform plan. Instead of accepting the Japanese demand, the Korean government on July 15, requested that both Chinese and Japanese troops be withdrawn from Korea, but this request was ignored by both countries. On July 19, Ōtori received an instruction from his government to "apply oppressive means" to find "justifiable causes for war" against the Chinese. Meanwhile, efforts made in mid-July by Karl Waeber met with Japanese opposition because of Japan's mistrust of Russian intentions. Efforts made by the British to geographically separate Chinese and Japanese troops met with Chinese rejection because of the favorable position held by the Japanese troops. Seoul had been occupied by Japanese troops, and 10,000 Japanese troops significantly outnumbered 5,500 Chinese troops.

On July 20, Ōtori sent two dispatches to the Korean foreign minister, Kim Yun-shik. One of them stated that "It is the duty of your government to protect Korea's independence and to observe the treaty concluded between Korea and Japan," that Korea make her independence from China clear, and that she abrogate all existing conventions and agreements with China. In another note, Ōtori threatened that "If your government delays in giving an answer, I have a decisive opinion on the matter which will be carried out.''

When, on July 22, Kim Yun-shik gave Ōtori an evasive answer, Ōtori delivered an ultimatum that unless a specific and satisfactory response was given to him by the Korean government Japan would resort to military force in defense of her rights and interests. The Korean government rebuffed the Japanese on July 22, and stated that the Chinese troops had come to Korea upon Korea's request and that they might stay as long as they desired.

Ōtori mobilized his troops and carried out his threat in early morning on July 23, and put the Kyŏngbok Palace, which was the king's residence, under Japanese occupation. After brief fighting, the Japanese quickly disarmed the ill-prepared Korean troops and drove them out. Ōtori sought out the Taewŏn-gun and put him in charge of the government, and Kojong, helpless in his palace occupied by Japanese troops, agreed to form a new administration. On July 24, a new Council of State was formed with Kim Hong-jip as its head, and the following day the king announced the abrogation of all agreements and treaties between his government and China.

The Sino-Japanese War commenced when, on July 25, in the Asan Bay, the *Naniwa* and other Japanese warships sank the *Kowshing* and other Chinese warships. China and Japan declared war on August 1. The Japanese troops quickly demolished the Chinese troops in the Asan area by July 29, and other Chinese units retreated northward.

Once the war began and when Japanese troops demonstrated their superiority over Chinese troops, the Korean government became helplessly domi-nated by the Japanese who established the military occupation in Korea. On August 20, Ōtori brought the Korean foreign minister, Kim Yun-shik, to con-clude the "Provisional Agreement" in which Korea agreed to accept Japanese advice on internal reform, to allow the Japanese to construct railway lines be-tween Seoul and Inch'ŏn and Seoul and Pusan; to promote trade with Japan by opening a port (Kunsan) in Chŏlla Province; and to raise no questions regard-ing the July 23rd incident which involved the Japanese invasion of the Kyŏngbok Palace. With this, the Japanese withdrew troops from the palace, and on August 26, the Korean government concluded a military alliance with Japan, and it legitimatized Japanese military occupation of Korea.

The capitulation of the Korean government to the Japanese demands changed the character of the *Tonghak* uprising into a rebellion and a war against the Japanese. The joint actions taken against the *Tonghak* insurgents by the Korean government and Japanese troops provoked a strong nationalistic reaction. Waiting until after the harvest, in October Chŏn Pong-jun and *Tonghak* in-surgents launched a war against the Japanese and the government controlled by the Japanese. The *Tonghak* forces marched northward toward Seoul, capturing Kongju, the capital of Ch'ungch'ŏng Province. At this juncture, the orthodox Northern branch of the *Tonghak* sect under Ch'oe Shi-hyŏng's leadership joined Chŏn's forces, and in November fierce battles ensued near Kongju.

However, the *Tonghak* forces were badly beaten at the end of November by a combined force of Korean and Japanese troops, and Chŏn's forces retreated southward to Chŏlla Province. Toward the end of December, Chŏn and most of the other leaders of the *Tonghak* army were captured and promptly executed, bringing the *Tonghak* movement to an end in January 1895.

Japanese troops of the First Army, commanded by General Yamagata Aritomo, won a major victory against the Chinese in the battle of Pyŏngyang in mid-September, and in October they crossed the Yalu River into Manchuria. Meanwhile, the Second Army of Japan, under commander General Oyama Iwao, landed on the Liaotung Peninsula and by the end of November captured key ports, including Lushun (Port Arthur) and Talien (Dairen). Contingents of the Second Army landed on the Shantung Peninsula and captured the port of Weihaiwei in early February. When the Western powers refused to assist China, the Chinese sued for peace and in late January 1895, peace negotiations began in Hiroshima. The Japanese forced Li Hung-chang himself to come to Japan, and on April 17 a peace treaty was concluded in Shimonoseki in which the Chinese recognized Korean independence, agreed to pay a large war indemnity, cede Taiwan, and lease the Liaotung Peninsula to Japan for twenty-five years.

The Kabo Reform

During the Sino-Japanese War, the Japanese imposed their reform measures upon Korea in the name of strengthening Korea's national security and promoting political stability, social order, and economic and cultural progress. At the same time, they demonstrated in various ways that they were determined to keep Korea under their control. The reform program which the Korean government implemented under Japanese direction was called the Kabo Reform.

 The Kabo Reform.   In order to carry out various measures proposed by the Japanese, the Deliberative Council (*Kun-guk Kimuch'ŏ*) was created on July 27, 1894, as the supreme organ of the state. Its key members were Kim Hong-jip, Ŏ Yun-jung, Kim Yun-shik, and Pak Chŏng-yang, all of whom were concurrently ministers of the Council of State. A new Security Agency called *Kyŏngmusa* was established, replacing old policing agencies. Until it was abolished on December 17, the Deliberative Council played a pivotal role in changing various systems of the country.

In certain ways, the Kabo Reform marked a radical departure from the past, however superficial. It not only had reconstructed the government system, but it also had curtailed the prerogatives of the monarch despite his objections. Among other privileges, the king lost his right to appoint high ranking officials in the government as well as his control over financial matters, including the ginseng monopoly, the gold mines, and the local taxes. Moreover, he was made to reign over the nation, and not to rule.

With the creation of the Deliberative Council, eight *amun* (ministries) were established under the Council of State: Home Affairs, Foreign Affairs, Finance, Justice, Military Affairs, Agriculture and Commerce, Education, and Industry. At the same time, the affairs of the court, including its financial matters, were separated from the government and were administered by the newly created Department of Royal Household Affairs.

Inoue Kaoru arrived in Seoul on November 20th as the new Japanese minister to Korea, replacing Ōtori. Immediately after his arrival, he presented a twenty-item reform plan to the king and his ministers. Meanwhile, Pak Yŏng-hyo and Sŏ Kwang-bŏm, both of whom had fled to Japan in 1884, were brought back to Korea, and they were made the Home and the Justice ministers, respectively. In the new Council of State headed by Kim Hong-jip, Kim Yun-shik remained as the Foreign Minister; Pak Chŏng-yang continued as the Education Minister, and Ō Yun-jung stayed as the Finance Minister. Yu Kil-chun, who published a book entitled *Sŏyu Kyŏnmun* (*Observations on a Journey to the West*) in 1895, was Home Minister, Yi Chun-yong, a grandson of the Taewŏn-gun, was sent to Japan as the Korean minister, and all criminal charges were dropped against those who had been involved in the 1884 coup. Kim Ok-kyun, who was assassinated in Shanghai in March 1894, was exonerated. In December, the Privy Council (*Chungch'uwŏn*) replaced the Deliberative Council.

On January 7, 1895, King Kojong took an oath before his ancestral shrine in Seoul. In his oath, which is often called "the 14-article constitution (*Hongbŏm shipsajo*)," the king pledged that he would establish firm national independence; improve education and technical training; strengthen the military; revise legal codes "in order to protect the lives and properties of the people;" and abolish class distinctions. A few days later, the Council of State was renamed as *naegak* (cabinet), and the royal titles of the king, the queen, and the crown prince and his wife were changed, patterning after those of Japan. In April, the administrative districts were redrawn, and eight provinces were replaced by 23 prefectures (*pu*) and 336 counties (*kun*).

The Kabo Reform also abolished the old class structure and slavery. Remarriage of widows, including those of the upper class, was legally permitted, and wearing Western clothes was encouraged. Thus, a certain egalitarian concept laid the foundation for a new social order. However, the time-honored social habits and conventions were not easily modified or discarded.

The reform program brought about the adoption of a new monetary system based on the silver standard, the payment of taxes in cash instead of goods, and the adoption of the Western system of weights and measures. A three million *yen* Japanese loan was secured in March 1895 to finance various reform projects, new silver coins were minted; and Japanese bank notes were permitted to circulate. The economic reform, however, failed to deal with the land tenure system, and brought no benefits to tenant farmers and sharecroppers.

The Kabo Reform also instituted military reconstruction. One of the items of the oath taken by the king in Janaury 1895 specified that "military officers shall be trained, a conscription system shall be adopted, and a firm foundation for the military shall be constructed." Accordingly, the Ministry of Military Affairs was established and the old military units were replaced by two new army battalions. One battalion was the Royal Guard, stationed in Seoul, and the other, for local security, had branches throughout the country. An American general, Charles LeGendre, who had been adviser to the Korean Foreign Office was dismissed because of his anti-Japanese sentiments, but another American general, William M. Dye, along with an American military officer who had been employed in the Korean government since 1888, were retained as instructors at the military academy, and more Korean soldiers were trained with modern weapons imported from Japan and the United States. Despite this, Korean troops were poorly trained, equipped, and paid, and they were numerically inferior vis-à-vis Japanese troops. The Korean navy was not modernized, and national security remained inadequate to either safeguard Korea's sovereignty and independence, or to withstand any foreign threats.

The Kabo Reform also brought about educational change. First of all it abolished the traditional civil service examination system. To be sure, Confucian studies continued under the government sponsorship at various institutions, including Sŏnggyun-gwan, but the Royal Edict proclaimed in February 1895 emphasized three principles, namely the development of ethics, the promotion of new knowledge, and strong body, establishing the three basic principles of education, namely *chi* (knowledge), *tŏk* (ethics and morality), and *ch'e* (body).

The Ministry of Education which was established in July 1894, promulgated seven ordinances concerning education and announced the plan for the establishment of normal schools and modern primary schools. Under these ordinances, Hansŏng (Seoul) Normal School was established in April to train primary school teachers, followed by the establishment of five primary schools in Seoul at the end of 1895. Primary schools were also established at other places. A Japanese language school had been established in June 1890 in Seoul, and following the promulgation of an ordinance concerning foreign language schools in May 1895, another Japanese language school emerged. New textbooks for modern curriculum were published in Korean mixed with some Chinese characters. However, no girls' schools were established.

The Collapse of Japanese Influence and the End of the Kabo Reform. All seemed well to the Japanese who defeated China and established a firm control over Korea. The Korean reform advocates also hoped for their country's steady modernization. But, suddenly, the influence of the Japanese collapsed, and the reformers faced increasing difficulties in the wake of the Triple Intervention and the October incident of 1895.

The leasing of the Liaotung Peninsula by Japan from China under the

Shimonoseki treaty which ended the Sino-Japanese War disturbed the Russians who detected Japanese intentions to establish a strong military position there with a naval base at Lushun (Port Arthur). Claiming that Japanese control over the Liaotung region made the independence of Korea illusory, the Russian government solicited the cooperation of France and Germany first, and then presented in May 1895, a joint demand to the Japanese government for the cancellation of the Liaotung lease. This action taken by three Western powers was known as the Triple Intervention. Japan had no choice but to meet the demand of the three powerful Western nations, and cancelled the lease.

The cancellation of the Liaotung lease by Japan, under the Triple Intervention, was regarded by the Koreans as a demonstration of Japan's weakness. Anti-Japanese sentiments grew in Korea, and the Japanese in May began to abandon its Korean projects. With this, the Korean cabinet which had included many Progressives was replaced by men with a pro-Russian orientation, forcing Pak Yŏng-hyo to flee to Japan for the second time. The new cabinet adopted a plan to disband a Japanese trained infantry regiment. By mid-July, Russian influence was strongly felt at the Korean court. Under Waeber's advice, General LeGendre was made private tutor to the crown prince and adviser to the Department of Royal Household Affairs. The influence of the Japanese declined sharply.

The Japanese assassination of Queen Min further weakened their influence in Korea. Miura Gorō, a new Japanese minister who replaced Inoue in September 1895, was determined to recover the position which Japan had held in Korea during the Sino-Japanese War. He believed that prompt and vigorous action would take care of the problems which the Japanese confronted in Korea, and his aim was to eliminate the leader of anti-Japanese, pro-Russian group in the government, namely the queen. In order to achieve his objectives, he solicited and won the cooperation of the Taewŏn-gun who hated the queen and was not happy with the situation in Korea. Being convinced that it was expedient, Minister Miura, in cooperation with other Japanese such as Okamoto Ryūnosuke, Sugimura Fukashi, and Ogiwara Hidejirō, as well as a few Koreans, carried out his plot against the queen.

At dawn on October 8, 1895, Queen Min was assassinated by a Japanese named Takahashi Genji. The Minister of Royal Household Affairs, Yi Kyŏng-shik, was murdered by two Japanese policemen, and two court ladies who attempted to protect the queen were killed by other Japanese and their Korean collaborators. The king and the crown prince were held captive in the palace surrounded by Japanese troops, and Kim Hong-jip, as a new prime minister, formed a new cabinet. This incident is known in Korean history as the *Ŭlmi sabyŏn*.

Although the death of the queen at the hands of the Japanese was not immediately announced, it could not be concealed; when it was made known, the Koreans were enraged and strong anti-Japanese feeling erupted. Miura and other Japanese who were involved in the incident were recalled to Japan and tried. In late October, a seasoned Japanese diplomat, Komura Jutarō, arrived in Seoul as the new minister, followed by Inoue Kaoru who went to Korea to assist Komura in settling the issues related to the Miura incident and to improve the relationship between Korea and Japan. However, the Japanese were unable to control the rising tide of anti-Japanese sentiment or to reestablish the Japanese influence in Korea, and the Kabo Reform came to an end.

The Kabo Reform had only modest success in modernizing Korean society. Although it dealt primarily with immediately pressing needs, it also adopted some long range plans and thereby made contributions by promoting public concerns regarding national affairs, as well as increasing the awareness of the need for economic development and social progress.

Domestic and Foreign Affairs After the Death of Queen Min.   When King Kojong recovered from the shock of the queen's death, he took both symbolic and practically significant steps. He established a special court, tried those Koreans who were responsible for the death of the queen, and executed them. He strengthened the palace guard. On October 11, the king granted a new title, Myŏngsŏng, to the deceased queen, and the state funeral was held a month later. On October 26, he promulgated an edict, adopting the Gregorian calendar; an ordinance concerning the establishment of modern elementary schools saw the appearance of four primary schools in Seoul in November, and in the same month, the ordinance concerning the smallpox vaccination was issued, followed by the establishment of more modern post offices. In December, he designated his reigning era as *Kŏnyang* ("Building Brightness"), and issued the ordinance concerning modern haircuts on December 30 and urged others to have their traditionally long hair cut, as he himself cut off his topknot.

Those pro-Russian officials, including Yi Pŏm-jin and An Kyŏng-su who had been dismissed with the formation of the new cabinet under Kim Hong-jip shortly after the death of the queen, felt that they must "rescue" the king and the crown prince from the pro-Japanese ministers, and on November 28, they attempted to kidnap the king and his son to the Russian legation, creating a more serious political crisis.

Although they were shaken by the events which took place in October and November, the reform minded ministers, such as Kim Hong-jip and Ŏ Yun-jung, pushed for more modernization. As a result, the king took those actions in November and December which have been discussed earlier. However, they encountered an increasing amount of internal and external problems. Immediately after the issuing of the haircut ordinance, riots of angry Confucianists who assailed the ordinance erupted in various places, the worst of which were in Ch'unch'ŏn and Ch'ungju where high magistrates and many other government officials were killed by mobs. Meanwhile, they encountered a growing pressure from Russia.

Arriving in Seoul in early January 1896, as the replacement of chargé d'af-faires Waeber, Alexis de Speyer stated that Russia did not have any aggressive policy toward Korea. He indicated that Russia had neither the intention of an-nexing Korea, nor establishing a protectorate over Korea. "We simply want," he said, "to eliminate the preponderant influence of the Japanese and establish order and tranquillity in Korea." However, he confessed that it was the Russian aim to increase Russia's influence in Korea. Both Waeber and de Speyer in-dicated that the main objective of Russia's policy was the removal of pro-Japanese officials from the Korean government and the support of anti-Japanese forces in the country.

The acquittal of Miura and other Japanese who were responsible for the death of Queen Min aroused strong anti-Japanese resentments in Korea, and the threat of an attack on the capital by the insurgents who were angered by the haircut ordinance, and rumors that the Japanese were plotting to force the king to abdicate in favor of his nephew, Yi Chun-yong (grandson of the Taewŏn-gun), all led Kojong to seek Russian help. On February 2, 1896, he sent a secret message to the Russian chargé d'affaires indicating that he was sur-rounded by traitors and that there was a threat to kill both him and the crown prince. He informed the Russians that he and his son wished to flee from the palace to the Russian legation, if they would have them. Without his govern-ment's consent, Waeber approved Kojong's plan and a new act of the tragic drama was ready to be played out.

6. The Demise of the Yi Dynasty and Korean Independence

Many events in the history of the Kingdom of Chosŏn might be considered the beginning of the demise of the Yi dynasty, but the most significant and crucial event was the king's flight to the Russian legation and the resulting aftermath. This event was the landmark which brought about intense rivalries and the power struggle in Korea between Russia and Japan, and when the Japanese won their victory in the Russo-Japanese War, Korea fell victim to Japanese colonialism.

Kojong's Flight to the Russian Legation. The pro-Russian Koreans carried out their second attempt to remove the king and the crown prince to the Russian legation, and this time they were successful. Early in the morning of February 11, 1896, with the help of the Russians they smuggled the king and his son out of the Kyŏngbok Palace, disguised them as court ladies, and took them to the Russian legation. As this bizarre event was taking place, some ministers such as Home Minister Yu Kil-chun, managed to flee to Japan, but Prime Minister Kim Hong-jip and Agricultural Minister Chŏng Pyŏng-ha were murdered in a savage mob assault; a few days later Finance Minister Ŏ Yun-jung was also killed. After the king established his residence at the Russian legation, a new cabinet was formed with a pro-American Pak Chŏng-yang as Acting Prime Minister. Yi Pŏm-jin, an ardent pro-Russian, was named the Minister of Justice; Yi Wan-yong became Foreign Minister, and Kim Hong-yuk, who spoke Russian, became the king's confidant.

During the period between February 11, 1896 and February 21, 1897, when Kojong resided at the Russian legation, Russia's influence grew rapidly as the 185 conservatives gained strength. King Kojong regained the power to appoint or dismiss high officials without the consent of the cabinet. In August 1896, Korea was divided into 13 provinces (*to*), 7 prefectures (*pu*), one special district called *mok*, and 331 counties (*kun*). Large provinces, such as Hamgyŏng, P'yŏng-an, Ch'ungch'ŏng, Kyŏngsang, and Chŏlla provinces, were divided into north and south, and along with Kyŏnggi, Hwanghae, and Kangwŏn provinces they constituted thirteen administrative districts. In September, the government structure was changed, and the old Council of State replaced the modern cabinet system. In October, the Minister of Education, Yi To-jae, published a book entitled *The Warp and Woof of Confucianism* in which he denounced the "barbarous teachings" of Christianity and criticized the Westerners, the Japanese, and the reform advocates.

Russo-Japanese Understanding. The ascendance of Russian influence in Korea that followed King Kojong's flight to the Russian legation led the Japanese to seek an understanding with the Russians. As a result, during the months of March and April 1896, the Japanese Minister to Korea, Komura Jutarō, negotiated with the Russian chargé Waeber in order to bring the Korean king back to the palace and to remove anti-Japanese ministers from th' Korean government.

On May 14, Komura and Waeber signed a memorandum and agreed that both Russia and Japan would advise the Korean king to return to the palace on "his own discretion and judgment" and when "no doubts concerning his safety could be entertained." They also agreed that they would advise the Korean king to appoint liberal and moderate men to the government. The Japanese agreed to remove three companies of Japanese troops from Seoul and to deploy 200 gendarmes to protect the Japanese telegraph line between Seoul and Pusan. The Russians agreed that two companies (no more than 200 men in each company) of Japanese troops might be stationed in Seoul, one company at Pusan, and one company at Wŏnsan for the protection of the Japanese settlements. They would, however, be withdrawn when peace and order were established by the Korean government. The Japanese recognized Russia's right to have the same number of troops as the Japanese in Korea, for the protection of the Russian legation, consulates, and properties. Under this agreement Russia gained an equal right to maintain troops in Korea.

The Japanese government sought high-level understanding with Russia, and they authorized General Yamagata Aritomo to negotiate with the Russians in order to establish understanding and agreements on a variety of issues concerning Korea. When Yamagata arrived in Moscow, in May 1896, to attend the coronation ceremony of Tsar Nicholas II, he held secret sessions with Russian Foreign Minister Aleksie B. Lobanov-Rostovskii.

On May 24, Yamagata presented a proposal to Lobanov, expressing Japan's interest in having a political agreement with Russia that would ensure the inde-

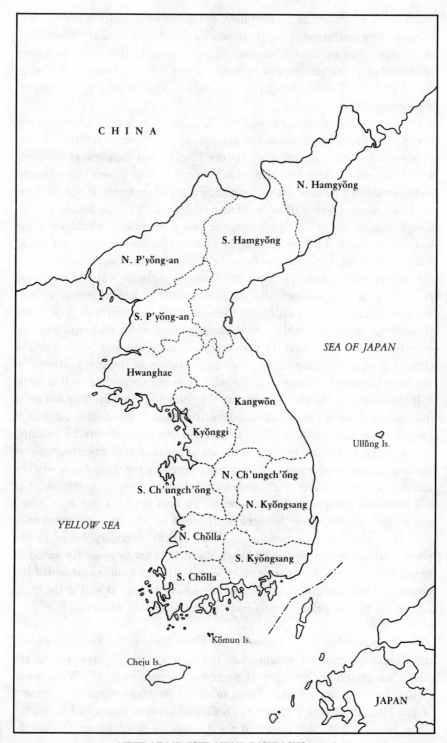

CHINA

N. Hamgyŏng

S. Hamgyŏng

N. P'yŏng-an

S. P'yŏng-an

SEA OF JAPAN

Hwanghae

Kangwŏn

Kyŏnggi

Ullŭng Is.

N. Ch'ungch'ŏng

S. Ch'ungch'ŏng

N. Kyŏngsang

YELLOW SEA

N. Chŏlla

S. Kyŏngsang

S. Chŏlla

Kŏmun Is.

Cheju Is.

JAPAN

NEW ADMINISTRATIVE DISTRICTS, 1896

pendence of Korea and maintain public peace and social order in the country. Lobanov, however, rejected the Japanese idea of having a mutual "guarantee" of Korean independence because, in his opinion, the joint guarantee amounted to a joint protectorate over the country. He was, however, willing to see that both Russia and Japan recognized and respected Korean independence.

On June 9, the Moscow Protocol (the Lobanov-Yamagata Agreement) was signed. The Protocol contained "public articles" and "secret articles." In the public articles, they agreed that: (1) the Russian and Japanese government would advise the Korean government so as to control superfluous expenditures, and to establish a balance between expenditures and revenues. If and when, as the result of the urgency of some reforms, it became necessary for the Korean government to secure foreign loans, the two governments would assist the Koreans by common efforts; (2) the Russian and Japanese government would leave it entirely up to Korea, insofar as the financial and economic conditions of the country would permit, to form and maintain indigenous armed forces and police in a number sufficient for the maintenance of general order, without foreign assistance; (3) in order to facilitate communication with Korea, the Japanese government would retain the management of the telegraph line now in its hands; and (4) should the above require more exact and detailed definition, or if other questions arose, the representatives of the two governments would be instructed to come to an amicable agreement regarding such matters.

In the secret articles, they agreed that: (1) "Should the tranquillity and order in Korea be disturbed or seriously endangered as the result of some internal or external cause and should the Russian and Japanese governments, by common accord, judge it necessary to come to the aid of the local authorities by means of sending troops in addition to the number necessary for the security of their nationals and the protection of their telegraph lines, the two. . . governments. . . will determine the sphere of action reserved for each in such a way as to leave a space free of occupation between the troops of the two governments," and (2) "Until the formation in Korea of the necessary forces. . . the provisional agreement signed by Waeber and Komura to maintain an equal number of troops in Korea remains in force." The Protocol left unsettled the question of military instructors for training a Korean army as well as the question of the Korean government's employment of foreign advisers.

Russo-Korean Relations.   Following the king's flight to the Russian legation, the Korean government sought close ties with Russia. A Russian language school was established in April 1896, and a Korean envoy, Min Yŏng-hwan (1861–1905) was dispatched to Russia to attend the May coronation ceremony of Tsar Nicholas II as well as to seek an alliance between Korea and Russia.

On June 5, 1896, Min presented the Russian Foreign Minister, Aleksie B. Labanov-Rostovskii, with his government's proposal which included a warning that any agreement between Russia and Japan to extend joint influence in Korea would lead to conflict between them and cause a new national calamity for the country. The Korean government asked Russia for the following: (1) Russian protection of the king until the creation of a new Korean army, (2) Russian instructors for the military and the police, (3) three Russian advisers—one each for the Royal Household, the cabinet, and industrial and railroad enterprises, (4) a three million *yen* loan to repay a Korean debt to Japan, and (5) the establishment of telegraph lines between Korea and Russia.

Almost a month later, on July 2, the Russian government agreed: to send some military personnel to protect the Korean king, to negotiate further for Russian military instructors, to make a loan to Korea, and to construct telegraph lines. Dissatisfied with the Russian promise, Min negotiated further with Foreign Minister Lobanov, but he did not receive fully satisfactory promises from the Russians. In mid-August, however, Lobanov finally decided to dispatch an adviser for the Korean government along with several military instructors, and also provided the requested loan.

When Min Yŏng-hwan returned to Korea, in late October, Colonel Putiata and a dozen Russians arrived in Seoul; they drew up a plan to establish a 40,000-man army over a three year period and requested their government to send 150 instructors. Although the Russian government did not approve Putiata's plan in its entirety, the Korean government, after a stormy debate, decided in April 1897, to invite a few Russian military instructors. Meanwhile, a plan to create a new 3,000-man Korean army was approved by the Russian government, and a dozen more military instructors arrived in Seoul late in July. In late September, Kir A. Alekseev arrived in Seoul from Russia as the financial adviser just as preparations for the establishment of the Russo-Korean Bank were in progress.

While the Korean king resided in the Russian legation, and immediately after his move to the Kyŏng-un (now Tŏksu) Palace on February 21, 1897, the Russians and other Westerners secured many concessions from Korea with the help of the Russians. First of all, the railway concession which had been given to the Japanese on August 20, 1894, to construct the Seoul-Inch'ŏn line, was revoked and was given to James Morse of the United States on March 29, 1896. However, the American sold the partially completed line to the Japanese in 1899.

Major concessions which the Korean government made to the foreigners during that period included: a railway concession on July 3, 1896, to a French syndicate, Fives Lille, to construct the Seoul-Shinŭiju line, (the French sold the concession to the Japanese with the consent of the Korean government on August 11, 1896); a concession granted in April 1896, to an American, James Morse, to mine gold at Unsan, North P'yŏng-an Province; and a concession given on April 22, 1896, to a Russian named Nisichensky, to mine minerals in the northern part of Hamgyŏng Province and to construct a railway there for the purpose of mining. A concession was granted in April 1897, to a German, E. Meyer & Company of C. Walter, to mine gold, silver, copper, and coal; and another concession was granted, on August 28, 1897, to a Russian, Jules Bryner of Vladivostok, to timber in the Musan region along the Tumen River as well as on Ullŭng Island in the Sea of Japan.

A cordial relationship between Korea and Russia, and Korean dependence on Russian advice and assistance were carefully cultivated by the able diplomat Waeber, and such a relationship lasted even after the king left the Russian legation and moved to the Kyŏng-un Palace. Some Russian guards provided protection for the palace as well as for the ministers after that date.

As Russian influence grew, the Japanese were disturbed. The Korean government's granting of concessions to Russia and other Western powers—particularly Korea's cancellation of the earlier concession given to the Japanese for the construction of the Seoul-Pusan railway line and the simultaneous granting of the same right to an American company—annoyed them. The Japanese decided to discredit the Russians, and in March 1897, they made public the contents of the Komura-Waeber Memorandum and the public articles of the Moscow Protocol. Moreover, Foreign Minister Ōkuma Shigenobu informed the Korean government that the Russo-Japanese protocol signed in Moscow contained secret articles for the possible partition of Korea in the future.

The reaction of the Korean government to this information was surprisingly mild, if not ambivalent. Perhaps the Korean officials did not realize the gravity of such an understanding between the two imperialist powers.

The Reformist Movements and Domestic and International Politics

At this critical juncture in Korean history, the voice of nationalist reformers rose, and it looked as though Korea might regenerate herself and safeguard her own sovereign rights and national independence. But the reformist movements collapsed as suddenly as they had risen, and politics in Korea returned to "traditional behavior" as the twilight of the Yi dynasty approached.

The Independence Club and Reform Advocates.   In the midst of an unsettled domestic and international situation, young reform advocates emerged and preached the gospel of nationalism and social progress. Among them were Yi Sang-jae (1850–1927), Yun Ch'i-ho (1865–1945), Namgung Ŏk (1863–1959) and Syngman Rhee (Yi Sŭng-man, 1875–1965), all of whom were critical of the imperialist powers and of their own inept government.

Dr. Sŏ Chae-p'il (1866–1951), a young revolutionary who had fled to Japan in 1884 when the reform government collapsed, and then migrated to the United States, returned to Korea in January 1896. Having studied medicine and earned a medical degree, he returned to Korea as a naturalized American citizen, with the Anglicized name of Philip Jaisohn, in order to "teach the people and to cultivate leadership'' for independence and the modernization of Korea.

After declining a post offered in the cabinet by Prime Minister; Kim Hong-jip, Dr. Jaisohn accepted an advisory position in the Privy Council (*Chungch'uwŏn*) which had replaced the Deliberative Council in December 1895. His primary goal was the education of the people toward new political and social concepts for the promotion of democracy in Korea. In order to do these, he established and published the first purely Korean-language newspaper, with an English language section, named *Tongnip Shinmun*, or *The Independent*, printed three times per week. The editorial of the first issue printed on April 7, 1896, stated that Korea was for Koreans, and that the paper's intention was to speak in the interest of Korea. Its circulation grew from 300 in April 1896 to 3,000 by the end of 1898.

A short time after the beginning of publication of *The Independent*, Dr. Jaisohn helped young reform advocates form the *Tongnip Hyŏp'oe*, or The Independence Club, which emerged in Seoul in July 1896. Its founding members included a few government officials and many ex-officials. Among its active leaders were Yun Ch'i-ho, Yi Sang-jae, Syngman Rhee, and Chŏng Kyo.

The purposes of the Independence Club were to protect national sovereignty, to reform politics so as to reflect public opinion, and to elevate the cultural and social level of the people. It advocated, like *The Independent*, that Koreans develop the spirit of independence and protect the sovereign rights of the country not by relying on this or that power, but by promoting national unity, economic and military strength, and modern culture. Within a short time after it was established, branches were established in many places and membership grew.

The voice of the reform advocates grew louder with the establishment of the Independence Club. It launched educational and cultural campaigns, and sponsored lectures and debates in order to arouse public concern and interest in reform movements. At the same time, it emphasized the need for moral and social reforms as well as the development of democratic ideals. Above all, it advocated the promotion of the spirit of independence for individuals and for the nation. In 1896 many patriotic poems and songs were written. In addition to the *Patriotic Song* by Yun Ch'i-ho, such songs as the *Song of United Hearts* by Yi Chung-wŏn and the *Song of Independence* by Ch'oe Pyŏng-hyŏn, urged the people to develop the spirit of independence and progressivism. The first stanza of the *Song of United Hearts* reads as follows:

Let us wake up, wake up
From a 3,000-year dream.
All nations of the world have met
And the Four Seas became neighbors.
Let us be free from troublesome old age,
And promote common virtues
With united hearts.

Dr. Jaisohn and his colleagues advocated the destruction of the Yŏng-ŭn Gate, a gate erected outside the West Gate of Seoul, where Korean kings welcomed diplomatic envoys from Peking. The gate had been a symbol of Korea's subservience to and dependence on China. The new Nationalists solicited funds to construct an independence arch, tore down the Yŏng-ŭn Gate, and in November 1896, the Independence Arch was dedicated as the symbol of the spirit of Korean independence. Meanwhile, the name of the China Adoration Hall, where Chinese envoys had been entertained lavishly by Korean officials, was also renamed as the Independence Hall, and it was used as the place where public lectures and debate sessions were held by the Independence Club.

The members of the Independence Club were extremely critical of the conservatives who controlled the government which lacked the spirit of independence and reformism. They also implored the king to leave the Russian legation and return to the palace.

On February 20, 1897, the king left the Russian legation and established his residence at the Kyŏng-un Palace, and inaugurated many reform measures advocated by the Independence Club. In August, he adopted a new era name of *Kwangmu* ("Illustrious Strength"), and on October 12, he held a solemn coronation ceremony at the Altar of Heaven in downtown Seoul, and he pledged to his ancestors' spirits that he would protect the independence of the nation and promote the welfare of the people. At the same time, he renamed Korea *Taehan Cheguk*, (Empire of Great Han) and he assumed an imperial title (*hwangje*) for the first time in Korean history. The late queen was also given a new title: Empress Myŏngsŏng.

Riding the rising, favorable tide, the Independence Club held a mass meeting at Chongno, Seoul on February 20, 1898, and demanded that the granting of concessions to foreigners be stopped. They bitterly criticized the leasing of Chŏllyŏng (Deer) Island to Russia and the way in which de Speyer had gained the concession; they also demanded the termination of the Russo-Korean agreement and the dismissal of Russian financial and military advisers. Under such pressure, the Korean emperor declined to employ a large number of Russian military instructors as Waeber had proposed and he cancelled his plan to form a palace guard with some 30 foreign soldiers.

Reaction to the growing influence of Dr. Jaisohn and the pressure from the Independence Club was bound to take its toll. The government, controlled by reactionaries and conservatives such as Foreign Minister Cho Pyŏng-shik, agitated for Dr. Jaisohn's dismissal from the Privy Council and his deportation from Korea. Under pressure from both the Korean and the American governments, Dr. Jaisohn and his wife left Korea in May 1898. It seemed to a foreign observer in Seoul at that time that the collapse of the reform sentiment within the Korean government was complete and that the situation was hopeless.

The Collapse of Russian Influence.   The cordial relationship between Korea and Russia which Waeber had carefully cultivated suddenly collapsed in the spring of 1898. The new Far Eastern policy of Russia was initiated with the adoption of what is known as the "Port Arthur Orientation" after Russia leased the Liaotung Peninsula from China on March 27, 1898. This reduced Russia's interest in securing ice-free ports in Korea. At the same time, the arrogance and the lack of diplomatic tact of Alexis de Speyer undermined the Russian position in Korea.

De Speyer arrived in Seoul on September 2, 1897, to replace Waeber, and even before he officially replaced him, de Speyer demanded that the Korean emperor promptly settle the issue pending between Russia and Korea. At the same time, he conspired to replace the British commissioner of .he Korean Maritime Customs Service, John McLeavy Brown, with Kir A. Alekseev. Only a few days after his arrival, de Speyer was able to force the retirement of the War Minister, Shim Sang-hun, who opposed the employment of a large number of Russian military instructors as proposed by Putiata. In early November, de Speyer forced the Korean emperor to dismiss the Finance Minister, Pak Chŏng-yang, who opposed the replacement of Brown with Alekseev. On November 15, the new Finance Minister, Cho Pyŏng-shik, made Alekseev the Financial Adviser and the commissioner of the Korean Maritime Customs Service.

The British Minister, J. N. Jordan, antagonized by the dismissal of Brown, brought the Asiatic fleet of Great Britain to Inch'ŏn and displayed its might thereby threatening the security of Korea. When this threat was posed, the Korean government, on January 19, 1898, appointed Brown as financial adviser to the Korean government and in March, when Russian influence collapsed, he was reinstated to his former position.

De Speyer was not only responsible for bringing about a threat of British military action, but also in February 1898, he pressured Kojong to dismiss Foreign Minister Yi To-jae, because of his attempts to block the Russian leasing in February 1898 of land on Chŏllyŏng Island in Pusan harbor to be used as a Russian coaling station. After Yi's departure from the government, the Russians were able to secure the lease, but his plan was frustrated by the Japanese who quickly bought up all possible sites for coal depots on the island.

The overbearing tactics employed by de Speyer aroused anti-Russian feelings. An ardent pro-Russian, Kim Hong-yuk, was attacked on February 22, but he escaped from his would-be assasin. It was at this juncture that de Speyer proposed to his government that Russian troops occupy the northern provinces of Korea. However, his government rejected the proposal. De Speyer even attempted to lure Emperor Kojong back to the Russian legation.

In March 1898, the Russian government instructed de Speyer to seek clarification of the Korean government's desire for Russian assistance. Employing rash tactics, on March 7, de Speyer delivered an ultimatum to Foreign Minister Min Chong-mok, demanding that the Korean government resolve without delay the issue related to the employment of Russian military instructors, and give a reply "within twenty-four hours." On March 8, he had an audience with the Korean emperor and pressed him to reply concerning Russian protection.

De Speyer's tactics backfired when, on March 12, the Korean foreign minister, after a series of heated sessions of the ministers, thanked Russia for help and other favors, and politely indicated that "we will not employ any foreign military instructors or advisers." "Your officials have accomplished their work," Min's statement said, "and it is convenient for us to have them relieved from our service." Without his government's positive support for a direct action, de Speyer had no choice but to carry out what he had indicated in his ultimatum: the Russo-Korean Bank, which opened on March 1, closed its doors; and some 60 Russian military instructors and advisers departed from Korea by late March. In April, Nicholai Matunine replaced de Speyer, but he was unable to recover the influence Russia had briefly enjoyed.

New Russo-Japanese Agreement.   Certain of no more than the moral support of Great Britain against the advance of Russia in the Far East, in January 1898, the Japanese initiated a movement in search of détente in Russo-Japanese relations. The Russian government also showed its interest in lessening Japanese antagonism toward Russia.

On January 15, 1898, the Russian Minister to Japan, Roman R. Rosen, met the Japanese Foreign Minister, Nishi Tokujirō, and told him that Russia was prepared to assist Japan, as far as possible, in her commercial and industrial interests in Korea. Nishi remarked that it was difficult to reach a satisfactory understanding with Russia "unless Russia was ready to abandon her position on the subject of the drilling of the army and the engagement of a Financial Adviser" in Korea. It was at this time that Nishi proposed Russia's recognition of the "preponderance" of Japanese interests in Korea, and introduced the scheme to exchange Korea for Manchuria—or the so-called *Mankan kōkan* idea in which Russia recognized Korea as within the Japanese sphere of influence in return for Japan's recognition of Manchuria as being within the Russian sphere of influence.

Nishi did not succeed in establishing the *Mankan kōkan* understanding, but recognizing the recent attitudes of the Russian government, which displayed its "desire to conciliate us in order to make an enemy less," he carried out negotiations, and brought about the Nishi-Rosen Protocol of April 25, 1898. In it, it was agreed that: (1) both Japan and Russia "definitively recognize the sovereignty and entire independence of Korea, and mutually engage to refrain from all direct interference in the internal affairs of that country;" (2) desiring to avoid every possible cause of misunderstanding in the future, the governments of Russia and Japan would not "take any measure in the nomination of military instructors and financial advisers, without having previously come to a mutual agreement on the subject;" and

(3) Russia would "not impede the development of the commercial and industrial relations between Japan and Korea." It is significant to note that such an understanding was established only after the withdrawal from Korea of Russian military instructors and a financial adviser and only after Russia leased the Liaotung peninsula on March 27.

Korea at the End of the Nineteenth Century

After Dr. Jaisohn left Korea, Yun Ch'i-ho took over the Independence Club as many government officials resigned from the Club for one reason or another. The publication of *The Independent* became increasingly difficult, although Dr. Appenzeller helped Yun to continue its publication. Yun was able to cultivate a cordial relationship with the emperor, and when he had an audience with the emperor, he proposed a series of reform measures and requested that the Independence Club be recognized as a liaison between the government and the people. In July 1898, Yun and three other members of the Independence Club were appointed to the Privy Council.

The pro-Russian Koreans were extremely unhappy with the collapse of Russian influence. In August 1898, An Kyŏng-su, the former war minister, attempted to force the emperor to abdicate in favor of his son, and on the Emperor's birthday, September 11, 1898, pro-Russian Kim Hong-yuk, who had resigned in March from the government, attempted to assassinate the emperor with poisoned coffee which was to be served with special Western food prepared for the occasion.

Meanwhile, the Korean government granted more concessions to foreigners, giving more precious natural resources away. On September 27, 1898, a British subject, Pritchard Morgan, received concessions to mine gold, silver, copper, iron ore, coal and other precious minerals at Unsan in North P'yong-an Province. On March 29, 1899, the government granted a whaling concession to a Russian, Count Henri Keyserling, and agreed also to lease land at Ulsan and Changjin on the east coast and on Chinp'o Island to be used to build fishing facilities and storehouses. The Japanese themselves secured on September 8, 1898, the concession to construct the Seoul-Pusan railway line and on August 16, 1900, Shibuzawa Eiichi and Asano Sōichirō acquired a mining concession at Chiksan in North Ch'ungch'ŏng Province.

The Last Phase of the Reform Movement.   While the Independence Club championed Korea's independence and cultural and social progress, at the end of the era, other Koreans and certain Western missionaries contributed much toward the modernization of Korea with their newspapers, schools, and various educational and cultural programs.

As a successor to the society newspaper *Hyŏpsŏng Hoebo,* published in early January 1898 by students of Paejae School—a mission school for boys, the first Korean-language daily newspaper, the *Maeil Shinmun* appeared in February of the same year. One of its reporters was Syngman Rhee. The paper ceased to exist when the government ordered its abolition in late 1898 because of its radicalism and anti-government attitudes.

In March 1898, Yun Ch'i-ho and other patriotic people published a newspaper named *Kyŏngsŏng Shinmun* (*The Seoul News*). It was renamed once in April, and then in September it became the *Hwangsŏng Shinmun* (*The Imperial Capital News*) which promoted nationalism and the spirit of progress under the leadership of such Nationalists as Namgung Ŏk and Chang Chi-yŏn.

The first Christian Korean-language newspapers were the *Chosŏn Kŭrisŭdoin Hoebo* (*The Korean Christian Society News*) of the Methodist Church, which began its publication in February 1897, and the *Kŭrisŭdo Shinmun* (*The Christian News*) of the Presbyterian Church which emerged in April. Although the publication of the English-language journal *The Korean Repository* ceased in 1898, American missionaries who had established it in 1892 left many valuable source materials on Korean history, culture and the society of the late Yi period.

More modern schools were established by patriotic leaders and by Christian missionaries. A Russian-language school and a German-language school, plus a medical school were established in 1896, 1898, and 1899, respectively. Korean noblemen, Min Yŏng-hwan and Min Yŏng-shi, each established a private school in 1895 and 1896, respectively. American Presbyterian missionaries established a primary school, named Chŏngjin, for girls in Pyongyang, and Kyŏng-ok School for girls in Seoul, in 1896. A secondary mission school named Sungshil for boys was established in Pyongyang in 1897 by the Presbyterian Mission.

Between 1895 and 1898, more modern post offices were established throughout the country, and in September 1899, the Seoul-Inch'ŏn railway was partially opened for traffic. When the modern bridge over the Han River was constructed, in July 1900, Inch'ŏn was linked with Seoul by railway. Streetcar operations in Seoul began in 1899.

Attempts made in the 1898–1902 period by the Korean companies, such as the Southwest Perimeter Railway Company of Pak Ki-jong in Pusan, the Korea Railway Company, as well as a government agency under Yi Yong-ik to construct a local line in South Kyŏngsang region, Pusan-Ŭiju and Seoul-Wŏnsan-Hoeryŏng railways failed due to lack of funds. However, in 1900 the Korea Joint Mail and Shipping, the Inch'ŏn Mail and Shipping, and the Inhan Steamship companies of the Koreans emerged as cargo carrying lines.

The members of the Independence Club and other patriotic people were critical of the government, which made many concessions to foreigners and seemed void of reform spirit and effective leadership, and they demanded the dismissal of several reactionary high government officials. On October 11,

1898, the Independence Club mobilized several hundred students and staged a mass demonstration in front of the palace. The weak and vacillating emperor gave in to pressure and dismissed the accused ministers. The leaders of the Independence Club met with key officials of the new cabinet and presented a request for the reorganization of the Privy Council. In it, they asked that twenty-five seats, or one-half of the expanded Council, be filled with popularly elected representatives of a "people's assembly." It was a revolutionary scheme which attempted to introduce the system of popular participation in government affairs. On October 15, the Independence Club brought about a new mass organization called Ten Thousand People's Cooperative Association, or the People's Assembly.

The Independence Club, on October 27, 1898, mobilized some 8,000 persons and held a Joint Conference of the Government Officials and the People, at Chongno, Seoul. At this time they adopted a resolution which included the following six items:

1. That both officials and people shall determine not to rely on any foreign aid but to do their utmost to strengthen and uphold the Imperial prerogatives.
2. That all agreements with foreign nations concerning mining, timber, railways, loans, military aid and treaties must be countersigned by all the Ministers of the State and the President of the Privy Council.
3. That all trials for felony should be open to the public, and grave offenders should be given an ample opportunity to defend themselves.
4. That all sources of revenue and methods of collecting taxes shall be under the control of the Finance Ministry, and other ministries and private firms shall not be allowed to interfere, and that the annual budget and balance shall be made public.
5. That His Majesty shall appoint his ministers only with the concurrence of the majority of the Cabinet.
6. That the existing laws and regulations shall be faithfully enforced without fear or favor.

The emperor and his government did not adopt these resolutions, but in November an imperial decree permitted the Independence Club to elect twenty-five members to the Privy Council. As far as the leaders of the Independence Club were concerned, everything seemed to be in their favor.

The Rise of the Women's Movement.   The emergence of women's organizations constituted a significant historical development. Encouraged by nationalism and the spirit of social reform which the Independence Club advocated, the first Korean women's association named *Ch'angyanghoe*, otherwise known as the Society for the Promotion of Sunsŏng School emerged in Seoul, established a private school, and on September 1 it made public the "Notice on the Establishment of a Girls' School." In its notice, it manifested a new vision and aspirations of Korean women, seeking social equality and educational opportunity. "Why should our women be kept at home as if they were fools, with their ears deaf and their eyes blindfolded?" it said, "Are there any differences between men and women in their bodies, arms and legs, or ears and eyes?" It declared that in enlightened countries both men and women are equal; boys and girls go to school early in their childhood, learning various skills and principles and broadening their vision." "We must establish girls' schools," it declared, "abolish our old customs and follow the new ways so that our girls can learn various skills and principles, and the methods of making life successful."

On October 11, 1898, the *Ch'angyanghoe* submitted a memorial to the throne, urging the monarch to establish schools for girls. "A school is where competent persons are educated and knowledge is propagated," it said, "We women. . . founded the Society with the aim of making our country prosperous. . . with loyalty and patriotism." In its memorial, the new Korean women said:

We kneel before Your Majesty asking Your Majesty to issue an imperial ordinance. . . to establish schools for girls so that Korea could become a civilized country. . . and be entitled to enjoy the equal treatment that is accorded other countries. . . .

The memorial submitted by the *Ch'angyanghoe* led to the adoption by the government of a budget for the purpose of establishing a girls' school, and in May 1899, a 13-article ordinance for a girls' school was promulgated.

While supporting the work of the Independence Club, the *Ch'angyanghoe* was endeavoring to strengthen the women's movement for educational equality and social justice. When the members of the Independence Club were arrested, the members of the *Ch'angyanghoe* took part in an overnight sit-down demonstration in front of the palace, appealing to the throne for the release of the arrested persons. They regarded their action as honorable and right for the sake of the nation, and they displayed their determination and willingness to be imprisoned for the right cause.

The government, dominated by narrow-minded conservatives, rejected the plan to establish a girls' school in January 1900. But one Mrs. Kim (Yanghyŏndang) maintained the existence of Sunsŏng School as its principal. Although it seems that the support of the *Ch'angyanghoe* ceased to exist, she moved the school from Sung-dong to Kye-dong, and renamed it in 1902 Chŏngsŏn School. After the death of Yanghyŏndang in March 1903. Mrs. Yi (Chayangdang) took over the school and operated it for a brief period.

The self-awakening of Korean women brought about the emergence of other Korean women's associations, such as the Society of Women Friends, founded in 1899 by Chŏng Hyŏng-suk, and the Protection Society, founded in 1900, by a group of Protestant women. These groups promoted a new life movement for women which advocated the improvement of the women's position and their enlightenment.

The Collapse of the Independence Club. While the emperor made such a concession to the reform advocates, the reactionaries in the government carried out their plans against the reformers. The Imperial Association, which had been organized by the reactionaries sometime in October 1898, brought members of the peddlers' guild to Seoul. Meanwhile, Cho Pyŏng-shik, an archenemy of the Independence Club, brought charges against the club members alleging that they had a plot to overthrow the monarchy and establish a republic. As a result, the Independence Club was declared subversive; its seventeen leaders were arrested on November 5; an imperial decree ordering its dissolution was issued, and Yun Ch'i-ho went into hiding.

Day and night, mass rallies were held in Seoul demanding the release of the arrested club leaders and the repeal of the imperial order. When the leaders of the club were released, the demonstrators rushed to the palace and pressed for further reform. They passed a no-confidence resolution against the government and demanded the resignation of the ministers in the name of the "people's assembly."

The reactionaries unleashed mob action by inciting peddlers against the demonstrators, and several days of bloodshed followed. Merchants closed their shops and joined the demonstration. Bloody fighting from November 21–23, resulted in heavy casualties and created near anarchy in Seoul.

Acting upon "strong urging" from foreign diplomatic representatives in Seoul, the emperor personally appeared before the demonstrators and brought the bloodshed to an end. On November 26, the emperor promised that the peddlers' guild would be dissolved, the persons who manufactured the fabrications against the Independence Club members would be punished, the Independence Club would be reestablished, and the resolution of six items of the people's assembly would be gradually implemented.

Emperor Kojong not only failed to carry out his promise, but he also ordered the dissolution of the Independence Club in late November. As a result, the Independence Club was crippled; many of its leaders fled to other countries, and the publication of *The Independent* ceased. With this, the Nationalists' reform movement collapsed, and Korea missed its last chance to preserve sovereignty and independence.

The emperor was too weak to overcome the conservatives' opposition, and in March 1899, he took steps to revive Confucianism. At this point Confucian scholars even attempted to restore the old civil service examination system. As the American minister to Korea William F. Sands observed, the imperial court was crowded with greedy favor seekers, and "sorcerers and witches were among the frequent visitors to the palace," and "the court was full of idle, hungry native place [job] hunters."

Meanwhile, the race between Russia and Japan continued; in 1899, the Japanese purchased the Seoul-Inch'ŏn railway line from an American company; Aleksandr I. Pavlov, who succeeded Matunine in January 1899, attempted to lease a strip of land near Masan on the southern coast not far from Pusan, but the preemption of the desired land by the Japanese frustrated his plan.

The Twilight of the Yi Dynasty

During the critical period between 1900 and 1904, Russian and Japanese antagonism and rivalries increased, culminating in a war. The Korean government, dominated by unenlightened and inept officials, failed to see the ominous signs and the gathering war clouds, and did virtually nothing to strengthen the national defense.

To be sure, the momentum of modernization continued. The modern bridge over the Han River was completed in July 1900, enabling the complete operation of the Seoul-Inch'ŏn railway line, and electric lights were installed in Seoul. A monetary reform was instituted in 1901, and the circulation of paper money, including that of the Japanese bank, increased. In 1902, a German musician, Franz V. Echert, composer of the Japanese national anthem, arrived in Korea and became a government employee, organizing the Imperial Military Band. Missionaries of the Seventh-Day Adventist Church arrived in 1903, and established a press, and initiated, in October 1910, the publication of a monthly journal, *Shijo* (*Signs of the Times*), which became the longest surviving monthly Korean language journal. In October 1903, the Young Men's Christian Association emerged in Seoul, and the number of Christians steadily grew to 40,000 by 1905.

The Nationalists adopted the melody of *Auld Lang Syne* as the music for a patriotic song in 1902. Needless to say, their purpose was to arouse patriotism and national consciousness. This *Patriotic Song* written by Yun Ch'i-ho became a national anthem of the Koreans. Its first stanza reads:

> *'Til Mt. Paektu wears away*
> *And the Eastern Sea dries up,*
> *May our country live long,*
> *Ten thousands of years*
> *Under God's protection.*
> *This is the beautiful garden of*
> *The Rose of Sharon;*
> *Let us preserve the Korean people*
> *In the land of Korea.*

Despite the Nationalists' efforts, political morality declined and corruption was rampant; government agents roamed the country selling public offices, and corrupt officials collected special taxes to enrich themselves. The tax burden fell heavily on the people and the famine in 1901 severely affected most parts of the country, particularly the south. At this juncture, Koreans began emigrating to Hawaii. After two Koreans emigrated to Hawaii as farm workers in 1900, some 7,300 Koreans emigrated to Hawaii between 1903 and 1905. Korean emigration to the United States ceased in 1905 when the Japanese stopped it.

The poverty-stricken peasants organized secret societies, such as the *Hwalbindang,* or the "party for the livelihood of the poor," and created disturbances in 1901 and 1902. Some of them were the *Tonghak* believers. The violent uprising of 1901 erupted on Cheju Island. Korea at this time was void of reform spirit, and her resources were exhausted. The twilight of the Yi dynasty was at hand.

The Russo-Japanese War and Its Impact on Korea.   The Korean govern-
ment failed to take steps either to establish a strong tie with Russia against Japan, or to form a concrete understanding with Japan to preserve Korean sovereignty and independence. Instead, it put its trust in, or relied on nonexistent American good will, for Korea's national security. The Russo-Japanese War was disastrous for Korea, to say the least. During the war, the Japanese forced the Korean government to conclude a series of agreements favorable to their aggressive designs and actions in Korea. The Japanese imperialists were not content with gains made in Korea during the war, and in November 1905, following the end of the war, they transformed Korea into their protectorate.

Attempts made by the Russians to establish their naval bases in Korea increased Japan's apprehension. After failing to lease land in the port of Masan in South Kyŏngsang Province in 1899, Pavlov again failed to lease an island near Mokp'o on the south coast in 1900. He was able to lease land at Yulgumi, near Masan in March 1900, but then the Russians abandoned the lease shortly thereafter, discovering its unsuitability for naval purposes. Be that as it may, Russian actions continued to increase the Japanese suspicion. Jules Bryner, who had managed to secure timber concession in the Tumen River area in 1896, also secured a timber concession from Korea in the Yalu River region in 1900.

Serious Japanese antagonism against Russia developed when Russian troops occupied Manchuria in conjunction with the Allied military intervention in China in 1900 as the Boxer Uprising threatened lives of foreign residents in Peking and its vicinity. After occupying Manchuria in January 1901, Russia proposed a plan to Japan to neutralize Korea under the joint guarantee of the Powers. Japan turned down the proposal because from her point of view, the Russian occupation of Manchuria made Korean independence illusory just as Japan's leasing the Liaotung peninsula in 1895 had been regarded by the Russians as a threat to Korea.

The Japanese continued to seek a free hand in Korea and to secure Russian recognition of their "preponderant" position in the peninsula. Thus the plan to exchange "Manchuria for Korea," or the so-called *Mankan kōkan* idea of Foreign Minister Nishi was reintroduced. The Japanese hoped to establish an understanding under which Japan would recognize Manchuria as within the Russian sphere of influence in return for Russia's recognition of Korea as within the Japanese sphere of influence, although the Japanese believed that Russian encroachment in Manchuria might lead to encroachment in Korea. The Japanese minister in London, Hayashi Tadasu, stated that "it was a matter of life and death" for Japan to keep Russia out of Korea. In late 1901, Itō Hirobumi himself went to Moscow to establish an understanding with the Russians regarding Korea, but his efforts brought no satisfactory results. Consequently, Prime Minister, General Katsura Tarō, supported by General Yamagata Aritomo and his military clique, concluded the Anglo-Japanese Alliance on January 30, 1902. Needless to say, Japan's primary objective was to keep Russia out of Korea. In the agreement, England recognized that "Japan. . . is interested in a *peculiar degree*, politically as well as commercially and industrially, in Korea." Japan, however, pledged to honor Korean independence in the agreement.

Russia concluded an agreement with China on April 11, 1902, agreeing to withdraw her troops from Manchuria in three stages. In October, Russian troops in the Liaosi region were relocated in the Liaotung region instead of evacuating from Manchuria, and when the time came, in April 1903, for Russia to carry out the second stage of the agreement, she showed no intention of doing so, in defiance of the powers which were interested in establishing the Open Door in Manchuria.

A series of events that took place in Korea accelerated the coming of the war. In 1903, the Russians revived their interest in the timber available in the Yalu River region, and their activities in that area increased. Pavlov secured a new concession from the Korean government to expand Russian logging areas in the region.

In April 1903, some 60 Russian soldiers, accompanying about 40 Chinese coolies, arrived in Yong-amp'o, a Korean port on the mouth of the Yalu River, where they purchased a large amount of land. They began building barracks and telegraph lines between Yong-amp'o and a Manchurian town across the Yalu River. Concurrently, Pavlov asked the Korean government to lease the entire port of Yong-amp'o to Russia. The joint action taken by the British, the American, and the Japanese representatives in Seoul against Russia's lease request frustrated Pavlov's plan in Korea for the second time. While the action taken by the Japanese angered the Russians, Japanese suspicion of Russia's intentions in Korea became more intense; and Prime

Minister Katsura concluded that war with Russia was unavoidable.

In order to accomplish their objectives in Korea short of going to war with Russia, the Japanese government presented a five-item proposal to Russia on August 12, 1903, seeking Russia's recognition of Japan's "preponderant" interests and complete freedom of action in Korea. Russia, however, was not willing to agree, and presented a counterproposal on October 3rd, in which the Russians indicated that they would allow the Japanese to assist Korea only with "advice and instruction in the interest of reform and good government in Korea." Russia also proposed the establishment of a neutral zone in Korea between the 39th parallel and the Yalu-Tumen border. Moreover, Russia insisted that Japan give them prior notification when troops were to be dispatched to Korea; in no case would Russia permit Japan to use Korea for military purposes.

None of these Russian proposals were acceptable to the Japanese, and Russo-Japanese negotiations deadlocked. Meanwhile, the October 8th deadline for the implementation of the third stage in the Russian troop withdrawal from Manchuria passed without any troop movement.

In further negotiations, Russia was willing to admit Japan's "preponderant" interests in Korea, at the same time ignoring the Japanese ultimatum for troop withdrawal from Manchuria. The Japanese cabinet resolved to sever relations with the Russians as of February 6, 1904. Meanwhile, on January 21, the Korean government declared its neutrality.

During the night of February 8 Japanese naval vessels launched their attack against Russian ships in Port Arthur, and the following day Japanese troops landed at Inch'ŏn, rushed to Seoul, and in violation of the Korean neutrality, they put the Korean capital under their occupation. In the afternoon of the 9th, the naval battle began between the Russian and the Japanese naval vessels off Inch'ŏn, and the following day, Japan declared war against Russia.

Korean Misunderstanding Regarding the U.S.-Korean Treaty. According to a report submitted by an American legation official in Seoul on December 17, 1884, the Korean king had "danced with joy," when American minister Foote arrived, for he and his ministers "viewed the Shufeldt treaty of May 22, 1882, as a wedge to free Korea from Chinese domination." The Koreans held the mistaken notion that the good offices clause in the American-Korean treaty (Article 1) was an American promise, if not a guarantee, to protect Korea's sovereignty and independence. Some Americans in Korea directly or indirectly encouraged the Koreans to develop such a notion.

The Koreans failed to learn a lesson from the American casual attitudes toward the encroachment of the powers against Korea. In 1885, when the British occupied the Korean island of Kŏmun, the Korean government formally invoked the good offices clause in the U.S.-Korean treaty, but the

American government made it clear that the United States had no intention of interfering on Korea's behalf. When the Sino-Japanese War began and the Japanese encroachment in Korea increased, the Korean government requested American help. Although the American government sent a polite diplomatic note to the Japanese government, requesting that Korea be treated as a sovereign nation, it rejected the British suggestion that the U.S. intervene in behalf of Korea in cooperation with France, Germany, and Russia.

Despite the historic unwillingness of the United States to become involved in Korean affairs in order to support the Koreans in maintaining their independence, Kojong and his ministers continued to believe that the United States would protect Korea. For example, on the eve of the Russo-Japanese War, Kojong was said to have expressed his belief that America's good office would protect Korean independence. Prime Minister Yi Yong-ik reportedly said to Frederick A. McKenzie, a British reporter in Seoul, that his country had "the promise of America. . . to protect" Korean independence. In February 1904, American Minister Allen wrote to the State Department that the Korean "Emperor always turns to me and the more they [Japanese] scare him the more eager he is to turn everything over to the Americans." In April, he wrote to the Secretary of State that the Korean emperor expected that the American government would "do something for him. . . to retain as much of his independence as. . . possible." But, when the Korean envoy in Washington informed Secretary of State John Hay that Korea was in a serious situation and asked for some help, Hay told him that the United States had "friendship and good wishes for Korea," but American interests were commercial rather than political, and he rejected the Korean request.

Between September 1904 and December 1905, the Korean government made several appeals to the American government, asking for help, but the Americans did nothing. Consequently, Korea suffered because of misunderstanding regarding the U.S.-Korean treaty of 1882, and because of her reliance on the good office of the United States, which did not exist.

U.S.-Japanese Understanding on Korea.   Whereas Korea had expected American help in preserving her independence, President Theodore Roosevelt and his administration neither had such willingness, nor such a plan. On the contrary, the American president actually encouraged the Japanese to become aggressive in Korea in order that he might secure their consent for the Open Door policy in China.

First of all, Roosevelt, was a believer in Social Darwinism and "Big Stick diplomacy" in international affairs. He had neither respect for Korea, which in his opinion had shown "its inability to stand by itself," nor sympathy for the Korean people, who could "not strike one blow in their own defense." Secondly, being an expansionist himself, he in many ways admired the

Japanese people, and had even indicated that he was pro-Japanese.

As early as 1900, when the American government circulated the so-called Open Door notes to the European powers, Roosevelt contemplated giving Korea to Japan in order to gain Japanese cooperation in establishing the Open Door policy in China, particularly in Manchuria. When the Russo-Japanese War began, William W. Rockhill, a confidant of Roosevelt, wrote a letter in February 1904 to Minister Allen, in Seoul, and said that it was clear that the Japanese would settle the Korean question at the end of the war. "The annexation of Korea to Japan," he wrote, "seems to be absolutely indicated as the one great and final step westward of the extension of the Japanese Empire. I think when this comes about it will be better for the Korean people and also for the peace in the Far East." Meanwhile, Roosevelt had concluded that since America could not prevent Japan's absorption of Korea, the next best thing to do was to recognize the inevitable and gain something in return. As a result, he pursued his plan—"Korea for Manchuria (*Mankan kōkan*)"—to give Korea to the Japanese in exchange for an open door in Manchuria.

Baron Suematsu Kenchō of Japan visited Washington in March 1904 and talked with Roosevelt about Korea and the war in the Far East. During their talks, Roosevelt told the Japanese that Japan should have a position in Korea "just like we have with Cuba," meaning that the Japanese should have control over Korea's external affairs as a protector. When, in early June, Baron Kaneko Kentarō and the Japanese Minister to Washington, Takahira Kogorō, had a luncheon with Roosevelt, they were told that Japan should establish "a paramount interest in what surrounds the Yellow Sea, just as the United States has... in... the Caribbean...," and Korea should be entirely within Japan's sphere of interest. It was at this time that the Japanese told Roosevelt that all talk about Japan's even thinking of seizing the Philippines was nonsense.

In many ways, Roosevelt made it clear to the Japanese that the United States would not interfere with the Japanese in Korea, and in August, 1904, he told the German Ambassador, Speck von Sternberg, in Washington that Korea should be a Japanese protectorate. By January 1905, Roosevelt concluded that Japan ought to have a protectorate over Korea, and in March he informed Japanese Prime Minister Katsura Tarō through George Kennan that Japan should hold Korea. In April, Roosevelt replaced Minister Allen who was regarded as anti-Japanese with Edwin V. Morgan who arrived in Seoul in June. To date there exists a persistent misconception regarding the Taft-Katsura Memorandum. It has been viewed as a secret pact between the United States and Japan regarding Korea and the Philippines, insisting that, for the security of the American colony, the United States gave Korea to Japan. But it was neither an agreement nor a secret pact between Japan and the United States, and it was certainly not the only time that the Americans expressed their belief that

Japanese control over Korea was inevitable and/or desirable.

The Taft-Katsura Memorandum was an official record of the July 27, 1905, conversations between the American Secretary of War, William Howard Taft, and Japanese Prime Minister Katsura Tarō, who exchanged their personal views regarding the situation in the Far East, including those in Korea and the Philippines. Although Taft had neither a mandate to negotiate with the Japanese, nor instructions from Roosevelt to exchange opinions with the Japanese premier, he met Katsura upon the insistence of the Japanese in an unscheduled meeting when he stopped over in Tokyo, on his way to the Philippines.

After "positively stating that Japan did not harbor any aggressive designs whatsoever on the Philippines," Katsura observed that Korea was the direct cause of our war with Russia, and stated that "Japan feels absolutely constrained to take some definite steps with a view to precluding the possibility of Corea falling back into her former condition and of placing us again under the necessity of entering upon another foreign war." In response to Katsura's statement, Taft "fully admitted the justness of" Katsura's observations, and made a remark that in "his personal opinion" the Japanese establishment of a suzerainty over Korea so that she could not conclude any treaties without the consent of Japan "was the logical result of the present war and would directly contribute to permanent peace in the Far East." Feeling uneasy about his talks with Katsura, Taft sent a telegram on July 29 to the new Secretary of State, Elihu Root, requesting Roosevelt's concurrence. Taft received Roosevelt's concurrence to his opinion a few days later.

Roosevelt knew in August 1905, that in the agreement between Great Britain and Japan, renewing their alliance which was concluded in 1902, the British had already given up Korea to the Japanese. Unlike the 1902 agreement, the new treaty dated August 12, 1905, did not contain a Japanese pledge to honor Korea's sovereignty and independence. Instead, it included British recognition of Japan's paramount political, military, and economic interests in Korea, and the Japanese were accorded "the right of guidance, control, and protection over Korea."

The securing of Japan's consent for an open door in Manchuria and Japan's abandoning of demands for a large war indemnity and territorial concession from Russia became Roosevelt's imperative in late August 1905, as peace talks between Russia and Japan, which he had initiated in Portsmouth, New Hampshire, faced imminent collapse. It was at this juncture that Roosevelt and Kaneko Kentarō, who was a member of the Japanese peace commission, had a secret meeting. According to a secret memoir of Kaneko, which is still unpublished, Roosevelt during their conversations, urged the Japanese to "take over Korea—not right away, but sooner or later," instead of demanding money and territorial concession from Russia. A short time later, the Japanese accepted Roosevelt's peace plan and, on September 5, signed the Portsmouth Treaty ending the Russo-Japanese War.

Japanese Aggression in Korea During the War.   The Russo-Japanese War was disastrous for Korea. Korea's January 21, 1904 declaration of neutrality was completely ignored by Japan, and the Japanese troops which landed on February 9 quickly occupied Seoul. During the war, the Japanese forced the Korean government to conclude a series of agreements favorable to Japan's own designs and actions in Korea. Their intention was to convert Korea into a Japanese protectorate.

The importance of the two protocols which the Japanese forced the Korean government to sign in 1904 was overlooked by many. Contrary to a common notion that the Japanese established a protectorate in Korea with the signing of the agreement on November 17, 1905, it was the protocol signed on February 23, 1904, by the Korean foreign minister *ad interim* and the Japanese minister to Korea (see Appendix B.) which in effect established a Japanese protectorate in Korea. In it, the Japanese guaranteed the independence and territorial integrity of Korea (Article 3). The Japanese government agreed to "immediately take such necessary measures as circumstances require" in the event that the welfare of the Korean imperial house or the territorial integrity of Korea was endangered by the aggression of a foreign power or by internal disturbance (Article 4), and both governments agreed that they would not conclude with a third power any arrangement as might be contrary to the principles of the protocol (Article 5). In order to discharge their obligations, the Japanese secured the right to occupy certain places in Korea "as may be necessary from strategic points of view." (Article 4). This protocol legitimized the Japanese military occupation of Korea, and Korean ministers who opposed this agreement were dismissed. In the unsettled situation that developed following the signing of this protocol, a plot by a few Koreans who attempted to dethrone the emperor was uncovered in March, and on the eve of April 14, a fire broke out in the Kyŏng-un Palace and destroyed several buildings.

In May 1904, two months after Baron Suematsu Kenchō, son-in-law of Ito Hirobumi, talked with President Theodore Roosevelt of the United States, the Japanese cabinet resolved "to take possession of the real powers of protection in political and military matters of Korea and to promote the development of our economic rights and interests in Korea." Accordingly, they adopted a concrete plan which included the following objectives: continuation of the military occupation of Korea even after the conclusion of peace with Russia; imposition of Japanese supervision and the veto over Korea's foreign affairs; employment by the Korean government of an adviser for foreign affairs who would take orders from the Japanese, as well as a Japanese financial adviser; encouragement of emigration of Japanese farmers to Korea; construction of railways and management of major railway lines and communication facilities in Korea; and acquisition of more economic concessions.

In May, the Korean government nullified all existing treaties and agreements with Russia and cancelled concessions which had been given to the Russians. At the same time, the Japanese increased their fishing rights in Korean waters, as well as gained the right to construct the Seoul-Shinŭiju and the Seoul-Wŏnsan railways.

Six months after the signing of the February 23rd protocol, the Japanese took one more step toward the establishment of their protectorate in Korea. As a result, on August 22, 1904, (two months after President Roosevelt encouraged the Japanese, Baron Kaneko Kentarō, to establish Japan's control over Korea), the Japanese brought the Korean government to sign another agreement with them. This was an agreement which was signed by the Acting Foreign Minister of Korea, Yun Ch'i-ho, and Japanese Minister Hayashi Gonsuke. The Japanese refer to this agreement as "the first Korean-Japanese agreement" which established a direct control of the Japanese over the Korean government.

In the new agreement, the Korean government agreed to employ a Japanese as financial adviser (Article 1) and a foreigner (non-Japanese) who was recommended by the Japanese government as an adviser on foreign affairs (Article 2). Article 3 stipulated that the Korean government "shall consult the Japanese government previous to concluding treaties or conventions with other powers, and in dealing with other important diplomatic affairs such as the granting of concessions to, or contracts with foreigners." Following the signing of this agreement, a Japanese, Megata Tanetarō, became financial adviser to the Korean government, and took over the Maritime Customs Service. In November 1904, an American, Durham White Stevens, who had been a Japanese agent for a long period, became an adviser on foreign affairs of the Korean government.

Rapidly the Japanese increased their control over Korea. The Japanese gendarmerie exercised police power and suppressed all Korean anti-Japanese activities, and in December 1904, Japanese policemen were assigned to supervise the Korean police. In January 1905, a Japanese-sponsored financial reform was carried out and new monies were coined. The Daiichi Bank of Japan became the central bank of Korea, and Japanese currency, including the notes of the Daiichi Bank, became legal tender. In April 1905, the Japanese took over management of the postal, telephone, and the telegraph services, and a Japanese adviser on police matters plus another Japanese adviser on educational matters were employed by the Korean government.

Meanwhile, a pro-Japanese association called *Ilchinhoe,* or the Society for United Advancement, emerged under the leadership of Song Pyŏng-jun and Yun Shi-byŏng. As this group and another pro-Japanese society, known as the Progressive Society of Yi Yŏng-gu, merged in August 1904, actively advocating the union of Korea and Japan, it became a tool for the Japanese expansionists such as Tōyama Mitsuru and Uchida Ryōhei of the *Kokuryūkai,* or the Black Dragon (Amur) Society.

Korea Becomes a Japanese Protectorate.   Although in the Portsmouth treaty of September 1905, which officially ended the war between Russia and Japan,

Japan recognized Korean independence, the Japanese had no intention of perpetuating Korea's sovereignty and independence. On October 4, 1905, the *Kokumin Shimbun*, in Tokyo, an organ of the Japanese government, published an article which stated that the Taft-Katsura Memorandum was a secret pact in which the United States gave Korea to Japan in exchange for Japan's guarantee for the security of the Philippines. Roosevelt was disturbed by the newspaper article, but he could do nothing except disagree that it was a secret agreement. Meanwhile, the Japanese government decided to conclude a treaty with Korea, making Korea a Japanese protectorate. When early in November, Prime Minister Katsura informed Roosevelt in strict confidence, that Japan was going to take charge of Korea's external affairs, Roosevelt raised no objections, and promptly ordered the American minister in Seoul to prepare to leave Korea.

Hard pressed by the Japanese, Kojong asked his confidant, Dr. Homer B. Hulbert, who was in Washington in late October 1905, to solicit American assistance in countering the Japanese demands, but Roosevelt refused to see Hulbert. Arriving at the State Department on November 15, Hulbert waited outside Secretary of State Root's office for several days in order to see him. But it was only after the Korean-Japanese agreement was forced upon the Korean ministers by the Japanese that Hulbert met Root and was told that there was nothing the United States could do on behalf of the Koreans.

On November 9, Itō arrived in Seoul to carry out Japan's plan. He had an audience with the Korean emperor on November 15, and presented a draft agreement, demanding that the Korean government accept it immediately. Both Itō and the Japanese Minister in Seoul, Hayashi Gonsuke, put intense pressure on the Korean government. Meanwhile, the Japanese troops in Seoul displayed their strength on the main street leading to the old palace and Japanese gendarmes as well as police were mobilized to control the excited Koreans who filled the street. Emperor Kojong was virtually under house arrest in his palace surrounded by the Japanese.

Acting Prime Minister Han Kyu-sŏl refused to approve the agreement and other ministers, including Foreign Minister Pak Che-sun, were powerless to stop the Japanese altogether. With a few minor changes, the convention providing for control of Korean foreign relations by the Japanese government and the establishment of the Japanese Residency-General "primarily for the purpose of taking charge of and directing matters relating to diplomatic affairs" of Korea was drawn up. This agreement, dated November 17, 1905, was signed by the Korean foreign minister, Pak Che-sun, and the Japanese minister, Hayashi Gonsuke, (See Appendix C). The Koreans called the agreement simply "the 1905 agrement" or "the 5-article agreement." The Japanese called it the "treaty of protection (*hogo jōyaku*)," although it said nothing about Japan protecting Korea. Because of this, many were misled to believe that it was indeed a treaty of protection.

The agreement stipulated that (1) the Japanese Foreign Ministry was to have control and direct the external relations of Korea, and the diplomatic and consular representatives of Japan would have charge of the subjects and interests of Korea in foreign countries; (2) the Japanese government would administer the existing treaties and agreements between Korea and the other Powers, and Korea would not conclude any act or engagement having an international character, except through the medium of the Japanese government. (3) a Japanese resident-general was to be stationed in Seoul under the Korean emperor as the representative of the Japanese government "primarily" for the purpose of managing the diplomatic affairs of Korea and he was to enjoy the right to have private audiences with the Korean emperor; (4) Japan was to station residents at the treaty ports and other places in Korea wherever necessary; (5) all existing agreements and treaties between Japan and Korea were to be maintained provided that they had no conflict with this treaty; and the Japanese government was to maintain the welfare and dignity of the Korean imperial house.

Even though the agreement was never ratified by either the Korean or Japanese emperor, and was therefore invalid, the Japanese still established the Residency-General (*Tōkanfu*) in Seoul in February 1906, and Itō returned to Seoul in March as the first Resident-General (*Tōkan*). With this, the Japanese took over not only the administration of Korea's foreign affairs, but step by step transformed Korea into a Japanese colony. A new Korean cabinet headed by Pak Che-sun emerged, which included Education Minister Yi Wan-yong. Needless to say, there was no foreign minister in the Korean government. All foreign missions departed from Seoul—the American legation was the first one to withdraw from Korea.

Such Korean patriots as Min Yŏng-hwan and Cho Pyŏng-se committed suicide in 1905, protesting the establishment of the Japanese protectorate, and tens of thousands of Koreans, refusing to live under Japanese domination, emigrated to Manchuria, Russia, or the United States. In Korea, a vast number of people engaged in a desperate but futile struggle to prevent this final disaster to the nation and its people. Riots and uprisings against the Japanese erupted everywhere in 1905 and 1906. The more celebrated rebellions were those of Min Chong-shik in South Ch'ungch'ŏng Province, Ch'oe Ik-hyŏn in North Chŏlla Province, and that of Na In-yŏng in South Chŏlla Province.

Final Movements for National Survival

The New Nationalists.   Encountering these unprecedented threats to national survival, the Nationalists arose and launched new campaigns to prevent the demise of their nation. They were keenly aware that unless the old conventions and customs which inhibited cultural and social changes were replaced by new values and new concepts, Korea's survival would be impossible. They expressed a strong faith in the potential strength of the people, and they believed that only the enlightenment and unity of the people would bring about a political, economic, social, and psychological reconstruction that could protect national independence.

Many reform societies emerged at this critical juncture in Korean history, preaching the gospel of nationalism as they accelerated a self-strengthening movement. Among these groups were the Korean Self-Strengthening Society (*Taehan Chaganghoe*) of Chang Chi-yŏn (1864–1921), which was formed in April 1906, the Northwest Education Society of Yi Kap, the Corps for the Advancement of Individuals (*Hŭngsadan*) of Yu Kil-chun, and the New People's Society (*Shinminhoe*) of An Ch'ang-ho (1876–1938), which emerged in 1907. Young Christian leaders such as Yi Sang-jae, Syngman Rhee, and Namgung Ŏk, who established the YMCA in Seoul in 1903 in cooperation with American missionaries, promoted nationalism and the self-strengthening movement among Christian youth.

Scholars such as Chang Chi-yŏn, Pak Ŭn-shik (1859–1925), Chu Shi-gyŏng (1876–1914), and Shin Ch'ae-ho (1860–1936) initiated a national culture movement, advocating the study of Korean history and language in order to arouse the spirit of nationalism and pride. Historical essays and biographies of past heroes were published. In July 1904, Yang Ki-t'ak (1871–1938) and an Englishman named Ernest T. Bethell, published a newspaper, the *Taehan Maeil Shinbo* (*The Korean Daily News*), which had both Korean and English editions, and promoted a patriotic debt redemption drive until in 1908 it was forced by the Japanese to terminate its publication. Yang and his associates collected a large sum of money to repay Korean debts (13 million *yen*) owed to the Japanese as a means to strengthen Korean independence.

The educational movement which the enlightened women launched withered, but the new spirit they fostered persisted. When, in December 1904, Yi Chun, president of the Society for Mutual Progress (*Kongjinhoe*), was arrested because of his accusation against the pro-Japanese ministers, his wife, Yi Il-chŏng, sent a letter to the vice-president of the *Kongjinhoe*, urging that all members of the society unite and strive for the protection of national sovereignty and for the introduction of civilization. She even made a patriotic speech before the members (all male) of the *Kongjinhoe*.

An increasing number of Korean women became involved in the enlightenment and patriotic movement. When Yang Ki-t'ak of the *Taehan Maeil Shinbo*, and others launched their campaign for national debt redemption in 1907, Korean women in Seoul, Taegu, Kanggye and elsewhere joined the campaign, raising money in various ways. The spirit of reform and nationalism was demonstrated in a statement issued in 1907 by a group of Korean women in Taegu quoted in part below:

. . . There is no difference between men and women, in loving one's own country and in discharging one's duties as a citizen. . . [our men] were resolved to stop smoking for three months to repay the national debt. . . but women are excluded from this movement. Are women not citizens of the country, and are they not human beings?

Meanwhile, such women's patriotic organizations as the *T'arhwanhoe,* or the Ring-Removing Society, and a Protestant women's society named *Kungmi Chōksōnghoe* emerged, and became involved in the nationalistic movement. The Ring-Removing Society declared that all human beings were created equal by God, and urged Korean women to sell their gold and silver rings and other ornaments to raise money to repay national debt "not only to restore our national sovereignty, but also to regain equality with men by demonstrating our ability." The *Kungmi Chōksōnghoe* declared: ". . . we will avoid the destiny of becoming slaves but restore our freedom and independence by repaying our national debt by saving (and donating) rice."

To be sure, the number of Korean women who were inspired by the new spirit of enlightenment, reform, progress, and patriotism was small at the dawn of the twentieth century. But the rise of women's organizations, together with the appearance of women such as Yi Il-chōng and others clearly showed the significant changes that were taking place in values, aspirations, and national consciousness among the Korean women.

Although press laws of July 24, 1907 and April 20, 1908, which the Korean government promulgated under Japanese pressure, drastically reduced the freedom of the press, many Western books were still translated into Korean. Some of these were *Gulliver's Travels, Aesop's Fables,* and John Bunyan's *Pilgrim's Progress.* More important, however, were those books which dealt with the concept of liberty and rights of the people, and the dangers of imperialism, giving warning to the people regarding the growing threats to national survival. They were: *A History of American Independence, A History of Italian Independence, A History of the Independence of Sweden, A History of the Fall of Poland,* and *A History of the Fall of Vietnam.*

Many new leaders in literature, such as Yi In-jik (1854–1915) and Yi Hae-jo (1885–1950), promoted a new "literature of enlightenment." They launched a frontal attack against traditional social thoughts and habits, including the evils of superstition and social injustice, as well as traditionalism in literature. Yi In-jik's novels such as his *Tears of Blood* and *Devil's Voice,* and Yi Hae-jo's *Liberty Bell* established landmarks in the new literary movement for the construction of a new Korean society.

In 1908, Ch'oe Nam-sōn (1890–1957) organized a publishing house named Shinmun-gwan and published the first magazine for children named *Sonyōn* (*Children*). In the first issue of *Sonyōn,* published in November 1908, Ch'oe said: "We must make Korea the country of young people." Until the publication permit of *Sonyōn* was suspended in August 1910, Ch'oe and other writers published many articles in it, encouraging Korean children to develop nationalism and a new social consciousness. With the publication of his poem entitled "From the Sea to Children," Ch'oe introduced a new form of *shijo* while advocating the development of a strong self-image among Korean children. In it, Ch'oe said in part:

> *The sea — a soaring mountain —*
> *Lashes and crushes mighty cliffs of rock.*
> *Those flimsy things, what are they to me?*
> *"Know ye my powers?" The sea lashes*
> *Threateningly, it breaks, it crushes.*
>
> *   *   *
>
> *Who has not bowed his head*
> *Before my sovereignty, let him come forth.*
> *Princes of earth, challenge me if you will.*
> *First Emperor, Napoleon, are you my adversary?*
> *Come, come then, compete with me.*

Like Ch'oe, Yi Kwang-su (1892–?) expressed strong patriotic and reform sentiments in his poems entitled "Our Heroes" and "To My Little Friends," which were also published in *Sonyŏn*.

Western music introduced by missionaries and by Echert grew increasingly popular at the turn of the century. Concurrent with the development of Western music, a new form of song called *ch'angga* developed and many nationalist leaders wrote new songs such as *The Student Song* (*Haktoga*) and *The Athletic Song* (*Undongga*), urging the students to develop patriotism, the spirit of enlightenment, industriousness, and a strong body for the sake of the future of their country.

The patriotic Korean leaders sensed the urgency to educate and train more Korean youth in conjunction with their self-strengthening and national regeneration movement. Yi Sŭng-hun (Namgang, 1864–1930), who had a brassware manufacturing company, founded Osan School, a private secondary school for boys, in 1907 in Chŏngju, North P'yong-an Province. In 1908, he established the Pyongyang Ceramic Company, and used the company profits to support the school. An Ch'ang-ho returned from the United States in February 1907. Immediately after that, in cooperation with such Nationalists as Yi Kap, Chang Chi-yŏn, Yi Sŭng-hun, and Shin Ch'ae-ho, he established the New People's Society. In 1908, the New People's Society founded a private secondary school named Taesŏng in Pyongyang with Yun Ch'i-ho as its principal. In March of the following year, An established the Young Student Fraternal Society whose key officers were Yun Ch'i-ho and Ch'oe Nam-sŏn. It was the New People's Society which established bookstores named T'aegŭk Sŏgwan in Pyongyang, Seoul, and Taegu in conjunction with the new cultural and self-strengthening movement.

Many other private secondary schools were established by the Korean patriots between 1905 and 1909. Among them were Chung-ang, Chungdong, Hwimun, Posŏng, and Yangjŏng for boys, and Chinmyŏng, Sookmyung, and Tongdŏk for girls. Meanwhile, more secondary mission schools such as Sung-ŭi Girls' School in Pyongyang, the first co-educational secondary school named Ŭimyŏng in Sunan, Russi (Lucy) Girls' School in Wŏnsan, and Hoston (Holstin) Girls' School in Kaesŏng were established. Some 2,000 private primary and secondary schools were established by 1910.

A new women's organization named the Chinmyŏng Women's Society founded by the leaders of Korean women's movement, such as Shin So-gan and Pak Yŏng-ja, emerged in 1907, and promoted patriotism as well as social consciousness among women.

Meanwhile, Cho Pyŏng-t'aek and others established a new bank named Hanil in 1906 in Seoul, joining then the existing Korean banks of Taehan Ch'ŏnil (founded in 1899) and the Hansŏng (Seoul, founded in 1903). The Hansŏng (Seoul) Chamber of Commerce and Industry, which was established by Korean entrepreneurs in July 1905, and its journal, *Sanggong wŏlbo*, which was established in December 1910, played an important role in the development of Korean entrepreneurship.

The Fall of the Yi Dynasty and the End of Korean Independence

The establishment of Japan's protectorate over Korea and the steadily growing domination of the Japanese foretold the eventual loss of Korean independence. Emperor Kojong made futile efforts to secure the help of the United States and other powers in order to regain his sovereignty rights. In 1907, Kojong again sent Dr. Homer B. Hulbert to Washington to solicit American assistance, but Hulbert failed to achieve his objectives. At the same time, Kojong sent Yi Sang-sŏl, Yi Chun, and Yi Wi-jong, who was Secretary of the Korean legation in St. Petersberg, to the second Peace Conference held in June 1907 in The Hague in order to enlist the help of the Western powers in recovering Korea's sovereignty and preserving her independence, but they too were unable to achieve their objectives. The end of the Yi dynasty approached rapidly.

The Abdication of Emperor Kojong.   The Japanese became annoyed by Kojong's actions. As a result, in July 1907, the elder statesmen and the Japanese cabinet resolved that Japan should seize all government powers in Korea. Meanwhile, the *Ilchinhoe*, a pro-Japanese society, in collaboration with Japanese expansionists, clamored for the emperor's abdication. Its leader was Song Pyŏng-jun, the Minister of Agriculture, Commerce, and Industry in the pro-Japanese cabinet of Prime Minister Yi Wan-yong, which emerged in May 1907.

Under heavy pressure from the Japanese and pro-Japanese ministers, the helpless emperor decided on July 18 to abdicate the throne in favor of his son. Rumors regarding the impending abdication of Kojong spread quickly, and thousands of people gathered on the night of the 18th, demonstrating against his abdication as they clashed with Japanese police. Some angry Koreans attacked the residence of Prime Minister Yi Wan-yong and burned it down. Meanwhile, the plot of Pak Yŏng-hyo, Minister of the Imperial Household, to carry out a coup and eliminate pro-Japanese ministers who in collaboration with the Japanese forced Kojong to abdicate, was discovered. Pak Yŏng-hyo was arrested and exiled to Cheju Island.

On June 22, 1907, Kojong abdicated, and retired with a new title of Yi T'aewang. Following this, Itō Hirobumi brought Prime Minister Yi Wan-yong to conclude perhaps the most damaging agreement concerning the administration of Korea, dated July 24, 1907, further strengthening the Japanese control in Korea. In the name of promoting "the wealth and strength of Korea" and "the prosperity of the Korean nation," the agreement stipulated that: (1) in all matters relating to the reform of the administration, the Korean government shall receive instruction and guidance from the Resident-General; (2) in all matters relating to the enactment of laws and ordinances and in all matters of administration, the Korean government must obtain the preliminary approval of the Resident-General; (3) in all appointments and removals of high officials the Korean government must obtain the consent of the Resident-General; (4) the Korean government shall appoint Japanese subjects recommended by the Resident-General as Korean government officials; and (5) the Korean government shall not appoint any foreigners to be government officials without consulting the Resident-General. With this agreement, the Resident-General became the *de facto* ruler of Korea. A press law, decreed on the same day, outlawed all nationalistic books, and abolished several Korean newspapers. On July 31, the 9,000-man Korean army was abolished, and the Japanese took over the administration of police affairs and the judicial institutions in Korea.

The coronation ceremony for Emperor Sunjong (Yi Ch'ŏk, 1874–1926, son of Kojong) was held on August 27, and in October the Japanese crown prince (late Taishō emperor), accompanied by Prince Arisugawa Takehito, General Katsura Tarō, and Admiral Tōgō Heihachirō, went to Seoul and paid a visit to the Korean emperor. Shortly thereafter, the Korean crown prince was taken to Japan to be "educated."

The new emperor, who became a Japanese puppet, adopted Yunghūi ("Rising Brightness") as the name of his reigning era, and on November 18 he took an oath before his ancestor's shrine and pledged that he would bring about *yushin,* or "revitalizing reform" in order to promote the unity of the people, develop agriculture, commerce, and industry to enrich the nation, abandon old habits and foster new ethics and principles, reform the administrative system and recruit men of talent in the government, and promote practical education. Early in 1909, he toured the southern and northwestern part of his empire and inspected the conditions of his country. It was the first time that a Koren monarch had toured his country and investigated the people's conditions.

The Uprisings of the Righteous Armies.   Rumors regarding the impending abdication of Emperor Kojong aroused Koreans' indignation, and on July 19, 1907 armed clashes occurred between Korean soldiers and Japanese police, signaling the beginning of the armed uprisings of the Koreans. A plot to assassinate Korean ministers on July 20 failed, but on that day, the angry mob burned down the residence of Premier Yi.

Following the abdication of Emperor Kojong and the disbanding of the Korean army, riots and uprisings of the *Ŭibyŏng*, or "The Righteous Armies" erupted everywhere. Those in Kyŏnggi, Kangwŏn, and North Ch'ungch'ŏng provinces were particularly serious and bloody. Such conservative Confucian scholars as Ch'oe Ik-hyŏn and Hŏ Wi were leaders of the movement of the Righteous Armies, and most of the men who led military actions against the Japanese were former officers or troops of the defunct Korean army.

Some 50,000 insurgents in small groups of 100, 200, or 500, engaged in 2,820 military campaigns against the Japanese military and the police between 1907 and 1909. Their patriotic battles did not prevent the demise of Korea's independence, but in their last armed struggle against Japanese imperialists, some 17,690 gallant Koreans, including Ch'oe Ik-hyŏn, who died in a Japanese prison on Tsushima Island in January 1907, gave their lives for the country.

Japanese Annexation of Korea.   The Japanese had resolved to seize the Korean nation as early as July 12, 1907, and believing that they "had to move gradually toward annexing Korea," the Japanese, who had already secured a free hand in Korea from Great Britain and the United States, initiated negotiations with Russia. As a result, on July 30, 1907, a secret agreement was signed between the Japanese Minister to Russia, Motono Ichirō, and the Russian Foreign Minister, A. P. Izvolsky. In a separate secret article, the Japanese gained Russian acquiescence to Japan's annexation of Korea, in return for a Japanese pledge of noninterference with Russia's special interests in Outer Mongolia. On April 20, 1908, another press law was declared to check the activities of Korean Nationalists.

Song Pyŏng-jun of the *Ilchinhoe*, who was the Minister of Home Affairs in 1908, pressured Itō to move faster to bring about the merger of Korea and Japan. Itō, however, being cautious, was reluctant to give his unqualified support to Song and the *Ilchinhoe*. Uchida Ryōhei, a founder and president of the Black Dragon (Amur) Society (*Kokuryūkai*), and author of an essay entitled "Japan's Asia (*Nihonno Ajia*)" in which new Japanese expansionism was advocated, was in Korea as an adviser to the *Ilchinhoe*. He also complained that Itō was too cautious and too slow in implementing Japanese plans in Korea. Unable to gain Itō's support, Song resigned his post in February 1909 and went to Tokyo to press for Itō's resignation.

Itō, who argued against an outright annexation of Korea because of his belief that Japanese annexation of Korea would not bring more benefits to Japan, went to Tokyo in June 1909 in order to dissuade Generals Yamagata and Katsura from their annexation plan. However, he was shown a plan which they had already adopted on July 6, and he realized that it was not possible for him to stop them from implementing their plan for Korea. Thereupon, he resigned as Resident-General on June 15, and returned to Korea to take leave of the Korean emperor. Meanwhile, Sone Arasuke, the former finance minister of Japan who had been Vice-Resident-General since September 1907, was selected by the Katsura clique to succeed Itō.

Itō, who briefly returned to Seoul, negotiated another agreement with the Koreans in behalf of the Japanese government, and the memorandum, signed on July 12, brought about the abolition of the Korean ministries of Justice and Defense, along with the officers training school, as the Japanese took over the administration of judicial affairs and prisons.

Korean antagonism against the Japanese and their collaborators grew strong as the Japanese were steadily taking over the prerogatives of the Korean emperor and the power of his government. The Nationalists were desperately seeking ways and means to preserve their national independence, and some of them violently demonstrated their patriotism. Two Korean students in America, Chang In-hwan and Chŏn Myŏng-un, shot Durham White Stevens in San Francisco on March 23, 1908, and Stevens died two days later. Stevens had been employed by the Korean government as an adviser on foreign affairs, but he spied for the Japanese and worked against the Koreans during the critical year of 1905. After the signing of the November 17th treaty, referred to as "the treaty of protection" by the Japanese, he remained in the Korean government as an adviser, but he was also a consultant to the Japanese Resident-General under a secret arrangement made with the Japanese government. In March 1908, Stevens traveled to the United States to justify steps taken by the Japanese in Korea and to influence American public opinion regarding the "beneficial" results of Japanese rule in Korea. The Koreans at home and abroad, however, regarded Stevens as a traitor.

On October 26, 1909, in Harbin, Manchuria, another young Korean patriot, An Chung-gŭn (1879–1910), an officer of the Righteous Armies, who had been engaged in the independence movement in Manchuria and Siberia, assassinated Itō Hirobumi. Regarded by the Koreans as an architect of Japanese aggression in Korea, Itō had gone to Harbin for the purpose of securing the reaffirmation of Russia's acquiescence concerning Japanese annexation of Korea. On December 22, a would-be assassin attacked Prime

Minister Yi Wan-yong, who was also regarded by the Koreans as a traitor.

Neither the armed uprising of the Righteous Armies insurgents, nor the killing of Stevens and Itō, discouraged the Japanese imperialists from taking their final actions against Korean independence. In May 1910, Sone resigned, and in late July, General Terauchi Masatake, the former war minister of Japan, arrived in Seoul as the new Resident-General. His mission was to terminate Korean independence. On June 24, General Akashi Motojirō, commander of the Japanese gendarmerie in Korea, concluded an agreement with the Korean government, increasing Japanese military control in Korea.

No sooner had General Terauchi arrived in Seoul than he put Korea under a Draconian rule. All political discussion and assembly was banned; all newspapers, whether they were Japanese or Korean, that criticized the Residency-General or carried any articles concerning the annexation were suspended; individuals suspected of being dangerous to the Japanese plans were arrested; all Korean organizations were placed under constant police surveillance; and the capital was under undeclared martial law. A British reporter in Seoul, Frederick A. McKenzie, observed that the "entire Korean peninsula was turned into a military camp," and Terauchi's "extreme military dictatorship gave the impression that Korea had returned to the medieval authoritarian regime."

As forces of destiny were working against Korea, a Korean poet, Ch'oe Nam-sŏn, reflected the sullen mood, as well as the strong national spirit and pride of the Koreans in the following poem:

We have nothing,
Neither sword nor pistol,
But we do not fear.
Even with an iron rod
They cannot prevail.
We shoulder righteousness
And walk the path without fear.

We have nothing to call our own,
Neither dagger nor [gun] powder,
But we do not fear.
Even with the power of the crown
They cannot prevail.
Righteousness is the spade
With which we maintain the path.

We have nothing to hold in our hands,
Neither stone nor club,
But we do not fear.
Even with all the wealth of the world,

They cannot prevail.
Righteousness is the sword
With which we watch over the path.

The final act of the Korean tragedy was played out. On August 16, 1910 Terauchi presented the draft treaty of annexation to the Korean ministers. Following this, he mobilized troops, surrounded the palace, and forced Emperor Sunjong to approve the Treaty of Annexation dated August 22, 1910, which was already signed by Prime Minister Yi Wan-yong and Terauchi. The treaty which contained eight brief articles was made public on August 29. It brought about the end of the Yi dynasty and the demise of Korean independence, as 14.7 million Koreans were put under a reign of terror. All treaties and agreements which the Korean government had concluded with other foreign powers became null and void. Both the Korean emperor, who lost his nation, and the Japanese emperor, who took over Korea, issued on August 29 their edicts concerning the merger of Korea and Japan. In protest, many Koreans committed suicide while others mourned the demise of their nation, or fled from their fatherland.

PART III

KOREA UNDER JAPANESE RULE
AND THE FIGHT FOR FREEDOM

7. Korea Under Japanese Colonial Rule

Korea was forcibly deprived of its sovereign rights and its people were subjected to Japanese colonialism from August 22, 1910, to August 15, 1945. The Japanese called Korea *Chōsen* and the Koreans *senjin*, in order to differentiate them from the Japanese whom they called *naichi-jin*, or the "homeland people." Japan was called *naichi* (inner land), and colonies such as Korea and Taiwan were called *gaichi* (outer land).

In 1910 Japan began to see her role in international affairs in light of her "mission." In that year, the Japanese Ministry of Education revised the elementary school textbooks, stressing Japan's special interests and special responsibilities in East Asia. Japan's mission, according to the Ministry of Education, was to "enlighten" and "civilize" the East Asian people, and establish "peace" in East Asia. A Japanese poem entitled "Fifty Million Countrymen" said: "The God given mission of peace in East Asia rests on the shoulders of such a people as we. Japan has a heavy responsibility in advancing the civilization of the East."

The Imperial Rescript of the Japanese emperor issued on August 29, 1910 stated that the Koreans would be treated as if they were Japanese subjects and would enjoy rights and privileges under the "benevolent rule" of the Japanese emperor. However, the Korean people were actually put under a militaristic rule which drove them into slavery in the suffocating atmosphere of fear. They lost not only their national independence, but also their lands, their rights, and every aspect of their lives came under the control of Japanese rules and regulations.

There were three periods of Japanese colonial rule: the first was the period of subjugation, suppression and appropriation that lasted until 1919, the second was the period of "accommodation and appeasement" between 1920 and 1931, which brought about some relaxation of colonial control and allowed the educational and cultural development of Korea, and the third was the period of Japanization and industrial development from 1931 to August 1945.

During the entire colonial period, a variety of momentous changes took place in Korea. Some were voluntary, and others were forced upon the country. In either case, these changes in large measure brought about the end of feudalism as Korea's education and culture, as well as economic and social systems, were transformed, communication and transportation systems were modernized, and a monopolistic capitalism and new industries developed.

The Japanese aims in Korea were to exploit human and natural resources in order to aid the economic development of Japan. They planned to assimilate the Koreans into Japanese culture and to construct a strong logistic base for Japan's continental expansionism. In order to achieve these objectives, the Japanese inaugurated many programs: the use of the Korean language was at first discouraged and later forbidden; the study of Korean history was forbidden; and the Koreans were forced to abandon their traditional family and given names and adopt Japanese style names. The very soul of the Korean people faced the danger of extinction.

The Japanese called Korea "a thriving land," but to the Koreans Japanese rule symbolized oppression and exploitation. The Korean people, their land, and natural resources were ruthlessly exploited by the Japanese capitalists. If Korea was thriving, it was doing so for the imperialistic ambitions of Japan and not for the Koreans.

Government and Politics

Government Structure and Administrative Districts.   Korea was ruled by the Government-General of Korea (*Chōsen Sōtokufu*), which was established in Seoul and headed by a Governor-General (*Sōtoku*). Seoul became known as Keijō. The Governor-General was appointed by the Japanese emperor and was responsible to him as well as to the prime minister of Japan. He was empowered to issue laws, ordinances, and regulations, and to mobilize Japanese troops in Korea, and to send them to Manchuria, if necessary. Therefore, all the governors-general, with the exception of a retired admiral, were army generals on active duty. The Government-General was supervised by the premier, the ministries of Home Affairs, the Army, the Navy, and the Colonization of the Japanese government, and its financial affairs were controlled by the Japanese Diet.

The Governors-General in Korea were as follows:

General Terauchi Masatake	October	1910–October	1916
General Hasegawa Yoshimichi	October	1916–August	1919
Admiral Saitō Makoto	August	1919–December	1927
General Yamanashi Hanzo	December	1927–August	1929
Admiral Saitō Makoto	August	1929–June	1931
General Ugaki Kazushige	June	1931–August	1936
General Minami Jirō	August	1936–May	1942
General Koiso Kuniaki	May	1942–July	1944
General Abe Nobuyuki	July	1944–August	1945

From April 14 through October 1, 1927, while Admiral Saitō was on leave, General Ugaki Kazushige acted as temporary Governor-General.

The Governor-General was assisted by the Director-General of Administration (*Seimu Sōkan*), who was appointed by the Japanese prime minister. In the beginning, the Government-General consisted of the Secretariat, and five departments: General Affairs, Internal Affairs, Finance, Agriculture-Commerce-Industry, and Justice. The Secretariat consisted of six bureaus: Police, Investigation, Railway, Monopoly, Communication, and Land Survey. In 1912 four new bureaus were added to the Secretariat, namely, General Affairs, Education, External Affairs, and Construction. Other changes followed within the year: the Department of General Affairs was abolished, and the Department of Agriculture-Commerce-Industry was divided into two departments of Agriculture-Forestry and Production (mainly rice). The Government-General also separated police matters from the Secretariat, established an independent Department of Security, and inaugurated the system of gendarmerie and enforced the Security Law which had been promulgated in 1907. In 1917, a new criminal law was issued, and in April 1919, the law concerning political criminals was decreed.

The Japanese gendarmerie and the civil police became two powerful arms of the Government-General. There were some 20,000 regular and 20,000 assistant gendarmes commanded by General Akashi Motojirō. The Department of Security established branches in each provincial capital, and a centralized police system emerged as more police stations and sub-stations were established in cities, towns, and villages. The number of policemen grew from 5,683 in 1910 to 7,100 in 1912. With the abolition of the system of gendarmerie in 1920, the number of policemen increased to 21,800 by 1931. There were some 60,000 policemen (one to every 400 people) in Korea in 1941.

In September 1910, the Central Advisory Council was established to assist the Governor-General. A few Koreans, who had helped the Japanese in the past, were among the 65 council members. Judicial matters were controlled by judges who were appointed by the Governor-General.

All the highest positions and those positions above the rank of clerk in both central and local governments were held by Japanese—none of them spoke the Korean language. Koreans were employed only in the lowest levels of governmental units and in the police force. As late as 1936, 52,270 out of 87,552 officials in the central, municipal, and other governmental units and agencies were Japanese. More than 80 per cent of the highest ranks, 60 per cent of the intermediary ranks, and about 50 per cent of clerical positions were held by Japanese.

During the first Saitō administration, the structure of the Government-General was modified. The departments became bureaus and two new bureaus of Education and Police were added in 1920; and a new Bureau of Monopoly was established in 1921, followed by the creation of the Bureau of Railways in 1925.

Administrative Districts.   Korea was divided into thirteen provinces each of which was divided into counties. Each county consisted of districts, villages and hamlets. Each province was headed by a provincial governor, each large city by a mayor, each county by a superintendent, and each district by a chief. All these officials were appointed by the Government-General, except chiefs of districts and villages who were appointed by county superintendents. No officials were elected.

Occasionally, one or two Koreans were appointed as provincial governor, and the number of Korean county superintendents increased somewhat after 1919. Most district and village chiefs were Koreans. The Japanese citizens in Korea enjoyed self-rule with their own organizations such as school associations, which were governed in accordance with the Japanese constitution.

Politics of Suppression and Appropriation.   No sooner had the colonial government been established than the Japanese proceeded to put the Koreans under their strict control as they suppressed anti-Japanese and nationalistic activities. They ordered all Korean political organizations to be dissolved and prohibited all meetings, debates, and public speeches by the Koreans. All Korean and some Japanese newspapers were ordered to cease publication under a new press law. On December 16, 1910, the possession of firearms and other weapons, including swords and knives, by Koreans was prohibited.

In December 1910 and January 1911, some 700 Koreans were arrested in connection with the alleged assassination plot of a Korean, An Myŏng-gŭn, (brother of An Chung-gŭn who assassinated Itō), against Governor-General Terauchi Masatake. Among those arrested were Korean Nationalists, most of whom were Christian leaders, such as Yun Ch'i-ho and Yi Sŭng-hun. This event became known as the Case of 105 Persons because of 700 individuals arrested, 105 were prosecuted. Although only five were given prison sentences, the Japanese made it clear that any anti-Japanese movement would be severely dealt with. Between August 1910 and 1918, over 200,000 Koreans, classified as *fiutei senjin* (malcontent and rebellious Koreans), were arrested and tortured.

The Land Survey.   In order to appropriate farm and forest lands, the Government-General established a Bureau of Land Survey in 1910, and the Land Survey Ordinance was put into effect immediately. The ordinance required all Korean landowners and tillers to report their legal ownership or their legal rights to cultivate the land.

A large number of Koreans lost their land because they failed to report as a result of being either uniformed or being unable to prove their legal ownership or right to cultivate. All lands which belonged to these Koreans were confiscated, whether they were those of individuals or of clans. The land survey, which was completed in 1918, led to the government ownership of 21.9 million acres or 40 per cent of farm and forest lands; of these 10.8 million acres were cultivated. Some Korean landlords took advantage of the ordinance to expand their ownership one way or another.

Some of the land appropriated by the Government-General was turned over to the Oriental Development Company (established in 1908) and other Japanese firms such as the Fuji Industrial Company. The Oriental Development Company alone held 73,500 acres of land in 1910, and by 1931 its ownership increased to 292,800 acres.

An increasing number of Japanese farmers were brought into Korea and were given free lands or were allowed to purchase a large amount of farmland at a low price. The Japanese population in Korea grew from 171,543, at the end of 1910 to 424,700 in 1925, and to 650,100 in 1939. In 1939 some 45,000 Japanese were engaged in agriculture as landowners. The amount of land owned by the Japanese citizens increased from 217,150 acres in 1910, to 820,750 by 1923.

Early Economic Change.   Under the protective Company Law issued in December 1910 (to be effective on January 1, 1911), the Japanese seized opportunities to dominate commercial and industrial fields. The law required that all commercial and industrial companies in Korea have Japanese either as co-investors or as managerial staff, in order to obtain government licenses. Japanese-owned firms were not subjected to this law.

As a result of this law, while the number of Japanese companies engaged in trade, mining, fisheries, and manufacturing grew from 109 in 1911, to 262 by 1918, the number of Korean companies (primarily small ones) grew only from 27 in 1911, to 39 in 1918. The number of Japanese-owned factories increased from 185 in 1911, to 650 in 1916, whereas the number of Korean-owned factories grew from 66 to 416. The gross value of production of Korean-owned factories increased from 1,969,000 *yen* in 1911 to 5,429,000 *yen* in 1916, while that of Japanese factories increased from 16,920,000 to

47,173,000 *yen* during the same period. Korea became a lucrative market for goods manufactured by the Japanese, who rapidly dominated commercial activity.

Several new taxes were added and old tax laws were revised, in order to increase the government revenue. Among those paid by the Koreans were taxes on liquor, corporations, land, tobacco, sugar, stamps, property, as well as head taxes. Old Korean monies, except copper coins, were replaced either by Japanese paper and other monies or by new paper money of the Bank of Korea (*Chōsen Ginkō*). Dominating the financial market were newly established Japanese banks, such as Chōsen Industrial, Mitsubishi, Mitsui, and Yasuda banks, and savings and loans associations.

Politics of Appeasement.   The March First Movement of 1919, (see next chapter), in which the Korean people displayed their displeasure with Japanese rule and sought national independence, forced the Japanese to alter their tactics and methods of control, although their basic policies remained unchanged.

In August 1919, the Japanese emperor issued an Imperial Rescript, and the Japanese government stated that it would bring about reconciliation between Japan and Korea, and that the policy of the government would be based on the principle of nondiscrimination between the two countries. The Japanese government also declared that it would no longer appoint only army generals as governors-general, that it would respect native culture and customs, spread education and develop industry, and employ more talented Koreans in the government. In order to implement the new principle and to bring about harmony between Japan and Korea, Premier Hara Kei appointed a retired admiral, Saitō Makoto, to the position of governor-general. Upon his arrival in Korea in September, Saitō announced that henceforth Korea would be administered under a more enlightened policy and he inaugurated what came to be known as the "civilized rule" of the Japanese in Korea.

Accordingly, in October 1919, the pay scale for Korean employees in the government was revised to make their wages the same as those of the Japanese, but, 60 per cent of the monthly wage given to Japanese employees as a bonus was not given to Koreans. A special ordinance of December 1920, opened the door for Koreans to be appointed to certain positions as "special employees." As a result, in 1921, some 330 Koreans were appointed to government positions.

A new civil code was promulgated, effective December 1, 1921, and a new family registration law, promulgated in December 1922, went into effect on July 1, 1923. With this a population census was taken every five years, beginning 1925. The following table shows the population increase in Korea since 1910:

Year	Total	Japanese
1910	14,766,000	171,543 (39,000 in 1906)
1920	17,764,000	346,000
1925	19,020,945	424,700
1930	20,438,000	527,016
1935	22,208,000	619,000

The rate of population growth of the Koreans between 1925 and 1930 was 15.29 per cent, and between 1930 and 1935 was 16.90 per cent.

A parole system was inaugurated in 1921, and a new criminal code was issued in December 1923. The judicial reform of August and December 1921 provided a comparable power to Korean judges and prosecuting attorneys as that of the Japanese when they were given authorization to deal with civil cases. Some 54,350 Korean convicts were paroled between 1920 and 1926. On the other hand, the number of policemen increased with the recruitment of 3,000 Koreans and the importation of 3,000 Japanese policemen, bringing the total number to 20,771 in 1922. Of these, 73.3 per cent were Japanese. Although the Japanese gendarmerie system was abolished, the gendarmes in the Japanese Army continued to affect the lives of the Koreans. The application of the Peace Preservation Law of May 1925, only made the police rule stronger.

Cultural Policy and Programs. The early cultural policy of the Government-General was aimed at the destruction of Korean nationalism and racial consciousness. In 1910 all speeches and public assemblies were banned, all Korean newspapers and many magazines were forced to cease publication, all school textbooks written by Koreans were banned, and hundreds of private schools were closed. There remained only one Korean-language and one English-language newspaper published by the government and a few Japanese language newspapers for Japanese in Korea. The government adopted various programs to promote Korean acceptance of the Japanese policy through the use of publications and the promotion of public speaking tours by officials and educators.

Even a Japanese reporter from the *Tokyo Nichi Nichi Shimbun.* commented on the absence of the freedom of speech and press in Korea in an editorial on October 2, 1910:

Newspapers were checked one by one; controls on companies were exercised to an extreme, unsatisfactory companies being destroyed one after the other. Reporters and writers were at their wit's end, gasping. If one grumbled, he would be arrested. . . . I felt as if I were in hell.

As an aftermath of the March First Movement of 1919 (see next chapter),

Saitō authorized, in January 1920, the publication of Korean language newspapers. As a result, five Korean newspapers emerged between March 1920 and November 1931. Among them were the *Tong-a Ilbo* (*The Oriental Daily*) and *The Chosŏn Ilbo* (*The Korean Daily*), which were established in Seoul in 1920, and the *Chung-ang Ilbo* (*The Central Daily*), which was established in Seoul in November 1926, under the editorship of a well-known left wing Nationalist. The *Tong-a Ilbo* was established by a group of right wing Nationalists. In 1933, *The Central Daily* was renamed as *The Korea Central Daily*. The contents of Korean newspapers were censored by the police, and any anti-Japanese remarks or articles led to the confiscation of certain issues or the suspension of publication.

In December 1922, the colonial government organized the Committee for Compilation of Korean History, and the *History of Korea* was published. However, it contained many fabrications and distortions, which were aimed at justifying the actions taken by the Japanese before and after 1905, as well as the policy of the colonial government.

Politics of the Critical Times   The official history of the Government-General of Korea described the third period that began shortly before the Japanese aggression in Manchuria as "the period of constructive change," which coincided with what the Japanese called the "critical times." All efforts were concentrated on making Korea serve Japan's nationalistic and aggressive ambitions. General Ugaki began his administration of Korea in June 1931, in the atmosphere of crisis with tighter political, economic, and thought control, in order to make Korea contribute more to the "fulfillment of the sacred aims" of the Japanese empire. Among his slogans was "Unity in Spirit and Increase in Production."

The structure of the government remained the same, but a few new sections and auxiliary organizations were created to meet the wartime needs. Among these important sections that were added were the Gold Production Section in the Bureau of Industry, the Animal Husbandry Section in the Bureau of Agriculture and Forestry, the Economic Police Section in the Bureau of Public Security, and the External Police Section which was established to cope with the increasing anti-Japanese activities of the Koreans in northeastern Korea and southwestern Manchuria. Among important new auxiliary organizations, which were established between 1931 and 1939, were the Korean Defense Association, the Association for the Study of Policy Dealing with the Critical Situation, the Anti-Communism Association, and the Korean Association for the Imperial Rule Assistance.

Ugaki launched the Movement for the Promotion of National Spirit in November 1932, so as to nurture among the Koreans the "awareness of being the subjects of His Imperial Majesty of Japan." However, his efforts to establish an equal pay scale for Japanese and Korean officials and to end the bonus system for Japanese officials met strong opposition from the Japanese, and he abandoned both plans.

General Minami Jirō, who succeeded Ugaki, stated in Tokyo in August 1936, that his administration would develop the strength and promote the welfare of the Koreans. He pledged that his energies would be devoted to ending discrimination against the Koreans and to promoting reconciliation between Japan and Korea. He stressed the importance of "mutual existence and mutual prosperity" for the Japanese and the Koreans. Upon his arrival as the Governor-General of Korea, Minami stated that his objectives were (1) the clarification of national policy; (2) the unity of Korea, Japan, and Manchuria; (3) the promotion of education and culture; (4) administrative innovation; and (5) the parallel development of agriculture and industry. Over and over, Minami stressed the importance of guiding public opinion and controlling the press. He was most anxious to pursuade the Koreans to develop an awareness of the "critical situation," the spirit of Imperial subjects and anti-Communist spirit, and to fulfill the goals of "the sacred war" in China. "Now is the time when we should be competely united into one body and overcome our common difficulties," said Minami in his instruction to the provincial governors in April 1937. He pointed out the critical importance of unifying the people and clarifying "our ideas and our national policy" in order to magnify the "achievements of our Emperor and extol His Imperial Way." He emphasized the importance of promoting national faith among the Koreans and their understanding of the objectives of the Japanese government.

Both Ugaki and Minami tightened public security measures, particularly against the Communists; additional security units were created and deployed along the Tumen River regions against Korean Nationalists and Communists in Manchuria. The role of the High Section (thought control section) of the police was expanded to check the resurgence of Korean nationalism and left wing movements.

In September 1937, Minami established the Patriotic Day and accelerated the promotion of the national spirit, which only meant the destruction of Korean nationalism and the Korean identity. Meanwhile, he made some efforts, in collaboration with the pro-Japanese society called the National Association of the Koreans, to induce the Japanese government to extend the Japanese franchise laws. Since 1921, the House of Representatives of the Japanese Diet had passed resolutions extending the franchise to Korea. The 74th Diet (1938–1939) passed a similar resolution, but the Tokyo government made it clear in 1939 that it had no intention of applying the Japanese constitution in Korea. The resolution passed by the 75th Diet (1940) likewise was vetoed by the Japanese cabinet whereas the new Japanese Peace Preservation Law of December 1941 was extended to Korea.

In order to promote the unity of Japan and Korea, more Koreans were recruited into high positions in the Government-General. The total number of high ranking Korean officials in the central government grew from 316 in 1931, to 416 in 1940, but the actual percentage of Koreans in this category decreased from 24.5 per cent in 1931, to 19.3 per cent, due to the increase in the number of high ranking Japanese officials. The number of Korean junior officials grew from 10,154 in 1931, to 14,224 in 1940; Koreans accounted for 35.4 per cent of junior officials in the central government. The number of Korean prosecutors remained small: 7 in 1931 and 11 in 1937, in contrast to the number of Japanese prosecutors numbering 80 in 1931, and growing to 87 in 1937.

Municipal governments, particularly those in large cities such as Seoul and Pusan, were almost completely dominated by the Japanese. As more Japanese officials were called into the military, the percentage of Korean officials in the government increased from 29.9 per cent in 1931, to 52.7 per cent in 1941.

Mobilization and Japanization of Korean Names.   Governor-General Minami believed that his historic mission was to achieve the complete union of Korea and Japan. Consequently, while preaching the common ancestry of the two peoples, he instituted numerous programs to assimilate the Korean with Japanese ideologies and culture. With the outbreak of the Sino-Japanese War in 1937, and as the need grew to mobilize the Korean people, promoting understanding among Koreans regarding Japan's fundamental national polity and Japan's aims for the New Order in East Asia became urgent. It was Minami's belief that the more the Koreans contributed to war efforts and showed their patriotism, the greater the chances were for a "more perfect union" between the Japanese and Koreans.

Following the policy of Prime Minister Konoe Fumimaro, Governor-General Minami launched a movement to promote such Japanese political ideologies as *hakkō ichiu* ("the eight recesses of the universe under a single roof") and *kyōzon kyōhei* ("co-existence and co-prosperity"). At the same time, he preached the concept of *naisen ittai* ("the united body of Japan and Korea") and *naisen yūwa* ("reconciliation between the Japanese and the Koreans").

In order to achieve his goals, he established a system of Army Special Volunteers, under the Imperial Ordinance No. 95 of February 22, 1938, and he created military training centers throughout Korea. In 1938 and 1939, 15,294 Korean youths "volunteered," but only, 1,280 were accepted into the centers. Those who successfully completed their military and political training were inducted into the Japanese infantry. The system of Army Special Volunteers continued to exist until 1943 when the military conscription system was imposed.

In July 1938, in response to the Movement for General National Spiritual Mobilization, which started in Japan in late 1937, Minami formed the

Korean Association for General National Spiritual Mobilization, headed by General Kawashima Yoshiaki, Commander of the Japanese Garrison in Korea. Meanwhile, he also initiated an anti-Christian campaign, requiring all Christians to participate in the Shintō rituals.

The government also organized a "Serve the Nation Labor Corps." Some 750,000 units of the Corps were established, and hundreds of thousands of Korean youth (both men and women) were mobilized to work in mines and factories. In September 1939, the government established the Rise Asia Service Day (*Kōa hōkōbi*), combining it with the Patriotic Day which had been established earlier. The first day of each month was designated as the Rise Asia Service Day, and the people were required to perform certain tasks for the sake of the development of a new Asia. They were also required to visit Shintō shrines and pray for Japan's fulfillment of her "sacred mission" in Asia and her victory over China. They were encouraged to eat less, work harder, and buy more national bonds. Some 350,000 "patriotic units," also known as "neighborhood units," were established throughout Korea in 1940. Each unit consisted of ten households and functioned as a semi-governmental unit, handling monetary and other contributions, distributing food and other commodities and discharging security duties.

Under the labor mobilization system begun in 1939, hundreds of thousands of skilled workers were mobilized and sent, first to various industrial sites in Korea and Japan, and later to the theaters of war in the Pacific. Thousands of young Korean women were forced to go to war zones to perform their patriotic duties to Japanese soldiers.

While accelerating Japanization efforts through education and propaganda, Minami took a significant step to Japanize the Koreans. On November 10, 1939, he issued the Ordinance No. 20, which, as of April 1940, "allowed" (required) the Koreans to change their family and personal names to a Japanese form in order to bring about "a more perfect union" between Japan and Korea. Under the supplementary regulations of December 1939, however, they were not allowed to copy names of Japanese emperors, aristocrats, or certain other important figures past or present. Fearing retaliation against those who refused to change their names, 84 per cent of the Koreans (population 25,133,352 in 1944) changed their family names, or the reading of their family names, as well as their given names, to a Japanese style. Under this ordinance, the Koreans "lost" their names and their Korean identity. The adoption of Japanese names did not, however, serve to conceal Korean identity or to eradicate discrimination, for all public documents, family registration records, and school and job applications required the Koreans to indicate their original family and given names and the place of the clan origin.

The Last Stage of Japanese Colonial Rule.   In 1942, in the heat of World War II, the final phase of Japanese rule in Korea began. This phase was

characterized by the desperate mood of both the Koreans and the Japanese—
the Japanese in pursuance of an impossible victory over the Allied powers,
and the Koreans striving for survival, waiting for the arrival of a new dawn of
freedom and independence.

Both Governors-General Koiso Kuniaki, "The Tiger of Korea," and Abe
Nobuyuki pursued three particular goals: (1) to inculcate thorough moral
training; (2) to increase production and production capacity; and (3) to
renovate government functions and improve communication between the
government and the people. Their overall objective was to make Korea
render greater assistance to Japan in her pursuance of war aims.

The most crucial task of the Japanese was to establish control over the
Korean mind. In order to tighten political control and check the resurgence
of Korean nationalism and all kinds of rumors, the Japanese strictly enforced
the Korean Temporary Security Ordinance of December 26, 1941. They
complained that, although most Koreans were giving spiritual and material
cooperation to the war efforts, there were growing "rumors and dangerous
anti-war talks." Rumors concerning the approaching doomsday of an
imminent defeat of Japan at the hands of the Allies spread widely, especially
after October 1943, when the war was going against Japan.

An increasing number of Koreans were arrested and convicted as "thought
criminals," "undesirables" or "rebellious" persons. Some 5,600 Koreans
were imprisoned between 1940 and June 1944 as "thought criminals," and
many other Koreans, as well as Chinese, were imprisoned as spies for the Allies.

In view of the growing demand for manpower in the military, the Government-General accelerated its efforts to "recruit" selected Korean youths into
the Japanese Imperial Army. Consequently, the Army Special Volunteer
Ordinance was promulgated in February 1938, and 17,664 Koreans out of
802,047 "volunteers" were trained and inducted into the Japanese Imperial
Army between April 1938 and March 1943. On August 1, 1943, the military
conscription law was applied in Korea. Under this law, some 214,000 Korean
youths took the physical examination, and 25,000 were inducted into active
military service in 1944. Meanwhile, the Navy Special Volunteer System was
introduced in July 1943, and in 1944, some 3,000 out of 90,000 applicants
were inducted into the Navy.

When in June 1943 the Tokyo government made military service mandatory
for all college students in Japan except those in scientific and medical studies,
some 5,000 of the 6,500 Korean college students in Japan were forced into
the Japanese Army. Many fled from their schools, dodging the draft, and
went into hiding either in Korea or in Manchuria. Most of them were caught
and inducted into military service. Although some undoubtedly joined the
Japanese Army to prove their loyalty to Japan, and some enlisted in order
"to receive military training and gain experience so as to be useful in the
future" when Korea would become an independent nation, the majority

became Japanese soldiers involuntarily.

The total Korean population was 25,133,352 in 1944, (there were 712,583 Japanese civilians in Korea); the birthrate was 34.1 persons per 1,000 and the deathrate was 17 per 1,000. This huge population had no right to participate in the constitutional process, with the exception of a small number of privileged Koreans who had voting rights in provincial, municipal, and district councils.

Realizing that the continued and increased Japanese demand that the Koreans fulfill their duties while simultaneously denying them their rights as Imperial subjects was creating greater discontent, Koiso made efforts to extend Japanese constitution and election laws to the Koreans. He also suggested that some Koreans be appointed to the House of Peers of the Japanese Diet. As of 1944, there was only one Korean who was an appointed member of the House of Peers, and in 1944 only one Korean in Japan was elected to the House of Representatives from an electoral district in Tokyo where he had resided. There were 54 Koreans who were appointed to the Central Privy Council of the Government-General in Korea.

Under an imperial injunction given at the opening ceremony of the Diet in 1944, the Japanese Diet passed a bill in December extending the Japanese constitution and election laws to Korea and Taiwan effective October 1946. At the same time, sixteen Koreans were recommended as candidates for the House of Peers. Under the bill, Koreans who were above the age of twenty-five and paid an annual direct tax of fifteen *yen* would have elected twenty-three members of the House of Representatives. Be that as it may, it was too late, for the end of Japanese colonial rule was approaching rapidly.

Meanwhile, the Koreans as a whole remained under Japanese rule without the right to participate in politics or to enjoy constitutional protection. They patiently waited for the arrival of a new dawn for the Korean nation.

Changes in the Korean Economy

The basic economic policy of the Japanese was to induce Korea to produce more foodstuffs, particularly rice, for Japan, supply cheap raw materials and labor for expanding Japanese industries, and be a lucrative market for Japanese investors. To be sure, the thirty-six years of colonial rule and the introduction of an enormous amount of Japanese capital and modern technology brought about some economic transformation as both heavy and light industries developed, modern commercial and financial institutions were established, modern communication and transportation systems were installed, and new methods of farming and modern farm implements were introduced. The Japanese advertised Korea as a "thriving land," but the colonial characteristics of the Korean economy prevailed in every sector.

In appearance Korea was "thriving," and casual and unwitting foreign travelers visiting certain areas or riding on an express train from Pusan to Seoul and then to Shinŭiju would have been led to believe so. But, had they traveled in rural areas or examined economic conditions carefully, they would have been startled by the stark contrast between modern and traditional sectors of the economy, as well as between the economic condition of the Japanese and Koreans. They could not have failed to notice the desolate condition of the Koreans under Japanese rule.

Agriculture.   When the land survey was completed in 1918, there were 10.8 million acres of cultivated land. There were 2,641,154 farm families at that time. Of these, only 66,391 families were either absentee landlords or cultivators, 538,195 owned some land and rented land from landlords, 1,073,360 were tenants with less than 2.45 acres of farmland, and 971,208 were sharecroppers. About 2.5 per cent of farm families owned 64 per cent of the farmland in 1918. The percentage of owner-tenants fell from 35.5. per cent in 1918 to 24.9 in 1932, and another per cent between 1932 and 1939. In 1938, 38.4 per cent of farmers tilled less than 0.74 acres, most of them as tenants or owner-tenants, and 24.9 per cent tilled betwen 0.74 and 1.26 acres; 30.6 per cent tilled between 2.45 and 7.35 acres, and only 6.1 per cent tilled 7.4 acres or more.

Fruit growing and cash crop farming (mostly cabbage, horseradish, garlic and green onions) became increasingly important, but animal husbandry and dairy farming were unknown, although most owner-farmers raised a few cows, pigs, and chickens. One of the most important sources of additional income for farm families was the cultivation of silkworms.

Under pressure to produce more rice, Korean agriculture was modernized during the 1930's, and the rice growing area was expanded. However, modernization was limited to areas where large rice lands were located and rich landlords and owner-farmers were numerous. The main rice growing areas were the plains in the northwestern region of North and South P'yŏng-an provinces, the west-central region in Hwanghae and Kyŏnggi provinces, the southeastern region of North and South Kyŏngsang provinces, and the south-western region of South Ch'unch'ŏng and North and South Chŏlla provinces. These rice bowls were located along such large rivers as the Taedong, the Imjin, the Han, the Naktong, and the Kŭm.

As the rice shortage in Japan grew acute, the pressure to produce more rice in Korea increased. In 1919 alone, some 10.2 million bushels of rice were exported to Japan out of the 64.7 million bushels produced in Korea. The demand for more rice was also increasing in Korea as the Korean population grew.

In view of this growing need for more rice, in November 1919 the Government-General adopted an ambitious plan to increase rice production. It was aimed at the production of 41.8 million more bushels of rice in Korea with the increase of the acreage by 1.9 million acres by 1938, so that at least 25.5

million bushels would be available to Japan per year. But only 186,200 acres of land were added by 1925. A second and more realistic 12-year plan, begun in 1926, projected the expansion of the rice growing area by 875,000 acres in twelve years, and an additional 23.9 million bushel increase in rice production. Some 301,350 acres of land were actually reclaimed, producing 8,833,000 additional bushels of rice.

The 12-year plan was terminated in 1934 when too much rice was exported to Japan, bringing the decline of the rice price there. However, in response to the growing need for rice following the 1937 outbreak of the Sino-Japanese War, a five-year plan was adopted in 1938 to produce 10.2 million additional bushels per year, and in 1939, a seven-year plan replaced the 1938 plan to produce more rice per year.

In order to accomplish Japan's goals, new land improvement, irrigation, and land development sections were created in the Bureau of Industry of the Government-General in cooperation with the Oriental Development Company. The construction of reservoirs and irrigation networks was encouraged; new improved seeds were introduced, and allied projects, such as flood control, prevention of landslides and erosion, and reforestation, were carried out. In conjuction with agricultural planning, the Government-General established the Korean Agricultural Association. Meanwhile in 1933, some 10,000 Japanese households were brought into Korea under the sponsorship of both the Oriental Development Company and the Japanese Ministry of Colonization, resulting in an increase of the Japanese population in Korea from 346,000 in 1920, to 527,016 in 1930, to 752,823 in 1942, and then a decrease to 712,583 in 1944.

Various land reclamation projects increased the total cultivated area of Korea from 10.8 million acres in 1919, to a little over 11 million acres (20.3 per cent of the total area of Korea) by 1938. The area of paddy fields where rice was grown increased from 3,680,000 acres in 1919 to 4,290,000 acres by 1939. Although the area of paddy fields irrigated by water supplied by some 190 irrigation associations grew as of 1938, 1.3 million acres of paddy fields were dependent upon rainwater.

Iron plows, better farm implements, modern huskers and thrashers, and better methods of farming were introduced, but most Korean farmers continued to harvest rice in the traditional way. The supply of commercial fertilizer increased with the production of chemical fertilizer at the Hŭngnam plant of the Chōsen Nitrogen Fertilizer Company, which was established by the Japanese in 1927 with the capacity to produce 500,000 tons of chemical fertilizer per year, but most Korean farmers had no money to purchase it. The amount of fertilizer used grew from 8.2 million tons in 1919, (only 48,100 tons were chemical fertilizer and 6.4 million tons were compost) to 30,268,000 tons by 1938 (only 367,000 tons of which were commercial fertilizer). The stepped-up labor mobilization drained labor power from rural areas, and the shortage of commercial and other fertilizers, coupled with the lack of skill, capital, and incentive on the part of Korean farmers, combined to reduce rice production. In 1940, the amount of rice produced in Korea was only 73.4 million bushels. In 1943, 20.4 million fewer bushels of rice and 10 million fewer bushels of other grains were produced than in 1938.

The landless peasants who refused to till the lands owned by absentee landlords, or those who live in areas where farmlands were scarce, became *hwajŏnmin*, or cultivators of fire-fields (*hwajŏn*). Fire-fields were created by burning wastelands and hillsides in order to plant corn, sweet potatoes, and millet. A government publication of 1935 stated that ''these poor people are driven by hunger from place to place, making shelters in log cabins and keeping their bodies and souls together by planting grains and vegetables on the hillsides.'' In 1931, some 27,000 families were living off 303,800 acres of unproductive fire-fields, and by 1939, the number had grown to 340,000 families (1,870,000 persons) and the acreage of *hwajŏn* to 1.8 million acres.

In 1933, Ugaki inaugurated a ten-year economic plan with the slogan: ''cotton in the south, sheep in the north.'' It emphasized the diversification of agriculture and called for a greater production of cotton and wool to meet the growing demand for these commodities by the Japanese military and industries.

Korea had 238,200 acres of cotton growing area in 1933, and under the plan the area grew to 618,850 acres by 1939, and therefore it steadily increased. Cotton production rose from 159.3 million pounds in 1933 to 213.3 million by 1939 when some 160 million pounds were shipped to Japan. The second stage in the plan was by 1952 to produce 700 to 800 million pounds of cotton.

Ugaki designated the Kaema Plateau in the border region of South Hamgyŏng and South P'yŏng-an provinces as the main sheep grazing area, and imported Australian and New Zealand sheep. His 1933 plan called for increasing the number of sheep to 100,000 (400 Mongolian and 200 Australian sheep had been imported, and there were 5,473 sheep in 1934) to produce more wool and skins in order to meet the growing military needs. But the number grew to only 27,450 by 1939. In 1937 Minami adopted a 15-year plan to increase the number to 500,000, and his 1939 plan was to increase the number to 650,000. However, all three plans failed to achieve their goals.

Increasing the cotton growing area meant decreasing the dry cereal-growing area, which worsened the food shortage. In order to relieve the mounting hardships of Korean farmers, Ugaki encouraged the Koreans to migrate into the Kando region of southeastern Manchuria. For this and various other reasons, the number of Koreans in that area increased from 630,980 in 1931 to 876,692 by 1936.

In January 1934, Ugaki inaugurated the Movement for Rural Revival with emphasis on self-regeneration through self-reliance and self-help. He stated that the ways to bring about self-regeneration were to eat less, work harder, be thrifty (balance one's income and expenditure), not borrow money, and save. He also launched a campaign to prevent the Koreans from wearing "uneconomical" white clothes. Many had to dye their clothes when they were smeared by campaign workers with ink and other materials. But the majority of Koreans, paricularly farm families whose living standard was far below the subsistence level, could not bring .about self-regeneration no matter how hard they tried. The rural revival movement made no tangible contributions so far as Korean farmers were concerned. Korean tenants suffered much during the colonial period due to various factors, including the high rent they paid to landlords. Some paid one third of their harvest as rent, but others paid between 58 and 90 per cent; a common rate was 50 per cent of the harvest, paid in cash or in goods. In addition, tenants usually paid land tax, water fees to irrigation associations, transportation costs, and other fees. They were frequently left with less than 25 per cent of the harvest to live on, and the landlords provided their tenants with little or no money.

The number of landlord-tenant disputes grew from 667 cases in 1931, to 1,975 in 1933, 7,544 in 1934, and 25,834 in 1935. The Tenancy Dispute Arbitration Ordinance of December 1932, and the Law on Agricultural Land of October 1934, were enacted to promote "a spirit of harmony and coopera-tion between landlords and tenants." But, contrary to claims made by some writers, these ordinances did not improve the economic conditions of tenants or promote a spirit of harmony and cooperation.

Although Korean agriculture was modernized in some ways and Korea was producing more grains, the peasants received no benefit from their hard work, and always faced the threat of starvation. Ugaki himself remarked in 1933 that the shortage of food forced the Koreans "to dig out and eat the roots of trees on the mountains and fields or . . . beg from every door to keep themselves alive." In short very few Korean peasants could hope to succeed in the future on account of their poverty in the past and their suffering in the present. According to government study in 1931, some 2.3 million households in 71,888 villages, and approximately 11 million out of a total of 21.5 million individuals, needed economic relief. But no relief came for them.

Despite the increase in food production, the average annual rice con-sumption per person was reduced from 3.5 bushels in 1921 to 1.7 bushels by 1939. Per capita annual consumption of other grains decreased likewise. Mean-while, the exportation of rice to Japan increased annually. In the 1927–1931 period, 30.6 million bushels were exported, 48.8 million in 1936, and 54.5 million or 40 per cent, of the 138.9 million bushels produced in 1937. In order to lessen the food shortage in Korea, Chinese millet was imported: 76,500 bushels in 1915, 6,477,000 in 1927, and 8,200,600 in 1932. In 1933, it drop-ped to 5,334,600 bushels and thereafter remained below the 1932 level.

With the outbreak of the Sino-Japanese War in 1937, the shortage of food increased sharply. While Korea was exporting more than 5.6 million bushels of rice to Japan, the Japanese imported rice from Taiwan for the Koreans. Meanwhile, in order to maintain a minimum supply of rice, as well as to meet the export quota, the system of price and black-market control was tightened and compulsory sale of rice to the government was enforced. Farmhouses were searched to discover hidden grains, and brewing rice wine and producing rice cakes and other pastries were strictly forbidden.

Fishery.   About 6,000 miles of Korean coastline, including its offshore islands, bays and inlets, contained rich fishing grounds—particularly the northeastern coast. Mackerel, herring, sardines, cod, whiting, and "yellow-fish" comprised the major catch, and many varieties of shellfish as well as tons of edible seaweed were also harvested from the sea. The fact that next to grain dealers Korean markets had more fish dealers than any other merchants attested to the importance of fish in the Korean diet.

In 1910 fishing underwent a modern development. Many Koreans turned to fishing after 1910, particularly after many lost their farms or rights to farm. Thus the number of Korean fishermen grew from 242,000 in 1915, to approximately 480,000 by 1932. Meanwhile, the number of Japanese fishermen in Korea increased from 23,486 in 1912, to 74,349 in 1918. As Japanese commercial and industrial enterprises increased in Korea, the number of Japanese fishermen declined to 15,913, but the improvement of Japanese fishing boats and tools kept the amount of their catch much higher than that of Korean fishermen.

The value of sea products increased from 8.5 million *yen* in 1921 to 87.1 million in 1938, and 96.8 million in 1939. The quantity of fish caught in Korean waters was almost 1.65 million tons, plus some 162,100 tons of shellfish and seaweeds, in 1938, and 1.7 million tons in 1941. Among the many sea products were dried, salted, and canned fish, fertilizer and oil.

The *yen* value of the catch of Korean fishermen was always far below that of Japanese fishermen. For example, in 1918, 74,349 Japanese fishermen caught 18.2 million *yen* worth of fish, but 272,680 Korean fishermen caught only 14.7 million *yen* worth. In 1932, the value per catch for Korean fishermen was only 102 *yen* as compared to 1,910 *yen* for the Japanese. This was so primarily because Korean fishermen had fewer boats (one boat for every thirteen as compared to one boat per two Japanese fishermen); their boats were small with premodern equipment and they fished near the shore. They also lacked the capital and modern technology to engage in deep-sea fishing.

The Fishery Law of 1912, (revised in 1929), benefited the Japanese more than the Koreans, for many regulations imposed upon the Koreans engaged in fishing and related industries severely restricted their activity. Whereas Korean fishermen had almost no organizations, the Japanese formed, as early as 1912, associations which aided their fishermen in a variety of ways, including financial and marketing assistance.

The expanding fishing industry did not benefit the Koreans, for less than one-fourth of the fish caught and less than half of the manufactured sea products in 1938 were used for food. Furthermore, because they were primarily engaged in non-industrialized sectors of the fishing industry, the income of Korean fishermen remained low.

Commercial Development.   With the arrival of the Japanese *zaibatsu* firms, modern commerce and financial business developed. Under the protective Company Law of 1910, however, the commercial economy and financial markets were completely controlled by the Japanese, although a handful of Korean firms and one bank were allowed to emerge. The Korean firms, mostly small and individually owned, maintained a traditional commercial philosophy and methods of trade.

Nearly all modern stores in Seoul and other large cities like Pyongyang and Pusan were Japanese-owned. Such large department stores as Mitsukoshi, Jōjiya and Minakai and their branches in key cities virtually monopolized the large-scale retail trade. The only department store which both catered to and was owned by Koreans was the Hwashin Department Store in Seoul, with branches in several other cities.

The establishment of large commodity markets in urban areas provided better opportunities for Korean merchants to market their goods, but the economic modernization hardly touched small towns and rural areas. The traditional once-in-five-days local markets remained important places for commodity exchange. As the number of stores and market places increased in urban areas, the number of peddlers dwindled there, but the rural population still depended on the visits of peddlers to their villages. With the growth of a cash economy, the barter system of trade completely disappeared.

The financial market was dominated by the Japanese Bank of Korea (Chōsen Ginkō), which was the only agency of the Government-General authorized to issue bank notes (legal tender), and the Yasuda, the Sumitomo, the Mitsui, the Mitsubishi, and the Industrial (Shokusan) banks. The only Korean-owned and operated bank that was allowed to remain after 1910 was the Hanil Bank of Seoul. Other commercial institutions that came into being were savings and loan associations and the government operated postal savings systems. The traditional Korean financial mutual-aid organizations known as *kye* maintained its importance in Korea.

As economic conditions changed and a new way of life developed, new and modern commercial establishments such as shoe stores, clothing stores, meat markets, barbershops, public bathhouses, and new types of restaurants increased in number. However, in 1939 only 7.9 per cent of the Korean population was engaged in commerce contrasted with 23 per cent of the Japanese population in Korea.

The Pattern of Industrial Development.   The development of heavy and light industries and of communication and transportation systems constituted the most conspicuous modern transformation of the Korean economy. However, the industries that developed were in reality an extension of the Japanese economy, although some contributions were made by the Japanese toward the modernization of the Korean economy.

The revision of the Company Law of 1910 in April 1920 did not accelerate the growth of Korean industrial enterprises. Some believed that the Company Law was abolished, but it was only revised so as to allow some Koreans with less than 50,000 *yen* captial to form their own commercial and manufacturing firms without having Japanese participating as investors or managers. The revision, actually, helped the Japanese more than the Koreans. For example, there were 544 companies of various kinds with an investment capital of 180 million *yen* in 1920. Of these, only 99 were owned by Koreans, 22 were jointly owned by Koreans and Japanese, 414, or 76.1 per cent, were owned by Japanese, and the rest were owned by other foreigners.

By 1930, the number of companies grew to 1,768. Of these, 363 were owned by Koreans, 165 were owned jointly by Koreans and Japanese, and 1,237 (70.1 per cent) were owned by Japanese. Moreover, whereas most of the Japanese-owned companies had a large amount of investment capital and did business in profitable mining and manufacturing industries, most Korean-owned firms had little capital and did business mostly in small commercial ventures.

Out of 1,199 factories in Korea in 1931, 479 or 39.9 per cent were for food processing and 140 were textile factories of varying kinds and sizes. These industries were followed by printing firms (111), earthenware firms (94), chemical companies (88), and machine and tool factories (63). In 1931, some 14 gas and coal-generating power plants established by the Japanese constituted Korea's "heavy" industry.

The development of heavy industries began in 1926 when the Noguchi *zaibatsu* of Japan established the Chōsen Hydroelectric Company on the Pujŏn River and the Chōsen Nitrogen Fertilizer Company at Hŭngnam in South Hamgyŏng Province. However, it was the Manchurian war that began in September 1931 which gave the real impetus to the development of heavy industries as Korea became the critical logistic base for the Japanese expansion on the Asiatic mainland. The development of mining to produce more strategic raw materials, including coal, gold, and iron ore, and the production of iron and steel in Korea became crucial, particularly after the outbreak of the Sino-Japanese War in July 1937. In that year, the Heavy Industry Control Law of Japan was applied to Korea, and a "North Korea Development Plan" was adopted by the Government-General. Various Japanese plans created two economic zones in Korea—the north as a heavy industrial zone and the south as a light industrial zone. The following table shows the regional differences in economic change in Korea:

INDUSTRIAL ORIGINS OF COMMODITY-PRODUCTS
1934–1940
(in percentage)

Category	The South		The North	
	1934–35	1939–40	1934–35	1939–40
Agriculture	72.6	59.9	62.3	46.8
Fishery	5.0	9.7	4.4	6.5
Forestry	6.6	7.9	8.6	8.2
Mining	1.7	3.5	8.8	12.7
Manufacturing	14.1	19.0	15.9	25.8

Source: Sang-chul Suh, *Growth and Structural Changes in the Korean Economy, 1910–1940* (1978), p. 139.

The percentage shared by various sectors in the Korean economy shifted between 1931 and 1939 as the following table shows:

Category	1931	1936	1939
Agriculture	63.1	51.8	42.0
Fisheries	6.9	7.0	8.0
Forestry	5.3	5.1	5.0
Mining	2.0	4.8	6.0
Industries	22.7	31.3	39.0

Source: Hatada Takashi, *A History of Korea,* tr. and edited by Warren W. Smith, Jr. and Benjamin H. Hazard (1959), pp. 120, 122.

Although some Korean-owned manufacturing firms were established, all heavy and most light manufacturing industries were in the hands of the Japanese *zaibatsu,* such as Mitsui, Mitsubishi, Noguchi, Sumitomo, and Asano. While the Shimizu Gumi dominated the field of heavy civil engineering and large construction projects, the Kanebo firm dominated the field of textile manufacturing.

Between 1931 and 1939, some 30 industrial companies of Japanese *zaibatsu* were established in Korea, most of which were engaged in heavy industry. Two Japanese construction firms, Kajima and Shimizu, virtually monopolized the construction of large industrial plants and hydroelectric facilities and dams.

Mining.   The Japanese knew that Korea had large mineral reserves, including gold, iron, and coal deposits. One of the three categories of heavy industries which the Government-General encouraged was mining, and it provided large subsidies to Japanese mining companies. The Japanese had a monopoly on gold mining after 1939, when an American company, which had been mining gold at Unsan since 1896, was forced out of existence. Various government regulations and laws, such as the Company Law of 1910, as well as lack of capital prevented the Koreans from mining gold.

The output of gold was valued at 3.7 million *yen* in 1910, 9 million in 1931, and 38 million in 1934. Between 1941 and 1944, 1,300 million *yen* worth, or 42,668 kg., of gold was mined in Korea. Among the important gold mines were the Unsan and the Taeyudong mines in North P'yŏng-an Province, the Hamhŭng and Changjin mines in South Hamgyŏng Province, the Ongjin and Suan mines in Hwanghae Province, along with a half dozen others where in the 1930s and early 1940s, over one million *yen* each of gold was produced annually.

Because traditional mining techniques proved to be costly and unsatisfactory as the demand for gold increased after 1931, the Japanese brought in new techniques. Alluvial gold (sand gold or gold dust) was discovered in North and South Chŏlla and South P'yŏng-an provinces. Dredgers were used by the Mitsubishi Company to "mine" the alluvial gold as early as 1929, and after 1933 over 40 dredgers were installed at Kimje, Chiksan, Sunan and other locations. It was reported that Sunan Mine in South P'yŏng-an Province alone annually produced 30 gold bars.

With the increase of gold mining, refineries were established at Chinnamp'o, Munp'yŏng and elsewhere by such Japanese companies as the Nihon and Sumitomo Mining corporations, and the Noguchi firm. Millions of *yen* of government subsidy were provided to these firms after 1937. Meanwhile, millions of acres of good farmland were ruined by the mining of alluvial gold, and the new method of gold mining left deep scars on the beautiful landscape of Korea.

The production of pig iron and steel was particularly emphasised in 1941. As with gold, most of the iron ore deposits were found in the northern part of Korea, the most important one being at Musan in North Hamgyŏng Province. The Mining Law of September 1934, along with the Gold Production Ordinance of 1937, accelerated the mining of mineral resources. In 1933 alone, some 522,000 tons of iron ore were mined in Korea, and by 1944 the tonnage grew to about one million.

Coal mining was unknown in Korea until the arrival of the Japanese. Like other mining industries, it became monopolized by Japanese firms because of the protection of the Company Law and other regulations of the Government-General and because the Koreans themselves lacked capital and technology. The dominant coal firms were the Chōsen Coal Industrial Corporation of the Noguchi group, the Samch'ŏk Development Corporation of the Mitsui group, the Chōsen Anthracite Company of the Mitsubishi group, and the Meiji Mining Company.

Anthracite deposits were discovered primarily in the northern part of the peninsula, although some were also found in the south. Many soft coal deposits were also found in the north. Important coal mines were the Aoji mine and others in North Hamgyŏng Province, the Hamhŭng mine in South Hamgyŏng Province, the Anju and Sunch'ŏn mines in South P'yŏng-an Province, and the Pongsan mine in Hwanghae Province.

Korea's coal reserves were estimated at 42 million tons in 1932, and with the discovery of more coal deposits, they were estimated at 1,340 million tons of anthracite and 410 million tons of soft coal in 1939. With the introduction of Japanese capital and technology, coal production increased rapidly. In 1920, the output of anthracite in Korea was 289,000 tons, but by 1930 it increased to 884,000 tons. Under the five-year plan adopted in 1937, it grew to 2.3 million tons by 1938. The rapidly developing coal industry allowed the Japanese to establish various kinds of related industries such as synthetic oil, gas, petroleum, fertilizer, synthetic fibers, paraffin, bakelite and others. The supply of coal for fuel also became more abundant for Japanese industrial plants.

The mining of tungsten, lead, nickel, zinc, copper, magnesite, phosphate and mica was initiated by Japanese *zaibatsu* firms. The total value of mining output in Korea grew from 24.7 million *yen* in 1936 to 445.5 million *yen* by 1942.

Iron and Steel Production and Machine and Tool Industry. Korea had about 20 million tons of high grade iron ore and over one billion tons of low grade ore. Iron ore deposits were discovered at such locations as Musan, Kyŏmip'o, Kaech'ŏn, Tanch'ŏn and Iwon—all in the northern part of Korea. The only ironworks, which was established in 1916, was located at Kyŏmip'o, Hwanghae Province. It stopped operating in 1920, but with the emphasis given to the development of heavy industries in 1934, it was reopened by the Japan Steel Corporation. The production of pig iron at this plant increased from 42,700 tons in 1918 to 155,500 tons in 1936. Thus the production of pig iron and steel became an important industry in Korea.

Steel production began in 1934, when 59,700 tons were produced. This grew to 83,000 tons by 1936. In 1943, 456,000 tons of pig iron and 101,060 tons of steel were produced at the Kyŏmip'o plant. Meanwhile, other mills were established at Ch'ŏngjin, Musan, and Hŭngnam by the Japan Steel Corporation and the Japan High Frequency Heavy Industrial Corporation.

With growing iron and steel production, machine and tool manufacturing industries developed under the auspices of such Japanese corporations as the Chosen Industrial Metal Company which had its plant in Inch'ŏn near Seoul. The Yŏngdŭngp'o district of Seoul across the Han River and the Yongsan ward of Seoul became centers of these industries. Machine and tool manufacturing, including the production of vehicles and ships, accounted for only 2.3 per cent of the total industrial production in 1938. However, the number of workers employed by the machine and tool factories increased steadily from little over 4,000 in 1931 to 17,058 in 1938. It continued to grow, particularly after 1941, when the Japanese firms were forced to transplant their factories from Japan to Korea as the Allied bombing of Japan increased in intensity.

Electric Power Production.   The production of electricity developed slowly. In 1917, only 8,000 kw. of electricity was produced, mostly by coal, by the Keijō (Seoul) Electric Company. The potential capacity to produce electricity by water-power was originally estimated to be only 57,000 kw., but it was reestimated in 1926 to be 2,250,000 kw. and later at five million kw., including one million kw. which could be generated by using the water-power of the Yalu and Tumen rivers.

Following the establishment of the hydroelectric power plant on the Pujŏn River by the Chōsen Nitrogen Fertilizer Corporation of the Noguchi firm in 1926, and another plant on the Changjin River in 1933, the generating capacity of the hydroelectric power plants grew by 1938 to 522,300 kw. Plants which produced power by coal increased their generating capacity to 145,800 kw. Four more hydroelectric plants were established between 1937 and 1939 with a combined capacity to produce an additional 800,000 kw., and in 1943 various plants produced a total of 1.5 million kw. Most hydroelectric power plants were located in the north in such places as Sup'ung on the Yalu River. The only hydropower plant in the south was located at Ch'ilbo in North Cholla Province. Despite the increase in power generation, only about 20 per cent of Korean homes, mostly in large and medium size cities, had electrical service.

Other Industries.   Although fertilizer was the most important product of the chemical industry, other aspects developed such as the manufacture of cotton, fish products, vegetable and mineral oils, drugs, hemp, gunpowder, paint, matches, ammonia, and sugar. The number of chemical firms grew rapidly, from 393 in 1929 to some 6,000 by 1940. However, the only significant Korean-owned chemical companies were a few drug companies and rubber shoe manufacturing firms. The gross value of chemical products, with the exception of fertilizer, increased from 17.4 million *yen* in 1929 to 319 million *yen* by 1940. The number of workers employed by chemical firms grew to 51,000 by 1940.

The ceramic industry expanded with the increasing demand for cement. The amount of cement produced grew from 67,000 tons in 1929 to 1,675,500 tons in 1940. Cement production was monopolized by Japanese firms such as the Onoda Cement Company of the Mitsui group, the Chōsen Asano Cement Corporation and the Yalu River Hydroelectric Company. Among the pottery firms were the Japan High Quality Ceramic Ware Company, and the Korean-owned Koryo Ceramic Company which produced mostly domestic goods. Brick manufacturing was monopolized by the Nihon Magnesite Corporation.

The paper and pulp industry was completely in the hands of the North Korea Paper Manufacturing Company, a branch of the Ōji Paper Company of

Japan. In 1939, its plant at Kilchu had the capacity to produce 30,000 tons of paper. Another pulp plant was built in 1939 in Shinūiju by the Kanegafuchi Corporation of Japan.

Light Industries.   Among light industries, the most important ones in value were food processing and textile manufacturing—fields in which the Koreans played a major role. In 1930, the food processing industry accounted for 57.9 per cent of gross value of commodity production, while the textile industry accounted for 12.8 per cent. The textile industry's share of gross value of commodity production remained relatively steady after 1930, but the food processing industry percentage suffered due to shortages of raw materials, fuel, capital and technology, as well as the greater importation of processed food from Japan. As a result, its share in gross value in production declined to 45.2 per cent in 1936, and then to 19.0 per cent in 1943. However, as of 1937, the food processing industry employed the third largest group (35,000) of industrial workers.

The textile industry managed to sustain its importance because the need for the supply of cotton clothes increased sharply after 1931. As a result, the number of spindles increased from 15,000 in 1934 to 213,000 by 1939. Raw silk, cotton yarn, wool, hemp, flax and other synthetic fiber goods were the main textile products. Wool production became more important after 1937. The silk industry, however, nearly collapsed toward the end of the Japanese period. There were six large textile companies in Korea, but only one was Korean-owned. The textile industry employed the second largest group (35,600) of industrial workers. The gross value of textile production rose from 38,211,000 *yen* in 1929 to 164,821,000 in 1938.

Communication and Transportation.   The departments of Communication and Railway of the Government-General expanded and modernized communication and railway networks. Their work accelerated after 1931, and by 1938, the telephone and telegraph systems, established as a government monopoly, extended telegraph lines to 5,630 miles and the telephone lines to 7,100 miles. However, only 53,000 telephone units were installed, and only 14,489, or one out of 306 Koreans, had telephone service in contrast to one out of four Japanese. Only Seoul had an automatic telephone exchange system. Long distance telephone, as well as telegraph services were handled by post offices, which were located only in large cities or in towns where county seats were situated. There were 1,031 post offices in Korea in 1938.

A government sponsored radio station and a wireless communication system were installed in 1927. The main radio station (JODK) was established in Seoul in 1926, and broadcasted in Korean and Japanese, but after 1941, Korean language broadcasting was terminated. A vast majority of Korean families had no radios, and to them the wireless communication system was irrelevant.

Air passenger service began in Korea in 1927, when the Japanese air line company opened the Fukuoka-Ulsan-Seoul-Dairen air line. Subsequently, such cities as Taegu, Shinŭiju, Wonsan, and Hamhŭng were connected with the main route originating in the Japanese city of Fukuoka in Kyūshū. Almost all air passengers were Japanese.

The first railway line in Korea was the Seoul-Inch'ŏn line, whose construction had been begun by an American company and was taken over by a Japanese company. This line, which was completed in 1899, was joined by the Pusan-Seoul line (280 miles) and the Seoul-Shinŭiju line (310 miles), which were built by the Japanese in 1905 and 1906, respectively.

Between 1910 and 1920, many railway projects were completed. They included the Seoul-Wŏnsan line (139 miles) and the Taejŏn-Mokp'o line (162 miles). Later, many branch lines, as well as the Wŏnsan-Hoeryŏng line, were constructed. Until 1925, the Korean railways were under the management of the South Manchuria Railway Company. These new rail projects were included in a twelve-year plan adopted in 1927, which aimed at the construction of 830 miles of lines in various regions of Korea, particularly in the north, which was designated as an industrial zone.

As Korea became more and more a "critical logistic base" for Japan in relation to her continental expansionism, the importance of railways grew. Many branch lines, as well as a major line between Pyongyang and Wŏnsan, were built between 1931 and 1938. Meanwhile, the Pusan-Seoul and Seoul-Shinŭiju lines became double-track lines. The government ordinance of February 1920 encouraged private companies to increase railway mileage. Needless to say, the largest private company in Korea, the Chōsen Tetsudō Kabushiki Kaisha, as well as all other private railway companies, was that of the Japanese.

By 1943, the total railway mileage increased to 6,376 km. of which 1,628 km. was owned by private companies. The rest was owned and operated by the Government-General. The railway project (200 miles) to link cities on the east coast from Wŏnsan to Pusan, via P'ohang, undertaken in 1941, was not completed.

Korean highways were modernized somewhat, and their total length grew to 9,000 miles by 1938, but all were narrow and unpaved. Bus transportation was available only to those who resided along the main highways.

Port facilities were modernized and expanded to improve the shipping industry. But of some 200 ports, only a dozen had modern facilities in 1940. Among the more important ones were Chinnamp'o, Wŏnsan, Ch'ŏngjin, Sŏngjin, and Najin in the north, Inch'ŏn in the center, and Kunsan, Mokp'o, Yŏsu, Masan and Pusan in the south.

Evaluation of Economic Change.   The structural changes and development of the Korean economy under Japanese monopolistic capitalism created new hardships for the Koreans. As was mentioned earlier, the economic conditions of Korean farmers were bleak and desolate, and those of Korean workers were as bad.

The number of Korean factory workers increased, but their wages were low. In 1931, for example, when a Japanese male factory worker's daily wage was 1.89 *yen*, a Korean's was only 0.85 *yen*; a Japanese female worker's wage was 0.85 *yen*, but a Korean's was only 0.46 *yen*; these wage differentials remained constant. All high and middle level commercial and industrial workers were Japanese, and Korean employees were either lower-level clerks or low wage earning blue-collar employees. For example, in 1944, out of 1,214 engineers and technicians in the metal industry, only 133, or 11 per cent, were Koreans; of 2,004 in the chemical industry, only 222, or 12 per cent, were Koreans. The total number of engineers, technicians and skilled Korean workers was 1,632, or 20 per cent of the total of 8,478. Per capita income of the Koreans was 211 *yen* as compared to 701 *yen* of the Japanese. Korea had a lower per capita income than Taiwan (243 *yen*). The gross national product of Korea in 1944 was estimated at 4,860 million *yen*, or 11.8 per cent of the total gross national product of Japan, which was 4.1 billion *yen*.

Various economic factors combined with the maltreatment of Korean workers by the Japanese brought about growing labor unrest and tenant disputes. The organization of labor unions was not prohibited, but no labor laws were enacted by the Japanese. The number of tenant disputes grew from 15 in 1920, to 176 in 1923, and 1,590 in 1928. There were 4,490 tenant disputes between 1920 and 1931. Meanwhile, the number of labor strikes increased from 84 in 1919, involving some 8,000 Korean workers, to 119 in 1929, 160 in 1930, and 204 in 1931. Some 17,000 Korean workers were involved in the strikes of 1930 and 1931.

The ever escalating price of consumer goods and the declining price of rice, coupled with increased taxes, created a serious situation for Korean wage earners and farmers alike. Among the new taxes were an income tax (1920), stamp taxes (1928), business and gambling taxes (1930) and a school tax. In March 1938, tax laws were revised and some twenty new taxes were added, and in 1940 tax laws were again revised and more new taxes were added. As of 1944, 23 per cent of the government income came from 38 different taxes, 27 per cent from the sale of bonds and loans, 42 per cent from government monopolies such as salt, tobacco, and ginseng, and 8 per cent from miscellaneous sources. The compulsory donation of money, labor and materials which the Koreans were forced to make, in order to bring about the successful conclusion of Japan's "sacred war" in China, worsened their economic conditions.

Major government expenditures of 1944 (2.3 billion *yen*) were for the expansion and maintenance of the communication and transportation systems (37.1 per cent) and for subsidies given for gold production, mining and other industries (15.6 per cent). Only 0.3 per cent was for education, while as of 1944, 5 per cent was allocated for experimental stations and other programs.

The growing inflationary trends made economic conditions desperate and dangerous. Prices were driven up by the ever increasing supply of the Bank of Korea (Chōsen) and other Japanese bank notes in order to finance first the China war and then World War II. The total amount of bank notes issued increased from 100.0 million *yen* in 1931, to 448.5 million in 1940, and 2 billion in August 1944. The price index in Seoul was 145 in 1931 (1900 = 100), but it rose to 312 in April 1941. The inflationary trends grew worse after December 1941 as the shortage of food and commodities grew.

The National Labor Registration Ordinance of January 1939, which required all workers to register, was followed by the National Labor Mobilization Ordinance of September 30, 1939. The latter depleted the labor force from rural areas and light industries in order to meet the increasing demands for labor by newly established heavy (war) industries. Those who hid were hunted out and forcibly shipped from villages and towns to various industrial sites. In 1938, some 26,588 Korean workers were relocated from rural areas to industrial sites, but in 1939 and 1940 the number expanded to 160,000.

In addition, many Korean workers were mobilized to meet the labor shortage in Japan. From 1939 to 1945, close to one million Korean youths were shipped to mines and factories in Japan. As a result, the Korean population in Japan jumped from 690,502 in 1936 to 2,400,000 at the end of the colonial period. Moreover, tens of thousands of young Korean women were sent to war fronts to provide sexual services to Japanese troops.

When Korea's twenty-five million people were liberated from Japan, Korea was an exhausted land, its natural resources and manpower had been ruthlessly exploited, and its energies had been sapped for Japan's vain dream of dominating all of Asia.

Educational and Cultural Change

Education Policy.   The colonial government issued an education ordinance in August 1911, which stated that the purpose of education in Korea was to produce "loyal and obedient" and useful subjects of the Japanese emperor. It adopted a system of four-year primary education, a four-year secondary school program for boys and a three-year secondary curriculum for girls. However, only a handful of schools were established during this time while a large number of private schools were closed. The ordinance made the study of the Japanese language compulsory at all approved schools and banned instruction in Korean history and geography. All textbooks which had been previously used in Korean schools were confiscated and only those approved by the government were allowed.

In 1919, 84,306 or 3.7 per cent of Korean children and 42,732 or 91.5 per cent of Japanese children attended Korean public primary schools in Korea. Some 245,000 Korean children attended 25,524 traditional village schools called *sŏdang* and studied the Chinese language and Confucian classics. There were only five public and seven approved private high schools for Korean boys and only two public and four private high schools for Korean girls. The number of nonaccredited (unapproved) schools decreased from 1,317 in 1912 to 690 in 1919.

The only liberal arts colleges, Sungshil (Union Christian) College established by the U.S. Presbyterian mission in Pyongyang in 1906, the nondenominational private Posŏng College founded by Koreans, and the college division of the missionary-established Ewha School for girls, lost their college status under the 1911 ordinance. There was not one liberal arts college in Korea in 1915. However, in 1917, a new liberal arts college for men called Yŏnhŭi (Chosŏn Christian) College and Severance Medical College were established by American mission boards under a new 1915 regulation. In 1918, public professional schools established before 1910 were elevated to colleges; they were Keijō (Seoul) Law College, Keijō Medical College, Keijō Industrial College—mainly for the Japanese, and Suwŏn Agricultural and Forestry College for Korean students.

A handful of private schools were given accreditation and were allowed to remain open, but they were constantly watched by the Japanese police, and they were often closed or certain classes were cancelled under the slightest suspicion of anti-Japanese or pro-Korean activity. Having been denied educational opportunities in Korea, an increasing number of young Koreans went to Japan to attend school.

When Saitō replaced Terauchi, certain policy changes were made regarding education and culture. A new Special Committee of Educational Investigation adopted several principles, "liberalizing" existing regulations. They stated that "*so far as the people permit*, Korean education should be in uniformity with that of Japan proper" and "*so far as the circumstances of the people permit*, educational facilities shall be provided to meet the growing desire of the Korean people for education.*" Based on these principles, on February 5, 1922, a new educational ordinance was promulgated. All public, or approved high schools for Korean boys and girls were renamed boys' or girls' high common schools. The length of primary education for Korean children was extended from four to six years, so long as local conditions allowed, although primary education was not made compulsory as it was in Japan. The length of secondary education was extended from four to five years for Korean boys and from three to four years for Korean girls.

Accommodating the wishes of the Koreans and of the American missionaries, the government somewhat liberalized education in November 1920, requiring instruction in Western languages and in science for all secondary students. But instruction in Japanese language, history, and geography was also made compulsory at all schools. Religious instruction was permitted at unaccredited private (mission) schools only.

The Growth of Educational Institutions.   Following the establishment of Keijō Normal School in 1921, other normal schools and short-term teachers' institutions were established. The length of education required for teacher preparation was extended to six years for men and five years for women. Most teachers at Korean primary schools were Korean and most teachers at secondary schools for Koreans were Japanese.

In 1929, a plan was adopted to establish one public primary school in each geographic unit comprising three districts (*myŏn*) and one public high school in each of the thirteen provinces. Between 1919 and 1935 approved private secondary schools increased from 18 to 45 and the number of students from 2,781 to 3,841. The number of children attending primary schools grew from 88,827 to 186,145, but this was only about 2.2 per cent of the school age population. In rural areas 579 two-year primary schools were established, permitting some 35,700 Korean children to receive basic education. The number of unaccredited primary and secondary schools decreased from 778 in 1918 to 406 with 79,998 students in 1935. In 1935 while only one out of 2,200 Koreans attended secondary schools, all Japanese students did so.

The development of vocational and technical schools was emphasized, and the length of vocational education was extended from two to five years. Along with more secondary level public vocational and technical schools, the government established more lower-level (two-year) vocational and technical schools. The number of new private vocational and technical schools increased as establishing them was made easier. As a result, Korean students who were unable to attend liberal arts secondary schools could receive some liberal arts education, as well as vocational and technical training, at these schools. Between 1919 and 1935 the number of vocational and technical schools grew from 21 to 72, and the number of students grew from 1,872 to 9,233. The number of two-year schools increased from 67 to 91 and the number of students from 1,252 to 3,595.

Under the Education Ordinance of 1922, three new private liberal arts colleges for Korean students were established in 1925. They were Sungshil (Union Christian) in Pyongyang, which regained its college status, and Ewha Woman's College and Posŏng College in Seoul. All private colleges which existed in 1925, except Posŏng College, were established by American mission boards. For all practical purposes, all other professional schools such as Keijō Law, Keijō Medical, and Keijō Engineering colleges were for Japanese students. Virtually no Japanese students attended private colleges in Korea.

Efforts made by several Koreans in the early 1920s to establish a Korean university in Seoul did not materialize. Not only was educational opportunity for Korean students limited, but facilities and the quality of instruction at public and private Korean schools were in most cases inferior to those of Japanese schools, or of schools which were more or less for Japanese students. Class size of Korean schools was usually larger than those of Japanese schools.

The Education Ordinance of May 1924 established Keijō Imperial University and its preparatory school. The two-year (3-year after 1934) preparatory school was opened in 1924 with 71 students, and in May 1926 two departments—law and literature, and medicine—were opened at the university. But the hopes of the Koreans were frustrated when it became clear that the only university in Korea was primarily for the Japanese. For example, out of 308 students in the preparatory school in 1927 only 104 were Koreans and only 89 Korean students were enrolled in the university compared to 220 Japanese students.

The situation remained the same after 1927, and the ratio between Japanese and Korean students remained almost constantly 2.5 to 1. When the College of Engineering and Technology was established in the university in 1941, 16 Korean and 23 Japanese students were admitted; in 1942, there were 25 Korean and 65 Japanese students in the college. The medical schools also had an unfavorable ratio for Korean students. Even after two existing medical institutes in Taegu and Pyongyang were elevated to medical colleges in 1933, the chances for Korean students entering those schools did not significantly improve.

Because it was difficult for Koreans to go to the United States or to European countries to study, more of them went to Japan or China. All Korean students who wished to travel to Japan had to have police clearance and a permit.

New textbooks were introduced and the quality of teachers improved during the 1920s and early 1930s, but chances for Korean students to receive high-level training in law, economics, engineering and technology were extremely limited.

The unhappiness and dissatisfaction of the Korean students was reflected in an article which appeared in the *Korean Student Bulletin* in December 1928:

.... every position of possible income here is occupied by the Japanese. Even the running of a street car is done mostly by the Japanese.... In turn, masses of able Koreans are out of work. Even many of the well-educated Koreans just returning from abroad are lingering around, simply because there is no place to work..... All this economic and political pressure has led the people to a state of unrest and anarchy.... Education means nothing here. The young people are going to school because they have nothing else to do in the village or the city... The graduation from a school in itself brings them nothing....

Chances for Koreans who graduated from unapproved private high schools to higher educational institutions were very poor throughout the colonial period. Most graduates of private colleges became teachers in private schools.

Education for the Japanization of the Koreans. The Manchurian Incident of September 1931 and the second Sino-Japanese War that began in July 1937 increased the need to promote Japanization and to train skilled Korean workers. As a result, while giving emphasis to industrial development, both Ugaki and Minami placed a high priority on educational and cultural indoc-trination of the colonial people. A new educational policy was adopted in line with the Imperial Rescript on Education of October 30, 1931. On November 10, 1933 Ugaki pointed out the importance of promoting the spirit of the Imperial subjects, so that "His Majesty's subjects could pay back one ten-thousandth of sacred benevolence." Accordingly in 1935, new textbooks were published and a new school curriculum was adopted. Instruction in Japanese ethics, language, and history was given particular emphasis. Meanwhile, teaching and speaking the Japanese language was forced upon the Koreans.

The cultural policy of the colonial government after 1931 was aimed at the rapid Japanization of the Koreans. Accordingly, it adopted many slogans and programs to assimilate Koreans into Japanese ideology and culture. The Japanese emphasized the importance of the transformation of Koreans into Im-perial subjects (*kōminka*) and assimilation (*dōka*). The term *kōminka* implied the political indoctrination of the Koreans to make them believe that they were truly the subjects of the "benevolent and august" emperor of Japan. Loyalty and obedience were the two cardinal principles for Imperial subjects (*kōmin*). The *dōka* policy essentially meant the obliteration of the racial and cultural heritage of the Koreans, not convergent assimilation between the Korean and Japanese cultures and peoples. Racial amalgamation was not prohibited, but it was not encouraged, and only a few Japanese learned the Korean language, studied Korean culture, or married Koreans.

With new magazines, pamphlets and other propaganda materials, including movies, the Japanese made various efforts to convert the Koreans to the Japanese ideology and way of life. While touring groups visited towns and villages with propaganda films, the government radio station JODK in Seoul and its local stations participated in the movement for cultural assimilation. The drive to make the Koreans speak Japanese was accelerated.

One of the most ambitious programs of Ugaki was to change the Korean custom of wearing white clothes, which symbolized their racial consciousness. The Japanese wished to destroy this symbol. Propaganda against the "un-economical" aspects of white clothes met conscious or intentional resistance from the Koreans. As a result, the government resorted to forceful measures, and police and other officials went about wherever people congregated spatter-ing ink or paint on their white clothes, forcing them to dye their ruined clothes. This effort, however, failed to obliterate the spirit of the Koreans as being "the people of white clothes."

The colonial government published many biased reports, pamphlets, and books concerning the Koreans, justifying the rule of Japan in Korea. For exam-ple, the book entitled *Chōsen-shi no shirabe (An Inquiry into Korean History)*, published by the Government-General in 1935 to commemorate the

25th anniversary of the annexation, made numerous subtle hints that the Koreans lacked organizational ability, innovative skills, and forward-looking attitudes.

In the name of assimilation, Korean language instruction was first simply discouraged while the movement for the use of Japanese was stepped up; in 1938 it was abolished in all public schools. By both covert and overt means, the use of the Japanese language was forced upon the Koreans. Failure to speak Japanese denied the Koreans many rights and privileges, including that of securing ration cards and public certification.

After 1935, compulsory attendance at Shintō ceremonies created numerous problems for Korean Christians. An increasing number of ministers and members of Christian churches were imprisoned because of their refusal to participate in the Shintō rituals, and a growing number of Korean private schools and social and cultural organizations were closed.

In 1936 Yagi Nobuo, Chief of the Education Section, Bureau of Education, stated that education was to serve Shintō nationalism and the fulfillment of Japan's "sacred mission" in Asia. He indicated that Korea was a military bastion of Japan for continental expansion and must discharge her economic and military obligation as "an integral part of the Japanese empire."

On March 4, 1938, another new educational ordinance was issued, and in a statement concerning it, Minami pointed out that the three fundamental educational objectives were: (1) the clarification of national policy; (2) the achievement of the unity of Japan and Korea, (3) the development of character and the training of mind and body to endure hardships.

This ordinance brought about the following changes: the names of Korean primary and secondary schools were made identical to those in Japan; schools for Koreans and Japanese were put under unified regulations; and separate normal schools for Koreans and Japanese were replaced by integrated normal schools. Elementary schools for Korean children became "citizens' schools," and high common schools for boys became middle schools and those for girls became girls' high schools.

In order to develop Japanese national consciousness among the Koreans, Minami himself took the lead in creating what became known as the "Pledge of the Imperial Subjects" which was officially adopted in October 1937 and henceforth was recited at all public gatherings whether they were political, religious, educational or social. Two versions of the pledge were to be recited—one by those with elementary students and the other by the students above the secondary level and by adults.

Type A. 1. We are the subjects of the great empire of Japan.
        2. We shall serve the Emperor with united hearts.
        3. We shall endure hardships and train ourselves to become good and strong subjects.

Type B. 1. We, the Imperial subjects, shall serve the nation loyally and faithfully.
2. We, the Imperial subjects, shall, through trust and love, cooperate to strengthen our unity.
3. We, the Imperial subjects, will endure hardships and train ourselves to promote the Imperial way.

The memorization of these pledges of the Imperial Subjects was required of all Koreans, and the memorization of the Imperial Rescript on Education (proclaimed in 1890 by the Meiji emperor) was required of all students. The picture of the Japanese emperor was placed in each classroom, and on each campus a stone structure which contained his picture was erected in the eastern corner of the campus. The practice of bowing in the direction of Tokyo became a standard ritual of all schools' activities.

A ten-year school expansion plan (it later became a six-year plan) was adopted in 1937 to accommodate 430,000 more Korean children at six-year public primary schools. Plans were also adopted to establish 220 new short-term (two-year) primary schools to accommodate 150,000 additional children, aimed at increasing the attendance rate of Korean children to 60 per cent by 1943.

Anticipating the increased demand for teachers, six new normal schools were established between May 1936 and April 1940, bringing the total number to ten. More short-term (one-year) teacher training schools were established to train 1,300 new teachers' helpers. Many Japanese teachers were imported to Korea. By the spring of 1941, the number of public six-year primary schools increased to 2,973 with 1,507,339 pupils. The number of two-year primary schools grew to 1,000 with some 60,000 pupils by 1941.

The colonial government showed only minor interest in promoting secondary and higher education for the Koreans. Thus only 12 new public middle schools for boys and 14 high schools for girls were established bettween 1937 and 1941, with a greater number of Japanese than Koreans taken into them. Among 23 new vocational and technical middle schools which were established during that period, nine were agricultural schools. In 1938, Keijō Mining College and a Confucian college were established by the government, bringing the total number of public colleges to nine, plus one university. In 1941, 1,360 Korean students attended public colleges as compared to 2,492 Japanese; 455 Korean and 729 Japanese students attended Keijō Imperial University.

As before, private institutions provided a significant amount of educational opportunity to Korean youths after 1936. The number of approved private primary schools remained small (134 with 57,878 pupils in 1940), the number of approved private high schools for boys increased slightly to 13 with 8,491 students, and those for girls grew to 13 with 5,035 students by 1941. After two private colleges—Taedong Industrial College and Sookmyung Women's College—were added in 1938, there were eleven private colleges with 2,580 Korean students in 1940. In that year, some 516 Japanese students attended private medical, dental and pharmaceutical colleges in Korea.

In 1941, there were 226 unapproved private primary schools, 35 unapproved private secondary schools, and 7 unapproved private colleges with a total of 71,591 Korean students. Most unaccredited schools were those established by Christian denominations. Had there been no private schools, over 150,000 Korean youths would have been deprived of any education as of 1941. Gates to public and private schools were narrow, and competition to enter them was intense. Some 20,844 Korean students attended various schools in Japan in 1941.

In order to indoctrinate Korean youth with the spirit of Shintō nationalism, in 1938 the colonial government established such organizations as the Korean Federation of Youth Organization, Local Youth Leadership Seminars, and Training Institutes for Children's Organization.

Textbook revision was carried out during the Minami period in order to develop Shintō nationalism and loyalty to the emperor and the state. The 1938 education ordinance abolished the teaching of the Korean language at all public schools, and Korean language instruction at private unaccredited schools was made "voluntary" and consequently, more schools dropped the Korean language course from their curriculum. The teaching of Korean history had long been abolished. English language instruction at public secondary schools was abolished in 1941.

The educational policy of the Government-General after December 1941 was directly affected by the growing war atmosphere. The primary educational objective remained the same, but new emphasis was given to promoting understanding of the Imperial Way and of those aspects of Japanese history that had "brought forth a superior national character and the special quality of [our] culture." Meanwhile, students of all levels were mobilized to provide labor assistance to war efforts. As a result, studies in academic subjects became less and less important. Physical education was strengthened at all levels as was military training at secondary schools and colleges.

After 1941, classroom instruction was sharply curtailed when students were required to (1) visit Shintō shrines to display loyalty to the emperor and pray for the empire, (2) go to railway stations to send off Japanese soldiers to war fronts, (3) participate in street parades celebrating "victories" on the battlefields, (4) work at construction sites such as roads, airfields, and other military installations, and (5) work on farms and in factories to lessen the labor shortage. They spent a vast number of hours collecting "patriotic monies" or materials such as gold and silver, brass, iron utensils, tin cans, and scrap iron. The Student Labor Mobilization Ordinance of April 28, 1944 virtually cut school schedules in half.

The number of public primary schools was 4,146 in 1944 with an enrollment of 2.1 million Korean children. This meant that only about 40 per cent of all Korean children (5,100,613) between the ages of 7 and 14 attended the first grade. There were 1,563 two-year rural schools.

As of April 1944, there were 75 public and private middle schools for Korean boys with 41,000 students, and 76 public and private high schools for Korean girls with 32,500 students. There were 18 public and private colleges. Less than 0.13 per cent of Koreans received secondary education and 0.07 per cent college education. The number of vocational schools increased to 268 with over 60,000 students. Some 61,590 students attended 268 unapproved private schools of various kinds and levels.

As the Pacific War intensified, the Government-General became more sensitive to what private schools taught and what efforts they were making toward the Japanese fulfillment of the "sacred mission" in Asia. Some private schools had been forced to change their names, and eventually they were taken over by the Japanese. There were no mission schools in Korea in 1944. Meanwhile, many Korean teachers were expelled from both public and private schools because of their "dangerous thoughts" or un-cooperative attitudes. In 1944 all liberal arts colleges became leadership training institutes.

More and more Korean publishers and authors suffered as press censorship became tightened. Three major Korean language dailies suffered frequent suspension of publication or censorship (blacking out, or removal of pages). Any editorials or news articles which would inflame Korean nationalism were blacked out, and the circulation of newspapers and magazines was often suspended. The deletion of the Japanese emblem from the uniforms worn by two Korean medalists (first and third) in the Berlin Olympic marathon in 1936, when their pictures were printed in Korean newspapers, was regarded by the Japanese as an expression of Korean racial nationalism. Therefore, in August 1936, the colonial government ordered the suspension of publication of the *Tong-a Ilbo* while another newspaper suspended its publication before it was ordered by the Japanese to do so. The *Tong-a Ilbo* was allowed to resume publication in June 1937, but its existence was precarious. The directive of the Book Section of the Bureau of Police on June 30, 1939, further restricted the activity of Korean newspapers, and in August 1940 all Korean language newspapers, except one (the *Mae-il Shinbo*) which was a government organ, were abolished. Some twelve Japanese language newspapers, including the *Keijō Nippō,* were published in Korea until the end of the Japanese colonial period. Meanwhile, after 1942, the Korean language instruction and the publication of Korean language books were banned.

Korea at the End of Japanese Colonial Rule

In August 1945 Korea was much different in many ways from what she had been in 1910. The thirty-six years of Japanese rule transformed the country: her political and judicial systems were modernized, her economy was transformed from that of an agrarian to one of a semi-industrial in nature. The acreage of land under cultivation increased, her farm production rose, her railway mileage expanded, her industrial output increased, and her mining output grew vastly. Modern educational institutions which were established brought about an increase in the educated population, and the rate of illiteracy decreased. With economic development and the increase of the number of high school and college graduates, the middle class, which hardly existed in the past, emerged, the age-old social structure was overthrown, and the urban population grew.

None of the modern commercial and industrial facilities which were mostly established by Japanese firms were damaged during the Pacific War, thanks to the decision made by the American government not to bomb Korea. Only a few bombs were dropped "accidentally" by American warplanes in the Kimje area in North Chŏlla province. But when the country was liberated from Japanese colonial rule, Korea was an exhausted land. Her natural resources and manpower had ruthlessly and indiscriminately been exploited, her energy was sapped, and her time and creativity were wasted for Japan's vanity and greed. Many changes notwithstanding, Korea was an underdeveloped nation with a variety of problems. Korea's government and politics were autocratic in character, her people were socially unsophisticated, and the economy was basically agrarian. During the Japanese period, the percentage of tenant farmers grew, and the percentage of owner-cultivators and part-owner/part-tenant declined. A majority of young people were uneducated, and the shortage of capital, scientists and technicians, and trained political and social leaders was quite evident.

Both the policy to amalgamate Korea and Japan into a single body (*naisen ittai*) and to bring about reconciliation between Koreans and the Japanese (*naisen yūwa*), together with the policy for the Japanization of the Koreans (*kōminka*) failed to achieve their objectives. The Japanese slogan, "co-existence and co-prosperity (*kyōzon kyōei*)" was primarily for the economic enrichment of Japan. Korea remained a Japanese colony (*gaichi*), her people enjoyed no freedom or rights, and her farmers and laborers were exploited to fatten Japanese capitalists.

The Japanese in Korea, who constituted a distinctive, segregated minority group at the beginning of Japanese colonial rule, remained separated from the Koreans until the end of their domination over Korea. Although some of them attended Korean schools, only a few of them had friends who were Koreans. Very few Koreans, including students, had any Japanese friends despite the fact that in 1944 some 10.8 per cent of the students in the schools primarily for the Japanese, were Koreans. Social contacts between the Koreans and the Japanese were infrequent, or almost nonexistent.

Although the Japanese found Koreans to be "acceptable and sociable" toward the end of the colonial period, according to a publication of the Government-General of Korea published in 1940, *Shisei 30-nen-shi* (*History of 30-Years' Administration*), as of December 1937 there were only 664 Japanese who married Korean women, and only 474 Koreans who were married to Japanese women. There were about 630,000 Japanese in Korea in that year. The number of Koreans who were adopted into Japanese families through marriage increased from 21 in 1928, to 48, while the Japanese who were adopted into Korean families through marriage grew from two in 1928 to 22 by 1937. This situation remained virtually unchanged until the end of the Japanese colonial period. The Koreans and the Japanese were neither united, nor amalgamated.

According to a Japanese source, as of December 1943, only 5,677,448, or 23.2 per cent of the Korean population (24.5 million) comprehended the Japanese language. Of this, 4,149,923 were male, and 1,527,525 were female. Only 12.3 per cent of the total number of Koreans who comprehended Japanese spoke Japanese "without difficulties." Despite Japanese repression in Korea and Japanese efforts to replace the Korean language with the Japanese language, at the end of the Japanese colonial rule, more than 50 per cent of the adult population of Korea could read Korean script.

8. The Liberation and Reconstruction
Movements at Home and Abroad

The dominant impulse in Korea under Japanese rule was fear—pervasive, oppressing, and strangling fear of extinction. Some Koreans believed that the restoration of Korean independence was out of the realm of possibility for the time being and therefore they advocated a "more perfect union" between Korea and Japan. However, the majority refused to accept Japanese colonial rule, and the human instinct for survival led them to struggle against their oppressors.

Despite extremely unfavorable circumstances, the Koreans at home and abroad carried out their struggles to liberate their country as they made tenacious efforts to bring about the regeneration of the people and the reconstruction of their society. At the same time, they fought not only to preserve their racial and cultural heritage, but also to bring about cultural and social progress. For these purposes, they formed various societies and launched a struggle against oppressive alien rule.

The Struggle of the Early Period

Many freedom fighters formed underground organizations immediately after August 1910; among these were the Council of Righteous Soldiers for Independence, the Society for the Restoration of the Korean Nation, and the League for the Restoration of National Authority. The New People's Society, which had been organized by An Ch'ang-ho before his flight to the United States, continued its fight for freedom as branches of Syngman Rhee's United States based Korean National Association (*Kungminhoe*) emerged in Korea. 261

Meanwhile, many women, educated at mission and other private schools, joined the national liberation movement. In 1913, Hwang Shin-dŏk (1898–1933) and others established a woman's association called The Pine and Bamboo Society and promoted patriotism among women.

Some of these societies in Korea advocated the violent overthrow of Japanese colonial rule, and within a few months after August 1910, thousands of Korean insurgents were killed. On December 11, some 700 Koreans, among whom were 123 Christian leaders, were arrested for their alleged plot to assassinate Governor-General Terauchi. Between 1910 and 1913, some two thousand armed clashes occurred throughout Korea between Korean insurgents and Japanese troops, but the Koreans were unable to change the course of history.

Tens of thousands of Koreans left their fatherland, either refusing to submit to humiliating Japanese rule, or to fight for Korea's liberation, and they formed various organizations in Siberia, Manchuria, China, Japan, and the United States. Those Koreans who remained at home suffered greatly as more and more of them were imprisoned on various charges, including anti-Japanese activities. The resentment of the people grew steadily and their anger mounted, but they were unable to reverse the tide of Japanese oppression and exploitation and therefore they suffered.

The March First Movement

In late 1918, some Koreans came to know of President Woodrow Wilson's "Fourteen Points," and the gospel of self-determination inspired them to take steps to regain the independence of Korea, believing that militarism was now a thing of the past, that the age of reason and peace had arrived, and that Korea had the right to reclaim her independence.

Preparations.   At least four separate groups of Koreans discussed the ways to achieve independence in late 1918. They were the Ch'ŏndogyo group, led by Son Pyŏng-hŭi, O Se-ch'ang, Kwŏn Tong-jin, and Ch'oe Rin, the Presbyterians in the north led by Yi Sŭng-hun, the Methodists in Seoul, and the Chung-ang High School group which included Kim Sŏng-su, Song Chin-u, and Hyŏn Sang-yun. In early 1919, all of them learned that the Korean Nationalists abroad were submitting their petition to the Paris peace conference for Korean independence and that the Korean students in Tokyo were planning to take an action in behalf of Korean independence on February 8. In such a situation they felt that it was their obligation to act.

The Ch'ŏndogyo group failed to solicit the participation of old government officials, but with the help of Ch'oe Nam-sŏn and Song Chin-u it pursuaded toward the end of February Christians and Buddhists to take a united action. At this juncture, the ex-emperor Kojong died. The official announcement, which recorded the date of death as February 22, gave no cause of his death, thus creating rumors. One said that he was poisoned, and another said that he committed suicide. The furneral was scheduled to be held on March 3, and tens of thousands of mourners were expected to be in Seoul, as sadness engulfed the people. The leaders of the movement decided to take a solemn action on March 1.

After settling their differences, the leaders asked Ch'oe Nam-sŏn to write the declaration of independence, and when he finished writing it, Han Yong-un, a Buddhist monk, added at its end three covenants which emphasized the non-violent principles of the movement. (See Appendix D) They selected thirty-three "national representatives" to sign the declaration of independence and a petition to be sent to the U.S. government, the Japanese government, and the Paris peace conference. Among the signers were 16 Christians, 15 Ch'ŏndogyo leaders, and two Buddhists. Various sources indicate that the leaders did not plan for a mass uprising. It was to be a dignified, non-violent action taken by a small group of national representatives, expressing the desires of the Koreans to be free from Japanese rule in accordance with the principle of self-determination. They printed thousands of copies of the declaration and shipped them to various localities. Originally, they plan to read the declaration at Pagoda Park at 2:00 p.m., on March 1, but fearing that some disturbances might interfere they selected a restaurant located near the park to do so at the February 28th meeting of the signers of the declaration. Only 29 of 33 signers attended the meeting.

The Movement.   In the morning of March 1, the citizens of Seoul read copies of a manifesto issued by a radical (separate) group named National Congress (*Kungmin Taehoe*) posted at various points in Seoul. Asserting that Kojong has been assassinated, the manifesto urged the Koreans to avenge his death as well as that of Queen Min, who was killed by the Japanese in 1895, inflaming the people and changing the character of the March First Movement.

Thousands of people, including students, who congregated at Pagoda Park to hear the declaration of independence read, waited until 2:00 p.m. When no leaders arrived, a school teacher from Haeju who had a copy of the printed declaration went up on the pavilion and read it. When he had finished, he shouted "Long Live Korea! Long Live Korean Independence!" The crowd joined him. After that they marched into the Chongno Street, singing the *Song of Patriotism* and waving the Korean national flag, both of which had been banned by the Japanese. Tens of thousands of citizens of Seoul and mourners from local areas participated in the demonstration for Korea's liberation and independence.

Similar events took place throughout the country. The cry "Long Live Korean Independence!" was heard everywhere. Some half million (a source said over 2 million) Koreans from all walks of life, young and old and men and women participated in the demonstrations throughout the months of March,

April, and May. Although some violent incidents, either provoked by the Japanese, or instigated by the National Congress, did occur at some places, most demonstrators expressed their long-cherished desires for freedom and national independence in a peaceful manner. It was neither an "uprising," nor a "rebellion" as the Japanese had alleged.

Aftermath.   The Japanese response to the independence movement was immediate and brutal. They arrested and imprisoned the signer of the Declaration of Independence, as well as thousands of others who took part in the movement. They outlawed all assemblies and street demonstrations, restricted traffic, closed markets, searched houses, schools, and even churches for men and documents.

Actions taken by the Japanese produced heavy casualties; some 1,200 Koreans were killed and 16,000 were wounded. A total of 715 houses were burned down, and 447 church buildings and many Korean schools were destroyed. In one area in Suwŏn, Kyŏnggi Province, alone, the Japanese burned down 270 houses and killed over 40 Koreans by locking them in a church and then setting fire to the building. Over 19,500 Koreans were arrested and of these 2,656 were given prison terms. A sixteen-year-old girl student named Yu Kwan-sun was arrested, tortured, and died in prison. Six gendarmes, two policemen, and one Japanese were killed, and about 130 Japanese were wounded during the entire period of the March First Movement.

The March First Movement did not restore Korean independence, but it made the whole world know that the Koreans were not happy under Japanese rule and that they desired freedom and independence. It along with what the Japanese did to suppress it, discredited the Japanese in the eyes of the Western leaders. It even moved conservative Confucianists, such as Kim Yun-shik and Yi Yong-ik, ex-high-ranking officials who were given ranks of nobility at the time of annexation, to demand at the end of March the independence of Korea "in accordance with the wish of heaven." Other Confucianists did likewise, sending their petition to the Paris peace conference. At the same time, it forced the Japanese to change their policy toward Korea. Meanwhile, many nationalists fled to China to continue their struggles for Korea's freedom.

New Nationalist and Reform Movements after 1919

The March First Movement did not achieve its immediate objective, but it did succeed in making Koreans aware that if they were to survive, maintain their heritage, and improve their conditions, they must adopt different methods of doing so. As a result, there developed a "New Life" movement which was sponsored by various societies. These groups strove to lay a new foundation for social and cultural progress and to improve the people's economic circumstances. Others who refused to suffer degradation and humiliation under the Japanese left their homeland in search of peace and a new life elsewhere.

Now and then, Korean nationalism was expressed in violence against the Japanese. For example, when Saitō Makoto arrived in Seoul in September 1919, as a new Governor-General of Korea, a Korean youth attempted to assassinate him at the Seoul railway station. However, the majority of the Nationalists devoted their energies to fostering the people's strength and capabilities.

The Self-Strengthening Movement.   Yi Kwang-su, a young Nationalist, said in an article published in a journal named *Kaebyōk* (*The Dawn*) in 1921 that:

Independence cannot be attained by outside help or by pure luck. . . . Even if the happiness of the Korean people should depend solely upon political independence, this will not be mailed in a package either by the League of Nations or by the disarmament conference. . . . Only when the Korean people, individually or as a nation, have the ability to carry out a civilized life, will they be able to decide whether they should be assimilated, be autonomous, become independent, or carry out a movement of great historical significance.

Therefore, he insisted that the Korean people must regenerate themselves in order to bring about the strengthening of the people and economic and social progress.

Although some Nationalists, particularly those in *Ch'ŏndogyo,* as well as some Socialists, advocated violent anti-Japanese movements, such Nationalists as Chang Tŏk-su (1894–1955), Cho Man-shik (1882–?), Kim Sŏng-su (1891–1955), and Song Chin-u (1889–1945), preached *minjokchuŭi,* or "racialism," and a nonviolent resistance (nonreconciliation) movement. At the same time, they advocated self-regeneration, the self-strengthening movement, as well as unity and a spirit of cooperation, in order to safeguard the interests of the people.

In general, the Nationalists endeavored to foster industrious habits and thriftiness, education and the elimination of illiteracy, and the spirit of self-reliance and self-reconstruction. They firmly believed that the economic life of the people must be improved and social reform must be carried out if the Koreans were to gain self-respect first, and ultimately gain freedom and rights.

Many new Nationalist organizations emerged. Among them were the Korean People's Fraternal Society founded in 1921, the Self-Production Society and the Korean Women's Association for the Use of Native Products founded in 1922, the Korean Association for the Encouragement of Production of Goods founded in 1923, and the Korean Studies Society and the Society for the Study of the Korean Situation founded in 1925. Since the Japanese prohibited the use of historic names for Korea, such as Han-guk or Taehan, all Korean associations and organizations used Chosŏn for Korea in their organizational names.

In an editorial on November 13, 1922, the *Tong-a Ilbo*, a leading Nationalist paper both praised Mahatma Gandhi's strategy, and pointed out the various weaknesses of the Korean economy. It concluded that "our only means of survival is to restrict foreign commodities and encourage the use of native products." The Self-Production Society advocated that (1) Koreans must be united and use only commodities produced by Koreans, (2) they must produce all necessary goods themselves, and (3) they must avoid mortgaging or selling their farmlands. Meanwhile, the Korean branches of *Hŭngsadan* (The Corps for the Advancement of Individuals) which was founded in the United States, urged the Koreans to nurture their inner strength and capabilities, industriousness and thrifty habits, and the spirit of cooperation, so as to bring about self-regeneration and the self-reconstruction of the society and economy. Yi Kwang-su, who returned from Shanghai in 1921, published a book in 1923, entitled *Korea's Present and Future*, which imbued many Korean students with a strong national consciousness.

The Rise of the Women's Movement.   Thousands of women and young girl students participated in the March First Movement. The tragic case of Yu Kwan-sun has been mentioned earlier. In the wake of the March First Movement, some 471 women and young girls were arrested, and many were imprisoned. The rise of the women's movement since the end of the 19th century has contributed significantly to the social transformation of Korea.

Na Hye-sŏk (1896–1946), who studied in Tokyo, initiated the women's nationalist and reform movements. In 1914, after graduating from Chinmyŏng Girls' School, she went to Tokyo to study painting. But she became highly motivated by patriotism and social consciousness, and began advocating the liberation of women from feudal bondage. As a young student, she published an article entitled "Ideal Woman" in the December 1914 issue of *Hakchi-gwang* (*The Light of Learnings*), a magazine published by Korean students in Japan. In it, she attacked the traditional concept of "good girl" or "good women," claiming that these concepts enslaved women under male domination. She insisted:

We too know how to make judgments in matters concerning life. . . . We too know what beauty is, what dirty things are. . . . We too think. . . . We wish to smile and express the true beauty of women.

Na Hye-sok returned to Korea in 1918 and participated in the preparation for the March First Movement in cooperation with other women of Chinmyŏng Girls' School. After 1919, she taught at girls' schools and planted the seeds of patriotism and of the woman's social consciousness in the hearts of young girl students.

After drinking a bitter cup in March 1919, O Hyŏn-ju and others established a women's society named the Hyŏlsŏng Puinhoe (Devoted Women's Society) in April. Another women's society named the Great Korean Patriotic Women's Association emerged shortly thereafter. These two organizations merged and became the Korean Patriotic Women's Association. In October, the Association was reorganized under the leadership of Kim Maria (1892–1945) and Hwang Shin-dŏk (1898–1983). Kim Maria was a graduate of Chŏngshin Girls' School who went to Tokyo to study in 1914. She returned to Korea in February 1919, and took an active part in preparing for the March First Movement in association with her former classmates. She was imprisoned until August, but after being released from prison she continued her nationalistic activities until she was again imprisoned in November. After being paroled in May 1920 because of her poor health, she fled to Shanghai in 1921, and joined other Nationalists there. Another organization named the Korean Women's Association for the Use of Native Products emerged in 1922, and promoted the resistance movement.

Many journals for women appeared after 1919, among them were *The New Women, The Modern Women*, and *The Women's World*. These and many other journals contributed much, not only to the promotion of patriotism, but also to the development of social and self-consciousness, and the awareness among women of the need for greater education and cultural development.

The Hyŏngp'yŏng Movement.   When the new Nationalist and Socialist groups were actively promoting their movements, Yi Hak-ch'an, a butcher in Chinju, South Kyŏngsang Province, formed the *Hyŏngp'yŏngsa* (The Society for Equality) and launched the equality movement in April 1923. Its aim was to liberate Korean social outcasts (mostly butchers), enabling them to enjoy the same social status as other Koreans. It published a journal called *Segwang,* and formed regional branches as well as women's and student groups. In 1925, the Society claimed a membership of over 400,000.

Much like other Korean organizations, the Society for Equality was affected by internal disunity and sectionalism when it was split into the Seoul and the Chinju factions. To make matters worse, the Communists infiltrated the Society, politicizing it. In the end, the movement collapsed.

The Rise of the Socialist Movement

After the March First Movement an increasing number of Koreans became attracted to Socialism, and the Far Eastern Bureau of the Comintern, which was established in Shanghai in 1919, trained Koreans, as well as Chinese and Japanese, and sent those who were indoctrinated with Socialism back to their countries. Several Korean students who studied in Japan before and after 1919 were influenced by Socialism.

The Rise of the Leftist Societies.   Following the emergence in November 1919 of the first leftist society—the League of Great Unity—whose objective was "the full implementation of socialism" in Korea, another socialist society named the Mutual Aid Society of Korean Laborers was established by Ch'a Kŭm-bong in April 1920. They were followed by the appearance of another leftist society named the New People's League which emerged in March 1921. It became the Fraternal Society of the Proletariat shortly thereafter, and with the emergence of the All Korea Youth League in March 1922, the leftist movement became more active. At the same time, many leftists infiltrated the right wing Nationalist organizations.

Yi Tong-hwi, the founder of the People's Socialist Party in 1918 at Khabarovsk in Siberia, went to Shanghai, and in May 1920, the Shanghai branch of his party sent agents into Korea to organize the Korean branch of his party. In competition with Yi's group, the Korean Communists in the Soviet Union, who moved their party from Khabarovsk to Irkutsk in early summer of 1920, dispatched Kim Chae-bong and others to Korea in April 1923, and organized the New Thought Research Society in Seoul in July of that year. Hong Myŏng-hŭi was a key member of this society which quickly established branches in various cities. It was at this juncture that Cho Pong-am (1898-1959), a Korean Communist, arrived in Seoul from China as a Comintern agent. The name of the New Thought Research Society was changed to the Tuesday Society on Tuesday, November 19, 1924, in commemoration of Marx's birthday.

Meanwhile, Kim Yak-san, an agent of the Korean Communists in Japan who had formed the North Star Society, arrived in Korea and organized the North Wind Society in Seoul in 1924. Soon after that, the North Wind Society established subordinate groups such as the Saturday Society, the Builders' Society, and the New Rising Youth League. Thus in 1924, three Communist factions—the Tuesday Society of the Korean Communist Party at Irkutsk, the Seoul branch of the Korean Communists in Shanghai, and the North Wind Society of the North Star Society of the Korean Communists in Japan—were competing against one another for the leadership of the leftist movement in Korea while combating both the Korean Nationalists and the Japanese. Another Communist faction, the Marxist-Leninist (the M-L faction), emerged in 1924.

The police broke up the leftist organizations as fast as they were organized while the unending ideological conflicts and power struggle among the leftists also weakened their effectiveness. After the December Thesis of the Comintern was issued in 1924, the intellectualism of the Communist movement in Korea was rejected, and a worker-farmer oriented movement was launched.

In April 1925, Cho Pong-am, Pak Hŏn-yŏng and others formed the Korean Communist Party in Seoul and organized the Korean Communist Youth Association which claimed a membership of 32,000 in 224 branches. At the

Girl students in the March 1 Movement, 1919.

Japanese execution of demonstrators in the March 1 Movement, 1919.

A demonstration on March 1, 1919 at the Poshin-gak, Seoul.

Officials of the Provisional Government of Korea around 1930.

A delegation to the first Congress of the Korean Independence League which met in Philadelphia, marches through Philadelphia's Independence Square.

A poster of the *Itti v narod* Movement sponsored by the Tong-a Ilbo Press.

270

Troops of the Korean Liberation Army in China.

The Koreans celebrating the liberation and welcoming American troops. 271

January 1946 anti-trusteeship demonstration of the people.

Inauguration ceremony for the government of the Republic of Korea.

South Korean women mourn for their relatives massacred by the North Korean aggressors.

North Korean aggressors in Seoul with a Russian tank during the Korean War.

Professors joined in anti-government demonstration of the students on April 25, 1960.

President Rhee Syngman (1875–1965).

President Park Chung-hee (1917–79).

A tank unit of the May 16th Military Revolution moves in.

273

Traditional ceramic art in modern form created by O Ch'ŏn-hak.

"An Archeress," a modern statue by Yun Hyo-jung.

"Autumn," a modern painting of a rural scene by Kim Ki-ch'ang.

"Farm Hut," a modern landscape painting by Kim Hwa-gyŏng.

Traditional "Monk's Dance."

Yi Sŏn-ok's modern form of traditional dance.

A mosaic of tradition and modernity.

Korean-made cars exported to all corners of the world.

New Community Movement and modernization of agriculture.

same time, they sent 21 students to the Communist University of the Toilers of the East in the Soviet Union.

The first Communist Party formed in Korea collapsed following the Shinŭiju Incident of November 1925. Two members of the party, carrying a letter from Pak Hŏn-yŏng to Yŏ Un-hyŏng (1885–1947) in Shanghai, became involved in a fight with a Japanese policeman and a lawyer in Shinŭiju, a Korean city on the Yalu River. The incident led to the arrest of many key members of the Party in Seoul. A new Communist Party was formed in early December, but it was quickly demolished by the police. Another one, which emerged under the leadership of Kim Tan-ya and Hŏ Chŏng-suk in late December 1925, also collapsed following the June 10th Incident of 1926, when some 100 Communists were arrested.

An increasing number of Korean women, influenced by Socialism, pursued more immediate objectives, and advocated more direct action against the Japanese. Among their organizations were: the Society for the Encouragement of Education for Korean Women founded in 1920 by Na Hye-sŏk and others who studied in Japan; the Korean Women's Sorority Society founded in 1924 by Hŏ Chŏng-suk; the March Society founded in 1925 by Hwang Shin-dŏk and her associates; the Korean Girls' League for the Liberation of Women and the Proletarian Women's League founded by Kim Kyŏng-ok in 1926 (she founded both organizations), and the Seoul Young Women's League founded in 1926 by Hŏ Chŏng-suk and her associates. Na Hye-sŏk, who fled to Manchuria with her husband, wrote a poem entitled "Nora" and published it in 1925. She said in part:

> *I was a doll.*
> *A doll who was a daughter of my father;*
> *A doll who was wife of my husband.*
> *I was a doll which was their playmate.*

> *Let Nora go.*
> *Let me go.*
> *Break down the walls,*
> *Open the doors,*
> *And let Nora go*
> *Into a free world.*
>
>   *   *   *
>
> *O, my beloved young girls,*
> *Be awakened and follow me.*
> *Rise up and show your strength.*
> *The light of the new day shines.*

In August 1925, Yi Hyŏn-gyŏng and other Socialist women who returned from Tokyo launched a movement, in cooperation with Hwang Shin-dŏk, to establish a united front of rightist and leftist women. As a result, the Central Young Women's League emerged, but the women leaders failed to achieve a unity of goals and methods.

The June Tenth Incident.   Both the Nationalists and Socialists, openly or secretly, carried out activities against the Japanese as well as against pro-Japanese Korean organizations. As of 1925, there were some 180 politically oriented societies, 128 labor organizations, 44 youth societies, 300 religious youth societies, and various other organizations which advocated political, economic, and social reforms. However, the Japanese Peace Preservation Law of May 4, 1925, and the ordinance of April 1926, of the Government-General, severely handicapped Korean organized movements whatever their nature. But,undaunted, the Koreans, including students of both sexes, continued their struggle against the Japanese.

One of the most spectacular anti-Japanese actions taken by the Koreans after March 1919 was that of June 10, 1926, which came to be known as the "Second March First Movement." Sunjong, the last Korean emperor, died on April 25, and his funeral was to take place on June 10th, in Seoul. Tens of thousands of Koreans poured into the city to witness the funeral.

Fearful of an uprising, the Japanese took various precautionary measures, but the Socialists, under the leadership of Kim Tar-yŏng of the Tuesday Society, in collaboration with a *Ch'ŏndogyo* faction, brought about a mass demonstration on June 10. The outlawed Korean national flag along with the Red flag waved in the hot summer air, while the people shouted "Long Live Korea!," or "The Price of Freedom is Blood," or "Drive Out the Enemy!" Thousands of students, including girls, participated in the demonstration. In the wake of the incident, many, including Kwŏn Tong-jin of *Ch'ŏndogyo* and some 100 Communist Party members, were arrested and imprisoned. But the incident once again demonstrated that the spirit of independence was very much alive in Korea.

The United Front of the Nationalists and Socialists

Facing many difficulties in promoting their resistance movements, both the Nationalists and Socialists felt the need for a united movement against Japanese colonialism. However, it was the members of the North Star Society, a socialist organization of the Koreans in Japan, who returned to Korea and took the initiative to form a united front of all anti-Japanese people. One of them, Kim Sam-gyu, issued the so-called *"Chŏng-uhoe* Declaration" of November 15, 1926, which stated that Korea's nationalist movement of the past was ineffective because of the factionalism created by ambitious status seekers. "The future of our movement," it stated, "depends largely on the unity and mass awareness" of the revolutionaries. At the same time, it pointed out that the "social movement must depart from a narrow economic struggle" and adopt "a politically oriented struggle which must embody class and mass consciousness." Kim advocated "a change in direction" as well as the formation of a united front with the Nationalists. Neither the Tuesday Society, nor other Socialist groups agreed with Kim because his ideas contained certain "revisionist" elements and demonstrated an "inclination toward the right." But "for the sake of unity," they reluctantly supported this movement.

As a result, the *Shin-ganhoe* (The New Shoot Society), emerged on February 15, 1927, as a united body of the Nationalists and Socialists. Its leaders were Yi Sang-jae, An Chae-hong, Shin Sŏg-u, and Kwŏn Tong-jin on the right, and Hong Myŏng-hŭi on the left. It quickly established some 140 local chapters, and its membership grew rapidly to 22,000 within a few months. Many radical leftists refused to join the Society, but such leading Socialists as Hŏ Hŏn joined it in the hope of enhancing the mass movement of workers and peasants under the banner of a united front and of eventually wresting the leadership of the Society from the rightists.

The basic objective of the Society was to implement practical plans for the ultimate solution of Korea's political and economic problems by rejecting the ideology of compromise and opportunism. Its platform stated that it would promote political and social awakening among the people and unify all anti-Japanese elements in Korea.

In the spring of 1927, the Society dispatched Ch'oe Rin, Hŏ Hŏn, and others to anti-imperialism and anti-colonialism conferences, held at Brussels and Cologne, where they presented the Korean people's grievances and their desire for freedom from Japan.

Many radical Socialists criticized the aims and tactics of the *Shin-ganhoe* as too limited and mild. The Tokyo branch of the *Shin-ganhoe,* for example, at a meeting in December 1927, drew up a proposal calling for the amendment of the platform and the tactics of the Society, resulting in the adoption of a new platform which reflected a more radical ideology. It called for the exemption of school fees for children of poor families, and it demanded the withdrawal of Japanese establishments, such as the Oriental Development Company, from Korea. It opposed the Japanese emigration policy and advocated the abolition of all laws, ordinances, and regulations which deprived the Koreans of freedom of speech, press, and assembly. It called for an end to all discriminatory Japanese policies in Korea and complete freedom of political action for the Koreans.

Meanwhile, women leaders, realizing that division within the women's movement was undesirable because it made the movement ineffective, sought a solution for the problem which they faced. In late May 1927, Kim Hwal-lan, representing the Nationalists, and Pak Wŏn-hŭi, representing the Socialists, met with some 80 other representatives, and resolved to form a united body of all women's organizations in Korea. A united body of all women's organization named the *Kŭnuhoe* (The Society of the Friends of the Rose of Sharon) emerged in March 1928, as a sister organization of the *Shin-ganhoe*. Its branches were established in many places and there began a more aggressive women's movement, preaching the establishment of the equality of the sexes, the freedom of marriage, property rights for women, and the elimination of old customs and ethics which were disadvantageous to them. Unfortunately, however, when the Society became radicalized, it became a "society of bickering leftist women" as almost all right wing women Nationalists withdrew.

Although the *Shin-ganhoe* was radicalized, the Socialists constantly charged that the Society was an organization of petty bourgeoisie which undermined the revolutionary cause. The December Thesis of 1928 of the Comintern provided the Socialists with more effective tools to destroy the Society. It instructed that in "all their work and action the Communists of Korea must strictly preserve the full independence of the revolutionary labor movement" and it warned of the danger of "a fusion of the Communist movement with the bourgeois-revolutionary movement." The alliance with the Nationalists, it said, may be permissible "if the action of the bourgeois. . . can be utilized for the development of a mass movement, and if such agreement will in no way restrict the freedom of the Communist party."

The collapse of the *Shin-ganhoe* was inevitable. The growing influence of the Communists within the Society led more Nationalists to withdraw from it while police suppression also grew. After the Red Flag Incident of November 1929, involving many students under the instigation of Hŏ Hŏn, the police banned meetings of the *Shin-ganhoe* and arrested its 44 leading members, including Hŏ himself, in early 1930. The arrest and imprisonment of radical leaders allowed the rightists to gain control of the Society, but it could not survive long. While the Japanese increased their surveillance with regard to the activities of the Society, the Communists insisted that it no longer served the interests of the working class, and advocated its dissolution. Many local chapters of the Society in the southern provinces had already been abolished by 1930.

Cho Man-shik, a Christian Nationalist, attempted along with others to preserve the *Shin-ganhoe* movement by purging all radical elements from the Society, believing that without it the Korean Nationalist movement could not be effective. But they were too late. Acting under the Comintern directive, the Communists adopted a resolution to dissolve the *Shin-ganhoe* while many Nationalists had already left. In May 1931, both *Shin-ganhoe* and the *Kŭnuhoe* were abolished, and no organized Nationalist movements reemerged after that. Many Nationalists were either growing older and discouraged, or were in prison as Japanese control became ever tighter after September 1931.

The New Communist Movement.   A new Communist Party was formed in February 1928, but in April the police arrested many of its members, including

Pak Hŏn-yŏng. Another Korean Communist Party was formed by Ch'a Kŭmbong shortly thereafter and gained membership in the Comintern in September. The new Communist Party accepted the December Thesis of the Comintern of 1928, which pointed out the past mistakes of the Korean Communists, and instructed the Korean Communists to incite workers and peasants to develop class consciousness and to launch the struggle against the "Nationalist reformist bourgeoisie." However, it too collapsed in early 1929.

The graduates of the Communist University of the Toilers of the East attempted in late 1929 and early 1930 to re-establish the Korean Communist Party. They formed the Korean Communist Re-establishment Preparation Society in Manchuria and dispatched Kim Tan-ya and others to Korea in the summer of 1929, but their purpose was not achieved. They did, however, establish the Leftist Labor Union National Council Preparation Society in Hamhŭng, South Hamgyŏng Province, in March 1931, as well as the Korean Communist Party Consultant Council in April.

After the arrest of Pak Hŏn-yŏng, many Korean Communists left Korea for Manchuria or China, and those who remained resorted to individual efforts to influence the students, frequently taking isolated terroristic actions.

The Peasant and Labor Movement.   Korean workers and peasants who were influenced by the leftist ideologies brought about many violent labor and farm disputes and strikes in the 1920s. Some outstanding examples were those of the Hamhŭng Ōya Printing Company of 1927, the Yŏnghŭng Mining Company, the Shinhŭng Mining Company, and the Wŏnsan Munp'yŏng-ri Petroleum Company of 1928. A dock workers' strike in Wŏnsan directed by the Wŏnsan Federation of Labor Unions from January to April 1929, involving 32 local chapters and 1,600 workers, was a landmark in the Korean labor movement. There were 6,000 labor disputes in 1927, and 5,000 in 1929. The Pusan Textile Company case of 1930, the Hamhŭng Federation of Labor Unions case of 1934, and the 1936 case involving the Korean Federation of Labor Unions were among the most celebrated labor strikes of Korean workers.

Korean peasants were also mobilized by the leftists to carry out their struggle against Korean as well as Japanese landlords, particularly against large landowning Japanese companies. They fought losing battles, but such cases as the peasant struggle of 1929 in Kowŏn against the Oriental Overseas Company, the peasant dispute against the Land Development Company in Taegu, in which some 6,500 tenants were involved, the Fuji Farm case, and the Tanch'ŏn Farmers' Incident of 1930, clearly reflected the peasant unrest in Korea. After 1931 all organized peasant and labor movements virtually ceased to exist because of the ever tightening Japanese control.

The Development of Nationalist Entrepreneurship

Because of the Company Law (promulgated in December 1910 becoming effective of January 1, 1911), which restricted the development of Korean commercial and industrial enterprises, only a handful of Korean financial institutions and manufacturing firms were established. Among them were the Kyŏngsŏng (Seoul) Fabric Company founded in 1911, the Bank of Kup'o (in 1915 it was renamed Kyŏngnam Bank, in Pusan) and the Bank of Taegu founded in 1912, the Paeksan Company (in 1918 it was renamed the Paeksan Trading Company) established by An Hŭi-je in Pusan in 1914, the Kaesŏng Electric Company founded by Kim Chŏng-ho in 1917, and the Honam Bank established in Kwangju in 1918, and the three firms established in 1919, namely the Taech'ang Trading Company of Paek Yun-su, the Tongyang Merchandising Company of Kim Yun-myŏn, and the Kyŏngsŏng (Seoul) Spinning and Weaving Company of the Kim clan of Koch'ang, North Chŏlla Province.

The influx of Japanese capital and entrepreneurs and the growing monopolistic tendencies of Japanese capitalism in Korea promoted the rise of "reactive nationalism" among Korean entrepreneurs. But it was not until the revision of the Company Law that the Koreans were able to establish companies with small assets and without Japanese on their managerial staff.

At a conference held in Seoul in 1920, and attended by Japanese capitalists from Japan, Manchuria, and Korea (some Koreans attended the conference), Governor-General Saitō Makoto emphasized the need to promote the Korean economy and what he called "Japanese-Korean joint enterprises (Nai-sen kyōdō jigyō)." In September 1921, Saitō announced a new policy to promote the Korean economy. The Company Law was revised in 1920, the Mountain and Forest Association was established in 1921 for the purpose of preserving forest lands, the Forest Experimental Station was established in 1922, and in 1924 the Marine Products Association was established. Between 1914 and 1927, 9,104 Japanese farm households were imported to Korea. Although the importation of Japanese farmers was suspended in 1927, in 1933, 695 more Japanese farm households were brought to Korea.

When the Company Law was revised, an editorial in the April 27, 1920 issue of the newly established Tong-a Ilbo (The Oriental Daily) stated:

We have suffered for ten years under the Company Law which created the greatest obstacle to our industrial and commercial development. Korea became a market for Japanese consumer goods. . . . Now all-Korean companies can be established without much difficulty.

Although the revised Company Law removed some obstacles to the development of Korean commercial and industrial enterprises, it did not bring about the establishment of these institutions by Koreans "without much difficulty." Shortage of capital, trained managerial staff, and skilled workers constituted the major problem for the Koreans. Moreover, the economic policy of the Government-General, notwithstanding Saitō's policy statement, only encouraged the development of such "desirable" industries as those which manufactured mats, lacquerware, wicker goods, straw goods, bamboo baskets, alcoholic beverages, animal oil, and other agricultural products.

The revised Company Law did, however, allow some Korean commercial and industrial firms to emerge. Some of the large firms that appeared after 1920 were:

The Pak Sŭng-jik and Company	(1921)
The Songdo Ceramic Company	(1922)
The T'aech'ang Textile and Silk Manufacturing Company	(1924)
The Songdo Rubber Goods Industrial Company	(1927)
The Kaesŏng Ginseng Industrial Company	(1936)

The Tong-a Rubber Industrial Company and the P'yŏng-an Rubber Industrial Company were the two largest Korean-established rubber footwear manufacturing firms, and the textile factory of the Kyŏngsŏng Spinning and Weaving Company at Yŏngdŭngp'o and the textile factory of the T'aech'ang Textile and Silk Manufacturing Company located at Sung-in-dong, Seoul were the two largest Korean-established textile factories. These Korean firms fought their patriotic battles against Japanese manufacturing firms of rubber and textile goods.

In July 1928, the Bank of Taegu and the Kyŏngnam Bank merged into the Joint Bank of Kyŏngsang. Unfortunately, the Kaesŏng Electric Company was taken over by a Japanese electric power company in 1936, and the Honam Bank in Kwangju was forced to be absorbed by another bank in 1942 because it refused to use the Japanese language, employ Japanese, and make loans to the Japanese or Japanese firms.

Among the Nationalist entrepreneurs were members of the Kim clan of Koch'ang, North Chŏlla Province. They were Kim Kyŏng-jung, who authored a 17-volume Korean history; his brother Kim Ki-jung, who had been an active member of the Korean Self-strengthening Society and the founder of a private school named Yŏngshin; Kim Sŏng-su, a graduate of Waseda University in Tokyo, who founded a private high school named Chung-ang for Korean boys in Seoul in 1915, published the *Tong-a Ilbo* in 1920, and established a private liberal arts college named Posŏng (now Koryŏ or Korea University) in 1922; and Kim Yŏn-su, Kim Sŏng-su's brother who after graduating from Tokyo Imperial University established an educational foundation in 1935, and became a key leader of the industrial corporation of the Kim clan. In 1932, Kim Sŏng-su took over financially troubled Posŏng College.

Brand names of the products of the Kims' textile firm bore distinctive nationalistic trade marks such as "The Star of Supreme Ultimate"—symbolism which was akin to that of the outlawed Korean national flag. The profit they made from their business was spent in promoting education and culture, providing scholarships to students, better jobs and wages to workers, and improving the economic and social conditions of their fellow Koreans.

The case of Pak Hŭng-shik is another example of successful Korean entrepreneurship. Born a poor man in Kangsŏ, South P'yŏng-an Province, Pak started a small business and accumulated capital. In 1926, he formed a stock company, and in 1934 he established a modern department store named Whashin, at the Chongno Square in the heart of Seoul. After some 300 chain stores of the Whashin had been established, it competed with Japanese-owned department stores, such as Mitsukoshi, Chōjiya, and Minakai. In 1939, Pak consolidated all of his enterprises into a gigantic Whashin Enterprise Corporation whose managers, staff, and sales personnel, as well as messengers were Koreans.

Among successful Korean entrepreneurs was Pang Ŭi-sŏk, who owned an auto-transportation company in South Hamgyŏng Province. Like other Nationalist entrepreneurs, An Hŭi-je, founder of the Paeksan Trading Company, established the Kimi Education Foundation in 1919, and founded several schools. A group of Nationalist businessmen in Kaesŏng took over a mission school named Hanyŏng School (founded in 1904), headed by Yun Ch'i-ho as its principal, and reorganized it into Songdo High School for Korean boys in 1916.

The steadily growing Korean population increased demand for consumer goods, and these and other Korean firms found lucrative markets both in Korea and Manchuria where a large number of Koreans resided.

KOREAN POPULATION, 1910–1944

Year	Population (1,000 persons)	Percentage Increase
1910	14,766 (13,310)	—
1915	15,958	8.0
1920	17,254	8.3
1925	19,020	10.4
1930	20,428	7.4
1935	22,208	8.6
1940	23,547	6.0
1944	25,133	6.7

KOREANS IN JAPAN, 1920–1943		KOREANS IN MANCHURIA/ CHINA, 1920–1942	
1920	41,000	1920	600,000
1930	419,000	1940	1,400,000
1940	1,199,000	1942	1,600,000
1943	1,832,000		

Sources: Kondō Kin-ichi, ed., *Taiheiyō sen ka no Chōsen oyobi Taiwan* (Korea and Taiwan under the Pacific War). *Chōsen Sōtokufu Kankei Jūyo Bunsho Senshū* I. Tokyo Chōsen Shiryō Kenkyū-kai, 1944, pp. 2-3, 75; Sang-chul Suh, *Growth and Structural Changes in the Korean Economy, 1910-1940.* Cambridge; Council on East Asian Studies, Harvard University, 1978, p. 40. The number given in parenthesis was taken from Kondo's work.

Regarding the managerial policy of Korean entrepreneurs, a Japanese publication, *Nenkan Chōsen (Korea Yearbook)*, of 1942, observed that a thorough employee training program was the most notable feature of Korean firms. The training programs of these Korean firms, the yearbook said, included the fostering of self-respect and pride among Korean workers under Korean management.

Although Korean entrepreneurship may have been quantitatively as well as qualitatively inferior to that of the Japanese, these nationalist enterprises laid the foundation for modern Korean society and economy while making positive contributions to Koreans' economic life during the colonial period.

The Korean Students and the Resistance Movement

Throughout the colonial period, Korean students of both sexes, who developed strong political and social consciousness, organized many societies of their own, and carried out their struggle against Japanese colonialism and imperialism. The student participation in the March First Movement of 1919 and in the June 10th Incident of 1926 has been discussed earlier in this chapter.

Student Organizations and Activities.   A new student movement began in Seoul with Chang Tŏk-su's formation of the Conference of Korean Students in May 1919. Its membership included college and high school students, and its aims were to promote patriotism, student unity, to encourage the use of native products, and to break down localism. In May 1921, the police forced the Conference with a membership of 23,000, to become a smaller association of Korean students, by eliminating the membership of high school students and restricting its activities. After failing to organize the General Federation of Korean Students in 1924, the Socialists formed the Mutual

Study Society in May 1925. Although it was forced by the police to disband only six months later, its founders remained active among students.

Although no open and organized student movement against the Japanese could flourish, students at various schools engaged in a variety of secret activities, such as reading banned books, discussing the problems of the Koreans, or studying ways and means to liberate Korea. Among many secret societies were the Society of Korean Students for the Study of Social Science, the Seoul Student League, the Anti-Imperialism Alliance, and the Pro-Gandhi Society. The Student Department of the *Shin-ganhoe* as well as the Korean YMCA and other Christian student groups were actively engaged in new social and cultural movements.

Korean students demanded, among other things, freedom of speech and assembly, better quality education, textbook revision, educational process without police interference, and a greater educational opportunity for Korean youth. They also demanded instruction in Korean history. They carried out many school strikes to achieve their objectives. Of some 386 school strikes carried out between 1920 and 1926, nearly 80 per cent were directed against pro-Japanese Korean teachers and poor educational facilities. There were 55 such strikes in 1926, and 72 in 1927.

In May 1927, some 400 students of Sookmyung Girls' High School in Seoul carried out a strike demanding the dismissal of certain Japanese administrators, improvement in the treatment of students, and employment of more Korean teachers. Students of Chinmyŏng Girls' High School in Seoul also carried out a strike in support of the girls of Sookmyung. The strikes lasted until August. While some of their conditions were met, a large number of students were either expelled or suspended from the schools.

Students belonging to various organizations, whether rightist or leftist, participated in oratorical contests and anti-illiteracy campaigns sponsored by political organizations as well as by newspapers such as the *Tong-a Ilbo* and the *Chosŏn Ilbo* (*The Korean Daily News*). The first large-scale touring oratorical group sponsored by the *Tong-a Ilbo* held its first meeting in Pusan in July 1929. The topics which the students most frequently discussed included the necessity of cooperation among the people and the urgent need for more education, cultural progress, and freedom of speech and press.

Meanwhile, many Korean students in colleges and universities in Japan returned to Korea during their summer vacation and participated in various activities, including the campaign against illiteracy. They took advantage of every possible opportunity to contribute to the development of national and social consciousness. When the *Chosŏn Ilbo* sponsored a summer vacation school project in 1929, with the slogan "Knowledge is strength—We must learn in order to survive," hundreds of students volunteered their services as teachers in villages and hamlets. When the *Tong-a Ilbo* launched a summer school project the *Itti v narod* ("Go Among the People") movement in

1931, over 400 returning students along with others in Korea, with certain political aspirations, took part in the anti-illiteracy campaign. Until these movements were stopped by the police in 1934, some 5,750 students participated in the summer projects, which were held at 1,321 places and were attended by some 46,221 men and 35,964 women.

The Kwangju Student Movement.   The most spectacular nationwide anti-Japanese student movement occurred in the winter of 1929–1930, as an aftermath of the Kwangju Incident of October–November 1929, in which Korean students in that city and its neighboring towns were involved in bloody fights with Japanese students.

There were three secondary schools for Korean students in Kwangju, the capital of South Chŏlla Province. They were Kwangju High Common School, Kwangju Agricultural School, and Kwangju Normal School. All were public schools and had inferior teachers and facilities as compared to those of Japanese schools. Kwangju High Common School had been established as a private school in 1920 by Korean Nationalists, but in 1923 the Japanese converted it into a public institution. With this change, various grievances grew among its students against the restrictions on freedom of speech, assembly, and instruction, and a strike occurred in that school in 1923.

Following the "first struggle" in 1923, leftist influence permeated the students when the Society for Awakened Progress in 1925 and the Reading Club in 1926 were established at the three Korean schools in Kwangju. In 1927 and 1928, several student strikes were carried out in that city. One of the strikers' demands was for "decent treatment of Korean students by the Japanese instructors." The Korean students also resented Japanese students who called them "barbarians," and Japanese male students who mistreated Korean female students led to bloody fights in late October and early November 1929.

News of the fighting between Korean and Japanese students in Kwangju and its vicinity incited Korean students elsewhere, and the arrest of students involved in the incident provoked other riots throughout the country. The nationwide anti-Japanese movement lasted for five months and involved some 54,000 Korean students from 194 schools. Most were college and high school students, but many primary school students also carried out strikes against the Japanese. Thousands of girl students in all parts of Korea became involved in the movement. Nearly all of the 310 students of Ewha Girls' High school, and some 2,000 students of girls' schools throughout Korea took part in anti-Japanese demonstrations and school strikes.

Korean students demanded the end of police interference in school activities, abolition of the colonial educational policy, release of students arrested in connection with the Kwangju Incident, release of all imprisoned students, and reinstatement of all students who had been expelled or suspended from

schools. The leaflets distributed by some students said "Down with Imperialism," "Long Live Proletarian Revolution,"—all indicated the growing leftist
influence among them.

In the wake of the Kwangju Student Movement, a large number of Korean
students were either imprisoned or expelled from their schools. Many valiant
student societies were either broken up or went underground. However,
anti-Japanese activities continued to disrupt campus activities and many
Korean teachers joined the students. In 1933 alone, some 550 high school
and college students were involved in anti-Japanese activities.

The Resistance Movement of Korean Christians

Christianity, particularly Protestantism, became from its inception an integral
part of the Korean enlightenment and progressive movement. The Christian
concepts of freedom, rights, and equality became a catalyst for Korean nationalism. Most foreign missionaries maintained political neutrality or aloof-
ness in the Korean struggle against the Japanese, but many of them, such as
Drs. Homer B. Hulbert, Frederick W. Schofield, and George S. McCune,
became deeply involved in Korea's fight for freedom.

Schools established by foreign mission boards produced a large number of
the leaders of the Nationalist and the social reform movement. The involvement of Christian ministers and elders in the March First Movement has
already been discussed in this chapter. After March 1919, more and more
foreign missionaries pursued the policy of noninvolvement in political affairs
in Korea, but the Korean Christians did not abandon their non-violent
struggle for freedom and rights, as well as for the restoration of the independence of their country. They made various efforts to let the world and Christians everywhere know that Korea still existed and that its people would not
give up their hopes and aspirations for national liberation.

Korean Christian Movement.   Many Korean Christian church groups participated in international conferences after 1919. Having a delegation at international gatherings became increasingly important to Korean Christian Nationalists. A delegation from Seoul participated in the 1921 World General
Conference of the YMCA, and many Nationalists, such as Shin Hŭng-u, Yu
Ŏk-kyŏm, and Yun Ch'i-ho participated in the subsequent international
conference of the YMCA as Korean delegates, and kept alive the concern of
Christians elsewhere for the Korean situation. With the establishment of the
Korean YWCA in 1922, contacts increased between Korean Christian women
and those in other countries.

Despite ever increasing difficulties, the Protestant churches in Korea continued to promote educational opportunities for Koreans, as well as to
support social reform movements. Mission schools were expanded and their

educational quality and facilities were improved, and graduates of these schools became leaders in all areas of Korean society, including the national reconstruction movement. One of many Christian women leaders was Kim Hwal-lan (Helen, 1899–1975). She was born as Kim Ki-dŏk, graduated from Ewha Girls' School, and took an active role in the March First Movement. She then studied at Columbia University and earned the degree of Doctor of Education. She returned to Korea in 1925, and later became President of Ewha Woman s College.

Whereas instruction in the Korean language at public and approved private schools was discouraged, those mission schools which either refused or failed to receive government accreditation continued to teach the Korean language until 1938. All churches conducted their services and published journals in the Korean language, thus preserving one of the most precious of the Korean cultural heritages.

Korean Christians and the Japanese Policy.　　The Japanese aggression in Manchuria, together with the Japanization drive initiated by Ugaki and accelerated by Minami, created many serious problems for Korean Christians. The Japanese increased their pressure on the Korean Christians to display patriotism toward the Japanese emperor and "encouraged" them to participate in Shintō ceremonies.

Japanese persecution of Korean Christians began in 1935. The most serious issue was the participation of the Christians in Shintō rituals. It became an explosive political issue in November 1935, when George S. McCune, President of Sungshil College, and Miss V. L. Snook, principal of Sung-ŭi Girls' High School in Pyongyang, as well as heads of other mission schools, refused to take part in the Shintō ritual at a conference of educators sponsored by the Japanese governor of South P'yŏng-an Province. In December, pastors of the Northern Presbyterian Church also refused to attend a Shintō ritual. Their rejection of what the Japanese called "a patriotic act" brought about retaliatory actions against Christian churches. A report of the Thought Section of the police complained that "most of the Christians had an inclination to loathe joining the patriotic movement." In some areas not only the Christians, but also the students of Christian schools totally abstained from participating in such events as seeing off the soldiers at railway stations. A police report said that the Christians "take anti-war, or anti-state attitudes. . . . Also there are many who refuse to bow in the direction of the imperial palace or worship at shrines."

The Shintō issue split Korean Christian churches. One group of Christians was willing to accept the Japanese political interpretation of Shintō rituals, but the majority refused to do so. George McCune was forced to leave Korea in 1936 as Korean Christian leaders engaged in bitter dispute over the Shintō issue.

While some Christian church leaders accepted the Japanese demand and participated in Shintō ceremonies, the conservative and fundamentalist Christians refused to bend. Rather than betrayed their convictions, they closed their churches and schools, including Sungshil College. The Japanese unleashed a wave of terrorism on them, but could not break the spirit of the Christian resistance movement, a fact exemplified by the case of the Sanjōnghyōn Presbyterian Church in Pyongyang under Pastor Chu Ki-ch'ōl and Elder Cho Man-shik.

Realizing that Christianity in Korea could not be destroyed altogether, the Japanese carried out the Japanization of Korean Christian churches. As a result, in October 1938, the Methodist Church of Korea became a division of the Japanese Methodist Church, certain portions of the Bible were removed and certain hymns were banned, services were conducted in Japanese, and various patriotic rituals were performed before religious services began.

However, those Christians, who refused to follow the new guidelines and directions of the Japanese or who refused to participate in Shintō ceremonies, launched a new movement in 1938 under the leadership of Pastor Yi Ki-sōn and Elder Pak Kwang-jung of the Presbyterian Church. This movement precipitated Japanese retaliation. A total of 2,000 pastors of various denominations were arrested and some 200 churches were closed down in 1938 and 1939. The number of Christians declined from 700,000 in 1938, to about 250,000 by 1941. By the middle of 1941, almost all foreign missionaries left Korea.

Those who were willing to cooperate with the Japanese, in order to save Christianity in Korea, formed the Korean Reform Christian Corps in March 1942, and in May 1943, the Presbyterian Church of Korea was reorganized into the Korean Presbyterian Church Corps of the Japanese Christian Church. In October 1943, the Korean Methodist Division also became a branch of the Japanese Christian Church.

Because the conservative and fundamentalist sects and the conservative members of the Methodist and Presbyterian churches resisted Japanese pressure to the end, all their churches and schools were abolished in 1944. The largest Methodist Church in Chōngdong in Seoul became the "Cultural Hall of the Imperial Way" in the fall of 1944. In August 1945, when all Protestant churches were amalgamated into the Korean Christian Corps of the Japanese Christian Church, and when the Seventh-Day Adventist Church refused to accede, the Japanese abolished it and confiscated its properties. Meanwhile, hundreds of Christian ministers, elders and laymen of all demonimations were imprisoned for various reasons, but the Japanese could not destory their Christian faith or their spirit of nationalism and resistance.

The New Cultural Movement

Darkness descended in Korea with the establishment of the Japanese colonial rule. In 1910, Yi Hae-jo wrote a novel entitled *The Liberty Bell,* but the liberty bell stood mute for the Koreans. The political and social environment in Korea was hostile and the cultural climate was bleak. All Korean newspapers, except the government operated one, were abolished, all books written by the Nationalists were outlawed, and many schools were closed. Such Nationalists as Syngman Rhee, Shin Ch'ae-ho, Chang Chi-yŏn, Pak Ŭn-shik and Kim Kyu-shik, fled from their country to the United States, China, or Vladivostok. However, those patriotic people who elected to remain in their fatherland carried out their struggle, even under the shadow of Japanese colonialism, not only to preserve their own cultural heritage, but also to promote a new Korean culture.

Poets, writers, dramatists, musicians, and other cultural leaders actively participated in the new cultural movement hoping to regenerate the people and revitalize the society. After drinking a bitter cup in the March First Movement of 1919, as the new cultural leaders with leftist orientation emerged, many disillusioned and discouraged leaders abandoned their nationalistic aspirations. Although they were not able to achieve their nationalistic objectives, their poems and songs, literary works, and magazines brought about a cultural transformation in Korea. In many ways, they sustained the hopes and aspirations of the Koreans who hungered for freedom and rights and the restoration of Korean independence during the dark period.

The Literary Movement for National Reconstruction. The angry young men of letters, who had initiated attacks against the feudalistic way of life, and advocated the concepts of liberty, equality, justice, and modernization before 1910, continued to play an important role in the literary movement for self-awakening and self-reconstruction after the Japanese annexation of Korea. In the early stage of the literary movement Ch'oe Nam-sŏn and Yi Kwang-su paid particular attention to the development of new ideas and ambitions among young Koreans, promoting what the Koreans called "instructional literature."

Yi Kwang-su collaborated with Ch'oe Nam-sŏn who published a new Korean-language magazine named *Sonyŏn* (*Children*), renamed later *Ch'ŏngch'un* (*The Youth*). Yi contributed many of his articles to the magazine, among which were: "My Credo," "The Creation of the New World," "Theory of Self-help," "Democracy," and "Problems Related to the Liberation of Women." It was Yi who laid the cornerstone of a new vernacular literature in such novels as *The Heartless* (*Mujŏng*, 1917) and *The Pioneer* (*Kaech'ŏkcha*, 1971–1918), and such short stories as *The Sorrows of the Youth* (*Sonyŏnŭi Piae*, 1917), *Wandering* (*Panghwang*, 1918), and *The Story of Yun Kwang-ho* (*Yun Kwang-ho*, 1918), which were published before his flight to Shanghai following the March First Movement of 1919. These works, and an article entitled "To My Young Friends" published in the July 1917 issue of *The Youth*, left deep imprints in the new literary movement.

After the March First Movement of 1919, many disillusioned writers gave up their political struggle against the Japanese and in the early 1920s promoted Romaticism and Naturalism as their literary vehicles. Influenced by European writers such as Emile Zola, Guy de Maupassant, and Oscar Wilde, they advanced "pure literature" or art for art's sake. The leaders of the pure literature movement, collectively known as the White Tide group, published such journals as *The Ruin* in 1920, and *White Tide* in 1922. Among the leading members of the group was Yŏm Sang-sŏp, author of short stories entitled *The Dark Night*, the *New Year's Eve Watch*, and *The Green Frog in the Laboratory*. In the *New Year's Eve Watch*, Yŏm's hero lamented the harsh realities of the Koreans:

The sun is long gone. The moon still has a long way to come. Millions of stars are beautiful but they are too far away and too small. Doves in the field are shivering in the cold frost. And the peacock, chained by the neck, only cries, stamping its feet.

Other representative works by members of the group included: *The Sorrows of the Weak* and *Potatoes* by Kim Tong-in; *The Face of Korea* by Hyŏn Chin-gŏn; and *The Sinking of the Sun* by Hwang Sŏg-u.

The emergence of the leftist Torch Society in 1922, signaled the coming of the proletarian literature movement as they advocated "the struggle for liberation of the proletarian class" in their short-lived journal called *The Torch*. However, it was only after the emergence of a group of writers who became collectively known as the PASKYULA that the full-fledged New Direction Movement in the leftist Korean literature developed. PASKYULA was an acronym of the initials of the last names of Pak Yŏng-hŭi and other members of the New Direction group.

In 1923, Pak Yŏng-hŭi with a few other members of the White Tide group revolting against "art for art's sake," launched a movement for "art for the people," and published journals. Yim Chong-jae's article, "A Letter to Writers," published in the July 1923 issue of *The Dawn* (*Kaebyŏk*), stated that "our future may be dark and there may be many hidden rocks in our voyage. But we do not fear them. We shall endure persecution and humiliation. . . and march forward bravely. We shall ring the bell [for liberty]." This declaration of purpose initiated a new struggle against Japanese imperialism and "the socialist struggle for the liberation of the proletarian class." With the rise of the New Direction Movement, the Korean literary world became a battlefield for Nationalists and Socialists. Among the leading members of the New Direction Movement were Pak Yŏng-hŭi, author of a short story entitled *The Struggle*, Ch'oe Hak-song (Ch'oe Sŏ-hae), author of *The Madness*, and Kim Ki-jin, author of *The Red Rat*, all of whom emphasized heroism and the revolutionary struggle in their works.

In July 1925, the PASKYULA and the Torch Society merged into the Korea Artista Proleta Federatio, better known as KAPF, and the leadership of the New Direction Movement fell into the hands of radical writers such as Ch'oe Hak-song, Han Sŏr-ya, and Lim Hwa, who regarded the arts as a weapon to win a "final and total victory of the proletarian class." After the formation of the KAPF, a movement began to include all proletarian artists in this body. On September 1, 1927, the KAPF officially adopted a charter, and it became a united group of socialist writers, painters, actors, and musicians, with branches established in many places. In its official publication, *The Arts Movement*, KAPF stressed the promotion of "socialist realism." One of its members, Kim Ch'ang-sul expressed his confidence in the new movement in his poem entitled "The Grand Stride."

> *We are striding on broad streets with arms spread wide*
> *Toward endless and great thoughts,*
> *Looking up at the clear blue skies.*
> *We are striding, on and on,*
> *Staring at the dust-covered market places*
> *And faces of all the people.*

Among the major works of the KAPF members were such short stories and novels as *The Starvation and Slaughter* and *The Naktong River* by Cho Myŏng-hŭi, *The Death of a Young Idealist* by Kim Ki-jin, *Murder* by Chu Yo-sŏp, *The People's Village* and *Field Fire* by Yi Ki-yŏng, and a historical novel entitled *The Legend of Lim Kŏ-jŏng* by Hong Myŏng-hŭi.

From its inception the KAPF suffered much at the hands of the police, and in 1935 it was dissolved with a final mass arrest of its members. However, many works by Karl Marx and other Socialists, including those of Mao Tse-tung, were translated into Korean and secretly published by this group.

In 1926, Yang Chu-dong and others, inaugurated a new movement for national literature in search of the real spirit of Korea. Their aims were first to combat the literature of the Socialists who "ignored national tradition and disowned Korean life and thought," and secondly to inspire the development of a national literature which would "continue the Korean tradition and purify and enrich the Korean language." Their slogans were "Let Us Return to Korea's Korea," and "Let Us Rediscover Korea."

No matter how noble their aims, they could not promote national literature as such under Japanese colonial policy. Therefore, it was only logical for them to search for the true identity of the Korean people in their tradition and history. As a result, they produce many historical novels and short stories related to the shaman culture. Among those historical novels written during the period were *The Tragic Story of Tanjong, Yi Sun-shin,* and *The Prince in Linen Garment* by Yi Kwang-su; *Young People* and *Spring of the Unhyŏn Palace* by Kim Tong-in; *Blood on Silk Garment* by Pak Chong-hwa, and *The Posterity of the Hwarang* by Kim Tong-ni. Yi Kwang-su's *The Soil* dealt with the soul of the Korean peasantry; and Kim Tong-ni's *The Rock* and *Portrait of a Shaman,* and Chŏng Pi-sŏk's *The Village Shrine,* depicted traditional Korean character and emotions. Yu Ch'i-jin, who wrote many historical plays, depicted in *The Mud Hut* and *The Village with Willow Trees*, the subhuman living conditions of the Korean peasantry.

The literary movements of the Nationalists as well as the Socialists suffered much in the 1930s, and by 1937 their activities virtually ceased.

The Poetry of the Oppressed People.   A sense of hopelessness and gloom dominated the Korean people following the March First fiasco. However, not all Korean poets wrote sorrowful poems. Kim Chŏng-shik (1903–1934), better known as Kim Sowŏl), author of such poems as "The Azalea" was called "a poet of nature and folk tradition" and found solace in aestheticism, and such poets as Chŏng Chi-yong wrote many masterpieces reflecting "sensuous beauty and imagery" and later promoted religious poetry.

Kim Ŏk heralded the arrival of the era of the poetry of the oppressed people of Korea in his poem written in 1918, entitled "Spring is Fading." The poetry of the oppressed people developed as a legacy of the Japanese oppression. Pak Chong-hwa epitomized the mood of the Koreans during this period in his poem entitled "A Song of the Hunted Man" written in 1920. In that year, O Sang-sun wrote a poem entitled "Difficult Times and Sacrifices" and said:

> *Our land is the wasteland.*
> *Korea is a ruin.*
>
> *Our age is an epoch*
> *Of despair and sorrow—*
> *Darkness and death are overwhelming us all around:*
> *Destruction and death reign over our ruined land.*

In his 1926 poem entitled "Does Spring Come to Stolen Fields," Yi Sang-hwa said:

> *The land is no longer our own.*
> *Does spring come just the same*
> *To the stolen fields?*
> *On the narrow path between the rice fields*
> *Where the blue sky and green fields meet and touch,*
> *Winds whisper to me, urging me forward.*

Countless sorrowful poems were written as quiet protests against Japanese colonialism. Rain became the symbol of the tears of sorrow of the downtrodden Korean people. Yang Chu-dong depicted the sorrow of the Koreans who were forced to leave their native land in his poem entitled "I Hear the Train Whistle."

> *In the night rain*
> *I hear the whistle of a distant train.*

A sharp shrill sound trailing off to the north,
North, north across the fields.

Where are they going, those travelers,
Packed in coaches through the night?
How many have said good-bye to the country,
Wandering souls filled with blighted hopes?

This is that time of year,
Seeing one off, alone, is worse than death.
Deep in the night, the rain sounds unceasing,
The whistle that is heard is
Like sleep that will not come.
It is fall, the night rain steadily falling.

Another poet, Yi Ŭn-sang wrote the following poem, expressing the sadness of the Koreans who for one reason or another were forced to emigrate to Manchuria.

Ah, I am forced to flee
To the fields of Kando and Liaotung,
The lands I had dreamed of. . .
Holding my hungry life,
I am forced to flee.

One Korean who fled to Manchuria expressed his homesickness in the following poem:

The flowers that bloom in my birthplace
Also bloom here:
The birds that sing in my birthplace
Also sing here.
Moments of happiness are here
As well as there.
But, why is my heart bursting in sadness
When the songs of birds of my birthplace
Echo in my ears?
Ah, when will it be my homecoming?

Although a majority of poems written by Koreans during the colonial period expressed the discontent and sorrows of the subjugated people, many expressed patriotism, and even hopes for the future. Two examples are given below:

"The Resurrection" by an unknown author:

When the bitter winds of Siberia cover the earth,
The land seemed to have died.
But, look, life in that land.
Crawlers and insects are wriggling,
Waiting for the return of a new spring!

Yang Chu-dong, who launched a movement for national literature in 1926, expressed his hopes and patriotic sentiments in the following poem entitled "I am a Son of This Land."

The people of this land—
Their minds poorer than their homes,
Loving peace and freedom as their brethren—
I am a son of this land!

Although they are lonely and alone,
Although they are weary and tearful,
They are the people of this land
With life and breath in their bodies—
Ah, I am a son of this land!

Magazines and Newspapers.   Despite a multitude of difficulties, the Koreans published magazines and newspapers in order to preserve their language and cultural heritage, to sustain their hopes and aspirtation for national liberation and reconstruction, and to enlighten the people and promote their social consciousness and nationalism.

The first monthlies which appeared after August 1910, were the *Monthly of the Ch'ŏndogyo* sect (formerly *Tonghak*) which appeared in August and *Shijo (Signs of the Times)* published by the Seventh-Day Adventist Church in October 1910. These two magazines not only printed religious articles, but also other pieces which contributed to the dissemination of new medical concepts as well as knowledge about economics, society, and sanitation. The *Monthly of the Shich'ŏn* sect (a branch of the *Tonghak* sect) appeared in March 1911, followed by the Korean Buddhists' *Monthly,* which dealt primarily with religious subjects.

Sonyŏn (Children) was the first Korean-language magazine published by a nonreligious organization named Shinmun-gwan, which was formed in 1906 by Ch'oe Nam-sŏn. Its publication was suspended in August 1910, but Ch'oe was allowed to revive its publication in December. After that, it changed its name several times, and finally, in November 1917, it became *Ch'ŏngch'un (The Youth),* a magazine for young men published by Ch'oe's new society named Chosŏn Kwangmunhoe.

Between November 1914 and February 1919, the publication of eight nonreligious magazines was permitted by the Japanese colonial government.

Among them were a legal magazine, a medical journal, and the first magazine for women, *Yŏjagye* (*The Women's World*). The first literary magazine named *Ch'angjo* (*The Creation*) was published by Kim Tong-in in February 1919. However, with the coming of the March First Movement, publication of all these magazines was suspended.

Other than one government newspaper in the Korean language, there were no Korean-language newspapers until March 1920. With the inauguration of Governor-General Saitō's so-called "civilized rule" in 1920, the publication of several magazines and a handful of Korean newspapers was permitted. The first magazine to appear was *Kaebyŏk* (*The Dawn*), published in 1920 by the *Ch'ŏndogyo* sect. It advocated the unity and regeneration of the people and the struggle against the Japanese, until it was ordered by the police to cease its publication in August 1926. After the appearance of *The Dawn*, over seventy Korean magazines were published between 1920 and 1937. However, only a few survived Japanese censorship and harassment, and by 1937 most of them had disappeared one by one.

The name of Korean magazines generally reflected the hopes and dreams of the people, although a few of them, such as *The Ruin* and *Proletarian*, published by the Socialists, preached the violent overthrow of colonialism and the system of exploitation. A majority of them used the word "new" in their names, for example, *New Women, New Life, The New World, New Light, New Society,* and *New People*. The two most popular magazines were *The Eastern Light* (*Tongmyŏng*), published by Ch'oe Nam-sŏn in 1922, and *Korea's Light* (*Chosŏn-ji-gwang*), published by Chang To-bin who had a leftist orientation. They were joined by monthly magazines published by the three major Korean-language newspaper presses, which were established after 1919, promoting enlightenment and the self-strengthening movement. They were *Shindong-a* (*New East Asia*) for men and *Shin-gajŏng* (*New Homes*) for women, published by the Tong-a Ilbo Press, *Chogwang* (*The Morning Light*) for men, *Sonyŏn* (*Youth*), and *Yŏsŏng* (*Women*), published by the Chosŏn Ilbo Press, and *Chung-ang* (*The Center*), for men, and *Sonyŏn Chung-ang* for young people, published by the Chung-ang Ilbo Press. There were three other magazines for women, in addition to those mentioned above. They were *New Women, Modern Women,* and *Korean Women*. Some periodicals such as *Haksaenggye* (*The Student's World*), *Haksaeng* (*Students*), and *Saedongmu* (*New Friends*) were for young people in which children's stories (*tonghwa*) such as Pang Chŏng-hwan's "Half Moon" and "Snowy Day" were published. In addition to the above mentioned, a popular magazine named *Samch'ŏlli* (*Three Thousand Li*), appearing in 1929, played a significant role in the Korean cultural and social movement.

There was only one Korean-language newspaper between 1910 and 1920. It was the *Maeil Shinbo* (*The Daily News*), which was an organ of the Japanese colonial government. In 1920, the new dawn of Korean journalism arrived when the colonial government gave permits to three groups of Koreans to publish daily newspapers. Consequently, three Korean-language newspapers appeared: the *Chosŏn Ilbo* (*The Korea Daily*) on March 6, and on April 1, the *Tong-a Ilbo* (*The Oriental Daily*) and the *Shisa Shinmun* (*The Current News*). Both the *Chosŏn Ilbo* and the *Shisa Shinmun* reflected certain pro-Japanese sentiments, but the *Tong-a Ilbo,* which was established by staunch Nationalists, such as Yi Sang-hyŏp, Kim Sŏng-su, and Chang Tŏk-su, emerged as the voice of the Koreans. The *Chosŏn Ilbo,* however, abandoned its pro-Japanese position with the resignation of its president and publisher in August 1920.

In its first issue, the *Tong-a Ilbo* stated its three primary objectives: (1) fulfillment of its obligation as a self-appointed voice of the Korean people, (2) promotion of democratic ideals and systems, and (3) promotion of culture and the principle of civility. From the outset, the *Tong-a Ilbo* was critical of Japanese policy. Consequently, even under Saitō's "policy of accommodation" it suffered frequent suspension, censorship, and confiscation. Between 1920 and 1925, an average of 15 daily issues per month were confiscated. In 1920 alone 56 daily issues were suspended, and in the 1930s almost 50 issues were confiscated each year. However, the *Tong-a Ilbo* endured government suppression and financial hardships until it and the *Chosŏn Ilbo* were closed down on August 10, 1940.

The *Chosŏn Ilbo* whose ownership and editorial character changed in August 1920, particularly after 1924 when such Nationalists as Shin Sŏg-u, Yi Sang-jae, An Chae-hong, and Min T'ae-wŏn took over the management and editorial department of the paper, became critical of Japanese policy and suffered a similar fate to that of the *Tong-a Ilbo* until its publication permit was revoked and its press was abolished.

Meanwhile, Ch'oe Nam-sŏn, who suffered a three-year prison term in connection with the role he played in the March First Movement, established a press and published, first a magazine named *Tongmyŏng* (*The Eastern Light*) in 1922, and then a daily newspaper, the *Shidae Ilbo* (*The Times Daily*) in March 1924, expressing a variety of negative views on Japanese policy.

When the publication permit of the *Shidae Ilbo* was revoked by the colonial government, Yi Sang-hyŏp and others established a press and published a new daily named the *Chung-oe Ilbo* (*Domestic and Foreign News*) in November 1926, but after suffering both financial difficulties and government harassment, it was re-organized in October 1931 as the *Chung-ang Ilbo* (*The Central Daily*), under a new publisher and staff. In early 1933, when it was renamed the *Chosŏn Chung-ang Ilbo* (*The Korean Central Daily*), a left wing Nationalist, Yŏ Un-hyŏng, who was arrested by the Japanese police in Shanghai, and suffered a prison term in Korea, became its president and made the paper one of the three major newspapers of the Koreans. It advocated the restoration of Korean rights and freedom until its right to publish was withdrawn by the colonial government in November 1937.

All Korean newspapers made special efforts to bring about cultural advancement of the people, they published monthly magazines for the adults and young people to enlighten them, and they serialized novels by Korean authors who aroused social consciousness of the people through their works. Both the *Tong-a Ilbo* and the *Chosŏn Ilbo* sponsored various cultural events to increase national consciousness and promote culture, and they encouraged the students to participate in anti-illiteracy campaigns of the 1929–34 period, which they had sponsored. The *Tong-a Ilbo* sponsored essay contests for the students, and hundreds of essays written in Korean and dealing with economic and social issues were submitted. Among many exhibitions which the *Chosŏn Ilbo* sponsored were those on "Native Arts (*Hyangt'o Yesul*)" and "The Discovery and Preservation of Native Culture (*Hyangt'o Munhwa Palgulgwa Pojŏn*)." which were held in April 1938.

In addition to constant press censorship exercised by the colonial government, an increasing amount of police harassment led to confiscation of daily issues of these papers, blacking out of certain sections in the papers, or suspension of their publication. The slightest suspicion on the part of the Japanese regarding the paper's intentions, or unfavorable presentation of Japanese policy, their actions either in Korea or in China, brought about government retaliations against these papers in various ways. Many of their editors-in-chief, reporters, and staff writers were forced to resign and given prison sentences. The most celebrated case was the "case involving the eradication of the Japanese flag" from the uniform of a Korean member of the Japanese Olympic team.

The Japanese were extremely sensitive to the slightest expression of Korean nationalism or anti-Japanese sentiment in Korean publications, particularly newspapers. Because of this attitude, Korean magazines and newspapers were frequently confiscated or their publication was suspended. Despite this fact, the *Tong-a Ilbo* and the *Chung-ang Ilbo* published a photograph of a Korean, Son Ki-jŏng, who won first place in the 1936 Berlin Olympic marathon race, along with another Korean, Nam Sŭng-yong, who won third place. When they printed the photograph of Son they deleted the Japanese national flag from his uniform, as an obvious nationalistic gesture. This brought about a swift retaliation from the Japanese against the *Tong-a Ilbo*, and its president, Song Chin-u, its editor-in-chief, Sŏl Ui-shik, along with five reporters were interrogated and forced to resign, and the publication of the paper was suspended indefinitely. This suspension lasted from August 1936 until June 1937.

Meanwhile, the *Chosŏn Chung-ang Ilbo*, rather than waiting for Japanese orders, voluntarily suspended its publication, but even so, many of its staff members were also interrogated. The upshot was the resignation of many key staff members from the paper, and the paper lost its publication right in November 1937 and ceased to exist.

In April 1938, the *Maeil Shinbo* became a non-government newspaper with

Koreans as its president, vice-president, and editor-in-chief, but its executive director and the head of management department were Japanese. It too suffered police harassment, and many of its staff members and reporters were forced by the police to resign in 1928 and 1939. When, in 1941, its president, Ch'oe Rin, resigned and another Korean took over the paper, it became a propaganda instrument of the Japanese, remaining as the only Korean newspaper until the end of the Japanese colonial period.

Both the *Tong-a Ilbo* and the *Chosŏn Ilbo*, which renewed their publication in June 1937 encountered increasing problems. Then, in December 1939, the Japanese colonial government brought its pressure upon the *Tong-a Ilbo* and the *Chosŏn Ilbo* in order to bring about "voluntary" dissolution of the two presses. Their struggle to survive was in vain, and on August 10, 1940 both of them published their last issues as they were abolished outright by the Japanese.

The Korean-language newspapers which appeared after 1919 and survived until 1940 contributed much to the increase of literacy and the expansion of the public's awareness of Korea's social and economic ills and nationalistic cultural interests, particularly the struggle of the Koreans to preserve their own language. A significant aspect of Korean journalism was the development of the role which women played as reporters and columnists. Ch'oe Ŭn-hŭi and Yun Song-sang of the *Chosŏn Ilbo*, Hŏ Chŏng-suk and Ch'oe Ŭi-sun of the *Tong-a Ilbo*, Hwang Shin-dŏk of the *Shidae Ilbo*, Kim Mal-bong of the *Chung-ang Ilbo*, and Kim Myŏng-sun and No Ch'ŏn-myŏng of the *Maeil Shinbo*, along with many other women reporters made a significant contribution not only toward the strengthening of women's role, but also toward the enlightenment of women through their writings.

Academic Societies.   The most significant academic societies established by Koreans were the Korean Language Research Society and the Chindan Academy which, in addition to the Chosŏn Kwangmunhoe of Ch'oe Nam-sŏn, were critical of biased and distorted Japanese interpretations of Korean history. Ch'oe, who believed that the cultural history of Korea possessed a particular significance and value to the Koreans, supported the revival of the Korean's spiritual strength. The publication of the *History of the Three Kingdoms* by Ch'oe's society led to its dissolution.

The Korean Language Research Society, organized in December 1921 by Nationalist scholars such as Chang Chi-yŏng and Shin Myŏng-gyun for the purpose of promoting studies of the Korean language, published a journal named *Han-gŭl (Korean Letters)*. The expressed purpose of the society was to purify, systematize, and standardize the Korean langague, but its real aim was to preserve the Korean language. In January 1931, it was reorganized into the Korean Linguistics Society, losing many of its nationalistic characteristics, but it was able to revive *Han-gŭl*, the publication of which had been suspended by the police since 1928. Beginning October 29, 1933, it published books on

Korean grammar and linguistic studies, sponsored seminars and colloquiums on the Korean language, and adopted a new official system for spelling Korean words. Until 1942, when its existence was terminated by the police and its leaders such as Yi Kung-no and Ch'oe Hyŏn-bae were imprisoned, it struggled not only to preserve Korean linguistic heritage, but also to advance Korean language studies.

The Korean Language Association, another linguistic society, was organized in June 1931, by Nationalist scholars such as Yi Yun-jae and Yi Hūi-sūng to promote the study of the Korean language and literature. Its life was cut short in 1933 by the police.

In May 1924, some 24 Nationalist scholars, including such prominent historians as Yi Pyŏng-do and Yi Sŏn-gūn and a literary leader named Yi Sang-baek, organized the Chindan Academy in order to promote studies of Korean literature and history. The leaders declared that "we must promote studies on Korean culture by ourselves." "Although our ability is limited," they stated, "it is our mission and obligation to cultivate and promote Korean culture." They published a journal named *Chindan Hakpo*, which published many articles on Korean literature, history and folklore, striving to revive the spirit of the Korean people. Because of its nationalistic aspirations, Korea's only academic society was abolished by the police in September 1943.

Because the study of Korean history and publication of history books by Koreans was either discouraged, or prohibited by the police, Korean historians and others wrote biographical studies of prominent Koreans of past centuries. Interest in the study of *Shirhak* thoughts, particularly of Tasan Chŏng Yag-yong grew in the 1930s.

Educational and Anti-Illiteracy Campaign. The Education Ordinance of 1911 made the establishment of new private schools extremely difficult and a small number of new private schools were established after that date. Meanwhile, the number of existing private schools decreased from 1,717 in 1912, to 1,320 in 1919. In 1919, there were only 412 public primary schools for Korean children, and 84,306 (or 3.7 per cent) school age Korean children were able to attend public schools. There were only five public secondary schools for Korean boys (with 1,705 students) and only one secondary school for Korean girls with 578 students. The opportunity for Korean children and other students to obtain modern education was extremely limited.

To make matters worse, the Education Ordinance of 1913 imposed further restrictions on private schools, making the survival of those schools even more difficult. Sungshil (Union Christian) College for men, established in Pyongyang by the Presbyterian Mission in 1906, and the college department of Ewha School both lost their status. As a result, there was not a single liberal arts college in Korea, as of 1916. In 1917, however, American mission boards established two colleges for men—Yŏnhūi (Chosŏn Christian) and Severance

Medical—in Seoul. By 1925, the total number of private schools had decreased to 604.

The Korean leaders were keenly aware not only of the need to increase educational opportunity for Korean students, but also the need to counter Japanese educational policy. Taking advantage of the revised education ordinance of November 1920, the Korean Nationalists established more schools, and by 1943 the number of secondary schools for boys grew to 26, and that of girls to 16, with a total enrollment of 20,540.

The new Education Ordinance of 1922 led such Nationalists as Yi Sang-jae, Yi Sŭng-hun, and Song Chin-u to establish in November a foundation for the purpose of creating a private Korean university, but they failed to achieve their objectives due to financial difficulties and Japanese policy against it. In 1925, American mission boards, however, successfully reestablished Sungshil College for men and established Ewha Woman's College. In that same year, a nonsectarian, liberal arts college for men named Posŏng with departments of law and business emerged. In 1938, the Nationalists established Sookmyung Women's College, the first nonsectarian liberal arts college for women, providing Korean women with more educational opportunity. Although student enrollment in Korean colleges was small (2,013 in 1943), Posŏng and Sookmyung, along with other colleges established by American mission boards, nevertheless, produced new leaders in the field of education, law, arts, medicine, and business.

The Nationalists launched anti-illiteracy campaigns, thereby initiating what is known as the "*kyemong* (enlightenment)" movement. In 1929, the Chosŏn Ilbo Press launched the movement using the slogan, "Knowledge is strength. We must learn in order to survive." Students were organized into small groups and sent into villages to teach reading and writing, as well as to enlighten villagers with new ideas. In 1931, the Tong-a Ilbo Press began the *Itti v narod* ("Go Among the People") movement, and during their summer vacation students were mobilized to establish summer schools in villages and hamlets for the purpose of eradicating illiteracy, enlightening the people in rural areas. Until the movements initiated by these two presses were stopped by the Japanese in 1934, some 5,750 students participated in the movement at 1,323 locations, and about 83,000 men and women learned how to read and write, being indoctrinated by the students as well.

Christian Nationalists also accelerated the Sunday School movement after 1922, and also organized summer Bible schools in order to teach reading and writing to Korean children who were unable to attend school. Some 423,000 Korean children learned how to read and write at the Sunday Schools, and at summer Bible schools. 116,518 children were taught until the movement was stopped by the Japanese in 1933.

Musicians and Composers.   Many musicians particiapted in the nationalist movement. Kim In-shik advocated both the preservation of Korean music, and its development; in 1913 he established the Institute for Korean Traditional Music for this purpose. In that year, he also established the Kyŏngsŏng (Seoul) Oratorical Society, in cooperation with Hong Yŏng-hu (1897–1941, better known as Hong Nanp'a) in order to contribute to the modernization of the Korean society through music. The German musician, Franz Echert, assisted them until his death in 1916.

A number of Koreans studied music in America, Japan, and Europe. Upon returning to Korea they endeavored to bring about the modernization of Korean music as well as trying to popularize Western music. Among these students were vocalists An Ki-yŏng, Hyŏn Che-myŏng, Chŏng Hun-mo, and Kim Wŏn-bok, pianists Pak Kyŏng-ho and Kim Maeri, and violinist Kim Saeng-yŏ and Kye Chŏng-shik. Chŏng Hun-mo, Kim Maeri, and Kim Wŏn-bok were outstanding women musicians who as teachers at Korean colleges for women contributed much toward the development of musical talents among women.

Many composers produced Korean lyric songs (*kagok*) using poems written by Korean poets, and their music provided spiritual comfort and a psychological uplift for the Korean people. One such composer was Hong Nan-p'a, who wrote many children's songs (*tongyo*) as well as such lyric songs as *The Night of the Sŏngbul Temple* with words written by the outstanding poet, Yi Ŭn-sang. Some major works of Korean composers were: Kim Tong-jin's *I Wish to Go*, using a nostalgic poem written by Yi Ŭn-sang about the place where he once lived; Pak T'ae-jun's *Homesickness*, with Kim Sowŏl's poem, and *Thinking About Friends* with Yi Ŭn-sang's poem; Yun Yong-ha's *Wheat Field*, with Pak Hwa-mok's poem; and Hyŏn Che-myŏng's *In Front of that House* with Yi Ŭn-sang's poem, and *Gentle Breeze* with Chŏng In-sŏp's poem. Hyŏn left behind many other beloved songs such as *To the Land of Hope*, *Longing for Friends*, and *The Autumn Wind*.

Many of the Korean musicians were engaged in the resistance or protest movement in a variety of ways. Because of this, they suffered. Hong Nanp'a, who had been imprisoned because of his involvement in the February 1919 independence movement of Korean students in Japan, returned to Korea in 1920, and established a musical society in 1926. In 1931, he organized the Association of Korean Musicians.

A lyric song, *Pongsŏnhwa* (the "Touch-me-not Flower"), composed by Hong Nan-p'a using Kim Hyŏng-jun's poem, became known as the hymn of the resistance movement. It reads:

> O, Pongsŏnhwa, *in the shadow of the wall,*
> *You look pitiful.*
> *All summer long you have delighted*
> *Pretty maidens with your charms.*

> *Summer is gone suddenly,*
> *And autumn wind stirs the air.*
> *O, Pongsōnhwa, my sweet flower,*
> *Sorrow is ours when your petals fall.*

> *Although you seemed perished*
> *Under bitter, heartless winds,*
> *Your soul is still alive, dreaming peaceful dreams.*
> *May your life return in the warm spring breeze.*

This song, along with the *Patriotic Song* written by Yun Ch'i-ho, was banned by the Japanese police. Meanwhile, a song, composed by Yun Kŭg-yōng in 1924 and entitled *The Blue Skies and the Milky Way* (*P'urūn Hanŭl Ŭnhasu*), became one of the most popular songs sung by the young and old alike.

Korean musicians were actively engaged in the social and cultural reconstruction and the modernization movement of the Koreans. Accordingly, they formed many societies and groups in order to achieve their objectives. In 1926, Hong Nanp'a and others organized the Central Musicians Association Symphony Orchestra, and the first college orchestra was formed at Yōnhŭi College in 1929. In 1934, the formation of the Seoul Symphony Orchestra and the Seoul Radio Broadcasting Orchestra contributed much toward Korea's musical modernization.

Popular song writers produced countless popular songs called *yuhaengga*, which reflected the mood of the unhappy Korean people as well as their spirit of resistance. The vitality and hopefulness in the songs of the pre-annexation period disappeared after 1910, and a pessimistic and sad sentiment became dominant. Most of the popular song writers either lamented separation of family members and friends, or the people's generally sad state of affairs.

Among the popular songs of the 1920s were *The Ancient Ruin*, *Three Friends* and the *Hymn of Death*. Those of the 1930s were *Life in a Foreign Land*, *The Tear-soaked Tuman River*, and *The Sorrows of a Traveler*. Many popular songs, such as *The Ancient Ruin* and *Three Friends* were banned by the Japanese. The two stanzas of *The Ancient Ruin* read:

> *As the night falls over the ancient ruin,*
> *The silent moon sheds its light over it*
> *As if it evokes now forgotten memories.*

> *Ah, pitiful is this body of mine.*
> *Why are you wandering in the endless dream-road?*
> *What is it that you seek?*

Many Christian hymns, such as *Abide With Me* (*Eventide*) and *Rock of Ages, Cleft for Me*, became favorite hymns of the Koreans who sought comfort, hope, and solace in the words. Among the most favorite hymns was *Bright Road to Heaven*, which was adapted from a Western hymn, *Bright Heavenly Way*, and sung to the tune of a Scottish song, *Annie Laurie*. Its first stanza in the Korean version reads:

> *The bright road to heaven is before me.*
> *Thought I witness many sorrows and always suffer;*
> *As the brightness of the heavenly glory*
> *Disperses the dark shadow,*
> *I always see the light by leaning to the deeds of Jesus.*

One of the Christian hymns which expressed Korean patriotism was *Samchŏlli kangsan kŭmsu kangsan* ("Three Thousands Leagues of Beautiful Garden"), otherwise known as *"Let Us Go To Work,"* written by a patriot, Namgung Ŏk. It said:

> *Let us go to work,*
> *Let us march to work,*
> *To the beautiful garden which*
> *God had given to us.*
>
> * * *
>
> *Let us go to work,*
> *Let us march to work.*
> *There is much work to be done;*
> *The call for workers is loud.*
>
> *Let us go to work.*
> *Let us march to work,*
> *To this beautiful garden, for*
> *We have received God's command.*

To be sure there were many other favorite hymns, but none was sung as often or as enthusiastically as this one. Whereas others conveyed sadness and lamentations, this song reflected determination on the part of the Koreans to work for their native land and to rebuild their lives.

When, in 1931, the Tong-a Ilbo Press sponsored a "Song of Korea (*Chosŏnŭi Norae*)" contest, many songs were submitted. The first stanza of the top winner of the contest reads as follows:

> *Mt. Paektu stretches into the peninsula of 3,000 li;*
> *The history of this garden of the Rose of Sharon is 5,000 years long.*
> *We are thirty million people who have lived in this land generation after*
> *generation;*
> *Blessed is the name of the land that is Korea.*

Together with musical societies, the Korean newspaper presses, such as the *Tong-a Ilbo*, the *Chosŏn Ilbo*, and the *Chung-ang Ilbo*, sponsored recitals of Korean musicians, as well as performances by foreign musicians and musical groups, contributing to the elevation of Koreans' cultural standard in urban centers. The modernization in the field of music in Korea owed much to the efforts made by the societies of Korean musicians and newspaper presses.

Nationalism and the Theatrical Groups, Dramatists, and Other Artists.   The Wŏn-gaksa Theatre in Seoul was the first modern theatre established in Korea, in July 1908, and the performance of *Ŭnsegye* (The Silvery World) written by Yi In-jik at this threatre marked the beginnings of the modern drama movement in Korea. After the Japanese annexation, the first theatrical groups which arose, promoting the patriotic movement and performing plays written by Korean playwrights, were the Hyŏkshindan of Lim Sŏng-gu, which emerged in 1911; the Yuiltan of Yi Ki-se, which was formed in 1912; and the Munsusŏng of Yun Paeng-nam, which was organized in 1913. Yi and Yun jointly organized another group named Yesŏngjwa, and in April 1916 it performed Leo Tolstoy's *Resurrection* (better known in Korea as "Katiusha") in Seoul.

The Japanese colonial authorities paid close attention to Korean theatre groups in order to check the expression of nationalism through plays. Many plays were banned and theatrical groups which had emerged disappeared quickly under police order. Meanwhile, in the 1920s, when the leftist movement grew, new groups, such as the Theatrical Art Society and the People's Drama Group, emerged and performed Western drama as well as plays written by Korean writers. Among leftist theatrical groups were the Street Theatre in Taegu, the Mass Theatre in Kaesŏng, the Drama Theatre in Haeju, and the New Construction Group in Seoul. While promoting national culture, most of them were involved in the ideological struggle against the Japanese as well as economic and social issues.

Korean students who returned from Japan organized such societies in the early 1930's as the Research Association of Theatrical Arts for the promotion of interest in drama and theory of play production. This group formed a performing group named the Experimental Stage in November 1931, and produced *The Inspector General* by Nikolai Gogol, *The Cherry Orchard* by Anton Chekhov, and *The Merchant of Venice* by William Shakespeare. Meanwhile, Korean playwrights, such as Yu Ch'i-jin, wrote *The Mud Hut, The Scenery of the Village with Willow Trees, The Cow,* and *The Slum,* all of which depicted the suffering of the Korean farmers. After suffering a prison term, Yu produced nonpolitical plays, such as *A Sacrificial Rite, Sisters,* and a historical play, *The Prince in Hemp Clothes,* in the second half of the 1930.

Among many actors and actresses, two people of singular importance were an actor named Na Un-gyu and an actress named Pok Hye-suk. Na had a profound effect as an actor, director, and producer of many plays, and became a legend in his own time. After suffering a prison term because of his nationalistic activity, Na joined a theatrical group called Kyerimhoe, and studied briefly at a Japanese-established Chōsen Kinema Company in Pusan. When Yun Paeng-nam established his own motion picture firm named the Paengnam Production in 1925, Na joined him and played the leading role in *The Tale of Shim Ch'ŏng*, a popular story about a filial daughter who sacrificed her life to give sight to her blind father. Na, along with Pok Hye-suk, played in a film entitled *The Bird in the Cage*. His fame reached a peak when he played the leading role in *Arirang*, which was produced in 1926. This film epitomized the Koreans' antagonism toward and hatred of the Japanese police. It was an exposure of the inhumane and harsh Japanese rule, as well as of the economic and social miseries suffered by a subjugated and exploited people. The performance of *Arirang* was quickly banned by the police.

Na Un-gyu also played in *Samnyong, the Mute*, a film which gave a satirical view of society, and other plays such as *The Gold Fish, The Adventurer*, and *The Field Rat*. He formed his own motion picture firm, and produced such memorable films as *Farewell* and *Across the Tuman River*. All of the films which he produced or in which he acted were banned by the police.

Among several motion pictures and dramas dealing with Korean history was the *Strange Story of the Party of Enlightenment and Progress (Kaehwadang-imun)*. This film portrayed the life of Kim Ok-kyun who launched the nationalist movement in the late 1870s and carried out a coup in December 1884. Korean theatre and drama lost much of its nationalistic and reformist fervor as well as its Korean identity after 1937, due to an increasing Japanese pressure.

Korean dancers joined the new cultural movement for national reconstruction in the 1930s. The Institute for the Study of Korean Dance was established in 1934 by Han Sŏng-jun who elevated the level of folk dances. His goal was not only to revive traditional Korean dance in order to preserve Korean cultural heritage but also to popularize and modernize Korean dance.

Several Koreans went to Japan to study dance, and emerged as leaders in the art in the early 1930s. Among them were a male dancer named Cho T'aeg-wŏn and a female dancer named Ch'oe Sŭng-hŭi, both of whom introduced a new style of dance for traditional pieces and created many new dances related to the cultural heritage of the Koreans. Whereas Cho created new dances from *The Tale of Ch'unhyang*, Ch'oe created new dances and gave them such names as *India's Sadness, Those Who Seek Liberation, They Who Search for the Sun*, and *Sorrows of a Wanderer*.

The Decline of the Nationalistic Cultural Movement.   Following such events as the Mukden Incident of September 1931, and the Marco Polo Bridge Incident of July 7, 1937, which initiated the second Sino-Japanese War, Koreans found it increasingly difficult to participate in a nationalist movement. The slightest suspicion on the part of the Thought Section of the Japanese police led to arrest and imprisonment, and by 1937 politically oriented Korean societies and organizations one by one ceased to exist.

However, the spirit of the resistance did not perish. Continued noncooperative attitudes of the Koreans were summed up in a police report which stated in part:

When the China incident occurred in July 1937, they [the Koreans] saw it as the precursor of a world war and asserted that Japan would be economically ruined and eventually defeated. This kind of propaganda is evident. . . there are those who assert that the government policy is merely to uproot the traditional Korean culture. . . .

The report concluded that it would be "wrong to interpret the tranquility as an indication of their trust in the Imperial government, or intention to become loyal subjects." Indeed, Korean nationalism, as well as the works of Marx and Mao Tse-tung which had been translated into Korean and published secretly, continued to influence young Koreans. Between 1939 and 1944, some 5,600 Koreans were arrested and imprisoned either as anti-Japanese subversives or revolutionaries.

In November 1943, the heads of three Allies (U.S., Great Britain, and China) met at Cairo, and on December 1 they made public a communique (the Cairo Declaration), stating that "in due course Korea shall become free and independent." Shortly after this, anticipating the imminent defeat of Japan at the hands of the Allies, Yŏ Un-hyŏng, representing the reformist (Socialist) Nationalist group, formed in 1944 a secret society called the Alliance for Korean Independence in cooperation with moderate Nationalists such as An Chae-hong and a few Communists.

Although ideological unity did not develop, the Koreans tenaciously showed their determination to maintain their racial separateness and cultural distinction, as well as their desire to regain freedom and independence. When, on July 24, 1945, a pro-Japanese organization held an oratorical meeting in Seoul, a member of the underground organization named the Korean Patriotic Youth Society threw two bombs into the Citizens' Hall where the meeting was held, displaying his anti-Japanese sentiments.

The National Liberation Movements of the Koreans Abroad

Many Nationalist societies were organized abroad by the Koreans residing in China, Manchuria, Siberia, and the United States during the period of 1905 to 1910 and after. The New People's Society and the Mutual Aid Society of the Koreans emerged in Hawaii along with two other societies in California, and their branches were established in the Vladivostok area of Siberia and the Chientao (Kando in Korea) region in southeastern Manchuria where some 300,000 Koreans lived around 1910. The first anti-Japanese organization of the

Korean Nationalists, which appeared in the Maritime Province of Siberia where over 100,000 Koreans lived, was the Righteous Army which was established by Yi Pŏm-jin. These organizations established schools in Manchuria and Siberia to educate Korean children, published newspapers to promote anti-Japanese feelings, and provided military training to Korean youth as they engaged in various anti-Japanese activities.

After the Japanese annexation of Korea, many more organizations were established by overseas Koreans in China, Manchuria, Siberia, and the United States for the purpose of liberating Korea. A total of twelve declarations of independence were issued before the March First Movement Declaration of Independence of 1919 by various groups and individual Koreans overseas. The first was issued in November 1918 by a group of Korean Nationalists in the Manchurian-Siberian border region, and the second on February 8, 1919, by Korean students in Japan. Others were issued by Korean Buddhist monks in China and one by Korean women in Chientao, Manchuria. However, being in foreign lands, having military forces neither large nor strong enough to overthrow Japanese colonialism in Korea by force, lacking the support of Western powers, and being divided between the Nationalists and Communists, overseas Koreans were unable to achieve their primary objective, although they demonstrated their patriotism and nationalism in various ways.

The Korean Nationalist Movement in America.   The Koreans in Hawaii and San Francisco provided financial support to a Korean who went to Seoul in 1907 to assassinate Korean Prime Minister Yi Wan-yong, who was regarded as a traitor. Meanwhile, two Korean students in San Francisco, Chŏn Myŏng-un and Chang In-hwan, shot and killed, in March 1908, Durham White Stevens, an American who betrayed the Korean trust as a Japanese spy.

In February 1910, several Korean societies in the United States were united into the Korean National Association (*Kungminhoe*), whose headquarters were in Los Angeles and which provided funds to defend Chang In-hwan and Chŏn Myŏng-un. But the Koreans encountered many problems. First of all, the number of Koreans in America was small and their economic ability to carry out an effective movement was negligible. Moreover, neither the American government, nor the majority of American people showed any interest in the Koreans' liberation movement. Be that as it may, Pak Yong-man, one of the leaders of the Korean National Association, established Korean military schools in Nebraska and Hawaii shortly after 1910 to train freedom fighters. Syngman Rhee, who was expelled from Korea, arrived in the United States in 1912, and launched his national liberation movement.

As early as July 1917, An Ch'ang-ho issued a six-point manifesto in which he advocated the establishment of a supreme organ of overseas Koreans to lead the struggle for regaining Korean independence, and his proposals were supported by such Nationalists as Shin Kyu-shik, Shin Ch'ae-ho, Pak Ŭn-shik, and Cho So-ang.

In March 1919, Syngman Rhee, the leader of the Koreans in America, and another leader named Chŏng Han-yŏng (Henry Chung), sent a petition to President Woodrow Wilson, asking him to initiate steps at the Paris Peace Conference to put Korea under the mandate of the League of Nations as a first step toward the eventual restoration of Korean independence. Meanwhile, An Ch'ang-ho (1878–1938) organized the Corps for the Advancement of Individuals (*Hŭngsadan*). According to An, its purpose was to unite the people, prepare them spiritually as well as militarily, and continue propaganda activities to win the support of the powers for Korean liberation.

Shortly after the March First Movement in Korea, the first Korean Congress was convened in Philadelphia in April 1919, under the leadership of Drs. Syngman Rhee and Philip Jaisohn. The Korean Congress, which was attended by hundreds of representatives of Korean organizations in the United States, issued an "Appeal to America," stating that Korea was a victim of Japan and that the Korean people were struggling to be free from Japanese domination. It stated, "Our cause is a just one before the laws of God and Man. Our aim is freedom from militaristic autocracy; our objective is democracy for Asia; our hope is universal Christianity." The Korean Congress adopted a ten-point resolution entitled "Aims and Aspirations of the Korean," established the Korean Information Bureau in Philadelphia in order to promote American understanding of, and sympathy for Korea's struggle against the Japanese, and published its organ, *The Korean Review*.

In September 1919, Dr. Rhee, the elected president of the Korean Provisional Government, which was created in April 1919 in Shanghai by the Korean Nationalists, established the Korean Commission in Washington, D.C., and Kim Kyu-shik (1881–1950) arrived from Shanghai as its director. The Korean Commission sent appeals to the U.S. government on behalf of the Korean people, and sponsored the publication of books such as *Korea's Fight for Freedom* by Frederick A. McKenzie and *The Case of Korea* by Henry Chung. In 1920, Dr. Rhee organized a new society named Comrades Society (*Tongjihoe*).

Some U.S. Congressmen showed their interest in the Korean situation. In October, a resolution expressing American sympathy with the aspirations of the Korean people for freedom and national independence was introduced by Senator James D. Phlan of California, and an identical resolution was introduced by Representative William E. Mason of Illinois. Neither resolution was adopted by the Congress, but Senator George W. Norris, of Nebraska, strongly defended the Korean cause in his speech before the Senate at that time.

When the Washington Disarmament Conference met in November 1921, the Korean Commission, under the direction of the Korean Provisional Government, prepared a "Brief for Korea" and presented it to Secretary of State Charles Hughes. It included an appeal for Korean independence.

However, the Korean question was not debated at the conference, although the head of the Japanese delegation promised Hughes that Japan would change its policy toward Korea.

The small number of Koreans in the United States, mostly poor, and scattered in Hawaii, San Francisco, Los Angeles, New York, and Chicago, had neither political influence nor effective means to promote American support for the Korean independence movement. Moreover, because of their inability to take cooperative actions they could not gain the support of the American government for Korean liberation or its recognition of the Korean Provisional Government in China. When disputes developed between Dr. Rhee and the radical leaders who controlled the Korean Provisional Government, Dr. Rhee was impeached by his critics in the government, the Korean Commission was abolished in 1923, and Kim Kyu-shik returned to Shanghai. In 1933, Dr. Rhee went to Geneva and presented two petitions for Korean independence to the League of Nations, but his efforts bore no fruit.

Responding to the unification movement of the Korean Nationalists in China in the spring of 1940, the United Society and the Patriotic Corps of the Korean Nationalists in Hawaii became the Hawaiian branch of the new Korean Independence Party which was formed in China, and in April 1941, delegates of nine Korean Nationalist organizations met in Honolulu, organized the United Korean Committee in America, and declared its support for the Korean Provisional Government in China. But its unity was broken in 1943 when Dr. Rhee's Comrades Society (*Tongjihoe*) withdrew from it.

The Atlantic Charter of August 1941, in which President Franklin D. Roosevelt and Prime Minister Winston Churchill asserted, among other things, the right of national self-determination, induced Korean Nationalists to accelerate their efforts. The commencement of World War II in the Pacific gave them a greater hope and impetus, and they sought immediate recognition by the American government of the Korean Provisional Government in China. Their hope rose high in April 1942 when the Chinese Nationalist government in Chungking proposed to the American government that it recognize the Korean Provisional Government "without delay." However, they were disappointed when the American government refused to do so. It was at this juncture that Dr. Robert T. Oliver, an American college professor, became Dr. Rhee's close associate and aide.

Meanwhile, Kim Yong-jung and his associates established the Korean Affairs Institute in Washington, and initiated in November 1943 the publication of a bi-weekly newspaper called *The Voice of Korea* "in order to set the record straight." Around this time, the Korean Pacific Press and the Korean Research and Information Office were established producing a considerable amount of reading material on Korea. Dr. Oliver's book, *Korea: Forgotten Nation*, was published in 1944 in behalf of Korea's fight for freedom. In April 1945, when the United Nations Conference was held in San Francisco, the Korean leaders in America attempted to participate in it as Korean delegates, but they were not allowed to do so. The United States continued to refuse its recognition for the Korean Provisional Government even after the end of World War II.

Nationalist Movement of the Koreans in China.   The nationalist movement of the Koreans in China began in the summer of 1918 with the establishment of the Nationalist Korean Youth Association in Shanghai by Chang Tŏk-su and Yŏ Un-hyŏng. After this, the Korean Provisional Government was established in April 1919, and many other Korean Nationalist and Communist organizations emerged in China making efforts to liberate Korea from Japan.

One of the most important actions taken by the Korean Nationalists was the establishment of the Provisional Government of the Republic of Korea in April 1919 in Shanghai. There were some 40 Koreans in Shanghai in early 1919, and after March 1919 many Nationalist refugees arrived in Shanghai from Korea and Japan, as well as from Siberia and the United States, bringing the Korean population in Shanghai to about 700. Dr. Syngman Rhee, who was in the United States, was elected premier, and when the government was reorganized he became president. An Ch'ang-ho, who was also in the United States, Kim Kyu-shik, who was in Paris, Yi Tong-hwi, who was in Siberia, Yi Shi-yŏng and two others in China were elected cabinet ministers. Meanwhile, a provisional legislative assembly composed of representatives of the eight provinces of Korea and all the overseas Koreans was established. The official organ of the Korean Provisional Government was *The Independence News.*

In May 1919, Kim Kyu-shik, as Foreign Minister of the Korean Provisional Government, submitted the "Petition of the Korean People and Nation for Liberation from Japan and for the Reconstruction of Korea as an Independent State" and the "Claims of the Korean People and Nation" to the peace conference held in Paris. He was unable to speak to the Allies, but he gained a significant number of sympathizers for the Korean cause among foreign delegates. Meanwhile, the Korean Provisional Government established the Korean Commission in Washington, D.C., and sent Kim Kyu-shik as its head.

The Korean Provisional Government was hampered by conflicts between the Nationalists and Socialists, as well as by disunity within the Nationalist camp. Personality conflicts, ideological discord, tactical differences, and financial problems constituted major impediments to the Korean government in exile from the beginning. Dr. Rhee's leadership was undermined by a dispute over the petition which he had submitted to President Wilson in March 1919 in which he asked that Korea be placed under the mandate of the League of Nations as a first step toward its full independence.

Yi Tong-hwi, a Socialist who became premier in October 1919, sent a mission to the Soviet Union and received the latter's financial support, but his secret motives were to socialize the Korean government. The inability of Korean leaders to achieve unity made the efforts of the Korean government in exile ineffective. Realizing that he should lay firm ideological guidelines for the government, Dr. Rhee went to Shanghai in December 1920, but was unable to accomplish his objectives and returned to the United States. A new cabinet was formed with Shin Kyu-shik as premier in January 1921, but the situation remained unchanged. The leaders of the government amply displayed their inability to overcome differences and take united action for the sake of Korean liberation. Disillusioned, Yi Kwang-su returned to Korea while An Ch'ang-ho resigned his cabinet post and made efforts to unify the Nationalists in China.

The radical Korean Nationalists, such as Pak Ŭn-shik and Shin Ch'ae-ho, as well as Socialists, denounced the Provisional Government from its inception for a varity of reasons. Both Pak and Shin first said that the establishment of the Provisional Government was a mistake, and then in February 1921 they advocated its reorganization. In April, they held the Military Unification Conference in Peking, advocating direct military actions against the Japanese.

The rapidly growing conflict among the Nationalists and between the Nationalists and Socialists led An Ch'ang-ho to resign from the government, and in May 1921, he launched a new independence movement of all the overseas Koreans. He felt that it was absolutely necessary for the Koreans to be united and to initiate a new unified movement for national liberation, and he advocated fostering military capabilities to drive the Japanese out of Korea.

President Warren G. Harding of the United States invited Great Britian, Japan, France, Italy and other powers to a disarmament conference in Washington in 1921 to discuss, among other things, the "Pacific and Far Eastern question." In August 1921 Nationalists in Shanghai formed the Association to Support the Diplomatic Work of the Korean Commission in the United States at the conference, and raised funds to this end. Meanwhile, in 1922 the ultrarightist Koreans organized the Korean Labor-Soldier Association in Shanghai under the leadership of Kim Ku (1876–1949). Its purpose was to train a large number of Korean soldiers to liberate Korea.

From 1922 to 1925 radicals such as Pak Ŭn-shik, controlled the Provisional Government and increased the division between the moderate and radical Nationalists. The two moderate leaders, An Ch'ang-ho and Yŏ Un-hyŏng, brought about the convening of the National Representative Conference in Shanghai in January 1923, to unify the anti-Japanese Koreans of all political orientations. It was attended by 113 delegates of 61 anti-Japanese organizations of Koreans in China, Manchuria, Siberia, and the United States. However, An and Yŏ were unable to achieve their objective. In 1923, Shin Ch'ae-ho wrote the Declaration of the Korean Revolution. Short time later, he was arrested by the Japanese, and died in 1936 in a Japanese prison in Port Arthur, Manchuria.

Shin Ik-hŭi (1892–1956) and Kim Ku (1876–1949), both of whom were right wing Nationalists, took over the leadership of the Provisional Government in 1926, but they were only able to maintain a precarious existence for the government, experiencing disunity and bitter discord as well as severe financial difficulties. Some Nationalists and Socialists took a new initiative to form a united front of all anti-Japanese Korean organizations and people, and in March 1927 they established in Shanghai the Association for Promotion of the United Korean Independence Party. It included such prominent Nationalists as Kim Ku and Cho So-ang, but other Nationalists refused to join. An Ch'ang-ho, a moderate Nationalist, did not join because he was fearful that the united movement would be dominated by "the Communists. . . who have a considerable degree of theory behind their movement."

In the early stage, the Korean Communists collaborated with the Nationalists in hoping to change the direction of the Nationalist movement along Socialist lines. However, following the collapse of the United Front of the Chinese Nationalists and Communists in 1926, they launched a separate anti-Japanese national liberation movement. After Yi Tong-hwi left Shanghai, the Foreign Liaison Center was founded in April 1926 by those Korean Communists who had fled from Korea. Shortly after that, the Center was replaced by a Korean section of the Far Eastern Bureau of the Comintern with Cho Pong-am as its head until April 1927. Some time in 1928, the Korean Communists organized the Restoration League of the Korean Communist Party and the Lenin Political School in Peking which trained and sent young Korean Communists back to Korea. Kim Wŏn-bong was one of the active members of the group of Korean Communists in Peking until his departure to Nanking in the spring of 1932.

When efforts were made by the Nationalists and Socialists to form a united front in the 1928–1929 period, the Korean Communists in Shanghai established the League of Korean Independence Movement Workers. In early 1930, the Korean Independence Party, which moved from Manchuria to Shanghai, supported Kim Ku, and took the initiative to revive the Provisional Government which had badly deteriorated.

The Japanese aggression in Manchuria in September 1931 and the Shanghai Incident of January 1932 gave a new impetus to the Korean Nationalists in China as anti-Japanese sentiment was rising among the Chinese. Sensing the growing urgency for all anti-Japanese Koreans to unite and struggle for Korean liberation, the Nationalists with Socialist orientation, such as Kim Kyu-shik and Kim Tu-bong, made efforts to bring about a united party. As a result, in July 1932, the Korean Anti-Japanese Front Unification League was formed, but many right wing Nationalist organizations, including the Korean Independence Party of Kim Ku refused to join it.

The Korean Independence Party carried out terrorist activities against the Japanese. On January 8, 1932, Yi Pong-ch'ang, one of its members, attempted to assassinate the Japanese emperor at the Sakurada Gate in Tokyo, and another member, Yun Pong-gil, threw bombs at the Japanese attending a celebration of the Japanese emperor's birthday at Hungk'ou Park in Shanghai on April 29, 1932, wounding many prominent Japanese such as Shigemitsu

Mamoru, General Shirakawa Yoshinori, and Admiral Nomura Kichisaburō. Shirakawa and another Japanese died of wounds. It was at this time that An Ch'ang-ho was arrested and sent to a prison in Korea.

With the help of some members of the Chinese Nationalist Party, Kim Ku's followers were trained at the Chinese Nationalists' Loyang Military Academy, and in 1934 Kim Ku formed the Korean Independence Army Special Duty Unit "to arm every Korean for the Korean revolution and destroy the Japanese imperialism." Among the Korean military leaders in China were Chi Tae-hyŏng (alias Yi Ch'ŏng-ch'ŏn, 1888–1959), Yi Pŏm-sŏk (b. 1900), and Kim Wŏn-bong. Meanwhile, the Korean Independence Party, which supported Kim Ku, disintegrated toward the end of 1933 under heavy Japanese pressure.

Kim Wŏn-bong, the founder of the Righteous Fighters Corps (*Ŭiyŏltan*) in Manchuria in November 1919, who had been active in Peking, arrived in Nanking in the spring of 1932, and contacted Chiang Kai-shek, receiving the latter's financial support. Subsequently, a Korean military unit (the Sixth Route Unit) of the Chinese Nationalist Army headed by Kim Wŏn-bong was formed under the supervision of the Chinese Military Commission. The Korean military unit was later renamed the Korean Volunteer Corps.

Following the signing of the Sino-Japanese (the Ho-Umezu) Agreement of July 1935, in which the Chinese capitulated to Japanese demands, the collaboration between the Koreans and the Chinese Nationalists declined. As a result, the acceleration of the anti-Japanese movement and the unity of the Koreans became more important.

In early July 1935, representatives of nine Korean Nationalist organizations of overseas Koreans met in Shanghai, and established the Korean National Revolutionary Party as a united body of the Koreans under the leadership of Kim Wŏn-bong, Kim Kyu-shik, and Cho So-ang. Many Korean Communists in central and southern regions of China joined it, but Kim Ku's rightist party did not. Among its aims were destroying Japanese imperialism and bringing about the Korean independence, purging all feudal and other anti-revolutionary forces and establishing a democratic regime in Korea, eliminating the economic system under which the majority are exploited by the minority, instituting universal suffrage, granting the people freedom of speech, press, and assembly, granting equal rights to women, punishing and confiscating the properties of traitors, and maintaining close ties with the liberation movements of the oppressed people of the world. It established a military arm under the direction of Kim Wŏn-bong and Yi Ch'ŏng-ch'ŏn. It was at this juncture that Kim Ku formed his own Korean Nationalist Party.

Cho So-ang, who reactivated the Korean Independence Party in April 1937, and Yi Ch'ŏng-ch'ŏn and his followers, who defected from the Korean National Revolutionary Party and revived the Korean Revolutionary Party in May, allied themselves with Kim Ku's Korean Nationalist Party, bringing the long sought unity of the Korean Nationalists in August. With this, they issued a "Joint

Declaration of the Korean Restoration Movement Organizations" which stated that the Provisional Government was the legitimate successor of the spirit of the March First Movement and that it was the "public weapon of our people." It also stated that "It is the absolute duty of the Nationalists to support it."

Shortly after the Japanese brought about the Marco Polo Bridge Incident on July 7, 1937, which marked the beginning of the Sino-Japanese War, the Chinese Nationalists revived their alliance with the Korean Nationalists. Kim Ku and Kim Wŏn-bong met them near Nanking and agreed to form a united front against the Japanese, and the training of Korean soldiers at the Shengtze Military Academy began in December.

When the Japanese invaded the Shanghai-Nanking area at the end of 1937, most of the Korean Nationalists and Communists left that area. After staying briefly in Changsha, Hunan Province, they went to Chungking. Some Koreans remained behind as underground agents. Sometime in 1938, Kim Ku organized a small military contingent named the Revolutionary Front Combat Area Maneuvering Unit.

Radical Communists who became disenchanted with the leadership of Kim Wŏn-bong and the policies of the Korean National Revolutionary Party, defected from it, and in June 1938 they formed their own Korean Youth Wartime Service Corps, which was renamed the Korean Youth Vanguard League in 1942. The founders of the Corps proposed moving to north China to fight the Japanese in alliance with the Chinese Communists. Some Communist leaders, such as Cho Pong-am, Hong Nam-p'yo, and Pak Hŏn-yŏng, could not agree on ideology and purpose while radical Communists bitterly criticized their leaders who collaborated with the Nationalists and advocated a complete disassociation from the Nationalists. Ch'oe Ch'ang-ik, who led the separatist movement, took a large number of members of the Korean National Revolutionary Party to Shansi Province in north China in 1938, where he formed the North China Branch Unit of the Korean Volunteer Corps.

With the arrival of more Korean Communists from Chungking to Shansi Province, the Korean Communists formed the North China Korean Youth Federation in January 1941. It was renamed the North China Korean Independence League in August 1942. The Federation stated that its aims were to struggle against imperialists of the world, liberate Korea and its oppressed people, and establish a Socialist state in Korea. Kim Tu-bong and Ch'oe Ch'ang-ik became the leaders of the Korean Communists in north China. During 1943 and 1944, the Korean Communists in south China, who had been fighting the Japanese as well as the Chinese Nationalists, retreated to Yenan, joined a Korean group under a Korean Communist named Mu Chŏng, and remained there until the end of World War II. Mu Chŏng was a former commander of a Korean unit of the Eight Route Army of the Chinese Communists. He fled from Kiangsi Province with Mao Tse-tung in the Long March, and after arriving in Yenan he organized a new military unit of the Koreans with the graduates of the Anti-Japanese Military-Political Institute at Yenan. After August 1945, many Korean Communists went to Manchuria, entering North Korea in late 1945 and early 1946.

In 1929, Kim Wŏn-bong who arrived in Chungking at the invitation of the Chinese Nationalists met Kim Ku, and in May the two Kims issued an "Open Letter to Comrades and Compatriots," in which they confessed their past errors and urged all Koreans to unite and fight the Japanese. However, their followers, particularly those Nationalists in the United States who supported Kim Ku, vehemently opposed the merger, and the two Kims failed to form a united body. As a result, the two Korean groups collaborated separately with the Chinese Nationalists.

In April 1940, the Korean Nationalists in Chungking dissolved their parties and formed a new Korean Independence Party under Kim Ku, and in September Kim Ku formed the Restoration Army with the assistance of the Chinese Nationalists. The Restoration Army was reorganized in July 1942 when it merged with the Korean Volunteer Corps of Kim Wŏn-bong. It consisted of three divisions, headed by Yi Ch'ŏng-ch'ŏn, Yi Pŏm-sŏk, and Kim Wŏn-bong. Thus at last the long sought unity of the Nationalists and the Communists in Chungking seemed to have been achieved in form if not in spirit. However, evidence shows that the Koreans were unable to transcend their differences to achieve their ultimate goal.

Some fifty Korean college students, who had been mobilized into the Japanese Army in 1943 and 1944 and were sent to China, deserted their units and went to Chungking in early 1945. They were warmly welcomed by the Nationalists there. But soon they became bewildered when they witnessed the disunity and factionalism among the Nationalists, as well as between the Nationalists and Communists. Chang Chun-ha, one of the Korean students who arrived in Chungking, remarked that the Korean leaders looked like "a roaring beast fighting for a piece of meat." He stated that "This ugly scene went from bad to worse as days went by." These students were sent to Sian to join the Second Division of the Restoration Army under Commander Yi Pŏm-sŏk, and they received training under the Americans there.

National Restoration Movements of the Koreans in Manchuria and Siberia.
The anti-Japanese activities of the Koreans in the Vladivostok area and southeastern Manchuria accelerated after 1910, particularly after the March First Movement, as thousands of Koreans emigrated to the Chientao region. The number of Koreans in southeastern Manchuria swelled to about 600,000 and those in the Maritime Province of Siberia to 200,000 by early 1920. Southeastern Manchuria was destined to become the main theater of Korean Nationalists' anti-Japanese military activities because of its proximity to Korea, the presence of a large number of Koreans, and its terrain, which was favorable to guerrilla activities.

The first anti-Japanese organization of Korean Nationalists that appeared in Manchuria after the Japanese annexation of Korea was the Korean Revolutionary Corps which was established in 1915 by the radical Nationalists Pak Ŭn-shik and Yi Tong-hwi. It collaborated with the Righteous Army of Korea which had been established by Yi Pŏm-jin in Siberia. Many Korean Nationalists were lured by military and financial aid offered by the Bolsheviks after 1917.

In June 1919, Yi Tong-hwi organized the Korean People's Socialist Party at a Soviet-Manchurian border city of Khabarovsk. Shortly thereafter, Yi went to Shanghai, became premier of the Korean Provisional Government, and established the Koryŏ (Korean) Communist Party there in May 1920. Meanwhile, his followers who remained in Siberia also renamed their party in April 1920, and moved it to Irkutsk. As a result, Yi's party was often called the Shanghai faction, while the group that settled in Irkutsk was referred to as the Irkutsk faction, of the Korean Communist Party. The latter group established a military academy with the help of the Soviet Bolsheviks.

In November 1919, Kim Wŏn-bong who was known as a Nationalist-Communist established an organization named *Ŭiyŏltan* of the (Righteous Fighters Corps), which sent trained agents into Korea and China. Although it was a small group, every member swore to fight the Japanese and liberate Korea with his blood. Kim too went to China a few years later, but most of the members remained in Manchuria and carried out guerrilla activities against the Japanese and the Koreans who were regarded as Japanese collaborators. One of its members attempted to assassinate General Tanaka Giichi of Japan who was in Shanghai in March 1922.

Meanwhile, more anti-Japanese associations of Korean Nationalists appeared in Manchuria in early 1920. Among them were the Korean People's Association in West Chientao and the North Chientao Great Korean National Association. Some 3,000 to 4,000 Koreans armed themselves and engaged in military actions against the Japanese across the Tumen River. Many of them had fought against the Japanese as members of the Righteous Army at the end of the Yi period.

The increasing number of Korean military units and their anti-Japanese activities led the Japanese to take punitive actions against them. Although a Manchurian warlord, Chang Tso-lin, did not meet the earlier requests of the Japanese to subjugate or expel the Korean Nationalists in Manchuria, he sent his troops, accompanied by Japanese advisers, to Chientao in 1920 and then allowed Japanese troops to patrol the Korean-Manchurian border area. As a result, some 1,200 Korean Nationalists were arrested and 80 of them were shot to death by the Japanese.

In response to the Japanese pressure, the Korean military groups stepped up their counter moves, and in June 1920, they inflicted heavy casualties on

Japanese troops. Thereupon, the Japanese dispatched a large number of troops from Korea to Manchuria to destroy the Korean Nationalists and their military units, forcing the Koreans to retreat into rugged mountain regions. But before the Koreans took refuge in the mountain regions, a military unit of 1,800 men under Kim Chwa-jin (1889–1929), commander of the Korean Independence Army, won a memorable victory against 10,000 Japanese troops at Ch'ingshan-li (Ch'ŏngsan-ri in Korean) in Chilin Province on October 21, 1920. The Korean victory in Ch'ingshan-li left a landmark in Korea's national liberation movement.

As large units of Japanese troops were mobilized against them, the Korean military units moved into rugged hills in southern Manchuria, and at Mishan some 3,500 men formed in late 1920 the United Greater Korean Independence Army Corps. In March 1921, it and other Korean groups in Siberia formed the Greater Korean Volunteer Army consisting of two brigades. One of their commanders was Kim Chwa-jin. A military school was established by the Koreans in the vicinity of Alekseyevsk, Siberia, in the summer of 1921, in order to train more soldiers.

A tragedy struck the Korean Nationalists in Siberia in the summer of 1921. The Soviets wished to put all Korean Nationalists and their military units under the control of the Korean Communists in Irkutsk. When the Irkutsk group organized the Korean Revolutionary Military Council in June 1921, with the Russian assistance, the Nationalists refused to go along with the Russian scheme. Thereupon, the Irkutsk faction and Soviet troops surrounded the Korean Nationalist troops located at Alekseyevsk and fighting broke out between the Nationalist and Communist troops. This is called the "Free City Incident" of June 27, 1921, in which several hundred Nationalist troops were killed or wounded and nearly a thousand were captured. Those who survived the ordeal fled back to Manchuria, but the military strength of the Nationalists was drastically curtailed. Meanwhile, the Koreans in Siberia were completely Sovietized as Chang Tso-lin's campaign against the Korean military and political organizations in Chientao was intensified.

Facing growing problems, the Korean Nationalists and Communists attempted to form a united front in Manchuria. However, their goals were not achieved, and in the end a new political organization named *Kungminbu,* or the "National Center" with a military branch, was established by a few Nationalists and Communists in April 1929. Its aims were to restore Korean independence, establish justice and the equality of man, and confiscate the properties of the enemies of the people. It acted as the self-governing agency of the Koreans; its branches were established in other parts of Manchuria; and it sent agents into Korea to establish its branches there. Although for strategic reasons it did not specifically so state, its intention was to establish a Socialist republic of Korea. The National Center, known also as the Korean Revolutionary Party, became one of the main anti-Japanese Korean forces in Manchuria. Meanwhile, Korean

Nationalists who refused to cooperate with the Communists, formed in July 1930 their own association called the Korean Independence Party, but it was overshadowed by the Communist dominated National Center and its Korean Revolutionary Army which won a minor victory against Japanese troops in March 1932 at Hsinpin. The Korean Independence Party moved to Shanghai early in 1933. In February 1933, the Korean Revolutionary Army joined the Liaoning Save-the-Nation Association of the Chinese Communists, and the combined forces of the Koreans and the Chinese won a major victory at Hsingching, Manchuria, in October 1933, but their strength was drastically depleted.

The Japanese stepped up their military actions against the Korean Nationalists and Communists after the establishment of a new state of Manchukuo in 1932. The Korean Revolutionary Army of some 3,000 men continued to struggle against the Japanese in collaboration with the South Manchuria Committee of the Chinese Communist Party and its First Route Army of the Northeast Anti-Japanese Volunteer Army. In September 1933,. when it was renamed the Northeast People's Revolutionary Army, many Koreans joined it. It consisted of six armies in 1934, and its Second Army consisted mostly of Koreans under a Korean commander. A Korean woman named Yi Hong-gwang was commander of the First Division of the First Army. It was at this juncture that the name Kim Il-sŏng became widely known as a Korean hero.

There were four Koreans who were engaged in anti-Japanese guerrilla activities in Manchuria and assumed Kim Il-sŏng as their alias, including the present North Korean president. The first Korean to do so was Kim Kwang-sŏ who was born in 1887. After graduating from a Japanese military academy in 1911, he turned against the Japanese and engaged in anti-Japanese guerrilla activity in Manchuria. His other alias was Kim Kyŏng-ch'ŏn. Perhaps it was he who was sent by the Russian Communists to Korea in 1920 and who died in 1922. The second Korean who assumed Kim Il-sŏng as his alias was Kim Sŏng-ju, who was born in South Hamgyŏng Province in 1901. A graduate of a Communist College in the Soviet Union, he was a staff member of the Northeast People's Revolutionary Army of the Chinese Communists. It was he who led the Korean Communists and attacked the Japanese in a small town in Korea named Poch'ŏnbo, in 1937.

The third Kim Il-sŏng may have been the one who led a group of Communists and in May 1930 destroyed the town of Yongjŏng (Lungching in Chinese) in Chientao where there was a large Korean population. He may have died in that year. The fourth Kim Il-sŏng is the present North Korean president who was born in 1912 as Kim Sŏng-ju in South P'yŏng-an Province. His earlier alias was Kim Yŏng-hwan, but perhaps in 1937, after the death of the hero of the Battle of Poch'ŏnbo in 1937, Kim Sŏng-ju adopted Kim Il-sŏng (Kim Il-sung) as his new alias. He was a low ranking officer in the Third Detachment of the First Company of the Second Army of the Northeast People's Revolutionary Army of the Chinese Communists. He took part in the battle against the Japanese at Millim in late 1939 and early 1940, was wounded, and after recovering he fled to the Soviet Union in December 1940.

Encountering growing difficulties as the Japanese increased their military pressure, the Korean Nationalists reorganized the Korean Independence Party in the spring of 1934, but they fought uphill battles and suffered many heartbreaks. In the meantime, the Korean Communists felt it necessary to form a united front of all anti-Japanese Koreans in Manchuria, and in May 1936 they brought about the establishment of the Fatherland Restoration Association of the Koreans in Manchuria as a united party of the Nationalists and the Communists.

The Fatherland Restoration Association of the Koreans in Manchuria published its periodicals named the *March First Monthly* and the *Fire-field People*. The platform and the ten-point program of the Association clearly showed that it was pursuing Nationalist rather than Socialist goals for the time being. It stressed the anti-Japanese campaign and Korean independence, and expressed no Socialist aims. It established branches in northern Korea in cooperation with the leaders of the *Ch'ŏndogyo* sect in Korea.

The Koreans in the military units of the Chinese Communists in Manchuria fought guerrilla wars against the Japanese in cooperation with the guerrillas of the Fatherland Restoration Association of the Koreans in Manchuria. In June 1937, a detachment of guerrillas led by Kim Il-sŏng attacked the Japanese police station at Poch'ŏnbo, South Hamgyŏng Province, killed a few Japanese policemen, destroyed the town, and kidnapped many Koreans. This is what the North Koreans celebrate today as the "Great Victory of Marshal Kim Il-sŏng at the Battle of Poch'ŏnbo," but the evidence shows that it was not Kim Il-sung of North Korea, but another Kim Song-ju whose alias was Kim Il-sŏng who carried out the attack.

The Japanese accelerated their anti-guerrilla campaign, and by early 1938 many members of the Fatherland Restoration Association of the Koreans in Manchuria fled either to China or to Siberia, and the Association was virtually destroyed by the Japanese. However, in May 1939 today's Kim Il-sung of North Korea led a Partisan band and attacked Japanese establishments in Musan, North Hamgyŏng Province. When the military units of the Chinese Communists were decimated by the Japanese in 1939 and 1940 and many Communists were arrested, the Korean Communists, including Kim Il-sung, fled to Khabarovsk in December 1940. Thus, by 1941 all anti-Japanese Korean associations and military units had been destroyed, or forced to go underground, or had fled to Siberia.

Nationalist Movement of the Koreans in Japan. The national liberation movement of the Koreans in Japan was initiated by Korean students who were studying at various colleges and universities in Tokyo and other cities. Before

1920 the Korean movement was by and large that of the Nationalists, but after 1920 it became dominated by radicals such as Socialists, Communists, and Anarchists, who changed it into a violent anti-Japanese and terroristic movement. The suppression of the movement by the Japanese police, particularly after the imposition of the Peace Preservation Law of 1925, brought about the sharp decline of the Koreans' liberation movement in Japan. As a result, it virtually ceased to exist as such, while the leftists engaged in an ideological and labor struggle on behalf of Socialism and Communism.

There were some 300 Korean students in Japan in 1910. Syngman Rhee (Yi Sŭng-man), who was expelled from Korea in 1911, stopped over in Tokyo on his way to the United States, and he encouraged the Korean students to promote the national liberation movement at a secret meeting held at the Korean YMCA at Kanda, Tokyo. The Korean YMCA was the center of the Nationalist movement in Japan at that time.

There were seven Korean student organizations, including the Fraternal Society of the Korean Students in Tokyo, which published a journal named *The Light of Learning;* the Korean Academic Association of Yi Kwang-su, Shin Ik-hŭi, and Chang Tŏk-su; the Society for the Encouragement of Learning among Korean Women, which was led by two women students, Kim Chŏng-ae and Na Hye-sŏk; and the Student Society of *Ch'ŏndogyo* under the leadership of Ch'oe Rin, which published a journal called *The Eastern Light.* Other Nationalist Korean student leaders were Yi Sang-jae, Cho Man-shik, An Chae-hong, Song Chin-u, and a woman student named Kim P'il-lye.

Inspired by President Wilson's Fourteen Points, which included the principle of self-determination by subjugated peoples, in January 1919, Korean students in Tokyo organized the Korean Youth Independence Corps, and on February 8 some 600 Korean students met at the Korean YMCA and drafted, under the guidance of Yi Kwang-su, Chang Tŏk-su, and Yŏ Un-hyŏng, (who arrived from Shanghai with instructions from the Korean Nationalists in China), a student declaration of Korean independence and a "Petition for the Convening of a National Congress." They sent printed materials to Japanese cabinet members of the Diet, and the Japanese Governor-General in Korea, as well as to Japanese newspaper presses, magazine publishers, and scholars, calling for Korean independence. A few of them went to Korea to promote the independence movement among students and others there. Many Korean students were promptly arrested and nine were imprisoned, and several student leaders fled to Korea or to Shanghai.

When the March First Movement took place in Korea, Korean students in Japan also demonstrated in Tokyo, Osaka, Kyoto, and other cities. As the Japanese police rounded up some of those who participated in the demonstrations, some 500 Koreans (359 of them were students) fled from Japan. Those students who remained carried out another demonstration in Tokyo in early November, demanding the liberation of Korea from Japan.

With the departure of right wing Nationalist students from Japan in 1919 and shortly thereafter, the Korean national liberation movement in Japan fell into the hands of Korean leftists and Anarchists. In March 1922, the Koreans carried out another demonstration in Japan calling for the liberation of Korea.

Among the extremist Korean organizations in Japan was the Black Current Society which was organized in 1921. It split into the Wind and Lightning Society of the Anarchists and the North Star Association of the Socialists. The Wind and Lightning Society, which in 1922 was renamed the Black Comrades Society, was under the leadership of an Anarchist named Pak Yŏl. Pak's plot to assassinate the Japanese crown prince (present Emperor Hirohito) on his wedding day in October 1923 was uncovered by the police, and he and his conspirators were arrested in September, crippling the Korean Anarchist group. The Black Comrades Society was renamed the North Wind Society in 1927.

The North Star Association was under a Korean Socialist named Kim Yak-su. This Association, which stressed the theoretical basis of the mass movement, received ideological guidance and financial support from Japanese Communists. It sent its representatives to Korea and formed the Saturday Society and the North Wind Society in Seoul, promoting the Socialist movement in Korea. At the same time, in January 1925, it established a study group in Tokyo named the January Society, which attracted many young Korean students.

The politically oriented Korean students in Tokyo formed a theatrical society named *Kŭgyesul Hyŏp'oe* in the spring of 1922, and it toured in Korea during the summer of 1922, performing such plays as *The Death of Kim Yŏng-il* written by Cho Myŏng-hŭi and *The Last Handshake* written by Hong Nanp'a, in addition to an Irish play, *The Glittering Gate* written by Lord Dunsany. When the society was dissolved under the order of the Japanese police in August, Korean students in Tokyo formed, in the same year, another theatrical group named *T'ōworhoe* and performed such plays as *Resurrection* by Leo Tolstoy. It performed several plays written by Korean playwrights, such as *The Bird in the Cage*. When, in November 1929, it performed a nationalistic play, *Arirang kogae* (The Arirang Pass), written by Pak Sŭng-hŭi, the Japanese police promptly dissolved the group.

The radicalism of Korean movements grew in the wake of the Japanese massacre of some 20,000 Koreans following the great earthquake of September 1923 in the Kantō region. The General Federation of Korean Labor Unions in Japan was established by Korean Socialists in November 1923, and its membership grew from 1,220 in that year to 23,530 by 1929. Meanwhile, the Tokyo branches of the *Shin-ganhoe* and the *Kŭnuhoe,* which emerged in Korea in 1927, were established and attempted to promote unity among the Koreans in order to achieve their nationalist objectives.

Korean students in Tokyo organized, in 1934, a new dramatic group named Tokyo Student Artists for the purpose of resurrecting national spirit through theatre, and performed in the summer of 1935, *The Cow,* a play written by Yu Ch'i-jin. At the same time, it published its journal, *Mak (The Curtain),* but its existence was cut short by the police.

The Korean population in Japan increased from 26,506 in 1919 to 276,061 in 1929, and to 537,695 in 1934. The number of Korean organizations grew from 165 in 1929 to 1,027 in 1934 with a total membership of 149,632. According to Japanese police reports, seventy-four of these organizations with 5,261 members were Communist groups, 4 with 165 members were Socialist, 19 with 2,048 members were moderate Socialist with Nationalist inclinations, 11 with 616 members were Anarchist, and 230 with 18,036 members were classified as right wing Nationalist groups. In 1929, a journal named *Musanja (Proletariat)* of the leftist Korean students appeared and a Marxist study group called *Tong-jisa* (The Comrades Society) was established in 1931.

With the outbreak of the Mukden Incident in September 1931, which marked the beginning of a new Japanese imperialistic expansion in China, censorship of the press and control over associations was vastly tightened. However, the Koreans continued to struggle against the Japanese with their cultural movements for the purpose of preserving Korean national and racial consciousness. In January 1932, a young Korean Nationalist named Yi Pong-ch'ang, who came from Shanghai, attempted to assassinate the Japanese emperor and attempted to bomb him at Sakurada Gate in Tokyo.

The Korean Socialists established the People's Front for Cultural Movement in 1933, and launched the Proletarian cultural movement. Meanwhile, various drama groups such as the Samil (March First) Drama Society, the Koryŏ Drama Society, and the Student Art Society emerged. The Japan branch of the Korean Artista Proleta Federatio, better known as the KAPF, emerged in Tokyo in 1937. However, they were engaged more in promoting Socialism, including anti-imperialism and anti-colonialism, than in furthering the national liberation movement.

After the Sino-Japanese War began in July 1937, the anti-Japanese and national liberation movement of the Koreans was brought to a halt by the Japanese, and the number of organizations, including those which had been promoting better relations between the Koreans and the Japanese, declined. Most leftist organizations were broken up while those of the Nationalists became fraternal or mutual aid groups. When the Pacific War began in December 1941 there were virtually no Korean organizations in Japan engaged in the national liberation movement.

Efforts made by the Koreans at home and abroad to liberate their fatherland from Japanese colonial rule did not bring about their desired objective. However, the Korean freedom fighters, whether they were rightists or leftists, sustained the hope and aspirations of the Koreans for their national independence. It is true that, by the end of the colonial period, more than 85 per cent of the Koreans had Japanese-style names, but the people as a whole remained

Korean in spirit and action, and their desire for independence increased, rather than diminished.

Those who stayed in Korea to carry out their struggle to reconstruct the Korean society, enlighten and strengthen the people, and preserve their cultural heritage, accomplished many remarkable things. Despite Japanese repression and the efforts they made to replace the Korean language with the Japanese language, more Koreans learned how to read Korean script, and the literacy rate rose above the 50 per cent level. Many Koreans received modern education, thanks to many private schools established by both Korean Nationalists and foreign mission boards. Despite various hardships to which they were subjected, the Korean people contributed significantly toward the reconstruction of their own society and economic life as well as to the promotion of a culture uniquely their own, always with a longing for freedom and justice.

PART IV

THE LIBERATION AND MODERN TRANSFORMATION

9. Korea Under the Allied Occupation

Korea was liberated from Japan at the end of World War II, but it did not become free and independent. Instead, it was partitioned along the 38th parallel, with American troops occupying the area south of the line and Soviet troops occupying the area to the north. The Allied occupation of Korea lasted officially until August 1948. Soviet troops, however, did not leave North Korea until the end of 1948, and U.S. troops did not withdraw from South Korea until the end of June 1949.

The Liberation and Partition

Agreements of the Allies on Korea.   At Cairo, in November 1943, British Prime Minister Winston Churchill, American President Franklin D. Roosevelt, and China's Generalissimo Chiang Kai-shek held a conference and issued the Cairo Declaration dated December 1, which stated that "in due course Korea shall become free and independent." The phrase "in due course" was presumed by the Koreans to mean, "when Korea was liberated from Japan." Roosevelt, however, maintained that Asian colonial peoples, including the Koreans, were not ready to enjoy freedom and independence, and therefore needed to be educated and trained, under the tutelage of the Allied Powers over a considerable length of time, in order to enjoy democratic rights and institutions.

At the Teheran meeting of the Allied leaders in late November 1943, Joseph Stalin accepted the decision made at Cairo by the other three Allied leaders; and at the Yalta meeting in February 1945, he agreed to join the Allies in a war against Japan three months after the German surrender. It was the opinion of American policy makers that the United States could not defeat the Japanese without Soviet assistance, for they grossly overestimated the strength of the Kantō Army of Japan in Manchuria as well as the presumed Japanese determination to fight against the Allies "to the last person."

At the Potsdam Conference of the United States, Great Britain, and the Soviet Union in July 1945, the Allies decided to deliver an ultimatum to Japan for its unconditional surrender. Simultaneously, the American and Soviet Chiefs of Staff worked out an agreement to synchronize military operations against Japan should Japan refuse to accept the Potsdam ultimatum. In accordance with the Yalta agreement, on August 8 the Soviet Union declared war on Japan, and immediately began military actions against the Japanese.

The Partition of Korea.   Following large-scale Soviet attacks against Japanese troops in Korea on August 10, Soviet forces landed at Ch'ōngjin and Nanam on the northeast coast. It seemed as though the Soviets could penetrate deep into the southern part of the peninsula while American troops were still more than 600 miles away from Korea. The American government saw it as both expedient and desirable, therefore, to propose that a military demarcation line be established in order to stop the Soviet advance.

The United States government not wishing to see all of Korea occupied by Soviet troops, decided hurriedly, without giving due consideration to the possible consequences, to establish the military demarcation line along the 38th parallel. Stalin accepted the American proposal without objection. Accordingly, Soviet troops disarmed the Japanese troops and occupied the area north ·of the line, and American troops, which arrived in Korea in early September, did likewise in the area south of the line, with the agreement that after the Japanese surrendered a joint control of the Allies was to be extended throughout Korea.

When Korea was partitioned, the Russian zone contained 55 per cent (48,240 sq. miles) and the American zone contained 45 per cent (37,060 sq. miles) of the total area. According to the Japanese census, taken by the Japanese in May 1944, the population in the south was 15,944,000 whereas that of the north was 9,170,000. Thousands of workers were mobilized from the south and sent to industrial sites in the north, and as a result, by the time Korea was liberated from Japan, the population of the north had grown to about 9.5 million.

The Emergence of the People's Republic of Korea.   When the Japanese were about to accept the Potsdam ultimatum, Endō Ryūsaku, Director-General of Administration of the Government-General, approached Yŏ Un-hyŏng, a prominent left wing Nationalist who had organized in 1944 an underground secret society named the Alliance for Korean Independence,

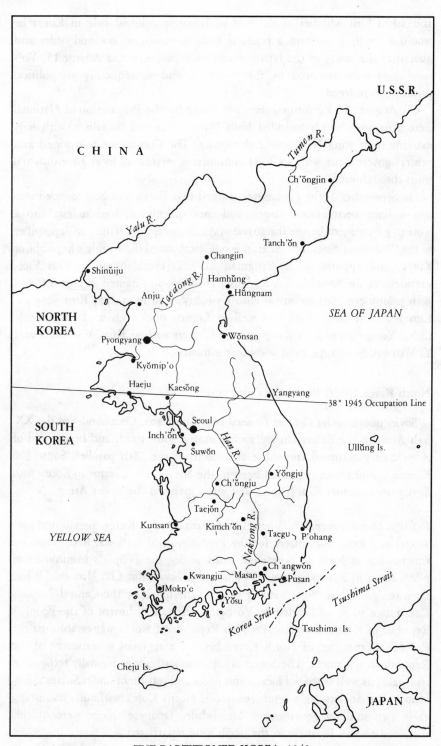

U.S.S.R.

CHINA

Tumen R.

Ch'ŏngjin

Yalu R.

Tanch'ŏn

Changjin

Shinŭiju

Taedong R.

Hamhŭng

Anju

Hŭngnam

NORTH
KOREA

SEA OF JAPAN

Pyongyang

Wŏnsan

Kyŏmip'o

Haeju   Kaesŏng

Yangyang

———— 38° 1945 Occupation Line

SOUTH
KOREA

Seoul

Inch'ŏn

Han R.

Ullŭng Is.

Suwŏn

Ch'ŏngju

Yŏngju

Taejŏn

Naktong R.

Kunsan   Kimch'ŏn

Taegu   P'ohang

YELLOW SEA

Ch'angwŏn

Kwangju   Masan

Pusan

Tsushima Strait

Mokp'o

Yŏsu

Korea Strait

Tsushima Is.

Cheju Is.

JAPAN

THE PARTITIONED KOREA, 1945

and asked him whether at the end of Japanese colonial rule in Korea he would be willing to form a political body to maintain law and order and guarantee the safety of the Japanese and their property. On August 15, Yo's conditions were accepted by the Japanese, and subsequently all political prisoners were freed.

On August 16, Yŏ formed the Committee for the Preparation of National Reconstruction, which included both Nationalists and Socialists, with only extreme right wing Nationalists abstaining. The Committee functioned as a central government with its local committees serving as local governmental units throughout Korea.

On September 2, the Committee learned that Korea had been divided into two military occupational zones; and they quickly resolved to establish a Korean government before the arrival of American troops. Thus, on September 6, the "National Assembly" met in Seoul, established the People's Republic of Korea, and appointed Dr. Syngman Rhee as President and Yŏ as Vice-president of the Republic. A Socialist, Hŏ Hŏn, was named as premier, and such prominent Nationalists as Kim Kyu-shik, Cho Man-shik, Kim Sŏng-su, Kim Ku, and Shin Ik-hŭi, as well as Communists such as Yi Kwan-sul, Ch'oe Yong-dal, and Yi Kang-guk, and others such as Kim Wŏn-bong and Yi Man-gyu were appointed as cabinet ministers.

North Korea Under the Soviet Occupation

Soviet troops under Colonel General Ivan Chistiakov, Commander of the XX-Vth Army of the Soviet Union, swiftly moved southward, and by the end of August they occupied the entire area north of the 38th parallel. Some 300 Korean Communists, who had been in the Soviet Union, came to Korea with Soviet troops under Kim Il-sung who was a major in the Soviet Army.

Political Development.   When the Russians invaded Korea, they found provincial and local committees for the Preparation of National Reconstruction functioning as local governmental units under the People's Committee of North Korea in Pyongyang headed by Christian Nationalist Cho Man-shik. It had been recognized as the top ruling body in the north by the Central People's Committee in Seoul headed by Yŏ before the establishment of the People's Republic of Korea. Once the People's Republic of Korea was established the People's Committee of North Korea became a regional government of the Republic in the north. The Soviet occupation authorities formally recognized its legality as well as that of local committees and put them under Soviet supervision. The Soviets, as a result, governed North Korea without establishing their own military government. Meanwhile, Japanese troops were quickly disarmed and all Japanese in the north were repatriated.

The People's Committee of North Korea was reorganized first into the Temporary Five Provinces People's Committee, and then on October 19, 1945, with the approval of the Soviets, into the Five Provinces Administrative Bureau. Known as "Gandhi of Korea," Cho Man-shik was respected by the majority of the people in Korea, and his popularity was such that the Soviet occupation authorities found it expedient to appoint him Chief of the Executive Committee of the Five Provinces Administrative Bureau.

Meanwhile, the Soviets began eliminating all vestiges of Japanese rule; they printed new money, abolished the old educational system, removed many industrial plants along with much equipment which had been installed by the Japanese, and imposed tight economic controls. Thousands of Koreans fled to the south. In November, Cho Man-shik formed the Korean (Chosŏn) Democratic Party whose membership was largely composed of Christians, Nationalists, intellectuals, the middle class property owners, and anti-Communist students. Meanwhile, in February 1946, the *Ch'ŏndogyo* sect established a rightist political organization named the Ch'ŏng-udang, or the *Ch'ŏndogyo* Fraternal Party.

The Rise of Kim Il-sung.   Kim Il-sung returned to Korea with Soviet troops sometime in early September as a major in the Soviet 28th Military Group which was commanded by Colonel General Terenti F. Shtykov. Kim led about 300 men collectively known as the Partisan (or the Kapsan) faction. He moved quickly to establish his power with the support of the Soviets. In late September, Hyŏn Chun-hyŏk, leader of the "domestic faction" of Korean Communists was assassinated. The members of this group were those Communists who were in Korea during the Japanese period. The Soviets put their hopes in Kim Il-sung and supported him. On October 14, they introduced him to the people in Pyongyang as "a national hero." Those who saw Kim for the first time were surprised to see such a young man (age 33), because the Kim Il-sung about whom they had heard had been described as a man in his 50's. Be that as it may, Kim soon became the First Secretary of the 4,530-member North Korean Bureau established on October 15 of the Korean Communist Party.

Shortly after assuming his office, Kim took steps to establish more local Communist parties. This resulted in a series of bloody clashes occurring between the rightists and leftists in Yong-amp'o, and in the anti-Communist uprisings which erupted in late 1945 in Shinŭiju in North P'yŏng-an Province, Pyongyang in South P'yŏng-an Province, and in Hamhŭng in South Hamgyŏng Province. Students, factory workers, and other young Koreans in opposing camps took up arms and caused more than 1,000 deaths. Between November 1945 and the early spring of 1946, the Korean Communists, supported by the Soviets and Security Guard members, dealt ruthlessly with the Nationalists and others who opposed them. Small uprisings and riots of anti-Communist Koreans occurred later, but each time, the Soviets and the Korean Communists suppressed all opposition by killing hundreds and forcing hundreds of thousands of Koreans to flee to the south. As a result, an atmosphere of fear prevailed everywhere. A new form of terrorism became the rule in North Korea, and the people who were freed from Japanese colonial rule were put under an even more oppressive rule by the Communists. As the politics of intimidation emerged in the north, Soviet troops became increasingly unpopular. Meanwhile, Kim Il-sung strengthened his power with the support of the Soviets as well as his own Partisan faction. He conspired to eliminate the Nationalists under Cho Man-shik as well as the Ch'ŏng-udang of the *Ch'ŏndogyo* sect.

Toward the end of 1945, some 22,000 Korean Communists who belonged to the North China Korean Independence League and who had been with Mao Tse-tung at Yenan (thus they were called the Yenan faction) entered North Korea via Manchuria. They were, however, permitted by the Soviets in consultation with Kim Il-sung to enter North Korea only after they were disarmed. In December 1945, some leaders of the Yenan faction, including Kim Tu-bong, went from China to South Korea, but soon after arriving in the south Kim and his followers migrated to the north and joined their former comrades. Since the Yenan faction was no longer allowed to exist as a military unit, it was first renamed the Korean Independence League and then in March 1946 it became the New People's Party with Kim Tu-bong as chairman.

The Moscow Agreement and the Fall of the Nationalists.   The Nationalists in North Korea encountered many difficulties under the Soviet occupation, and ultimately their opposition to the Allied Powers' Moscow Agreement brought about their downfall in early 1946, as Cho Man-shik was put under house arrest and many Nationalists were forced to flee to South Korea.

In mid-December 1945, when the foreign ministers of Great Britain, the United States, and the Soviet Union met in Moscow to deal with postwar problems, they agreed on certain matters concerning Korea. The American Secretary of State James F. Byrnes proposed that immediate actions be taken to abolish the separate zones of military administration as a first step toward the establishment of an independent and unified Korea. At the same time, Byrnes recommended that Korea be put under a five-year Allied trusteeship following the establishment of a Korean government. Foreign Minister V.F. Molotov of the Soviet Union agreed with Byrnes, and proposed that a joint commission of the occupation authorities be established to deal with problems related to economic unification, the new government, and a four-power trusteeship. As a result, the December 24 Moscow Agreement stated that (1) with a view to the reestablishment of Korea as an independent state. . . there shall be set up a provisional Korean democratic government, (2) a Joint Commission composed of representatives of the United States and the Soviet occupation powers shall be established in order to assist the formation of a provisional Korean government, (3) the Joint Commission, with the participation of the Provisional Korean Democratic Government and of the Korean democratic organizations shall work out measures to help the Koreans to achieve political, economic, and social progress, and (4) a five-year trusteeship of the United States, the Soviet Union, Great Britain and China, shall be established in Korea.

It is not clear why the American government proposed a five-year Allied trusteeship instead of a longer one as President Roosevelt had envisioned. Perhaps it was because the Americans believed that the Soviet Union would not agree to such a plan. Regardless, the entire trusteeship idea was a United States proposal, and as Byrnes stated on December 30, the Americans naively believed that "the Joint Soviet-American Commission [might] find .it possible to dispense with the trusteeship." Some Americans believed that only a trusteeship could check possible Soviet domination in Korea. At any rate, the Moscow Agreement failed to abolish the barrier between the two occupied zones. Consequently, the partition of Korea was perpetuated.

The Moscow plan of the Allies met strong Korean opposition from Nationalists and Communists alike. Suddenly, however, the Communists in both zones changed their minds and accepted the plan without reservation, perhaps in order to gain time to strengthen their power base, and perhaps due to Soviet pressure. Whatever their motives, the opposition of the Nationalists to the Moscow plan provided a convenient pretext for the Soviets and Kim Il-sung to crush the Nationalists in the north. The Korean Democratic Party was taken over by Ch'oe Yong-gŏn, a Communist who opposed Kim Il-sung, and the Ch'ŏng-udang was taken over by other Communists. These organizations were kept to present a democratic façade, or as a deception to its current members.

Consolidation of Kim Il-sung's Power.   Following the fall of the Nationalists, Kim Il-sung strengthened his power with the help of the Soviets, particularly that of Major General Romanenko, head of the political arm of the Soviet occupation authorities. When the North Korean Provisional People's Committee was established in February 1946, replacing the Five Provinces Administrative Bureau as the central government of North Korea, Kim became its chairman. Meanwhile, the membership of the North Korean Bureau of the Korean Communist Party grew under Kim's chairmanship from 4,530 in December 1945, to 276,000 in August 1946. At the same time, Kim Il-sung carried out various measures in order to eliminate as many Communists belonging to the "domestic faction," as well as his own men, including An Kil, and Mu Chŏng, who showed tendencies of insubordination.

In late August 1946, the 276,000-member North Korean Bureau of the Korean Communist Party and the 90,000-member New People's Party merged into a single party, taking the name of the North Korean Workers' Party. A short time prior to this, Pak Hŏn-yŏng, chairman of the Korean Communist Party in Seoul, changed the name of his party to the South Korean Workers' Party. By August 1947, the membership of the merged party grew to 680,000. Although Kim Tu-bong was elected chairman and Kim Il-sung and Chu

Nyŏng-ha became vice-chairmen of the united party, the real power was in the hands of Kim Il-sung who had the unqualified support of the Soviets. When the first local elections were held in November to choose the members of provincial, city, county, and district People's Committees (local governmental units) of the North Korean Provisional People's Committee (the central government of North Korea), many supporters of Kim Il-sung were elected. Thus, Kim was able to increase his power both within the North Korean Workers' Party and within the government units.

In mid-February 1947, the General Congress of People's Committees met in Pyongyang, and established the North Korean People's Assembly (a ratifying but not a legislative body). The People's Assembly of 237 members met on February 21 and 22; it established the Presidium, headed by Kim Tu-bong; approved a judicial system for North Korea; and replaced the Provisional People's Committee with a permanent People's Committee composed of the various ministries and bureaus. Of the 22-member People's Committee, 16 were leaders of the North Korean Workers' Party; Kim Il-sung was named its chairman. As head of the executive organ of North Korea and as vice-chairman of the North Korean Workers' Party, Kim vastly increased his power.

Military Development.   The establishment of the Public Security Officers' Training Battalion Headquarters in Pyongyang under Ch'oe Yong-gŏn sometime in September 1946, marked the beginnings of North Korea's military development. By the end of the year, two divisions of Security Forces emerged becoming the forerunners of the Korean People's Army which was established in February 1948. The First Division headquarters was located at Kaech'ŏn, South P'yŏng-an Province and the Second Division headquarters was located at Nanam, North Hamgyŏng Province. The military center established at Chinnamp'o (renamed Namp'o), became the headquarters for the Coast Guard.

A large portion of the Security Force was composed of Korean troops who returned from China, Manchuria, and Siberia. The commanders and officers of the Security Forces were associated with Kim Il-sung. No official conscription system was adopted, but under the "volunteer system," a growing number of youths were recruited from villages, and they were given military training at various training centers. Every recruitment district was obligated to fill the quota with "volunteers." Some 20,000 received military training by the end of 1946 at various centers to which Soviet advisers were assigned.

The Communization of North Korea: Economic Change.   The Soviets, who up until the early spring of 1946, had no long-range plans for Korea, saw the need to establish a pro-Soviet government there. As a result, they hastened to establish an indigenous regime molded after the Soviet political system. In February 1946, the Provisional People's Committee for North Korea emerged as a central government, with Kim Il-sung as its chairman and Kim Tu-bong as its vice-chairman. After that, the process of communization of North Korea was rapid.

In several stages North Korea's economy changed toward Socialization. Three economic plans were implemented after March 1946. The first plan dealt with the eradication of the "colonial deformity of economy" and the construction of a foundation for a Socialist economic structure. The economic plan adopted in 1948 called for an expanded production and a complete removal of what the Communists called "the one-sidedness and backwardness of the colonial economy" in order to establish an independent national economy. The Two-Year Plan adopted in January 1949 laid the foundation for industrial development. A significant aspect of this plan was the reconstructing of the "damaged south Korean industry" which was to follow the reunification of the country. Evidently, the North Korean Communists were confident that during this time period the country would be unified.

The Law on Land Reform issued on March 5, 1946, heralded the beginning of the Communization of the North Korean economy. Kim Il-sung reported that, as of 1946, between 6 and 7 per cent of the farmers owned 54 per cent of the cultivated land, some 51.5 per cent of farmers owned only 5.4 per cent, and 41.5 per cent of farmers were tenants who owned no land. The Communists confiscated farmlands and other lands which had been previously owned by the Japanese, Korean landlords, Christian churches and their schools, Buddhist temples and monasteries, or by those who were classified as "traitors" and "compradors." Of 2,572,500 acres (1,050,000 *chŏngbo*) of farmlands confiscated, 9.5% was those of the Japanese, 2.1% was those of Korean "traitors," 62% was those of large and middle landlords, 25% was those of small landlords, and 1.4% was those of Christian churches and Buddhist temples. Some 70,000 landlord households lost not only their farms, but also 175,846 acres (71,770 *chŏngbo*) of orchards, 8,410,993 acres (3,432,936 *chŏngbo*) of forest lands, 14,477 houses, 4,658 cows, and 116 horses. The upper limit of acreage of privately owned farmland was set at 12.25 acres (5 *chŏngbo*), but some farmers who had less than that amount lost their lands for various reasons. Meanwhile, some 44,000 former landlords were forcibly relocated elsewhere.

The confiscated land was distributed to the tilling farmers. Some 2.4 million acres were given to 724,522 farm households, free of charge, each household receiving 3.20 acres of farmland. Farmers donated 25 per cent of their products to the government as tax. The farm population in 1946 comprised 74.1 per cent of the total population, but this percentage declined to 69.3 by 1949 and continued to decrease as industries grew.

The Communists encouraged laborers and peasants to form unions, and such unions mushroomed. In January 1946, the 430,000-member General Federation of Trade Unions and the 400,000-member Federation of Peasants Unions emerged. The Labor Law for Workers and Office Employees, which was promulgated on June 20, 1946, established an equal wage system and an eight-hour day. All factory and office workers were enrolled in the General Federation of Trade Unions which had power to deal with special wages, extra working hours, and workers' compensation. On July 30, a law was issued, guaranteeing equal rights to women.

As the state-controlled sector in the economy grew, the number of factory and office workers increased from 18.7 per cent of the total population in 1946 to 26.0 per cent in 1949. By 1950, as more factories began operation, the number of blue-collar workers grew to about 600,000. The Law Concerning the Nationalization of Industry, Railroads, Transportation, Communication, and Banks was decreed on August 10, 1946. Under this law, over 1,000 industrial enterprises, or 90 per cent of all the industry in North Korea, became state-owned; small-scale enterprises owned by so-called "nationalist capitalists" were permitted to exist, but their output steadily declined from 13.4 per cent of the gross national product in 1947 to 7.0 per cent in 1950, and 3.0 per cent in 1958. In 1968, all private enterprises were abolished.

The North Korean economy began to improve, particularly during the Two-Year Plan period of 1949-1950. The 212 million rubles of Soviet economic aid made a significant contribution to the economic growth, and it was reported that the gross national product doubled in 1949 as compared with 1946. The cultivated area increased from 4.7 million acres in 1946 to 5.7 million in 1949, and 6.6 million in 1950. The amount of food grains produced increased from 1,898,000 tons in 1946 to 2,654,000 tons in 1949. National income (1946 = 100) grew to 209, gross value of industrial products increased to 337, production of consumer goods to 288, and gross value of agricultural products to 151.

The Rise of Social Organization. Regimentation of the people began with the organization of various Socialist groups which were put under the guidance of the Party. All children between the ages of 9 and 13 were organized in June 1946, and placed in groups in the organization named the Korean Young Pioneers, for the purpose of creating "a new type of human beings who can champion the cause of the Party and the Revolution."

The Communist Youth League was organized in January 1946, and all young men and women between the ages of 14 and 30 became members. The aims of the League were to make the youth become "honor bodyguards and death-defying fighters." They were to defend the Party and execute the order of the leader (Kim Il-sung) on behalf of "the Korean Revolution" and the unification of the country.

In November 1946, all women between the ages of 30 and 50 were organized into the North Korean Democratic Women's League, which was established to mobilize women, give them strong political indoctrination, stimulate them to support the Party, and make them produce more as factory workers and farmers. Equality of the sexes was established under the July 30, 1946 law which guaranteed equal rights to women. With this, the traditional role of women changed dramatically.

Cultural and Educational Change.   After the partition, a radically different educational system and culture emerged in North Korea. Both the philosophy of education and the content and form of culture became revolutionary in character, and the purpose of education and the objectives of cultural activities were designed to promote what the North Korean Communists called "the Korean revolution."

A North Korean publication stated that "only when we eliminate all vestiges of the old ideas remaining in the heads of the people, educate them with the ideology of Communism, and constantly exalt class consciousness and the revolutionary spirit, can we allow them to express their conscious zeal and creative power, and. . . successfully promote revolution. . . ."

The educational goal of the North Koreans was "to arm youth with Communist ideology" and prepare them to be "the builders of a developed Socialism-Communism." Regarding the duties of the teachers, Kim Il-sung said:

Our Party. . . entrusts the people's teachers with the honorable task of educating the younger generations. . . to make them the builders of a developed Socialism-Communism. The Party arms the teachers with the ideology of Marxism-Leninism and cultivates in them an uncompromising spirit against the reactionary thought of the bourgeois. . . it is the first function of teachers to educate youths to be Red warriors.

In other words, "Teachers are not simply the conveyors of knowledge, but the disseminators of Communist ideology and Red propaganda for the Party."

Educational reform measures abolished all private schools, purged all vestiges of Japanese education, and required new textbooks to be published without any Chinese characters. Primary schools were renamed *inmin hakkyo,* or "people's schools." With the adoption of an educational reform law in December 1946, a 5-3-3-4 system of education was implemented, reducing the length of primary education from six to five years. It established 3-year middle schools, 3-year high schools, 3-year junior technical middle schools, and 3-4-year vocational high schools. In July 1946, Kim Il-sung University was established along with 2-year technical and 4-5-year colleges. Some 620 college students were sent to the Soviet Union to receive further education in 1949. The implementation of the plan announced in March 1946 to introduce a system of universal compulsory primary education was postponed until September 1956. In June 1947, day-care nurseries were set up in order to free mothers of young children to work in factories.

The growth statistics for schools and students between 1945 and 1950 were as follows:

	Number of Schools		Number of Students (unit = 1,000)	
	1946–47	1949–50	1947–49	1949–50
Total	2,731	5,069	1,289	1,969
Primary	2,482	3,882	1,183	1,474
Middle Schools	217	920	73	353
High Schools	28	69	30	58
Colleges & Universities	4	15	3	18

All schools were tuition free, but secondary school graduates had no choice as to schools they wished to attend or the curriculum in which they wished to enroll.

Freedom of speech, religion, press, and assembly disappeared rapidly as Socialist culture grew and the Communists permitted the circulation of newspapers and magazines published only in the north. The *Rodong Shinmun* was published by the Korean Workers' Party as its organ. Meanwhile, many new revolutionary songs were produced to arouse patriotism as well as to glorify Kim Il-sung.

South Korea Under American Military Rule

The unexpected suddenness with which Japan surrendered to the Allies caught the Americans by surprise. The United States XXIVth Corps of the Eighth Army, which had fought in the Okinawa campaigns, was ordered to go to Korea and accept the surrender of the Japanese in the area south of the 38th parallel line. On September 6, a month after Soviet troops invaded Korea 72,000 American troops under Lt. General John R. Hodge landed at Inch'ŏn, and proceeded to Seoul and other localities. The next day, Governor-General Abe Nobuyuki surrendered to the Americans. The Japanese troops were quickly disarmed without any incident.

The American occupation forces arrived in Korea without any plans other than to disarm the Japanese troops and evacuate the Japanese from South Korea. They had no knowledge of Korean history, culture, or economic and social conditions, and none spoke the Korean language.

Political Development.   At the outset General Hodge made a serious blunder, when, under the instruction of General Douglas MacArthur, he announced that Japanese officials, including Governor-General Abe, would be retained in office temporarily in order to facilitate the administration of South Korea. This meant that some 70,000 Japanese officials, who were despised by Koreans, remained in the government. General Hodge outlawed the People's Republic, and established the United States Army Military Government in

Korea (USAMGIK) in September as the only government in South Korea. Yŏ Un-hyŏng resigned from his post in the disallowed government and formed the Working People's Party, providing the more radical elements with a means to fight for the People's Republic.

The Korean people, who enthusiastically welcomed American troops as their liberators, were disappointed and understandably their resentment against the Americans rapidly grew. Their dissatisfaction with the American actions was so great that, on September 12, the Japanese Governor-General was relieved of his duty and Major General Archibald V. Arnold replaced him as Military Governor. Most Japanese officials in the American military government were gradually replaced by Koreans and Americans, but as late as January 1946, as many as 60 remained in high ranking positions. Freedom of thought, speech, press, religion, and assembly was restored, but policy decisions were made by General Hodge and his military governor, not by the Koreans. Communists and Socialists flourished with the new freedom as they established their political and social organizations, and published propaganda materials.

In order to soften the constantly increasing Korean antagonism, General Hodge, on October 5, 1945, created a Korean Advisory Council headed by Kim Sŏng-su, a moderate Nationalist, to assist the American military government. The Americans, unfamiliar with Korean history, psychology, or heritage, made vain attempts to bring about a unity of moderate Nationalists and leftists who were not Communists, and thereby antagonized the conservative right wing Nationalists. Meanwhile, the number of political parties and social organizations with various political ideologies grew by 1947 to 350 creating a chaotic political situation.

The two dominant right wing parties were the Korean (Han-guk) Democratic Party of Kim Sŏng-su, Song Chin-u, and Chang Tŏk-su, which was supported by landlords, bankers, industrialists and businessmen, and the National Party headed by An Chae-hong, who was a moderate rightists. The two major left wing parties were the Working People's Party of Yŏ Un-hyŏng and Pak Hŏn-yŏng's Korean Communist Party, which had a large number of labor and youth organizations affiliated with it.

The Nationalists made several attempts to consolidate various right wing groups into a more effective political body, but it was not until Dr. Rhee returned to Korea from the United States in mid-October 1945, that a united association of the Nationalists emerged. Under American advisement, Dr. Rhee returned to his native country as a private citizen and not as a former president of the Provisional Government. He was nevertheless welcomed as a national hero by both Koreans and Americans, and he enjoyed the high respect of the people, for he, who authored a book entitled *Spirit of Independence*, was regarded as the embodiment of the spirit of the Korean independence movement.

Dr. Rhee did not affiliate with any one group, because he wanted to unite all right wing organizations. In October, he brought about the formation of the Committee for Rapid Realization of Korean Independence (*Tongnip Ch'oksŏng Hyŏbŭihoe*), which was joined by some 50 Nationalist political parties and social organizations. The leftists did not join the group for obvious reasons, and continued to carry out their own schemes. Meanwhile, in late November, Kim Ku, president, and Dr. Kim Kyu-shik, vice-president of the Korean Provisional Government, returned to Korea from China. Unfortunately, Dr. Rhee and the two Kims did not find common grounds for cooperation and their personality clashes caused serious problems within the right wing camp.

The Moscow Agreement and South Korean Politics.   The Allies of Moscow Agreement, which has been discussed earlier, caused serious political repercussions in South Korea. The Moscow plan was not only opposed by the right wing, but also by the leftists, and as a matter of fact, was opposed by all Koreans. The *Tong-a Ilbo*, a leading daily newspaper which reemerged after August 1945, described the Moscow Agreement as "a second Munich," "another mandatory rule," "an insult to Korea," and "a violation of international treaties." It warned that such a plan would subject the Koreans to "international slavery." The Korean people, having suffered an alien colonial domination for thirty-six years, absolutely refused to accept another foreign rule whether it was for a short period or a long period of time. Never has there been more Korean unity than at the time of the anti-trusteeship movement that began on December 28, 1945.

Nationwide strikes, including the government employees strike, encouraged by Dr. Rhee, worsened his relationship with General Hodge which had never been cordial. This, plus the violent storm of opposition to the Moscow Agreement, paralyzed the nation, leading Hodge to seek the cooperation of moderate Nationalists such as Kim Kyu-shik and An Chae-hong and a moderate leftist Yŏ Un-hyŏng, although they too were against the Moscow plan.

Encountering such unified, determined, and hostile opposition to the Mocow Agreement, Hodge made an unsuccessful attempt to convince the Koreans that it was "designed to give aid and protection to Korea in establishing itself as an independent nation," and that the four-power trusteeship was different from an international mandate. He created the impression that the trusteeship plan was authored by the Soviet Union. Meanwhile, on October 30, the American government stated that the Joint Comission, working with the new Korean government, might find it possible to dispense with a trusteeship. President Truman in his State of the Union message of January 14, 1946, declared that the purpose of the American government was "to provide as rapidly as is practicable for the restoration of Korea and the establishment of a democratic government by the free choice of the people of Korea."

On December 30, 1945, in the midst of the political turmoil that developed in connection with the anti-Moscow plan activities, Song Chin-u, a key leader of the conservative Nationalist group, was assassinated, marking the beginning of a series of tragic events in South Korea.

None of the American statements satisfied the Koreans. Whereas the Communists in the north and south suddenly changed their position and supported the Moscow Agreement from January 3, 1946, the Nationalists who followed Rhee, along with others, vehemently rejected it. General Hodge felt that it was necessary to soften Korean criticism against the United States and the American military government which was described as autocratic and incompetent. Realizing the extent of Rhee's prestige, Hodge sought to improve relations with him. He announced that a new advisory council, composed of Koreans, would be established in order to "provide the Koreans a greater degree of self-government," and on February 14, 1946, a 25-member Democratic Council of Representatives of South Korea (*Namjosŏn Minju Ŭiwŏnhoe*) was formed with Rhee as its chairman. However, the right wing dominated Council was boycotted by both liberals and leftists, the relationship between Hodge and Rhee did not improve, and some 40 left wing organizations formed the Korean Democratic National Front (*Chosŏn Minjujuŭi Minjok Chŏnsŏn*) in order to counteract the American's pro-rightist policy. Hodge and the new Military Governor, Major Geneal Archer L. Lerch, meanwhile issued warnings that continued demonstrations against the Moscow Argeement would create in the United Nations an unfavorable impression of Korean political capabilities and would delay the attainment of Korean independence.

The rightist leaders reluctantly ordered the strikes ended, but they continued to protest against the Soviet Union and the Communists, accusing them of delaying the independence of Korea. Witnessing the growing anti-Soviet feelings in South Korea, Colonel General Terenti F. Shtykov, arriving in Seoul in January 1946 as head of the Soviet delegation to the Joint Commission, issued a press release on January 26, and stated that the United States was primarily responsible for the adoption of the Moscow Agreement. The Soviet press release was a damaging blow to the Americans in South Korea, and the Korean people were shocked and dismayed. The Americans were discredited and their prestige fell sharply. General Hodge became an innocent victim, primarily because of his lack of knowledge regarding what had actually occurred at the Moscow conference. He made various attempts to restore the Korean confidence in the American plan even though the policy makers at the State Department were vacillating. They were torn between the conviction that only a trusteeship could protect Korea from being completely dominated by the Soviet Union and their fear that any form of trusteeship would arouse more violent Korean opposition to the plan in South Korea.

The Moscow Agreement and U.S.-Soviet Relations

The Joint U.S.-Soviet Commission.   On January 15, 1946, the Soviet delegation of 73 persons, headed by Colonel General Terenti F. Shtykov, arrived in Seoul to convene the Joint Commission. Preliminary meetings of the Commission held at the Tōksu Palace on the following day immediately encountered various roadblocks. The American delegation, headed by the former Military Governor, Major General Arnold, expressed its desire to unify the operation of railroads and communication systems, to establish a single currency throughout Korea, to allow the free flow of goods, and the free passage of certain categories of persons across the 38th parallel. In effect, the Americans were concerned with the elimination of the 38th parallel. The Soviets, however, showed no desire to abolish this line of demarcation, although they were willing to discuss limited subjects such as the exchange of northern electric power for southern rice, the exchange of a limited number of commodities and equipment, and the re-establishment of rail and automobile traffic between the two zones.

Three weeks after the preliminary talks began, certain nonpolitical agreements were reached. They include guidelines for (1) railroad, motor, and coastal water-borne transportation; (2) movements of certain groups of Korean citizens between the two zones; (3) exchange of mail; (4) radio broadcasting frequencies; and (5) the establishment of a liaison between the two commands. The Joint Commission, however, failed to agree to allow free passage of Koreans across the parallel, or to establish a uniform currency, or a unified telecommunication system, or to permit the free circulation of newspapers. However, the Americans failed to secure Russian consent to supply South Korea with North Korean electricity, raw materials, fuel, industrial equipment, and chemical fertilizer.

When the Joint Commission held its opening ceremony on March 20, 1946, General Hodge pointed out its grave responsibility:

Today is an important day in Korean history. It is a day to which all Koreans have looked forward with great hope for the future of their nation and should be a day Koreans will celebrate in the future as the start of a new era in Korean history. The eyes of the entire world, as well as of the Korean people, will be watching our deliberations here. . . . Our successful results in the councils of this Commission will have a lasting effect upon the peace and happiness of the world as well as the future of Korea.

He concluded by saying that he was confident that the joint efforts of the two powers "will be able to solve amicably and justly all Korean problems presented, whether they be political, economic or adminsitrative."

In contrast to General Hodge's businesslike remarks, expressing high hopes for a successful conclusion of the negotiation, General Shtykov's speech praised Korea's ancient culture and her "vividly expressed national self-consciousness, year after year suffering hardships and the humiliation of colonial slavery." "The people deserve," he said, "the best future possible. With their blood and innumerable sufferings, the Korean people earned the right to independence and a free way of life." After presenting a picture of the Soviet Union as the champion of oppressed peoples, and complimenting some of the people of Korea who had "shown their determination to create, with the help of the Allies, a free democratic Korean government" and those who formed "their democratic parties, public organizations, people's committees as organs of democratic self-government," he condemned "the furious resistance of reactionary and anti-democratic groups and certain elements whose object is to undermine the work of creating and firmly establishing a democratic system in Korea." Moreover, he indicated in strong terms that the Soviet Union would seek cooperation for the establishment of a unified provisional government of Korea *only from those "democratic parties and organizations supporting the decisions of the Moscow Conference of the Ministers of Foreign Affairs" of the Allies.*

The Impasse.   The Americans should have known that the Soviets were rejecting all political parties and social organizations which did not accept the decision to establish the trusteeship in Korea. Futile efforts were made by the Americans, who insisted that freedom of expression was an essential aspect of the democratic process, and that Koreans ought to be entitled to express their feelings against the trusteeship plan. The Russians did not waver until they made all of the Joint Commission's efforts useless and inconsequential. On May 8, 1946, the Joint Commission adjourned *sine die*, accomplishing almost nothing. No sooner had the Soviet delegation departed for Pyongyang, than General Hodge communicated with General Chistiakov, Commander of Soviet forces in North Korea, seeking to resume the talks. He even indicated his willingness to travel to Pyongyang to meet with General Shtykov. His May 9 letter received no reply. On June 15, he again wrote to the Russians indicating the American willingness to resume negotiations "in order to carry out the Moscow decision in accordance with the principles of freedom of expression as enunciated in the Atlantic Charter to which both of our governments have adhered."

Not until August 6 did General Chistiakov reply to General Hodge by stating that the Soviet delegation was "motivated by the necessity for the exact fulfillment of the Moscow Decision. . . the only document in which is laid out the program of the Allies" for the establishment of a democratic government in Korea. He completely disregarded Hodge's argument concerning freedom of expression for the Koreans. He insisted on having consultation only with those parties and organizations and their representatives which "duly, without any reservations, support this decision and did not compromise themselves by active opposition to this decision.''

General Hodge stood firm on the question of freedom of expression. In his August 12 letter to Chistiakov, he stated that the American delegation could not be a party to any "arbitrary, exclusive, punitive tactics" in dealing with legitimate Korean organizations. He insisted that "there is nothing in the Moscow Decision that prohibits Koreans in conferences with the Commission or elsewhere from expressing freely their wishes and desires in formation of their own government.

The two commanders exchanged charges and countercharges until November 26, 1946, when General Chistiakov hinted at the Soviets' willingness to resume talks. He did not, however, change his position regarding those parties and organizations which had expressed opposition to the Moscow Agreement. The Soviets were not even willing to consult with South Korean parties and organizations which had accepted the Communique No. 5 of the Commission, dated April 18, 1946, which required any organizations wishing to participate in the Joint Commission work to sign pledges not to obstruct the work of the Commission.

By April 1947, it became increasingly clear that the Korean dilemma could not be solved by occupation authorities alone. As early as March 1946, the head of the American delegation had expressed the view that "if anything is done, it must be on a higher level." When General MacArthur and General Hodge expressed a similar view to President Truman he instructed his Secretary of State, George C. Marshall, to negotiate with Soviet Foreign Minister V.M. Molotov to reopen the Joint Commission in an attempt to remove the impasse.

Finally, on May 21, 1947, the Joint Commission reconvened in Seoul. The new American delegation was headed by Major General A.E. Brown while General Shtykov led his delegation. As the first session of the Commission opened at the Tŏksu Palace, the right wing conservatives, who rejected the trusteeship plan, refused to participate in the meeting. The moderates headed by Dr. Kim Kyu-shik and the Communists who were affiliated with the National Democratic Front declared their support of the Commission.

Although a better beginning was made when the Joint Commission agreed to limit its work to the adoption of a formula to create the provisional democratic government in Korea, the examination of the parties and organizations to be invited to the meetings led to the insolvable problem of defining the meaning of "democratic organizations."

Encountering the unwavering opposition of the Soviet delegation, the Americans agreed in the Joint Communique No. 1 of the second session of the Joint Commission, dated June 12, 1947, to exclude from consultation Koreans who actively opposed the Moscow Agreement, even though this might be regarded as an abridgement of freedom of opinion. Meanwhile, the Soviet delegations agreed to accept for consultation many Korean parties and organizations which had earlier opposed the Moscow decision, but only those which were willing to sign the Communique No. 5 of April 18, 1946.

In June, 38 parties and organizations in North Korea and 425 in South Korea turned in their applications for consultation. However, the Soviet delegation insisted that the Joint Commission accept only those applicants which the Soviets classified as social organizations and certain others which met their own criteria. American opposition brought about no changes in the Soviet attitude, and all attempts made by the Americans failed to change the position of the Soviets regarding "democratic parties and social organizations."

Knowing full well that the acceptance of the Russian plan would allow the Communists to dominate Korea, the American negotiators attempted to break the deadlock by suggesting that the Russians and the Americans consult separately with the Korean parties and organizations in their respective zones without examining the validity of their membership claims. On July 29, the Soviets flatly rejected this proposal.

On August 12, the American delegation further attempted to fulfill the mission of the Joint Commission by proposing to the Soviets that a general election be held throughout Korea in order to elect the members of the national legislature under "international supervision" so as to establish a provisional government. The Soviets in turn suggested the creation of a "provisional assembly," with equal representation from the north and south, of those parties which "fully support the Moscow Agreement."

The American reaction was such that an assembly could not be reconciled with the disparity in the populations of the two areas: South Korea's population was estimated to be about 21 million, whereas that of the north was estimated at not more than 9 million. On August 26, the Acting Secretary of State, Robert A. Lovett, proposed to the Russian Foreign Minister a substitute for the Moscow plan to the effect that: (1) separate elections shall be held in each zone to choose a wholly representative provisional legislature for each zone; (2) voting shall be by secret multi-party ballot on the basis of universal suffrage; (3) the provisional legislatures shall choose representatives in numbers which reflect the proportion between the populations of the two zones in order to constitute a national provisional legislature; (4) the legislature shall meet at Seoul to establish a provisional government for the united Korea; and (5) the resulting Provisional Government shall meet in Korea with representatives of the four Powers adhering to the Moscow Agreement to discuss what aid and assistance is needed to place Korean independence on a firm economic and political foundation.

This proposal was accepted by Great Britain and China, but Molotov in his letter of September 4 not only stated that the American proposal was not acceptable to the Soviet Union, but complained that the United States took unilateral action in calling for a four-power conference in which Great Britain and China would participate. Moreover, he charged that the impasse was due primarily to "the position adopted by the American delagation" in the Joint Commission regarding the selection of democratic parties and social organizations. Thus, the impasse remained and the establishment of a provisional government and the creation of a new independent and united Korea remained only a remote possibility, if not an unattainable goal.

The Moscow Agreement and its aftermath constituted a key and tragic juncture in Korea's recent history. It marked the growth of a sharp division between the parties on the right and those on the left. Prior to January 1946, most of the parties were still in an embryonic stage as the desire to create a united and independent government overshadowed all other considerations. However, the Moscow Agreement gave a strong impetus to the parties on both sides of the line to consolidate their positions and sharpen their ideologies. National interest became secondary to their own political ambitions as political polarization fostered the possible perpetual division of Korea, and Korea became a victim of the rapidly growing power struggle between the United States and the Soviet Union.

By the spring of 1947, American attitudes toward the Soviet Union changed drastically as American foreign policy shifted from the position of accommodation to one of containment in dealing with Communist power. The Truman Doctrine was enunciated on March 12, and the Marshall Plan was announced soon thereafter. When Greece and Turkey were threatened by the Soviet backed revolutionaries, President Truman declared in March that it was the policy of the United Sates "to support free peoples who are resisting attempted subjugation by armed minorities or by outside countries," initiating the Cold War.

Whatever the reasons for the failure of the Joint Commission to activate the Moscow plan, General Shtykov, as he departed from Seoul in May 1946, informed Hodge that "the main reason the Soviet Delegation insisted on barring certain persons from consultation is that Russia is. . . interested in establishing in Korea a provisional democratic government which would be *loyal to the Soviet Union.*" He further stated that if those Koreans who objected to the Moscow Agreement and "raised their voice against the Soviet Union, slandered the Soviet Union and smeared it with mud. . . seized power in the government, *the government would not be loyal to Russia*, but its officials would be instrumental in organizing hostile action on the part of the Korean people against the Soviet Union." This Soviet view remained unchanged if not hardened in August 1947, and eventually brought about the prolonged, if not a permanent, partition of Korea.

South Korean Development

Hodge's Search for Solutions.   In order to gain Korean support for the American military government and the American efforts at the Joint U.S.-

U.S.S.R. Commission, and in order to soften Dr. Rhee's criticism of the American policy, General Hodge established the 25-member Representative Democratic Council in February 1946, with Rhee as its chairman, but the extreme leftists refused to cooperate with the Americans, denouncing the American plan.

The relationship between Hodge and Rhee did not improve even after Rhee was named chairman of the new council. Rhee charged that the moderate leftists, such as Yŏ Un-hyŏng, used the council for their own political gain and bitterly criticized the Russians. Moreover, when Hodge had someone censor all of Rhee's speeches, prepared for delivery over the Korean radio network, and deleted all critical remarks against the Soviet and Communists, the relationship between the two men reached the point where reconciliation seemed impossible.

General Hodge lost patience with the conservative rightists. At the same time, he cracked down on the Communists who caused serious problems in South Korea. In October, he closed three Communist newspapers, and arrested many Communist leaders who were printing counterfeit money. He also ordered the arrest of Pak Hŏn-yŏng and other key Communist leaders, of the South Korean Workers' Party, and widespread Communist-inspired strikes and riots in southern cities ensued. Riots in Taegu and Chŏnju and other cities in South Chŏlla Province were particularly serious as more than 2,000 Communists were arrested. Some 1,500 of them were prosecuted, 500 were convicted, and 16 were sentenced to death. Pak, Yi Kang-guk, and other key Communists fled to North Korea.

The antagonism between Hodge and Rhee grew even more bitter when Hodge, in October 1946, gave his strong support to Kim Kyu-shik and Yŏ Un-hyŏng, who formed the Coalition Committee of the Rightists and the Leftists (*Chwau Hapchak Wiwŏnhoe*), composed of moderate Nationalists and Socialists. Kim and Yŏ realized the futility of Korean opposition to the Moscow plan and the work of the Joint Commission, and declared that they would establish "a democratic transitional government" in cooperation with the Joint Commission and secure Korean independence by unifying the rightists and leftists.

Angered by Hodge's pro-moderate stand, Rhee went to Washington, D.C. in December 1946 to convince the American government of the urgent need to establish an interim Korean government ignoring the Moscow Agreement. He hoped that such a government once established in South Korea, would join the United Nations and negotiate with the United States and the Soviet Union for a solution to Korea's dilemma.

The Koreanization of the American Military Government.   General Hodge desperately sought the support of moderate Nationalists and Leftists, and at the same time, he felt that it was necessary to Koreanize the administration. To these ends, in mid-October 1946, he disclosed his plan to eatablish the South Korean Interim Legislative Assembly (SKILA), to replace the Representative Democratic Council.

The first election in South Korea was held in October–November 1946, to elect 45 members of the 90-member SKILA. Some 38 conservative rightists, 2 moderate leftists, and only one moderate Nationalist were elected. Four seats were left unfilled. Half of the members of the SKILA were appointed by General Hodge. Dr. Kim Kyu-shik, the only moderate Nationalist elected, was named chairman of the SKILA, which was organized in December. Dr. Rhee was greatly annoyed at the appointment of Dr. Kim.

The SKILA held its first session in January 1947, and antagonism between Hodge and the rightist members grew rapidly. The rightist members not only refused to cooperate with the Americans, but also condemned Hodge's policy and the Moscow plan by a vote of 44 to 1, with 9 abstentions in a resolution passed on January 15. Many members were absent from the session when this resolution was adopted. At the same time, the conservative Nationalists launched a movement to make the Provisional Government, which had returned to Korea from China in November 1945 when Kim Ku and Kim Kyu-shik returned to Korea, the *de jure* government with Dr. Rhee as its president and Kim Ku as its vice-president. The SKILA accomplished virtually nothing, except the passage of a limited land sale act and a franchise law endorsed by Major General William F. Dean, the new Military Governor, in August 1947.

Hodge encountered many difficulties in dealing with the Koreans as well as with the Soviets, and became frustrated. Meanwhile, a majority of the Americans in Korea lost interest in helping the Koreans and wished to go home. To most American GI's, Korea was simply "a piece of worthless real estate," and they totally lacked concern for the Korean people's future. Realizing the futility of trying to solve the Korean question by negotiating with the Soviets, Hodge took further steps to Koreanize the American military government, perhaps with the hope of bringing an early withdrawal of American occupational forces.

General Hodge adopted a plan to establish the South Korean Interim Government (SKIG). An Chae-hong, a moderate Nationalist who was a close associate of Dr. Kim Kyu-shik, was designated in early February 1947, as Civil Administrator. The SKIG was established in May and became the counterpart of the American military government headed by the Acting Military Governor, Brigadier General Charles G. Helmick. Following this, more Koreans replaced Americans in high government positions but remained under American advisers. Only after SKIG was established were all Japanese officials, retained in the government since August 1945, removed. However, the Americans' control of South Korea did not diminish, for neither the SKILA nor the SKIG had any independent decision making power. As of

August 1947, there were 3,231 Americans in the military government, of whom 2.594 were military officers and 637 were civilians. In the midst of clamor against the Americans as well as the Moscow plan and the Communists, Yŏ Un-hyŏng, who had been mentioned as a possible candidate to head the proposed provisional Korean government, was assassinated on July 19, 1947 in broad daylight.

Internal and National Security Forces.   Law and order was maintained by the Counterintelligence Corps (CIC) and the Criminal Investigation Division (CID) of the U.S. Army, assisted by the poorly trained and poorly paid National Police. Many Korean policemen and officers had been in the Japanese police force and learned police tactics from the Japanese. Police brutality and corruption were widely reported, and contributed to the people's alienation from the government. There were some 30,185 policemen toward the end of the American occupation period. The judiciary branch, including the courts, was dominated by the graduates of Japanese law schools. The Americans did not carry out any significant judicial or legal reforms.

In order to train the South Koreans to maintain their own security, General Hodge created, in November 1945, an Office of National Defense in the American military government. In January 1946, the Constabulary of 25,000 men and the Coast Guard of 2,500 men were established. Both of these organizations were supplied with military equipment left behind by the defeated Japanese troops. The Constabulary had no tanks or heavy military equipment, and its members were not given any American weapons. The Coast Guard had only a meager number of small, light craft, mostly for offshore duties; it was not given any American vessels until the end of the American occupation period. There was no air force.

Despite these deficiencies, the Constabulary and the Coast Guard were the embryo of what later became the South Korean army and navy. Meanwhile, an officers' training institute (often called the Military English Language School), which was established in the fall of 1945, recruited Koreans who had previously been in the Japanese or the Chinese army, and many who graduated from this school later became high ranking military officers.

Economic Conditions.   South Korea was in economic chaos after the collapse of Japanese rule and the partition of the country. Before the division of Korea, the south had been primarily an agricultural region, producing 63 per cent of the nation's food grains, and containing most of the country's light industry and about 24 per cent of heavy industry. Almost all electric power had been generated by the hydroelectric plants on the Yalu and other rivers (0.5 per cent came from plants in the south), and the entire supply of chemical fertilizer came from the Japanese-established plant at Hŭngnam on the northeast coast. When the northern supply of chemical fertilizer stopped, farm production in the south declined sharply, creating a serious food shortage. Because of the lack of power, many industrial plants were shut down.

Meanwhile, a variety of left wing labor organizations affiliated with the All Korean Labor Council created serious economic problems further aggravating the poor economic conditions that had existed since August 1945. Communist-directed labor strikes became widespread, and terrorism ran rampant with support from leftist organizations as well as from organizations such as the Korean Federation of Labor Unions and General Yi Pŏm-sŏk's rightist youth group named the Korean National Youth.

The shortage of food, fuel, clothing, electricity, and other consumer goods, coupled with the rapidly rising unemployment rate, caused many serious problems. To make matters worse, the severity of the winter of 1945–1946 was record breaking. The U.S. Assistant Secretary of State John H. Hildring warned, in late 1945, that "if we are to prevent Korea's becoming a danger spot again, a cause of war and an aid to aggression, we must make certain the establishment of a free, democratic and sovereign country which will become an active factor in maintaining stability in the Orient." In reality, however, the most urgent task of the American military government was to sustain the economic life of the people and improve the economy in order to create a social atmosphere more congenial to political improvement. As Secretary of State, George C. Marshall, said, "When a people starve they are unprepared to learn democracy."

The Rising Inflation.   The ever increasing volume of bank notes in circulation, coupled with the commodity shortage, drove prices high, creating rampant inflation. The Japanese had issued bank notes in enormous amounts before the end of their colonial rule, and the trend which they had established continued after August 1945. The total amount of money supply grew from 4,698 million *wŏn* (*wŏn* = 100 cents) in July 1945, to 7,988 million in August, 10,333 million in July 1946, 18,638 million in July 1947, and 30,500 million by July 1948. Consequently, money became worthless.

The wholesale price index (1947 = 100) grew from 143 in December 1947 to 185 in August 1948. The retail prices of essential commodities grew as follows:

RETAIL PRICES OF ESSENTIAL COMMODITIES
August 1945–1948 (In *wŏn*)

Items	Unit	Aug. 1945	May 1946	May 1947	May 1948
Polished Rice	14.6 kg.	220	500	1,000	1,460
Wheat Flour	22 kg.	130	1,100	1,400	2,250
Beef	600 g.	16	70	180	280

Sugar	600 g.	15	75	140	320
Cotton Sheet	yard	13	100	300	750
Silk	yard	170	500	2,000	3,900
Rubber Shoes	pair	40	80	200	210
Firewood	2.3 cu.m.	300	650	3,100	4,500
Laundry Soap	piece	4	25	150	220
Sesame Oil	2.1 g.	60	130	1,000	2,000
Charcoal	22.5 kg.	45	60	250	500

Many factories in the south were closed due to the shortage of skilled workers, technicians, electric power, and raw materials, making the economic situation worse. Moreover, the influx of some 1.5 million refugees from China, Manchuria, Japan, and North Korea between August 1945 and August 1946 created additional problems. The population of South Korea, which was about 16 million in August 1945, grew to 19,369,170 in September 1946, and 21 million in 1947. The population of Seoul was a little over 700,000 in August 1945, but by the spring of 1947, it jumped to 1.2 million. This rapid population growth increased the housing shortage as well as shortages of essential commodities, resulting in many social problems.

As a sense of frustration overwhelmed the people, moral and ethical standards declined. Their dream of establishing an independent nation was broken, their hopes for a free and better way of life were dashed, and the danger of starvation caused them to develop a profound apathy, indifference, and a sense of hopelessness. In 1946, an eyewitness reported: the "situation is getting worse. There is a rampant inflation. Consumer goods and coal are virtually nonexistent. Food distribution is inequitable. . . Transportation equipment is breaking down. Unemployment is rising to dangerous proportions. . . . Hunger is rapidly spreading and will probably result in starvation in many areas by midsummer. . . ."

Economic Policy and Planning. The American military government searched in vain for solutions to remedy this grave situation. A few American economic missions went to South Korea, and in late May 1946, the American military government adopted the Emergency Economic Program, which included a ten-point rehabilitation project. However, due to insufficient funds, lack of skilled administrators and workers, and low incentives on the part of politically preoccupied authorities, there was no economic improvement. The prevention of widespread starvation and epidemics seemed to be the primary concern of the American military government.

The United States provided a $25 million loan and $409.3 million relief funds between 1945 and 1948. The relief funds of the Government Appropriation for Relief in Occupied Areas (GARIOA) of the United States prevented the starvation and the death of many. Some GARIOA funds were used to support an agricultural recovery program and to import chemical fertilizers from the United States. This program resulted in the increase of food grain production from 45.7 million bushels in 1947 to 58.6 million bushels in 1948. American wheat flour was imported, and along with $1 million worth of relief goods, such as dried milk, medical supplies, and clothing, of the United Nations Relief and Rehabilitation Agency (UNRRA) saved the lives of thousands of children and elderly persons.

Due to the stubborn opposition of the members of the SKILA who were, by and large, landlords themselves, the American military government failed to adopt a land reform act. The Americans had neither the desire to confiscate farmlands from landlords and redistribute them to the tenants, nor funds to purchase farmlands for the purpose of selling them to the farmers. The American military government did, however, carry out a rent reform, prohibiting landlords from collecting more than 33.3 per cent of the annual harvest from their tenants. At the same time, it did sell farmlands which were taken over from the Oriental Development Company and other large Japanese farms through a newly created New Korea Company. Under the land sale program, which was administered by the National Land Administration created in March 1948, some 686,965 acres of farmlands were sold to some 588,000 tenant households whose family members totaled 3.4 million, or 25 per cent of the farm population in South Korea. The average parcel of farmland sold to them was 4.9 acres.

The Korean economy began to improve in the fall of 1947, but the shortage of food, fuel, clothing and other consumer goods, including medical supplies, persisted until the American occupation ended in August 1948.

Education and Cultural Development.   Perhaps it was in educational and cultural fields that the Americans made their most significant contributions. The granting of the freedom of thought, speech, and press (however, this freedom might have been curtailed later) at last liberated the Koreans from various laws and restrictions, which had been detrimental to the development of education and culture. Despite many problems which beset the American military government, as well as the people of South Korea, a remarkable progress was achieved in these areas.

The Bureau of Education of the American military government created several educational commissions and committees. According to the stated purposes and objectives of the National Committee on Educational Planning in March 1946, the primary aim was to establish democratic education in South Korea. Particular emphasis was given to scientific and technical training, but the most significant change was the introduction of Korean language and Korean history as part of the curriculum. The development of national consciousness and pride, ethical and wholesome character, and the sense of social responsibility was emphasized.

All private colleges which had been confiscated and closed by the Japanese toward the end of World War II were reopened. Some American personnel along with Koreans took over the Keijō Imperial University from the Japanese and reorganized it into Seoul National University, and other public colleges were also reopened under Korean administrators and teaching staff. Seoul National University incorporated many professional colleges, becoming a bona fide university. However, like primary and secondary schools, Seoul National University and other public and private colleges suffered from the shortage of qualified professors and other teaching staff, and from lack of funds, educational facilities, and classroom space. Nevertheless, the Koreans witnessed a tremendous educational growth during the period of the American occupation, thanks primarily to their own eagerness and efforts to educate their children.

Changes in Pattern of Education.   In September 1946, the American Military Government put into permanent effect the 6-3-3-4 system, which had been adopted earlier in March by the National Committee on Educational Planning. This system was recommended by American educational missions after visiting Korea and conducting educational surveys.

The names of primary schools were changed to *kungmin hakkyo,* or "people's schools." The curriculum and textbooks were revised. Many new elementary schools were established, and the number of primary school students increased from 1,366,024 in September 1945, to 2,666,917 in the spring of 1948. Due to a shortage of buildings and classrooms, most of these primary schools had a two-shift system, overloading the teachers with work.

Many 3-year normal schools were established to train more qualified primary and secondary teachers, and at the same time in-service teacher training institutes were established to increase the quality of teachers.

In 1945, there were 252 secondary schools in the south with an enrollment of 62,136 students. At the end of 1947, the number increased to 415 with an enrollment of 277,447 students. Like the primary school curriculum, the secondary school curriculum was revised to promote democratic education and provide more scientific and technical training. Physical education and studies in mathematics were given special attention. The creation of *hong-ik in-gan,* or "a person with enlightenment who benefits humanity," became the slogan which embodied the purpose of South Korean education.

The number of colleges and universities grew. In 1945, there were 18 colleges and one university, with a total enrollment of 3,000 students, most of whom were Japanese. In November 1947, there was one national university, 4 national colleges, 3 provincial colleges, and 21 private institutions of higher education. Three private colleges, Yonhūi, Koryō (formerly Posōng), and Ewha Woman's received new charters in 1946, and became the leading universities in South Korea. College enrollment grew from 6,111 in late

1945, to 20,545 by the end of 1947, and steadily increased thereafter. The quality of higher education, however, remained low.

Efforts were made to increase literacy. When the Japanese period ended, 7.9 million, or 77 per cent of Koreans above the age of twelve, were illiterate. Some 90 per cent of the adult population had had no formal education. Some 30,538 "folk schools" were established throughout South Korea which were attended by a total of 1,625,340 persons. By the end of the American occupation, illiteracy decreased to 9.5 million persons, or 42 per cent of the population. The "folk schools" made significant contributions, not only by reducing the rate of illiteracy, but also by increasing the general knowledge of government affairs, Korean history, geography, economy, and vocational subjects. Shortly before the termination of American military rule, various educational ordinances were issued in order to promote local control over primary education, but these efforts which were made to establish local control over education were not successful.

Cultural Development.   The freedom of press which the Korean people enjoyed for the first time since 1910 brought about highly satisfactory results. Many Korean language newspapers, including the *Tong-a Ilbo,* reemerged, and the Korean radio network began to play a significant public role. By July 1947, 21 newspapers (many of them leftist papers) were published in South Korea. The papers had a small circulation (480,000 in July 1947), were printed on poor quality paper, and had only a few pages (normally four), but they played an important role in the shaping of public opinion.

Among some 325 publications in 1947, 4 per cent were semi-weeklies, 23.8 per cent were weeklies, 43.4 per cent were monthlies, and 22.7 per cent were daily newspapers. Many religious journals and other general publications were revived.

With the restoration of religious freedom, Christian churches sprang up all over South Korea, and Christianity once again became a dominant factor in cultural and social progress. Japanese Shintō shrines and Japanese Buddhist temples were torn down. The Protestant churches continued to play an important role in promoting education through their private schools.

Meanwhile, the newly introduced American culture—songs, dance, and motion pictures—brought about a considerable Americanization of Koreans, and for many young Koreans, "GI Joe" became a symbol of modernity and freedom.

The Emergence of the Two Korean States

The failure of the Joint U.S.-U.S.S.R. Commission, led the United States to seek a different solution to the Korean question, and it turned the issue over to the United Nations. The U.N.'s failure to satisfactorily settle the Korean question led ultimately to the emergence in 1948 of the two separate Korean states.

The United Nations Decisions on Korea.   In September 1947, the American government submitted the Korean problem to the United Nations. Despite the strong opposition of Andrei Vyshinsky, head of the Soviet delegation at the United Nations, the General Assembly voted on September 23, to place the Korean question on its agenda and referred it to the First Committee for consideration and report. The Americans rejected a counter-proposal which the Soviet Union made three days later to the Joint Commission to withdraw all foreign troops from Korea in 1948, and to permit the Koreans to organize their own government without outside assistance.

Disregarding a poll taken in Korea indicating that 57 per cent of the participants favored the Soviet proposal, the United States, on October 17, proposed that elections be held by the occupation authorities under United Nations supervision not later than March 13, 1948, to elect the members of the Korean National Assembly which would first form a government of united Korea and then negotiate with the occupation authorities for the withdrawal of their troops from Korea.

Despite the objections raised by Andrei Gromyko of the Soviet Union, on November 5, the First Committee of the United Nations adopted by a vote of 46 to 0 (4 abstentions) a resolution based on the American resolution. Subsequently, on November 14, the United Nations General Assembly passed the resolution recommended by the First Committee, despite Soviet objections, by a vote of 43 to 1 with 6 abstentions. With this, the idea of trusteeship of four Allies in Korea died. The resolution stated that "the Korean question. . . is primarily a matter for the Korean people themselves and concerns their freedom and independence, and this question cannot be correctly and fairly resolved without the participation of representatives of the indigenous population." The United Nations thereby decided to conduct national elections in Korea and to that end created the United Nations Temporary Commission on Korea (UNTCOK).

Dr. Kumara P. S. Menon of India was named chairman of UNTCOK, but he failed to enlist the assistance and cooperation of the Soviet government. The Soviet occupation authorities refused to grant permission to UNTCOK to conduct elections in North Korea. Facing a Russian boycott, UNTCOK sought the advice of the Interim Committee of the General Assembly in February 1948. Despite vigorous objections from the Soviet government and its bloc nations in the Interim Committee, and in spite of the fear expressed by some of its members of creating two permanently separate nations in Korea, the Committee adopted a resolution on February 26, by a vote of 31 to 2 with 11 abstentions, to hold elections in South Korea alone.

The UNTCOK in an informal meeting on February 28 in Seoul unanimously decided to implement the Interim Committee's resolution and issued a state-ment the following day that it would observe elections not later than May 10, 1948, in such parts of Korea as were accessible. The elections were to be held on the basis of adult suffrage, by secret ballot, and in a free atmosphere wherein the democratic rights of freedom of speech, press and assembly would be upheld.

On March 1, the Memorial Day for the March First Movement of 1919, General Hodge issued a proclamation stating that elections would be held in South Korea on May 10.

The First Korean Reunification Attempt.   The reaction of the Koreans to the Interim Committee's resolution was sharply divided. The right wing conser-vatives, aligned with Dr. Rhee's National Society for Acceleration of Korean Independence, supported it without reservations. They claimed that North Korea had a population of about 10 million and that South Korea's population was 22 million, or more than two-thirds of Korea's total population. There-fore, they maintained that the National Assembly and the new government of Korea, which was to be established following the May elections, could rightly claim to be a national government.

The United Nations decision to hold separate elections only in South Korea created a dangerous situation there. The open warfare between the rightists and leftists, and the bitter conflict between the conservative and moderate Na-tionalists brought about an extremely unstable political atmosphere. The alliance between General Hodge and Dr. Kim Kyu-shik, who resigned the chairmanship of the SKILA, was broken because of the latter's opposition to the United Nations plan, resulting in a strange and unnatural alliance between Hodge and Rhee. Meanwhile, the relationship between Dr. Rhee and Dr. Kim continued to deteriorate and a sharp division emerged between the supporters of Dr. Rhee and Kim Ku.

The radical Korean leftists not only challenged the November 14 resolution of the General Assembly, but also contended that the UNTCOK was "a tool of American imperialism," and rejected the resolution. The Communists charged that UNTCOK's plan to hold elections in South Korea was an American attempt "to cut through the middle, chop off the arms and legs of our homogeneous nation and tramp down our beautiful land with iron boots of im-perialism." The moderates under the leadership of Dr. Kim Kyu-shik and An Chae-hong strongly objected to the resolution on the ground that such elec-tions would perpetuate the division of the country, if not make it permanent.

In October 1947, Dr. Kim and An Chae-hong organized the Democratic Independence Party with the moderate leftist Hong Myŏng-hŭi as its head, hoping to strengthen the position of the moderates against the United Na-tions plan. Meanwhile, Kim Ku, one of the most respected and powerful rightist leaders, came to regard the United Nations plan as certain to perpetuate the division of Korea. As a result, he mobilized the forces of his own Korean (*Han-guk*) Independence Party in opposition to the American and the United Nations plan to create a separate government in South Korea.

The major groups supporting the United Nations plan to hold elections in South Korea alone and establish a Korean government were Dr. Rhee's National Society for Acceleration of Korean Independence, the Korean (Han-guk) Democratic Party of Chang Tŏk-su and Kim Sŏng-su, and the Korean (Chosŏn) Democratic Party of the refugees from the north in South Korea, along with their auxiliary youth, women's and labor organizations. The departure of Kim Ku and his party from the right wing camp weakened the rightists' position against the leftists, particularly against the Communists. In the midst of a bitter political struggle, on December 2, 1947, Chang Tŏk-su, chairman of the Political Section of the Korean (Han-guk) Democratic Party, was assassinated by policemen who were allegedly Kim Ku's supporters.

In February 1948, Kim Ku and Dr. Kim Kyu-shik established an understanding that the Korean problem should be solved by the Koreans. They were joined by Cho So-ang, Yŏ Un-hyŏng and Hong Myŏng-hŭi. They formed the National Independence Federation, a loosely knit coalition of the rightists and leftists who opposed the United Nations plan. On March 12, they issued a joint statement pledging their determination to achieve Korean independence and vowed not to participate in the forthcoming elections which "would result in murder in a family." These opponents of the United Nations plan proposed convening a joint conference of political leaders of the two zones to achieve Korean independence and to allow the Koreans themselves to establish a democratic national government of united Korea.

The idea of holding a joint conference between North and South Korean leaders to establish national independence was not new. As early as December 1947, Dr. Kim Kyu-shik, and Kim Ku and others, realizing that the Korean question could not be settled either by the Allies adhering to the Moscow Agreement or by the United Nations, gave serious thought to convening a joint conference of political leaders of both zones to map out plans to achieve Korean independence without external interference. Dr. Kim had hoped that the Joint Commission would do so and even suggested the implementation of certain programs as a prerequisite for such a conference. But the Joint Commission paid no attention to his suggestions.

The opponents of the United Nations plan sent a message to Kim Il-sung, chairman of the North Korean People's Committee, proposing a joint conference of Korean leaders for the early establishment of Korea's territorial unification and a national government. The North Korean leaders reacted quickly and favorably to the proposal, and they had the Central Committee of the Democratic National Coalition Front of North Korea invite all parties and organizations in South Korea who were opposed to the United Nations plan to come to Pyongyang for a conference in April. Following the March 25 broadcast of Kim Il-sung's statement over Radio Pyongyang in which the invitation to the joint conference was issued to South Korean leaders, Kim Il-sung sent a personal message to Dr. Kim, inviting 15 right wing leaders to attend the conference. Dr. Rhee's name was not included in Kim Il-sung's list, nor were the names of the members of his organizations or those of the Korean Democratic Party, which had fled from the north to the south.

Prior to his departure for Pyongyang, Dr. Kim was concerned that while only 15 moderate rightists were attending the conference, a great many leftists from South Korea had been invited to attend. He was also concerned with the personal safety of the rightist participants. Shortly before his departure, he issued a statement which contained five principles as a basis for discussion to which Kim Il-sung agreed.

Dr. Kim's five principles for national reconstruction were:

1. Any form of dictatorship shall be rejected and a truly democratic government should be established.
2. Monopolistic capitalism shall be rejected and private property ownership should be recognized.
3. A united central government shall be established through a general election of the entire nation.
4. No military bases shall be allowed to any foreign power.
5. Regarding the early withdrawal of the two occupation forces, the powers concerned should immediately open negotiations for reaching an agreement as to the time and conditions of withdrawal and make a definite pronouncement to the world.

Dr. Kim was equally concerned with the possibility of northern aggression if the simultaneous withdrawal of American and Soviet troops came before South Korea was militarily capable of repelling such an attack. He believed that there were some 250,000 well-trained and well-equipped North Korean troops, and therefore, he opposed immediate withdrawal of all foreign troops without a guarantee of nonaggression from the north, and urged the Americans to recruit and train at least 200,000 or 300,000 men for the security of South Korea. Meanwhile, he was satisfied with Kim Il-sung's acceptance of the five principles which he had proposed.

North-South Joint Conference.   Kim Il-sung opened the conference in Pyongyang on April 19 before all the leaders of South Korea arrived. It was attended by 695 representatives from 16 political parties and other organizations from both zones, most of whom were North Koreans. The conference heard Kim Il-sung's criticism that the work of UNTCOK would result only in "disaster and unhappiness to Korea," and that the United Nations plan was to collaborate with the Americans to "colonize Korea." The Russian Communist Party organ, *Pravda*, also charged that the Americans were aiming to dismember Korea in order to make South Korea "a base for American expansion in the Far East."

From the beginning, it was apparent that Kim Il-sung and his cohorts were determined to push through their own plans. Each of the participating group representatives was allowed to present a statement regarding Korean independence to the planning committee headed by the North Korean Workers Party chairman, Kim Tu-bong. There was to be no discussion on any question, and voting was done by a show of hands. Decision after decision was adopted without debate. Dr. Kim's dinner speech was distorted and broadcast over radio. In this manner, after the two-day meeting the conference adopted three resolutions and a joint communiqué was issued on April 30. The main points of the communiqué were as follows:

1. The only solution for Korea under the present situation is the immediate and simultaneous withdrawal of foreign troops from Korea.
2. Leaders of both the North and South will never permit an outbreak of civil war or any disturbance which might militate against Korean desire for unity after the withdrawal of foreign troops.
3. Following such withdrawal, a political conference of all of Korea will be convened for the purpose of establishing a democratic provisional government, which in turn will "elect" a United Korean Legislative Organ on the principles of universal, direct and equal elections and on the basis of a secret ballot. This legislative organ will then adopt a constitution.
4. The signatories of this declaration will never acknowledge the result of a separate election in South Korea nor support the separate government so established.

Both Kims were disappointed by the way in which the conference dealt with many crucial issues, and both refrained from personally affixing their names to three resolutions passed by the conference. (Their names were signed by their secretaries.) On May 5, a few days after the two Kims returned to Seoul, they reported to the people that the conference was fruitful in many ways, and that Kim Il-sung agreed not to establish a separate government in the north. Furthermore, they reported that the supply of North Korean electricity to the south would continue and the famed nationalist Christian leader, Cho Man-shik, who was under house arrest, would soon be released. At the same time, they urged their followers to continue to oppose the forthcoming election. General Hodge, however, warned the Koreans against heeding the counsel of Dr. Kim and Kim Ku, saying that they were "blind men" who had been "baited by the Communists."

The glory of the champions for the North-South collaboration for Korean independence was short-lived, for less than two weeks after their joint statement was issued in Pyongyang, the supply of electricity from the north was suddenly cut off. Meanwhile, on May 1, the North Korean Supreme People's Assembly adopted a new constitution for all Korea, arousing strong suspicion in the minds of the supporters of the two Kims who realized that the North Koreans were preparing for the establishment of a separate government in the north just as was Dr. Rhee's group in the south. As a result, a strong sense of being tricked and betrayed grew in the minds of those Nationalists who participated in the Pyongyang conference as well as those who nurtured high hopes for the movement launched by the two Kims and their associates. Realizing their dismal failure, the two Kims reluctantly acquiesced to the separate election in the south and prosposed that the north elect 100 representatives to the National Assembly to be set up in Seoul.

Prelude to Disaster.   The stuggle between the groups supporting the United Nations' plan and those opposing it intensified. On January 24, 1948, an attempt was made by the members of South Korean Workers' Party to assassinate Chang T'aek-sang, Director of the Metropolitan Police of Seoul, in February, a Communist-inspired armed uprising occurred in Miryang, South Kyŏngsang Province, and in early April a large-scale armed rebellion of the Communists occurred on the island of Cheju, causing a large number of casulaties and the destruction of more than 12,000 houses. Throughout the south many other bloody events took place.

The UNTCOK discussed the subject of the elections, and on April 28, 1948 it adopted a resolution, with five votes in favor and 2 abstentions, stating that the Commission would observe the elections to be held on May 10. They insisted that the elections were to be held in a free atmosphere and the democratic rights of speech, press and assembly were to be respected and observed. The responsibility of preparing for the elections and conducting them fell upon the American military government.

The Communists in the south, acting under instructions from the north, had embarked on an intensive campaign of terrorism to obstruct and sabotage the elections. The American military government intensified its campaign for public education on one hand and military preparedness on the other to encounter the Communist movement. The entire Korean Constabulary was alerted for possible hostile actions from the North Koreans, and the Community Protective Corps, a civilian organization, was organized to meet the Communist challenge. Meanwhile, the Communists increased their terroristic activities in order to discourage the eligible voters from registering or preventing the shipment of ballots and ballot boxes. A week before the election day, in Pusan harbor, they bombed a ship carrying election materials and ballot boxes being sent to Cheju Island.

The Establishment of the Republic of Korea.   In spite of the Communist terrorism, the election preparations were carried out, and by April 9, the last day of registration, 7,837,504 eligible voters, or 79.7 per cent of the Koreans above the age of 21 had registered. Of this number, 51 per cent were men and 49 per cent were women in 200 electoral districts with 13,407 voting places. Each district was to elect one member of the constituent assembly, and 842 candidates, including 17 women, ran for the office.

Although some 44 persons, including many candidates, were killed, nearly 100 wounded, and 68 voting booths were attacked by leftist terrorists, "the actual mechanics of voting was generally satisfactory and the secrecy of the balloting was, on the whole, ensured," according to the U.N. observers. The UNTCOK indicated that a reasonably free atmosphere existed wherein the democratic rights of freedom of speech, press, and assembly were recognized and respected during the election process. In this first democratic election in Korean history 7,487,649 or 95.5 per cent of the registered voters participated in the voting. Considering the lack of experience in democratic elections, the prevailing political conditions, the presence of terrorism, and the short time which was available to educate the voters, the May 10 elections amply testified the conscientiousness of the Korean people and their desire for a free and democratic way of life. It was a great victory for democracy and an undeniable repudiation of opportunism and Communism.

No party won a clear-cut majority. Dr. Rhee's National Society for Acceleration of Korean Independence won 54 seats; the Korean Democratic Party of Kim Sŏng-su, 29 seats; the Taedong Youth Corps, 13 seats; the National Youth Corps, 6 seats; the Korean Labor League, 2 seats; and the People's Unity Party and others won 10 seats; and the remaining 83 seats were taken by "independents." Nearly half of the 198 men elected (the National Assembly was to have 300 members of whom 200 were to be elected in the south while 100 in the north) were avowed members of right wing groups, and a large number of the remaining members were suspected of being left wing sympathizers. On June 25, the UNTCOK certified that the elections were "a valid expression of the free will of the electorate in those parts of Korea which were accessible to the Commission and in which the inhabitants constituted approximately two-thirds of the people of all Korea."

The National Assembly held its first meeting on May 31, and Dr. Rhee was elected as its chairman. On June 3, he informed UNTCOK that a temporary liaison committee of the National Assembly had been created and he invited UNTCOK's consultation with the Assembly. On June 12, a democratic constitution was adopted, and on June 20, Dr. Rhee was elected the first president of the Republic of Korea by an overwhelming majority. Dr. Philip Jaisohn was as popular among the Assembly members as Dr. Rhee, but his American citizenship disqualified him from holding the office of President in the Republic.

On August 12, the American government stated: "it is the view of the United States government that the Korean government so established is entitled to be regarded as the Government of Korea envisaged by the General Assembly resolution of November 14, 1947," and designated John J. Muccio as Special Representative, with the rank of ambassador, to the Republic of Korea. The government of the Republic of Korea was inaugurated on August 15, 1948, the third anniversary of Korean liberation.

On December 12, 1948, the U.N. General Assembly adopted a resolution declaring that there has been established, under the U.N. mandate, "a lawful government" of the Republic of Korea "having effective control and jurisdiction over that part of Korea where. . . the great majority of the people of all Korea reside. . . ." Thus, the government of the Republic of Korea gained the status of being the only legitimate regime in Korea, and it was so recognized by the nations of the non-Communist world. At the same time, the General Assembly established the Commission on Korea, replacing the Temporary Commission on Korea, in order to achieve the objectives set forth in the resolution of November 14, 1947, as well as to assist the development of the new nation.

The Emergence of the Democratic People's Republic of Korea.   The North Korean Communists continued their politics of deception, and in June they called for a second conference of the leaders of North and South Korea at Haeju, Hwanghae Province. No leaders in the south accepted their invitation, and the conference was held on June 29 in Pyongyang without any south Korean representation. Regardless, on July 5, the conference resolved that it would not recognize the election results in the south, but that it would conduct nation-wide elections on August 25 to establish a "Korean Supreme People's Assembly." Both Dr. Kim Kyu-shik and Kim Ku denounced the resolution and gave their unqualified disapproval of this unilateral move on the part of the Communists.

The North Koreans claimed that "secret elections" were conducted in South Korea sometime in August and elected 360 South Korean representatives for the 572 member Supreme People's Assembly. According to them, 77.2 per cent of the 8,681,745 eligible voters in South Korea took part in the secret elections, while 99.97 per cent of the voters in the north exercised their "democratic rights."

The Supreme People's Assembly met on September 3, 1948, in Pyongyang, ratified the constitution, and elected Kim Il-sung premier. Pak Hŏn-yŏng, former chairman of the South Korean Workers' Party, was elected vice premier and Minister of Foreign Affairs. On October 12, the Soviet Union, followed by its satellite countries, formally recognized the North Korean regime. General Shtykov, who had successfully prevented the Joint U.S.-U.S.S.R. Commission from achieving its goals, was appointed ambassador of the Soviet Union to Pyongyang.

Thus, during the months of August and September 1948, the Korean people witnessed the emergence of two governments, each claiming to be the legitimate government for all Korea. The military demarcation line between the American and the Soviet occupation zones became an international boundary as a new "iron curtain" descended across the Korean peninsula. The die was cast. More tragedies were yet to visit the Korean people because of the division of the land.

The Allied occupation achieved its primary aim, that of defeating and disarming Japanese troops in Korea and the liberation of Korea from Japanese colonial rule. However, it failed to implement the Moscow Agreement. When they withdrew their troops from the Korean peninsula, they left a nation which was still divided.

The outcome of the American occupation of South Korea was quite dissimilar from that of the American occupation of Japan. Having no clear-cut policy or plans for Korea, the American occupation left behind no particular imprints, or notable accomplishments. When the Americans ended their occupation, South Korea was politically unstable, socially chaotic, and an economically bankrupt country.

The Soviets, on the other hand, achieved much more in North Korea, although they too had no policy or plans for Korea in the early stage of their occupation. In contrast to the Americans in the south, the Soviets promoted cordiality with the North Korean Communist leaders, established a coherent political structure, and fostered a well-equipped military force capable of launching an aggressive war to unify the divided country.

10. The Communist State of North Korea

Various measures implemented by the Soviets and the Korean Communists during the period of the Allied occupation initiated the Communization of the northern half of Korea. Following the establishment of the Communist regime in 1948, the new government discarded all traditional systems, changed the people's way of life and their culture, and North Korea became one of the most regimented and closed societies in the world.

The State and the Ruling Organs

Chosŏn Minjujuŭi Inmin Konghwaguk, or the Democratic People's Republic of Korea (DPRK), commonly called North Korea, was inaugurated on September 9, 1948. Its size (48,948 sq. miles, or 122,380 sq. kilometers) was slightly larger than the state of Pennsylvania, and much larger than the Republic of Korea in the south. When it emerged, it consisted of six provinces, namely North and South Hamgyŏng, North and South P'yŏng-an, most of Hwanghae, and the northern half of Kangwŏn.

The North Korean Communists claimed that the territory of the DPRK covered the entire Korean peninsula, and called South Korea "the southern half of the Republic." They designated Seoul as the nation's capital in 1948, and Pyongyang as a temporary national capital and a special city administered directly by the central government. Each province was divided into counties, consisting of districts, and each district included towns and villages. North Korea's population in 1948 was about 10 million.

The Supreme People's Assembly.   The Supreme People's Assembly (SPA) was established on August 25, 1948, as the supreme organ of the state, and its delegates were elected by all citizens 18 years of age or over for a four-year term. The number of delegates of the First SPA in 1948 was 572 (212 representing North Korea and 360 representing South Korea), each delegate representing 50,000 constituents (30,000 since 1962). It was headed by the Standing Committee (Presidium), whose chairman was the chairman of the SPA and acted as the chief of state. The Standing Committee was created as "a permanent executive body" of the SPA, and its officers included a chairman, two vice-chairmen, a secretary, and 20 members. It was empowered to convene the regular and special sessions of the SPA, examine bills, and amend laws and ordinances when the SPA was not in session. Needless to say, the members of the Standing Committee were top personnel of the Korean Workers' Party. In 1948, provincial, municipal, county, and district people's assemblies were established as bodies representing the people.

ADMINISTRATIVE DISTRICTS OF THE DEMOCRATIC
PEOPLE'S REPUBLIC OF KOREA (1948)

Although the constitution adopted in September 1948 stipulated that the SPA was given exclusive legislative power, it had no legislative power as such since all laws were originated in the Central Committee of the Korean Workers' Party. The SPA, however, exercised the power to approve or amend the constitution, laws, and ordinances, approve the appointment of top government personnel, such as premier, vice-premiers, and ministers, as well as approve domestic and foreign policies proposed by the Party. The elections for the Second SPA were not held until August 1957.

The Central and Local Governments.   The central government was headed by a premier. He was originally the chief administrative official of the State Administrative Council (cabinet), but under the 1972 constitution, the president of the DPRK, elected by the Supreme People's Assembly, became the head of the government and the state. In 1948, it consisted of one commission and 15 ministries. Kim Il-sung was premier, and he was assisted by three vice-premiers. The two other top state organs were the Supreme Court and the Supreme Procurator's (Attorney-General) Office. The local organs of the government were the provincial people's committees, the municipal and districts people's committees, local courts, and the local procurators' offices.

The Korean Workers' Party.   In 1949, the North Korean Workers' Party and the South Korean Workers' Party merged and formed the new party named the Korean Workers' Party (KWP) with a membership of about 790,000. The KWP, whose General Secretary was Kim Il-sung, became the most powerful political institution in North Korea. Kim Il-sung said that ''the Workers' Party is a combat unit and the vanguard of the working masses. We must fight with our utmost to maintain the Party's purity, unity, and iron discipline,'' and the Party will exercise an absolute power in order to complete ''the Korean revolution.''

In addition to the Central Party in Pyongyang, each province, municipality, county, district, the town and village, as well as each military unit, factory, and school established a Party branch.

The top organs of the KWP were the Secretariat and the following committees: Central, Military Affairs, Foreign Affairs, Inspection, and Central Auditing. Of these, the Central Committee was most powerful. Although its membership was small (12 full members and 6 alternate members up to 1961) in reality it was the ruling body not only of the Party, but also of the nation. The Political Committee (Politburo) of the Central Committee was where the power was concentrated and where all major policy decisions were made and laws and ordinances were originated. Of the departments of the Central Committee, the Organization and Guidance Department and the Propaganda and Agitation Department were the two most important ones.

All top ranking Party members, who had also occupied top positions in the

Supreme People's Assembly and the State Administration Council concurrently, were members of the so-called Partisan (Kapsan) faction of the Korean Workers' Party until about 1975. The members of the Kapsan faction, such as Ch'oe Hyŏn, Kim Ch'aek, Pak Sŏng-ch'ŏl, O Chin-u, and Ch'oe Yong-gŏn, were those who were with Kim Il-sung in Manchuria and Siberia before their return to Korea. Two exceptions were General Nam Il and Ho Ka-i, Russian-born Koreans who elected to stay in North Korea when Soviet troops withdrew from there in December 1948.

By 1980, nearly all members of the Kapsan faction have died. Some of its key members were killed during the Korean War, or eliminated by Kim Il-sung after 1953. Many younger Communists who had no ties with the Kapsan faction have been elevated to high ranks to fill the vacancies in key positions. Among them are Sŏ Ch'ŏl, Lim Ch'un-ch'u, O Kŭk-yŏl, Chŏn Kŭm-ch'ŏl, and Kim Chŏng-il (Kim Jong-il), the first son of Kim Il-sung by his second wife, Kim Chŏng-suk, who died in 1949.

Obtaining a party membership was difficult. Only those who were 18 years and older and who were regarded as having a "good origin" were admitted into the Party. Sons of former landlords, those Koreans who had been pro-Japanese, and those who failed to demonstrate their enthusiasm and unquestionable loyalty to Kim Il-sung and the Party were rejected. Intense recruitment campaigns were conducted in order to increase the Party membership, and in June 1950, a year after the North Korean Workers' Party and the South Korean Workers' Party merged, the Party membership increased to 820,000. When the two parties merged, Kim Il-sung became the chairman of the new party, and Pak Hŏn-yŏng and one other were elected vice-chairmen. The Party Congress met twice before the Korean War—in August 1946 and in March 1948. Some 801 delegates attended the first Party Congress, and 999 delegates participated in the second Party Congress.

The Military.   The People's Army is a powerful instrument of the Korean Workers' Party through which it absolutely controls the state and the people. The North Korean Communists consciously fostered a strong militarism and created a huge military machine in order to carry out what they called the "liberation of the southern half of the Republic" and to complete the so-called Korean revolution.

The Korean People's Army was created in February 1948 with some 20,000 members of the Security Force who were trained by the Soviets. Kim Il-sung himself had some 300 seasoned fighters who constituted the Partisan group. There were also about 2,200 Communists who had been with the Chinese Communists at Yenan and returned to Korea in late 1945, and about 3,000 Koreans returning from Siberia under Hŏ Ka-i and An Kil. In March 1948, a Soviet-Communist-China-North Korea Joint Military Council was established in Pyongyang, and both the Soviets and the Chinese Communists helped

North Korea's military. Sometime in 1949, about 22,000 Korean Communist troops who fought against the Chinese Nationalists in Manchuria under Communist Commander Lin Piao, entered Korea and formed the three strongest divisions in the Korean People's Army. Among the top military leaders, in addition to Kim Il-sung, were Kim Il, Mu Chŏng, Kim Ch'aek, Ch'oe Yong-gŏn, and O Chin-u as well as Soviet-born Korean generals such as Nam Il, Hŏ Ka-i, and An Kil.

Kim Il-sung said that the Korean People's Army was the Korean Workers' Party's armed force and its guiding ideology included "Marxism-Leninism and the policies and principles of our Party." He said "it guards and protects, with a spirit of sacrifice. . . the course of revolution proposed by the Party, and considers these duties its sacred work."

The number of troops in the People's Army increased rapidly after 1948 as they were intensely indoctrinated with political ideology and militarily trained. The Soviet occupation forces withdrew from North Korea in December 1948, but some 2,300 Soviet military advisers and technicians remained there and trained North Korean troops. At the same time, an increasing quantity of Soviet weapons were brought into North Korea.

The People's Army had consisted of "volunteers" who were recruited under a quota system. Each district had a quota to meet, and these "volunteers" were actually conscripted into military services. From March 1948, some 20,000 young men between the ages of 18 and 22 were recruited annually into the military. As a result, the People's Army grew from two divisions and one mixed brigade in 1948, to 24 infantry divisions of 135,000 troops, 4 mixed brigades, and a tank brigade by June 1950. The tank brigade of 8,800 troops had 500 Russian-built T-34 and T-70 tanks, the 2,300 men Air Force had 211 Yak and MIG planes built in the Soviet Union, and the Navy of 15,270 men had 35 military crafts of various kinds.

The Korean War

With the vastly strengthened military power and an ambition to unify Korea and put it under communist rule, Kim Il-sung, however reluctantly abetted and approved by the Soviets, launched a war against South Korea in June 1950. The war lasted for three years, but Kim failed to accomplish his objectives. The tragic war caused tremendous hardships for the people in both zones, it destroyed a vast number of lives and properties, and it made the peaceful reunification of Korea difficult, if not virtually impossible.

Prelude. The unification rhetoric from both Pyongyang and Seoul was belligerent, each threatening to march and take over the other and each stating that unification of the nation must be achieved. The South Korean government insisted that as long as the border along the 38th parallel was not dismantled, true independence of Korea and true peace between the East and the West would not be possible. President Rhee expressed his determination to "move into North Korea" to American ambassador John Muccio in February 1949. Meanwhile, the North Korean Communists emphatically stated that without the "liberation of the southern half of the Republic" the Korean revolution would not be completed.

By the spring of 1949, all efforts made by the Pyongyang regime to gain support for its membership in the United Nations Organization failed to achieve their objectives; the General Assembly of the United Nations had adopted a United States resolution and recognized the Republic of Korea as the only legitimate government in the Korean peninsula. In March 1949, Kim Il-sung, Pak Hŏn-yŏng and a few top ranking North Korean Communists visited Moscow and concluded cultural and economic agreements as well as a secret military aid agreement. Evidently, it was at this time when Kim Il-sung secured Stalin's consent to his plan to launch an attack against South Korea.

On June 28, 1949, the Democratic Front for the Unification of the Fatherland was founded in Pyongyang, and it announced the so-called "peaceful unification formula," advocating the formation of an election committee of representatives of political parties and social organizations of the north and the south to conduct general elections throughout the peninsula for the establishment of a unified national legislature.

Between May and August 1949, many border clashes between the troops of the south and the north occurred at such places as Kaesŏng, as well as Paekch'ŏn and Ongjin in Hwanghae Province and near Ch'unch'ŏn in Kangwŏn Province. Meanwhile, the South Korean Workers' Party leaders who migrated to the north and formed the Democratic Front for the Unification of the Fatherland in June 1949, sought cooperation of anti-Rhee elements in the south, and initiated a guerrilla war against the south in cooperation with the remnants of the rebels who had brought about the Yŏsu-Sunch'ŏn Rebellion in South Chŏlla Province in the south in October 1948.

The Democratic Front for the Unification of the Fatherland sent several guerrilla units into South Korea in the fall of 1949, and the North Korean guerrillas established their eastern base at the Odae mountain area in Kangwŏn Province. The second guerrilla base was established in the Chiri mountain area in the border region of North Chŏlla and South Kyŏngsang provinces, and in August they infiltrated the Andong area in North Kyŏngsang Province in order to establish their base. In October and November, North Korean guerrillas, supported by their allies in the south, launched a large-scale winter offensive at Andong, Chinju, and P'ohang, and the fighting continued throughout the winter months. But the counterattack launched by South Korean troops destroyed most of the North Korean guerrillas and their allies by March 1950.

Kim Il-sung was "much excited" when informed of the American Secretary of State Dean Acheson's January 1950 speech at the Press Club in Washington,

D.C. regarding the "defense perimeter" of the United States in the Pacific, and he also learned that the U.S. Congress had cut off Korean aid. Realizing that North Korean guerrilla movements in the south were virtually wiped out and there was no hope of the South Korean government being overthrown by the subversive activities of the South Korean Workers' Party, the North Korean Communists decided to launch the war, for by the spring of 1950, a conventional military attack was the only alternative left to Kim Il-sung for achieving Korean unification. All his policy options had been tried and had failed.

Sometime in April or May, the North Koreans resolved to launch an all-out attack against the south, and their propaganda against the South Korean government was stepped up. The North Korean regime employed various tactics to disguise their hostile intentions thereby misleading the South Korean government and people. On June 7, the Central Committee of the Democratic Front for the Unification of the Fatherland proposed the holding of "free elections" throughout Korea between August 5 and 8 in order to unify the country peacefully. At the same time, it called for the convening of the conference of representatives from all political parties and social organizations of the north and the south between the 15th and 17th, either at Kaesŏng or Haeju. Radio Pyongyang said on June 10 that the North Korean regime was dispatching its delegates to Panmunjom. That day, three North Korean officials arrived at Panmunjom and transmitted a written statement of the North Korean government to a member of the United Nations Commission on Korea. However, they refused to take back with them the United Nations plan for Korean unification.

When the South Korean government ignored North Korean proposals as mere propaganda, on June 11 Radio Pyongyang again announced that, since the South Korean government did not send its delegates to negotiate with the North Korean delegates, the North Korean government was sending three officials to the south. When they came across the 38th parallel, they were promptly arrested by South Korean guards, and were interrogated. Those North Koreans denied that North Korea had any hostile intentions against the south. On June 19, the Supreme People's Assembly made a proposal calling for the merger of the two Korean legislative assemblies into a single body.

In early June 1950, the North Koreans evacuated all the residents along the 38th parallel and deployed combat ready troops there. Meanwhile, a large number of heavily armed guerrillas infiltrated the south with an order to organize uprisings in cooperation with members of the South Korean Workers' Party who had gone underground. The timing of the uprising was to be coordinated with the North Korean attack against the south. The first battle order written in both Korean and Russian was issued on June 22 to the 4th Infantry Division which was one of the major attack forces of North Korea.

Between October 1949 and June 25, 1950, at least six warnings of the possible North Korean attack were issued by U.S. military intelligence and the

Korean government. The Central Intelligence Agency of the United States had also warned of a possible North Korean attack in the wake of the U.S. troop withdrawal from Korea. In October 1949, General Hodge issued a warning about a possible North Korean attack; in October 1949 and February 1950, General MacArthur's headquarters warned that the North Koreans might launch a war in March or April 1950; in April 1950 the U.S. Air intelligence units stated that the Soviet Union had ordered North Korea to attack the south; on May 10, 1950, the southward movement of North Korean troops was detected; and South Korea's Defense Minister reported that North Korean troops were moving southward toward the 38th parallel and that there was imminent danger of invasion; and in early June the southward movement of North Korean troops was confirmed. On June 19, the U.S. Central Intelligence Agency also reported active North Korean troop movements near the border. All these warnings were either ignored or they were given perfunctory attention by Washington.

The Northern Aggression.   The inherent weakness of South Korea, particularly its military weakness, coupled with certain steps taken by the United States government, contributed to North Korea's launching of the war. In the first place, the United States, because of President Truman's demilitarization program, withdrew U.S. troops from South Korea in 1949 without adequately preparing South Korean troops to defend their national territory. The United States regarded South Korea strategically less important than Greece, Italy, and Iran in dealing with Soviet expansionism. Secondly, President Truman did not believe that the Soviet Union would permit a North Korean invasion for military conquest of the entire peninsula. He believed that the Soviets would continue their efforts through infiltration and underground activities. Above all, the United States government, specifically Secretary of State, Dean Acheson, wanted to make Korea a testing ground for the policy of containment of the United States, and therefore misled the North Koreans to believe that the United States had abandoned South Korea.

Some suspect, and there is some evidence supporting the suspicion, that Secretary of State Dean Acheson deliberately omitted South Korea from the United States defense perimeter between the Aleutians and the Ryukyus when he spoke at the Press Club in Washington, D.C. on January 12, 1950, about American defense in Asia. His intention was said to have been to test the will of the Soviets. Acheson, as Under Secretary of State, was one of those who in 1947 strongly voiced the importance of securing Korea for the free world and the drawing of a line between "the Russians and ourselves."

To be sure, containment of Soviet expansionism was a factor which led to the establishment by Dean Rusk and others of the State-Army-Navy Coordinating Committee, in early August 1945, of a military demarcation line between Soviet and American occupation forces in Korea. However, it was between 1947 and

1950, that the internationalism of President Roosevelt was discarded or suspended by the Truman administration which pursued instead a containment policy in the context of a Cold War. There was, however, no consensus among the policy makers behind the containment policy as of early 1950. If North Korea started a war, then the containment policy would be justified and it would create a consensus supporting the policy. Whatever Acheson's motives may have been, many argue that he deliberately misled Kim Il-sung and lured the North Korean Communists into launching a war against South Korea. Some believe that Acheson "wishing to shape defense [in Asia], created a situation in which the offense would blunder."

On the other hand, Stalin may have not ordered the North Koreans to launch an attack in June 1950, but sometime in 1949 he gave tacit approval to the North Korean invasion, however reluctantly he might have done so. Some believe that Stalin gave his reluctant approval so that Kim Il-sung, who wanted to launch "a civil and revolutionary war," would "stew in the juice of his own provocation." Be that as it may, it was widely acknowledged that the Korean War came because the United States never made a conclusive decision to hold Korea, and failed to make a credible military threat to the Soviet Union.

On early Sunday morning, June 25, 1950 (Korean time), the North Korean government launched a war against South Korea, and over 56,000 North Korean troops, supported by Soviet-built tanks, crossed the 38th parallel. Several tens of thousands more North Korean troops poured into the south. Four days later, North Korean troops captured Seoul, and the aggressors quickly demolished South Korea's resistance as they occupied more than half of the territory of the Republic of Korea. Kim Il-sung said in his speech to the soldiers on August 15, 1950 that:

The national liberation struggle, which the Korean people are waging for the freedom and independence of their fatherland against the U.S. imperialists who attempt to enslave them, does not arise from a transient or temporary cause, but from the fundamental national aspiration of the Korean people who do not wish to become slaves again to foreign imperialists. . . .

President Truman, who received the news from Seoul about North Korea's aggression, ordered American ground, air, and naval support for South Korean troops on June 27. American forces arrived in Korea on June 30 and encountered the invaders, but they too were pushed back. Meanwhile, the United Nations Security Council condemned North Korea as aggressors, and ordered the North Koreans to withdraw beyond the 38th parallel. When the North Koreans refused to do so, the United Nations in June formed U.N. forces with troops provided by the United States and 15 other nations. President Truman appointed General Douglas MacArthur as commander of the U.N. forces.

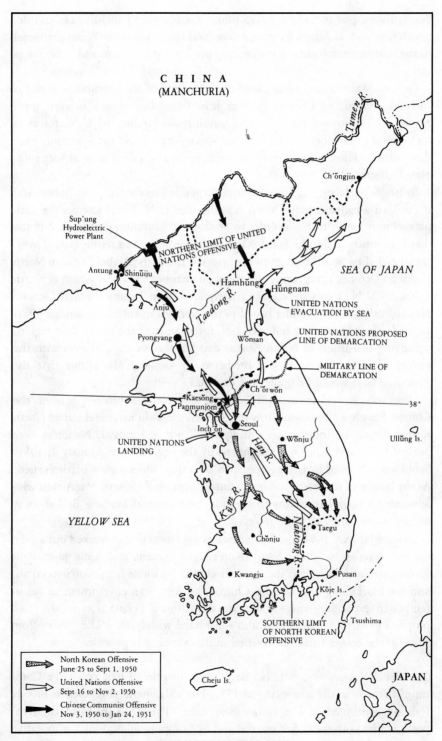

THE KOREAN WAR MAP

South Korea put its armed forces under his command in July. Meanwhile, South Korean and American troops took their last stand in the Pusan perimeter in the southeastern corner of the country until more American and U.N. forces arrived.

General MacArthur contemplated the launching of an amphibious assault at Inch'ŏn, Haeju, or Chinnamp'o in July 1950, but it was delayed until September. Following the successful amphibious landing by U.N. forces at Inch'ŏn on September 15, 1950, Seoul was recovered and the aggressors were driven back. Those aggressors in between Seoul and Pusan were almost completely destroyed.

In late September, the United States suspended its containment policy, and it initiated a rollback policy when it authorized U.N. forces to cross the 38th parallel into North Korea in order to destroy the Communists and reunite the divided country under the South Korean government. As a result, U.N. forces, spearheaded by South Korean troops, crossed the 38th parallel line into North Korea on October 1, capturing its capital on October 20. The invasion of North Korea by U.N. forces took place shortly after Kim Il-sung ignored General MacArthur's call to surrender issued to the North Koreans on September 30. It seemed, when Pyongyang fell and U.N. forces reached the upper Yalu region, occupying two-thirds of North Korea, that the war would end soon with the victory of U.N. forces. It was predicted by General MacArthur that the American boys would be home by Christmas.

However, sometime in mid-October, 200,000 "volunteers" from the Chinese People's Liberation Army had crossed the Yalu River and joined North Korean forces, beginning "an entirely new" war in Korea. U.N. forces were pushed back, and Seoul was recaptured by the aggressors on January 4, 1951. Seoul was recovered by U.N. forces soon after that, but a seesaw battle ensued. At the height of the war, President Truman dismissed General MacArthur who advocated a complete victory in the war, and General Mathew B. Ridgeway became commander of U.N. forces.

In early January 1951, the United States government had worked out a plan for the evacuation of the South Korean government and some prominent Korean civilians, as well as the evacuation of U.N. forces from Korea to Japan, and the blockading of mainland China. The American government also contemplated expanding the war to mainland China if Peking rejected the truce proposal of U.N. forces, and it also considered withdrawing U.S. forces from Korea if the Soviet Union intervened in the war on a large scale.

The Korean Armistice.   U.N. forces were unable to halt two large Communist attacks in the late spring of 1951, but a stalemate developed as bloody fighting continued in the eastern war zone. The Truman administration, pressured by both the U.S. Congress and by European allies, took the initiative for a negotiated settlement in Korea, and began secret talks with the Chinese government through an intermediary. However, the Chinese proposal for a simultaneous withdrawal of U.N. forces and Chinese troops from Korea created a roadblock in the truce talks.

The deadlock was broken when Soviet Deputy Foreign Minister Jacob Malik indicated that the Soviets wanted peace, and hinted on June 23, 1951, that the Soviet government might intervene in the truce negotiations provided that a new truce line would not radically alter the then existing division of Korea along the 38th parallel. It was acceptable to U.N. forces. As a result, General Ridgeway issued an invitation to the Communists on June 30, and on July 10, truce talks between the representatives of U.N. forces and those of China and North Korea began at Kaesŏng, a South Korean city which had been captured by North Korea.

The negotiators encountered many obstacles and fighting continued with each side attempting to capture more territory. One of the troublesome issues was related to the repatriation of Communist prisoners-of-war. Another issue was the establishment of a truce line. The Communists insisted upon the repatriation of all prisoners-of-war, whereas U.N. forces insisted upon voluntary repatriation. The Communists attempted to reestablish the 38th parallel as a line of division in Korea whereas U.N. forces proposed to make the existing battle line the line of division between the north and the south. Meanwhile, truce talks were suspended between August and October 1951.

Talks resumed in late October at a new place named Panmunjom, an obscure hamlet located in between Seoul and Kaesŏng. However, the negotiators reached an impasse as soon as they met. Thereupon, General Mark Clark, the new American and U.N. commander who replaced General Ridgeway, in May ordered massive air attacks against targets in North Korea, including Pyongyang. These air attacks of May, July, and August did not bring the Communists to accept the proposals made by the U.N. Command. Meanwhile, the United States presidential candidate, General Dwight Eisenhower, said in his campaign speech that he would go to Korea himself and end the war.

The death of Stalin in March 1953 and the unyielding stand of U.N. forces brought Kim Il-sung to end the war he could not win. The South Korean President's release on June 18 of some 25,000 prisoners-of-war who did not wish to be repatriated to their countries almost wrecked truce talks. However, Kim Il-sung knew that he could not continue the war. Arduous negotiations with the Communists at Panmunjom, conducted by Admiral C. Turner Joy, brought about the Korean armistice on July 27, 1953. Some 82,500 Communist prisoners-of-war, including 6,700 Chinese were repatriated to their homelands, while 50,000, including 14,700 Chinese, chose not to go back to their countries. Meanwhile, Chinese troops withdrew from North Korea.

The Korean War caused 157,530 American casualties, including 33,625 deaths, 14,000 casualties of other U.N. forces, and 257,000 South Korean soldiers who were either killed, wounded, or missing. Some 244,000 South

Korean citizens were killed, over 229,000 were wounded, and 303,000 were listed as missing. Some 129,000 South Koreans were massacred by the Communists during their occupation of South Korea, and over 84,000 South Koreans were forcibly marched off to the north while 200,000 South Korean youths were forced to join the North Korean military. Among those who were known to have been kidnapped to the north were such prominent leaders as Kim Kyu-shik, An Chae-hong, Cho So-ang, and Yi Kwang-su.

Pyongyang, the North Korean capital, was completely destroyed and many industrial facilities and hydroelectric plants in the north were either destroyed or badly damaged. The casualties on the part of the North Korean and Chinese forces were estimated at 520,000 and 900,000, respectively. Civilian casualties were not reported by the North Korean regime.

When the Korean armistice was ready to be concluded, the South Korean government, either disregarding, or failing to realize possible long-term consequences, refused to sign the truce document with the North Koreans and the Chinese. By doing so, the South Korean government refused to recognize either North Korea or Communist China, and created a serious problem related to the establishment of diplomatic relations with the People's Republic of China in the future, as well as any amicable negotiations between Seoul and Pyongyang for peaceful reunification of Korea.

The war which Kim Il-sung launched to annex the south did not bring about his intended result. Korea remained divided along a new truce line—a three mile wide demilitarized zone (DMZ) which zig-zags across the peninsula. Panmunjom became a truce village where a joint security area of North Korean and U.N. forces was established. North Korea lost a considerable amount of its mountainous eastern territory, but it gained a small but more economically and strategically valuable coastal region of the west central area of the peninsula, including the city of Kaesŏng.

The Postwar Reconstruction and Development

North Korea was badly damaged during the war, particularly toward the end of the conflict. The destruction of cities and industries in the north was more severe and extensive than that in the south. Be that as it may, the North Korean Communists devoted their energies to rebuilding their party, military, economy, and society after 1953 with assistance given to them by the Soviet Union, the People's Republic of China, and other socialist countries.

Strengthening of Kim Il-sung's Power.   Kim Il-sung rapidly increased his dictatorial power during and immediately following the Korean War. On various grounds he purged a large number of his opponents, including Pak Hŏn-yŏng. Pak was charged with misleading Kim to believe that if North Korean troops invaded the south, the people there would rise up, overthrow their government, and create a situation in which unification of the country could be achieved. Moreover, Pak was charged as an American spy and as an agent of General Hodge. Although Pak was not formally tried, he was executed in December 1955.

Conflict among the surviving top Communist leaders did not end, however. Kim Tu-bong, the leader of the Yenan faction, was a formidable figure. The attack made against the personality cult of Stalin in the Soviet Union encouraged the Korean Communists, particularly those of the Yenan faction, to take similar actions in 1956 against Kim Il-sung's one-man-rule.

Kim Il-sung in turn launched a vicious counterattack against his critics, forcing some of them to flee either to China or to the Soviet Union. Many were imprisoned or killed. Moscow and Peking interposed and effected a temporary truce between Kim Il-sung and his opponents. However, Kim either eliminated his adversaries completely or forced them to accept his rule without question. Kim Tu-bong himself became a victim in 1956.

It was imperative for Kim Il-sung to establish the legitimacy of his leadership and strengthen his authority. In order to do so, in 1955 he introduced what he called *chuch'e* (*juche*) ideology. *Chuch'e* means self-orientedness or self-reliance. Kim claimed that it was a creative application of Marxist-Leninist thoughts. He complained in 1955 that "some people say that the Soviet way is best or that the Chinese way is best...." He responded by saying "have we not now reached the point where we can construct our own?"

Kim Il-sung emphasized the importance of making the North Korean regime "suit the characteristics of the country," and advocated the adoption of a self-oriented and independent domestic policy in order to carry out "a strictly Korean revolution." He made tenacious efforts to make his *chuch'e* ideology the standard of the Party and that of the Korean revolution. In 1960, he said that whatever the Korean Communists studied about the histories of the Soviet and the Chinese revolution, all must direct them toward the completion of the Korean revolution. Kim Il-sung used the *chuch'e* thought as the ideological basis for the his absolute leadership as much as Mao Tse-tung had done in Yenan with his Clean Wind campaign in 1940, Kim said in 1961 that:

In the course of our persistent struggle against the anti-Party factional elements and their evil ideological influence, the Party has been able to extirpate factionalism... and has completed the historic task of achieving the complete unity of the Korean Communist movement.

Thus, with the *chuch'e* ideology, Kim Il-sung not only made North Korea a monolithic state and the *chuch'e* thought a new religion of the people, but also strengthened his dictatorial power. Meanwhile, the North Korean historians

compiled a fictitious biography of Kim Il-sung and a history of the Communist movements of Kim and his followers in Manchuria, glorifying the
ingenuity and achievements of Kim Il-sung.

In October 1966, Kim Il-sung abolished the post of vice-chairmanship of
the Korean Workers' Party, thereby strengthening his control over the Party
as its general secretary. When the Socialist Constitution was adopted by the
Supreme People's Assembly in October 1972, the *chuch'e* ideology was
declared the "guiding principle of the Republic." Kim, without relinquishing his general secretaryship of the Party, was elected president of the DPRK
under the new constitution, and he was reelected president in 1976 and
1982. On April 15, 1982, North Korea held a week long, nationwide celebration
for his 70th birthday.

Administrative Reconstruction.   In 1953, the administrative districts were
redrawn either by reducing the size of the existing provinces or by dividing a
province into two in order to make the number of provinces equal to that of
South Korea. As a result, at present, there are nine provinces, namely, North
and South Hamgyŏng, North and South P'yŏng-an, Yanggang, Chagang,
North and South Hwanghae, and Kangwŏn. Two large cities (Ch'ŏngjin and
Kaesŏng) strategically located were designated, like Pyongyang, as special
cities administered directly by the central government. The city of Sŏngjin on
the northeast coast was renamed Kimch'aek, in honor of Kim Ch'aek, former
comrade of Kim Il-sung. The number of counties was increased from 97 to
173 in December 1952, and sub-administrative units (districts) of each
county were abolished when, in 1958, workers' districts and collective farm
districts replaced the then existing sub-administrative units of each county.

The government structure remained basically unchanged, but the 149-
article Socialist Constitution, which was adopted on December 22, 1972, by
the Supreme People's Assembly, created the offices of the president and two
vice-presidents. With this change, Kim Il-sung, who had been premier, was
elected the president of the DPRK. The constitution, however, did not make
the president accountable to the SPA. In 1980, the number of vice-presidents
was increased to three. The number of deputy-premiers was increased to six
in 1957, to eight in 1962, to nine in 1967, to ten in 1980, and in 1982 it
increased to thirteen. In 1962, the office of the first deputy-premier was
instituted.

The State Administrative Council grew in size after the Korean War.
Between 1957 and 1962, there were 2 commissions (Planning and Construction) and 22 ministries, but between 1962 and 1967 the number of commissions grew to 3 and that of ministries to 25. Since then, the number of commissions has increased to 7 and that of ministries to 31.

The 1972 Socialist Constitution created the Central People's Committee as
a policy making body of the central government. With this, the State

Administrative Council became a purely executive branch of the central government. As of November 1980, the 14-member Central People's Committee was headed by President Kim Il-sung, and its membership included three vice-presidents and 10 others, one of whom was its secretary. The commissions which were directly supervised by the Central People's Committee were: Internal Policy, Foreign Policy, National Defense, Justice and Security, Legislative, Economic, and Judicial Life Guidance commissions.

The Supreme People's Assembly. The first postwar elections, which established the second Supreme People's Assembly (SPA), were held on August 27, 1957, electing 251 deputies. Significantly, in 1957 elections no "delegates" from the "southern half of the Republic," namely South Korea, were elected. The election dates for the SPA and the number of deputies elected since 1948 were as follows:

Term	Date of Elections	Number of Deputies
1	August 25, 1948	572
2	August 27, 1957	215
3	October 8, 1962	383
4	November 25, 1967	457
5	December 12, 1972	541
6	November 11, 1977	579
7	February 28, 1982	615

In 1962 the number of constitutents per delegate was reduced from 50,000 to 30,000.

In the first elections for the SPA held in 1948, 157 members of the Korean Workers' Party of both the north and the south were elected; the remaining 415 seats were filled by the representatives of other North Korean parties and organizations. However, in the second, third, and fourth SPA, the number of deputies representing the Korean Workers' Party increased to 178, 371, and 442, respectively, thus dominating the SPA. The total number of deputies representing other parties and organizations decreased to 37, 12, and 15 in the second, third, and fourth SPA, respectively. In the 4th SPA established in 1967, 7 deputies representing the General Federation of Korean Residents in Japan were elected for the first time. The number of deputies representing the Korean Workers' Party in the 5th, 6th, and the 7th SPA constituted more than 95 per cent of the total number of deputies.

The deputies who were workers constituted a majority (347 out of 541), followed by those who were office workers (122) until 1972, but in the sixth elections 267 office workers (mostly scientists and technicians), or 46.2 per cent of the total number of deputies (579), were elected while 248 (42.8 per cent) workers were elected. The number of peasants who were elected to the

GOVERNMENT STRUCTURE OF DEMOCRATIC PEOPLE'S REPUBLIC OF KOREA
(November 1980)

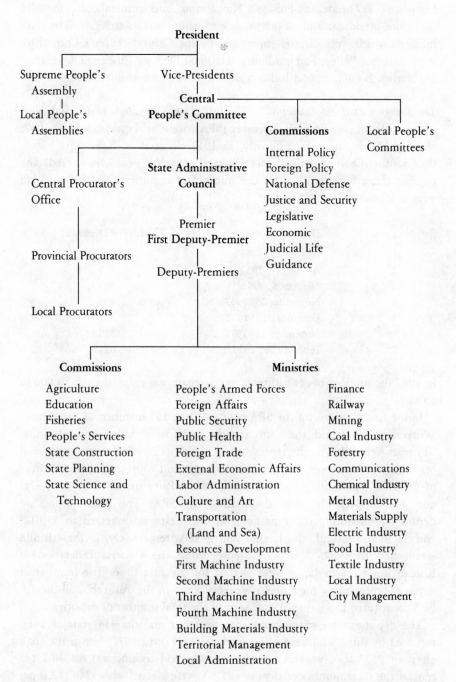

President

Supreme People's
Assembly

Local People's
Assemblies

Vice-Presidents

Central
People's Committee

State Administrative
Council

Premier
First Deputy-Premier

Deputy-Premiers

Commissions
Internal Policy
Foreign Policy
National Defense
Justice and Security
Legislative
Economic
Judicial Life
Guidance

Local People's
Committees

Central Procurator's
Office

Provincial Procurators

Local Procurators

Commissions	Ministries	
Agriculture	People's Armed Forces	Finance
Education	Foreign Affairs	Railway
Fisheries	Public Security	Mining
People's Services	Public Health	Coal Industry
State Construction	Foreign Trade	Forestry
State Planning	External Economic Affairs	Communications
State Science and	Labor Administration	Chemical Industry
Technology	Culture and Art	Metal Industry
	Transportation	Materials Supply
	(Land and Sea)	Electric Industry
	Resources Development	Food Industry
	First Machine Industry	Textile Industry
	Second Machine Industry	Local Industry
	Third Machine Industry	City Management
	Fourth Machine Industry	
	Building Materials Industry	
	Territorial Management	
	Local Administration	

SPA was always small—72 (13 per cent) and 64 (11 per cent) in the fifth (1972) and the sixth elections (1977), respectively.

The 1972 constitution further curtailed the significance of the SPA when the office of the president of the republic was created, and the chairman of the Standing Committee of the SPA no longer served as head of the state. Although some members (mostly low ranking) of the Central Committee of the Korean Workers' Party were elected to the Standing Committee of the SPA, none of the members of the Standing Committee of the SPA were elected to the powerful Political Committee of the Central Committee of the KWP, or appointed as members of the State Administrative Council. Currently, there are four committees of the SPA, namely the Standing, the Budget, the Bills, and the Credentials committees. Local people's assemblies were established in provinces, municipalities, and counties.

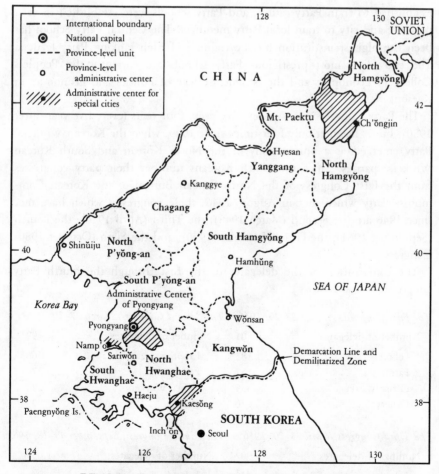

DEMOCRATIC PEOPLE'S REPUBLIC OF KOREA (1982)

Reconstruction of the Party.   The Korean Workers' Party was badly damaged and it lost many of its members during the Korean War, and the rebuilding of the Party became imperative. As soon as the armistice was signed, Kim Il-sung initiated the reconstruction of the Party and he launched an intense campaign to recruit new Party members.

The regulations governing the admission of new Party members were revised in 1956 without relaxing the membership qualification. As a result, the Party membership jumped to 1,164,945 in 1956 from 725,762 in 1948, and it grew to 1.3 million in 1961, to 1.6 million in 1970, and to about 2.7 million in 1982. North Korea became the country having more Communist party members per capita than any of the other Socialist countries. About 12.5 per cent of the population of 18.5 million in 1982 were Party members.

The newly recruited members were intensely indoctrinated and trained to fulfill their duties and obligations. Absolute loyalty to Kim Il-sung and obedience to the Party were required of all members. Special schools were established to train Party cadres, and Party schools were established in each province and city to train local Party members. The Central Party School has been the highest institution for the training of high ranking Party leaders. The two other most prestigious Party schools are currently the People's College of Economics and the Songdo College of Politics and Economics in Kaesŏng.

The Party Congress was to meet once every four years (every five years after 1980), but it has met only four times since 1949, when the Korean Workers' Party emerged as a united body of the North Korean and South Korean Workers' parties. Since the North Koreans number their party congresses from the First Congress of the North Korean Bureau of the Korean Communist Party which met in August 1946, these congresses which have met since 1946 are the Second (March 1948), the Third (April 1956), the Fourth (September 1961), the Fifth (November 1970), and the Sixth (October 1980) Congress.

The composition of the delegates to the first through the fourth Party congresses was as follows:

The First Congress, August 22-29, 1946

Number of delegates: 801

Laborers 183
Farmers 157
Office Workers 385
Others 76

The Second Congress, March 27-30, 1948

Number of delegates: 999

Laborers 466
Farmers 270
Office Workers 234
Others 29

The Third Congress, April 23-29, 1956

Number of delegates: 907

Laborers 439

The Fourth Congress, September 11-18, 1961

Number of delegates: 1,657

Laborers 944

Farmers 192	Farmers 451
Office Workers 246	Office Workers 191
Others 39	Others 71

The number of delegates to the fifth and the sixth Party congresses was 1,871 and 3,222, respectively, but the breakdown of categories of delegates was not given. It was assumed that the percentage of the "Others" category which included military personnel increased in view of the trend shown in the past.

The reconstituted Central Committee of the KWP consisted of 116 members (71 full and 45 candidate members) who were elected by the Third Party Congress in April 1956. The membership of the Central Committee steadily increased to 135 (85 full and 50 candidate members) in 1961, to 172 (117 full and 55 candidate members) in 1970, and to 248 (145 full and 103 candidate members) in 1980.

The reconstructed Political Committee of the Central Committee of the KWP consisted of 12 full and 6 candidate members until 1961. In 1966, the number of full members grew to 16 and that of the candidate members to 12. The membership of the Political Committee fluctuated between 1966 and 1970. In 1970, there were 11 full and 4 candidate members, and as of November 1980, there were 19 full and 15 candidate members in the Political Committee.

In October 1980, the Sixth Party Congress created a 5-member Standing Committee (*Presidium*) of the Political Committee of the Central Committee of the KWP as the highest decision making body within the Party, concentrating power in the hands of such leaders as Kim Il-sung, Kim Il, O Chin-u (O Jin-u), Kim Chŏng-il, and Yi Chong-ok. The 10-member Military Committee of the Central Committee, headed by Kim Il-sung, remained a powerful unit of the Party.

Military Reconstruction.   It was necessary for the North Koreans to recon-struct their armed forces which were almost completely annihilated by U.N. forces. For this reason, North Korea sought and received a tremendous amount of military assistance from the Soviet Union and the People's Republic of China. Efforts made by them to rebuild their military strength led to the rise of a large military force, well indoctrinated with political ideology and equipped with up-to-date weapons.

In 1957, a universal compulsory military system was inaugurated, and all able-bodied males between the ages of 18 and 25 were conscripted into the military. In 1965, the lower age limit was changed to 20, and all draftees remained on active duty for 5 or 6 years, and were discharged at the age of 27.

With the adoption of a compulsory military system, the number of troops

STRUCTURE OF THE KOREAN WORKERS' PARTY
(1982)

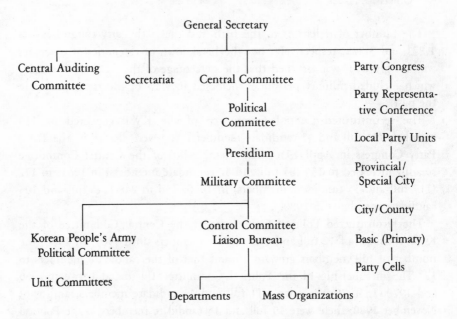

grew rapidly from 420,000 in 1955 to 678,000 in 1979. There were 600,000 in the Army, 31,000 in the Navy, and 47,000 in the Air Force. Since 1979, it has been reported that the number of troops in the Army has grown to 780,000. The People's Army was well equipped with about 2,500 Soviet-made tanks, 700 Soviet warplanes, 120,000 artillery units, 450 naval vessels, including 16 submarines, and 16 military airfields in 1979. The Navy Headquarters were established at Namp'o (formerly Chinnamp'o) on the west coast, near Pyongyang, and two regional naval headquarters were established at Wŏnsan on the east coast and Haeju on the west coast. North Korea now maintains the largest armed forces per capita in the world today, and it had the fourth largest armed forces in the world as of 1980.

Military officers have been trained at two war colleges, three military academies, and five military schools of the various branches. All military matters have been absolutely controlled by the Military Affairs Committee of the Central Committee of the Korean Workers' Party through the Ministry of People's Defense in the government.

Under the mutual military assistance agreements signed in 1961 with the Soviet Union and the People's Republic of China, North Korea received a considerable amount of military assistance from both countries, particularly from the Soviet Union. The Soviets provided not only a major portion of war equipment, but also technical assistance. All of North Korea's military-related industries were established by foreign assistance programs, especially

Soviet-sponsored programs. In 1975, Kim Il-sung visited Peking in order to request new military assistance from China to launch a new war against the south in the wake of the fall of South Vietnam, but failed to achieve his goal.

Immediately after the new Sino-American treaty was concluded in 1979, a North Korean vice-president visited Moscow seeking greater military assistance from the Soviets, and it was reported that in July 1978 North Korea had offered the port of Najin near Ch'ŏngjin on the northeastern coast as a Soviet naval and missile base. Meanwhile, North Korea received an increased supply of oil and MIG-21 planes from China.

North Korea s military spending was low until 1966, but it spent a tremendous amount of money for the military since 1967, perhaps beyond its capacity. Its military budget was 30.4 per cent of the 1967 annual national budget. Between 1967 and 1971, North Korea spent an average of 24.3 per cent of its annual budgets for the military. In terms of dollars, North Korea's military spending in 1967 was $466 million, and $1,378 million in 1979. The military budget of 1980 was $1,478 when the annual national budget was about $9,500 million. It was reported that North Korea allocated an average of 25 per cent of the GNP per year to the military during the decades of the 1970s.

In addition to the regular armed forces, North Korea had over 2 million highly trained and well indoctrinated men and women in the Workers' and Peasants' Red Militia as of 1980. All able-bodied men between the ages of 18 and 45 who were not on active military duty, and all single women between the ages of 18 and 35 have been given compulsory military training at least two hours per week by military officers. Political indoctrination was provided to them by Party cadres. The members of the red militia have been trained to participate in combat activities on a short notice. All members of the red militia participate in annual as well as occasional mock combat exercises. Young secondary school students, including girls, have been trained to drive trucks and man communication equipment in order to augment the military. The North Korean Communists proudly claim that the entire nation has become an indestructable fortress with underground air and submarine bases and storage facilities manned by highly indoctrinated and well drilled defense forces.

Economic Reconstruction and Development

It was estimated that about 80 per cent of the North Korea's productive capacity was destroyed by the war. Some 806,500 acres of farmland, 250,000 head of cattle, 330,000 pigs, and 90,000 fruit trees were reported to have been destroyed. Many industrial plants at Ch'ŏngjin, Hamhŭng-Hŭngnam area, and South P'yŏng-an and Hwanghae provinces were badly damaged, and many hydroelectric plants on the Yalu, the Changjin, and other rivers were severely damaged.

During the Korean War, industrial output decreased as follows:

DECLINE OF INDUSTRIAL PRODUCTION

	1949	1953
Electric Power (million kwh)	5,924	1,017
Coal (1,000 tons)	4,005	708
Pig Iron (1,000 tons)	166	—
Steel (1,000 tons)	401	—
Cement (1,000 tons)	537	27
Paper (1,000 tons)	17	4

The production of grains decreased from 2,654,000 tons in 1949 to 2,327,000 tons in 1953.

Development Plans.   In order to reconstruct the economy, the North Korean regime carried out various plans. The postwar economic reconstruction policy was aimed at (1) the rapid reconstruction and rehabilitation of the war-shattered farm implement factories and the farms and irrigation system, (2) the acceleration of the socialization of agriculture, and (3) the development of heavy industries. Five economic development plans were implemented after 1953: the Three-Year Plan of 1954–1956, the Five-Year Plan of 1957–1960, the first Seven-Year Plan of 1961–1967 (which became a 10-year plan ending in 1970), the Six-Year Plan of 1971–1976, and the second Seven-Year Plan of 1978–1984. The Three-Year Plan was designed for postwar reconstruction, and the subsequent plans were aimed at industrial development.

Factors Related to Economic Development.   North Korea achieved a faster and greater economic recovery and development than South Korea between 1954 and the mid-1960s. After 1965, its economic development slowed down as it encountered many problems.

What brought about the early recovery and faster development in North Korea? First of all, it had a stronger industrial base built by the Japanese during the colonial period. Secondly, about 80 per cent to 90 per cent of all known mineral deposits, particularly coal, iron ore, lead, zinc, tungsten, magnesite, and gold were located in the north, which also had a plentiful supply of electric power. Third, its population was small and it had less population pressure than the south. Fourth, its managed (socialistic) economic structure was able to mobilize manpower better than that in the south.

Foreign economic and technical aid was a major factor in North Korea's rapid economic recovery and growth in the early period. The Soviet Union provided 2 billion *rubles* in grants and credits, several thousand technicians, and sponsored some 40 industrial projects between 1954 and 1960. The People's Republic of China provided 1.8 billion *rubles* in grants and credits before 1960, and $500 million in 1960. China cancelled all wartime debts which North Korea had incurred. Other Socialist countries, including East Germany, provided 11,400 million *rubles* between 1954 and 1956. The Mongolian People's Republic provided a large number of farm animals.

Economic Achievements.   The North Korean government made efforts after 1953 to construct a socialist economy, emphasizing the growth of heavy industries, and the increase of military related industries. Large industries and financial institutions were nationalized in 1956. Some privately owned factories, enterprises, and commercial establishments not nationalized at that time were gradually nationalized between 1947 and 1956.

During the period of the Three-Year Plan (1954–1956) the reconstruction of the war torn economy to the pre-war level, and "priority development of heavy industry with simultaneous development in agriculture and industry" was given emphasis. Its aim was to raise industrial output by 1956 to 2.6 times that of 1953, and to increase grain production by 11.3 per cent of that of 1949 by recovering and reconstructing "idle land" and by the higher utilization of land and expansion of irrigated area.

During the 1954–1956 period, most of the damaged industrial plants and hydroelectric dams were rehabilitated. With the initial recovery, North Korea's industrial production increased as follows: electric power to 5,120 million kilowatt hours, coal to 3,968,000 tons, steel to 190,000 tons, cement to 597,000 tons, paper to 77,000 tons, and food grains to 2.3 million tons. The production of pig iron reached the 231,000 ton level, chemical fertilizer production grew to 195,000 tons, and textiles to 77.1 million meters by 1956.

According to the North Koreans, the Three-Year Plan brought about an increase of gross national product (GNP) from $320 million in 1953 to $732 million in 1956 (with an exchange rate of 2.4 *wŏn* to one U.S. dollar). North Korea's per capita income increased from $41 in 1953 to $85 by 1956. Most transportation networks were rehabilitated and most agrarian reconstruction was completed.

After achieving most of its primary objectives, thanks to foreign aid provided by Socialist nations, North Korea implemented the Five-Year Plan (1957–1961). Its major aims were the complete elimination of any remnants of a colonial industrial structure and the establishment of a firm foundation for industries, as well as solving problems of food, shelter, and clothing. Its plan was to raise industrial output to 2.6 times that of the 1956 level, and to bring about complete collectivization of farms as well as Socialization of private enterprises.

North Korea

Although the slogan known as *Ch'ŏllima undong* ("The Flying Horse Movement") was not widely used until September 1958, it actually began in conjunction with the Five-Year Plan. Some one million workers were mobilized and organized into *Ch'ŏllima* work teams by the end of 1970s. During the period, all private enterprises were absorbed by the state sector and private ownership of land and business was completely wiped out. The percentage of privately owned business vis-à-vis the state sector had decreased from 13.4 per cent in 1947 to 9.8 per cent in 1949, and to 4.0 per cent by 1956.

Contrary to North Korean claims that the Five-Year Plan was successfully completed and that its goals were met, ahead of time in 1959, evidence shows that many of its goals were not met with the exception of the complete Socialization of the economy. For example, the production of iron ore and steel in 1959 was behind the goal by 36.0 per cent and 43.0 per cent, respectively, and the production of chemical fertilizer and carbide was also below the intended level by 12.0 per cent and 10.0 per cent, respectively. The amount of chemical fertilizer produced in 1959 was approximately 500,000 tons. Regardless, the North Koreans reported that the GNP growth rate during the period was 21.0 per cent, and per capita GNP increased from $85 in 1956 to $152 by 1960.

Using 1960 as a buffer year, North Korea set out on the first Seven-Year Plan (1961–1967). The development of heavy industry remained its targeted priority, and particular emphasis was given to the development of the machine-building industry. Its goals were to raise national income 2.7 times, industrial output 3.2 times, and agricultural output 2.4 times that of the 1960 level. The North Korean regime, however, was compelled to extend the plan three additional years, to the end of 1970. The decrease of foreign aid was one of major causes for its failure to achieve its goals. The proportion of foreign aid in North Korea's revenue was 18.5 per cent in 1953, 31.4 per cent in 1954, 21.6 per cent in 1955, but it dropped to 12.2 per cent in 1957, 4.2 per cent in 1958, 2.7 per cent in 1959, and finally to 2.0 per cent in 1961. In 1961 it was only 1.9 per cent. On the other hand, military spending increased enormously between 1966 and 1970. During that period, North Korea spent an average of 24.3 per cent of its annual budget for the military. The shortage of technology and skilled workers, in addition to the bureaucratic nature of the managerial staff and lack of incentives on the part of the people constituted major problems.

Be that as it may, North Korea claimed that the national income in 1967 was 8.6 times that of 1953 with an annual growth rate of 16.6 per cent during the period. With the slow increase in population, annual per capita income grew by 21.0 per cent to $218 in 1967. The gross national product in 1967 amounted to $2.6 billion. However, Kim Il-sung disclosed in his speech to the 5th Party Congress in late 1970 that the goal of raising the national income to 2.7 times that of the 1960 level was not achieved. Kim Il, the First Vice-premier also stated in November 1970 that compared to the development of heavy industry, light industry lagged far behind and the quality of North Korea's consumer goods was relatively low. He complained that "Daily necessities and processed foods lack both the variety and quantity of production." Judging from their statements, the Six-Year Plan, which became a de facto 10-year plan ending in 1970, did not in many respects accomplish its objectives.

In 1971 the Six-Year Plan was launched in order to consolidate and "carry forward the accomplishments of industrialization and advance technical revolution to new heights in order to cement further the material and technical foundations of socialism. . . ." Its goal was to raise national income 1.8 times and industrial output 2.2 times that of the 1970 level, respectively, and to produce 7 to 7.5 million tons of grains, including 3.5 million tons of rice. Adopted at the 5th Party Congress, it was aimed at the achievement of an average annual growth rate of 14.0 per cent. In order to accomplish their objectives, the North Koreans introduced billions of dollars of foreign capital from Western countries and Japan. The plan was also extended by one year, ending in 1977.

Information regarding the accomplishments of North Korea under the Six-Year Plan became scarce. The keeping of economic secrets was tightened by the North Koreans after 1970, and most rates of increase were given in percentage over "the previous year."

Although North Korea achieved industrial growth during the period of the Six-Year Plan, many of its goals were not attained. For example, electric power production reached the 22 billion kwh mark, 6 billion kwh below the minimum target.

With 1977 as a "year of adjustment", the second Seven-Year Plan was implemented in 1978 with particular emphasis given to railway construction, the production of electric power, and improvement of the mining industry. North Korea's economy historically had been heavily reliant on railroads, and the plan to build more highways and trucks was put into action.

The repayment of debts ($560 million) to the Soviet Union was rescheduled in 1981 when the Soviet Union provided new credit to North Korea in the amount of $235 million. China, which had been supplying an increasing amount of crude oil to North Korea in the 1970s, further increased its oil supply to its neighbor. In 1981 alone China sold $146 million worth of crude oil to North Korea at the reduced price of $32.9 million. With this foreign assistance, Kim Il-sung launched a new "struggle for speedy achievement" in July 1982.

Overall Assessment of Economic Development. Various economic development plans and efforts made by the North Koreans between 1953 and 1982 brought about a rather remarkable economic development. While achieving a complete Socialization of agriculture and industries, North Korea increased its agricultural and industrial products, along with the complete elemination of private ownership of any properties in these areas. Several major industrial centers arose in North Korea: Taean near Pyongyang, Sŏngnim (formerly Kyŏmip'o), and Shinŭiju in the west, and Hamhŭng, Hŭngnam, Kimch'aek (formerly Sŏngjin), and Ch'ŏngjin along the east coast. North Korea's largest oil refinery and petrochemical plants were established at Ponghwa.

The following table shows the rate of GNP and per capita GNP growth between 1953 and 1982:

Year	GNP (in U.S. $ million)	Per Capita GNP (in U.S. $)
1953	320	41
1956	732	85
1960	1,703 (1,520)	145 (137)
1965	2,050 (2,340)	174 (192)
1970	3,000 (3,980)	220 (286)
1975	6,300 (9,350)	398 (579)
1980	13,500	758
1982	13,600	736

Sources: Naeoe Press, Seoul, Korea, *Economic Development in the Republic of Korea—in Comparison with North Korea*, 1977, p. 17. The figures in parentheses were from *A Comparative Study of the South and North Korean Economies*. National Unification Board, Republic of Korea, 1984, pp. 30–31.

Agricultural Development.   Kim Il-sung announced in late 1953 a three-stage agricultural development policy: (1) the cooperative farm stage between 1953 and 1954; (2) the mass production stage of 1954–1956; and (3) the collectivization stage of 1957–1958. After that time, the number of cooperative farms grew from 806 in 1953 to 10,098 in 1954, and to 16,032 in 1957 (its number was reduced to 13,309 by consolidation in late 1957). The average number of households in a cooperative farm district in 1957 was 80 with an average of 305 acres per cooperative farm. In 1958, 13,309 cooperative farms were replaced by 3,843 agricultural cooperative unions with an average of 300 households in each union. Each union had an average of 494 hectares (1,225 acres) of farmlands and 300 households.

The farming population in each agricultural cooperative union was divided into brigades of 70–80 persons each, and each brigade into squads of 20 farmers. Some were grain production brigades, some were fruit growing brigades, some were vegetable growing brigades, and some were livestock brigades. All of the farm population belonged to farm cooperative unions.

Efforts made by the North Korean people, together with land reclamation projects of the government brought about an increase of cultivated area. The relocation of farmhouses from farmable areas to hillsides also helped to increase the farm acreage. Consequently, the acreage under cultivation increased from 4.9 million acres in 1946 to 5.9 million in 1949, and to 6.3 million by 1975. The North Korean government claimed that its total acreage of cultivated area in 1975 was 8.9 million; however, the acreage of paddy fields was 607,030 hectares (1.5 million acres) at the end of 1982.

The acreage of irrigated paddy fields also increased. In 1949 there were 376,800-acre irrigated fields, or 33 per cent of paddy fields where rice was grown, and it increased to 560,350 acres in 1954, 830,000 acres in 1957, 1.2 million acres in 1961, and 1.2 million acres in 1975. The North Korean government announced in 1982 that all paddy fields were irrigated. The acreage of corn cultivation grew as corn production became important as an alternative to rice consumption, or as a means of meeting the steadily increasing demand for food grains. The acreage of corn growing area increased from 578,200 in 1954, to 2,022,700 in 1958, and to about 5 million by the end of 1982, due to the growing importance of corn as substitute for rice. Some 735,000 acres (297,443 hectares) of salt flats were reclaimed and converted into rice paddies between 1957 and 1982.

An increase in the production of chemical fertilizers, expansion of irrigated paddy fields, a greater use of insecticides, and a growing number of farm and garden tractors helped the North Koreans to increase food production, and reduce the shortage of food grains. The amount of chemical fertilizers produced increased to 1.8 million tons in 1979, and, the acreage where chemical fertilizers were applied increased vastly from less than two million in 1956, to 3.6 million in 1965, and to 6 million in 1979. North Korea reported that 1.5 tons of chemical fertilizers were used per 2.45 acres in 1979.

More farm tractors (28 horsepower and 75 horsepower) and garden tractors (12 horsepower) were produced. In 1953, there were 372 Russian-built tractors, and, according to North Korean reports, the number of tractors manufactured in North Korea per year increased from 500 in 1953 to 710 1959, 20,000 in 1964, and 60,000 in 1970. In 1981, an average of 6 to 7 tractors per 24.5 acres of land were available, according to North Korean sources.

Improvements in farming methods and the reduction of bureaucratism in farm management also contributed to agricultural development. In February 1960, Kim Il-sung visited a small farm village named Ch'ŏngsan-ri in Kangsŏ district, near Pyongyang, and he gave an "on-the-spot" instruction to the Party cadres and leaders of the farm cooperative union. In 1961, the Korean Workers' Party adopted a policy entitled "For the Correct Management of the Socialist Agrarian Economy," giving birth to what became known as the Ch'ŏngsan-ri Method. It was aimed at increasing the enthusiasm and technical skills of lower level cadres assigned to collective farms, eliminating their bureaucratism, formalism and "commanderism," developing scientific farm management skills, and increasing the production capacity and zeal of the farmers.

Kim Il-sung encouraged the cadre with his "on-the-spot" guidance to go out from the office, observe actual conditions, and to draw up comprehensive practical plans to increase the willingness of the farmers to produce more foodstuffs. The Ch'ŏngsan-ri farm union became a model for all collective farm unions. The Ch'ongsan-ri farm union was larger than the average collective farm, composed of 600 households with 3,100 persons, its farm acreage was 3,917 and it was better equipped with modern farm implements (it had 110 tractors in 1981).

The Mongolian People's Republic helped the increase of North Korea's livestock industry during the immediate postwar reconstruction period by donating 6,054 horses, 19,760 sheep, 18,693 goats, 446 dairy cows, and by an additional gift of 17,000 horses in 1972.

North Korea's reports regarding the increase of food grain production are not reliable since the amounts produced were usually inflated in order to show that the goals of various development plans had been met. Be that as it may, the estimated increase in food grain production was as follows:

FOOD GRAIN PRODUCTION
NORTH KOREA CLAIMS (In 1,000 tons)

(Estimation in parenthesis)*

Year	Total	Rice	Corn
1949	2,654 (1,500)	1,158	224
1951	2,260 (2,100)	–	–
1954	2,327 (2,230)	1,225	–
1956	2,873 (2,782)	1,392	1,130
1961	4,830 (3,378)	1,919	1,606
1970	5,600 (3,500)	–	–
1975	6,300 (4,224)	–	–
1979	8,000 (5,600)	3,500 (2,400)	4,000 (3,200)

*Estimated by various South Korean and United States sources.

Although food grain production has increased since 1954, various sources indicate that a food shortage persists in North Korea. Between 1955 and 1969, North Korea imported 2.6 million tons of food grains from the Soviet Union and other socialist countries. At the same time, North Korea exported a large amount of rice to east European countries in order to purchase a greater amount of wheat from them in exchange for rice. Between 1970 and 1976, North Korea imported $126 million worth of foodstuffs, of which $112 million was for grain.

Industrial Development.   After the completion of the Three-Year Plan, which involved "sweeping up the rubble" of the war, acquiring the critical materials for reconstruction, and the training of skilled personnel, North Korea, between 1956 and 1970, achieved a rather remarkable industrial growth. Following this period, the industrial growth slowed down.

The North Korean Communists gave lip service to a balanced growth of heavy and light industries and agriculture. However, they spent more funds for the development of heavy industry, neglecting commodity production. During the Three-Year Plan period, heavy industry expanded twice as fast as light industry. The average growth rate of heavy industry was about 4.1 times and light industry about 2.1 times the 1953 level. The average rate of industrial growth during the period was claimed to be 41.7 per cent. According to a North Korean source, national income rose between 1953 and 1958 from 70 per cent to 285 per cent (1940 = 110). Every able-bodied man and woman who was not on active military duty was mobilized in the industrial or agricultural sector.

During the period of the Five-Year Plan launched in 1957, complete Socialization of the economy took place when all privately owned enterprises were taken over by the state under the policy of laying "the ground work for socialist industrialization." It was during this period that the *Ch'ŏllima* ("Flying Horse") work teams involving some one million workers were organized by the end of 1962. The number of *Ch'ŏllima* workers grew after May 1963 to 3.2 million when the *Ch'ŏllima* movement was expanded to include factory workers, farmers, office workers, and students. The *Ch'ŏllima* movement was a North Korean version of the "Great Leap Forward Movement" of China. Its aim was to increase industrial and agricultural production and the motto was "Let Us Ride the Flying Horse."

The development of heavy industry was given priority despite opposition from some Party leaders who argued in favor of focusing on light industrial growth. As a result, the percentage of the growth of heavy industry was much higher than that of consumer industries. Between 1957 and 1960, the production of electric power grew from 6,908 million kilowatt hours (kwh) to 9,139 million kwh, coal from 4,984,000 tons to 10,630,000, pig iron from about 250,000 tons to 853,000, steel from 277,000 tons to 641,000, and chemical fertilizers from 323,000 tons to 561,000.

With the exception of textiles, the quantity of consumer goods produced lagged far behind. The production of fabrics increased from 91,000,000 meters in 1957 to 189,659,000 in 1960. According to the North Koreans, the average growth rate of industry between 1957 and 1960 was 36.6 per cent, somewhat lower than that of the Three Year Plan period of 41.7 per cent.

After 1961, North Korea encountered increasing problems in industrial development. In order to overcome these problems, the Taean System in industry was inaugurated in 1960. At the Taean Electric plant near Pyongyang, Kim Il-sung gave his "on-the-spot" advice in December 1960 and initiated the Taean System for industrial development. In it, he emphasized the elimination of the one-man management of the director of the plant and the promotion of the collective leadership of the Party committee of the plant. At the same time, he urged the Party cadres to rouse workers to increase production by superior workers assisting inferior workers, to accelerate ideological education programs, and to mobilize the workers to revolutionary tasks. The system which Kim inaugurated at the Taean plant became the model for all other industrial establishments, creating an impact similar to that of the Ch'ōngsan-ri Method in agriculture.

Raising the living standard of the people and expanding the industrial base by promoting a major technological revolution were two main objectives of the first Seven-Year Plan which began in 1961 and ended in 1970. Kim Il-sung called it "a decisive period in the Socialist construction of our country." He emphasized the capturing of "six hills," namely the production of more goods in six areas: grains, textiles, marine products, steel, coal, and housing units for the workers.

In view of the fact that the first Seven-Year Plan was extended by three years, ending in 1970, it was obvious that North Korea failed to achieve its goals by 1967. Despite a negative 3 per cent growth in 1965, the North Koreans claimed that between 1961 and 1967 they made over a 17 per cent average annual growth. Kim Il-sung reported in December 1967 that industrial production in that year was 1.4 times greater than that of 1962. Records show that in 1970 North Korea's industrial output of key items was as follows: electric power 16,500 billion kwh (500 million kwh short of goal), coal 27,500,000 tons (2,500,000 tons over the goal), crude steel 2,200,000 tons (100,000 tons short of goal), fabrics 400 million meters (100 million meters short of the target), chemical fertilizer 1,500,000 tons (200,000 tons below the intended level), and cement 4,000,000 tons (300,000 tons short of goal). Kim Il, the First Vice-Premier of North Korea, disclosed in November 1970 that North Korea's annual average industrial growth rate between 1961 and 1969 was 12.8 per cent, and not 17 per cent as previously claimed by the North Koreans.

It became increasingly difficult to obtain reliable economic information from North Korea after 1970. As a result, the achievements of the Six-Year Plan (1971–1976) and of the early stage of the second Seven-Year Plan (1978–1984) cannot be adequately ascertained. Available sources do, however, indicate that the economic growth of North Korea slowed down considerably, achieving less than 6 per cent annual growth after 1971, "the struggle for speedy achievement" (*soktojōn*), notwithstanding.

The industrial output in 1976 and the targets of the Second Seven-Year Plan (1978–84) were as follows:

	1976 *	*Targets* **
Electric power (billion kwh)	21.8	50–60
Coal (million tons)	39.5	70–80
Crude steel (million tons)	2.7	7 – 8
Chemical fertilizer (million tons)	0.6	5
Cement (million tons)	11.9	12–13
Textiles (million sq. meters)	450	800
Pig iron (1,000 tons)	?	6.4
Tractors (1,000 units)		200
Trucks (1,000 units)	10	?

*These figures are from National Foreign Assessment Center/CIA, *Korea: The Economic Race Between the North and the South,* 1978, p. 11.
**These figures are from *The Korea Herald,* October, 24, 1979.

With the development of industries, the number of industrial workers increased from 524,000 in 1953 to 829,000 in 1956, and to 1.5 million by the end of 1979.

As a result of great emphasis and the large allocation of funds, heavy industry developed faster than light industry after 1953. The increase in major industrial products between 1953 and 1980 are as shown below:

MAJOR INDUSTRIAL PRODUCTS
(1953–1980)

	1953	*1956*	*1961*	*1970*	*1976*	*1978*	*1980*
Electric power (million kwh)	1,017	5,120	10,418	16,500	21,800	24,600	49,900
Coal (1,000 tons)	708	8,908	10,620	27,500	39,500	50,000	
Cement (1,000 tons)	27	597	2,263	4,000	5,000	8,000	95,000
Crude steel (1,000 tons)	4	190	641	2,200	2,750	4,000	
Pig Iron (1,000 tons)			931	2,300			
Chemical fertilizer (1,000 tons)		195	662	1,500	1,600	1,800	
Textiles (million meters)	22	77	187	418	450		

Source: Communist Block Research Center ed., *North Korea's Economic Statistics,* 1953, p. 194; National Foreign Assessment Center/CIA, *Korea: The Economic Race Between the North and the South,* 1978, p. 11; Economic Planning Board, the Republic of Korea, *Report,* 1978; Joseph S. Chung, *The North Korean Economic Structure and Development,* 1974, pp. 86–87; *The Korea Herald,* March 15, 1980.

Economic Problems.   North Korea achieved much economic recovery and development after 1953; however, it also experienced many economic difficulties. Among the more prevalent problems were the low incentives of the people, the shortage of funds and a lack of trained scientists and technicians, a trade imbalance, and the ever persisting food shortage.

The people were forced to work and produce more goods without receiving adequate monetary and material compensation. They were mobilized not only into industrial and agricultural teams, but also into various politically oriented social organizations. Their working days were long, holidays were too few, and political indoctrination was heavy. Overworked and inadequately fed people developed no high incentives. Although the government constructed more and often better housing units for the workers and farmers than they had before, rationed food supply and consumer goods, and low income which did not allow them to purchase nonrationed goods did not motivate the people. The so-called luxury goods were beyond their ability to acquire. In an essay concerning the economic situation of North Korea, published in the May 1978 issue of *Kŭlloja,* an official magazine published by the Korean Workers' Party, Kim Il-sung himself complained that there was not enough garlic, cooking oil, red pepper, notebooks, watches, belts, and clothing. He also pointed out that there was a shortage of refrigerators and commercial trucks.

An average monthly wage for North Korean workers was between $35 and $45 in 1982, which could purchase only two meters of high quality silk. Items, regarded as luxury goods, such as women's Korean silk dresses ($25), men's polyester jackets ($31), 19-inch black and white television sets ($275), electric phonographs ($150), accordions (small, $200 and large, $340) were beyond the reach of average workers in North Korea. A fountain pen was sold for $9.

Underfed and overworked, the North Korean farmers and workers were exhausted. Free medical care and education has helped the people, but the high pressure politics, combined with the slow rise in the living standard and various threats of punishment for anti-state and anti-Party activities, as well as the mere suspicion of anti-state activities, has fostered a strong discontent among the people. The calorie intake per person per day was about 1,500 in 1974 when the author visited North Korea, and it has since improved only slightly.

The balance of trade was always unfavorable to North Korea. Its balance of trade between 1951 and 1976 was as follows (in million U.S. dollars):

Year	Exports	Imports
1951	160	167
1970	315	395
1975	400	1,075
1982	1,500	1,800

The Soviet Union and China were two major trade partners, and after

FOREIGN TRADE

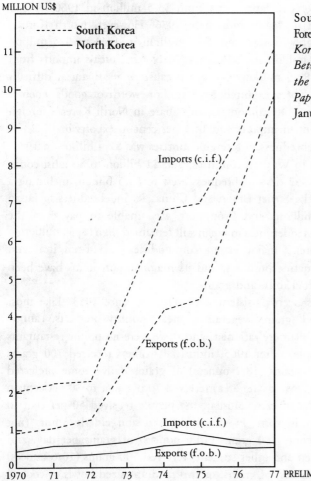

Source: U.S. National Foreign Assessment Center, *Korea: The Economic Race Between the North and the South: A Research Paper.* Washington, D.C., January 1978, p. 9.

1970 Japan became an important trade partner. The percentage of imports-exports to and from the Soviet Union and China was as follows:

	U.S.S.R.		China	
	Imports	*Exports*	*Imports*	*Exports*
1968	53.2	48.6	24.9	19.2
1975	24.3	27.3	17.3	19.4
1982	36.9	48.5	17.6	21.6

The total amount of North Korea's exports to the non-Socialist nations (there was no trade with the United States or South Korea) increased from $260 million in 1974 to $306 million in 1982 while its imports from the Western nations grew from $535.1 million to $669.6 million during the same period.

North Korea's exports to Japan grew from $3.5 million in 1960, to $33 million in 1970, and to $64.8 million in 1976. However, North Korea's imports from Japan grew faster: from $4.5 million in 1961 to $25 million in 1970 and to $251 million in 1974. In 1976 North Korea's imports from Japan declined to $180.6 million, perhaps because of its financial difficulties. In 1980, North Korea exported $171 million worth of goods when it imported goods worth $340 million. Japan's share in North Korea's foreign trade was 27.9 per cent in imports and 14.1 per cent in exports in 1982.

North Korea's indebtedness to foreign countries was $2.4 billion in 1976. It owned $1.4 billion to Western countries, and $1 billion to Socialist countries. At the end of 1982, its indebtedness grew to $3.5 billion, including a $1.2 billion debt to the Soviet Union and China. Its indebtedness to Japan in 1980 was $520 million, and Pyongyang was unable to pay even the interest on its loans. Its indebtness to Japan still remained high ($330 million in in 1982). North Korea's major export commodities have been iron and steel, clothing, and marine products, and its major import items have been industrial materials, fuel (oil), and grains.

Grain shortage has been persistent and pervasive since 1953. Like most consumer goods, food (grains, vegetables, meat, poultry products, canned food, sugar, cooking oil) were rationed, and there were no public restaurants for the common people. After 1965, industrial workers received 700 grams (24.7 ounces) to 800 grams (28.2 ounces) of grains daily. Some preferred workers (mostly in the Pyongyang area) received 70 per cent to 80 per cent in rice and the remainder in corn. Most of the people received 50 per cent in rice and 50 per cent in corn. Preschool children and elderly adults (not working) were given only 300 grams (10.6 ounces) of grains per day, and primary school children and other students received 500 grams (10.6 ounces) to 700 grams (17.6 ounces) of grains, or two medium sized bowls of cooked rice.

A total of 2,636,000 tons of grains were imported from the Soviet bloc nations during the 1955–1969 period alone. Rice shortage became so critical that the North Koreans coined a new word, *kangnangssal*, or "corn-rice" which describes a grain consisting of some rice flour with corn flour. The possibility of solving the grain shortage is not in sight as of 1982.

Communication and Transportation.   The communication system developed last. Although telegraph and telephone systems have been expanded since 1953, the ordinary citizens have not been benefited by it. The state owned and operated telephone services have been available only to public institutions, schools, factories, collective farm district offices, and certain Party members. A public telephone (payphone) system has not been established.

The Korean Workers' Party imposed strict information control. No foreign language books, newspapers, and magazines have been sold. The state owned and operated Central Broadcasting System and Radio Pyongyang have remained the two broadcasting networks, and one or two channel radios have been made available to nearly all North Korean homes. There were only 5,000 black and white television sets in North Korea in 1975, and the number has increased since then.

The transportation system has expanded since the end of the Korean War. At the time when Korea was liberated from Japan, there were 2,624 kilometers (1,681 miles) of railroads in North Korea, and most of the railroads were destroyed during the war. After 1953, particularly under the Five-Year Plan that began in 1957, railway transportation expanded vastly, and the total railway mileage increased to 4,280 km (2,659 miles) in 1978, and to 4,590 km (2,852 miles) in 1982. Electrification of certain main lines (militarily and industrially important ones) began in 1957. The main railway lines are those between Kaesŏng and Shinŭiju, Pyongyang and Wŏnsan, Wŏnsan and Ch'ŏngjin, Wŏnsan and Kaesŏng, Pyongyang and Manp'o, and Haeju and Namp'o. The Pyongyang-Shinŭiju line, the Pyongyang-Wŏnsan line, and the Wŏnsan-Ch'ŏngjin line are electrified. All railroads are standard single tracks.

Most North Korean highways were narrow (narrower than two lane highways in the United States) and were not paved. After 1972, main highways between Pyongyang and Kaesŏng, Pyongyang and Namp'o, and Pyongyang and Wŏnsan have been paved. The mileage of paved highways increased from 20,755 km (12,862 miles) in 1978 and to 23,000 km (13,291 miles) in 1982.

A majority of cities have had no public transportation system. Only in a few cities was a local bus transportation system installed, and there has been no development of long-distance bus routes. Only a handful of privileged individuals have owned private automobiles. The capital city of Pyongyang has had by far the most extensive public transportation system, which includes a subway line and several electric bus lines. Almost all passenger cars have been state owned. Air transportation was available only between Pyongyang and Peking or Pyongyang and Moscow as of 1980.

Education and Culture

We have noted in the previous chapter that the philosophy and contents, as well as the pedagogy of education, and the content and form of culture have been revolutionized during the Soviet occupation of North Korea. Since the Korean War, educational and cultural reconstruction and development programs have been carried out along the socialist revolutionary line.

Educational Reconstruction.   In 1954, a new 4-3-3-4 system was adopted, reducing the length of primary education from five to four years, and in September 1956 compulsory education at the elementary level began. A seven-year compulsory education plan (4-year primary and 3-year middle) was implemented in November 1958. In order to accelerate educational and cultural development, the Ministry of Education and Culture was divided in 1959 into ministries of General Education, Higher Education, and Culture. At the same time, the 3-year-senior middle schools were replaced by 2-year vocational schools, and the plan adopted in 1961 brought about a 9-year compulsory education system (4-year primary, 3-year middle, and 2-year senior vocational) in 1967 when 3-year middle schools and 2-year senior vocational schools were combined into 5-year technical high schools. In 1973, the length of the 5-year technical education at the secondary level was extended to six years, and a 10-year compulsory education system (kindergarten through technical school) was inaugurated.

In April 1976, the Law on the Rearing and Education of Children was adopted by the Supreme People's Assembly and it made preschool education mandatory. All preschool age children were accommodated in crèches and kindergartens. The law stated that "All children should be brought up to be *chuch'e*-oriented revolutionaries, loyal to the Leader Kim Il-sung; the first words to be learned by members of the new generation born in this land should be the glorious, respected General Kim Il-sung; the first song to learn is the one devoted to General Kim Il-sung. . . ."

The philosophy of education of North Korea was to train the builders of socialist society and make the young people absolutely loyal to Kim Il-sung. Hong Myŏng-hŭi, vice-premier, stated in 1959 that the basic policy of the party was to strengthen the connection between education and productive work. He pointed out the need to educate and cultivate the younger generation to become the builders of Socialism-Communism, and more able and practical scientists and technicians. A North Korean paper, *Minju Chosŏn,* stated in its editorial of August 25, 1959, that the function of teachers is "to bring up the younger generation to be warriors faithful to Comrade Kim Il-sung." Accordingly, when senior middle schools were replaced by 2-year schools, and all secondary schools were made into vocational schools in 1959, liberal arts courses were drastically reduced. The study of the *chuch'e* ideology and the study of the history of the Korean revolution were given top priority. Foreign languages (Russian and Chinese in the beginning, and some English recently) are taught at the college level only. North Korean students pay no tuition fees at any level, but graduates of secondary schools have no freedom of choice as to colleges they attend, or the curriculum in which they enroll.

The new educational policy adopted by the Fourth Party Congress in September 1961 included the following objectives:

1. The creation of a new type of Communist man.
2. Combining of theory and practice, learning and production.
3. Intensification of technical education.
4. Emphasis on revolutionary traditions so far as to foster the spirit of collectivism, ability to think, speak and act as the Communist Party would have them do.
5. Intensification of adult education so that every citizen will possess the basis for a general cultural revolution.
6. Implementation of the compulsory mobilization of students and encouragement of self-initiated projects for expanding school facilities.
7. Strengthening of Party guidance to promote the loyalty of teachers and students to the Party.

The nature of socialist pedagogy was defined in the Socialist Constitution of 1972 as "a discipline dealing with the principles and methods of educating and cultivating the rising generation to be revolutionaries and Communists armed solidly with the monolithic ideology of our Party and infinitely loyal to the great leader Comrade Kim Il-sung. . . ." Similar views were expressed in the "Theory of Socialist Education" published in 1975 and the "Thesis on Socialist Education" of 1977. In regard to training youth, the "Theory of Socialist Education" stated:

We have to inculcate in our future generation the absolute authority of the leader, the indisputable thoughts and instructions of the leader so that they may accept them as faith and the law of the land. We must cultivate them as infinitely loyal and self-reliant Communist revolutionaries who will forge ahead with no reservations and give everything for the leader in full demonstration of ultimate readiness for devotion and sacrifice.

All secondary school students were required to work at least 8 or 10 weeks per year in factories and other industrial establishments.

In addition to regular schools, factory colleges were established in order to provide technical training for workers who received no high school or college education. In 1965, there were 37 such colleges with over 12,000 students, and by 1975 the number grew to 80 with over 23,000 students. Kim Il-sung University (established in October 1946), the Academy of Science, and the Academy of Social Science are the top three academic and research institutions.

The North Korean Communists saw a great need to educate the people and eradicate illiteracy. At the time when Korea was liberated from Japan, only about 35 per cent of school age children were able to attend primary schools. The situation was even worse in the north. About 85 per cent of the people in the north were illiterate. In order to achieve their objectives, adult night schools were established throughout the country, and illiteracy was virtually wiped out in North Korea.

The growth of the number of schools and students is as follows:

NUMBER OF SCHOOLS

	1956–57	1964–65	1970	1980
Total	5,352	9,020	9,235	9,613
People's Schools	3,777	3,985	4,064	4,160
Middle Schools	1,247	2,827		
Technical Schools	227	1,644		
Senior Middle Scholls	82		4,542	4,750
High Technical Schools		466	500	516
Colleges	19	98	129	187

NUMBER OF STUDENTS (1,000)

	1956–57	1964–65	1970	1980
Total	2,107	2,468	3,500	4,124
People's Schools	1,508	1,138	1,900	2,280
Middle Schools	445	704		
Technical Schools	68	285		
Senior Middle Schools	64		1,230	1,430
High Technical Schools		156	160	158
Colleges	22	185	210	256

Whereas there were 8,600 state-run crèches with 1.2 million infants and 6,800 kindergartens with 950,000 children in 1970, by 1980 the number of state-run crèches and kindergartens increased to 60,000 accommodating 3.6 million preschool age children.

Lacking high education institutions for technical education, North Korea sent a large number of students to the Soviet Union and other socialist states in eastern Europe. A total of 7,763 students were reported to have returned from study abroad by 1957.

Culture for Revolution.   A Socialist culture, nurtured and controlled by the Party, emerged in North Korea. North Korea's cultural exchanges were directed by the Culture and Arts Division of the Korean Workers' Party, and its policies were implemented by the Ministry of Culture, which was separated from the Ministry of Education and Culture in 1959. The primary aim of the Party was to make all forms of literature and arts reflect socialist realism, or partisan allegiance.

The Korean Workers' Party made it clear that "elements which cater to the taste and pleasure of the exploitative class should not be tolerated," and that "only such revolutionary literature and art conforming throughly to the course and policy of the Party will deserve the genuine attention of the masses, and only they (revolutionary art and literature) can prove an effective weapon of the Party to infuse Communist and revolutionary spirit into the working people.''

The idea of "art for art's sake" was discarded altogether, and the Party emphasized the elimination of old thoughts and the old culture. Its main objectives were to arm the people with ''the revolutionary spirit of the working class and Communist thought,'' and train them ''to be true intellectuals of the working class and ardent Communists.'' Meanwhile, Kim Il-sung stressed that revolutionary culture must be fostered to establish national identity in the fields of science and technology, as well as in art, history, music, dance, literature and other forms of culture with the *chuch'e* ideology.

The General Federation of North Korea Literature and Arts Unions, which was formed in 1946 as a united body of various unions of writers, artists, and musicians, has been the arm of the Party in developing a culture for revolution. In 1951, it dropped "North" from its me, and in March 1961, it was renamed the General Federation of Korean Literature and Arts. With this, the Party emphasized the promotion of a new culture which was "socialist in content and nationalist in form." It said that revisionism, doctrinism, and formalism must be combatted and rejected, and literature and arts must be freed from "the bourgeois literary and artistic ideas of anti-revolutionary nature." The guidance of the Party and the efforts made by the members of the Federation not only brought about a rapid cultural development, but also the personality cult of Kim Il-sung. Meanwhile between 1952 and 1962, many key literary figures and artists were purged because of their disagreement with the Party line, among whom were two writers named Lim Hwa and Han Sŏr-ya, and a woman dancer named Ch'oe Sŭng-hŭi.

Religion was totally discarded, churches were abolished, and all clergymen and monks were forced to join the labor force. The North Korean Communists defined religion as "the enemy of science and progress," and they condemned it as "an obstacle which hinders self-awakening and the purposeful fight for the construction of Socialism and Communism." They said that "the remnants of unscientific religion and superstition which remain with us must be rooted out." As a result, any form of culture which represented "reactionary bourgeois ideas, feudalistic Confucian ideas, and other outmoded ideas" have been eliminated. All Christian church buildings and most Buddhist temples were torn down. Some historic Buddhist temples have been restored in recent years for tourism.

The Federation of North Korean Buddhists (formed in December 1945), the *Ch'ŏndogyo* Association (formed in February 1946), were kept by the Communists for propaganda purpose. However, all religious services, ceremonies, and the propagation of religion were outlawed. These so-called religious organizations, which virtually ceased to exist after 1965, reemerged in 1972, and the Federation of North Korean Christians became involved in North Korea's drive to win the support of Korean Christians in foreign countries for its unification policy. It even made an attempt to join the World Council of Churches in August 1975.

Traditional musical instruments were retained, but all folk songs of the traditional period and popular songs of the Japanese colonial period were discarded. Many new songs and operas were produced in order to glorify the revolutionary achievements of the Communists, particularly those of Kim Il-sung, and to promote loyalty to Kim and the Party. Among these songs are "Marshal Kim Il-sung is Our Sun" and "Song of Marshal Kim Il-sung." The song, "Marshal Kim Il-sung is Our Sun," reads as follows:

> *The Sun of Hope of 30 million people.*
> *Marshal Kim Il-sung's affectionate love*
> *Makes us realize life's worthiness*
> *In his benevolent bosom of size unknown.*
> *Warm is his love, the Sun of Hope.*
> *Marshal Kim Il-sung is our Sun.*

The lyrics of the "Song of Marshal Kim Il-sung," which is required to be memorized and sung by all, read as follows:

> *Bright traces of blood on the ridges of*
> *Mt. Changbaek still gleam;*
> *Blood marks are still vivid*
> *In each bend of the Yalu River.*
> *Still do those hallowed traces*
> *Shine resplendently*
> *Over Korea ever flourishing and free.*
>
> *(Refrain)*
> *So dear to all our hearts is*
> *Our General's glorious name,*
> *Our own beloved Kim Il-sung of undying fame.*
>
> *Tell us, blizzards that rage*
> *In the wild Manchurian plains,*
> *Tell us, you nights in forests deep*
> *Where the silence reign,*
> *Who the Partisans are;*
> *Who the Patriot is.*
>
> *He severed the chains of the masses;*
> *He brought them liberty.*
> *He is the Sun of the new democratic Korea*
> *Where spring has come at last.*

> *We stand fast, united*
> *Under the Twenty Principles of the Party.*

Among the most popular children's songs were "We Are the Happiest Children in the World," "We Have Nothing to Envy in the World," and "We Are Grateful to the Great Leader Kim Il-sung for His Care and Love." The lyrics of the song entitled "We Have Nothing to Envy in the World" read as follows:

> *Skies are blue and my heart is joyful.*
> *Play the accordion.*
> *Wonderful is my fatherland*
> *Where the people live harmoniously.*
> *Our father is Marshal Kim Il-sung,*
> *Our abode is the bosom of the Party,*
> *We are brothers and sisters.*
> *We have nothing to envy in the world.*

This song is said to have been written by Kim Chŏng-il.

Numerous operas were produced. The most popular ones have been "The Sea of Blood," "The Flower Salesgirl," "The Maiden of Mt. Kŭmgang," and "O, Forest, Tell Us the Story," which depicted revolutionary activities of Kim Il-sung and others during the Manchurian days. A recent film, "The Star of Korea" depicted the early period of Kim's revolutionary activity. It shows his development of the *chuch'e* ideology and his composition of a revolutionary song entitled "The Star of Korea." Other most frequently performed operas and films were "The Fate of a Self-Defense Corps Member" and "The Story of a Detachment Leader." All of these have a common theme, namely the struggle of Kim Il-sung and other anti-Japanese guerrillas in Manchuria. More recent films include "Underground Front" and "Red Agitators."

The North Korean Communists insisted that literature must serve the policy of the Party. From time to time, different emphases were made in the literary movement in accordance with the prevailing conditions or in line with certain drives initiated by the Party. Thus, during the Korean War such short stories as *Tank Number 214* and *Wolves* were produced to arouse anti-American feelings as well as to encourage respect for Red troops. When the Flying Horse Movement began, the writers produced such poems as "Poem of Irrigation in South P'yŏng-an Province," and short stories such as *Unit Leader of Trade Union, Fatherland, Regimental Flag Bearer* and *A Boy Partisan*.

All North Korean newspapers have been published either by the Korean Workers' Party and its local units, or by the government and its agencies. Strict press censorship has been imposed by the Party, and no foreign newspapers or magazines have been sold in North Korea. The Korean-language *Rodong Shinmun* (*The Workers' Daily*), which is the organ of the Party, and a weekly, *The Pyongyang Times,* is the major English-language paper published by the Party. A monthly, *Kŭlloja* (*The Workers*) has been the major magazine, which the Party published. The state-owned and operated Foreign Language Publishing House in Pyongyang has been the only publisher of foreign language books.

Needless to say, there is no freedom of the press, and all newspapers, magazines, and books of all categories are published by state run presses or publishing houses. All radio and television broadcasting systems are state-run and, like newspapers and magazines, they are devoted to the praise of Kim Il-sung, the Party, and the Korean revolution.

Man-gyŏngdae, the birthplace of Kim Il-sung where his grandparents lived, Ch'ilgol, the birthplace of his mother, and another place near Man-gyŏngdae where his parents lived have become national shrines. People of all ages make pilgrimage to these and other places where various revolutionary museums and statutes of Kim Il-sung, his relatives, or his former wife have been erected.

Many museums were constructed throughout the country for propaganda purposes. Among them are the massive Museum of the Korean Revolution on the Mansudae Hill in Pyongyang, overlooking the Taedong River, the Korean War Museum, and the Museum of Arts, the Museum of History, the Man-gyŏngdae Museum of History, the Great People's Study House, and the People's Palace of Culture. The Children's Palace in Pyongyang became the national center for school children's revolutionary activities. A cultural hall was built in each city, town and village, as a center for indoctrination of the *chuch'e* ideology and other revolutionary activities of the people.

Kim Chŏng-il has been actively involved in a new cultural movement since August 1972, and he was said to have directed the production of such films as "The Star of Korea," "Our Burning Fire," "Always One Thought," and "An Chung-gŭn Kills Itō Hirobumi." Many films related to the Korean War have been produced recently. Among them are: "The Wŏlmi Island," "The Diary of a War Correspondent," and "The War for Liberation of the Fatherland." At the same time, several films such as "The Secretary of the Party in Charge of Military," "That Day's Pledge," and "The Blood Rose" were produced in order to promote military spirit. Some of them were specifically fabricated in order to create a new myth about Kim Chong-il.

The Society and People

North Korea has become a Spartan society with a Puritanic way of life ruled by the powerful and all-pervasive Party and its apparatus. It is a paternalistic society of corporate statism. Kim Il-sung is its father and the Party is mother. The people of this highly organized and closed society are regimented and thoroughly indoctrinated. Some 2.3 million, or approximately 12.5 per cent of the 18.5 million people were Party members in 1982, and the children, the young, and men and women of all ages and all walks of life belong to various politically oriented social organizations or trade unions, and must participate in a variety of movements and activities.

All boys and girls between the ages of 8 and 14 belong to a society called the Korean Young Pioneers (founded in 1946); all young people between the ages of 15 and 30 belong to the Korean Socialist Working Youth League (founded as the Communist Youth League in January 1946 and renamed in May 1964) with a membership of 2.9 million in 1980; and all women between the ages of 30 and 50 belong to the Korean Democratic Women's League (founded in November 1945 as the North Korean Women's Federation and renamed in 1951) with a membership of 2.7 million in 1980. All factory and office workers belong to the General Federation of Trade Unions formed in January 1946, and all farmers are members of the Korean Agricultural Workers' Federation. Various professional people, such as doctors, nurses, teachers, writers, composers, actors, dramatists, and film makers belong to their respective professional organizations.

Together with the military, these professional and social organizations became the arms of the Party under the dictatorial rule of Kim Il-sung. They have been frequently mobilized for various purposes; their members are constantly indoctrinated with Kim's *chuch'e* thought and the ideolgy of the Korean revolution, and they are required to take part in a variety of political activities. Uniformity of thought and action and conformity to the established code of conduct have been achieved through a carefully designed method of regimentation and pervasive surveillance against heretics.

The equality of man and sexual equality were proclaimed, and equal rights to women were guaranteed. Traditional social customs and habits and traditional seasonal holidays were abolished. All social activities have become solely related to the promotion of socialist ideology and the revolutionary way of life according to the *chuch'e* ideology. Traditional human relationships have also been radically altered as traditional filial piety has been replaced by loyalty to Kim Il-sung and the Party, and the historic kinship system has been abolished. Friendship has been replaced by the comradeship of revolutionaries.

The North Korean Communists regarded family as a feudalistic legacy. In their view, the home had been "the hotbed of outdated institutions, outdated ideology and outdated customs. . . ." The home, said Kim Il-sung, must be "a laboratory for practicing the revolutionary theories of socialism." The family has lost its economic function with the termination of private ownership of land and the inheritance system. Patriarchal authority lost ground together with the fortune of economic rights.

The extended family system was broken up, and children of 3 months old to age 5 are nurtured at state-run nurseries under the 1976 Law on the Rearing and Education of Children. In 1982, some 3.5 million infants and children were accommodated in state-run crèches and kindergartens where better medical care, as well as intensive ideological indoctrination and political socialization have been provided from early childhood to mold their personality of "a new Communist type." Children finish kindergarten at the age of six and proceeded to elementary school for formal education.

The Korean Workers' Party not only controls and manipulates the people's thoughts and behavior, but it has taken away their freedom of movement and travel, as well as their choice of profession, their freedom of speech, press, assembly, and religion. The people have no privacy, no right to disagree, and are not allowed to move their residence, change jobs, or travel without government permission. The Party established a new system of marriage by which males under 30 and females under 27 years of age are forbidden to marry, and divorce is possible only by government permission. Concubinage, premarital and extra-martial sexual activity is outlawed. Marriage has become regarded as a union of "ideological comrades," and most marriages are arranged. Wedding ceremonies have been simplified. Memorial festivities celebrating one's 60th or the 70th birthday have been abolished, and funeral rites have been simplified. However, performance of traditional rites (ancestor worship) at home and at grave sites has been tolerated, but they have also been simplified.

North Korea has become a closed and isolated society. The people are forbidden to travel abroad, and the travel of foreigners to North Korea and inside the country has been extremely restricted. State censorship, which does not permit the dissemination of news from abroad, keeps the people ignorant of world affairs.

North Korea's population grew from 9 million in 1953 to 18.5 million by 1982. Meanwhile, tens of thousands of persons have been relocated to remote areas for various (particularly security) reasons. It became known in 1982 that some 105,000 political prisoners were being held in concentration camps located in the Hoeryŏng area in North Hamgyŏng Province.

Unification Strategy and Hostile Actions

North Korea's commitment to the reunification of Korea explicitly stated that without the "liberation of the southern half of the Republic from U.S. imperialists," the Korean revolution would not be completed. Accordingly, the North Korean Communists made "the liberation" of South Korea their historic mission and the ultimate goal of the Korean revolution. The unification of Korea must be achieved one way or another.

In order to achieve their supreme goal, in July 1949, the North Korean Democratic National Unification United Front (formed in June 1946) and two organizations, which arrived from South Korea in April 1948, formed the

Democratic Front for the Unification of the Fatherland. The two South Korean organizations which emigrated to the north were the People's Republican Party of Kim Wŏn-bong (founded in July 1946) and the Democratic Independence Party of Hong Myŏng-hŭi (established in October 1947). The Democratic Front for the Unification of the Fatherland launched a vigorous campaign to unify the country and put it under Communist rule.

Unification Proposals.   As it has been mentioned earlier, the North Korean Communists made several proposals for the unification immediately before they launched the war against the south. After the Korean armistice was signed in July 1953, the first major unification conference dealing with Korea and Vietnam was held in Geneva in April–June 1954. However, after rejecting South Korea's 14-point proposal, which advocated step-by-step solutions to the Korean question, the North Koreans made a counterproposal calling for the establishment of an all-Korean Commission consisting of an equal number of representatives from both Koreas. North Korea's insistence on an equal number of representatives although her population was only a half that of South Korea precipitated the collapse of the conference.

After 1954, North Korea launched the so-called peace offensive, constantly preaching "peaceful unification" but actually seeking to create confusion and discord in South Korea and to overthrow the government in Seoul. Meanwhile, it made tireless efforts to bring about the withdrawal of U.N. troops from South Korea.

On August 4, 1960, Kim Il-sung announced an 8-point proposal which advocated "free general elections" throughout Korea "without any foreign interference" for the purpose of peaceful unification of the country. In it, Kim expressed the idea of establishing a confederation system in Korea. His proposal created serious political repercussion among young and idealistic students in the south who had forced President Rhee's cabinet to resign in April. While luring the innocent Koreans in the south to their "peaceful plans," the North Koreans launched their drive to isolate South Korea from the world community. In order to accelerate their peace offensive, the North Korean Communists formed, in May 1961, a government agency named the Committee for Peaceful Unification of the Fatherland. At the same time, they made tenacious efforts in the 1960s to foment political and social unrest and to instigate more uprisings in the south against the government.

In April and May 1971, the Supreme People's Assembly adopted another 8-point program, proposing the establishment of a "supreme national conference" composed of representatives of the governments of the north and south in order to solve the Korean dilemma. North Korea accepted proposals made by the South Korean National Red Cross in April 1971, and direct North-South Red Cross talks were initiated in order to reunite tens of thousand of families separated due to the division of the country and the Korean War. But, the North Koreans used these sessions as a platform for propaganda rather than solving the problems of millions of separated family members. In 1971, when Henry Kissinger was in China on a secret mission, Kim Il-sung was in Peking, perhaps to open channels for direct negotation with the United States in conjunction with a new Sino-American détente. However, it is not clear whether or not Kim met Kissinger.

Meanwhile, Kim Il-sung attempted to bring about wider contacts between the leaders of the north and the south through various political conferences, and through specific proposals. He indicated this desire for increased contact in his interview with a reporter from a Japanese daily paper, the *Mainichi Shimbun*, in September 1972, as well as his speech welcoming Prince Norodom Sihanouk of Kampuchea in April 1973. It is evident that Kim and other Communists believed that the more contacts made between the Koreans of the greater the possibility for them to convert the South Koreans to their views and increase the gap between them and their government.

North Korea had refused to recognize the legitimacy of the new South Korean government which was established in 1963. However, President Richard Nixon's trip to Peking in 1972 and a sudden change in the Sino-American relationship led both Seoul and Pyongyang to take unusual steps toward the unification process. As a result, Pyongyang agreed to the proposals made by the Director of South Korean Central Intelligence Agency, who secretly visited Pyongyang in May, and each government issued a statement on July 4, 1972, indicating that they would establish direct contacts and initiate dialogue in order to solve the Korean question, ''transcending differences in ideas, ideologies, and systems.'' In their statement, they also declared that they would achieve the unification of Korea peacefully by their own efforts without outside interference, and they pledged that they would not use force against each other.

The North-South Political Coordinating Committee was created in the summer of 1972 and several sessions of this committee were held in both capitals. Many South Korean officials and reporters visited Pyongyang on several occasions and conversely North Korean officials and reporters visited Seoul. However, in early 1973, the North Koreans abruptly suspended the talks unilaterally, and renewed their attacks against the South Korean government. Several proposals made by the South Korean government in 1973 and after were rejected by Pyongyang, which cut off the hot line between Seoul and Pyongyang in August 1976.

Shortly after the North Koreans suspended the talks between Seoul and Pyongyang, in June 1973, they disclosed a five-point plan for the reunification of Korea. In it, Kim Il-sung proposed the creation of a confederation of the north and the south (to be named as the Confederal Republic of Koryŏ) without abolishing the existing political, economic and social systems of each state, and the reduction of the armed forces of both Koreas to a 100,000-man level or less *after* the withdrawal of all U.S. troops from South Korea.

As a means to bring about the withdrawal of U.S. troops from South Korea, the Supreme People's Assembly proposed to the U.S. Congress in March 1974 the conclusion of a peace treaty between the United States and North Korea, replacing the armistice agreement. The North Koreans indicated that the withdrawal of U.S. troops could be achieved without losing face by the signing of a peace treaty, and they expressed their strong desire to establish direct contact between the United States and North Korea without the participation of South Korea. Meanwhile, they welcomed with enthusiasm and new expectations President Jimmy Carter's troop withdrawal plan, which was announced in late 1978. Kim Il-sung even called Carter "a man of justice."

After North Korea joined the nonaligned nations organization in 1975, it endeavored to secure its support for Pyongyang's own unification plan. Meanwhile, it sent many agents and commandoes into South Korea and encouraged the dissidents in the south to rise up and seize power from "American puppets" and drive out the "U.S. imperialists." Pyongyang refused to accept America's proposal for cross recognition between North and South Korea, as well as U.S. recognition of North Korea and Soviet and Chinese recognition of South Korea.

On January 12 1980, the North Korean premier proposed to open the North-South dialogue on the prime minister's level, but as soon as a new government was established in Seoul in March 1981, North Korea changed its mind. North Korea not only refused to recognize the legitimacy of the new government in Seoul, but it charged that the South Korean government was a "puppet of U.S. imperialists" and called for the withdrawal of U.S. troops from the "southern half of the Republic."

After demonstrating hostile attitudes toward South Korea in late 1979 and early 1980, Kim Il-sung presented at the 6th Korean Workers' Party Congress, which met in October 1980, a detailed ten-point proposal for reunification. He proposed the creation of a "supreme confederative national conference," consisting of an equal number of representatives of overseas Koreans, in order to establish the "Confederal Democratic Republic of Korea," or *Koryŏ Minju Konghwaguk*. He indicated that the confederated republic would be headed by (1) a supreme confederated assembly comprising an equal number of representatives of the north and the south and a certain number of the overseas Koreans, (2) a standing committee of the assembly would guide the existing government of the north and the south as regional governments, (3) each regional government would follow its independent policies, and (4) the confederated republic would be a neutral and nonaligned state with the repeal of all existing military alliances with other nations. However, his proposal was accompanied by a strong attack on the government of South Korea and President Chun Doo-hwan.

North Korea rejected the proposals made in January and February 1981 by the

President of South Korea and its Minister of the Unification Board. On January 12, 1981, the South Korean president proposed an exchange visit between the top government leaders of both sides. Kim Il-sung also rejected President Chun's June 6th proposal to have talks between the heads of two Koreas anytime and anywhere. Kim likewise rejected the proposal made by the South Korean president in January 1982. North Korea's attitudes and actions since 1981 seemed to indicate that under no circumstances would it negotiate any government-to-government talks. As in the past, Pyongyang rejected the idea of each Korean state securing a separate membership in the United Nations Organization.

Hostile Actions Against the South.   While advocating peaceful solutions to the Korean question, North Korea became increasingly belligerent as many hostile actions were taken after 1953 against South Korea as well as against American troops there. It seemed that the North Korean Communists were determined to bring about the collapse of South Korea one way or another, and they carried out a variety of clandestine operations in order to accomplish their objectives.

North Korea concluded a new military alliance with the Soviet Union on July 1, 1961, and with China on July 10, and took an offensive posture against the south. Although the warning given by the United States government to Pyongyang prevented the North Koreans from taking another reckless action against South Korea in 1961, in January 1968, 31 North Korean armed commandoes were sent to Seoul with the purpose of assassinating President Park Chung-hee of South Korea. Three days later, on January 23, the North Koreans captured an American intelligence-gathering ship, the *USS Pueblo*, on the high seas east of Wŏnsan. On April 15, 1969, a U.S. reconnaissance plane, EC 121, which mistakenly flew over North Korea near the demilitarized zone, was shot down by North Koreans and three of its four crew members were killed. The North Korean Communists made another attempt to assassinate President Park in 1970. In late September, a North Korean agent was killed while planting an explosive on the roof of the main gate of the National Cemetery. On October 1, which is the National Armed Forces Day, President Park and top government officials were to have a ceremony at the National Cemetery, and if the North Korean agent had been successful, the bomb planted on the roof of the gate would have exploded as President Park and others arrived there.

Between 1953 and 1969 the North Koreans created 6,814 incidents, and between 1970 and 1977 over 32,775 incidents occurred along the demilitarized zone. Sometime before 1970, the North Koreans, while pretending to pursue peaceful unification, began to dig infiltration tunnels under the demilitarized zone into the southern part. Three of these tunnels were discovered by in 1974, 1975, and 1978, respectively.

In August 1974, a pro-North Korean resident in Japan, who was presumed to have been guided by Pyongyang, made an attempt to assassinate South Korea's President Park. President Park avoided the assassin's bullets, but his wife was killed. Shortly after the fall of South Vietnam in 1975, Kim Il-sung sought Soviet and Chinese military assistance to invade South Korea, but he failed. Meanwhile, he sent a large number of spies and underground workers to the south to organize communist cells and prepared for a revolution there. North Korean naval vessels abducted several South Korean fishing boats between 1975 and 1980, and several South Korean citizens were abducted from Europen countries by North Korean agents.

On June 30, 1976, North Korean soldiers attacked and seriously wounded an American officer in the joint security area of Panmunjom, and on August 18, they killed two American officers at Panmunjom where American soldiers were engaged in a tree trimming operation. In July 1977, an American helicopter, which flew over the demilitarized zone by navigational error was shot down by the North Koreans, killing three crew members. Kim Il-sung in 1979, once again sought the support of either China or the Soviet Union to invade South Korea by taking advantage of the chaotic situation that developed there after the assassination of President Park in October.

A number of truce violations by North Koreans occurred along the demilitarized zone after 1977. On August 13, 1981, two MIG 21s flew over a South Korean island which is a northern-most security post, and on August 26, a North Korean missile base located near Haeju fired a surface-to-surface missile at an unarmed U.N. forces reconnaissance aircraft, which was navigating in the South Korean air space. In September 1981 and in June 1982, North Korean troops fired machine guns at the South Korean guardposts below the demilitarized zone in the eastern section. More commandoes were sent into the South in 1982, and many of them were killed by South Korean troops.

The Founding of the Kim Dynasty

Kim Il-sung, fearful of his post-mortem defamation or of any possible revision of his ideology or system which he had laboriously built, in the 1960s groomed his younger brother, Kim Yŏng-ju, to be his successor. However, Kim Yŏng-ju lost his brother's favor for a variety of reasons, including his failure to successfully implement anti-South Korean measures, and he disappeared from the scene in 1975.

Kim Il-sung took concrete steps in 1973 to make his son, Kim Chŏng-il, his successor. The young Kim was born in February 1942 in Manchuria to Kim Chŏng-suk, Kim Il-sung's second wife, who died in 1949. Kim Il-sung had previously been married to Han Sŏng-hŭi (alias Kim Hye-sun and Han Yŏng-suk), who had been chief director of the women's department of the Partisan group during the Manchurian days. She was arrested by the Japanese in 1940 and imprisoned in Korea.

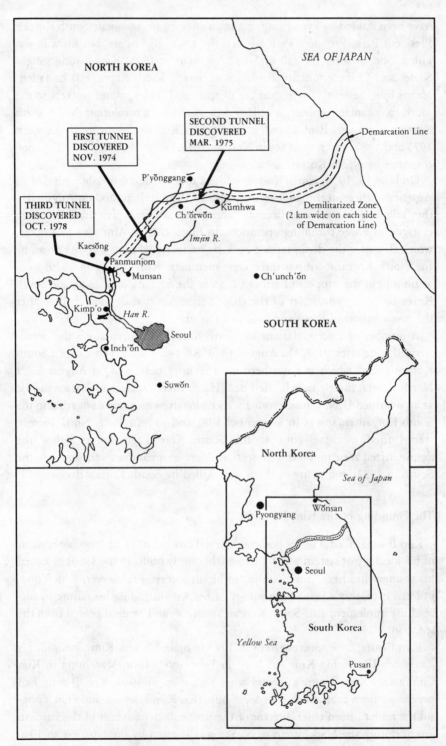

NORTH KOREA'S INFILTRATION TUNNELS

In September 1973, the Party Central Committee appointed the young Kim as an alternate member of the Political Committee and the Party secretary in charge of the Department of Organization and Propaganda, replacing his uncle, Kim Yŏng-ju. At the same time, the young Kim organized the Small Units for the Three Great Revolutions, which were the North Korean counterparts of the Red Guards in China during the Great Proletarian Cultural Revolution period. The Small Units for the Three Great Revolutions were organized in order to promote ideological, cultural and technical revolutions. Each unit consisted of 20 to 50 members, and each factory, school, and other organizations, including the military, established the Small Units for the Three Revolutions. These unit members pledged their absolute loyalty to the young Kim and promised to promote his leadership. Meanwhile, the young Kim himself endeavored to strengthen his position as heir-apparent.

In 1975, the young Kim's birthday (February 16) was declared a national holiday, as was the birthday (April 15) of Kim Il-sung himself. The young Kim's portraits were hung alongside those of his father in 1975. Many who opposed the naming of the young Kim as heir apparent were either purged or killed in 1976 and 1977. Many veteran politicians died in mysterious accidents: General Nam Il in March 1976, Vice-premier Hong Wŏn-gil in May, and Vice-president Ch'oe Yong-gŏn in September. Many, including General Yi Yong-mu, Chief of Political Bureau of the People's Army, Yang Hyŏng-sŏp and Kim Tong-gyu, members of the Political Committee of the Central Committee of the Party, were purged in July and August 1976 when Kim Il-sung carried out a purge against the group comprising those who studied in the Soviet Union. During the stormy period of purge, Kim Chŏng-il was attacked and he was seriously wounded in September 1977. When the 6th Supreme People's Assembly held its first plenary session in December 1977, and reorganized the Central People's Committee, reducing this powerful Committee's size from 25 members to 15, all those who opposed Kim Chŏng-il lost their memberships.

In 1977, Kim Chŏng-il became known as "an extraordinary hero and future leader of the Communist world," and the North Korean Communists called him in 1978 the "guiding star of national identity." Also he was referred to as "the Party Center." The April 1979 issue of *Kŭlloja (The Workers)*, a magazine published by the Korean Workers' Party, stated that a "positive struggle will be staged against any elements which attempt to oppose the unique guidance of the Party Center." The *Rodong Shinmun (The Workers' Daily)*, the Party organ, stated in February 1980 that the "Party Center" initiated an all-out campaign for the early realization of Korean unification, faithfully supporting the principles established by his father. The editorial of the *Rodong Shinmun* of February 5, 1980, stated that "the instructions of the Party Center should be unconditionally carried out." Kim Chŏng-il himself elevated the *chuch'e* ideology to Kim Il-sung-ism, consolidated the single-thought-structure, and strengthened the body politic's suppression of heterodoxy.

When the 6th Party Congress met in October 1980, Kim Chŏng-il emerged as an indisputable heir to his father's position. He was made the second-ranking member of the 10-member Secretariat of the Korean Workers' Party, the third-ranking member of the newly created 5-man Standing Committee of the Politburo of the Party, and the third-ranking member of the 10-men Military Affairs Committee of the Central Committee of the Party. Thus, the groundwork for a hereditary rule of the Kim dynasty was solidified. Now the North Korean children sing a song, saying: "We pledge allegiance to you [Kim Chŏng-il] as we do to our beloved leader Kim Il-sung." The young Kim became known as "our future sun!"

Kim Il-sung had been endeavoring for sometime to establish a hereditary rule of the Kim dynasty. Meanwhile, North Korean writers, particularly historians, carried out various schemes to glorify not only Kim Il-sung himself, but also his relatives, as they promoted his personality cult. During the 1960s and the 1970s, many books and other materials were published in North Korea glorifying the achievements of Kim Il-sung and his grandparents and parents as true and outstanding revolutionary heroes. Monuments and statues were erected in their honor, and their birthplaces were dedicated as sacred national shrines. Recently, Kim Chŏng-il's mother, Kim Chŏng-suk, was also glorified as a remarkable revolutionary heroine, her statues were erected, and a school in which she once taught and the county where she was born were named after her. All North Korean people were expected to make pilgrimages to Man-gyŏngdae (Kim Il-sung's birthplace), as well as to the birthplaces of his grandparents and parents.

A large number of Kim Il-sung's relatives held key positions in the Party and the government after 1948. Some of them were removed from influential positions in 1977 as a result of a power struggle between the pro and anti-Kim Chŏng-il factions. Nonetheless, many relatives of Kim Il-sung still remain in key positions as of 1982 as shown below:

Name	Relationship	Major Positions Held
Kim Sŏng-ae	Wife	Chairman, Korean Democratic Women's League
Kim Chŏng-il	Son	Member of the Secretariat, Standing Committee of the Central Committee, the Military Affairs Committee, and the Politburo of the Party
Kang Yang-uk	Cousin of a maternal grandfather	Vice-president of the state; Chairman of the Korean Democratic Party
Pak Sŏng-ch'ŏl	Son-in-law of Kang Yang-uk	Vice-president of the state; Member of the Politburo and

		the Central Committee of the Party
Kang Sŏng-san	Maternal relative	Member of the Central Committee and the Politburo of the Party
Kang Hŭi-wŏn	Maternal cousin	Member of the Central Committee and candidate member of the Politburo of the Party
Hŏ Tam	Husband of a cousin	Vice-premier; Foreign Minister; candidate member of the Politburo of the Party
Yi Yong-mu	Father-in-law of Kim Il-sung's daughter	Army general; chief of Political Bureau of the People's Army
Kim Chŏng-suk	Cousin: wife of Hŏ Tam	Vice-chairman, General Federation of Trade Union
Hwang Chang-yŏp	Nephew	Member of the Secretariat Central Committee of the Party; member of the Standing Committee of the Supreme People's Assembly
Kim Chung-rin	Paternal relative	Secretary of the Party; member of the Secretariat, the Politburo, and the Central Committee of the Party
Kim Pyŏng-ha	Husband of a niece	Chairman of Political Security Department of the Party

The reorganized Central Committee of the Party and the Central People's Committee have become completely dominated by Kim Chŏng-il's supporters such as Vice-presidents Kim Il, Kang Yang-uk, and Pak Sŏng-ch'ŏl, along with theorists named Lim Ch'un-ch'u and Chŏn Kŭm-ch'ŏl (Jon Gum-chol), and military leaders such as O Chin-u, O Kŭk-yŏl, and O Paek-yong. Although the young Kim was not officially named as successor to Kim Il-sung in 1980, his probable succession to power created bitter controversies between his supporters and opponents. The power struggle between the young Kim and his stepmother, Kim Sŏng-ae, and her allies, as well as between the young Kim and his uncle, Kim Yŏng-ju, and his supporters became intensified. It was reported that some twelve army generals were purged in 1982 because of their opposition to the young Kim, and some ten of them were said to have fled to Manchuria.

Be that as it may, the foundation for the Kim dynasty has been constructed in recent years, and barring unforeseen events or his poor health the succession of Kim Il-sung's position by this son seemed to have become only a matter of time. No matter who would be the successor to the aged dictator (age 70 in 1982), North Korea will exist as a Communist state and a threat to South Korea in the foreseeable future, its internal and external problems notwithstanding.

11. The Struggle for Democracy in the Republic of Korea: A Political History

The New Nation

Following the inauguration of Taehan Min-guk (The Republic of Great Han), known in the West as the Republic of Korea and commonly called South Korea, on August 15, 1948, with Dr. Syngman Rhee as its president, the people in South Korea launched movements to foster a free and democratic nation despite unfavorable circumstances. They wished for the reunification of the country and they were hopeful of building a better way of life after a long period of alien domination. The American government desired to make South Korea a "showcase of democracy."

Government and Administrative Districts. The constitution promulgated on July 17, 1948, established the framework of the government for democratic rule. Under the principle of the separation of power, it established the executive, legislative and judicial branches. It guaranteed the rights of citizens, equality before the law, the freedom of speech, press, and association, property rights, equality of the sexes, and other rights of a democratic state.

The legislative power was vested in the bicameral National Assembly. Members of the House of Representatives were elected for a four-year term by universal, equal, direct, and secret vote. The House of Councillors, which was not established until 1960, was to have members elected by popular vote for a six-year term of office. The National Assembly was given, in addition to legislative authority, the power to institute impeachment proceedings against the president, vice-president, members of the State Affairs Council (Cabinet),   421 judges, and other public officials designated by law.

The president who was elected by a two-thirds majority vote of the National Assembly for a four-year tenure received broad power under the Constitution. He was empowered to appoint the prime minister, ministers of the State Affairs Council, as well as justices of the Supreme Court and other high ranking judges. He was also given power to propose emergency measures restricting freedom of speech, assembly, and press under certain circumstances. The State Affairs Council was headed by the permier and it included ten ministers of Home Affairs, Foreign Affairs, Defense, Finance, Education, Agriculture, Commerce and Industry, Social Affairs, Transportation, and Communication. There were four offices of General Affairs, Public Information, Planning, and Legal Affairs which were attached to the Office of the Prime Minister. The vice-presidency was a ceremonial post. The National Police was under the direct

REPUBLIC OF KOREA (1982)

control of the Home Minister.

The judicial branch was headed by the Supreme Court, and the Chief Justice of the Supreme Court and other judges were appointed by the president. There was an Appeals Court, and many district and local courts. Questions involving the constitutionality of law were handled by a Constitutional Committee composed of the vice-president, five justices of the Supreme Court and five members of the National Assembly.

Administrative Districts.   The Republic of Korea (38,452 sq. miles, or 98,431 sq. km.) was slightly larger than the state of Indiana, and it was divided into nine provinces of Kyŏnggi, Kangwŏn, North and South Ch'ungch'ŏng, North and South Kyŏngsang, North and South Chŏlla, and Cheju. Seoul, its capital, and Pusan were designated as special municipalities directly administered by the central government. In 1982 Taegu and Inch'ŏn became special cities.

Each province was divided into counties, and each county into districts. No local autonomy law was enacted, and all provincial governors were appointed by the Home Minister, and all local government officials were appointed by the provincial governor.

The First Republic, 1948–1960

A rocky and uncertain future lay ahead for the young Republic with its unstable political conditions. Its social situation was chaotic and its economy was poor. Two months after the birth of the republic, a Communist-inspired military insurrection broke out in the Yŏsu-Sunch'ŏn area in the south-western region of the country, making the situation even worse for the promotion of democratic institutions and way of life.

The Growth of Autocratic Rule.   The relationship between President Rhee and his cabinet and the National Assembly steadily deteriorated. First of all, the National Assembly elected Yi Shi-yŏng who had a close tie with Kim Ku as vice-president by 133 votes out of 197. Kim Ku, who was vehemently opposed to Dr. Rhee, received 62 votes. Secondly, the National Assembly refused to approve the appointment of Yi Yun-yŏng, President Rhee's choice, as premier. At the same time, President Rhee was not willing to accept Kim Sŏng-su, the leader of the Han-guk (Korean) Democratic Party, as his premier. As a result, Yi Pŏm-sŏk was elected as a compromise candidate for premiership. Unable to receive the unqualified support of the National Assembly, and as the Communist activities and a general sense of national insecurity grew, President Rhee looked toward the police and the armed forces for support.

Meanwhile, criticism against President Rhee for his choice of cabinet ministers grew. No cabinet ministers were of the opposition parties such as the

Korean Independence Party or the Han-guk (Korean) Democratic Party. None of the ministers were adherents of the views of Kim Ku or Kim Kyu-shik. Most of his cabinet ministers were conservative rightists. The only exception was the Minister of Agriculture, Cho Pong-am, a former Communist, who was dismissed in February 1949. In general, President Rhee was criticized for not utilizing the best talents available, and his cabinet was regarded as incompetent.

A special law concerning the punishment of former Japanese collaborators passed by the National Assembly on September 12, 1948, and promulgated on September 22, and the investigative works conducted by a special commission, which was created to classify and punish former Japanese collaborators who were regarded as traitors, provoked bitter political conflicts. Some people who had obviously collaborated with the Japanese were on the list compiled by the commission, but many were unjustly accused. Meanwhile, charges and countercharges were exchanged between the accusers and those who were accused, contributing to the growth of social discord and mutual suspicion among the people. The social atmosphere was extremely unhealthy.

The growing criticism against the Rhee administration and an increasing antagonism between the President and the National Assembly, coupled with the Communist activities in the south, gave great impetus to the growth of President Rhee's autocratic rule and to the open suppression of civil liberties.

The Communists, who opposed the United Nations sponsored elections in South Korea in May 1948, instigated a rebellion on Cheju Island. The Cheju Rebellion, which had begun on April 5, 1948, resulted in the death of at least 30,000 persons, or 10 to 15 per cent of the population of the island by the time it was completely subjugated in the spring of 1949. While the rebellion in Cheju Island was in progress, an army regiment in Yōsu in South Chōlla Province, which was ordered to go to Cheju Island to subjugate the rebels, carried out an insurrection on October 19, 1948. The Communist-led mutiny which began in Yōsu spread into other areas, including Sunch'ōn. The Yōsu-Sunch'ōn Rebellion caused the death of 1,200 civilians and South Korean troops, 1,500 rebels and their supporters, and much property damage.

In the wake of the Yōsu-Sunch'ōn Rebellion, and as rumors of an imminent invasion from North Korea were circulating, the police rounded up several hundred persons. Meanwhile, a press control law and the National Security Law of December 1948 were promulgated. The directives of the Office of Public Information prohibited the printing of articles "contrary to the policy of the government," "detrimental to the Republic," approving either the Communist or the North Korean regime, or "having a detrimental influence on the public mind." The National Security Law made it a crime to seek to consolidate or form a group with the object of disturbing the peace in collusion with enemies of the state. Between October 1948 and April 1949, some 89,710 persons were arrested, and although 28,400 were released, politics of repression gained momentum. Between September 1948 and May 1949, the government closed seven newspapers and one news agency.

Facing the growing repressive tactics of the government, and looking toward the 1950 National Assembly elections, the Han-guk (Korean) Democratic Party merged with other groups and formed the Democratic Nationalist Party in February 1949. President Rhee's proposal made in March for the postponement of the 1950 elections for the National Assembly was soundly rejected as the increasing ties between the President and the armed forces nurtured more antagonism of his opponents. Meanwhile, factional rivalry that developed within the cabinet led President Rhee to dismiss three ministers, including Foreign Minister Chang T'aek-sang, who was regarded as a potential rival to Rhee. Other potential challengers, such as Cho Pyŏng-ok and Chang Myŏn, were given ambassadorial posts in Europe and the United States, repectively, and kept out of domestic politics.

The rebellion in the southern parts of the country was put down by the spring of 1949, but national security did not improve as economic and social conditions worsened. The Communists and their sympathizers in the south, and guerrilla units sent into the south by the North Korean Communists created unending security problems for the Rhee administration. A series of North Korean-provoked military incidents occurred in May 1949 near Kaesŏng as well as in Paekch'ŏn in Hwanghae Province, and during the months of May and June military clashes took place in the Ongjin region in Hwanghae Province as well. Military clashes between the troops of the south and the north occurred in the Kaesŏng and Ongjin area as well as near Ch'unch'ŏn in Kangwŏn Province during the month of August, causing the rise of concern for national security.

Meanwhile, North Korean-directed guerrilla activities became troublesome. The Democratic Fatherland Unification Front, which was established in June 1949 by the leaders of the South Korean Workers' Party who fled to the north, launched a guerrilla offensive against the south in alliance with the remnants of the Yŏsu-Sunch'ŏn rebels who had fled into the Chiri mountain region located in the border area of South Kyŏngsang and North Chŏlla provinces. North Korean guerrillas established their eastern base in the Odae mountain area in Kangwŏn Province, a southwestern base in the Chiri mountain region, and in August they penetrated into the Andong area in North Kyŏngsang Province in order to establish a third base.

Some three thousand guerrillas, assisted by several hundred supporters in South Korea, launched a winter offensive in October against such large towns as Andong, Chinju, and P'ohang. North Korean guerrilla units were unable to occupy these key towns, but their activities increased the sense of danger to national security as the Rhee adminstration became increasingly oppressive with liberal application of the National Security Law. Many, including ten National Assemblymen, were under arrest as of May–June 1949. In the midst of a growing anti-Rhee atmosphere, Kim Ku, the leader of the Korean Independence Party who had been in contact with Pyongyang in order to hold a

Peaceful Unification Conference, was assassinated by a South Korean Army officer on June 26, creating an extremely unstable political climate.

The long awaited land reform bill finally passed the National Assembly in May 1949 after causing the dismissal of Minister of Agriculture Cho Pong-am in February because of his liberal views. However, the rather liberal land reform bill was abrogated by the Rhee administration, and the conservative Land Reform Law which the Rhee administration proposed was adopted by the National Assembly in June. The Land Reform Law eliminated absentee land-lordism and forbade the holding of more than 7.5 acres of farmland by a cultivator.

In January 1950, the Democratic Nationalist Party proposed a constitutional amendment in order to make the cabinet responsible to the National Assembly and the president a ceremonial head of the state. The proposal was defeated, but it made President Rhee only more determined to increase his control. In the midst of the growing antagonism between the Rhee administration and the National Assembly, the government arrested No Il-hwan, Kim Yak-su, and eleven other Assemblymen, charging them with their Communist-linkage and with violation of the National Security Law. This was so-called the p'urakch'i (fraktsya in Russian) incident of February 1950.

No Il-hwan, Kim Yak-su and others who were collectively known as "the young faction" in the National Assembly had formed a political club named the Tongsŏnghoe, and it adopted a seven-point resolution which included: (1) complete withdrawal of all foreign troops, (2) release of political prisoners in the north and the south, (3) formation of a political conference of the representatives of political parties of the north and the south, (4) establishment of a new supreme legislative assembly of Korea by general elections, (5) establishment of a new Korean government by the supreme legislative assembly, (6) punishment of "anti-people persons" (former Japanese collaborators), and (7) reorganization of national defense forces.

The members of the Tongsŏnghoe were charged with the planning of the overthrow of the Republic in collaboration with the South Korean Workers' Party whose leaders had fled to the north. Many members of the South Korean Workers' Party who remained in the south and went underground had been engaged in subversive activities. Eleven members of the Tongsŏnghoe, including No and Kim, were given two to twelve-year prison sentences as the politics of intimidation began to gather force.

The internecine antagonism and rivalries between the Rhee administration and the Democratic Nationalist Party, as well as Rhee's own actions brought about their own defeat in the May 30 elections for the National Assembly. Some 91.9 per cent of the 8.4 million eligible voters cast their ballots, and the disenchanted voters elected only 12 of Rhee's National Society candidates and only 23 candidates of the Democratic Nationalist party. They lost 44 seats and 55 seats, respectively. Meanwhile, the Independents and moderate candidates won 127 seats, constituting a formidable opposition group against Rhee who could count only 57 votes in the National Assembly.

By March 1950, Communist guerrilla units were by and large demolished, thanks to a major counteroffensive launched by the South Korean military in the winter of 1949-1950. But certain mountainous areas, including those in Ch'ungch'ŏng Province, were harassed by the remnants of the guerrillas.

The War Time Politics. In the midst of political turmoil, the young Republic faced the most serious threat to its existence when the North Koreans launched a war against the south on June 25, 1950. The poorly trained and inadequately equipped South Korean military was unable to stop the aggressors, and the government fled first to Taejŏn and then to Pusan. The aggressors quickly occupied almost two-thirds of South Korean territory. Only after the arrival of more U.S. and U.N. forces, and following the successful amphibious landing of U.N. forces at Inch'ŏn in September did the security of the Republic seem to be assured. However, toward the end of October the tide of the war turned against U.N. forces with the arrival of Chinese troops to aid the North Koreans, and Seoul was retaken by the aggressors in early January 1951. Seoul was recovered by U.N. forces shortly thereafter, but the South Korean government remained in Pusan.

A number of events led to the decline of the people's confidence and the growth of their mistrust of the government. The flight of the government from Seoul without giving due warning to the people regarding its abandonment of the capital had already antagonized the people who suffered much as hundreds of thousands of refugees fled to the southern area. The killing of some 606 civilians of a small town in Kŏch'ang, South Kyŏngsang Province in December 1950 by troops of the 3rd Battalion, 9th Regiment, 11th Division of the South Korean Army, their burning down of 700 houses and their confiscation of cattle, and other violence committed against the people of Kŏch'ang in the name of a mopping-up operation against the Communists aroused tremendous anti-government feelings in the people. The attack of the national troops against the investigation team of the National Assembly which went to Kŏch'ang in March 1951 only furthered the anti-government sentiment of the people. The embezzlement of a large sum of defense funds by the commander of the National Defense Corps in 1951 caused considerable embarrassment on the part of the administration. Although Commander Kim Yun-gŭn was executed in August 1951, the mistrust of the people remained strong.

Korea was in the throes of war when the second presidential election neared. President Rhee, whose term of office was due to expire in August 1952, moved quickly to strengthen his chance for re-election, and in December 1951 he brought about the formation of his own Liberal Party (*Chayudang*). Realizing that it would be difficult, if not impossible, for him to be re-elected by the National Assembly, his party proposed a constitutional amendment to institute the system of electing the president and vice-president by popular votes. The bill also included the proposal to establish an upper house in the National Assembly. However, the proposal was soundly defeated in January 1952 by a vote of 143 to 19. President Rhee did not give up his fight for re-election.

During the Korean War, anti-government criticism increased and Rhee's politics of intimidation grew further. President Rhee declared martial law in the Pusan area on May 25, 1952, and employed strong pressure tactics, including police power and a terrorist group named the White Skeleton Corps which supported the newly appointed Home Minister Yi Pŏm-sŏk, who had been prime minister between 1948 and 1950. Some fifty Assemblymen who opposed any constitutional amendment were arrested on May 27, and four of them were imprisoned in connection with their alleged connections with international Communist organizations. On May 31, eleven more persons, including Chang Myŏn, prime minister who resigned from his office a short time before, were arrested on charges of plotting to assassinate Rhee. Chang T'aek-sang, former chief of Metropolitan Police of Seoul and foreign minister, became the new prime minister in May. The demand for the lifting of martial law was simply ignored by the administration as more anti-Rhee politicians were arrested. On July 5, all the opponents of the proposed bill were rounded up by the police and those who had been detained in jail were released to attend the Assembly session. That night, the National Assembly passed constitutional amendments proposed by Rhee and his party by a vote of 163 to 0, with three abstentions. The amendments provided for: (1) a direct, popular election of the president and vice-president, (2) creation of an upper house, (3) recommendation of cabinet appointees by the prime minister, and (4) limited authorization for the National Assembly to dissolve the State Affairs Council by a vote of no-confidence.

For the August 5, 1952 presidential elections, the Liberal Party nominated Dr. Rhee as its presidential candidate and Yi Pŏm-sŏk as its vice-presidential candidate. However, President Rhee, who feared the growing strength of Yi, instructed his supporters, through police channels, to vote for Ham T'ae-yŏng, an 81-year old independent candidate, for the vice-presidency. The major opposition, Democratic Nationalist Party, nominated Cho Pyŏng-ok as its presidential candidate, while a small Progressive Party nominated Cho Pong-am, former minister of agriculture, to oppose Rhee. Yi Shi-yŏng, former vice-president, also ran against Rhee. Some 7.3 million, or 88.0 per cent of eligible voters, cast their ballots, and Rhee won the election by an overwhelming majority 5,238,796 votes. Despite Rhee's secret instructions, Yi Pom-sŏk received two million votes against 2.8 million for Ham. Cho Pong-am received 800,000 votes, Yi Shi-yŏng 764,725, and Cho Pyŏng-ok 575,260 votes.

The way in which the constitutional amendment was carried out by the Liberal Party and the Rhee administration alienated the people and aroused their feelings against the government. At the same time, the monetary reform which the government implemented in February 1953 further antagonized the people, although it was done in order to cope with an astronomical inflation rate. The government set the exchange rate between the old currency (*wŏn*) to new (*hwan*) as 300 to 1, resulting in considerable financial difficulties for the people. Be that as it may, the growing inflation rate could not be arrested as politics by intimidation grew worse.

 ## The Korean War and U.S.-Korean Relations

Korean Policy of the United States.   The Joint Chiefs of Staff of the United States has ranked South Korea as the country 15th in importance after Japan (13th) and China (14th) in terms of American global politics. Secretary of War Robert Patterson said on April 4, 1947, that the United States should "get out of Korea at an early date." George F. Kennan, champion for the containment policy and head of the Policy Planning Staff of the State Department, said in late September 1947 that "our policy should be to cut losses and get out of there [Korea] as gracefully but promptly as possible."

Only the fall of the Nationalist Chinese led the United States government to adopt a policy to stay in South Korea a little longer. However, the United States decided to withdraw its troops from South Korea because it did not wish to involve American troops in a Korean war. Although it was discussed by American policy makers in June 1949, they adopted no plan to take military actions in Korea, even with U.N. sanction, in the event of a full scale invasion from North Korea subsequent to withdrawl of U.S. troops from South Korea. As mentioned earlier, the withdrawal of American troops was completed in June 1949.

The National Security Council of the United States adopted a policy in the fall of 1949 "to contain. . . the power and influence of the USSR in Asia," but the American government pursued no concrete plans in South Korea to safeguard its security. Moreover, no actions were taken by the United States government even after it adopted, in April 1950, a policy to "check and roll back" Soviet expansionism. This was mainly because the American policy makers did not believe that the Soviet Union would condone the North Korean Communists starting war, or that the North Koreans would start a war themselves. Nevertheless, the war launched by the North Korean Communists with the approval of Moscow, however reluctantly Stalin might have done so, came on June 25, 1950.

China's entry into the Korean War in October 1950, the growing unwinability of the war, together with the looming danger for a possible protracted war with Communist China, led the American government to seek a way to end the fighting. Many influential Americans, including General Omar N. Bradley, believed that the United States was fighting "a wrong war, at a wrong place, at a wrong time." The absence of the will to win the war and destroy Communist

North Korea was clearly demonstrated by the Americans.

The oppressive politics of the Rhee adminsitration and its stand against the Korean armistice plan won the enmity of the Amercians. President Rhee was bitterly critical of American policy to stop the war short of a complete destruction of Communist North Korea. He did not wish to let the golden opportunity to unify the country pass by. Moreover, he was concerned with the future security of South Korea if North Korea was allowed to exist under the Communist rule. Being unable to stop the U.N. Command from negotiating with the Communists to end the fighting, the South Korean government desired to obtain a bilateral security pact from the United States.

Korean Foreign Minister Pyŏn Yŏng-t'ae stated in early April 1953 that "such a pact would be the price for ROK[Republic of Korea]'s cooperation with armistice efforts." Meanwhile, President Rhee proposed that a mutual security treaty between the United States and South Korea accompany the simultaneous withdrawal of U.N. and Chinese troops from Korea. The Korean president also threatened to remove Korean troops from the U.N. Command.

Encountering Rhee's determined opposition to the truce, General Mark Clark devised in May 1953 a plan known as "Operation Everready." The plan included the abduction of Rhee to Japan and the establishment of a new government of South Korea under Chang T'aek-sang with the understanding of Gen. Paek Sŏn-yŏp, Chief of Staff of the Korean Army. In late May, U.S. policy makers, including U.S. Army Chief of Staff, General Lawton J. Collins, considered the following options: (1) the U.S. government would support General Clark's plan to establish a military government in Korea by taking Presidnet Rhee and his ministers into custody in the event Korean troops were withdrawn from the U.N. Command; (2) the U.S. government would agree to the withdrawal of the U.N. Command from Korea in the event that President Rhee refused to cooperate in reaching or implementing an armistice agreement; and (3) the American government would offer South Korea a mutual defense treaty if it accepted the armistic agreement. General Collins was in favor of taking the Korean president under "protective custody" rather than submitting to his "blackmail."

Although it was proposed to take President Rhee and other intransigent leaders of the South Korean government into custody and establish a military government in South Korea, President Eisenhower and Secretary of State John Foster Dulles as well as the Secretary of Defense did not approve the plan which amounted to an American-instigated coup d'état against the legally constituted government of South Korea.

President Rhee's release of 25,000 anti-Communist prisoners-of-war on June 18 without the knowledge or consent of the U.N. Command created new problems for the U.N. Command. A short time later, General Clark threatened Rhee that the U.N. Command would take such steps against him "as may be necessary." Meanwhile, a high-level conference of U.S. military and civilian officials was held in Tokyo, and it adopted a resolution and proposed to inform General Clark and American Ambassador Robert Murphy in Seoul that if Rhee remained intransigent, Rhee should be informed that the U.N. would get out of Korea without a U.S. guarantee for South Korean security. Furthermore, it proposed that Clark be informed that he should take proper steps if it became necessary to replace the present Korean government.

In late June, the Joint Chiefs of Staff of the United States approved a Korean Army coup against President Rhee and informed General Clark that "If no change occurs in Rhee's attitude, it would be our hope that influential political and military elements in South Korea would themselves take steps to induce the Korean Government to accept the armistice." At the same time, Clark was instructed to exploit the possibility of "quietly and adroitly creating an impression among Rhee and ROK leaders that the U.N. Command was preparing to withdraw."

The U.S.-Korean Mutual Defense Treaty. In late June 1953, Assistant Secretary of State for Far Eastern Affairs Walter Robertson went to Seoul to negotiate with President Rhee. In the meantime, General Maxwell Taylor, commander of the U.S. Eighth Army, implemented a plan which had been developed by General Clark "to induce, through covert means," President Rhee to accept the American peace plan. Robertson offered five pledges, namely (1) the promise of a U.S.-South Korean security treaty, (2) a loan of 200 million dollars, (3) an agreement on the part of the United States to withdraw from the political conference between the belligerents after ninety days if nothing constructive resulted in terms of Korean reunification, (4) American aid for the expansion of the South Korean Army, and (5) high level U.S.-South Korean talks related to the conference on Korean reunification to be held later. Meanwhile, President Eisenhower assured President Rhee that the United States would not renounce its efforts to unify Korea "by all peaceful means," and the American president threatened to carry out an atomic war on the Chinese mainland if the Communists did not end the war soon. President Rhee accepted the American pledges and grudgingly acquiesced to the U.N. armistice plan. At the same time, he agreed not to obstruct the armistice negotiation, and to keep South Korean troops under U.N. Command.

The Korean armistice was signed on July 27, 1953, and a three mile wide demilitarized zone (DMZ) zig-zagging across the peninsula was established, replacing the 38th parallel line as the national boundary between the two Korean states.

Disappointed and angry, and disregarding or being unaware of possible future effects, President Rhee refused to approve the signing of the armistice by the Korean government. By doing so, the South Korean government refused to recognize the existence of North Korea and the People's Republic of China, and it created a serious problem related to the establishment of diplomatic relations with the People's Republic of China on one hand, and any amicable negotiations between the two Korean governments for the reunification of Korea on the other.

The United States and the Republic of Korea signed the Mutual Defense Treaty on October 1, 1953, but it did not guarantee unconditional military actions on the part of the United States in behalf of the security of the Republic. Unlike the NATO agreement or the U.S.-Japan Mutual Defense Treaty, the implementation of the U.S.-Korean Mutual Defense Treaty required the advice and consent of the U.S. Senate. The treaty clearly stated in Article 3 that each party would act to meet the common danger in accordance with its constitutional process. Since the end of the Korean War and up to 1960, South Korea received a total of $40 billion in U.S. military grants.

The Postwar Politics

The 1954 Elections.   Shortly after the government returned to Seoul, elections for the National Assembly were held in May 1954. The Liberal Party nominated one candidate, who pledged his unconditional obedience to Rhee, in each Assembly district, while opposition and independent candidates ran against one another. The outcome was predictable, for candidates of the Liberal Party were given financial support by the government and police protection while many opposition candidates were terrorized by organizations supporting Rhee. Many opposition candidates were either arrested, or disqualified one way or another. A large number of newspaper reporters were arrested, and a variety of corruptive and illegal means were employed by the Liberal Party to win more seats in the National Assembly.

About 91.9 per cent of 8,466,509 qualified voters cast their ballots in the May 20, 1954 elections. As was expected, the Liberal Party won as many as 109 seats, whereas the opposition Democratic Nationalist Party won only 15. Despite many difficulties, opposition candidates such as Shin Ik-hŭi and Cho Pyŏng-ok won by an overwhelming majority over Rhee's candidates. The Independents won 79 seats, denying the two-thirds majority to the Liberal Party.

The Second Constitutional Amendments.   President Rhee's second term of office was due to expire in 1956 making him ineligible to run under the 1948 constitution which restricted a presidential tenure to two terms only. Needless to say, it was his wish to rule the country continuously and the Liberal Party was determined to keep the power under his leadership. Thus, on September 6, 1954, the Liberal Party proposed a series of constitutional amendments, including the elimination of the two-term restriction on presidential tenure, the abolition of the post of premier, and the instituting of the voters' right to recall legislators by petition. Such amendments would perpetuate Rhee's tenure and the corruptive politics of the Liberal Party.

However, the National Assembly defeated the bill on November 27 by a one vote margin. The bill received only 135 votes, one vote short of a two-thirds majority, and the presiding official who was a member of the Liberal Party declared the amendments defeated. But the next day, the Liberal Party declared the amendments passed under the principle of *sasa oip*, the rounding off of the fractional vote. It claimed that since there were 203 votes, only 135 votes were required for the passage of amendments. The important changes in the constitution included the exemption of Rhee from the two-term limitation, the succession of the elected vice-president to the presidency should the incumbent die, and the abolition of the post of prime minister.

The nation was stunned by such gimmickry, and the anger of the people rose. Meanwhile, the badly split Democratic Nationalist Party was reorganized as the Democratic Party in 1955 with the purging of those who had bettayed the party.

The 1956 and 1958 Elections.   In the May 15, 1956 presidential election, the opposition Democratic Party nominated Shin Ik-hŭi and Chang Myŏn as presidential and vice-presidential candidates, respectively. The sudden death of presidential candidate Shin assured an easy victory for Rhee, who was renominated by the Liberal Party. Therefore, the real contest was between Chang Myŏn and Yi Ki-bung, vice-presidential candidate of the Liberal Party.

As corruption among government officials and members of the Liberal Party and police pressures increased, a widespread desire for change grew strong, particularly among urban voters. The people's slogan was "We cannot make a living. Let us change!" About 94.4 per cent of the 9,906,870 qualified voters cast their ballots in the election, and reelected Rhee as president. However, Chang defeated Yi Ki-bung, Rhee's running mate, by winning over 4 million votes as against 3.1 million votes for Yi, despite various tactics employed by the Liberal Party and the police against Chang. A Socialist candidate, Cho Pong-am, won close to 2.2 million votes. The 1956 election clearly showed the antagonism of the people toward Rhee and his party. Whereas Rhee received 72 per cent of the votes in 1952, he won only 56 per cent of the votes in 1956. Through the May 15 election, the Korean people proved their capability in making rational judgments, and resisting pressure from the ruling group. The opposition Democratic Party became a power to reckon with for Rhee and the Liberal Party.

The upper house of the National Assembly was not established and Vice-President Chang Myŏn was given no power to exercise. However, the possibility that he might succeed Rhee in the event of the aged Rhee's sudden death gave rise to the hope of those who aspired for democracy while it made the Liberal Party more corrupt and led it to resort to more illegal means to suppress the opponents. An attempt was made to assassinate Chang by a pro-Rhee would-be assassin in 1956.

The stronger the opposition against the administration grew, the more desperate the government and the Liberal Party became. In January 1958, Cho Pong-am, former Minister of Agriculture and Chairman of the Progressive Party, and its several top leaders were arrested on alleged espionage charges. In February, a plane belonging to the Korean National Airlines was hijacked by the Japanese to North Korea, creating a tense atmosphere. Meanwhile, many writers, newspaper reporters and publishers, and magazine publishers were arrested. The cases of a popular monthly magazine named *Sasanggye* (*The World of Thoughts*) and such newspapers as *The Korea Times*, the *Kyŏnghyang Shinmun*, and the *Tong-a Ilbo* were more notorious examples of the suppression of freedom of speech and press.

In the May 2, 1958 National Assembly elections, the voters elected more candidates of the Democratic Party which increased the number of Assemblymen from 47 to 79. The Liberal Party won 126 seats, but 5 less than it had had. Some 28 Indepedents were elected, and they together with the members of the Democratic Party were in the position to block any bills proposed by the Liberal Party. As a result, the hope to promote a parliamentary democracy rose considerably.

It is significant to note that the voters in urban areas supported the opposition Democratic Party. In five key urban areas, the Democratic Party won a total of 29 seats whereas the Liberal Party won only five. In Seoul, only one candidate of the Liberal Party was elected while 14 candidates of the opposition party won. The results of the 1958 elections clearly showed that the Liberal Party had become a party of the unsophisticated and easily manipulated rural voters.

The Fall of the First Republic

The New National Security Law.   Looking forward to the 1960 presidential election, the Liberal Party set out to crush the opponents, and it introduced, on November 18, 1958, a new national security law ostensibly aimed against Communist propaganda. Cho Pyŏng-ok, the leader of the Democratic Party, attacked the bill as a transparent attempt to silence all criticism against the administration and the Liberal Party.

In order to block the passage of the bill, the opponents carried out a week-long sit-in strike in the National Assembly hall. Three hundred policemen were brought in, and the striking Assemblymen were forcefully carried out from the hall and locked in the basement. Meanwhile, members of the Liberal Party and those who were intimidated by them passed the new security law and many other bills, including a bill abolishing elections for local officials. Following this, the Liberal Party quickly filled politically important local posts with its own party members. Chiefs of police were also replaced with the supporters of the administration and the Liberal Party, as the Army became an effective political arm of the administration.

The new National Security Law was promulgated on December 26. The law was not only against any group of individuals or organizations which sought to overthrow the state in violation of the national constitution, but it was also against anyone who secured and/or divulged national secrets, or took actions for the purpose of "benefiting the enemy." The law also declared that anyone who disturbed "the people's minds by openly pointing out or spreading false facts," and those who "openly impaired the prestige of a constitutional organ by holding a meeting or by publishing documents," would be prosecuted. It specified that the "constitutional organ" included the President, the Speakers of the National Assembly and the Chief Justice. The penalties for violators of the law would be death or life imprisonment.

Needless to say, the public was outraged by the ways in which the new National Security Law was passed. Moreover, the liberal and progressive people became bitterly critical of the administration and its political arms. Be that as it may, the new National Security Law virtually killed any chance for democratization of politics as it deprived the people of most of their civil rights.

The 1960 Elections and Student Uprising. The 4th presidential election was set for March 15, 1960. The Liberal Party again nominated Rhee and Yi Ki-bung to run for presidency and vice-presidency, respectively. The Democratic Party nominated Cho Pyŏng-ok, as the presidental candidate and Chang Myŏn as the vice-presidential candidate. Three weeks before the election date, Cho, who became seriously ill and went to the United States for medical treatment, died in late January, assuring the re-election of Rhee.

The leaders of the Liberal Party mobilized the National Police, the Army, and corrupt means to assure the election of Yi. Popular reaction against the corrupt and fraudulent practices grew, and riots and student demonstrations erupted throughout the country, particularly in the southern cities such as Masan, culminating in the April 19 Student Uprising. The landslide victory of Yi by winning 8,221,000 votes against a mere 1,844,000 votes for Chang created a strong suspicion and astonishment on the part of the voters. The incumbent Vice-president Chang immediately resigned in protest over the March election.

On April 19, thousands of university and high school students, as well as professors, teachers, parents, and others, staged one of the most spectacular demonstrations against the government. The voters in Masan, South Kyŏng-sang Province, who were convinced that a fair election was impossible, had already carried out their demonstrations on the election day, producing at least seven dead at the hands of the police. Dozens of the people, including young students, were wounded. The discovery of the body of a student with a tear-gas shell imbedded in one eye touched off wild rioting. The government charged that the Masan uprising was the work of Communist agents.

The "Righteous Student Uprising of April 19," came in the wake of a large student demonstration at Korea University in Seoul on April 18 in sympathy with fellow students in Masan. The April 18 incident which was bloody, only infuriated the students more. Other students in Seoul joined those of Korea University, and violent riots occurred on April 19.

Martial law was declared and troops were mobilized when the police were powerless to control the situation. The mobilized troops, however, chose to remain neutral, refusing to take any actions against the demonstrators who were demanding the resignation of the president and his cabinet, the nullification of the March 15 election results, and a fundamental political reform to foster democracy, as well as the removal of corrupt politicians and profiteers from the government. The demonstrations and riots continued every day after April 19 until they forced the cabinet to resign.

Facing the inevitable, and under heavy pressure from the United States, President Rhee tendered his resignation on April 26, followed by the resignation of the Cabinet members. Yi Ki-bung's son, who was adopted by Rhee, shot his natural father, mother, and other family members first on April 28, and then he himself committed suicide. Thus, the First Republic, which began in great hope, collapsed in a violent uprising.

On April 27, the hastily convened National Assembly appointed Foreign Minister Hŏ Chŏng as the head of a caretaker government as the hope for the establishment of a clean, just, and democratic government grew. Dr. Rhee, who fought for the independence of his fatherland for some sixty years from the time he was a youthful high school student in the late 1890s, the man who led the country during those dark days of the Korean War, and "the Father of the Republic" who was rejected by the people, left Korea soon after the fall of the First Republic for Hawaii where he died in 1965.

The Legacies of the First Republic.   With the exception of the Land Reform Law of May 1949, and besides mere survival during the Communist-inspired rebellions of 1948 and 1949 and the Korean War, the government of the First Republic recorded no positive and beneficent success. It was a corrupt and oppressive government, its methods were undemocratic and its politics were unclean. It made no efforts to relax the tension between the north and the south, and it failed to settle the issues with Japan. Its economic programs were at best poorly designed and administered, and it paid no satisfactory attention to the welfare of the people. Its military became another political arm along with the National Police, and it failed to promote the confidence and unity of the people. Economic recovery did begin around the middle of 1959, but it was offset by the political corruption and profiteering of the officials and members of the ruling party. The only positive contribution which it made may be found in the development of education.

The Interim Government Period

Hŏ Chŏng was a friend of Dr. Rhee from their days in the United States, and he served as Minister of Transportation between 1948 and 1952, resigning when the political crisis of 1952 developed. After that he maintained his political independence (neutrality) until he was appointed by Rhee as Mayor of Seoul in 1958. However, he was replaced in 1959. He was regarded as "meek" and a man without political ambitions. He reluctantly assumed the foreign ministership shortly after the April 19 uprising, upon Rhee's insistence.

On May 3, Hŏ made it known that the primary task of his government was to restore political and social order, and he declared that he had no intention of prolonging the interim period. Meanwhile, many, including nine members of the Rhee administration and fifteen leading members of the Liberal Party, were arrested for the violation of election laws in March and other crimes against the people. Trials for those who were arrested on political and financial charges began on July 5. At the same time, some personnel change was made to remove highly political army generals.

The Amendment of the Constitution.   Despite much opposition to the legality of the then existing National Assembly, on June 15 the National Assembly adopted a series of amendments to the constitution in order to foster political democracy under a strong parliamentary system. First of all, a 58-member House of Councillors was to be established as a consultative body, and the minimum age of the candidates for the upper house was set at 35. The 233-member House of Representatives was to remain as primarily responsible for legislative process. The terms of the members of the upper house and the lower house were to be six and four years, respectively.

The amended constitution abolished the post of vice-president. It made the president a figurehead chief of state with a five-year tenure of office and eligible for re-election only once, and the National Assembly regained the power to elect the president of the nation.

The office of prime minister was resurrected, and the National Assembly was empowered to appoint the prime minister as head of the executive branch and responsible to the National Assembly. The House of Representatives was authorized to cast a vote of no-confidence against the State Affairs Council, and in such an event the State Affairs Council would resign *en bloc* or dissolve the House of Representatives and call for an election. The voting age was lowered from 21 to 20. Limited local autonomy was restored, and the system for electing the mayor of Seoul and provincial governors was established. The first election for local officials was held in December 1960.

The new constitution guaranteed (Article 13) that citizens shall not be subjected to any restrictions on the freedom of speech, press, assembly, and association. Article 27 guaranteed the political impartiality of public officials. It retained Article 28 which empowered the government to adopt laws imposing restrictions upon the liberties and rights of citizens "when necessary for the maintenance of public order or the welfare of the community." However, it stated that such restrictions should not infringe upon the essential substance of the liberties and rights, and no provisions should be made to impose censorship in freedom of speech, press, assembly and association. Article 75 ensured the impartiality of the police.

Taking advantage of newly gained freedom, in May school teachers organized the National School Teachers' Labor Union, which was a radical organization, and the radical students, particularly those of Seoul National University who participated in the April Uprising, formed the Student League for National Unification in July 1960. Meanwhile, radical "reformist parties" emerged. Among these were the Socialist Mass Party, which was organized by former members of the Progressive Party, and joined by Sŏ Sang-il and Yi Tong-hwa who had formed the Democratic Reformist Party, and the Korean Socialist Party led by a trade unionist Chŏn Chin-han.

The Establishment of a New Government.   On July 29, 1960, elections were held to establish a new bicameral legislative assembly. Some 1,562 candidates ran for the House of Representatives and 214 candidates for the House of Councillors. All the candidates pledged themselves to clean up corruption, oppose dictatorship, promote economic reconstruction, and continue a pro-American, anti-Communist foreign policy.

Despite the stormy weather on the election day, 82.6 per cent of eligible voters cast their ballots, demonstrating their desires for participation in the political process. A 58-member upper house, the House of Councillors, was created; 31 were from the Democratic Party, 23 were Independents, 4 members were of the Liberal Party, 1 was that of the Socialist Mass Party, and 1 was from the National League for Progress. The 233 seats in the lower house, the House of Representatives, were won as follows: 175 by the Democratic Party, 46 by Independents, 4 by the Socialist Mass Party, 1 by the Korean Socialist Party, 2 by the Liberal Party, and 5 by other splinter groups. The United Nations and other foreign observers stated that the July 1960 elections were clean and the least violent, manifesting the democratic spirit of the Korean people.

On August 12, the House of Representatives elected Yun Po-sŏn (1897–   ) a graduate of the University of Edinburgh, and the leader of the Old Faction of the Democratic Party, as the president of the Republic. Kim To-yŏn of the Old Faction of the Democratic Party was nominated for the premiership, but he failed to receive a majority vote of 114. Chang Myŏn (1899–1966), a graduate of Manhattan College, New York, and a key member of the New Faction of the Democratic Party, was elected as prime minister on August 19.

Prime Minister Chang organized a 14-man cabinet. All except one minister were members of the Democratic Party, and most of them were those belonging to the New Faction. All cabinet ministers, except Foreign Minister Chong Il-hyŏng, were those who had been educated at Japanese colleges or universities.

Kim To-yŏn's failure to win the premiership, and the composition of the Chang Myŏn's cabinet, created serious dissension and schism within the Democratic Party. Subsequently, in October 1960, Kim To-yŏn and the Old Faction members deserted the Democratic Party and formed the New Democratic Party with the purpose of "fostering parliamentary democracy." Meanwhile, certain dissatisfied members of the New Faction of the Democratic Party who called themselves the "young group" formed the New Breeze Society, further weakening the Democratic Party. Factional strife continued to weaken the effectiveness of the Democratic Party.

The Second Republic, 1960-1961

The inauguration of President Yun in August 1960 marked the beginning of the shortlived Second Republic in South Korea. The people of South Korea were provided with an unprecedented opportunity to promote democracy, and hopes were high to construct a democratic nation. However, the Second Republic was destined to fail in the struggle for democracy as political leaders were disunited, freedom and rights were abused by various groups of power seekers, social instability increased, and economic conditions deteriorated badly. The Second Republic was overthrown by the military revolution of May 1961.

The Weaknesses of the Administration.   The government of the Second Republic was hamstrung from the start. In the first place, it had no mandate from the people. Secondly, both President Yun and Prime Minister Chang were men of intellectual and scholarly interests, personal integrity, and mild dispositions, but they lacked fortitude and practical tactics. The Chang administration was indecisive in selecting a policy to deal with former leaders of the Rhee regime, and seemed too tolerant toward left wing radicals. It was unable to deal effectively with ideological and social cleavages between political and social groups and gained no support or loyalty from the people. Above all, the Democratic Party which dominated the National Assembly and the government was badly disunited as factional strikes weakened its power.

When a strong and charismatic leadership was required to restore order and confidence, neither Yun nor Chang furnished such a leadership. The sudden acquisition of power by the Democratic Party with the fall of Rhee's adminstration and his party created tension among various factions within the Party, resulting in sharp alignments. Neither Yun nor Chang could ameliorate the situation within their own party.

Parties and Politics.   Political rivalries among the factions of the ruling Democratic Party and between the leftist Popular Socialist Party on one hand, and the rightist Democratic Party and the Korean Independence Party created a serious political instability. Premier Chang reshuffled his cabinet three times in less than nine months between September 12, 1960 and May 3, 1961, but he neither strengthened his leadership, nor did he gain popularity.

The labor union movement became strong. The number of labor unions grew from 621 in April 1960 to 821 by September, and union membership increased from 307,415 in April 1960 to 373,735 by September. With the rise of the labor union movement, the leftist movement gained momentum, generated by such unions as the National School Teachers' Labor Union of 18,678 members which was formed in May 1960. The number of labor disputes in 1960 grew from 29 before April to 189 after April. Meanwhile, Seoul National University's Student League for National Unification, which was formed in July 1960, joined left wing labor unions in demanding radical reforms and an immediate unification of Korea. All of them advocated the withdrawal of all foreign troops from Korea, political, economic, and cultural exchange between North and South Korea, and the achievement of national unification on the basis of the principle of permanent neutrality of the unified Korea. Radical students demanded "revolutionary legislation" to punish ex-government officials and pro-Rhee politicians, school administrators and professors who supported the Rhee regime, and those who had committed crimes against students in March and April 1960.

Prime Minister Chang was caught in between the pro-revolution and anti-revolution groups. The liberal intellectuals and college students constituted the main core of the former group and those who desired stability and gradual change made up the second group. The pro-revolution group was strongly against the former leaders of the Rhee administration and the Liberal Party, and it demanded harsh punishments for those who committed crimes against the people. Some 48 former officials of the Rhee regime were tried in October, but some who regarded themselves as victims of the Rhee government were not satisfied with the outcome as most of them were either freed or received only short term prison sentences.

Under a growing pressure of the pro-revolutionaries, the Chang administration promulgated the Special Law adopted by the House of Representatives on October 31, 1960. Its purpose was to punish those who committed illegal acts in connection with the March 15, 1960 elections, as well as those who were responsible for wounding and killing citizens protesting the election frauds. Under the Special Law all those who performed clearly anti-democratic acts and/or amassed wealth through illegal means prior to April 26, 1960 were to be punished and be deprived of civil rights. Some 1,500 individuals were classified into the "automatic case" category of criminals and 40,000 others were to be investigated for their alleged crimes.

The process of prosecution of former politicians and racketeers began, causing an extremely unstable political and social condition. Some 2,217 ex-government officials, 81 police chiefs, and 4,000 police officers were purged by the end of December 1960. Meanwhile, the purification of the military began by removing politicized military officers. The plan to reduce the size of the Army by some 100,000 men was not carried out when the government met strong opposition from the United States and the Army itself.

In January 1961, Sŏ Sang-il and Yi Tong-hwa defected from the Socialist Mass Party and formed a reform party named Unification Socialist Party against radical reformists. Some time later, another reform party named the National Unification Party of the Socialists emerged. These, along with the Socialist Mass Party and the Korean Socialist Party, agitated for the withdrawal of all foreign troops from Korea while advocating various reforms. In order to achieve their objectives, each launched its own movement. When the Socialist Mass Party formed the Consultative Committee for the Nationalist and Independent Unification of Korea in January 1961, the Unification Socialist Party, allied with the General League for Realization of Neutralist National Unification agitated for the holding of a North-South dialogue in response to the March 24, 1960 North Korean proposal for national unification.

State of the Nation. The unrestricted freedom of speech and press granted under the new constitution permitted anyone to establish a newspaper press or magazine company with or without a printing press and/or intention to publish, or ability to do so. Consequently, the number of newspapers and periodicals increased from about 600 in early 1960 to 1,600 by April 1961. Although the circulation of these new newspapers and periodicals was small, there were some 160,000 reporters. The abuses of the freedom of association were widespread.

The 32,800-man National Police was impotent and the crime rate soared as groups of extortionists, black marketeers, gangsters and hoodlums emerged. Corruption and nepotism were rampant. Meanwhile, many colonels in the Army demanded the purification of the highly politicized military by removing inefficient and corrupt generals. In May 1960, Major General Park Chung-hee (1917–1979) in behalf of the reform minded military officers asked for the resignation of Army Chief of Staff General Song Yo-ch'an. In late May, Lieutenant General Ch'oe Kyŏng-nok replaced General Song as Army Chief of Staff, but the reform advocates within the Army were not satisfied. Meanwhile, the relationship between the new Army Chief of Staff and Lieutenant General Ch'oe Yŏng-hŭi, who was the chairman of the Joint

Chiefs of Staff, deteriorated.

A five-year development plan was adopted by the Chang administration, but it was not implemented. The government was unable to cope with the serious economic problems which were increasing. The exchange rate between the Korean currency (*hwan*) to U.S. dollar changed from 650 to 1 to 1,300 to 1. The unemployment rate grew from 24 per cent in the fall of 1960 to 26 per cent in early 1961. The wholesale price index grew from (1955 = 100) 158.7 in March to 193.3 by April 1961.

Some 2,000 demonstrations involving 900,000 persons erupted as the influence of the Communists in South Korea grew, particularly among the students. The student agitation to open direct negotiations with North Korean students for the reunification of the country caused much anxiety and turmoil. In mid-November 1960, Yŏnsei University students carried out a violent strike when the school administration refused to dismiss professors who had been Rhee's supporters, and it caused serious damages to the university.

In March and April 1961 some 74,000 teachers, students and workers of leftist organizations carried out anti-government demonstrations in Seoul, Taegu, Pusan, Masan and Kwangju. They condemned the government which could not "save the proletarian masses" while they advocated the achievement of an immediate national unification by direct negotiations between Seoul and Pyongyang. The absence of a clear majority party in the House of Representatives following the division of the ruling Democratic Party into three separate parties created many serious problems for the legislative assembly. The disappointed and disillusioned people became apathetic and indifferent. In the elections held in December 1960 for the mayor of Seoul and for provincial governors, only 38.2 per cent of the eligible voters participated.

A stronger party discipline was finally achieved by Prime Minister Chang in the early spring of 1961, and his administration made efforts to curb both corruption and public demonstrations. But it was too late as the economy plummeted and the food and job shortage worsened. The military became restless. In early May 1961, the Unified Committee of Anti-Communist Organizations was organized. It included 61 organizations of veterans, religious groups, and economic, social, and cultural groups. As the confrontation and conflict between the rightists and the leftists intensified, political atmosphere and social conditions became intolerable as the threats from the north grew.

Military Rule, 1961–63

In May 1961, a group of military officers carried out a coup and overthrew the Second Republic. With this, a military junta was established, and military controlled reform politics prevailed, bringing several significant changes.

The Military Revolution.   Many high ranking military officers became concerned with the chaotic situation that developed in the spring of 1961, and many of them were dissatisfied with the leadership of incompetent, corrupt, and highly politicized generals who crowded the top layer of the armed forces. These officers who promoted what became known as the "military purification" movement contemplated carrying out some sort of actions in early May 1960. Most of them were lieutenant colonels who were members of the 8th graduating class (1949) of the Korean Military Academy.

On May 8, 1960, they adopted a 5-item resolution for military purification. It included:

1. Punishment of top military officers who collaborated with members of the Liberal Party in rigging the 1960 presidential election.
2. Punishment of military officers who amassed wealth illegally.
3. Elimination of incompetent and corrupt commanders.
4. Political neutrality of the armed forces and elimination of factionalism within the military.
5. Improvement of treatment for military personnel.

These officers had been demanding the resignation of Army Chief of Staff Song Yŏ-ch'an. Their scheme was discovered, and six of them were investigated. Although some generals wished to punish them for their rebellious attitudes, they were quietly released. However, conflict within the ranking military officers of the Army led to the resignation of General Song on May 20, but the restlessness of the Young Turks did not subside. Instead, the military purification movement gained momentum.

In August 1960, eleven lieutenant colonels attempted to have a meeting with the Defense Minister and press for the removal of corrupt, inefficient, and highly politicized generals from the military, including Lieutenant General Ch'oe Yŏng-hŭi, chairman of the Joint Chiefs of Staff who resigned a short time later. But they were taken to the provost marshal's office and severely reprimanded for their behavior. Failing to find ways to satisfy their wishes through regular channels, they held a secret meeting in Seoul with Major General Park Chung-hee and resolved to execute a coup. One of the group was Lieutenant Colonel Kim Chong-p'il (1921–   ), better known as J.P. Kim, who was the husband of a niece of General Park himself.

In an attempt to achieve their purpose without resorting to bloody means, a group of sixteen officers who advocated military reform confronted the Army Chief of Staff on September 1960 and demanded his resignation. As a result, they were court-martialed, and in December one of them was sentenced to imprisonment, and some time later Kim Chong-p'il and one other colonel were put on reserve status. Meanwhile, General Ch'oe Kyŏng-nok resigned, and Lieutenant General Chang To-yŏng replaced Ch'oe as Army

Chief of Staff early in December 1960.

Actions taken by the Army Chief of Staff Ch'oe, before his resignation, against reform advocates only infuriated the rebellious Young Turks further, and plans were adopted by them to strike as they recruited Major General Kim Tong-ha, commander of the Marine Corps, and others into the movement. By early April 1961, some 250 revolutionaries were ready to strike under the leadership of General Park, then commander of the logistic base in Pusan.

In the predawn hours of May 16, 1961, some 1,600 troops, spearheaded by the Marines, moved into Seoul and occupied strategic points after minor clashes at the Han River bridge. Premier Chang fled from his residence and went into hiding at a Catholic convent. Seoul was quickly put under military occupation. The revolutionaries broadcasted over Radio Seoul that the military authorities had taken over the government. Martial law was declared along with a 7 p.m. to 5 a.m. curfew.

U.S. Minister Marshall Green and U.N. Commander General Carter B. Magruder learned about the military takeover by the information provided by Army Chief of Staff General Chang. After notifying Washington, they waited instructions from their government. Meanwhile, they announced that the United States supported the constitutional government of the Republic, and General Magruder urged President Yun to launch a counterrevolution as he showed his willingness to mobilize U.S. troops against some 3,500 rebel troops.

The revolutionaries organized the Military Revolutionary Committee consisting of five generals, and succeeded in soliciting the cooperation of General Chang, whose aim was to avoid bloodshed and control the revolutionaries so as to protect the constitutional system. Both President Yun and General Chang were concerned with the ever present threats of the North Korean Communists. In the morning of May 18, General Chang accepted the chairmanship of the Military Revolutionary Committee, announcing six revolutionary pledges. They were:

1. Positive, uncompromising opposition to Communism is the basis of our policy.
2. We shall respect and observe the United Nations Charter, and strengthen our relations with the United States and other Free World Nations.
3. We shall eliminate corruption, and eradicate other social evils which have become prevalent in our country; we shall inculcate fresh and wholesome moral and mental attitudes among the people.
4. We shall provide relief for poverty-stricken and hungry people, and devote our entire energies toward the development of a self-sustaining economy.
5. We shall strengthen our military power and determination to combat Communism, looking forward to the eventual achievement of our unchangeable goal of national unification.

6. As soldiers, after we have completed our mission, we shall restore the government to honest and conscientious civilians, and return to our proper military duties. As citizens, we shall devote ourselves without reservation to the accomplishment of these tasks, and to the construction of a solid foundation for a new and truly democratic republic.

While the president decided not to launch a counterrevolution, the commander of the First Army of the Republic, who could have crushed the revolutionaries, ordered his troops to maintain strict neutrality. Meanwhile, Premier Chang, who left his hiding place escorted by General Chang, held a cabinet meeting and decided to submit the resignations of his ministers *en masse*. With this the Second Republic ended its short existence.

On May 18, General Chang, chairman of the Military Revolutionary Committee, sent a message to President John F. Kennedy, explaining the motives of the military revolution and indicated the desire of the revolutionaries to maintain "the most friendly ties" with the United States. The message said in part that "Unable to let the situation deteriorate any further. . . we embarked upon the sacred revolutionary task of overthrowing the corrupt and inefficient regime and of saving the people and the country."

On May 19, Lincoln White of the U.S. State Department, read a statement, presumably approved by President Kennedy, that the United States wished to see the Korean people achieve, through the democratic processes, stability, order, constitutional government and the rule of law "without approving or disapproving the Korean revolution." However, it stated that "We are encouraged by the strong intent of the military leaders in Korea to return the government to civilian hands." A little over a week later, Minister Green informed the Korean Foreign Minister Kim Hong-il that the American government noted with satisfaction the expression of intention to return the government to civilian control. With this, any possibility of U.S. military intervention against the revolutionaries was dispersed.

The Junta Rule. The Military Revolutionary Committee was renamed the Supreme Council for National Reconstruction on May 30, and it was announced that the Supreme Council was the supreme governing organ of the nation. It was followed by the promulgation of the Law Regarding Extraordinary Measures for National Reconstruction on June 6. The revolutionary junta suspended the constitution, dissolved the National Assembly, forbade all political activities, imposed press censorship, and banned student demonstrations.

President Yun was persuaded to remain in office, and Yi Tong-wŏn was dispatched to Washington to solicit American understanding and support for the new government in Seoul. The new cabinet controlled by the junta included Premier Chang To-yŏng, Foreign Minister Kim Hong-il, and Home Minister Han Shin. Three ministers of Foreign Affairs who served in the military controlled government were Song Yo-ch'an, Ch'oe Tŏk-shin, and Kim Yong-shik, in addition to Kim Hong-il, between May 1961 to December 1963. Only Kim Yong-shik was a civilian.

The Supreme Council carried out clean-up campaigns, and some 41,000 civil servants were dismissed. Gangsters and hoodlums, along with leftists and those military officers who did not support the coup were arrested. The law promulgated on June 10 established the Central Intelligence Agency "for the purpose of countering indirect aggression of the Communist forces and to remove obstacles to the execution of the revolutionary tasks." Kim Chong-p'il became its first director. The Prosecution Law and the Anti-Communist Law were promulgated, and the Revolutionary Court was established, and a large sum of money was confiscated from some 60 individuals who amassed wealth through illicit means.

While the 30-member Supreme Council acted as a legislative body, the grip of the core group of the revolutionaries was tightened in June. General Chang, Chairman of the Supreme Council, who was concurrently the Chief of the Cabinet (premier), Minister of Defense, and Army Chief of Staff, resigned from these offices. General Song Yo-ch'an, who gave his support to the coup while in the United States, returned to Korea and replaced General Chang as Chief of Cabinet and Defense Minister in June. General Chang and three other members of the Supreme Council were arrested and tried in July. It was charged that General Chang and his supporters were engaged in the anti-revolutionary plot. General Chang was eventually given the death sentence, but was permitted to exile in the United States.

In July 1961, General Park took over the chairmanship of the Supreme Council, and in August, he announced that political activity would be permitted in early 1963 in order to pave the way for the restoration of civilian rule. His announcement was welcomed by the American government. Meanwhile, in June the Supreme Council adopted a 1962–1966 Five-Year Economic Development Plan with the goal of constructing a self-supporting economy with a 7.1 per cent annual rate of growth in the gross national product.

General Park visited the United States and Japan, and as he initiated talks between South Korea and Japan for the establishment of normal relations, he secured American support for his plans for Korea. In 1961 and 1962, South Korea received a total of $414.5 million in economic aid from the United States. Meanwhile, the government structure was modified and new ministries of Construction and Public Information, along with the Economic Planning Board, were created.

In order to accomplish what they hoped to be a "miracle on the Han River," the government carried out a currency reform in June 1962, replacing *hwan* with *wŏn*, and bank deposits were frozen temporarily. As political stability grew, economic conditions began to improve. However, the amount of currency in circulation increased by 70.2 per cent between June 1961 and

December 1963, increasing the growth rate of inflation. At the same time, large-scale financial scandals, such as "*Saenara* Datsun cases" involving a Japanese automobile firm and some members of the Supreme Council, as well as the stock market manipulations involving leading members of the junta, caused serious problems for the government.

Politics for Restoration of Civilian Rule.   In August 1961, General Park announced that a new constitution would be adopted in March and a general election would be held in May 1963 in order to establish a new government and return it to "honest and conscientious civilians." In order to accomplish this important task, on March 16, 1962, the Supreme Council promulgated the Political Activities Purification Law and banned political activities of "old politicians" for six years, until August 15, 1968. Under this law, the Political Purification Committee was established, and 2,641 persons were purged by the time the Political Purification Committee had completed its work in May 1962. Meanwhile, President Yun resigned in March in protest against the law, and General Park became acting president.

Martial law was lifted on December 5, and the revised constitution was offered for a public referendum on December 17. Hoping to achieve their democratic aspirations, 10,885,998 or 85.28 per cent of the 12.4 million registered voters cast their ballots, and the new constitution was approved by 8.3 million votes, or 78.8 per cent of votes cast. Some two million voters cast negative votes.

The amended constitution, which was promulgated on December 26, 1962, retained democratic aspirations and other democratic features of the government. However, it increased the power of the president and reduced the State Affairs Council (Cabinet) to a consultative body. The president was empowered to appoint or dismiss the prime minister without the consent of the National Assembly. He was also given the power to mobilize the military to maintain public safety and order. The term of office for president remained four years, the office of vice-president was abolished, and the office of deputy-premier was created. The new constitution also abolished the system of a bicameral legislature, and the National Assembly Election Law divided the nation into 131 single-member districts. Under the new system, 44 additional seats, or one-third of the elected membership were to be distributed in accordance with the proportion of votes received by various parties as at large seats.

The Political Party Law of December 31 was promulgated, and 273 former politicians who had been purged were freed in early 1963. With the revival of party politics, new political parties emerged in the spring of 1963. The first to emerge was the Democratic Republican Party (DRP), which was organized in the middle of January 1963 by Kim Chong-p'il with President Park as its president. Other parties which emerged were the Civil Rule Party with former President Yun Po-sŏn as its leader, the Party of the People with Hŏ Chŏng as its standard bearer, and the Justice of the People Party under the leadership of Pyŏn Yŏng-t'ae.

Two days after the new constitution was promulgated, on December 28, President Park announced that the Supreme Councillors would retire from active military duty and play an active role in the future civilian government. Meanwhile, the conflict between the hard-line group and the moderates within the junta developed. The hard-line group led by Kim Chong-p'il maintained that many revolutionary tasks had not been accomplished and it was necessary for the revolutionaries to participate in the new government as civilians. On the other hand, the moderates led by General Kim Chae-ch'un, argued against such a move insisting that the revolutionaries were obligated to honor the sixth item in the pledges which they had made in May 1961. General Song Yo-ch'an, who had supported the military coup while he was in the United States and became the Defense Minister after he returned to Korea, openly criticized General Park's intention to run in the forthcoming presidential election. Meanwhile, Marine Corps General Kim Tong-ha resigned from the Supreme Council in late January in an angry mood. The opposition groups in turn launched their attack against the military leaders and denounced the Democratic Republic Party as an illegal political organization because it was formed during the period when all political activities were banned.

In the midst of flurries of politics, President Park announced on February 18 that he would stay out of the civilian government and the presidential election would be postponed if all political parties would agree to (1) prevent reprisals against those who brought about the May 16 revolution after a civilian government was established, (2) allow retired military officers to run for public offices, (3) guarantee the status of those employed by the revolutionary government since the coup, (4) preserve the new constitution, and (5) cooperate in the Korean-Japanese negotiations for the normalization of relations.

Those conditions which President Park presented were met by civilian politicians on February 27 in an official ceremony. On that day, some 2,322 names of those who had been purged were removed from the blacklist, leaving 269 on the list. Meanwhile, Kim Chae-ch'un, leader of the moderate group within the junta who had replaced Kim Chong-p'il as director of the Central Intelligence Agency, announced on March 11 that twenty anti-revolutionaries, including Marine Corps General Kim Tong-ha, had been arrested for their plot to overthrow the revolutionary government.

A few days later, on March 15, some 90 officers and soldiers demonstrated in front of the Supreme Council building and urged the extention of military rule, the dismissal of Defense Minister Song, and General Park's participation in the presidential elections. The next day, President Park announced that military rule would be extended for four more years, and that he would ask the people's approval for his plan in a plebiscite. All political activities were once again banned and censorship of the press was imposed under a Law Concerning Temperary Measures Aimed at the Settlement of Critical Situations.

President Park's announcement and the actions taken by the government raised a storm of opposition as the U.S. government warned that prolongation of military rule in Korea could constitute a threat to stable and effective government. American Ambassador Samuel D. Berger delivered, on April 2, a reply from President Kennedy to President Park's letter in which the reasons for the proposed extension of military rule were explained. Needless to say, President Kennedy's letter was strongly opposed to President Park's plan.

Under strong American pressure and certain threats, President Park backed down, and on April 8, he lifted the ban on political activities and press censorship. On July 27, he announced that the transfer of government to civilians would be made within the year. At the same time, he made it clear that he would retire from active military duty and run for the office of president in the forthcoming election. Accordingly, he ran as the candidate of the Democratic Republican Party and former president Yun ran as the candidate of the Civil Rule Party in the 5th presidential election. Three other parties—the Democratic Party, the Liberal Democratic Party, and the Party of the People—also nominated candidates.

In the October 15, 1963 presidential election, 11 million, or 84.9 per cent of the 13 million eligible voters cast their ballots, and elected the incumbent president, who retired from active military duty a short time before, by a slim margin of 1.42 per cent. President Park received a total of 4.7 million, or 42.61 per cent of the votes cast, and his major opponent, former president Yun, received 4.5 million, or 41.19 per cent of the votes. The candidates of three other parties received a total of 831,944 votes, or 7.53 per cent of the votes cast. It is significant to note that the opposition candidates received a total of 5.3 million, or 48.72 per cent of valid votes. Had the opposition leaders been united and presented their combined front against President Park and the military junta by presenting a single candidate, they could have changed the course of political history of South Korea in 1963. Be that as it may, it was clear that the voters amply demonstrated their desires to see the development of democratic politics and the government in the hands of civilians.

The National Assembly elections were held on November 26. Some 9,622,000, or 72.1 per cent of the 13.3 million eligible voters cast their ballots. It was the lowest voter turnout in the history of the National Assembly elections.

The Democratic Republican Party won 110 (88 elected and 22 at large), or 62.9 per cent of the Assembly seats, seven seats short of the two-thirds majority. The Civil Rule Party won 41 (27 elected and 14 at large) seats, and three minor parties won a total of 24 (16 elected and 8 at large) seats. Some 24 candidates who won the Assembly seats were former military officers nominated by the Democratic Republican Party which became the ruling party and remained so until 1979.

The Third Republic, 1963–72

Civilian constitutional rule was restored on December 17, 1963, upon the inauguration of President Park Chung-hee, and with this the Third Republic was born. President Park vowed to free the nation "from century-old yokes," and to reform the nation, "with sweat, blood, and hard work."

Government and Politics.   President Park appointed a respected and an independent minded Ch'oe Tu-sŏn as premier and asked him to form a pan-national cabinet in order to unite the people, restore the people's confidence in the government, and bring about the reconstruction of the nation. Premier Ch'oe recruited able individuals into his cabinet which included Deputy-premier Kim Yu-t'aek, Foreign Minister General Chŏng Il-gwŏn, Home Minister Ŏm Min-yŏng, Finance Minister Pak Tong-gyu, Justice Minister Min Pok-ki, Education Minister Ko Kwang-man, and Minister Without Portfolio Kim Yong-shik. Only six out of fourteen ministers were members of the ruling Democratic Republican Party.

The government faced many difficulties in terms of winning the support of the people as economic conditions did not improve. The wholesale price index in Seoul rose (1960 = 100) to 113.2 in 1961, 123.8 in 1962, 149.3 in 1963, and then to 164.7 in 1964. Per capita income dropped from $87.71 in 1961 to $85.25 in 1962. The talks initiated by the military junta in 1962 in order to remove thorny issues and establish normal relations between South Korea and Japan caused serious problems for the government.

When the contents of the Kim-Ōhira Memorandum were known in March 1964, the opposition leaders and students raised havoc, accusing the government of taking a "low posture" and "humiliating stand" vis-à-vis Japan. The Kim-Ōhira Memorandum was signed by then director of the Korea CIA Kim Chong-p'il and Japanese Foreign Minister Ōhira Masayoshi following their conversations in October and November 1962. As the opposition leaders such as Yun Po-sŏn, Hŏ Chŏng, and others formed a pan-national committee in opposition to the talks between South Korea and Japan in early March, students in Seoul carried out wild demonstrations against the government and the Korean-Japanese talks during the months of March and April, and many of them were arrested.

Premier Ch'oe took conciliatory steps toward the demonstrating students and tension subsided toward the end of April when all arrested students were released. However, student demonstrations erupted again during the months of May and June following the resignation of Premier Ch'oe.

Facing many problems and under pressure from leading members of the Democratic Republican Party who advocated strong measures against the opponents of the government, President Park attempted to influence Premier Ch'oe to replace some ministers with members of the ruling party as well as to take strong measures to curb student demonstrations. Premier Ch'oe, however, refused to bend, and resigned on May 9, only four months after he formed a cabinet. President Park appointed General Chŏng Il-gwŏn (1917–   ), former Chief of Staff of the Korean Army and who had been the Minister of Foreign Affairs of the Ch'oe cabinet, to be new premier, and on May 11, a new cabinet emerged. It included Deputy-premier Chang Ki-yŏng, Home Minister Yang Ch'an-u, Foreign Minister Yi Tong-wŏn, and Education Minister Yun Ch'ŏn-ju. Finance Minister Park Tong-gyu who remained in the Chŏng cabinet was, however, replaced in June.

The resignation of Premier Ch'oe and the continued talks between Seoul and Tokyo antagonized the opposition leaders as well as politically oriented students. Despite the opposition, in late March, Kim Chong-p'il went to Tokyo to negotiate with the Japanese for a normalization treaty. Encountering growing opposition to the talks, President Park recalled Kim Chong-p'il, but student demonstrations became wilder and more widespread as students displayed anti-Japanese and anti-government attitudes and demanded the resignation of President Park himself. Tension mounted in late May, and in the evening of June 3, martial law was declared in Seoul following clashes between thousands of demonstrating students and the police during the day. Martial law was withdrawn on July 26, but the roots of anti-government movement of the students grew deeper.

In August 1964, the National Assembly enacted the Law Concerning the Security of Educational Institutions and the Law Concerning Press Ethics, causing bitter controversies between the government and the news media. The implementation of the Press Ethics Law and the creation of the Committee on Press Ethics was postponed in October due to strong opposition of the organizations of newspapers and magazine publishers, editors, and reporters, but the government established a tight control over the campus activities of the students as well as the press.

Meanwhile, the Central Intelligence Agency arrested some 40 persons in August, charging them with violation of the National Security Law. Thus, a pattern of political control by the Korean Central Intelligence Agency emerged as it effectively manipulated the students' Youth Thought Party (commonly called YTP). The YTP was originally formed in August 1960 as an anti-government secret political society of the students named the National Salvation Party (commonly called KKT), but its character changed after 1961, and it became a tool of the Korean CIA. In the midst of political turmoil, Kim Chong-p'il resigned from the chairmanship of the Democratic Republican Party.

In May 1965, the Civil Rule Party of Yun Po-sŏn and the Democratic Party of a dynamic woman political leader named Pak Sun-ch'ŏn merged, forming a new party named the Masses Party "in order to strengthen the people's struggle against corrupt and militaristic political power of the Park regime." It declared that it was "the vanguard of the struggle of the people for the restoration of freedom, and the accuser of corruptive power and economic favoritism" of the government of President Park.

Looking toward the 1967 presidential election, four opposition parties joined together and formed the New Democratic Party in February 1967 with Yu Chin-o, a respected legal scholar and president of Korea University, as its chairman. Both former president Yun and Yu Chin-o severely criticized the policies of the government. Yun, charging that the government was riddled with "corruption", irregularities and dictatorial authoritarianism," lashed out against the poor handling of economic problems and the favoritism for certain enterprises. He said that the government policy "made the rich richer and the poor poorer."

The trials of a former Seoul National University professor and others in March 1967 foretold the coming of a tough policy against dissidents. A group of Koreans, who were engaged in anti-South Korea, pro-North Korea activities in West Germany, had been abducted from West Germany in December 1966 by the agents of the Korean CIA, and death sentences were given to the leaders of the group commonly known as "the East Berlin Operation Team."

The government announced the Second Five-Year Plan for 1967-1971. This plan, like that of 1962-1966, emphasized the development of industries, particularly light industries, in order to provide more commodities which the people needed, while increasing food production. Foreign loans were sought and foreign investments in Korea were made easier so as to attract foreign investors.

In the May 3, 1967 presidential election, President Park defeated Yun, the candidate of the New Democratic Party, by a large margin (50.4 per cent to 37.7 per cent). A new National Assembly was elected on June 8, and a majority of seats were captured by the Democratic Republican Party. It secured a total of 129 seats (102 district and 27 proportional seats). The New Democratic Party won only 45 seats (28 district and 17 proportional seats). Charging election irregularities, the opposition party demanded the nullification of the election results and called for a new election. Failing in this, the members of the National Assembly belonging to the opposition party boycotted the Assembly sessions. A compromise was finally reached in early 1968 and the opposition party members returned to the National Assembly.

Meanwhile, a new cabinet was formed in June under Premier Chŏng Il-gwŏn, and in November a cabinet reshuffle took place. As of December 1967, the Chŏng cabinet included Deputy-premier Pak Ch'ung-hun, Home Minister Yi Ho, Foreign Minister Ch'oe Kyu-ha, and Justice Minister Kwŏn O-byŏng. The cabinet reshuffle which took place in May 1968 saw the appointment of Pak Kyŏng-wŏn as Home Minister, Yi Ho as Justice Minister, and Kwŏn O-byŏng as Education Minister.

Certain leaders of the Democratic Republican Party, such as Speaker of the National Assembly Yi Hyo-sang, Yun Ch'i-yŏng, and Kim T'aek-su launched a movement for a constitutional amendment in January 1969 so as to prolong "the strong and positive leadership" of President Park. However, many influential members of the ruling party, such as Kim Chong-p'il, vigorously opposed any constitutional changes. Meeting the strong opposition within and without the ruling party, particularly that of the opposition New Democratic Party and the students, Kim Hyŏng-uk, new director of the Korean CIA, exerted heavy pressure against those who were against the change and many members of the ruling party were expelled. In the midst of a new political crisis, Minister of Education Kwŏn O-byŏng was ousted in April, and in June Kim Chong-p'il himself resigned from the chairmanship of the ruling party and made another overseas trip. With this, the so-called "new main line" of the anti-J.P. (Kim Chong-p'il) groups gained strength and pushed for a constitutional amendment. Meanwhile, power struggle between the "old main line" of the J.P. groups and the "new main line" intensified.

The Amendment of the Constitution and Political Situation. The Democratic Republican Party officially approved the proposal for a constitutional amendment, and on the night of September 14, 1969, the National Assembly dominated by the members of the Democratic Republican Party and its allies passed certain changes in the constitution which allowed the incumbent president to run for a third term of office. In the national referendum held on October 17, 67.5 per cent of the voters approved the amended constitution, abolishing the two-term limitation for the presidency. The amended constitution was promulgated on October 21, and it also authorized members of the National Assembly to concurrently serve as cabinet ministers. The new constitution specified that the membership of the National Assembly was to be no less than 150 and no more than 250. It is significant to note that only 77.1 per cent of 15 million eligible voters participated in the referendum, making the turnout the lowest in the history of referendum in South Korea. Needless to say, the new constitutional amendment created bitter controversies between the ruling and opposition parties as it brought about a growing anti-government sentiments of the students who rapidly became cynical and disillusioned.

In a sudden move on October 22, 1969, President Park replaced Yi Hu-rak, chief secretary to the President, who was known as "the premier of the inner cabinet," and Kim Hyŏng-uk, director of the powerful Central Intelligence

Agency. Both of them were regarded as arch-rivals of Kim Chong-p'il, and the President's move was perhaps due to pressure coming from top leaders of the Democratic Republican Party who were the allies of Kim Chong-p'il. It was widely said that both Yi Hu-rak and Kim Hyŏng-uk were becoming too power-ful. Meanwhile, a cabinet reshuffle took place, and it was rumored that all those who were against the third term of office of the President were replaced. The new cabinet headed by Premier Chŏng Il-gwŏn included Deputy-premier Kim Hang-nyŏl, Foreign Minister Ch'oe Kyu-ha, Home minister Pak Kyŏng-wŏn, Justice Minister Yi Ho, and Education Minister Hong Chong-ch'ŏl.

Yu Chin-o, the aged chairman of the New Democratic Party, stepped down, paving the way for younger members to rise. Both Kim Yŏng-sam and Kim Tae-jung (Kim Dae-jung) sought the presidency of the party, but Yu Chin-san, a veteran politician defeated the two Kims as well as Chŏng Il-hyŏng and became the new president of the opposition party in January 1970. Be that as it may, Kim Tae-jung's star was rising rapidly, and he was nominated as presidential candidate of the New Democratic Party in September 1970 to run against the incumbent president in 1971. Kim Tae-jung campaigned vigorously, charging that the government of President Park was that of ''a highly militaristic'' and a South Korea turned into a ''police state.''

As party politics intensified, Premier Chŏng resigned in December 1970. President Park named Paek Tu-jin as new premier, and appointed Yi Hu-rak as director of the Central Intelligence Agency. Meanwhile, President Park was able to pursuade Kim Chong-p'il to return to the Democratic Republican Party and support his work for national development. In March 1971, Kim Chong-p'il became vice president of the ruling Democratic Republican Party.

The 1971 Elections.   In the 7th presidential election held on April 27, 1971, seven candidates ran for the office. A little over 12 million voters, or 83.6 per cent of the 15.5 million registered voters cast their ballots. Kim Tae-jung, nominee of the New Democratic Party, was narrowly defeated by the incumbent president by 51 per cent of votes. About 56 per cent of urban voters cast their ballots for Kim as the New Democratic Party became the party of the urban voters, particularly that of liberal intellectuals and students.

The 8th National Assembly elections were held on May 25, 1971. Some 696 candidates ran, and 11.4 million voters, or 73.2 per cent of the 15.5 million registered voters cast their ballots. The ruling party suffered a setback as it won only 113 seats (86 district and 27 proportional seats) while the major opposition New Democratic Party won 89 seats (65 district and 24 proportional seats), well over one-third of the 204 seats and became large enough to block the passage of any new constitutional amendments proposed by the ruling party.

Shortly before the inauguration of President Park for his third term of office on July 1, 1971, he appointed, on June 4, Kim Chong-p'il, as premier. The government adopted a new national slogan, which was *minjok chunghŭng,* or "the regeneration of the people," which emphasized the development of culture, economy, and a strong national spirit. The government pledged to build a strong foundation for the nation and to strengthen its defense capabilities.

During the Third Republic period, in addition to new ministries such as Construction and Public Information, which were established in 1961, the Ministry of Science and Technology, the National Security Council and the National Economic and Scientific Council were established in 1967, followed by the merger of the ministries of Public Information and Culture into Ministry of Culture and Information in 1968 and the establishment of the National Unification Board in 1969. All these additional new ministries and agencies reflected the emphasis made by the government in terms of national development, security, and the unification of Korea.

Foreign Affairs.   The Third Republic improved its relations with the United States and Japan. In May 1965, President Park visited the United States upon President Lyndon Johnson's invitation, and soon after that the agreement between South Korea and the United States regarding the dispatch of Korean troops to Vietnam was concluded despite vehement opposition of a large number of National Assemblymen, students, and intellectual and political leaders in South Korea. Although it was a losing proposition, the contribution made by several thousand South Korean troops toward American efforts made in the Vietnam War was highly praised and appreciated in the United States. For the first time, South Korea was regarded by the United States as a viable ally. Meanwhile, South Korea and the United States concluded in August 1965 an administrative agreement concerning the status of U.S. troops in Korea, thus resolving many thorny problems which had existed ever since the arrival of American troops.

The most significant accomplishment in foreign affairs was the conclusion of a normalization treaty with Japan on June 22, 1965, despite the vigorous opposition of tens of thousands of Koreans. This treaty, while settling many problems which had existed between South Korea and Japan ever since Korea was liberated from Japan, established diplomatic and economic relations between the two countries. Japan's payment of a $300 million indemnity and its $300 million long-term loan to South Korea helped the Korean government implement the new five-year economic development plan which began in 1967 and helped the economic development of South Korea.

The Third Republic expanded the foreign relations of South Korea by signing diplomatic treaties with many countries, bringing the total number of countries which established diplomatic relations with South Korea to 77. As of April 1961, only 17 nations had recognized the Republic of Korea and established diplomatic ties with her. Between May 1961 and December 1972, South Korea concluded diplomatic treaties with 60 nations, some of which were nonaligned countries. The signing of diplomatic treaties with the nonaligned nations of Asia and Africa was significant.

North-South Relations.   As the attempt made by North Korean armed commandoes to assassinate President Park on January 21, 1968 increased the animosity of the people of South Korea against the North Korean Communists, the capture of an American intelligence ship, the USS *Pueblo,* two days later by North Korean gunboats on the high seas east of the North Korean port of Wonsan created a war scare in South Korea. The situation became worse when the North Koreans shot down the U.S. reconnaissance plane EC 121, which due to a navigational error flew over North Korea near the demilitarized zone on April 15, 1969.

South Korea made various gestures to the north in order to reduce tension in the Korean peninsula. The South Korean Red Cross had been proposing to its counterpart in the north the opening of talks in order to reunite over 100,000 separated families. Some ten million people were reported to have been separated since 1945 owing to the partition of the country as well as the Korean War. The efforts made by the South Koreans resulted in an agreement, and on September 20, 1971, the representatives from each side met at Panmunjom and started negotiating.

Following a secret Pyongyang visit by South Korean CIA Director Yi Hu-rak in early May 1972, and the Seoul visit by North Korea's Second Deputy-premier Pak Sŏng-ch'ŏl in late May, on July 4 the two Korean governments issued historic statements regarding the opening of negotiations to achieve national unification by peaceful means and without outside intervention. Soon after that, the North-South Co-ordinating Committee was created, and subsequently several meetings were held in Seoul and Pyongyang in 1972 and early 1973.

The Fourth Republic, 1972–79

The Coming of the Fourth Republic.   The rapidly deteriorating situation in South Vietnam, a sudden change in U.S. Asian policy and her policy toward the People's Republic of China with the trip made by an American ping-pong team and Henry Kissinger's China visit in July 1971, coupled with the growing anti-government activities of the opposition parties and students, led President Park to take an extraordinary step in strengthening his power. Claiming that North Korea's threat to the Republic of Korea was vastly increased, on December 6, 1971, he proclaimed a National Emergency Decree in order to strengthen national defense. His action further curtailed human rights and the freedom of press. A storm of opposition against such a decree rose, but while the National Assemblymen of the opposition New Democratic Party were conducting a sit-in strike in the Assembly Hall, members of the ruling party and some Independents met in a separate room and approved the decree at 3 A.M. on December 27. All efforts made by the New Democratic Party to nullify the action taken by the ruling party and to restore parliamentary rule failed.

Many members of the ruling party and certain military leaders did not wish to see President Park step down, although he himself pledged in 1970 that he would do so after serving a third term if elected in 1971. The two five-year plans of 1962-1966 and 1967-1971 had laid a good foundation for further economic development by 1971. Many of his close advisers, including military officers, felt that the nation could not again afford to risk chaos under an untested leader who might endanger the nation's security. President Park himself may have changed his mind, and felt that he had to remain in office in order to achieve more toward national regeneration. Those who supported him argued that a strong leader with vision and dynamism should lead the nation. However, many of his own party members, including Kim Chong-p'il, did not agree with such a view.

Antagonism between the ruling party and the New Democratic Party grew as student anti-government activities increased. The New Democratic Party whose popularity was growing demanded the dismissal of the chairman of the Economic Planning Board, Home Minister O Ch'i-sŏng, and Justice Minister Shin Chik-su. Although they were able to oust only Home Minister O in October 1971, the government and the ruling party felt that their leadership was directly challenged. Some members of the ruling party who collaborated with the opposition leaders in ousting Home Minister O were expelled from the party.

The sudden changes in the international situation due to the radically altered Sino-American relations following President Richard Nixon's China visit in February 1972, and the new development in North-South relations with the issuance of the July 4th statement in 1972 by the governments in Seoul and Pyongyang to open talks between the two governments for peaceful reunification of the country, provided a convenient pretext to prolong President Park's rule. In a *coup de grâce*, the government proclaimed nationwide martial law on October 17, dissolved the National Assembly, and suspended the constitution in order to pave the way for President Park's continued rule. A new constitution proposed by the Extraordinary State Council on October 17 was put to a public referendum, and in November it received the approval of 14.4 million voters, or 91.9 per cent of the 15.7 million registered voters.

The new constitution, commonly known as the *Yushin* (Revitalizing Reform) Constitution, gave the president greatly expanded powers, authorizing him to issue emergency decrees and establish the National Conference for Unification as an electoral college. In December 1972, the 2,359 member National Conference for Unification was established, and it elected the incumbent president to serve a new six-year term. All but 2 votes were cast for President Park. With his inauguration on December 28, 1972, the Fourth Republic emerged.

Government and Politics.   The 9th National Assembly was established following the general elections held on February 27, 1973, under the new National Assembly Law of the *Yushin* Constitution. Some 399 candidates ran in the elections in which 11.2 million, or 72.9 per cent, of 15.7 million eligible voters cast their ballots and elected 146 Assemblymen, or two-thirds of the 219 seats, according to the provisions of the constitution. It was the lowest voter turnout in the history of elections for the National Assembly, reflecting the growing voter apathy. One-third of the seats were to be given to the members of a new political party called the *Yujŏnghoe,* or the Political Fraternity for Revitalizing Reform. The Democratic Republican Party won 73 elected seats, the New Democratic Party secured 52 elected seats and the Independents won 19 seats.

Meanwhile, the *Yujŏnghoe* was organized with President Park's blessings as a sister organization of the ruling party, and 73 of its members were elected by the National Conference for Unification on the president's recommendation to serve a three-year term in the National Assembly according to the provisions of the *Yushin* Constitution. Thus, President Park was assured an absolute majority of 134 legislators of the 219-member National Assembly.

Kim Chong-p'il remained in office as premier until December 1975, but frequent cabinet reshuffles took place, indicating political instability. The following list of selected cabinet ministers shows the high degree of instability of the government of the Fourth Republic.

Premiers:
Kim Chong'p'il, June 1971–December 1975
Ch'oe Kyu-ha (Acting Premier), December 1975–March 1976
Ch'oe Kyu-ha, March 1976–December 1979

Deputy-premiers:
T'ae Wan-sŏn, January 1972–May 1974
Nam Tŏg-u, September 1974–December 1978
Shin Hyŏn-hwak, December 1978–Decembe. 1979

Foreign Ministers:
Kim Yong-shik, July 1971–December 1973
Kim Tong-jo, December 1973–December 1975
Pak Tong-jin, December 1975–September 1980

Home Ministers:
Kim Hyŏn-ok, October 1971–December 1973
Hong Sŏng-ch'ŏl, December 1973–August 1974
Pak Kyŏng-wŏn, August 1974–December 1978
Ku Cha-ch'un, December 1978–September 1980

Finance Ministers:
Nam Tŏg-u, October 1969–September 1974
Kim Yŏng-hwan, September 1974–December 1978

Kim Yun-gi, December 1978–May 1980

Justice Ministers:
Shin Chik-su, June 1971–December 1973
Yi Pong-sŏng, December 1973–September 1974
Hwang San-dŏk, September 1974–December 1976
Yi Sŏng-jung, December 1976–December 1978
Kim Ch'i-yŏl, December 1978–December 1979

Education Ministers:
Min Kwan-shik, June 1971–September 1974
Yu Ki-ch'un, September 1974–December 1976
Hwang San-dŏk, December 1976–December 1977
Pak Ch'an-hyŏn, December 1977–December 1979

Only one (Education Minister Yu Ki-ch'un) was replaced because of illness. Both campus unrest and student demonstrations as well as anti-government activities of the opposition parties and groups caused frequent changes of the ministers of Education, Home Affairs, and Justice. The Ministry of Energy and Resources was established in 1977 in the wake of the oil shock.

Political and Social Turbulence.   During the Fourth Republic period, South Korea witnessed tremendous economic growth, with rapid industrial expansion and an increase in the gross national product and per capita income. The South Koreans called their economic achievement a "miracle on the Han River." However, the growing autocracy and bureaucratism of the government together with the misuse of power by the ruling Democratic Republican Party, as well as economic favoritism given to monopolistic industrial and economic institutions, caused the democratic movement to suffer much as freedom of speech and press and basic human rights were suppressed.

The government faced persistent demands for a new constitution (or the abolition of the *Yushin* Constitution), as it encountered various economic problems associated with the oil shock and a world-wide recession. The voice of the students and opposition leaders, which demanded the withdrawal of four emergency measures (decrees) which were proclaimed between January 9 and April 3, 1974, grew louder.

The kidnapping of Kim Tae-jung, the presidential candidate of the New Democratic Party who was narrowly defeated in the 1971 presidential election, by the agents of the Korean Central Intelligence Agency in August 1973 in Tokyo, created a bitter conflict between the government and the opposition New Democratic Party. Kim had been campaigning against the Park administration in the United States in 1972, and he went to Japan in the spring of 1973 and formed an alliance with anti-Park groups there, including a pro-North Korean group.

Kim Tae-jung who was abducted from Japan to Korea was imprisoned for

a long time. Needless to say, the case of Kim Tae-jung infuriated the opponents of the government as anti-government activities of the students grew
stronger. In the midst of political turbulence that developed in connection with
the kidnapping of Kim, a Korean from Japan who was allegedly sent by the
North Korean Communists to Seoul, attempted to assassinate President Park
on August 15, 1974, as he was making a speech commemorating the liberation
of Korea from Japan and the establishment of the Republic of Korea. The
assassin's bullets missed him, but Madame Yuk Yŏng-su, wife of President
Park, was killed.

In the wake of the tragic death of his wife, and for the sake of promoting
national unity, President Park repealed two of his emergency decrees in August
and two others in October. Following this, the opposition New Democratic
Party and certain other segments of the population pressed more strongly for a
new constitution and freedom of speech, press and assembly.

In January 1975, President Park announced that a national referendum
would be held to determine the fate of the 1972 constitution. His aim was to
end the debate over the *Yushin* Constitution and the legitimacy of his rule. He
said that if it was rejected by the people he would promptly resign. The
national referendum held in February affirmed his rule and upheld the 1972
constitution, but the opposition groups did not end their anti-government
activities. As a result, the National Assembly passed a bill forbidding the people
to criticize their government to foreigners as the Central Intelligence Agency
and the police tightened their control. On May 13, a new Emergency Measure
No. 9 was instituted by the government, banning any agitation for constitutional revision or anti-government activity.

The power struggle between the "old main line" of Kim Chong-p'il and the
"non-main line" group within the ruling party created many problems for
President Park. In the end, he dismissed Premier Kim in December 1975 and
appointed Ch'oe Kyu-ha, who had no party affiliations, as acting premier in
December, and made him premier in March 1976. Deputy-premier Nam Tŏg-
u remained in the office until December 1978 when he was replaced by Shin
Hyŏn-hwak. In February 1976, the National Conference for Unification elected
73 new *Yujŏnghoe* members to the National Assembly.

In July 1978, the National Conference for Unification reelected President
Park to serve six more years by a vote of 2,578. All the delegates cast their
ballots for President Park, making his rule seemingly perpetual. A storm of
criticism against his perpetual rule gathered force as public unrest, particularly
that of the students, grew. As campus demonstrations increased in number,
secret agents of the Central Intelligence Agency were planted at colleges and
universities, and clashes between the students and anti-riot units of the
National Police became frequent. A growing number of students were arrested
and prosecuted.

The general elections for the 10th National Assembly were held on

December 12, 1978, in a worsened political atmosphere. A total of 470 candidates ran for the 154 seats, or two-thirds of the expanded 231-member Assembly. One-third of them was to be filled by members of the *Yujŏnghoe*. Among the candidates were 77 of the Democratic Republican Party, 81 of the New Democratic Party, 60 of the Democratic Unification Party which was established in 1973, and the rest were Independents.

Only 77.1 per cent, or 15 million voters out of the 19.5 million registered voters, cast their ballots, and they gave a victory to the opposition New Democratic Party. The opposition party increased the number of its Assemblymen from 52 to 61 while the ruling Democratic Republican Party won only 68 seats, losing 5 seats. The significant fact was that the opposition party received 32.8 per cent of the vote cast against 31.7 per cent of the ruling party. Those who ran on independent tickets won 22 seats while the Democratic Unification Party won only 3 seats, one more than it had won in February 1973.

Foreign Affairs.   The fall of South Vietnam, the growing criticism of the Americans against human rights violations by the Korean government, and President Jimmy Carters's plan to withdraw the ground troops of the United States from South Korea caused grave concerns for national security. U.S.-Korean relations became strained in connection with the kidnapping of Kim Tae-jung, coupled with Congressional investigation of activities of Korean officials and businessmen in the United States in what became known as the Koreagate affair.

The Korean government made reluctant concessions to the American government, and it cooperated in Congressional investigations of Koreans such as former Ambassador to the United States, Kim Tong-jo, and a Korean businessman named Pak Tong-sŏn. With this, U.S.-Korean relations improved somewhat, but criticism of the United States against the South Korean government for its human rights violations did not cease. The Americans, particularly leaders of the Democratic Party, maintained their pressure on the Korean government as President Park displayed certain anti-American feelings. Following President Carter's Korea visit in June 1979, the thorny issue of troops withdrawal was solved to the satisfaction of the Korean government as President Carter withdrew his plan for troop withdrawal.

Be that as it may, the Fourth Republic expanded diplomatic ties with more countries, particularly with nonaligned nations. It concluded diplomatic treaties with four Asian nations, including India and Indonesia between 1972 and 1977, with five African nations, including Ghana and Sudan between 1976 and 1979, with Finland in 1973, with four states of south and central America, and with four nations of Oceania, bringing the total number of nations which recognized the Republic of Korea and established diplomatic relations to 95 at the end of 1979. Meanwhile, South Korea signed postal agreements with five Communist countries, including Yugoslavia and Czechoslovakia in September

1979, marking a significant turning point in South Korea's foreign policy toward Communist states. The government had earlier announced that it would establish ties with "non-hostile" Communist states, and it carried out its promise in 1979. Trade relations with the People's Republic of China were established on unofficial grounds and a few government officials visited the Soviet Union.

North-South Relations.   The unilateral suspension of the north-south political talks by the North Korean regime on August 28, 1973, shattered the hopes for easing tension in the Korean peninsula and an early peaceful reunification of the divided nation by the Koreans themselves. However, President Park repeatedly made appeals to the North Korean regime to resume the talks. The North Korean regime not only rejected President Park's August 1974 and January 1975 proposals, but also cut off the Seoul-Pyongyang direct telephone line in August 1976.

On January 19, 1979, President Park proposed bilateral talks "without any precondition, to be held at any time, at any place, and at any level." Pyongyang responded favorably, and delegates from both sides met at Panmunjom on February 17, but they accomplished nothing as the North Koreans called for wide representation from both the north and the south as well as from the overseas Koreans. At the same time, they insisted that the Democratic Front for the Reunification of the Fatherland of North Korea should be expanded so as to include South Korean delegates and some overseas Koreans and replace the defunct North-South Coordinating Committee.

The proposal made jointly in July 1979 by Seoul and Washington for the three-way talks to ease the tension was rejected by the North Korean regime stating that the problem of Korean reunification should be solved by the Koreans themselves without outside interference. Following this, North Korea accelerated its anti-South Korean propaganda as it increased subversive activities against the south. Meanwhile, North Korea sent several commando units into the south, causing bloodshed and property destruction.

The Fall of the Fourth Republic.   Despite unprecedented economic development and greater prosperity than the Republic had ever before experienced, the absence of certain political liberties, coupled with rising inflationary trends, caused the growth of political and social unrest, and of labor disputes. While the opposition New Democratic Party and certain student groups and religious leaders were promoting a political reform movement in order to secure more human rights and freedoms, factory and mine workers launched a drive to better their wages and working conditions.

The arrests in March 1979 of former president Yun Po-sŏn, Kim Tae-jung, who had been released from a prison in December 1978, a religious leader Ham Sŏk-hŏn, and a few others in connection with their anti-government activities, created a new political crisis. Meanwhile, the New Democratic Party elected Kim Yŏng-sam as its new president in June.

The police raid on the headquarters of the New Democratic Party in downtown Seoul brought about the August 11 Incident, heightening political tension. The police stormed the building which had been occupied by some 170 striking female workers of the Y.H. Trading Company who sought the help of the New Democratic Party, and carried out brutal actions against the workers. Bitter charges were lodged against the police, the government, and the ruling party which supported the police action. Public opinion was strongly critical of the police, as Kim Yŏng-sam, the outspoken new president of the New Democratic Party, launched a new attack against the government of President Park.

In a conciliatory mood, the government released some 871 political prisoners on August 15, including some 60 professors and college students, but the anti-government movement did not subside. In the meantime, the National Assembly, which had weathered a political storm in late March in connection with the election of Paek Tu-jin of the *Yujŏnghoe* as Speaker of the Assembly, encountered another storm in October when the Assemblymen of the ruling party and the *Yujŏnghoe* unanimously voted to expel Kim Yong-sam from the National Assembly, charging him with committing anti-state acts. In the wake of this unfortunate event, all lawmakers of the New Democratic Party and the Democratic Unification Party tendered their resignation *en masse* on October 13 in protest against the expulsion of Kim Yŏng-sam. Meanwhile, the government ordered the suspension of Kim Yŏng-sam's presidency of the party. With these actions the political situation rapidly deteriorated as economic conditions worsened due to the rise of oil price and the growth of world-wide recession.

Riding the new tide of political current, several thousand university students in Pusan first held campus rallies, and then poured into streets, clashing with the police on October 16. The situation in Pusan became worse, and martial law was proclaimed on October 17, following violent and bloody clashes between the police and students, which involved death and destruction of property. Student demonstrations spread to the other southern cities of Masan and Ch'angwŏn, and garrison decrees were issued in those cities. The nation witnessed the most serious student uprising in fifteen years after 1960.

Meanwhile, the opposition parties accelerated their anti-government activities, and college students in Seoul became restless while students in such cities as Taegu, Kwangju, and Ch'ŏngju launched anti-government movements. It was rumored that an unmanageable situation would develop in Seoul if tens of thousands of college and high school students in the capital joined students in other cities and initiated a new crisis.

In the midst of this tense situation, President Park was shot and killed by Kim Chae-gyu, director of the Central Intelligence Agency, on October 26.

Evidently, there had been a bitter power struggle between Ch'a Chi-ch'ŏl, chief of the Security Guard of the Blue House (presidential mansion), and Kim Chae-gyu. The worsening of the political situation in 1979, and the eruption of violent student demonstrations in southern cities brought about a serious political crisis within the government, and the director of the CIA was blamed for not being able to either prevent or control such violent student activities. Kim's possible dismissal was rumored.

When President Park was shot by Kim at a dinner, Ch'a was also killed by Kim, and a half dozen other staff members of the Blue House were assassinated. Kim Chae-gyu claimed that he killed the president in order to end the one-man rule and restore democracy in the country. A limited martial law was proclaimed, and Prime Minister Ch'oe Kyu-ha became acting president.

The news of the violent death of the President shocked and bewildered the people. A profound gloom engulfed the nation. The people mourned the death of the president, and they regretted that such violence should end the life of a man who had done so much for the nation, his authoritarian rule notwithstanding. Tension rose and the nation felt a threat of imminent military aggression by North Korea as its troop movements were widely reported.

The Interim Period, 1979–81

The restoration of national stability became the most urgent task. Whereas Acting President Ch'oe disclosed that a new president would be elected under the existing constitution, many, including Kim Yŏng-sam of the New Democratic Party, made it known that they would oppose such a procedure. They demanded the cancellation of the Emergency Decree No. 9, the abolition of the *Yushin* Constitution, and the immediate adoption of a new constitution. The ruling Democratic Republican Party, which had lost its helmsman, supported the government plan, and it elected Kim Chong-p'il as its new president. Meanwhile, the demands grew louder for the cancellation of the October 27 decree which closed the schools, for the release of all political prisoners, and for freedom of speech and press.

General Chŏng Sŭng-hwa, the Martial Law Commander, cancelled the school closing decree on November 16, as Acting President Ch'oe repeatedly made it known that a new president would be elected under a new constitution which would be adopted early in 1980. Meanwhile, many political prisoners, including Kim Tae-jung, Yun Po-sŏn, and Ham Sŏk-hŏn, who had been arrested in March, were released.

In early December 1979 the National Assembly unanimously approved a recommendation calling for the retraction of the Emergency Decree No. 9 of May 1975. In the midst of political turmoil and uncertainties, the National

Conference for Unification elected Ch'oe as the new president of the Republic on December 6, and Ch'oe quickly formed a new cabinet headed by Prime Minister Shin Hyŏn-hwak. With this, the Fourth Republic period officially ended.

On the night of December 12, Major General Chun Doo-hwan (1931–   ), Commander of the Defense Security Command, ousted General Chŏng Sŭng-hwa. General Yi Hŭi-sŏng replaced General Chŏng as Army Chief of Staff, and with the rise of General Chun as a new strong man in South Korea, many generals retired, paving the way for younger officers to move up to higher ranks. The December 12 incident raised a serious issue between the commander of the United States forces in Korea and General Chun because of his mobilization of troops without the authorization of the commander of the U.S.-Korean Combined Forces Command, which was established in November 1978, with the commander of the U.S. Eighth Army as commander of the combined forces. Therefore, any troop movement of Korean troops without the approval of the commander of the combined forces was regarded as illegal. However, the United States, recognizing particular situation in Korea, raised no serious objection.

Growing Problems.   The people on the whole displayed a remarkable degree of self-restraint, and political stability seemed to be restored. The political turmoil that followed the death of President Park, however, initiated a sudden economic crisis resulting from a sharp decline of production, a rise of prices, and a decline in exports. While General Chun was exercising power behind the scene, President Ch'oe and Prime Minister Shin seemed to be vacillating. Although President Ch'oe repeatedly said that a new constitution would be adopted and a new government would be established in early 1980, various indications were that he and Shin were attempting to prolong the life of the interim government in order to build their own political base, and possibly be re-elected. Meanwhile, the National Assembly and the government each claimed the right to write a new constitution. Public hearings on the new constitution were held in Seoul and elsewhere.

The people, particularly university students, became more and more impatient with the slow pace of the political reform program. Problems at various university and college campuses multiplied and became troublesome when those professors and students who had been expelled from universities during the Park period, because of their anti-government activities, were allowed to return to their former positions. "Campus-cleanup" was their slogan, as the students demanded the purgation of those professors who had collaborated with the Park government, the end of the practice of placing students under surveillance, and reform in the system of selecting corps commanders and staff members of the Student Defense Corps.

Minister of Education Kim Ok-kil, former president of Ewha Woman's

University and an outspoken champion of academic freedom and the independence of institutions of higher education from government interference, directly and indirectly encouraged democratization of university affairs. She met many of the students' demands, as their struggle to end the compulsory military training of students picked up momentum.

 In March 1980, full rights of citizenship were restored to 687 political prisoners who had been released after the "end of the *Yushin* rule." Included in this group were former President Yun, Kim Tae-jung, and Ham Sŏk-hŏn. Meanwhile, the rivalries among the "Three Kims"—Kim Chong-p'il, Kim Tae-jung, and Kim Yŏng-sam—became intense, each vying for the presidency of a new government that was to be established under a new constitution.

The political atmosphere became turbulent in the spring of 1980 as the two major political parties (the ruling Democratic Republican Party and the opposition New Democratic Party) were embroiled in the so-called purgation movement which was launched by younger members of both parties. The anti-establishment movement of the ruling DRP was highly damaging to the party itself as an open rebellion against the leadership of its president, Kim Chong-p'il, was followed by a retaliatory step taken by the party elders against the rebels in the party.

The general political situation became increasingly murky. Charges and countercharges were exchanged between the National Assembly and the government while the two major parties were locked in serious internal power struggles as well as against each other. All attempts to bring back Kim Tae-jung into the New Democratic Party failed as the rivalry between him and Kim Yŏng-sam grew bitter. At the same time, the appointment of General Chun as Acting Director of the Central Intelligence Agency (without relinquishing his post as Commander of the Defense Security Command) in April created a sharp reaction among politically conscious people and intellectuals. In an uncertain and confusing political atmosphere and rapidly deteriorating economic condition, some 3,000 coal miners at the Sabuk mine went on a rampage, clashing with the police in late April. The miners' strike, which caused a considerable amount of property damage, was settled, but labor unrest created an extremely serious situation. Between April and mid-May, some 80,000 workers of 176 industrial establishments staged sit-ins and strikes, worsening the already badly deteriorated economy.

The demands for the early adoption of a new constitution, the end of martial law, and the resignation of General Chun as Acting Director of the Central Intelligence Agency grew louder. Several thousand university students in Seoul, Chŏnju, and Taejŏn held campus rallies and clashed with the police in early May. On May 9, Kim Yŏng-sam and Kim Tae-jung, representing the voice of the opposition, urged the government to cancel martial law and suspend its plans to revise the constitution and to call a National Assembly session.

The government reply to these demands was vague, evasive, and unresponsive. It asked self-restraint and patience on the part of the people. Meanwhile, President Ch'oe left for a six-day tour of two Middle Eastern countries on May 10. On May 14 and 15, some 100,000 students from 45 universities in the country demonstrated in force and their street actions grew so strident and riotous as to paralyze public security.

Student disturbances peaked in Seoul on May 15, when about 72,000 students filled the City Hall and the Seoul Railway Station Plaza far into the night, raided police substations, burned police vehicles, and hurled stones and Molotov cocktails at policemen, injuring some 600 of them and killing one. The slogans shouted by rioting students grew more and more extreme. Some of them, such as "expel comprador capitalists and the military clique," "repeal the anti-Communist and National Security Laws," and "create a unified socialist state," clearly indicated that Communists operating in South Korea were among those who instigated student distrubances to foment uprisings and, ultimately, overthrow the Republic.

Student representatives from 55 universities and colleges met at Ewha Woman's University on May 16 and 17 and issued an ultimatum for the repeal of martial law by May 22, and they warned that failure by the government to meet their demand would bring about violent countrywide demonstrations and uprisings, even at the risk of clashes with the military. Meanwhile, it was reported that the two major parties were launching a movement to lift martial law and that the ruling Democratic Republican Party would call for the dissolution of the government's Constitution Revision Deliberation Council and advance the government's schedule for political reform.

Facing a possible collapse of law and order, the government extended its limited martial law to nationwide one, and the Martial Law Command issued the Emergency Decree No. 10 on May 18. Under this decree, political leaders such as Kim Chong-p'il and Kim Tae-jung were arrested, and Kim Yŏng-sam was put under house arrest. Some 26 other individuals were reported to have been arrested. With this, all political activities were prohibited, colleges were closed, and the National Assembly was indefinitely suspended.

The turmoil that erupted on May 18 in the city of Kwangju, capital of South Chŏlla Province, was the largest and severest regional disturbance in the history of the Republic after 1950. A demonstration started by some 200 students of Chŏnnam and Chosŏn universities in that city snowballed into an uncontrollable disturbance as citizens of Kwangju were aroused by the news of the arrest of Kim Tae-jung, whose political base was located in the province. From May 19 to 22, some 200,000 citizens and students clashed with police and military forces. The rebels occupied government offices, including the Provincial Administration Building and the Korean Broadcasting System building. They seized police stations and Homeland Reserve Force armories, and appropriated weapons and ammunition. A full-fledged rebellion began.

Efforts made by the rebels and the military to resolve the Kwangju case brought no satisfactory results. On May 20, the cabinet ministers resigned *en masse.* President Ch'oe hurriedly returned to Korea, and named Pak Ch'ung-hun to form a new cabinet. On May 22, paratroopers stormed Kwangju and subjugated the rebellion, but the insurrection resulted in the death of several hundreds and several hundreds were wounded. The tragic Kwangju incident wrote another bloody chapter in modern Korean history.

On May 24, Kim Chae-gyu and four others who had been involved in the assassination of President Park and his aide, were hanged. On May 22 the State Affairs Council formed the Special Committee for National Security Measures (*Kukpowi*) in order to facilitate cooperation and coordination between the government and the Martial Law Command. The Special Committee was composed of eight cabinet ministers, including the prime minister and deputy prime minister, director of the Central Intelligence Agency, chief secretary to the president, the Martial Law Commander, Chairman of the Joint Chiefs of Staff, Chiefs of Staff of the Army, Navy, and Air Force, Commander of the Defense Security Command and ten other members appointed by the president. General Chun Doo-hwan was appointed by the president as chairman of the Special Committee.

The Standing Committee of the Special Committee for National Security Measures was headed by the chairman appointed by the President from among the Special Committee members, and it had 13 subcommittees. Each subcommittee oversaw appropriate ministers of the government. General Chun was named chairman of the Standing Committee. The fundamental objectives of the Special Committee were: the buttressing of national security preparedness in the face of rapidly shifting situations at home and abroad, the paving of the way for political development by securing social stability, and the establishment of national discipline by eradicating corruption, irregularities and other social ills.

The Special Committee adopted measures to accomplish these objectives. One of its achievements was the elimination of those political leaders who were regarded as corrupt and had accumulated wealth through illegal means. Many key leaders of both major parties were indicted and were forced to retire from active political life. The Committee also launched an ambitious social purification drive to uproot corrupt and irregular practices and to create an atmosphere where political development could be accomplished. Some 2,000 government officials, and officials of state-financed organizations and other affiliated agencies were dismissed, some 2,000 hooligans, smugglers, mobsters, gamblers, and other lawbreakers were arrested and sent to reeducation centers, and the publication permits of some 172 "harmful" and "undesirable" periodicals were cancelled.

General Chun, who resigned the acting directorship of the Central Intelligence Agency in early June, stated in early August that the Republic needed a new generation of leaders to build a democratic welfare society. He insisted that without uprooting injustice, irregularities and corruption, the nation could not make progress and promote justice.

The Emergence of the Fifth Republic

Under the tight political control and stern social purification measures of the Special Committee, stability began to return as students remained inactive. Meanwhile, hunting for those who were responsible for the Kwangju insurrection began as the citizens of Kwangju themselves launched their restoration and reconstruction drive in cooperation with the government. Economic recovery was slow in coming due to various domestic and foreign factors. It was reported that the GNP growth of the first six months of 1980 was a negative 4.5 per cent. The rate of unemployment rose as did the price of commodities.

President Ch'oe suddenly stepped down from the presidency on August 16, 1980, taking the blame for the misfortune that struck the nation. In his farewell address, he stated that he decided to step down in order to "put an end to the unhappy political history by establishing the precedent of peaceful transfer of power," and "to provide a historic turning point for the building of a new, happy community of stability, morality and prosperity. . .". His intention was reported to be the shortening of the transition period. It was reported that his resignation was timed to coincide with "the emergence of a fresh and creative force which has played a decisive role in protecting the nation's survival amid numerous challenges and trials from within and without after the October 26 incident last year."

No sooner had President Ch'oe resigned than there was a movement to elect General Chun, who had recently retired from active military duty after being promoted to a four-star general. Members of the National Conference for Unification from various districts nominated General Chun, and on August 27 he was elected president by 2,524 votes cast by the delegates of the electoral college. One vote was declared invalid. On September 2, General Chun was inaugurated as the new president of the Republic, marking the beginning of a new era. On that day, an all-civilian cabinet emerged with Dr. Nam Tŏg-u, an American-educated economist, as premier.

In his inaugural address, President Chun reaffirmed that his goal was to build a "democratic welfare state" in the 1980s, and that a new "efficient constitution" would be put to a referendum in October at the latest, and elections under the new constitution would be conducted in early 1981 to inaugurate a new government and the Fifth Republic. He promised that political activities would be allowed to be resumed after the adoption of the new constitution, and martial law would be lifted as soon as the political situation became stabilized.

Meanwhile, Kim Tae-jung, who had been charged by the Martial Law

Command for his anti-state activities and his Communist connection, was indicted along with 23 conspirators by the general court-martial. They were specifically charged with the suspicion of plotting a rebellion and violation of the martial law decrees. Kim was also charged with the crime of inciting student uprisings in Seoul and elsewhere and inciting the Kwangju insurrection. He was given the death sentence on September 17 and others who were involved in the Kwangju incident received 2 to 20-year prison sentences.

In mid-September, all colleges and universities which had been closed since May were reopened, and students returned to their schools in a relatively calm atmosphere with an enthusiasm to make up the losses. The National Assembly, which had long been in recess, held its final full session on September 22, and after approving the appointment of the prime minister and the chairman of the Office of Audit, it went into recess. On September 30, the government made the draft of the new constitution public and announced that a national plebiscite would be held on October 22, on the new constitution, which would mark the beginning of the Fifth Republic. The government also announced that until the new legislative assembly was formed under the new constitution, a new Legislative Council for National Security would function as a legislative organ of the state.

In early October, the new constitution, which included 131 articles and 10 supplementary provisions, was offered to the voters for study. The overall aim of the constitution was the creation of "a democratic welfare society brimming with hope and vitality." It proposed to limit the term of office of the president to one seven-year term, increased the power of the National Assembly, curtailed certain emergency powers of the president, and strengthened the rights of the people. It was regarded as the most democratic constitution of the Republic of Korea.

On October 22, some 19.5 million (95.5 per cent) of the qualified voters participated in the plebiscite, and approved the new constitution by an overwhelming 91.6 per cent majority of 17.8 million votes. The voter turnout was the largest in the history of Korean elections.

Following the promulgation of the new constitution on October 27, 1980, the National Assembly, the National Conference for Unification (which had been an electoral college since 1973), the Special Committee for National Security Measures, as well as all existing political parties, were dissolved. It was disclosed that new political parties, including one of the government, would be formed before the presidential and National Assembly elections in the spring of 1981.

Meanwhile, the 81-member Legislative Council for National Security, which was established immediately after the promulgation of the new constitution, replacing the Special Committee for National Security Measures, began to function as a legislative body of the Republic. Its members, who were appointed by President Chun, included twenty politicians, eight legal specialists, eight religious leaders, four women representatives, one labor leader, nine cultural, educational, and social leaders, three journalists, two representatives of veterans' organizations, and ten who had been members of the defunct Special Committee for National Security Measures. It was a pan-national body.

Under the Special Law for Political Renovation of November 12, 1980, 835 persons among 7,066 individuals, who were screened by the Political Renovation Committee, were banned from participating in political activities until the end of June 1988. Among them were 210 ex-lawmakers, 254 office holders of political parties, and professors and writers. Noted persons on the blacklist were Kim Chong-p'il, Kim Tae-jung, Kim Yŏng-sam, Yi Hyo-sang, Chŏng Il-gwŏn, and Paek Tu-jin.

The Martial Law Command issued a proclamation on January 10, 1981, announcing the restoration of the freedom of political activity as of January 12. With this, the movement to form new political parties began, and the Democratic Justice Party emerged first as the dominant party with President Chun as its president. The Democratic Korea Party emerged as the major opposition party, and the Korean National Party was formed as the third voice in politics. Among the minor parties was the Democratic Socialist Party. Meanwhile, in early February, President Chun visited the United States on President Ronald Reagan's invitation, and he received the support of the American president for his plans to make South Korea a more progressive and better society for the people.

On February 11, elections were held to form a new electoral college—National Conference for Unification—of 5,278 members. Some 15.6 million voters, or 78.1 per cent of 19,967,267 eligible voters cast their ballots. As expected, the Democratic Justice Party won the majority in the electoral college, and on February 25 the incumbent president was elected by the body to serve a single seven-year-term of office as the first president of the Fifth Republic.

On March 3, President Chun was inaugurated and thereby the Fifth Republic emerged in South Korea. In his inaugural address, he reaffirmed his pledge to build a "democratic welfare society" and promised that he would regard it his sacred duty to free the nation and the people from what he called "three great evils"—the threat of war, political repression and abuse of power, and poverty. He also declared "we cannot let an individual or a small group alone bear responsibility for the destiny of our people and country." He added that new leaders must continually emerge if creation, innovation and progress are to be sustained. He concluded that "the days when an individual or a small group of leaders could shape the course of history are gone."

A special amnesty was issued, and 5,221 prisoners were freed; the death sentence which had been given to KimTae-chjung,was commuted to life imprisonment, ex-Army Chief Chŏng Sŭng-hwa who had been imprisoned was released, and the prison term of Kim Kye-wŏn, former secretary to the late President Park who had been implicated in Park's death, was reduced.

GOVERNMENT STRUCTURE OF THE REPUBLIC OF KOREA (December 1982)

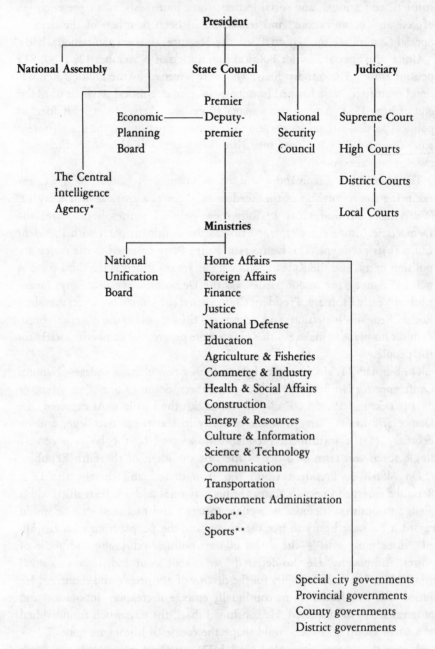

President

National Assembly   **State Council**   **Judiciary**

Premier

Economic————Deputy-   National   Supreme Court
Planning   premier   Security
Board   Council   High Courts

The Central   District Courts
Intelligence
Agency*   Local Courts

Ministries

National   Home Affairs
Unification   Foreign Affairs
Board   Finance
                      Justice
                      National Defense
                      Education
                      Agriculture & Fisheries
                      Commerce & Industry
                      Health & Social Affairs
                      Construction
                      Energy & Resources
                      Culture & Information
                      Science & Technology
                      Communication
                      Transportation
                      Government Administration
                      Labor**
                      Sports**

                                              Special city governments
                                              Provincial governments
                                              County governments
                                              District governments

*The Central Intelligence Agency was renamed in 1982 as the Agency for National
Security Planning.
**Established in April 1981 and March, 1982, respectively.

On March 25, elections were held to elect 276 members of the new National Assembly. Some 16 million voters, or 78.4 per cent of 19.9 million eligible voters cast their ballots. As a result, the Democratic Justice Party won 61 proportional representative seats and 90 district representative seats, thereby constituting the majority party in the National Assembly. The Democratic Korea Party won 24 proportional seats and 57 district seats each, and the Korean National Party won 7 proportional seats and 18 district seats each. The remaining 19 seats were taken by five minor parties and 11 Independents. The result of the 1981 National Assembly elections showed a certain change in generation in the political circle. Unlike in the past, the new National Assembly seats were taken by younger people. Those in their forties won 60.3 per cent of the seats whereas those in their fifties won 27.8 per cent. Those in their sixties won only 5.4 per cent of the seats, and only five per cent of the seats were taken by those in their seventies. Another significant fact which emerged in the wake of the National Assembly elections was that 181 persons, or 98.4 per cent of 184 district representatives were college graduates.

As younger people constituted a majority in the National Assembly, the posts of cabinet ministers and bureau chiefs in the government were also given to the persons in their forties and fifties. These trends clearly indicated that President Chun, who was 50 years old in 1981, had decided to let the new generation chart destiny of the Republic. Meanwhile, in the middle of April, Chŏng Nae-hyŏk was elected as Speaker of the National Assembly.

With the establishment of the Fifth Republic, a new struggle for democracy began, and the New Community Movement was accelerated to construct a democratic welfare society in South Korea.

12. National Development and Modern

Transformation in South Korea

Korea, which had been a feudal society, was kept by the Japanese as an underdeveloped country. Her people were politically untrained, her economy was backward, and her society was tradition-bound. This state of the Korean nation was one of the reasons for President Franklin D. Roosevelt to propose putting former colonies, including Korea, under allied trusteeships for 30 or more years in order to educate and train them to be able to enjoy their national independence and make political, social, economic and cultural progress.

Following the establishment of the Republic of Korea, however, the Koreans in the south brought about a remarkably rapid national development and modern transformation of their country despite its feudalistic heritage, shortage of trained personnel, and lack of resources and technology. Arduous and determined efforts made by the Koreans themselves, together with assistance given to them by the United States and other democratic nations enabled the Koreans to achieve what they proudly called "the miracle on the Han River" during the decades of the 1960s and 1970s. At the same time, they were able to make many changes in political, cultural, and social areas, making their country a modern and industrial nation.

Political Change

To be sure, South Korea did not become a "beacon of light of democracy" as some Americans hoped. The bureaucratic political heritage and the feudalistic social order of the past, the legacies of Japanese colonial rule, and the division of the country constituted insurmountable obstacles to the promotion of

474

democratic institutions and a new way of life. As an American writer pointed out in 1948, most Koreans were still "living with the mental heritage of the Yi Dynasty."

The authoritarian regime fostered a "guided democracy," and often the freedom and rights of the citizens were violated. However, the seeds of democracy planted in South Korea grew despite its hostile soil and stormy political climate. So long as their civil rights were guaranteed in the basic document of the nation, the democratic aspirations of the people persisted and the struggle for democracy continued.

Basic Problems for Democratization. It was generally anticipated that the Republic of Korea was to be a democratic nation, but there were many apparent and hidden obstacles. Some of them were historical in character, such as feudalistic patterns, as well as the legacy of Japanese colonialism; others were social and economic problems which were newly created by the division of the country.

The political atmosphere was always turbulent and unstable as were economic and social conditions. Korea's political culture which had long been associated with authoritarian rule was incompatible with democratic ideals. The gap between the idealistic aspirations and the realities was too wide to overcome, and such incongruity and disparity caused tension and disturbances rather than harmony and stability.

The constitution itself was the source of problems. Although it guaranteed basic freedoms and rights of citizens, it provided various tools for the president to use against the proponents of democracy. Article 13 stated that "citizens should not, *except as specified by law,* be subjected to any restrictions on the freedom of speech, press, assembly, and association." However, Article 28 allowed the government to enact laws restricting the liberties and rights of citizens *when necessary for the maintenance of public order or the welfare of the country*, and Article 57 gave the government the right to "issue orders having the effect of law" and to take necessary financial dispositions in time of civil war or other crises without the authorization of the National Assembly. President Rhee made liberal use of the latitude which these articles provided.

Because of these exceptions, the constitution became a mere democratic document, and disparity between what political leaders said and what their actions showed became greater, creating cynicism, distrust and outright antagonism among the people against the government and politicians. Democratic formalities were maintained and presidential elections and elections for the National Assembly were regularly held, even during the war. President Syngman Rhee himself habitually remarked that Korea was the "bulwark of democracy in the east." However, the lawmakers and government officials, as well as political party leaders were not equipped to accomplish democratic goals. Most political leaders were either born in the 19th century

and had been immersed in traditional political and social concepts and practices, or were born toward the end of the Yi dynasty and grew up and received
their indoctrination and training during the Japanese colonial period.

President Rhee, "the Father of the Republic," was born in 1875 as a distant
relative of the founding clan of the Yi dynasty. After fleeing to the United
States, he earned a bachelor's degree from George Washington University, a
master's degree from Howard, and a doctorate degree in International Relations from Princeton University when Woodrow Wilson was its president. Dr.
Rhee was an autocrat with rich democratic rhetoric. He was the president of a
republic with imperial trappings. He did not tolerate any opposition, ruling
the nation with his personal charisma. He was surrounded by men who were
willing to obey his commands, and he demanded absolute loyalty from his
followers. Many of his supporters were corrupt and incompetent, and they
freely exercised nepotism and favoritism.

Those who came after him did not tolerate any opposition either, and were
surrounded by men who were willing to obey their commands. They, like Rhee,
demanded absolute loyalty from their followers. New politicians were equally
corrupt, incompetent, dishonest, freely exercising nepotism and favortism. An
overwhelming self-righteousness (*toksŏnjuŭi* in Korean) was a trade mark of
political leaders.

Above all, the threats of Communism and the Korean War and its aftermath
created extremely unfavorable political, economic, and social conditions in
South Korea for the development of democracy. Since the emergence of a
Communist regime in the north, the supreme national concern had been the
security of the nation and not the promotion of democracy. Even economic and
cultural movements were intertwined with national security considerations.
Consequently, the people's struggle for democracy suffered.

Although its power was weak vis-à-vis the executive branch, the legislative
branch carried out its fight for a parliamentary democracy, however futile its efforts may have often been. Its determination to reflect the will of the people
could not be demolished, and its struggle continued.

The Rise of Party Politics.   Political modernization in post-liberation Korea
brought about a sudden birth of party politics. Political parties and politically
oriented social organizations mushroomed overnight. There were over one hundred such organizations in South Korea in 1945. By 1947, the number of such
organizations grew to 354. Some rose in the morning and went out of existence
by nightfall.

Following the establishment of the Republic of Korea, political organizations
were consolidated into more viable parties. The radical left wing parties were
either outlawed and went underground, or were abolished. The South Korean
Workers' (Communist) Party emigrated to the north. With the passage of
time, a multiple party system declined as a two major party system emerged,

although a few single-issue-oriented minor parties existed. Unfortunately, the ruling party became a tool of the administration as the major opposition party was intimidated by the administration and its agencies. The growing party politics accompanied the rise of the politics by violence and many outstanding political figures were assassinated.

The outstanding weakness of Korean political parties was that they were organized around a person rather than focusing on certain ideologies or programs. Thus, when the leader of the party either died or fell, the party collapsed. A fragile unity of party members pestered all political parties. Dispute and schism resulting essentially from differences in personalities, regionalism, and loyalties of the boss-follower type never ceased to exist within the party.

Another weakness of Korean political parties was their hunger for power. They were more interested in monopolizing political power and exercising it for their own benefits rather than solving national issues with the spirit of compromise. The leaders of political parties demonstrated no such spirit of compromise whether they dealt with the opposition parties or their intra-party matters. The spirit of compromise had not been the style of the politics of the Yi dynasty.

Most party leaders were primarily concerned with getting votes by clever and timely slogans and lavish bribery. Party members did not dare to challenge the ideas and policies of the leaders. Instead, they were mainly concerned with the distribution of top party positions or securing high government posts. When party leadership was weak, the members were split into bickering factions contending for power. Most parties behaved like social clubs of power-hungry and privileged individuals rather than those of men of ideals and principles, championing freedom, rights, social justice, and the economic welfare of the people.

The concern for national security and economic development had an overriding impact on political development. Facing constant threats and occasional violent actions from the north, the government tightened its restrictions on the freedom and rights of the people, and political parties acquiesced to the proposal made by the government.

Be that as it may, the people gradually became knowledgeable about their rights as well as the political process, they chose the party of their own view and they were eager to exercise their rights. Some came to believe that casting their ballot was a citizen's sacred duty. Gone was the people's political apathy, indifference, and cynicism. In the elections held since 1948, between 72 and 95.5 per cent of the qualified voters cast their ballots, participating in the democratic political process.

However, the people's perceptions of democracy did not develop adequately as they maintained the traditional mode of thinking and social behavior. While an increasing number of people criticized the prevailing concept and practices of *kwanjon minbi* (the government is superior and the people are inferior), the majority regarded obedience to the government as desirable and proper. They failed to develop the idea that the government is the servant of the people and that sovereignty resides in the people. Instead, they expected that the government should lead and they should follow.

By and large, the Koreans did not realize that democracy is what the people foster. Instead, the majority regarded democracy as something which the government could give to the people. Many regarded the president of the Republic as a new monarch and showed respect for the imperial presidency. Their resentment of "too much control" notwithstanding, the people supported the efforts of the government to improve national security and construct a strong economic foundation.

The politicization of the military that began during the early period of the First Republic overshadowed the development of the democratic process. The meaning and consequence of this politicization of the military were not fully understood until after the fall of the First Republic, but its threat to democratic development had already been demonstrated in 1952, when the government mobilized the military and the police to achieve its objectives. Thereafter, the impact of the military on political affairs steadily grew. The direct or indirect military intervention in political affairs during the First Republic, the overthrow of the Second Republic by the military coup of May 1961, the rise of the military junta which ruled the country until 1963, and the rise of former high ranking military officers to top political positions after 1963 undoubtedly created a certain negative impact on the democratic process.

The National Police, the CIA and Democracy.   Whatever the justifications may have been, the retention of the National Police, which had been strongly politicized, first by the American Military Government and then by the Korean government, created serious problems. Police intervention in the election process, violation of civil liberties, suppression of freedom, and misuse of power have been widely reported. The National Police became a powerful weapon for the government, hampering the development of democracy in South Korea. Indeed, the National Police, which had been an effective tool of the autocratic government, became a source of discontent and anti-government feelings of the people.

The politicization of the Central Intelligence Agency, which was created in 1961 "for the purpose of countering indirect aggression of the Communist forces and to remove obstacles to the execution of the revolutionary tasks," and its placement under the control of former military officers constituted another serious problem. Having no counterpart to the U.S. Federal Bureau of Investigation, the South Korean Central Intelligence Agency became deeply involved in domestic politics and the investigation of thoughts, beliefs, and private and public activities of a large number of individuals. Sometimes, it was called the "real" government, and indeed the director of the Korean CIA was the second most powerful person in South Korea. The assassination of Presi-

dent Park in October 1979 by the then director of the CIA, a former high ranking military officer who had been deeply involved in domestic politics, clearly
indicated the political impact of the Central Intelligence Agency on South
Korea's political development and democratization. The assassin claimed that
he had killed the president in order to "restore democracy" in the nation. The
Korean CIA was renamed in 1981 the Agency for National Security Planning,
but its power did not diminish.

Under these circumstances, it was futile to expect the development of
healthy and effective party politics or democratic institutions and a democratic
way of life in South Korea. Mindful of past political problems, the new government which emerged in August 1980 adopted various measures to improve the
political situation. First of all, it wrote a new constitution, and reduced the extraordinary power of the president, limited the president's term of office to a
single seven-year term, restored the habeas corpus system, and in principle the
inviolability of basic human rights. The Fifth Republic emerged in South Korea
under this constitution in March 1981 with the aim of creating a "democratic
welfare society."

Economic Development

Economic Conditions of the 1945–1948 Period.   The liberation of Korea
from Japanese colonial rule provided the Koreans freedom to reconstruct their
economy, but the economy of South Korea could not develop until the 1960s
due to many factors. First of all, the partition of the country had enormously
negative effects on the economy. The south had been primarily an agricultural
area with some industries. At the time of the partition, about 30 per cent of the
country's heavy industries and 85 per cent of its light industries were located
in the south. However, by and large the industries were small, and the dire
shortage of electric power and natural resources constituted one of the major
economic difficulties. It should be born in mind that about 90 per cent of electric power used by South Korea was supplied by the north.

Secondly, South Korea had virtually no highly trained scientists, technicians,
economic experts, or managerial personnel, thanks to the Japanese policy which
did not allow Koreans to be trained in these fields. Thirdly, political and social
conditions were not conducive to economic growth. Fourthly, the rampant
inflation that was created by the Japanese toward the end of World War II
plunged South Korea into a chaotic economic situation. Fifthly, South Korean
farmers had almost no fertilizer to apply to their fields when the supply of
chemical fertilizers from the north was cut off. Finally, the rapid population
growth due to a high birth rate and the influx of refugees from the north and
elsewhere brought about added economic problems. South Korea had almost
nothing to export, no money to import needed goods, and no capital to
develop industries. The shortage of food, fuel, and consumer goods grew pro-

gressively worse.

The American occupation authorities had no economic policy or plans for South Korea. American economic aid for the period of 1945 to 1948 amounted to $300 million, and it was used almost entirely on a relief basis, to secure essential supplies to stave off widespread starvation. The military government sold former Japanese properties to the Koreans, and instituted a commodity price control system which only made black-marketing worse as the amount of cereals produced in South Korea declined from 1,118 million bushels in 1944 to 760 million bushels in 1945. The amount of cereals produced grew slightly in 1947 to 891 million bushels, but it was far below the 1944 level. Although the military government established the New Korea Company to administer farmlands which had been owned by the Japanese, no land reform was carried out.

The decline in production of industrial raw materials followed the pattern of the decline in the amount of grain produced. Gold production declined from 225,000 fine ounces in 1944 to 3,466 in 1948; copper production declined from 2,302 metric tons in 1944 to 1,125 in 1948; lead ore production declined from 8,386 metric tons to 497 in 1944 and 423 in 1948; and tungsten production fell from 6,217 metric tons in 1944 to 1,179 in 1948. Only coal production made a gain from 270,000 metric tons of anthracite mined in 1946 to 299,385 metric tons in 1948.

Deficit spending on the part of the government made the economic situation even worse, and when North Korea cut off its supply of electricity in 1948, in-dustries in South Korea collapsed almost completely, creating severe economic problems. The shortage of food, fuel, and medical supplies threatened the livelihood of the people and created serious health problems. The American military government handed over the country in economic shambles to the Koreans in August 1948.

The rapidly increasing rate of population growth constituted another serious problem. With the influx of 2,384,533 Koreans from abroad between October 1945 and April 1948, South Korea's population grew to 20.1 million by 1949. Some 1.1 million Koreans returned from Japan, and 829,886 Koreans fled from the north to the south during that period. Over 2.5 million Koreans were reported to have fled from the north to the south between August 1945 and June 1950.

Early Economic Conditions, 1948–1953.   The young republic faced many economic problems. Uncontrolled spending by the government, particularly by agencies concerned with hunting down Communists, inadequate tax collection, and the shortage of the supply of food, fuel, and commodities constituted major problems. The steadily increasing amount of currency in circulation created rampant inflation, adding to the existing economic problems. Between December 31, 1948 and January 1950, the government printed some 150 billion *wŏn* of currency, making the money worthless.

The Korean government made various efforts to improve economic conditions in cooperation with the U.S. Economic Cooperation Administration. However, the U.S. economic assistance was too small to make any significant contribution toward economic recovery of South Korea. The U.S. Economic Cooperation Administration in Korea wished to have $350 million for a three-year period beginning in 1949 in order to help South Korea, but the U.S. Congress reluctantly appropriated only $110 million for South Korea to cover the fiscal year of 1949–1950.

The most significant economic program which the South Korean government carried out was a land reform. Under the Land Reform Act of June 22, 1949, all farmlands, excluding fields where special crops such as tobacco and ginseng were grown, not cultivated by the owners, as well as holdings of more than 7.5 acres by owner-cultivators were purchased by the government. The government paid 150 per cent of the value of the annual crop to landowners, and sold farmlands to farmers for 125 per cent of the same value. The poor farmers were given 30 per cent of the purchase price as government subsidy and they bought farmlands on a 15-year installment plan, without interest. Some 687,000 acres of farmlands were sold to 588,000 farm families soon after the Land Reform Act was implemented. Eventually, 1.5 million farmers acquired some 1.2 million acres of land, but the average amount of farmland per farm household was 2 acres, too small for any significant economic improvement of farm families. Be that as it may, with the implementation of the Land Reform Act, the Rhee administration gained political support of the rural population. In 1959, there were some 2.3 million farm households which had an average area of 2.23 acres of farmland. About 1 million had less than a half acre, while only 7,000 had 7 acres or more.

Although the Korean government failed to arrest runaway inflation, reduce deficit spending, or increase the production of consumer goods in any meaningful way, it managed to increase the agricultural output by 11 per cent. The amount of grain produced rose from 4.6 million tons in 1948 to 5.2 million tons by 1950. Three new railroad lines were constructed to provide access to coal areas not previously reached by rail, a number of irrigation and land reclamation projects were completed, and plans were completed to construct a cement plant and fertilizer plants, along with the production of more tungsten and other mineral raw materials. However, manufacturing industries made little progress, if any, due to the critical shortage of electric power and raw materials. Consumer goods production increased somewhat, but it was far short of even minimum domestic needs. Coal production increased about 40 per cent by June 1950. The per capita gross national product during the period of 1948 and 1950 reached the postwar high of 86 dollars. Any improvement which South Korea made in the economy was wiped out by the Korean War.

The war had a devastating effect on the Korean economy. The damage inflicted upon agriculture, transportation, and industrial facilities was estimated at $3 billion. Some five million people lost their homes as tens of thousands of schools and other buildings were destroyed or badly damaged. The rate of inflation grew faster as the currency in circulation increased from 71,383 million *wŏn* at the end of 1949 to 650,135 million by 1953. The wholesale price index (1947 = 100) grew from 334 in 1950 to 5,951 in 1953 and the retail price index (1947 = 100) rose from 331 in 1950 to 4,329 in 1953. Meanwhile, rice production decreased to less than 19 million tons. The war left 300,000 war widows, and 100,000 orphans, and it caused the separation of millions of members of families. Between October 1950 and July 1951 alone, some 90,000 North Koreans fled to the south, resulting in the separation of tens of thousands of families. The influx of North Koreans who fled from the Communist rule increased population pressure in the south while adding to food and housing shortages.

Economic Reconstruction, 1953–1961.   The government maintained the free enterprise system and made various efforts to bring about economic recovery after the war, but due to the shortage of funds, scientists, technicians, and skilled workers, plus shortages of electricity and raw materials, South Korea's economic recovery was slow at best. Without foreign aid, South Korea could not have made any progress in economic reconstruction, however insufficient that aid might have been.

During the war, the United Nations established two commissions—the U.N. Commission for the Unification and Rehabilitation of Korea (UNCURK) and the U.N. Korean Reconstruction Agency (UNKRA)—and raised $150 million (the U.S. share was $93 million) for long-range reconstruction projects at the end of the war. After the war, the United States and South Korea signed an economic cooperation agreement in 1954 and established the Combined Economic Board. Meanwhile, the U.S. Foreign Operations Administration (FOA), later redesignated as the International Cooperation Administration (ICA), contributed much toward the economic recovery and development of South Korea. Between 1953 and 1960, the United States spent a total of $1.8 billion in South Korea. These aid monies ($270 million per year average) enabled small business and manufacturing industries to initiate economic recovery and development. The American Public Law 480 also helped the Korean economy to develop.

Between 1954 and 1960, the U.S. ICA spent $444 million in South Korea, heavily concentrated in transportation and industiral reconstruction, and it imported $1,143 million worth of such needed commodities as chemical fetilizers, raw cotton, petroleum and other fuels, and foodstuffs. Total U.S. military aid to South Korea during these years was valued at $1,360 million.

The postwar reconstruction program was carried out under the Nathan (Robert R. Nathan) plan of the United Nations Korean Reconstruction Agency and the U.S. sponsored Tasca (Henry J. Tasca) plan of 1953. A three-year economic development plan of the Korean government adopted in 1960 was aborted when the First Republic collapsed in April 1960 following a student uprising.

In order to deal with the rampant inflation, in February 1953 the government carried out a monetary reform. and replaced *wŏn* notes with *hwan* notes. The exchange rate between *wŏn* and *hwan* was set at 100 to 1. At the same time, the exchange rate between U.S. dollar and *hwan* was set at 1 to 300. The rate of economic recovery between 1953 and 1956 was extremely slow, but from 1956 the Korean economy began to improve. The rate of GNP growth in 1953 was 1.0 per cent, but it grew to 5.9 per cent in 1960. Per capita income, however, remained below $100. South Korea's exports which amounted to $39.6 million in 1953 grew slightly to about $41 million in 1960.

With the increasing supply of American chemical fertilizers, grain production increased from 5.2 million tons in 1950 to 5.9 million tons in 1960. Of this, 2.3 million tons were rice. Marine products grew from 216,000 tons in 1950 to 340,000 tons in 1960; the amount of anthracite produced increased from 867,000 tons in 1953 to 5,350,000 tons in 1960, and the amount of electric power generated increased from 899 million kilowatt hours (kwh) in 1954 to 1,686 million kwh in 1960, thanks to coal production. Almost all electricity was generated at thermal power plants. With this, the GNP originating in agriculture-forestry, fisheries and mining-manufacturing industries shifted from 45.1 per cent and 54.8 per cent, respectively, in 1957 to 40.2 per cent and 59.8 per cent, respectively, in 1961. Be that as it may, the South Korean economy remained underdeveloped although many economic problems were solved. The steady population growth and the high inflation rate remained serious economic problems. South Korea's population increased from 20.1 million in 1949 to 21.5 million in 1955, and then to 24.9 million in 1960. The annual average rate of population growth was approximately 2.8 per cent. The wholesale price index (1947 = 100) grew from 5,951 in 1953 to 22,077 in 1959, and the retail price index rose from 4,329 in 1953 (1947 = 100) to 15,280 in 1959. The currency issued in 1953 was 22.3 million *hwan*, but it increased to 166.1 million *hwan* in 1961. The exchange rate between U.S. dollar and *hwan* changed from 1 to 300 in 1953 to 1 to 500 in 1961. The value of money steadily declined.

The short-lived Second Republic adopted a five-year plan, established the National Construction Service in order to inaugurate public works to reduce unemployment, and adopted a plan to devalue Korean currency of *hwan* to 1,300 to one U.S. dollar, but all these plans were aborted when it was overthrown by the May 16 military revolution. The Second Republic collapsed in a worsening economic situation.

New Economic Development Planning.   South Korea promoted a market economy during the First and the Second Republic periods, but in 1961 the military junta implemented strong measures, initiating a system of command economy which the Third and the Fourth Republic strengthened. The principle of market economy was not abandoned altogether, however. With this change, the public economic sector came under an increasingly unified economic system while the private sector maintained a market economy. Both of these systems brought about remarkable economic development, unparalleled in Korean history.

The Supreme Council for National Reconstruction established the Economic-Planning Board in July 1961, and adopted a monetary reform plan in utter secrecy. New monies were printed in England in early spring of 1962, and the new currency of *wŏn* replaced the *hwan* currency with the exchange rate of 1 to 100, respectively. The exchange rate between U.S. dollar and *won* was set at $1 to 130 *wŏn*.

The Supreme Council took several measures to improve the economic situation. It curbed speculative financial dealing and adopted an austerity program, and in January 1962 initiated a five year development plan for 1962-1966. Its main objectives were to reverse the declining rate of economic growth and to lay a foundation for long-range development. The concept of "guided economy" or "guided capitalism", like that of "guided democracy" in politics, became the cornerstone of the new economic plans of South Korea after 1961. The free enterprise system was kept but the government became deeply involved in the economic affairs of both public and private sectors.

The First Five-Year Plan called for an average growth rate of 7 per cent in GNP, 15 per cent in secondary industries, and 6 per cent and 4 per cent respectively in primary and tertiary industries. It was to reduce the rate of unemployment from 24 per cent to 15 per cent by 1966, and to expand trade. Two of its most ambitious projects were the establishment of a large iron and steel plant at Ulsan and a fertilizer plant in cooperation with American corporations. The plan anticipated that 44 per cent of its financial needs would be provided by U.S. aid.

The United States government approved a loan of $70 million for the first quarter of 1962, and the U.S. Agency for International Development (AID-the successor to ICA) indicated that the United States was planning a large-scale aid program for Korea totaling some $1.2 billion. A new agreement was signed in June 1962 to expand the PL 480 program of the United States. The Korean government secured a $14 million loan from the First National City Bank of New York and concluded a $37.5 million loan agreement with West Germany and a $120 million loan agreement with the Fiat Company of Italy in 1961.

South Korea implemented three successful five-year plans beginning in 1962: the aforementioned First Five-Year Plan of 1962–1966, the Second Five-Year Plan of 1967–1971, and the Third Five-Year Plan of 1972–1976. In 1977 the Fourth Five-Year Plan was launched, and substantial progress was made despite chaotic situations which followed the death of President Park in October 1979.

The basic aims of South Korea's development plans were to construct a self-sustaining economy, develop heavy industries without sacrificing the consumer economy, and to modernize the economic structure. The key slogan was "the harmonization of growth, stability and balance." The particular aims of the Fourth Five-Year Plan were to equalize income distribution between rural households and urban wage earners through rural development and to improve agricultural technology. Its targets were to increase GNP to $58.7 billion, per capita GNP to $1,512, and exports to $17 billion by the end of 1981.

The government paid particular attention to bringing about a balanced growth between heavy and light industries, securing of large foreign loans, and the development of mining and manufacturing industries. At the same time, it emphasized the increase in domestic saving and self-sufficiency in food supply.

Economic Accomplishments After 1963.   South Korea's economic development was slow and sluggish until 1963. However, after 1963, South Korea achieved an unparalleled economic record in many ways, elevating South Korea into an industrial state. The leaders proudly called their achievement "the miracle on the Han River." A strong government leadership, careful planning, increased funding and the industriousness of the people, contributed to astonishing economic achievements.

Significant progress has been made in the area of investment. Whereas between 1961 and 1976 Korea depended heavily on foreign aid funds for domestic investment, the increase in domestic savings has enabled the government to reduce this dependency. The United States economic aid (grants) decreased rapidly after 1963. Between 1953 and 1963, South Korea received $2,689 million in U.S. economic aid, but between 1964 and 1973 this amount declined to $920 million. In 1964, it received $149.3 million, $51.2 million in 1971, $10 million in 1974, and in 1976 the economic aid program of the United States virtually came to an end as the Korean economy developed. However, South Korea continued to secure loans from the United States. Meanwhile, the financing of industrial projects with domestic savings steadily increased from 3.9 per cent in 1961 to 18 per cent in 1975, and to 39.4 per cent in 1978. However, South Korea's borrowing from the World Bank, the International Monetary Fund, and foreign governments and firms (especially those of Japan) grew rapidly in order to expand industries. In 1982, South Korea's indebtedness to foreign creditors reached the $27.9 billion mark.

Along with the growing domestic savings, increasing exports, more foreign loans, and earnings from overseas economic activities (mostly construction works in the Middle East), South Korea's economic activities vastly increased. In 1976 alone, South Korean firms won contracts for construction and engineering projects worth $2.9 billion in the Middle East, the Pacific Area,

Southeast Asia, Africa, and Latin America. As of October 1978, 113,888 Korean workers earned $534,615,000 from overseas employment, and contributed to the growth of domestic savings.

As the economy developed, the ratio between the primary (agriculture, forestry, and fisheries) and secondary (mining and manufacturing) sectors changed from 40.2 per cent to 15.2 per cent, respectively, in 1961 to 25.4 per cent to 29.7 per cent in 1975, and 18.5 per cent to 39.7 per cent in 1981. As a result, the origin of gross national product (GNP) of the primary sector dropped to 18 per cent in 1981 and that of the secondary sector grew to 40.9 per cent. The number of workers engaged in the primary sector decreased from 63.1 per cent of the total work force in 1963 to 39.7 per cent in 1981 while the percentage of the work force engaged in mining and manufacturing increased from 8.7 to 26.1 during the same period. Meanwhile, as heavy industry grew, the ratio between light and heavy industries changed from 70.4 per cent to 29.6 per cent in 1961, and to 57.2 and 42.8 by 1978.

The gross national product grew from $12.7 billion in 1962 to $18.8 billion in 1975, and to $57.4 billion in 1980. This means that South Korea's GNP increased between 1962 and 1980 by 452 per cent. The average GNP growth during each plan period was as follows: 8.8 per cent during the 1962–1966 period, 10.5 per cent during the 1967–1971 period, 11.2 per cent during 1972–1976 period, and 5.0 per cent during the 1977–1981 period. The GNP growth rate in 1979 was 6.3 per cent, but it dropped to –6.2 in 1980. However, it rose by 7.1 per cent, or $63.2 billion in 1981 from $57.4 billion in the previous year. Despite the population increase from 25 million in 1961 to 38.7 million in 1981, South Korea made an unparalleled per capita GNP increase from $87 in 1961, to $532 in 1975, and to $1,735 in 1981.

Average annual income per farm household grew from $147 in 1962, to $735 in 1971, $1,800 in 1975, and $4,830 in 1979, while average annual income of urban wage earners increased from $190 in 1962, to $991 in 1971, $1,990 in 1975, and $5,460 in 1979. In 1976 average annual income of farm households was slightly higher than that of average urban wage earners.

The Korean economy which developed in such an astonishing way attracted an increasing number of foreign firms which confidently made direct investments (mostly in joint ventures) in Korea. Some 130 American firms, such as General Motors, Ford Motors, General Electric, and Westinghouse, became involved in the industrial developments of South Korea. Companies of Japan, Great Britain, West Germany, France, the Netherlands, and Switzerland were also among foreign investors.

The Ministry of Commerce and Industry recently reported that South Korea paid $681 million in royalties for imported know-how during the 1962-1982 period. The amount represented 47.4 per cent of the total investment foreign businesses made in South Korean industrial projects during the same period. Among the 2,281 cases of foreign technology transfer, Japan accounted for

1,287, worth $233 million, while the United States was responsible for 533 cases, worth $248 million. The United States and Japan provided 80 per cent of imported technical know-how to South Korea. Japan's share in foreign investments was 48 per cent and that of the United States was 28 per cent as of 1982. Needless to say, the transfer of technical know-how from advanced countries to South Korea, as well as direct investments by foreign firms in Korean industries contributed greatly to the economic development of South Korea.

The rampant inflationary trend that developed in the 1973–1974 period with the expansion of economic activities was brought down in 1977. But it grew again between 1978 and 1980, increasing economic difficulties of the people following the assassination of President Park. However, the efforts made after 1980 by the government benefited the people when both wholesale prices and prices of consumer goods were brought down by government regulations which included the control over interest rates.

INFLATION RATE 1974-82

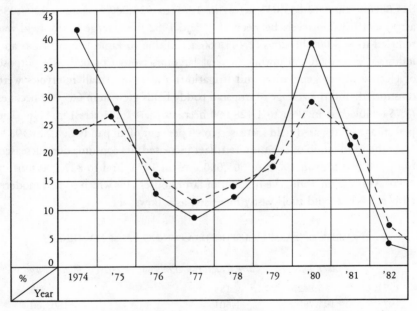

——— Wholesale price index

- - - - Consumer price index

Source: *The Korea Herald*, January 11, 1984.

As the above chart shows, the rise in wholesale prices stood at 42.1 per cent in 1972, 38.9 per cent in 1980, and 9.0 per cent in 1977 and the lowest 4.7 per cent in 1982. Consumer prices which rose by 26.6 per cent in 1975 as compared to 24.5 per cent rise in 1974, dropped to 10.1 per cent in 1977. Although consumer prices rose by 28.7 per cent in 1980, they dropped to 7.3 per cent in

1982, continuing toward the easing of the consumer economy.

Agricultural Development.   The Law on Land Improvement Projects and the Reclamation Law which were promulgated in 1962 had enormous effects on the consolidation of farmlands, relocation of farmhouses from cultivated areas to hillsides, and reclamation of tidal flats for rice production. These laws initiated a "Green Revolution" in South Korea. An increase in the supply of chemical fertilizer, chemical insecticides, and modern farm machinery and tools, enabled South Korean farmers to increase the production of foodstuffs.

Various land reclamation projects created 198,000 hectares (271,366 acres) of new farmland, increasing the total acreage of farmland from 2,033,000 hectares (5,012,540 acres) in 1961 to 2,231,111 hectares (5,758,010 acres) in 1977. More tidal flats have been converted to rice growing areas since then. The acreage of paddy fields (rice growing fields) increased from 1,211,000 hectares (2,992,381 acres) in 1961, to 1,303,000 hectares (3,225,710 acres) in 1977, and 1,311,512 hectares (3,239,435 acres) in 1982. The acreage of dry fields also increased from 823,000 hectares (2,033,033 acres) in 1961 to 928,000 hectares (2,294,088 acres) in 1977. However, between 1977 and 1982 the acreage of dry field was reduced to 868,000 hectares (2,143,660 acres) due to rapid urbanization and industrial expansion. Meanwhile, several large reservoirs (for both the purpose of electric power generation and irrigation) and many small reservoirs were constructed, and the acreage of irrigated paddy fields grew from 665,000 hectares (1,754,450 acres) in 1961 to 1,128,000 hectares (2,787,283 acres) in 1978. The percentage of irrigated field increased to 90 per cent of all paddy fields by 1982.

As the production of chemical fertilizer increased, its consumption increased from 308,000 tons in 1964, to 605,000 tons in 1975, and to 827,000 tons in 1980. At the same time, the number of farm households which owned modern farm machinery and tools vastly increased as follows:

NUMBER OF FARM HOUSEHOLDS OWNING FARM MACHINERY

	Power Tillers	Farm Tractors	Power Weeders	Water Pumps
1971	16,842	183	—	57,896
1978	194,780	1,601	148	180,660
1980	289,779	2,664	604	193,943

Source: Ministry of Culture and Information. Republic of Korea. *A Handbook of Korea,* 1982, p. 538.

Although South Korea has not achieved self-sufficiency in food grain production (about 85% self-sufficiency in 1980), the production of food grains has increased since 1962. Food grain production increased as follows (in 1,000 tons):

	Total	Rice	Barley	Wheat	Soy Beans	Irish Potatoes
1962	5,032	3,015	1,113	184	156	357
1971	6,792	3,998	1,510	205	229	589
1976	8,184	5,215	1,755	87	295	553
1980	5,014	3,550	811	95	216	342

Source: Ministry of Culture and Information, Republic of Korea. *A Handbook of Korea,* 1982, pp. 541, 542.

In 1982, 5,175,000 tons of polished rice was produced.

Lately, growing cash crops has become increasingly important to farm households. Some farmers have converted their rice paddies into vegetable growing areas while some begun double-cropping on their lands. Cultivation of fruits and vegetables—tomatoes, green onion, strawberries, and others—has become profitable. Vegetable growing acreage increased from 173,000 hectares (427,490 acres) in 1961 to 280,000 hectares (691,900 acres) in 1978. At the same time, fruit growing has become profitable, and thousands of acres of low hills and slopes have been converted into orchards. The production increase of fruits and vegetables was as follows (in 1,000 tons):

	Apples	Pears	Grapes	Peaches	Oranges	Chinese Cabbage	Radishes
1962	118	27	8	20	0.8	428	460
1972	261	50	48	80	11.9	826	821
1980	410	60	57	89	161.0	3,040	1,973

Source: Ministry of Culture and Information, Republic of Korea. *A Handbook of Korea,* 1982, p. 536.

The New Community Movement and Rural Economy.   The New Community Movement (*Saemaŭl undong*) was set in motion in 1971 to assist farmers to improve their economic and living conditions, and to promote diligence and the spirit of self-help and cooperation. It was also aimed at the modernization of agriculture and rural communities. Since its inception, it has become a major factor in rural development.

The movement accompanied the organization of cooperative societies in rural districts. All the farm households were urged to join the society. By 1973 some 34,665 villages joined the movement, and by 1976 all farm households became participants.

The government provided leadership, funds, and materials for the construction of a new rural economy and society while the villagers themselves made financial contribution to the movement. A total of $6.9 billion were spent for the movement by the end of 1980, including $3.5 billion contributed by the government. New Community schools and leadership training centers were established, New Community banks were established in each district, cooperative farming and cooperative projects were undertaken, and rural modernization projects, which included new housing, new road construction, sanitation, mechanization, flood control and farmland rearrangement projects, were carried out. Scientific farming and a greater application of chemical fertilizers and insecticides were emphasized.

Under local leadership and with the cooperation of the government, rural areas saw a rapid modern transformation. New houses, new roads, new bridges, new embankments of creeks and rivers, and numerous small reservoirs were constructed. Small farms were consolidated into larger units, and villages were removed from farming areas to hillsides so as to increase the area of cultivation. Meanwhile, the spirit of self-help, cooperation, and thriftiness increased among the people. Living standards of rural people improved, and income per farm household grew significantly. Rural electrification and new farmhouses changed the face of the Korean village.

Fisheries.   With the increase of shipbuilding and improvement of technology, the fishing industry developed rapidly. An increased consumption of fish and other marine products contributed to the growth of the fishing industry. Deep-sea fishing by large ships increased the supply of favored fish such as cod and tuna. Like the rural communities fishing villages organized cooperatives and participated in the New Community Movement.

The increase in the tonnage of fishing boats and catch are as follows:

	Number of Vessels	Total Tonnage	Catch (in 1,000 tons)
1962	45,504	161,709	702
1972	67,679	451,767	1,344
1980	77,574	770,688	2,410

Source: Ministry of Culture and Information, Republic of Korea. *A Handbook of Korea,* 1982, pp. 541, 542.

With the growth of the amount of fish harvested, exports of fishery products increased from $12.3 million in 1962 to $152.6 million in 1972, and to $871.4 million in 1980.

Industrial Development.   South Korea's industrial development was far behind that of North Korea until the middle of the 1960s. However, since about 1967, South Korea has accomplished a remarkable industrial growth, and its achievement has been widely recognized. With the implementation of the Second Five-Year Plan in 1967, industrialization was in high gear, and in 1980 South Korea's industrial capacity far surpassed that of North Korea.

The government allotted more funds and helped private corporations to secure foreign loans and establish joint ventures, aiming not only at becoming self-supporting in the supply of steel, cement, coal and chemical products, but also striving to increase exports. The government itself secured large amounts in foreign loans, and it established several large industrial estates (parks) and tax-exempt zones to attract more foreign investment, accelerate industrial development, and promote the economy in general. As a result, large industrial estates emerged at such places as Ulsan, P'ohang, Masan, Kumi, Yŏch'ŏn, and Ch'angwŏn. Giant multi-enterprise corporations arose, among which were the Hyundai, the Samsung, the Daewoo, and the Lucky Group. The petro-chemical complex at Ulsan, the iron and steel works at P'ohang, the Hyundai shipyard at Ulsan and others on the island of Kŏje, the Ssangyong cement plant at Samch'ŏk, the Honam Oil Refinery, and automobile, textile mills, electronic manufacturing plants, chemical fertilizer plants, and many other modern industrial plants changed the face of the country, transforming the backward economy into a modern, industrial one. Meanwhile, the industrial origins of GNP changed radically by 1980s as follows: agriculture/forestry/fishery, 16.9 per cent; mining and manufacturing, 30.7 per cent; and social services, 52.4 per cent.

Among the new modern industries which developed were automobile, electronic, petroleum, petro-chemical, shipbuilding, and manufacturing industries. Meanwhile, cement and textile production increased vastly. South Korea did not produce any automobiles until the latter part of 1960. Since then, aotomobile production increased as follows:

	Passenger Cars	Trucks	Buses	Total
1970	14,487	10,529	3,803	28,819
1976	26,605	19,219	3,468	48,292
1979	112,314	76,661	12,307	201,282
1980	57,037	52,169	11,854	121,060

Petroleum (gasoline) production increased from 4.6 million barrels in 1963 to 776 million barrels in 1976, the tonnage of ships built in Korea increased from 4.6 million in 1963 to 776 million in 1978; petro-chemical production grew from 17,000 tons in 1968 to 622,000 tons in 1973, 1,557,000 tons in 1978, and 2,071,000 tons in 1980. The dollar value of petro-chemical products in 1968 was $4 million, and it jumped to $171.5 million in 1980. Among petro-chemical products were ethylene, benzene, propylene, butane, and xylene. The manufacturing of radios and televisions (both color and black and white) constituted two major products in the electronics industry.

The production of cement greatly increased and brought about self-sufficiency. With this, the amount of cement exported increased from 90,000 tons in 1966, to 4,409,000 tons in 1980. Meanwhile, textile products earned an enormous amount of foreign currency: $340 million in 1970, $3,982 million in

INDUSTRIAL GROWTH

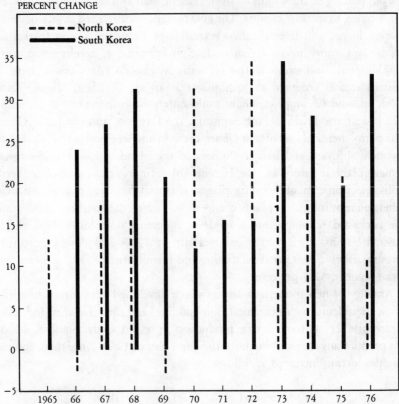

Source: U.S. National Foreign Assessment Center, *Korea: The Economic Race Between the North and the South: A Research Paper*. Washington. D.C., January 1978, p. 5. The percentage of North Korea's industrial growth in 1971 is not available.

1978, and $3,743 million in 1982.

Industrial development brought about a decline in the ratio of the population engaged in agriculture and fisheries to those in the industrial sector from 46 per cent in 1970 to 29 per cent by 1980. The number of farm households and farm population in 1970 was 2.5 million and 14.4 million, respectively, but in 1980 the number of farm households declined to 2.1 million with 10,830,583 people. More female than male workers migrated out of rural areas into nearby industrial areas during the period. The number of workers engaged in mining and manufacturing industries in 1980 was 3,095,000, or 22.6 per cent of the total population. The unemployment rate in 1980 was 5.2 per cent (749,000 persons) of the total population of 38,124,000. The rate of population increase in 1980 was 1.5 per cent.

The growth of the industrial population and labor problems, led the government to establish a new Ministry of Labor in April 1981, separating labor affairs from the Ministry of Health and Social Affairs. Be that as it may, the problems related to low wages paid to workers, long working hours, and inadequate medical care remained to be solved.

The chart below shows the increase in production between 1961 and 1980:

PRODUCTION INCREASE

	1961	1963	1972/73	1976	1978	1980
Grain (1,000 tons)	5,933	5,472	6,759	8,184	8,289	5,014
Fisheries (1,000 tons)		532	1,687	2,407	2,444	
Coal (1,000 tons)	7,444	8,858	13,571	16,427	18,056	18,624
Electric power (million kwh)	1,773	2,236	14,825	19,837	31,510	37,239
Iron ore (1,000 tons)	489	501	600	524	589	489
Zinc ore (1,000 tons)		23	96	153	133	132
Steel ingots (1,000 tons)			1,157	2,737	3,138	
Pig iron (1,000 tons)			455	1,186		
Gasoline (1,000 kilolitres)			1,039	1,186	1,271	
Chemical fertilizer (1,000 tons)	30	98	698	833	1,186	2,854
Cotton yarn (1,000 tons)˙		63	103	175	189	413
Textile (million meters)	111	153	223	444	620	635
Diesel oil (million kilolitres)			2,854	3,309	5,476	
Cement (1,000 tons)	720	778	8,175	12,775	15,136	15,573
Automobile (passenger cars)			14,480	26,605	12,314	57,037
Trucks			10,529	19,219	76,661	52,169
Plywood (million sq. ft.)			4,149	5,665		4,233

Source: Ministry of Culture and Information, Republic of Korea. *A Handbook of Korea*, 1982, pp. 535, 539, 559, 562, 563, 569, 581, 584, 605.

South Korea's rapid economic growth since 1963 has been attributed to the following factors; more well educated economic planners and top businessmen, extensive training facilities for upgrading the technical skills of a diligent labor force, freedom of opportunity, enterprise and economic activities, better economic planning, less spending on defense, importation of more efficient technology and equipment, and a dynamic export-oriented economy.

Improvement of Transportation Facilities. In order to bring about a rapid economic development, as well as to facilitate a greater mobility of people and goods, the government launched ambitious plans for highway and railway construction, harbor reconstruction, and rapid transit and air traffic expansion. As a result, the mileage of paved highways increased from 27,167 kilometers (17,398 miles) in 1961 to 44,905 (27,950 miles) in 1968, and 142,440 (115,575 miles) by 1979. Some 537 (333.6 miles) kilometers of four-lane expressways, such as the Seoul-Pusan Expressway, have been constructed since 1963.

In 1945 South Korea had 3,738 kilometers (2,318 miles) of railway. During the Korean War most of the railway tracks were destroyed as were 61 per cent of locomotives, 60 per cent of the passenger coaches, and 57 per cent of the freight cars. The railway reconstruction that began in 1953 brought about not only a recovery, but also an increase in railway mileage and modernization of rail transportation. The progress made since 1963 has been spectacular. As a result, the total railway mileage in the country grew to 5,860 kilometers (3,976 miles) by 1980. The Seoul-Pusan line, the Taejŏn-Mokp'o line, and the Kwangju-Pusan line are among the main trunk lines.

Harbor facilities of Inch'ŏn, Pusan, and other key ports were expanded and modernized. As the total tonnage of the merchant marine fleet of Korean flag carriers increased from less than 340,000 tons in 1961 to 2 million tons in 1968, to 6.3 million tons by 1980, Korean ports handled 93.9 million tons of export-import cargo in 1980.

The government-operated Korean Air Lines was turned over to a private company in 1969. Since then, the KAL fleet has grown and air routes have increased in number, linking Seoul's Kimp'o International Airport with most of the capitals of non-Communist countries of Asia and Europe, as well as with four American cities. It is now capable of handling 48 million passengers and 280,000 tons of cargo per year. While overseas routes increased in number and mileage, domestic routes also increased, vastly improving the mobility of people and goods.

Foreign Trade.   South Korea's foreign trade had occupied an insignificant position in its economy during the 1950s, and up to 1963, as she had little to export. During the same period, imports outweighed exports. Be that as it may, during the 1952 and 1976 period, the annual export volume increased by 235 times and the import volume by 38 times. In 1952 and 1963, the dollar value of South Korea's exports was $27.7 million and $84.4 million, respectively, while the dollar value of imports was $214.2 million and $560.3 million, respectively.

With the development of industry since 1963, South Korea's exports grew to $835 million in 1970 and $17.5 billion in 1980. Its imports also increased to $2. billion in 1970 and $22.3 billion in 1980. South Korea's export expansion was especially impressive between 1974 and 1979. In 1982, South Korea exported $21.9 billion worth of goods and imported $24.3 billion worth of commodities. The United States and Japan have been two major trading partners, Japan becoming a more important trading partner since 1965. The share of manufactured commodities in exports increased to about 190 per cent in 1980. South Korea's overseas earning in 1980 in construction projects amounted to $1.8 billion.

Major import items and share in percentage in 1980 were: raw materials

FOREIGN TRADE

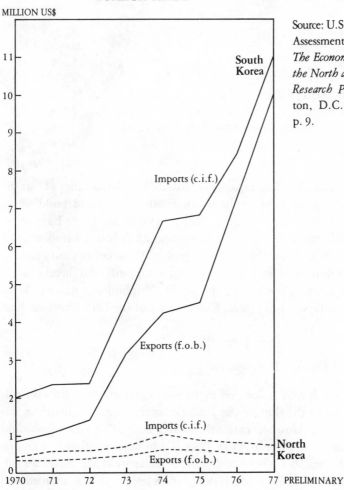

MILLION US$

South
Korea

Imports (c.i.f.)

Exports (f.o.b.)

Imports (c.i.f.)

Exports (f.o.b.)

North
Korea

1970   71   72   73   74   75   76   77 PRELIMINARY

Source: U.S. National Foreign
Assessment Center, *Korea:
The Economic Race Between
the North and the South: A
Research Paper.* Washington, D.C., January 1978,
p. 9.

(39.7%), crude oil (25.3%), capital goods (23%), consumer goods (6.5%), and grain (5.6%). The importation of crude oil increased from 5,835,000 barrels in 1964 to 182,861,000 barrels in 1980 as the demand for petroleum and petroleum products increased.

Textile products (mainly clothing), plywood, footwear, and marine products had been major export items. However, recently the export of electronic goods (radios and televisions), automobiles, steel, and machinery have become important. The dollar value of textile products exported increased from $334 million in 1970 to $5,014 million in 1980, that of plywood export grew from $176 million in 1972 to $304 million in 1980, and the dollar value of marine products exported increased from $124 million in 1962 to $871.4 million in 1980.

The chart below shows shares in exports by products in 1980:

Primary industry 9.1%
Textile products 29.9%
Footwear 5.0%
Chemicals 4.5%
Steel and metal products 14.4%
General machinery 2.1%
Electronics and electrical machinery 6.6%
Others 4.6%

The expanded shipbuilding capacity contributed to the earnings of foreign currencies. In 1972 the largest ship which South Korea could build was a 25,000 ton vessel, but since 1976 South Korea has become able to build ships of the one million ton class. Its shipbuilding capacity grew to 2.8 million gross tons in 1980. Only 4,636 tons of ships were built in 1962, but in 1980 a total of 654,931 tons of ships were built at South Korean shipyards, and thereby South Korea attained fourth place among the world's shipbuilding nations. With these economic achievements, South Korea launched the Fifth Five-Year Plan in 1982.

Educational and Cultural Development

Korea had been heavily influenced by traditional values and Confucian cultural ideology up to the time of the Japanese annexation, and then she was strongly affected by Japanese nationalistic and militaristic educational and cultural values until her liberation in 1945. To be sure, modern educational institutions and curricula emerged and Western influence changed Korean cultural patterns somewhat. However, educational development was retarded and cultural modernization was hampered. Only after the liberation, coupled with the influx of Western influence, were the Koreans able to promote modern, democratically oriented education and to provide educational opportunities to those who had been deprived of them. After 1945, the Koreans achieved remarkable success in the fields of education and culture, contributing to the modern transformation of the society and people.

The New Beginnings in Education.   In August 1945, there were in both the north and the south only 2,834 primary schools with a total enrollment of 1,366,024 pupils, 165 secondary schools with 83,514 students, and 19 institutions of higher education with 7,819 students when the population was 25 million. More than two-thirds of lower level schools and almost all institutions of higher education were located in the south. When the Japanese were repatriated, a majority of colleges and the only university (Keijō Imperial

University) in Korea virtually ceased to function. Three private institutions, such as Yŏnhŭi, Posŏng, and Ewha Woman's colleges, were reopened and in 1946 the Keijō Imperial University was reorganized into Seoul National University.

While expectations and opportunities in the years immediately following the liberation were plentiful, so were the problems. Among the difficulties Korea encountered was a serious shortage of experienced and qualified teachers on the secondary level and in institutions of higher education. Classroom shortages and inadequate school facilities also constituted serious problems.

Realizing the urgent need for educational development, the American military government formed the Korean Committee on Education in September 1945, and in March 1946 it elevated the Bureau of Education to the Ministry of Education. Meanwhile, the American military government introduced a new system of education under the advisement of U.S. educational missions. Under this system, there were established 6-year primary schools, 3-year middle schools, 3-year high schools, and 4-year colleges and universities. At the same time, efforts were made to provide democratic education under the principle of equal opportunity, and accelerated teacher training plans were implemented. Some Koreans were sent to the United States to be trained for Korean educational development.

Whereas the Americans emphasized the promotion of democratic educational philosophy and practices, the Korean leaders in the Ministry of Education and other government organizations emphasized the need to eradicate colonial residues in education and culture while recognizing the importance of promoting democratic education. Be that as it may, efforts made by the American military government brought about a rapid increase in the number of schools. There were, in August 1948, 3,443 primary schools with a total enrollment of 2,426,115 pupils, 380 middle schools with 287,572 students, 184 high schools with 110,055 students, and 31 colleges and universities with 24,000 students. During the American occupation, over fifteen million copies of new textbooks on various subjects were distributed.

Educational Development, 1948-1962. Following the establishment of the Republic in 1948, the Korean government promulgated the Education Law on December 31, 1949, making elementary education compulsory for children aged 6 to 12. Primary schools were called *kungmin hakkyo* (people's schools). At the same time, the Ministry of Education adopted the principle of *hong-ik in-gan,* which stressed the development of national spirit, the concept of righteousness and the principles of obligation and duty, knowledge and technical skills, courage, and the concept of one-people (*ilmin* in Korean), or the unity and harmony of all the people. It also set forth the ideal of education: all nations and people must contribute to the common prosperity of mankind by developing democracy and individuals to lead independent lives and become qualified citizens with altruistic ideals.

The educational progress that had just begun to have an impact was abruptly arrested with the outbreak of the Korean War, which destroyed over half of the school buildings. Educational activities were carried on in tents and makeshift barracks in the area not occupied by the Communist troops.

With the signing of the armistice that ended the war, rehabilitation of the educational system was undertaken vigorously with the help of the United States and the United Nations Korean Reconstruction Agency. The physical facilities and quality of teaching were restored within a few years to prewar levels. The most noted change which occurred was quantitative growth due to the desire of students and parents for education. Quality improvement lagged far behind the quantitative growth. Nevertheless, by 1960, the number of primary schools grew to 4,496 with a total enrollment of 3,621,267 students, the number of secondary schools increased to 1,693 with 792,177 students; the number of vocational schools to 282 with 99,071 students, and the number of institutions of higher education to 85 with 101,045 students. The establishment of national universities in the provinces was a significant aspect of higher education for men and women.

Education for National Reconstruction.   The Third Republic promulgated the Charter of National Education on December 5, 1968. It defined the following goals: (1) the construction of a spiritual base for the regeneration of the nation, (2) the creation of a new image for the Korean people, and (3) the promotion of knowledge of national history and issues. It emphasized the strengthening of determination of the people to counter the aggressive schemes of the Communists.

With the new goals defined, changes in the educational policy were undertaken. In 1969, the abolition of entrance examinations to middle schools triggered a rapid increase of primary school graduates into middle school. The percentage of primary school graduates advanced to middle schools rose from 58.4 in 1969 to 95.7 in 1980. Meanwhile, preparations were made in 1968 to extend the period of compulsory education from six to nine years by 1981, and teacher training institutions were expanded. The high school entrance examination was abolished in 1973 and a lottery system was established.

While promoting institutional growth and improving the curriculum the government emphasized active participation of the students in the process of national regeneration and social progress and the development of the "human factor" in national reconstruction.

The rapid economic growth in the 1960s and 1970s led to a greater educational investment. For example, the total educational budget for 1960 was 6,381,347 *wŏn*, and it increased in 1970 to 8,476,212 *wŏn*, and to 616,418,000 *wŏn* in 1978.| The percentage of educational budget in the annual national budget grew from 15.2 in 1960 to 23.2 in 1980.

The Korean government made systematic efforts to develop science and technology by realigning the administrative machinery. It emphasized the improvement of scientific and technical education, particularly on the secondary level and in institutions of higher education. As a result, in 1967 the Ministry of Science and Technology was created when the United States government-sponsored Korean Institute of Science and Technology was founded. In 1971, the Korean Advanced Institute of Science was established, and the Korean Atomic Energy Research Institute, the Korean Science and Energy Foundation, and many other research institutes emerged after 1973. In 1974, the Taedŏk Science Estate was created near Taejŏn in order to promote cooperation among research institutes and foundation.

With the adoption of the *Yushin* Constitution in 1972, a new policy was adopted to make Korean education reflect the new spirit of the nation. The new policy changed the content of education to increase technical and vocational training, and instructions in Korean history was strengthened in order to promote pride in the Korean cultural heritage. Meanwhile, the New Community (*Saemaŭl*) Movement which began in 1971 included the program of the New Community Education to elevate the educational, cultural, and scientific knowledge and standards of the rural communities. Radio and correspondence schools were made available to the rural people, and various levels of vocational schools were made accessible for out-of-school youth to learn specific trades. All efforts were channeled to fill the needs of an expanding industrialized society as well as to promote the new spirit of national reconstruction.

There were 57 special schools for handicapped children in 1980 with a total enrollment of 8,904 students. Between 1953 and 1980, a total of 14,503 Korean students attended universities in some 40 foreign countries and of these 13,942 have earned advanced degrees from American universities.

Such organizations as the National Academy of Science, the National Academy of Arts, the Academy of Korean Studies, the National Institute of Education, the Korean Educational Development Institute, and the Educational Broadcasting System helped to improve the quantity and quality of Korean education.

Among 85 four-year colleges and universities as of 1980 were 20 public and 65 private institutions of higher learning, all of them with graduate schools. A national university was established in each province (there are nine provinces). Seoul National University enjoyed the highest reputation.

Private educational institutions, as in the past, made a significant contribution toward educational development in South Korea. As of 1978, there were 79 private primary schools with 69,513 pupils, 730 private middle schools with 904,530 students, 623 private high schools with 840,460 students, 246 private vocational high schools with 327,546 students, and 58 private four-year colleges and universities with 198,582 students. Among the leading private universities which were founded by religious bodies were such coeducational institutions as

Yŏnsei and Sŏgang, and Ewha for women. Such coeducational private universities as Koryŏ (Korea), Hanyang, Hong-ik, Sŏnggyun-gwan, Han-guk University for Foreign Studies, Yŏngnam, Chung-ang, and Kyunghee, Kŏn-guk, and Sookmyung for women were leading nonsectarian educational institutions of higher education. The significant aspects of higher education were the growth of the number of women's colleges and universities and the increasing number of women entering into coeducational colleges and universities. Among a dozen of colleges and universities for women were Sŏngshim, Tongdŏk, Pusan, Tŏksŏng, Sangmyŏng, and Seoul colleges, in addition to aforementioned Ewha and Sookmyung universities for women.

Qualification of instructors and laboratory and library facilities of institutional higher education still need further improvement and the number of qualified faculty members in colleges and universities has to be increased. However, educational opportunities for Korean students have greatly expanded as the following tables show.

Cultural Development. Since the liberation, the Korean people have made great strides in cultural development. Although certain restrictions have been imposed on the freedoms of speech and press, mainly for national security and as a defense against propaganda of the North Korean Communists, in general cultural progress has not been hampered. Confucianism remained intact with its 232 shrines and a large number (4,124,760 in 1978) of followers.

Newspapers. Korean journalism has come a long way from the dark period during which no Korean newspapers, except one which was the mouthpiece of the Japanese, were allowed to be published. Since 1945, Korean journalism has achieved much, spearheaded by such prestigious daily papers as the *Tong-a Ilbo*, the *Chosŏn Ilbo*, the *Kyŏnghyang Shinmun*, and the *Han-guk Ilbo*. Twenty-eight major daily newspapers, including two English-language dailies —*The Korea Herald* and *The Korea Times*—have emerged, raising circulation to over nine million in 1980 from less than one million in 1945, thanks to the decline of illiteracy from about 25 to 0.5 per cent by 1978, as well as greater public interest in national and foreign affairs. The increase in paper production also helped the rise of circulation. News agencies, such as the Hapdong News Agency, played a significant role in the improvement of public knowledge about the situation abroad.

Religious. With the establishment of religious freedom in 1945, churches of many denominations and church-related educational institutions rose rapidly, particularly those of Catholicism and Protestantism. Confucianism remained intact with its 232 shrines and a large number (4,124,760 in 1978) of followers. Shamanism, which had been virtually rejected by the people, began its revival in 1945, as popular religious sects proliferated.

QUANTITATIVE GROWTH OF KOREAN EDUCATION 1945–1980

A. Number of Schools (the 1945 figures include both zones)

	1945	1960	1970	1980
Primary Schools	2,834	4,496	5,961	6,487
Middle Schools	166	1,053	1,608	2,100
High Schools	97	353	408	748
Vocational High Schools	68	282	481	606
Higher Education Inst.*	19	85	191	224
4-year Colleges and Universities	19	56	71	85

Source: Ministry of Culture and Information, Republic of Korea. *A Handbook of Korea,* 1982, pp. 686,689.
* Includes 4-year colleges and universities, junior colleges, teachers' colleges, and and junior technical colleges.

B. Number of Students (the 1945 figures include both zones)

	1945	1960	1970	1980
Primary Schools	1,366,024	3,621,267	5,749,301	5,658,002
Middle Schools	83,514	528,614	1,318,808	2,471,997
High School	50,343	164,492	315,367	932,602
Vocational High Schools	33,171	90,071	272,015	764,187
Higher Education Inst.*	7,819	101,045	201,436	611,394
4-Year Colleges and Universities	7,819	92,934	146,414	402,979

Source: Ministry of Culture and Information, Republic of Korea. *A Handbook of Korea,* 1982, pp. 686,689.
* Includes 4-year colleges and universities, junior colleges, teachers' colleges, and junior technical colleges.

By far the largest religious body was that of Buddhism, which became stronger after 1961 when the government provided more financial assistance to the Buddhist church. The birthday of Buddha was recently declared a national holiday. Many Buddhist temples which had been neglected have been repaired. There were 7,444 Buddhist temples in South Korea in 1980 with 12,329,720 followers. Two universities, Tongguk and Wŏn-gwang, were established by the Buddhists.

The modernization of the nation was accompanied by the growth of the Catholic and Protestant churches and their schools and other institutions. In 1980, there were 2,342 Catholic churches with 1,321,293 followers, among whom were many prominent political and social leaders. Protestantism, which suffered greatly during the later period of Japanese rule, made a remarkable recovery after 1945. Protestantism has been associated with modern civilization and democracy, and with the growing desire of the people for a modern way of life, the number of denominations, their churches, and other institutions grew rapidly. In 1980, there were over a dozen major Protestant denominations with 21,243 churches and 7,180,627 followers. A majority of Korean leaders had memberships in Protestant churches. The Protestant churches, which had made significant contributions to modern education for men and women, continued to have an important impact on education and culture. Among the top institutions of higher education established by Christian churches in Korea were such universities as Yŏnsei, Ewha, and Sŏgang.

The *Ch'ondogyo* sect did not make any significant progress. However, with its 249 churches and 1,153,677 followers it constituted an important religious body in South Korea. In a similar fashion, the religion called *Taejong,* which worships Tan-gun, the legendary founder of the Korean nation some 4,357 years ago, had only 80 temples with 316,000 followers in 1980. The most recently introduced Islam grew in a somewhat surprising way. The first mosque was built in Seoul in 1976, and the second has been recently dedicated in Pusan. The Islamic church had some 19,400 followers in 1980.

Radio and Television.   Radio broadcasting made remarkable progress. There was only one government-operated broadcasting system in Korea in 1945, when no private systems were allowed. After the liberation, there emerged five private radio broadcasting systems, and the network of the government-run Korea Broadcasting System (KBS) was expanded. Among the major systems were the KBS and such private systems as Munhwa Radio Broadcasting Company (MBC), the Dong-a Broadcasting System (DBS—absorbed by KBS in 1981), and the Tongyang Radio Broadcasting Company (TBC—absorbed by KBS in 1981) which emerged in the 1960s. FM broadcasting began in 1966.

The number of radio receivers increased from less than one million in 1950 to over 22 million by 1980. Even rural households in remote areas have radios since the electrification of rural areas.

Television broadcasting also grew rapidly after its introduction in 1956 by a privately owned station. In 1961, the official KBS-TV was set up in Seoul, and since then all other radio broadcasting system have established television networks, and television viewing became a daily activity of the people, including those in rural areas. The number of television sets increased from 25,000 in 1961 to 2.8 million by 1976 and to 6.3 million in 1980, or one TV set per household. Color television broadcasting began in 1982. The manufacture of radios and televisions in Korea greatly enhanced the development of a new news and cultural medium.

Movies.   The motion picture industry has made significant progress. In 1945, virtually no movie making was done by the Koreans. In 1955, the government exempted all domestic film makers from taxation in order to promote film production, and in the late 1950s the number of films produced reached about 100 per year. Since 1960, the number has increased to about 200 per year. Unlike North Korean films, the majority of films produced in South Korea include little, if any, political propaganda and are intended for commercial gain and popular entertainment. Lately, with the growing number of television viewers, Korean film production has decreased somewhat. However, the number of viewers of foreign films, particularly those of the United States, remained high. In 1970, some 53.8 million theatergoers filled 468 movie theaters. By 1979, South Korea became one of the top ten nations to produce full-length movies, and like radio and television, movies have become an important mass medium, contributing to the rise of Korea's cultural standards.

Magazines and Book Publishing. Popular magazines began to flood the market in the 1960s with the increasing availability of printing paper and the number of readers of all ages and both sexes. In 1976 alone, a total of 293 new magazines, including 176 monthlies and 45 quarterlies, were published. In 1980, some 640 magazines and journals were published in South Korea, many of them being for women and children, and they included materials on culture and homemaking, science fiction and popular stories. About 60 of them were academic journals. In 1980, some 64 million (21,000 titles) copies of books were published, making South Korea the fifteenth among large book publishing nations in the world. Among them were 4,779 school reference books and 2,565 books on literature, which were published by 1,346 publishing firms.

Libraries. A large number of public and private libraries have risen since 1945. Headed by the Central National Library and the National Assembly Library, along with university and college libraries, they enhanced the cultural development of the nation as they became crowded with readers. In addition to 108 public libraries, there are 4,100 school libraries, 96 special libraries, and 35,011 village libraries throughout the country. With the increasing number of radios and televisions, schools and libraries, and local newspapers in rural areas, the cultural gap between the urban and rural areas has narrowed considerably.

Other Cultural Developments. These developments, plus the growing number of literary circles, music societies, oratorio groups, symphony orchestras and popular music groups, concert halls, museums, theater groups, cinema theaters, Christian church activites and other cultural activities, enabled more and more Korean people to become exposed to modern culture. The newly established National Theater and the Sejong Cultural Center play important role for the development of Korean culture.

While promoting modern culture, the government also encouraged the revival of traditional (national) culture in cooperation with private institutions. The strengthening of the National Institute of Music and the formation of government-sponsored performing arts groups enhanced the revival of traditional painting, calligraphy, and music and dance. Folk arts and folk festivals became increasingly popular. Not only specialized institutions, but schools of all levels instituted various programs for the study of Korea's heritage, not only making the students knowledgeable regarding their heritage, but also enabling them to participate in traditional cultural activities. In order to foster the study of indigenous culture and promote awareness and pride in the heritage of the people, there was established in 1978 the Academy of Korean Studies with its graduate school.

Meanwhile, painters, dancers, and other artists created modern forms of traditional art, contributing to the development of modern culture in Korea. Their new styles of painting, calligraphy, dance and artistic creations fostered modernity within tradition.

Military Development and National Defense

The South Korean Armed Forces have their origins in the National Constabulary and the Coast Guard which had consisted of volunteers. They were established in January 1946 under the American Military Government. In March 1946, the Bureau of Military Affairs was separated from the Ministry of Home Affairs and made into the Department of Internal Security when the plan to establish a ministry of national defense was rejected. Most officers in the two branches of the South Korean military either had been in the Korean military units in China or were college and university students who had been drafted into the Japanese army as "student troops (*hakpyŏng*)" toward the end of World War II.

The American occupation authorities did little to establish an adequate South Korean defense posture: South Korean troops received only elementary military training with outdated Japanese weapons which had been surrendered to American forces. When the Republic of Korea was inaugurated in August 1948, there were five divisions of Constabulary with 50,000 officers and men, and 3,000 men in the Coast Guard, which had only small, light training ships. The formation of the National Defense Forces in August 1948 did little to strengthen the military. Facing the constant threats of the Communists, the South Korean government was anxious to expand and improve its military readiness, but lack of funds and the absence of a United States military assistance program retarded the process. Meanwhile, it had to deal with the Communist-inspired Yŏsu-Sunch'ŏn Rebellion which came shortly after the establishment of the Republic.

New Armed Forces.   In November 1948, headquarters of the Army and the

Navy were established, followed by the founding of various military training schools. In April 1949, the South Korean Marine Corps was created with 300 officers and men. It was not until October 1949 that the Air Force was formed, replacing the Reconnaissance Unit of the National Constabulary, which had been established by the Americans in April 1948.

All American troops were withdrawn from South Korea by June 1949, but some 500 American military advisers remained. The American Military Advisory Group did little to strengthen the defense capabilities of South Korea, however. The total amount of U.S. military aid (grants) up to 1952 was $12.3 million.

The government promulgated the Military Service Law on August 6, 1949, establishing a conscription system. All men above the age of 20, except those who were either physically handicapped, or only sons in the families, were subjected to conscription and active duty of two years in the Army or three years in the Navy. The maximum draft age was 40 in peacetime. The conscription law was modified several times after 1949. Draft evasion, inequity and partiality were major problems until May 1961, when corrective measures were taken by the military junta.

When the Korean War broke out in June 1950, the nation was totally unprepared to cope with the aggressors. Some 67,559 officers and men in the military were poorly equipped and inadequately trained. The Army (8 infantry divisions) had no tanks; the 6,474-man Navy and the 1,241-man Marine Corps had only small, light crafts, and the Air Force had only 22 planes which were trainers.

Military Reconstruction and Modernization.   Following the signing of the armistice agreement in July 1953, South Korea strengthened its military, aiming at the construction of a self-reliant defense posture. Various new academies of the military branches and a war college were established, and after the signing of the Mutual Defense Treaty with the United State on October 1, 1953 more U.S. military aid was received and troops became better trained and equipped. While training better qualified officers at military schools in Korea, the government sent a large number of officers to receive advanced training at U.S. military institutions.

Although South Korea's military strength increased during and after the Korean War, it was not until after the emergence of the Third Republic in 1963 that the national defense posture was noticeably improved. The government adopted several important measures to strengthen national defense, increased the number of divisions and units in the armed forces, and improved the training programs. In April 1968, the Homeland Reserve Forces were created, and in June 1975, a Combat Reserve Corps designed to counter enemy infiltration was established. In September 1975, male high school and college students were organized into the Student National Defense Corps, each school having its own unit. Military training programs for students, including the Reserve Officers' Training Corps (ROTC), were intensified in order to augment the national defense capability. At the same time, a Civil Defense Corps was organized in late 1975 in every community to protect lives and property of the people in times of enemy attack or in emergencies. All able-bodied male citizens between the ages of 17 and 50 were obliged to serve in the Corps. In 1969, the manufacturing of small arms, tanks, and guided missiles and rockets began, and Korean-made guided missiles, tanks and high-powered rockets were tested successfully in September 1978.

Military expenditure grew steadily after 1963, particularly after 1972, due to the shift in U.S. Asian policy and the international situation. The increased threats and guerrilla activities of the North Koreans and the discovery of infiltration tunnels that the North Koreans had constructed across the demilitarized zone into the south led to a sharp increase in military spending as U.S. military aid shrank.

Military assistance from the United States was a key factor in Korean military development. Between 1953 and 1961, the United States provided $1.6 billion, between 1962 and 1969, $2.5 billion, and between 1970 and 1976, $2.8 billion in grants and loans. Most of the early military aid was in the form of grants. However, after 1967, South Korea secured an increasing amount of military loans from the United States: $1 million in 1967, $15 million in 1971, and $59 million in 1978.

South Korea spent an enormous amount of money for the military. Its military budget had been an average of 4.5 per cent of GNP between 1960 and 1969 and 4.8 per cent between 1970 and 1979. In 1980, it grew to 6.6 per cent of GNP. In terms of dollars, the military spending grew from $226 million in 1960 to $307 million in 1969, to $943 million in 1975, and to $3.2 billion in 1980. In order to meet the increasing defense expenditure, the Defense Tax was instituted in 1975.

South Korea, which initiated the military modernization program, purchased $2.1 billion worth of arms from the United States between 1975 and 1979. South Korea was the 4th largest buyer among the countries which purchased military goods from the United States during that period.

In 1978, the Marine Corps became absorbed into the Navy, losing its independent status. In 1980, South Korean Armed Forces consisted of a 520,000-man Army, a 48,000-man Navy, and a 32,600-man Air Force with some 3.3 million reservists in the Homeland Reserve Forces.

The strengthening of the national defense posture notwithstanding, the growth of the size of the armed forces and their increased expenditures created economic burdens on the people, as well as social and personal problems for high school and college graduates because of the requirements for a long (3-year) active military duty. At the same time, the politicization of the military that began during and after the First Republic created numerous difficulties and problems in the process of democratization. Now and then, the military, directly or indirectly, has exerted powerful influence upon the politics of the nation while military domination over the government increased.

U.S. Forces in South Korea.　　The presence of U.S. troops in South Korea had been a deterrent against North Korean aggression since 1953. However, President Richard Nixon quietly removed about 10,000 American troops (ground force) in 1972, and some 3,400 were sent home in February 1979 under the Carter administration's military disengagement program to pull out 37,000 American ground troops over a period of four to five years beginning 1978.

The original plan of President Jimmy Carter was to withdraw 6,000 troops by the end of 1978, but mounting pressure against the plan both in the United States and South Korea first reduced the number to 4,300 and then, following President Carter's visit to Korea in 1979, the entire plan was discarded. Meanwhile, in order to compensate for the ground troop phase-out program, the United States increased South Korea's air defense capabilities by deploying a tactical air command squadron in Korea and replacing old-model planes with the latest models. Meanwhile, American military aid for the military modernization program of South Korea increased considerably. In November 1978, the Combined Forces Command of the United States and Korean forces was established, with the commander of the U.S. Eighth Army as commander of the combined forces, and an annual joint military exercise named "Team Spirit" was inaugurated.

Social Transformation

The Japanese colonial rule modified the traditional social structure of Korea somewhat when it reduced the power and privileges of the upper class (*yangban*) and created new conditions which allowed some commoners to rise and form a middle class. However, the Japanese rule made all Koreans second-rate citizens, as the feudalistic and hierarchical character of Korean society remained intact. Korea's class structure, feudalistic social practices, and social backwardness remained virtually unaltered despite the rise of a new educated class. There was an increasing social mobility, but Japanese rule and policies did not increase social mobility enough to transform Korea into a modern society. Be that as it may, as political, economic, and cultural conditions changed toward the end of the colonial period, the law of social evolution operating in Korea brought about inevitable alterations of the social structure and the people's social relations.

Beginning of Social Change.　　The liberation of Korea from Japanese control removed certain conditions which had been artificial, manipulative, and restrictive. Needless to say, they were detrimental to social and individual development. The Korean people at last gained the freedom to chart their own future and to shape their own destiny. At the same time, opportunities were provided to them to reform and reconstruct their social system and practices.

However, political, economic, and social conditions which the Japanese had left behind, and new conditions that developed as a result of the division of the country and its occupation by foreign troops, coupled with the social psychology and outlook of the people who were suddenly liberated from a highly controlled situation, did not permit a congenial and favorable social atmosphere to prevail. The breakdown of social cohesion and morality, together with the absence of a clear sense of direction created a chaotic social situation.

Be that as it may, with the gradual restoration of political order and economic improvement, social stability conducive to the normal process of social transformation developed, and Korean society began to change. The most significant changes that took place after 1948 were: (1) the decline of traditional (Confucian) concepts, (2) the growth of an industrial population, (3) greater social mobility and the emergence of a new elite class, (4) urbanization and the migration of rural population into urban centers, (5) the rise of a middle class, (6) the closing of the gap between urban and rural areas, (7) improvement of the position of women, and (8) the rise of a new social outlook and attitudes.

Population Pressure.   South Korea's population at the time of the partition was a little over 15 million, but it grew to 20 million by 1949, and to 21.5 million by 1955 with the influx of 3.5 million people who either fled from the north or had been repatriated from Japan and China. The birth rate was high. The population of South Korea was 25.7 million in 1961, 31.8 million in 1970, and 35.9 million in 1976. The growth rate between 1950 and 1966 was about 3.0 per cent, but it declined to 1.9 per cent during the period of 1966 and 1970. After 1970, it declined to 1.6 per cent, and it maintained the 1.5 per cent level after 1975, thanks to family planning programs promoted by the Ministry of Health and Social Affairs. The changing economic conditions also contributed to the lowering of the birth rate. In 1980, the number of households was 7,969,201 and the population was 38,197,000 with a population density of 378 persons per square kilometer. South Korea was the third most densely populated nation in the world in 1980. In 1980, 1,261,194, or 3.7 per cent of the population were above the age of 65, and 13.1 million, or 35.8 per cent, were below the age of 14. Persons between 14 and 65 years of age numbered 24,106,000. Approximately 58 per cent was urban population. South Korea's total population grew to 39.3 million in 1982. Between 1953 and 1982, a little over one million persons emigrated from South Korea to the United States, Canada, West Germany, and South America.

The life expectancy of the South Koreans increased from 55 years in the 1950s to 65 by 1982 as public health and welfare programs of the government and private institutions improved. The number of hospitals, medical and dental clinics, doctors, dentists, midwives and nurses grew. In 1979 there were 193 hospitals with 47,178 beds, 6,154 medical and 1,671 dental clinics, 17,848 physicians, 2,744 dentists, 8,154 midwives, and 26,947 nurses. However, they were mostly concentrated in large and medium-sized cities, and rural areas benefited little by these developments. The medical insurance law, a public relief program, and a social welfare program have been established lately, but most of the people are not yet included in these programs.

The composition of the population changed with the rise of commerce and industry. The composition by economic sectors was as follows:

	1966	1975	1978
Total Number of Employed Persons	9,110,000	11,934,000	13,968,000
Agriculture/Forestry/Fishery	5,414,000	5,473,000	5,137,000
Mining and Manufacturing	1,124,000	2,285,000	3,296,000
Social Services (Transportation/ Communication/and Others)	2,542,000	4,542,000	5,535,000

Urbanization and Modern Way of Life. The growth of educational and commercial institutions, as well as industrial establishments in and around large cities, brought about rapid urbanization, attracting more and more people away from rural areas. The urban population grew at an annual average of 5 per cent between 1955 and 1965, and more than 70 per cent of the growth in urban areas came after 1965 despite the efforts made by the government to curb the population growth in urban areas, particularly in Seoul.

The population of Seoul, which was about 700,000 in 1945, grew to 8.3 million by the end of 1980, that of Pusan grew from about 350,000 in 1945 to 3.1 million, and that of Taegu from less than 250,000 to 1.6 million by 1980. There were two cities (Inch'ŏn and Kwangju) which had about a million each in 1980, and some eight cities with more than 500,000 people each. With the development of industrial estates (parks) and the establishment of factories and military bases in rural areas, the population of many small towns increased rapidly as new medium-sized cities grew in number. For example, the population of the port of Ulsan, which was less than 10,000 before 1960, increased to 350,000 by 1980. The population of such other industrial towns as P'ohang, Masan, Kumi, and Ch'angwŏn likewise grew larger.

Urban areas saw a conspicuous transformation. The construction of high-rise commercial and smart apartment buildings and Western-style houses and boulevards and streets, and the expansion of a modern mode of transportation, the mushrooming of theaters, tea and coffee shops, modern restaurants, department and other stores, and cultural institutions such as museums and libraries had a profound influence on the social and cultural life of the people. As the social outlook of the urban population changed, the appearance of the people also changed. Although older women prefer traditional costumes, men (young and old) and young women prefer Western costumes, shoes, and hair styles. On holidays and certain other occasions young women wear the traditional Korean dress, but seldom are men in urban areas seen in traditional costumes in public.

With the growing number of high school and college graduates securing jobs in the rapidly expanding number of commercial and industrial establishments, as well as in educational and cultural institutions, a large middle class rose. Here and there in urban areas the so-called "middle class village" or "cultured people's village" of professional people and high ranking office workers emerged. Even in rural areas the increased number of high income earners created a distinctive new class with a "middle class outlook" which sought to improve its economic and social status.

Various new social and civic organizations of the upper and middle classes emerged. Among them were such groups as the Lions and Rotary clubs, Chambers of Commerce, fraternal societies of professional people, and other philanthropic and social service organizations. The taditional mutual-aid financial institution called *kye* was modernized as it became more and more a social club rather than a purely financial institution. With the increase of all these organizations, participation in social and civil activities grew rapidly.

The number of theatergoers and concert and opera audiences rose among the middle and upper classes. Automobiles, both privately owned and commercial, crowded city streets, creating traffic congestion everywhere. Electronic instruments and electric appliances such as televisions and other audio equipment, refrigerators, cooking and heating equipment, washing machines, and the like appeared in many homes. The consumption of beef, poultry and dairy products, including milk, increased vastly. "Eating out" became increasingly popular.

Western drinks—whiskey, wine, beer—became popular while Western-style tailor and dressmakers' shops, modern barber and hairdressers' shops, ready-made clothing stores, and packaged food stores became prosperous. A drastic change occurred in moral and ethical values and practices among urbanized Koreans as modern social relations and a modern way of thinking and acting became widely accepted. Dating, walking hand in hand or arm in arm, and divorce among young couples increased.Western-style dance halls, nightclubs and bars became popular among the affluent. Wealthy persons displayed their newly acquired taste for conspicuous consumption in their extravagant dwellings and life style.

Women in South Korea.   Although meaningful and satisfactory sexual equality has not yet been established, the position of women has improved considerably. Research institutes such as the Women's Research Center at Ewha Woman's University and others, along with the YWCA, the Korean National

Council for Women and the Korean Association of Women College Graduates, have contributed much to the promotion of the awareness of the need to improve women's status and have achieved some success in advancing women's political, economic and social rights.

The Constitution gave political rights to women and they exercised their newly gained privilege in the political process. Some were elected to the National Assembly and some have been ministers of the state and played important roles. An ever increasing number of young women attended colleges and universities and became judges, lawyers, physicians, dentists, writers, educators, scientists and technicians. Many women became military personnel, police officers, business women, office workers, and taxi drivers.

The old image of women has changed as has their social role. Although the women's rights movement has not yet fully developed, the voice of women has unmistakably risen. They have gained the right to sue their husbands for divorce and have acquired more influence over family matters. Be that as it may, the divorce rate is still low (1.5%).

Social dislocation and the decline of traditional sexual morality and ethics, as a result of the rise of modern values and attitudes, brought about new patterns of human behavior, particularly those of women who had hitherto been deprived of their freedom. Like the heroine in a novel, *The Free Lady* (*Chayu puin*) by Chŏng Pi-sŏk, which created a sensation when it was published in 1954, many liberated women openly displayed their feelings and carried on romantic affairs. Sexual permissiveness became widespread, and the number of children born out of wedlock increased. Although prostitution was outlawed and public houses of prostitution were abolished, this common element of human societies was not eliminated.

New Pattern of Family Life.   The Korean family has been the stronghold of the Confucian social order. Even city dwellers whose life styles have become modern in many respects still participate in the continuing vital areas of Korea's premodern tradition in their family and social life. Changes in any institution as basic as the family proceeded very slowly as traditional systems and practices stubbornly persisted. Yet, in urban areas, changes have taken place with the increase in the number of nuclear families and educated population. Consequently, the extended family system has declined sharply. The conjugal family has become popular, birth control has become widely practiced, and the birth rate has declined.

Under the law, parental consent for marriage had been required for men and women even those who were older than twenty one years of age until January 1979. Most marriages are still arranged by parents and go-betweens, but the choice by individuals has become increasingly important. A *de facto* marriage system still exists without the benefit of legal protection. However, the traditional concubinage system is almost completely extinct under the law banning it.

With the rise of a modern family system, relationships between parents and children and in-laws have changed. However, authoritarianism of fathers still remains strong. Most first sons stayed with their parents, but an increasing number of first sons have begun to establish separate households. Recent studies have indicated that a growing number of parents also wish to live separately from their children. Meanwhile, with the growing job opportunities for women, the relationship between husband and wife has changed. More and more women have become co-breadwinners, as many well-educated women seek professional positions. The concept of being a housewife among educated women is rapidly weakening. At the same time, the concept of freedom and equality, as well as rights, has grown as the notion of the attainment of happiness of individuals has replaced the traditional concept of obedience and propriety.

Changing Village Scene.   Village society changed considerably with the migration of the young and others into urban areas. The fabric of the tradtional society wore thin, and village solidarity began to crumble. In rural areas, the kinship system and family lineage and family ties have become less important. The abolition of traditional landlordism with the land reform law of 1949 did not entirely destroy the traditional social order of villages, but individuals became increasingly important.

The appearance of rural areas rapidly changed with the New Community Movement (*Saemaŭl undong*) that began in 1971. New houses, new roofs, and new roads were constructed, and new community centers and community enterprise profoundly changed the attitudes and way of life of rural Koreans as they became involved in various political, economic, and social and cultural activities, as well as in decision making processes. Thatched roofs on farmhouses have completely disappeared. The increase in the number of schools, libraries, radios and televisions, refrigerators, and reading materials elevated the cultural standards of the rural population. The New Community Movement also stimulated the growth of cooperation and communal solidarity and improved the sanitary and health standards of the people. The improvement and expansion of highway networks, and increased communication between rural and urban areas led to the development of a new outlook among the village dwellers.

The New Society and Social Patterns.   South Korea is a homogeneous society. It has no ethnic minorities other than a small number of Chinese who immigrated to Korea a long time ago and their family members who were born in Korea. There is no aristocracy, and there is no racial problem. However, it has become a society of classes—upper, middle and lower. Class status is based on educational achievement, political position, economic situation and participation in social activities. Birth no longer is a determining factor for one's social status, but it still is important in certain situations.

The newly emerged families of successful entrepreneurs, professional people, and political and military leaders constitute the new elite class in South Korea, replacing the traditional *yangban* class. Although some members of this class came from former *yangban* families, the majority were self-made men, rising from the commoner class of the past.

The emergence of a class of *nouveau riche* constituted a spectacular social phenomenon of the post-liberation era, particularly after 1961. A dozen members of the *chaebŏl* (capitalist clique who amassed enormous wealth) arose. Among them were such firms as the Samsung, the Lucky, the Daewoo, the Hyundai, and the Ssangyong enterprises. The best known cases are those of Yi Pyŏng-ch'ŏl of the Samsung Enterprises and Chŏng Chu-yŏng of the Hyundai Heavy Industrial Company, which clearly testifies that birth, family ties, and educational background had little or no relevance to one's success in the business world. Recently, the Lotte enterprise of another self-made Korean in Japan joined the *chaebŏl* group of South Korea when he made heavy investments in South Korea.

Despite numerous modern changes, South Korean society remains traditional in many respects: Although certain social customs such as marriage and funeral ceremonies have been modernized, Confucian, Buddhist, and Shamanistic influence on social customs remain strong. Seasonal holidays associated with Confucanism and religious heritage are still observed, traditional rituals for ancestors (*chesa*) and household spiritual (*kosa*) as well as Shaman rituals (*kut*) are still performed by a large number of people.

To be sure, egalitarian concepts grew, but the vast majority of Koreans maintain their traditional conservatism and behavioral patterns. Age still commands respect, and the relationship between seniors and juniors is not based on the principle of equality. Sons still would not smoke or sit cross-legged before their fathers, and sons and young people would hesitate to drink alcoholic beverages before their fathers or elderly persons. The pattern of language has changed somewhat, but the pattern of speech of elders to younger persons or of the young to their elders remains traditional, displaying the respect of the young to the aged.

Regionalism, family ties, and *sŏnbae-hubae* (senior-junior) ties remain strong. One's birthplace is still as important as who one's father or ancestors were. The sense of obligation on the part of *sŏnbae* (those who graduated from a school first) to ''look after'' or help their *hubae* (those who graduated afterwards) is still important. These three ties—regional, family, and school—have been clearly reflected in the composition of political, military, and economic groups. The rise of powerful political leaders and military officers from the southeastern provinces of North and South Kyŏngsang provinces, the regional solidarity of the people of North or South Chŏlla provinces, and the distinctive relations of the so-called KS people (those who graduated from Kyŏnggi High School and Seoul National University) clearly testify to this. ''He is so-and-so's son or grandson," "He is related to so-and-so," or "He is from such-and-such a region" are frequently used descriptions of persons in the process of advancement on the social and political ladders.

South Korean society and human relations are hierarchical although egalitarianism has grown. The traditional notion of *kwanjon minbi* (the government is superior and the people are inferior) still remains, although lip service has been given to the sovereignty of the people. The idea that the government (officials) is the servant of the people has not grown much. The concepts of benevolent bureaucratism or "guided democracy" are widely accepted and practiced. Human relations are still largely based on feudalistic ideas. Elders and parents, as well as politically powerful and economically affluent people enjoy traditional prestige and privileges although the traditional Confucian notion has been considerably weakened. Respect for age is still regarded as a cardinal virtue. The position of wife vis-à-vis husband, younger brother and sister vis-à-vis older brother and sister, student vis-à-vis teacher is hierarchical and feudalistic. One's way to success often depends on how well one observes this order which should not be violated if one wishes to advance in the hierarchical society. Although the position of women has considerably improved, most men refuse to recognize and treat women as equal, resulting in slow progress toward sexual equality.

Social dislocation and the decline of traditional values have created considerable unrest and discord. While the older generation was disturbed by the breakdown of time-honored social ethics and the family system, the many who missed out on the new prosperity, those who were critical of political and economic conditions, and young, idealistic univerity students brought about frequent social upheavals. South Korean universities have been storm centers of disgruntled youths, impatient with the prevailing situations.

The rapidly changing way of life, the rising standard of living, and the steady growth of the urban population created a critical housing shortage. Hundreds of modern apartment buildings were built by both the government housing authority and private firms, but the pace could not keep up with increasing demands. Some 1.5 million housing units have been built since 1961, but there is a housing shortage. Fortunately, urban ghettos, which accompanied urbanization and industrialization in other countries, did not develop in South Korea. Hundreds of shantytowns which had emerged in and around Seoul during and after the Korean War have been swept away as shantytown dwellers moved into government built apartments or acquired their own residences.

Despite tremendous social progress, there remain a number of problems. The disparity between the rich and the poor, the bureaucratic notions and practices of the government, the demand for democratization of politics, and the ever increasing expectations of the people for social justice and equality constituted major causes of social problems. At the same time, the decline of public morality and the breakdown of the traditional social code of conduct and the family system have already aroused serious concern.

Be that as it may, with the urban renewal and expansion plans of the government, most cities such as Seoul, Pusan, Taegu, Kwangju and Taejŏn were rebuilt, and their widened and paved boulevards, modern buildings, parks, and new private dwellings transformed Korean cities into large cosmopolitan areas. The metamorphosis of the cities and rural areas of South Korea during the short span of thirty-five years brought about a remarkable transformation from a "village country" into an urbanized nation.

These problems notwithstanding, with the growth of a modern economy and industries, the development of modern political concepts and systems, the growth of modern educational and cultural institutions and the increases of the number of educated population, the changes in the physical appearance of the people and cities, the development of a cosmopolitan culture, together with the rise of modern values, outlook, mentality, and practices, South Korea at last has joined the modern and developed nations in the world.

Chronology

ca. 30000–2333 B.C.	PREHISTORIC PERIOD
ca. 30000 B.C.	The appearance of the Paleolithic culture
ca. 5000 B.C.	The appearance of the Neolithic culture—pointed bottom pottery, as well as flat bottom pottery and the pottery with comb marking.
ca. 2333–108 B.C.	THE OLD CHOSŎN PERIOD
ca. 2333 B.C.	Traditional date of the founding of the Kingdom of Chosŏn by Tan-gun.
ca. 1200 B.C.	The beginning of the Bronze Age; appearance of black pottery and agricultural tools.
ca. 1122 B.C.	The establishment of Kija Chosŏn.
ca. 800–700 B.C.	The rise of the Chin state of the Han tribes in the south.
ca. 500 B.C.	The beginning of the Iron Age.
ca. 194 B.C.	The rise of Wiman Chosŏn in the north and the three federations of the Han tribes in the south.
109–108 B.C.	Invasion of Korea by Emperor Wu of the Han dynasty of China; the fall of Wiman Chosŏn.
57 B.C.–688 A.D.	THE THREE KINGDOMS PERIOD
57 B.C.	The founding of the state of Saro (later Shilla).
ca. 37 B.C.	The emergence of Koguryŏ.
ca. 18 B.C.	The emergence of Paekche.
313 A.D	The end of the Lolang commandery of China in Korea.
372	Official adoption of Buddhism and the establishment of a school for Confucian studies in Koguryŏ.
384	Official adoption of Buddhism in Paekche.
427	The establishment of the new capital of Koguryŏ at Wanggŏm-sŏng (now Pyongyang).
503	Saro renamed Shilla.
527	Official adoption of Buddhism in Shilla.
612–8	Invasions of the Sui (Chinese) forces; great military victories of the Koguryŏ forces.
644–668	Invasions of the T'ang (Chinese) forces.
663	The destruction of Paekche by the combined forces of Shilla and China.
668	The destruction of Koguryŏ by the combined forces of Shilla and China.
668–918	UNIFIED KOREA OF SHILLA
674	Adoption of a new calendar from T'ang China.
682	The establishment of a school for Confucian learning.
687	Shilla established 5 subcapitals and 9 districts.
699	The emergence of the Kingdom of Parhae in the north.

516

727	The return of Monk Hyech'o's from his pilgrimage to China and India.
ca. 750	The printing of Buddhist texts.
751	The reconstruction of the Pŏmnyu Temple, built in 528, and renaming it the Pulguk Temple.
846	Chang Po-go's rebellion.
895	The founding of the Kingdom of Later Koguryŏ.
900	The founding of the Kingdom of Later Paekche.
918–1392	THE KORYŎ PERIOD
918	The overthrow of Kungye and the founding of the Kingdom of Koryŏ by Wang Kŏn.
935	The surrender of the last Shilla king to Koryŏ.
936	The overthrow of the Later Paekche: reunification of Korea.
993	Invasion of the Khitans.
998	Adoption of the Chinese civil service examination system, and the land grant system.
1011	Publication of the *Tripitaka* with wooden blocks began.
1018	Second invasion of the Khitans.
1104	Invasion of the Jurcheds.
1135–1136	The rebellion of Myoch'ŏng and other rebellions.
1145	The completion of Kim Pu-shik's *Samguk sagi*.
1170	Chŏng Chung-bu's rebellion.
1196	Ch'oe Ch'ung-hŏn's coup; the establishment of dictatorship of the Ch'oe clan.
1231	The first Mongol invasion.
1232	The flight of the Koryŏ court to Kanghwa Island; the second Mongol invasion.
1234	The casting of movable metal type.
1235	The third Mongol invasion.
1251	Production of new printing blocks; publication of the *Tripitaka Koreana*.
1258	The end of dictatorship of the Ch'oe clan.
1259	Establishment of the peace with the Mongols; and acceptance of Mongol domination.
1270	The return of the Koryŏ court to Kaegyŏng; Korea's acceptance of vassalage to the Mongols; the rebellion of the *Sambyŏlch'o*.
1273	The end of the rebellion of the *Sambyŏlch'o*.
1274	The first Mongol-Korean expedition to Japan.
1281	The second Mongol-Korean expedition to Japan.
1285	The publication of Illyŏn's *Samguk yusa*.
1313	April, first population census.
1359–1361	First and second invasion, the Red Turbans.
1388	Coup d'état of General Yi Sŏng-gye.
1392	The end of the Koryŏ kingdom.
1392–1910	THE YI DYNASTY (CHOSŎN) PERIOD
1394	Hanyang (now Seoul) became the capital of Korea.

1403	The casting of new metal type.
1420	April, the founding of the Royal Academy of Scholars.
1432	Publication of *Geography of the Eight Provinces*.
1441	Installation of the first rain gauge.
1446	Promulgation of the new Korean script (*han-gŭl*).
1452	Publication of *History of Koryŏ*.
1453	Yi Ching-ok's rebellion.
1467	Yi Shi-ae's rebellion.
1470	Publication of a new code.
1498	First purge of scholars.
1502	Second purge of scholars.
1519	Third purge of scholars.
1545	Fourth purge of scholars.
1559	Lim Kŏ-jŏng's rebellion.
1592	April, invasion of the Japanese; July, construction of iron-clad war vessels (turtle boats); Admiral Yi Sun-shin's great naval victory.
1597	January, second Japanese invasion.
1598	October, withdrawal of Japanese troops from Korea.
ca. 1610	Introduction of Catholicism.
1624	Yi Kwal's rebellion.
1627	First Manchu invasion.
1628	The crew of a ship-wrecked Dutch vessel rescued off Cheju Island and taken to Seoul.
1636	December, second Manchu invasion.
ca. 1650	Beginning of the *Shirhak* movement.
1653	August, another Dutch ship, the *Sparrow Hawk*, wrecked off Cheju Island; its crew taken to Seoul.
1654	Korean rifle troops sent against the Russians in Manchuria in behalf of the Manchus.
1712	Establishment of the new Sino-Korean boundary line.
1728	Yi In-jwa's rebellion.
1776	Establishment of Kyujanggak (Royal Library).
1785	First anti-Catholic persecution.
1790	Publication of An Chŏng-bok's *Outline of History of Korea*.
1791	Second anti-Catholic persecution.
1801	Third anti-Catholic persecution.
1812	The rebellion of Hong Kyŏng-nae.
1815–1827	Anti-Catholic persecution.
1831	Establishment of Korean Catholic diocese; arrival of French Catholic priests.
1839	Proclamation of anti-Catholic edicts; persecution.
1845–1846	Arrival of British, American and French vessels.
1854	April, arrival of a Russian Admiral E.V. Putiatin.
1855	Introduction of vaccination against smallpox.
1864	Beginning of the reign of King Kojong and the regency of the Taewŏn-gun; April, execution of Ch'oe Che-u.

1866   February, beginning of a large-scale anti-Catholic persecution; August, the destruction of an American merchant ship, the *General Sherman;* September-October, invasion of French naval force.

1871   May-July, invasion of American troops; proclamation of policy of isolation.

1873   December, the end of the regency of the Taewŏn-gun.

1875   September, the *Unyŏ-kan* incident; landing of Japanese troops at Pusan.

1876   February, the arrival of six Japanese naval vessels; February 26, the signing of the Kanghwa treaty with Japan; April-July, a Korean mission to Japan; August 26, the signing of a supplementary treaty and the trade regulation with Japan.

1879   The opening of Wŏnsan to Japanese traders.

1880   May 1, beginning of trade at Wŏnsan; August-September, Kim Hong-jip's mission to Japan.

1881   January, establishment of the Office for the Management of State Affairs; sending of a mission to Japan.

1882   March, beginning of modern military training; May 22, the signing of the Chemulp'o treaty with the United States; June 9, beginning of the military insurrection and the abduction of the Taewŏn-gun to China by the Chinese; the signing of the Chemulp'o treaty with Japan; September 20, departure of a Korean mission headed by Pak Yŏng-hyo to Japan; December 26, establishment of the Foreign Office.

1883   January 1, renaming of Chemulp'o as Inch'ŏn; Adoption of national flag; June, the opening of Inch'ŏn; September, the departure of the first Korean mission headed by Min Yŏng-ik to the United States; October 30, the publication of the first Korean newspaper, the *Hansŏng Sunbo;* November 26, the signing of Korean-British and Korean-German treaties.

1884   June, the return of the Korean mission from the United States; June 21, the signing of the Korean-Italian treaty; July 7, the signing of the Korean-Russian treaty; September, arrival of first Protestant missionary, Dr. Horace N. Allen; December 4, the coup of the Progressive, Chinese military intervention, and the flight of the Progressives to Japan.

1885   January 9, the signing of the Korean-Japanese agreement; April 15, the occupation of Kŏmun Island by British marines; April 18, the signing of the Tientsin Agreement between China and Japan; October 5, the return of the Taewŏn-gun from China to Korea.

1886   January, publication of the *Hansŏng Chubo;* establishment of the first school for girls named Ewha; June 4, the signing of the Korean-French treaty.

1887   February 27, the evacuation of British troops from Kŏmun Island; October, the arrival of Pak Chŏng-yang in the United States as the first Korean minister.

1888   August 20, the signing of a Russo-Korean overland trade agreement.

1894   March, the beginning of the *Tonghak* uprising; July 25, the outbreak of the Sino-Japanese War; July 26, establishment of the

Deliberative Council and the beginning of the *Kabo* Reform; August 26, the conclusion of mutual defense agreement between Korea and Japan.

1895   January 7, the taking of an oath by King Kojong before his ancestors' shrine, and the proclamation of a royal charter, *Hongbŏm shipsajo;* January 18, establishment of the cabinet system; April 17, the signing of the Treaty of Shimonoseki and the end of the Sino-Japanese War; October 8, assassination of Queen Min; December 30, proclamation of the hair-cutting ordinance.

1896   January 1, adoption of the Gregorian calendar; arrival of Dr. Philip Jaisohn (Sŏ Chae-p'il) from the United States; February 11, the flight of the king and the crown prince to the Russian legation; April 7, the publication of *The Independent;* May 14, the conclusion of the Waeber-Komura Memorandum; June 9, the signing of the Lobanov-Yamagata Protocol; July 2, the conclusion of the Min-Lobanov agreement; the establishment of the Independence Club; August, division of Korea into 13 provinces; November 21, construction of the Independence Gate.

1897   February 20, return of King Kojong from the Russian legation; October 12, the renaming of Korea to Empire of Taehan, and the adoption of imperial title by the king.

1898   February 22, the death of the Taewŏn-gun; May 20, opening of Sŏngjin, Kunsan, and Masan; November 4, the arrest of the leaders of the Independence Club and the abolition of the Independence Club.

1899   May 4, the opening of street car operation in Seoul; partial operation of the Seoul-Inch'ŏn railway.

1900   April 10, installation of street lights in Seoul; November 12, the opening of the entire Seoul-Inch'ŏn railway line.

1901   March 23, the signing of the Korean-Belgian treaty.

1902   July 23, the signing of the Korean-Austrian treaty; July 15, the signing of the Korean-Danish treaty; August, adoption of national anthem.

1903   October, founding of the YMCA in Seoul and Seoul Medical School.

1904   February 8, the outbreak of the Russo-Japanese War; February 23, the signing of the Korean-Japanese protocol; August 22, the signing of the Korean-Japanese agreement; the formation of the *Ilchinhoe;* completion of Seoul-Pusan railway line.

1905   March 21, official adoption of Western weights and measures system; June, inauguration of a new monetary system; August 10, the publication of *The Korean Daily News;* September 5, the signing of the Portsmouth treaty and the end of the Russo-Japanese War; November 17, the signing of the Japanese-Korean agreement; November 29, the formation of the Corps for the Advancement of Individuals.

1906   January 28, the renaming of the *Tonghak* sect as *Ch'ŏndogyo;* February 1, the opening of the Residency-General; arrival of Ito Hirobumi as the first Resident-General of Korea; April, the opening of the Seoul-Shinŭiju railway line, August, promulgation of a new public school ordinance.

1907	May, formation of a new cabinet headed by Yi Wan-yong; June, adoption of a new cabinet system, and the arrival of Kojong's envoys at The Hague; July 20, the abdication of Kojong; July 24, the signing of a new Korean-Japanese agreement; promulgation of a new press law and the Public Security Law; July 31, disbanding of the Korean Army, and the beginning of anti-Japanese guerrilla war of the Righteous Armies; August 27, coronation of Emperor Sunjong; November 18, proclamation of a six-article imperial charter.
1908	April, promulgation of the ordinance concerning girls' schools; August, promulgation of an ordinance concerning private schools.
1909	February-April, promulgation of new tax laws; March 4, promulgation of the family registration law; April, the opening of the Seoul-Shinŭiju railway line; July 5, succession of Itō Hirobumi by Sone Arasuke as Resident-General; July 12, the assumption of judicial administration by the Japanese; July 31, abolition of the Ministry of Defense and the Korean military school; September 4, the signing of a treaty between China and Japan concerning Kando, and the establishment of new boundaries between Korea and Manchuria; October 26, assassination of Itō Hirobumi, November 24, the opening of the Bank of Korea.
1910	August 22, the signing of the Treaty of Annexation, and the end of the Yi dynasty and Korean independence; December, the Company Law promulgated.
1910–1945	JAPANESE COLONIAL RULE
1910	October 1, the establishment of the Government-General of Korea; beginning of land survey.
1911	January, the 105 Persons Incident, promulgation of the first Korea Educational Ordinance.
1914	August, the Seoul-Wŏnsan railway line opened.
1918	Completion of the land survey.
1919	January 22, ex-emperor Kojong died; February 8, Korean students in Tokyo issued the Declaration of Independence; March 1, beginning of the March First Independence Movement; April 11, establishment of the Korean Provisional Government in exile in Shanghai.
1920	March 5, publication of the *Chosŏn Ilbo;* April 1, publication of the *Tong-a Ilbo;* October 21, a victory of the Korean insurgents at Ch'ŏngsan-ri.
1925	April 18, founding of the Korean Communist Party in Seoul.
1926	April 25, death of former emperor, Sunjong; June 10, independence demonstrations in Seoul.
1927	February 15, Founding of the *Shin-ganhoe* and the *Kŭnuhoe.*
1929	October 30, the Kwangju student incident; November 3, beginning of the nation-wide anti-Japanese student movement.
1931	July, the Manbosan (Wanpaoshan) incident in Manchuria; anti-Chinese activities in Korea; September 18, the Mukden Incident.
1932	January 8, Yi Pong-ch'ang's attempt to assassinate the Japanese emperor at the Sakurada Gate in Tokyo; April 29, the bomb incident of Yun Pong-gil at the Hungk'uo Park in Shanghai.

1934	Korean Farmland Ordinance promulgated.
1938	February 26, enactment of the Special Army Volunteer Ordinance in Korea; March, promulgation of a new educational ordinance; October 1, beginning of labor mobilization.
1940	February 11, promulgation of the ordinance concerning the adoption of Japanese-style family and given names by the Koreans; August 10, abolition of the *Tong-a Ilbo*, and *Chosŏn Ilbo*, and other Korean language newspapers.
1942	May 8, mobilization of Korean youth into the Japanese imperial army; September 1, the case of the Korean Linguistics Society and the arrest of its leaders.
1943	October 20, mobilization of students into the Japanese army; December 1, the Cairo Declaration of the Allies regarding Korean independence.
1944	January 20, general mobilization of Korean youth into the Japanese armed forces.
1945	August 8, declaration of war by the Soviet Union against Japan; invasion of Soviet troops in Korea; August 15, Japanese acceptance of the Potsdam ultimatum; end of World War II, and liberation of Korea; establishment of the Committee for the Preparation of National Reconstruction.
1945–1948	THE ALLIED OCCUPATION PERIOD
1945	September 2, the division of Korea into two Allied military operational zones along the 38th parallel line; September 6, proclamation of the People's Republic of Korea; September 7, landing of U.S. troops; September 9, signing of the surrender document by the Japanese governor-general; September 11, establishment of the United States Army Military Government in Korea; September 16, the formation of the Korean (Han-guk) Democratic Party; October 21, establishment of South Korean national police; November 7, anti-Communist uprising of the students in Shinŭiju; November 10 and December 1, re-establishment of *Chosŏn* and *Tong-a* daily newspapers; December 27, the Moscow Agreement; eruption of anti-trusteeship demonstrations; December 30, assassination of Song Chin-u.
1946	January 3, nation-wide anti-trusteeship strikes and demonstrations; the fall of the Nationalists in North Korea; February 14, establishment of the Representative Democratic Council; March 13, anti-Communist-inspired labor uprising in Taegu; October 13, establishment of the South Korean Interim Legislative Assembly; November 23, renaming of the Korean Communist Party to the South Korean Workers' Party.
1947	February, establishment of the Supreme People's Assembly in North Korea; creation of the Central People's Committee as the central government of North Korea; June 3, establishment of the South Korean Interim Government in Seoul; July 19, assassination of Yŏ Un-hyŏng; November 14, adoption of the Korean resolution by the U.N. General Assembly; creation of the U.N. Temporary Commission on Korea; December 2, assassination of Chang Tŏk-su.

1948   January 7, establishment of compulsory elementary education system; April 19–21, journey of Kim Ku, Kim Kyu-shik and other to Pyongyang for a joint conference with the Communists; May 10, the U.N.-sponsored general elections in South Korea; May 14, North Korea's suspension of electric power supply to the south; May 31, Convening of the National Assembly in South Korea; adoption of a democratic constitution; election of Dr. Syngman Rhee as president of the Republic of Korea; August 15, inauguration of the Republic and its government; End of the Allied occupation of South Korea; September 3, Supreme People's Assembly's adoption of the constitution of the Democratic People's Republic of Korea; election of Kim Il-sung as premier; September 9, inauguration of the Democratic People's Republic of Korea and its government; October 19, the Yŏsu-Sunch'ŏn military insurrection; outlawing of the South Korean Workers' Party; November 30, promulgation of the law concerning the establishment of South Korean armed forces; December 9, U.N. recognition of the Republic of Korea; withdrawal of Soviet troops.

1949   February, formation of the Democratic Nationalist Party; June 26, assassination of Kim Ku; June 29, completion of U.S. troop withdrawal; July, emergence of the Korean Workers' Party; October 2, establishment of South Korean armed forces.

1950   May 30, National Assembly elections; July 14, South Korea's joining UNESCO; June 25, North Korea invasion of the South; the beginning of the Korean War; June 28, the fall of Seoul; the flight of the South Korean government first to Taejŏn and then to Pusan; July, formation of U.N. Forces under General MacArthur; September 15, amphibious landing of U.N. troops at Inch'ŏn; September 30, Oct. 1, U.N. troops crossed the 38th parallel line into North Korea; October 20, the fall of Pyongyang; October 2, the arrival of the "Volunteers" of China's People's Liberation Army in Korea officially acknowledged; November, withdrawal of U.N. troops from North Korea.

1951   January 4, the fall of Seoul for the second time; March 7, adoption of a new educational system; February 11, the Kŏch'ang incident; April 11, dismissal of General MacArthur as U.N. commander; July 10, the truce negotiations began; December, formation of the Liberal Party.

1952   January 18, the declaration of the Rhee (Peace) Line; July 4, the first constitutional amendment; August 5, re-election of President Rhee by popular votes.

1953   June 14, release by President Rhee of 25,000 Communist prisoners-of-war; July 15, the return of the South Korean government to Seoul; October 1, the conclusion of U.S.-Korean mutual defense treaty.

1954   May 20, general elections for the National Assembly; November 29, the second constitutional amendment.

1955   September 18, formation of the Democratic Party.

1956   May 15, presidential election, re-election of Dr. Rhee; election of Chang Myŏn of the Democratic Party as vice-president; September 28, assassination attempt on Chang Myŏn.

1958	May 2, general elections for the National Assembly; December 26, promulgation of the National Security Law.
1959	December 14, first group of Koreans shipped to North Korea from Japan.
1960	March 15, presidential elections; re-election of President Rhee; anti-government student demonstrations in Masan; April 19, student uprising in Seoul; June 15, adoption of responsible cabinet system; April 27, resignation of President Rhee and his cabinet; July 29, general elections for the National Assembly; August 23, the emergence of the Second Republic; December 31, passage of the Special Laws.
1961	May 16, the military revolution and the fall of the Second Republic; establishment of the Supreme Council for National Reconstruction; May 22, banning of all political activities; establishment of the Central Intelligence Agency.
1962	December 17, a national referendum on a new constitution; December 26, the promulgation of the new constitution.
1963	January 1, the lifting of the ban on political activities; November 26, general elections for the National Assembly; December 17, the emergence of the Third Republic with Park Chung-hee as president.
1964	March-April, student demonstrations against the negotiations for the establishment of normal relations between South Korea and Japan.
1965	June 3, promulgation of martial law in Seoul; June 22, the signing of the South Korean-Japanese treaty; December 18, establishment of diplomatic relations between South Korea and Japan.
1967	June 8, general elections for the National Assembly.
1968	January 21, North Korean commandoes attempt to storm the presidential mansion in Seoul and assassinate President Park.
1969	September 14, passage of constitutional amendment.
1970	March 31, Japanese hijacking of a South Korean passenger plane to North Korea.
1971	April 27, re-election of President Park; May 25, general elections for the National Assembly; December 6, promulgation of national emergency decrees.
1972	July 4, issuance of the statement concerning the opening of North-South political dialogue by Seoul and Pyongyang; August 30, first North-South Red Cross talks; October 12, first North-South political talks; October 17, emergency decrees proclaimed; November 21, a national referendum on the *Yushin* Constitution; December 27, North Korea's adoption of the Socialist Constitution; election of Kim Il-sung as president; December 15, establishment of the National Conference for Unification in South Korea; December 23, re-election of President Park by the National Conference for Unification; December 27, the emergence of the Fourth Republic.
1973	February 27, general elections for the National Assembly; August 8, abduction of Kim Tae-jung from Tokyo to Seoul; suspension of all North-South talks.

1974   January, proclamation of Emergency Decrees Nos. 1-3; April, proclamation of the Emergency Decree No. 4; August 15, assassination of President Park's wife, Madame Yuk, by a North Korean agent from Japan; August 23, cancellation of Emergency Decrees Nos. 1 and 4; October, cancellation of Emergency Decrees Nos. 2 and 3.

1975   February, a national referendum to reaffirm the 1972 *Yushin* Constitution; April 8, proclamation of Emergency Decree No. 7; May 13, proclamation of the Emergency Decree No. 9.

1976   August 18, the killing of two American army officers by North Korean troops at Panmunjom.

1978   April 30, declaration of the twelve mile limit; July 6, elections for the National Conference for Unification; July, Re-election of President Park for the Fourth term of office; December 12, general elections for the National Assembly.

1979   October, violent student demonstrations in Pusan and other southern cities; proclamation of a garrison decree; October 26, assassination of President Park; December 6, election of Ch'oe Kyu-ha as president by the National Conference for Unification; December 12, General Chun Doo-hwan's coup.

1980   May 13, mass student demonstration in Seoul, Pusan, and other cities; May 17, proclamation of the emergency Decree No. 10; banning of all political activities; dissolution of all political parties; arrests of key political leaders; May 18, the Kwangju uprising; May 31, formation of the Special Committee for National Security Measures; August 16, resignation of President Ch'oe; August 27, election of General Chun Doo-hwan as president by the National Conference for Unification; October 17, proclamation of martial law; October 22, a national plebiscite on the new constitution; replacement of the National Assembly by the Legislative Council for National Security; November 25, proclamation of the Political Renovation (Purification) Law and the purge of 835 persons from political life.

1981   January, promulgation of a new National Security Law; January 12, lifting of the October 17, 1980 martial law; February 11, elections for the National Conference for Unification; February 25, election of President Chun as the first president of the Fifth Republic; 470, March 3, inauguration of President Chun and the Fifth Republic; April 1, re-establishment of the National Assembly.

1982   January 3, cancellation of the 36-year-old midnight curfew; March, May, June, and July, cabinet reshuffles; August, the Fifth Five-Year Development Plan inaugurated.

APPENDICES

Appendix A

Major Dynasties and Rulers

Koguryŏ (Ko dynasty) 高句麗 고구려 (? 37 B.C. -668 A.D.)

1. Tongmyŏng Wang   東明王   동명왕 (37 B.C.-19 B.C.)
2. Yuri Wang   琉璃王   유리왕 (19 B.C.-18 A.D.)
3. Taemushin Wang   大武神王   대무신왕 (18-44)
4. Minjung Wang   閔中王   민중왕 (44-48)
5. Mobon Wang   慕本王   모본왕 (48-53)
6. T'aejo Wang   太祖王   태조왕 (53-146)
7. Ch'adae Wang   次大王   차대왕(146-165)
8. Shindae Wang   新大王   신대왕(165-179)
9. Kogukch'ŏn Wang   故國川王   고국천왕 (179-197)
10. Sansang Wang   山上王   산상왕(197-227)
11. Tongch'ŏn Wang   東川王   동천왕 (227-248)
12. Chungch'ŏn Wang   中川王   중천왕 (248-270)
13. Sŏch'ŏn Wang   西川王   서천왕(270-292)
14. Pongsang Wang   烽上王   봉상왕(292-300)
15. Mich'ŏn Wang   美川王   미천왕 (300-331)
16. Kogugwŏn Wang   故國原王   고국원왕 (331-371)
17. Sosurim Wang   小獸林王   소수림왕 (371-384)
18. Kogugyang Wang   故國壤王   고국양왕 (384-391)
19. Kwanggaet'o Wang   廣開土王   광개토왕 (391-413)
20. Changsu Wang   長壽王   장수왕 (413-491)
21. Munja Wang   文咨王   문자왕 (491-519)
22. Anjang Wang   安藏王   안장왕 (519-531)
23. Anwŏn Wang   安原王   안원왕 (531-545)
24. Yangwŏn Wang   陽原王   양원왕(545-559)
25. P'yŏngwŏn Wang   平原王   평원왕 (559-590)
26. Yŏngyang Wang   嬰陽王   영양왕 (590-618)
27. Yŏngnyu Wang   榮留王   영류왕(618-642)
28. Pojang Wang   寶藏王   보장왕 (642-668)

Paekche 百濟 백제 (? 18 B.C.-660 A.D.)

1. Onjo Wang   溫祚王   온조왕 (18 B.C.-28 A.D.)
2. Taru Wang   多婁王   다루왕 (28-77)
3. Kiru Wang   己婁王   기루왕 (77-128)
4. Kaeru Wang   蓋婁王   개루왕 (128-166)
5. Ch'ogo Wang   肖古王   초고왕 (166-214)
6. Kusu Wang   仇首王   구수왕 (214-234)
7. Saban Wang   沙伴王   사반왕 (234)
8. Koi Wang   古爾王   고이왕(234-286)
9. Ch'aekkye Wang   責稽王   책계왕 (286-298)
10. Punsŏ Wang   汾西王   분서왕 (298-304)
11. Piryu Wang   比流王   비류왕 (304-344)
12. Kye Wang   契王   계왕 (344-346)
13. Kŭnch'ogo Wang   近肖古王   근초고왕 (346-375)

14. Kŭn-gusu Wang 近仇首王 근구수왕 (375-384)

15. Ch'imnyu Wang 枕流王 침류왕(384 -385)

16. Chinsa Wang 辰斯王 진사왕 (385-392)

17. Ashin Wang 阿莘王 아신왕 (392-405)

18. Chŏnji Wang 腆支王 전지왕 (405-420)

19. Kuishin Wang 久爾辛王 구이신왕 (420-427)

20. Piyu Wang 毗有王 비유왕(427-455)

21. Kaero Wang 蓋鹵王 개로왕 (455-475)

22. Munju Wang 文周王 문주왕 (475-477)

23. Samgŭn Wang 三斤王 삼근왕(477-479)

24. Tongsŏng Wang 東城王 동성왕 (479-501)

25. Muryŏng Wang 武寧王 무령왕(501 -523)

26. Sŏng Wang 聖王 성왕 (523-554)

27. Widŏk Wang 威德王 위덕왕(554-598)

28. Hye Wang 惠王 혜왕 (598-599)

29. Pŏp Wang 法王 법왕 (599-600)

30. Mu Wang 武王 무왕 (600-641)

31. Ŭija Wang 義慈王 의자왕 (641-660)

Shilla (Pak, Sŏk, Kim dynasties)
新羅 신라 (57 B.C.-935 A.D.)

1. Hyŏkkŏse Kŏsŏgan 赫居世居西干 혁거세거서간 (57 B.C.-4 A.D.)

2. Namhae Ch'ach'aung 南海次次雄 남해차차웅 (4-24)

3. Yuri Isagŭm 儒理尼師今 유리이사금 (24-57)

4. T'arhae Isagŭm 脫解尼師今 탈해이사금 (57-80)

5. P'asa Isagŭm 婆娑尼師今 파사이사금 (80-112)

6. Chima Isagŭm 祇摩尼師今 지마이사금 (112-134)

7. Ilsŏng Isagŭm 逸聖尼師今 일성이사금 (134-154)

8. Adalla Isagŭm 阿達羅尼師今 아달라이사금 (154-184)

9. Pŏrhyu Isagŭm 伐休尼師今 벌휴이사금 (184-196)

10. Naehae Isagŭm 奈解尼師今 내해이사금 (196-230)

11. Chobun Isagŭm 助賁尼師今 조분이사금 (230-247)

12. Ch'ŏmhae Isagŭm 沾解尼師今 첨해이사금 (247-261)

13. Mich'u Isagŭm 味鄒尼師今 미추이사금 (261-284)

14. Yurye Isagŭm 儒禮尼師今 유례이사금 (284-298)

15. Kirim Isagŭm 基臨尼師今 기림이사금 (298-310)

16. Hŭrhae Isagŭm 訖解尼師今 흘해이사금 (310-356)

17. Naemul Maripkan 奈勿麻立干 내물마립간 (356-402)

18. Shilsŏng Maripkan 實聖麻立干 실성마립간 (402-417)

19. Nulchi Maripkan 訥祇麻立干 눌지마립간 (417-458)

20. Chabi Maripkan 慈悲麻立干 자비마립간 (458-479)

21. Soji Maripkan 炤知麻立干 소지마립간 (479-500)

22. Chijŭng Wang 智證王 지증왕(500-514)

23. Pŏp'ŭng Wang 法興王 법흥왕 (514 -540)

24. Chinhŭng Wang 眞興王 진흥왕(540 -576)

25. Chinji Wang 眞智王 진지왕 (576-579)

26. Chinp'yŏng Wang 眞平王 진평왕 (579-632)

27. Sŏndŏk Yŏwang 善德女王 선덕여왕 (632-647) (queen)

28. Chindŏk Yŏwang 眞德女王 진덕여왕 (647-654) (queen)

29. Muyŏl Wang 武烈王 무열왕 (654-661)

30. Munmu Wang 文武王 문무왕(661-681)

31. Shinmun Wang 神文王 신문왕 (681 -692)

32. Hyoso Wang 孝昭王 효소왕 (692-702)

33. Sŏngdŏk Wang 聖德王 성덕왕 (702 -737)

34. Hyosŏng Wang 孝成王 효성왕(737 -742)

35. Kyŏngdŏk Wang 景德王 경덕왕 (742-765)

36. Hyegong Wang 惠恭王 혜공왕(765 -780)

37. Sŏndŏk Wang 宣德王 선덕왕 (780- 785)

38. Wŏnsŏng Wang 元聖王 원성왕 (785-798)

39. Sosŏng Wang 昭聖王 소성왕 (798- 800)

40. Aejang Wang 哀莊王 애장왕 (800- 809)

41. Hŏndŏk Wang 憲德王 헌덕왕 (809 -826)

42. Hŭngdŏk Wang 興德王 흥덕왕(826 -836)

43. Hŭigang Wang 僖康王 희강왕(836 -838)

44. Minae Wang 閔哀王 민애왕 (838- 839)

45. Shinmu Wang 神武王 신무왕 (839)

46. Munsŏng Wang 文聖王 문성왕(839 -857)

47. Hŏnan Wang 憲安王 헌안왕 (857- 861)

48. Kyŏngmun Wang 景文王 경문왕 (861-875)

49. Hŏn-gang Wang 憲康王 헌강왕(875 -886)

50. Chŏnggang Wang 定康王 정강왕 (886-887)

51. Chinsŏng Yŏwang 眞聖女王 진성여 왕 (887-897) (queen)

52. Hyogong Wang 孝恭王 효공왕(897 -912)

53. Shindŏk Wang 神德王 신덕왕(912- 917)

54. Kyŏngmyŏng Wang 景明王 경명왕 (917-924)

55. Kyŏng-ae Wang 景哀王 경애왕(924 -927)

56. Kyŏngsun Wang 敬順王 경순왕 (927-935)

Koryŏ (Wang dynasty) 高麗 고려 (918-1392)

1. T'aejo 太祖 태조 (918-943)
2. Hyejong 惠宗 혜종 (943-945)
3. Chŏngjong 定宗 정종 (945-949)
4. Kwangjong 光宗 광종 (949-975)
5. Kyŏngjong 景宗 경종 (975-981)
6. Sŏngjong 成宗 성종 (981-997)
7. Mokchong 穆宗 목종 (997-1009)
8. Hyŏnjong 顯宗 현종 (1009-1031)
9. Tŏkchong 德宗 덕종 (1031-1034)
10. Chŏngjong 靖宗 정종 (1034-1046)
11. Munjong 文宗 문종 (1046-1083)
12. Sunjong 順宗 순종 (1083)
13. Sŏnjong 宣宗 선종 (1083-1094)
14. Hŏnjong 獻宗 헌종 (1094-1095)
15. Sukchong 肅宗 숙종 (1095-1105)
16. Yejong 睿宗 예종 (1105-1122)
17. Injong 仁宗 인종 (1122-1146)
18. Ŭijong 毅宗 의종 (1146-1170)
19. Myŏngjong 明宗 명종 (1170-1197)
20. Shinjong 神宗 신종 (1197-1204)
21. Hŭijong 熙宗 희종 (1204-1211)
22. Kangjong 康宗 강종 (1211-1213)
23. Kojong 高宗 고종 (1213-1259)
24. Wŏnjong 元宗 원종 (1259-1274)
25. Ch'ungyŏl Wang 忠烈王 충렬왕 (1274-1308)
26. Ch'ungsŏn Wang 忠宣王 충선왕 (1308-1313)
27. Ch'ungsuk Wang 忠肅王 충숙왕 (1313-1330, 1332-1339)
28. Ch'unghye Wang 忠惠王 충혜왕 (1330-1332, 1339-1344)
29. Ch'ungmok Wang 忠穆王 충목왕 (1344-1348)
30. Ch'ungjŏng Wang 忠定王 충정왕 (1348-1351)
31. Kongmin Wang 恭愍王 공민왕 (1351-1374)
32. U Wang 禑王 우왕 (1374-1388)
33. Ch'ang Wang 昌王 창왕 (1388-1389)
34. Kongyang Wang 恭讓王 공양왕 (1389-1392)

Chosŏn (Yi dynasty) 朝鮮 조선 (1392-1910)

1. T'aejo 太祖 태조 (1392-1398)
2. Chŏngjong 定宗 정종 (1398-1400)
3. T'aejong 太宗 태종 (1400-1418)
4. Sejong 世宗 세종 (1418-1450)
5. Munjong 文宗 문종 (1450-1452)
6. Tanjong 端宗 단종 (1452-1455)
7. Sejo 世祖 세조 (1455-1468)
8. Yejong 睿宗 예종 (1468-1469)
9. Sŏngjong 成宗 성종 (1469-1494)
10. Yŏnsan-gun 燕山君 연산군 (1494-1506)
11. Chungjong 中宗 중종 (1506-1544)
12. Injong 仁宗 인종 (1544-1545)
13. Myŏngjong 明宗 명종 (1545-1567)
14. Sŏnjo 宣祖 선조 (1567-1608)
15. Kwanghaegun 光海君 광해군 (1608-1623)
16. Injo 仁祖 인조 (1623-1649)
17. Hyojong 孝宗 효종 (1649-1659)
18. Hyŏnjong 顯宗 현종 (1659-1674)
19. Sukchong 肅宗 숙종 (1674-1720)
20. Kyŏngjong 景宗 경종 (1720-1724)
21. Yŏngjo 英祖 영조 (1724-1776)
22. Chŏngjo 正祖 정조 (1776-1800)
23. Sunjo 純祖 순조 (1800-1834)
24. Hŏnjong 憲宗 헌종 (1834-1849)
25. Ch'olchong 哲宗 철종 (1849-1863)
26. Kojong 高宗 고종 (1863-1907)
27. Sunjong 純宗 순종 (1907-1910)

Japanese Governors-Generals (1910-1945)

1. Terauchi Masatake 寺内正毅 (1910-1916)
2. Hasegawa Yoshimichi 長谷川好道 (1916-1919)
3. Saitō Makoto 齋藤實 (1919-1927)
4. Ugaki Kazushige 宇垣一成 (1927) (acting governor-general)
5. Yamanashi Hanzō 山梨半造 (1927-1929)
6. Saitō Makoto 齋藤實 (1929-1931)
7. Ugaki Kazushige 宇垣一成 (1931-1936)
8. Minami Jirō 南次郎 (1936-1942)
9. Koiso Kuniaki 小磯國昭 (1942-1944)
10. Abe Nobuyuki 阿部信行 (1944-1945)

Appendix B

Protocol Signed Between Korea and Japan (February 23, 1904)

Article 1.   For the purpose of maintaining a permanent and solid friendship between Korea and Japan and firmly establishing peace in the Far East, the Imperial Government of Korea shall place full confidence in the Imperial Government of Japan, and adopt the advice of the latter in regard to improvements in administration.

Article 2.   The Imperial Government of Japan shall in spirit of firm friendship ensure the safety and repose of the Imperial House of Korea.

Article 3.   The Imperial Government of Japan definitively guarantee the independence and territorial integrity of the Korean Empire.

Article 4.   In case the welfare of the Imperial House of Korea or the territorial integrity of Korea is endangered by aggression of a third power or internal disturbances, the Imperial Government of Japan shall immediately take such necessary measures as circumstances require, and in such case the Imperial Government of Korea shall give full facilities to promote the action of the Imperial Japanese Government. The Imperial Government of Japan may for the attainment of the above mentioned object occupy when the circumstances require such places as may be necessary from strategic points of view.

Article 5.   The Governments of the two countries shall not in the future without mutual consent conclude with a third power such an arrangement as may be contrary to the principles of the present protocol.

Article 6.   Details in connection with the present protocol shall be arranged as the circumstances may require between the Minister of Foreign Affairs of Korea and the representative of the Empire of Japan.

Yi Chi-yong / Seal /
Minister of Foreign Affairs *ad interim*
The 23rd day of the 2nd month of the 8th year of Kwangmu

Hayashi Gonsuke / Seal /
Envoy Extraordinary and Minister Plenipotentiary
The 23rd day of the 2nd month of the 38th year of Meiji

Appendix C

Korean-Japanese Agreement*(November 17, 1905)

The Government of Japan and Korea, desiring to strengthen the principle of solidarity which unites the two Empires, have with that object in view agreed upon and concluded the following stipulations to serve until the moment arrives when it is recognized that Korea has attained national strength:

Article 1.   The Government of Japan, through the Ministry of Foreign Affairs at Tokyo, will hereafter have control and direction of the external relations and affairs of Korea, and the diplomatic and consular representatives of Japan will have the charge of the subjects and interests of Korea in foreign countries.

Article 2.   The Government of Japan undertake to see to the execution of the treaties actually existing between Korea and the other Powers, and the Government of Korea engage not to conclude hereafter any act or engagement having an international character, except through the medium of the Government of Japan.

Article 3.   The Government of Japan shall be represented at the Court of His Majesty the Emperor of Korea by a Resident-General, who shall reside at Seoul, primarily for the purpose of taking charge of and directing matters relating to diplomatic affairs. He shall have the right of private and personal audience of His Majesty the Emperor of Korea. The Japanese Government shall also have the right to station Residents at the several open ports and such other places in Korea as they may deem necessary. Such Residents shall, under the direction of the Resident-General, exercise the powers and functions hitherto appertaining to Japanese Consuls in Korea and shall perform such duties as may be necessary in order to carry into full effect the provisions of this agreement.

Article 4.   The stipulations of all treaties and agreements existing between Japan and Korea not inconsistent with the provisions of this Agreement shall continue in force.

Article 5.   The Government of Japan undertake to maintain the welfare and dignity of the Imperial House of Korea.

In faith whereof, the Undersigned duly authorized by their Government have signed this Agreement and affixed their seals.

Hayashi Gonsuke /Seal/
Envoy Extraordinary and Minister Plenipotentiary
The 17th day of the 11th month of the 39th year of Meiji

Pak Che-sun /Seal/
The 17th day of the 11th month of the 9th year of Kwangmu

*This agreement was a convention providing for control of Korean foreign relations by Japan and the establishment of the Japanese Residency-General for the purpose of taking charge of and directing matters relating to diplomatic affairs of Korea.

The Korean called the agreement by several different names: the *Ŭlsa hyŏpyak* (The 1905 Agreement), the *Ojoyak* (The Five-Article Treaty), or the *Chei Han-Il hyŏpyak* (The Second Korean-Japanese Agreement of 1905).

The Japanese, on the other hand, called it the *Nikkan gitei-sho* (The Japanese-Korean Agreement), or *hogo joyaku* (The Treaty of Protection), misleading many to believe that the name of the agreement was as such.

Appendix D

Treaty of Annexation (August 22, 1910)

The Proclamation

Notwithstanding the earnest and laborious work of reforms in the administration of Korea in which the Governments of Japan and Korea have been engaged for more than four years since the conclusion of the Agreement of 1905, the existing system of government in that country has not proved entirely equal to the duty of preserving public order and tranquility; and in addition, the spirit of suspicion and misgiving dominate the whole peninsula.

In order to maintain peace and stability in Korea, to promote the prosperity and welfare of Koreans, and at the same time to ensure the safety and repose of foreign residents, it has been made abundantly clear that fundamental changes in the actual regime of government are absolutely essential. The Governments of Japan and Korea, being convinced of the urgent necessity of introducing reforms responsive to the requirements of the situation and of furnishing sufficient guarantee for the future, have, with the approval of His Majesty the Emperor of Japan and His Majesty the Emperor of Korea, concluded, through their respective plenipotentiaries, a treaty providing for complete annexation of Korea to the Empire of Japan. By virtue of that important act, which shall take effect on its promulgation on August 29, 1910, the Imperial Government of Japan undertake the entire government and administration of Korea, and they hereby declare that the matters relating to foreigners and foreign trade in Korea shall be conducted in accordance with the following rules. . .

The Treaty

His Majesty the Emperor of Japan and His Majesty the Emperor of Korea, having in view the special and close relations between their respective countries, desiring to promote the common weal of the two nations and to assure the permanent peace in the Far East, and being convinced that these objects can be best attained by the annexation of Korea to the Empire of Japan, have resolved to conclude a treaty of such annexation and have, for that purpose, appointed as their plenipotentiaries, that is to say, His Majesty the Emperor of Japan Viscount Terauchi Masatake, Resident-General, and His Majesty the Emperor of Korea Yi Wan-yong, Prime Minister, who upon mutual conference and deliberation have agreed to the following articles:

Article 1.   His Majesty the Emperor of Korea makes the complete and permanent cession to His Majesty the Emperor of Japan of all rights of sovereignty over the whole of Korea.

Article 2.   His Majesty the Emperor of Japan accepts the cession mentioned in the preceding article and consents to the complete annexation of Korea to the Empire of Japan.

Article 3. His Majesty the Emperor of Japan will accord to their Majesties the Emperor and ex-Emperor and His Imperial Highness the Crown Prince of Korea and their consorts and heirs such titles, dignity, and honor as are appropriate to their respective ranks, and sufficient annual grants will be made for the maintenance of such titles, dignity and honor.

Article 4. His Majesty the Emperor of Japan will also accord appropriate honor and treatment to the members of the Imperial House of Korea and their heirs other than those mentioned in the preceding article, and the funds necessary for the maintenance of such honor and treatment will be granted.

Article 5. His Majesty the Emperor of Japan will confer peerage and monetary grants upon those Koreans who, on account of meritorious services, are regarded as deserving such special recognition.

Article 6. In consequence of the aforesaid annexation the Government of Japan assume the entire government and administration of Korea, and undertake to afford full protection for the persons and property of Koreans obeying the laws there in force to promote the welfare of all such Koreans.

Article 7. The Government of Japan will, so far as circumstances permits, employ in the public service of Japan in Korea those Koreans who accept the new regime loyally and in good faith and who are duly qualified for such service.

Article 8. This treaty, having been approved by His Majesty the Emperor of Japan and His Majesty the Emperor of Korea, shall take effect from the state of its promulgation.

In faith thereof:

Resident-General Viscount Terauchi Masatake
Prime Minister Yi Wan-yong

Appendix E

Declaration of Independence (March 1, 1919)

We hereby proclaim the independence of Korea and the liberty of the Korean people. We announce this to the nations of the world in order to manifest the principle of the equality of man, and we pass it onto our posterity in order to preserve forever our people's just rights to self-preservation. We declare this in witness of our history of five millennia, and in the name of twenty million united people so as to insure the perpetual, permanent, and unrestricted progress of our people, and to join the great movement for the reconstruction of the world order, inspired by the conscience of mankind. This is in accordance with the command of Heaven, the great trend of the time, and a popular manifestation of the principle of coexistence of all mankind. Nothing in the world can stop or suppress this.

For the first time in the history of several thousands of years, our people for the past ten years have suffered, under alien domination, tyranny and oppression, which are the legacies of antiquity. How much of our right to life has been plundered? How much of our spiritual progress has been barred? How much of our honor and dignity have been violated? And, how much of our opportunity to contribute to the cultural progress of the world with our new visions and creativity has been lost?

If we are to make known to the world our past grievances, to deliver ourselves from our present sufferings, to remove future threats, and advance our national dignity and nobility, to cultivate the character of individual citizens, to prevent our children from an inheritance of shame, to assure a full and happy life for our posterity, our first urgent task is to secure the independence of the people. Today, twenty million hearts are dedicated to the attainment of this goal, and human nature and the sentiment of the age combine with the armies of righteousness and moral law support us. No barrier is too strong for us to break down and no goals unattainable.

We are not here merely to accuse Japan for her breach of numerous solemn agreements entered into since the Treaty of Friendship of 1876, nor are we here to reprimand Japan for her lack of integrity and faithfulness simply because her teachers in their classes and her politicians in their practices have regarded our civilized people as savages, seeking only the pleasure of the conqueror, and have shown contempt for the age-old tradition of our society. Indeed, the urgency of self-examination and self-innovation does not allow us time to find fault with others. Neither can we, who work at great speed to mend the wrongs of the present age, afford to spend time grieving over what is past and gone. Our critical task today lies only in self-reconstruction and not in the destruction of others. Our work is to chart the new destiny of our own in accord with the solemn dictates of our conscience and not to hate or reject others, swayed only by momentary emotions or resentments over the past. Our purpose is to correct and reform today's unnatural, illogical, and maladjusted conditions created by power-hungry and fame-seeking Japanese politicians who were bound by archaic ideas and force. Our aim is to restore conditions to be harmonious with just principles which are natural and logical.

Examine the result of the annexation brought about against our wishes. Under unjust and unequal treatment, the suffocating oppression, and the hypocritical and falsified statistics, the resentment of our people, which forever prevents the harmonious existence of the two people with opposing interests, is ever deepening.

Who cannot see that the shortest path to avoidance of disaster and to an invitation to mutual blessings between the two peoples is to take enlightened and courageous steps to redress past errors and cultivate new friendly relations based on true understanding and sympathy? To bind by force twenty million resentful people will not only impair forever peace in the Far East, but will also deepen the ever-increasing fear and suspicion toward Japan of four hundred million Chinese, upon whom the key to peace in the Far East rests. It will surely invite the tragedy of mutual destruction of the entire Far Eastern region. Therefore, the independence of Korea is to induce our people to pursue their rightful course for life and prosperity; at the same time, to enable Japan to escape from an evil path and fulfill her grave responsibilities as leader of the Far East, and to rescue China from every pressing anxiety and fear. Furthermore, our action is taken as a necessary step for the establishment of peace in the Far East and that of the world and for the promotion of happiness of all mankind. How could this be an outburst of emotion!

Behold, a new world unfolds before our eyes. The Age of Force is gone and the Age of Reason and Righteousness has arrived. The spirit of moral law and humanity, nurtured and perfected during past centuries, is about to shed its light of new civilization upon the affairs of mankind. The arrival of the new spring to the earth calls for the revival of all creatures. If the forces of the past have suffocated the people like the cold snow and ice of winter, then the force of the present age is the revitalzing breeze and warmth of spring.

Finding ourselves amid this age of restoration and reconstruction, and riding with the changing tide of the world, we neither hesitate, nor fear to complete our task. We must guard our distinctive rights to liberty and freedom, and pursue the happiness of a full life. It is our sacred duty to exhibit our indigenous creative energy, and crystalize and achieve our people's spiritual glory in a world filled with spring. For these reasons we have been awakened.

The conscience of mankind is with us; truth marches with us. Young and old, rise and come forward from your resting places; let us accomplish our tasks for a resurrection in harmony with nature. The spirits of our ancestors protect us from within, and the trend of the entire world assists us from without. Undertaking this task is success; let us march forward into the light before us.

Pledge of the Three Principles

1. Ours is an undertaking in behalf of life, humanity, righteousness, dignity and honor at the request of our people. Exhibit our spirit of liberty; let no one follow his instinct to agitate for the rejection of others.
2. Let each and every person demonstrate to the end our people's rightful wishes and desires.
3. Let all our actions be orderly and solemn so that our demands and our attitudes may be honorable and upright.

The First Day of March of the 4252nd
Year (1919) of the Kingdom of Korea

Son Pyŏng-hūi, Kil Sŏn-ju, Yi P'il-chu, Paek Yong-sŏng, Kim Wan-gyu, Kim Pyŏng-jo, Kim Ch'ang-jun, Kwŏn Tong-jin, Kwŏn Pyŏng-dŏk, Na Yong-hwan, Na In-hyŏp, Yang Chŏn-baek, Yang Han-muk, Yu Yŏ-dae, Yi Kap-sŏng, Yi Myŏng-yong, Yi Sŭng-hun, Yi Chong-hun, Yi Chong-il, Lim Ye-hwan, Pak Chun-sŭng, Pak Hŭi-do, Pak Tong-wan, Shin Hong-shik, Shin Sŏk-ku, O Se-ch'ang, O Hwa-yŏng, Chŏng Ch'un-su, Ch'oe Sŏng-mo, Ch'oe Rin, Han Yong-un, Hong Pyŏng-gi, and Hong Ki-jo.

*Translated by Andrew C. Nahm

Appendix F

Heads of Government of the Republic of Korea (1948–   )

1. Presidents

	Term of Office
Yi Sŭng-man (Syngman Rhee)	Aug. 48–Aug. 52
Yi Sŭng-man	Aug. 52–Aug. 56
Yi Sŭng-man	Aug. 56–Apr. 60
Hŏ Chŏng (Acting)	Apr. 60–June 60
Kwak Sang-hun (Acting)	June 1960
Hŏ Chŏng (Acting)	June 60–Aug. 60
Yun Po-sŏn	Aug. 60–Mar. 62
Park Chung-hee (Acting)	Mar. 62–Dec. 63
Park Chung-hee	Dec. 63–June 67
Park Chung-hee	July 67–June 71
Park Chung-hee	July 71–Dec. 72
Park Chung-hee	Dec. 72–Dec. 78
Park Chung-hee	Dec. 78–Oct. 79
Ch'oe Kyu-ha (Acting)	Oct. 79–Dec. 79
Ch'oe Kyu-ha	Dec. 79–Aug. 80
Chun Doo-hwan (Acting)	August 1980
Chun Doo-hwan	Aug. 80–Feb. 81
Chun Doo-hwan	Mar. 81–

2. Vice-presidents. (The Office of Vice President was abolished in 1960)

Yi Shi-yŏng	July 48–May 51
Kim Sŏng-su	May 51–May 52
Ham T'ae-yŏng	Aug. 52–Aug. 56
Chang Myŏn	Aug. 56–Apr. 60

3. Premiers (The Office of Premier was abolished in 1954; restored in 1960)

Yi Pŏm-sŏk	Aug. 48–Apr. 50
Shin Sŏng-mo (Acting)	Apr. 50–Nov. 50
Chang Myŏn	Nov. 50–Apr. 51
Hŏ Chŏng (Acting)	Apr. 51–Apr. 52
Yi Yun-yŏng (Acting)	Apr. 52–May 52
Chang T'aek-sang	May 52–Sept. 52
Paek Tu-jin (Acting)	Oct. 52–Apr. 53
Paek Tu-jin	Apr. 53–June 54
Pyŏn Yŏng-t'ae	June 54–Nov. 54
Hŏ Chŏng	April 60–Aug. 60
Chang Myŏn	Aug. 60–May 61

Chang To-yŏng	May 61–July 61
Song Yo-ch'an	July 61–June 62
Kim Hyŏn-ch'ŏl	July 62–Dec. 63
Ch'oe Tu-sŏn	Dec. 63–May 64
Chŏng Il-kwŏn	May 64–Dec. 70
Paek Tu-jin	Dec. 70–June 71
Kim Chong-p'il	June 71–Dec. 73
Ch'oe Kyu-ha (Acting)	Dec. 75–Mar. 76
Ch'oe Kyu-ha	Mar. 76–Dec. 79
Shin Hyŏn-hwak	Dec. 79–May 80
Pak Ch'ung-hun (Acting)	May 80–Sept. 80
Nam Tŏg-u (Acting)	September 1980
Nam Tŏg-u	Sept. 80–Jan. 82
Yu Ch'ang-sun (Acting)	January 1982
Yu Ch'ang-sun	Jan. 82–June 82
Kim Sang-hyŏp (Acting)	June 82–Sept. 82
Kim Sang-hyŏp	Sept. 82–Oct. 83
Chin Iee-jong	Oct. 83–Feb. 85

4. Deputy-premiers concurrenly Ministers of the Economic Planning Board

Kim Yu-t'aek	Dec. 63–May 64
Chang Ki-yŏng	May 64–Oct. 67
Pak Ch'ung-hun	Oct. 67–June 69
Kim Hak-ryŏl	June 69–Jan. 72
T'ae Wan-sŏn	Jan. 72–Sept. 74
Nam Tŏk-u	Sept. 74–Dec. 78
Shin Hyŏn-hwak	Dec. 78–Dec. 79
Yi Han-bin	Dec. 79–May 80
Kim Wŏn-gi	May–Sept. 80
Shin Pyŏng-hyŏn	Sept. 80–Jan. 82
Kim Chun-sŏng	Jan. 82–July 83
So Sŏk-chŭn	July–Oct. 83
Shin Pyŏng-hyŏn	Oct. 83–Jan. 86

Appendix G

Heads* of the Democratic People's Republic of Korea (1948–   )

Kim Tu-bong
Chairman of the Presidium of the Supreme People's Assembly, 1948–1957

Ch'oe Yong-gŏn
Chairman of the Presidium of the Supreme People's Assembly, 1957–1972

Kim Il-sung
President, 1972–

> *Chairman of the Presidium of the Supreme People's Assembly was head of state until the adoption in 1972 of a new constitution, which established a presidential system.

Selected Bibliography

A. ENGLISH LANGUAGE SOURCES

1. Anthropology and Sociology

Horace N. Allen, *Fact and Fancy*. Seoul: The Methodist Publishing House, 1904.

——————, *Things Korean: A Collection of Sketches and Anecdotes Missionary and Diplomatic*. New York: Fleming H. Revell, 1908.

Herbert Barringer, *Social Stratification and Industrialization in Korea*. International Liaison Committee on Republic of Korea (ILCORK), Work Paper No. 11. Seoul, 1971.

Vincent S. R. Brandt, *A Korean Village Between Farm and Sea*. Cambridge: Harvard University Press, 1971.

Charles Dallet, *Traditional Korea*. New Haven: Human Relations Area Files, 1954.

James S. Gale, *Korean Sketches*. Nashville: Publishing House of the Methodist Episcopal Church South, 1898.

Gordon Howes and Chin-hong Kim, *Korean Kinship Behavior and Structure*. Hamilton, N.Y.: Korea Research Associates, 1952.

Younghill Kang, *The Grass Roof*. New York: C. Scribner's, 1931.

Helen K. Kim, *Rural Education and the Regeneration of Korea*. New York: Columbia University, 1931.

Percival Lowell, *Chosen: The Land of the Morning Calm—A Sketch of Korea*. Boston: Tichnor and Co., 1888.

Robert J. Moose, *Village Life in Korea*. Nashville: Publishing House of the Methodist Episcopal Church South, 1911.

Cornelius Osgood, *The Koreans and Their Culture*. New York: Ronald Press, 1951.

2. Art and Art History

J. Barinka, *The Arts of Ancient Korea*, tr. from German by Iris Urwin. London: Peter Nevill, 1962.

Alan C. Covell, *Shamanist Folk Paintings: Korea's Eternal Spirits*. Seoul: Hollym Corp., 1984.

Andreas Eckhardt, *A History of Korean Art*, tr. from German by J.M. Kindersley. London: Goldstone, 1929.

G. St. G. M. Gompertz, *Korean Celadon and Other Wares of the Koryo Period.* London: Faber and Faber, 1963.

_____, *Korean Pottery and Porcelain of the Yi Period.* London: Faber and Faber, 1968.

William B. Honey, *Corean Pottery.* London: Faber and Faber, 1947.

Che-won Kim and G. St. G. M. Gompertz, *The Ceramic Art of Korea.* London: Faber and Faber, 1961.

Che-won Kim and Lena Kim-Lee, *Arts of Korea.* Tokyo: Kodansha International, 1974.

Evelyn McCune, *The Arts of Korea: An Illustrated History.* Rutland, Vt. and Tokyo: Charles E. Tuttle, 1962.

3. Culture: Education, Literature, Philosophy and Religion.

Charles A. Clark, *Religions of Old Korea.* New York: Fleming H. Revell, 1932.

Choi Min-hong, *A Modern History of Korean Philosophy.* Seoul: Songmunsa, 1978.

Chon Sin-yong ed., *Buddhist Culture in Korea.* Seoul: International Cultural Foundation, 1974.

Choo Young-ha, *The Education in the Yi Dynasty.* Seoul: Sudo Women's Teachers College, 1960.

Jon C. Covell, *Korea's Cultural Roots.* Salt Lake City and Seoul: Moth House and Hollym Corp., 1981.

Ha Tae-hung, *Folk Culture and Family Life.* Seoul: The Korean Information Service, 1958.

International Cultural Foundation ed., *Buddhist Culture in Korea.* Seoul, 1960.

_____, *Folk Culture in Korea.* Seoul, 1974.

_____, *Upper-class Culture in the Yi Dynasty Korea.* Seoul, 1974.

Roger Janelli, *Ancestor Worship in Korean Society.* Stanford: Stanford University Press, 1982.

Hugh A. W., Kang, ed., *The Traditional Culture and Society of Korea: Thoughts and Institutions.* Honolulu; Center for Korean Studies, University of Hawaii, 1975.

Hai-jin Kim, *Buddhism and Korean Culture.* New Delhi: The International Academy of Indian Culture, 1958.

Peter H. Lee, complied and edited, *Anthology of Korean Literature from Early Times to the Nineteenth Century.* Honolulu: The University Press of Hawaii, 1981.

_____, ed., *Flowers of Fire: Twentieth-Century Korean Stories.* Honolulu: The University Press of Hawaii, 1974.

_____, compiled and edited, *Poems from Korea: A Historical Anthology.*

Honolulu: The University Press of Hawaii, 1974.

Charlotte D. Meineske, *Education in Korea*. Seoul: Ministry of Education, Republic of Korea, 1958.

Frederick Starr, *Korean Buddhism*. Boston: Marshall James, 1918.

4. Economy, Economic History, and Geography

Patricia M. Bartz, *South Korea: A Descriptive Geography*. Oxford: Clarendon Press, 1972.

Cheng-siang Chen, *Agricultural Geography of Korea*. Hong Kong; Geographical Research Center, University of Hong Kong, 1970.

Hochin Choi, *The Economic History of Korea*. Seoul: The Freedom Library, 1971.

David C. Cole and Princeton N. Lyman, *Korean Development: The Interplay of Politics and Economics*. Cambridge: Harvard University Press, 1971.

Andrew J. Grajdanzev, *Modern Korea, Her Economic and Social Development Under the Japanese*. New York: Institute of Pacific Relations, 1944.

Hoon-koo Lee, *Land Utilization and Rural Economy in Korea*. Chicago: The University of Chicago Press, 1936.

Paul W. Kuznets, *Economic Growth and Structure in the Republic of Korea*. New Haven: The Yale Press, 1977.

Shannon McCune, *Korea's Heritage: A Regional and Social Geography*. Rutland, Vt. and Tokyo: Charles E. Tuttle, 1956

_____, *Views of the Geography of Korea, 1935–1960*. Seoul: The Korean Research Center, 1980.

Sang-chul Suh, *Growth and Structural Changes in the Korean Economy, 1910-1940*. Cambridge: Council on East Asian Studies, Harvard University, 1978.

V. T. Zaichikov, *Geography of Korea*, tr. by Albert Perry. New York: Institute of Pacific Relations, 1952.

5. History

Allen D. Clark, *History of the Korean Church*. Seoul: Christian Literature Society, 1960.

Soon Sung Cho, *Korea in World Politics, 1940-1950: An Evaluation of American Responsibility*. Berkeley and Los Angeles: The University of California Press, 1967.

Ching-yang Choe, *The Rule of the Taewŏn-gun, 1864-1883: Restoration in Yi Korea*. Cambridge: East Asian Research Center, Harvard University, 1972.

Bong-youn Choy, *Korea: A History*. Rutland, Vt. and Tokyo: Charles E. Tuttle, 1971.

Henry Chung, *The Case of Korea: A Collection of Evidence on the Japanese Movement*. New York: Fleming H. Revell, 1921.

Hilary Conroy, *The Japanese Seizure of Korea: 1868-1910—A Study of Realism and Idealism in International Relations*. Philadelphia: University of Pennsylvania Press, 1960.

Bruce Cumings, ed., *Child of Conflict: The Korean-American Relationship, 1943-1953*. Seattle and London: University of Washington Press, 1983.

_____, *The Origins of the Korean War: Liberation and the Emergence of Separate Regimes, 1945-1947*. Princeton: Princeton University Press, 1981.

Martina Deuchler, *Confucian Gentlemen and Barbarian Envoys: The Opening of Korea, 1875-1885*. Seattle and London: University of Washington Press, 1983.

James S. Gale, *The History of the Korean People*. Seoul: Christian Literature Society, 1927.

_____, *Korea in Transition*. Cincinnati: Jennings and Graham, 1929.

William Griffis, *Corea, the Hermit Nation*. New York: C. Scribner's, 1909.

Pyong-choon Hahm, *The Korean Political Tradition and Law: Essays on Korean Law and Legal History*. Seoul: The Royal Asiatic Society, Korea Branch, 1967.

Sungjoo Hahn, *The Failure of Democracy in South Korea*. Berkeley and Los Angeles: The University of California Press, 1974.

Han Woo-keun, *The History of Korea*, tr. by Lee Kyung-shik and ed. by Grafton K. Mintz. Seoul: Ulyu Publishing Co., 1969.

Fred H. Harrington, *God Mammon, and the Japanese: Dr. Horace N. Allen and Korean-American Relations, 1884-1905*. Madison: The University of Wisconsin Press, 1944.

Hatada Takashi, *A History of Korea.*, tr. by Warner S. Smith, Jr. and Benjamin H. Hazard. Santa Barbara: CLIO, 1969.

Gregory Henderson, *Korea: the Politics of Vortex*. Cambridge: Harvard University Press, 1968.

William E. Henthorn, *A History of Korea*. New York: The Free Press, 1971.

Homer B. Hulbert, *The History of Korea*. 2 Vols. Seoul: The Methodist Publishing House, 1905.

_____, *The Passing of Korea*. New York: Doubleday, Page & Co., 1906.

Wanne J. Joe, *Traditional Korea, a Cultural History*. Seoul: The Chung-ang University Press, 1972.

Sang-woon Jeon, *Science and Technology in Korea: Traditional Instruments and Techniques*. Cambridge: MIT Press, 1974.

John Karadoss, *An Outline History of Korean Drama*. Greenvale, N.Y.: Island University Press, 1946.

C.I. Eugene Kim and Doretha E. Mortimore, ed., *Korea's Response to Japan:*

The Colonial Period, 1910–1945. Kalamazoo: Center for Korean Studies, Western Michigan University, 1974.

C.I. Eugene Kim and Han-kyo Kim, *Korea and the Politics of Imperialism, 1876–1910.* Berkeley and Los Angeles: The University of California Press, 1967.

Se-jin Kim, *The Politics of Military Revolution in Korea.* Chapel Hill: The University of North Carolina Press, 1971.

Yung-chung Kim, ed. and tr., *Women of Korea: A History from Ancient Times to 1945.* Seoul: Ewha Woman's University Press, 1977.

Tae-hwan Kwak, et al., *U.S.-Korean Relations, 1882–1982.* Seoul: Kyungnam University, 1982.

Chang-soo Lee, ed., *Modernization of Korea and the Impact of the West.* Los Angeles: East Asian Studies Center, University of Southern California, 1981.

Chong-sik Lee, *The Politics of Korean Nationalism.* Berkeley and Los Angeles: The University of California Press, 1963.

Ki-baik Lee, *A New History of Korea,* translated by Edward W. Wagner and Edward J. Schultz. Cambridge and London: Harvard University Press, 1984.

Yur-bok Lee, *Diplomatic Relations Between the United States and Korea, 1861–1887.* New York: Hamilton Press, 1970.

George A. McCrane, *Korea's Tragic Hours: The Closing Years of the Yi Dynasty,* edited by Harold F. Cook and Alan M. McDougall. Seoul: Taewon Publishing Co., 1973.

George M. McCune and Arthur L. Grey, Jr., *Korea Today.* Cambridge: Harvard University Press, 1950.

Frederick A. McKenzie, *Korea's Fight for Freedom.* New York: Fleming H. Revell, 1920.

_____, *Tragedy of Korea.* London: Hodder & Stoughton, 1908.

E. Grant Meed, *American Military Government in Korea.* New York: Columbia University Press, 1951.

Andrew C. Nahm, ed., *Korea and the New Order in East Asia.* Kalamazoo: Center for Korean Studies, Western Michigan University, 1975.

_____, ed., *Korea under Japanese Colonial Rule—Studies of the Policy and Techniques of Japanese Colonialism.* Kalamazoo: Center for Korean Studies, Western Michigan University, 1973.

_____, ed., *The United States and Korea—American-Korean Relations, 1866–1976.* Kalamazoo: Center for Korean Studies, Western Michigan University, 1979.

Melvin F. Nelson, *Korea and the Old Orders in East Asia.* Baton Rouge: Louisiana State University Press, 1945.

John K. C. Oh, *Korea: Democracy on Trial.* Ithaca: Cornell University Press, 1968.

Robert T. Oliver, *Korea, Forgotten Nation*. Washington, D.C.: Public Affairs Press, 1944.

——————, *Syngman Rhee and American Involvement in Korea, 1942-1960: A Personal Narrative*. Seoul: Panmun Book Co., 1978.

Ernest Oppert, *A Forbidden Land: Voyages to Corea*. London: Sampson Low, Marston, Searle and Revington, 1880.

George L. Paik, *The History of Protestant Missions in Korea, 1832-1910*. Pyongyang: Union College Press, 1929.

James B. Palais, *Politics and Policy in Traditional Korea*. Cambridge: Harvard University Press, 1975.

W. D. Reeve, *The Republic of Korea: A Political and Economic History*. London: Oxford University Press, 1963.

John Ross, *History of Corea, Ancient and Modern: With Description of Manners and Customs, Language, and Geography*. London: Elliot Stock, 1891.

Sohn Pow-key, *Early Korean Typography*. Seoul: Korean Library Science Research Institute, 1971.

Sohn Pow-key, et al., *The History of Korea*. Seoul: The Korean National Commission for UNESCO, 1970.

Isidor Stone, *The Hidden History of the Korean War*. New York: Monthly Review Press, 1952.

Edward W. Wagner, *The Literati Purges: Political Conflict in Early Yi Korea*. Cambridge: East Asian Research Center, Harvard University, 1974.

Benjamin B. Weems, *Reform, Rebellion, and the Heavenly Way*. Tucson: The University of Arizona Press, 1964.

W. H. Wilkinson, *The Corean Government: Constitutional Changes, July 1894-to October 1895, with an Appendix on Subsequent Enactments to June 30th, 1896*. Shanghai: The Statistical Department of inspectorate-General of Customs, 1897.

Edward P. Wright, ed., *Korean Politics in Transition*. Seattle: The University of Washington Press, 1975.

6. Sources on North Korea

Tae-sung An, *North Korea: A Political Handbook*. Wilmington, Del.: Scholarly Resources Inc., 1983.

——————, *North Korea in Transition from Dictatorship to Dynasty*. Westpoint Conn.: Greenwood Press, 1983.

Ellen and Jacques Hersh Brun, *Socialist Korea: A Case Study in the Strategy of Economic Development*. New York: Monthly Review Press, 1976.

Joseph S. Chung, *The North Korean Economy: Structure and Development*. Stanford: The Hoover Institution Press, 1974.

C.I. Eugene Kim and B.C. Koh, ed., *Journey to North Korea: Personal*

Perceptions. Berkeley: Institute of East Asian Studies, University of California, 1983.

Chang-sun Kim, *Fifteen-year History of North Korea*. Washington: Joint Publications Research Service, 1963.

Ilpyong J. Kim, *Communist Politics in North Korea*. New York: Praeger, 1975.

Byung-chul Koh, *The Foreign Policy of North Korea*. New York: Praeger, 1969.

Chong-sik Lee, *The Korean Workers' Party: A Short History*. Stanford: The Hoover Institution Press, 1978.

Lim Un (pseud), *The Founding of a Dynasty in North Korea: An Authentic Biography of Kim Il-sung*. Tokyo: Jiyusha, 1982.

Andrew C. Nahm, *North Korea: Her Past, Reality and Impression*. Kalamazoo: Center for Korean Studies, Western Michigan University, 1978.

Koon Woo Nam, *The North Korean Communist Leadership, 1945–1965: A Study of Factional and Political Consolidation*. University: University of Alabama Press, 1974.

Jae-kyu Park and Jung Gun Kim, ed., *The Politics of North Korea*. Seoul: The Institute for Far Eastern Studies, Kyungnam University, 1979.

Philip Rudolph, *North Korea's Political and Economic Structure*. New York: Institute of Pacific Relations, 1959.

Robert A. Scalapino, and Jun-yop Kim, eds., *North Korea Today: Strategic and Domestic Issues*. Berkeley: Institute of East Asian Studies, University of California, 1983.

_____ and Chong-sik Lee, *Communism in Korea*. 2 Vols. Berkeley, Los Angeles, and London: University of California Press, 1972.

Dae-sook Suh, *The Korean Communist Movement, 1918–1948*. Princeton: Princeton University Press, 1967.

B. JAPANESE AND KOREAN LANGUAGE SOURCES

Cho Ki-chun, et al., *Ilche ha ŭi minjok saenghwal-sa* (A History of the Life of the People under Japanese Imperialism). Seoul: Minjung Sŏgwan, 1971.

Cho Tong-kŏl, *Ilche ha ŭi Han-guk nongmin undong-sa* (A History of the Movement of Korean Farmers under Japanese Imperialism). Seoul: Hangilsa, 1979.

Cho Yong-man, *Ilche ha ŭi munhwa undong-sa* (A History of Cultural Movement under Japanese Imperialism). Seoul: Minjung Sŏgwan, 1970.

Ch'oe Chun, *Han-guk shinmun-sa* (A History of Korean Journalism). Seoul: Ilchogak, 1960.

Ch'oe Yŏng-hŭi, et al., *Ilche ha ŭi minjok undong-sa* (A History of Nationalist Movement under Japanese Imperialism). Seoul: Minjung Sŏgwan, 1971.

Chŏng In-bo, *Chosŏn-sa yŏn-gu* (A Study of Korean History). 2 Vols. Seoul: Seoul Shinmunsa, 1947.

Chŏng Kyo, *Han-guk kyenyŏn-sa* (A History of the Last Years of the Yi Dynasty). 2 Vols. Seoul: Kuksa P'yonch'an Wiwŏnhoe, 1957.

Chŏng Yo-sŏp, *Han-guk yŏsŏng undong-sa—Ilche ha ŭi minjok undong ŭl chungshim ŭro* (A History of Korean Women's Movement—Focusing on Nationalist Movement under Japanese Imperialism). Seoul: Ilchogak, 1979.

Chōsen Sōtokufu, *Shisei 30-nen* (Thirty-Years of Administration), Keijō (Seoul), 1940.

Chosŏn Minjujuŭi Inmin Konghwaguk. Sahoe Kwahagwŏn. Yŏksa Yŏn-guso edited, *Kim Ok-kyun*. Pyongyang: 1964.

Fujishina Unai and Hatada Shigeo, *Kindai Chōsen ron* (Discourses on Recent Korea). Tokyo: Keisō Shobō, 1966.

Han Ki-ŏn, *Han-guk kyoyuk-sa* (A History of Korean Education). Seoul: Pagyŏngsa, 1963.

Han Ki-ŏn, et al., *Ilche ha ŭi munhwa ch'imnyak-sa* (A History of Cultural Aggression under Japanese Imperialism). Seoul: Minjung Sŏgwan, 1970.

Hwang Hyŏn, *Maech'ŏn yarok* (Unofficial Records of Maech'ŏn). Seoul: Kuksa P'yŏnch'an Wiwŏnhoe, 1955.

Hyŏn Sang-yun, *Chosŏn yuhak-sa* (A History of Korean Confucianism). Seoul: Minjung Sŏgwan, 1949.

Imanish Ryū, *Kōrai-shi kenkyū* (A Study of the History of Koryŏ). Keijō (Seoul): 1943.

Itani Zen'ichi, *Chōsen keizai-shi* (An Economic History of Korea). Tokyo: Osumikaku, 1928.

Kikuchi Kenjō, *Kindai Chōsen-shi* (A History of Recent Korea). 2 Vols. Tokyo, 1940.

Kang Chae-ŏn, *Kindai Chōsen no henkaku shisō* (Reform Thoughts of Recent Korea). Tokyo: Nihon Hyōronsha, 1973.

_____, *Chōsen kindai-shi kenkyū* (A Study of Recent Korean History). Tokyo: Nihon Hyōronsha, 1970.

Kim Chae-wŏn and Yi Pyŏng-do, *Han-guk-sa* (A History of Korea). Seoul: Chindan Hak'oe, 1959.

Kim Chŏng-hak, ed., *Nikkan kodai kokka no kigen* (The Origins of Ancient Japanese and Korean nation-states). Tokyo: Rokuko Shuppan, 1980.

Kim Kwang-su, *Han-guk minjok kitokkyo paengnyŏn-sa* (One-hundred-year History of Christianity of the Korean People). Seoul: Han-guk Kyohoe-sa Yŏn-guwŏn, 1978.

Kim Mun-shik, et al., *Ilche ha ŭi kyŏngje ch'imnyak-sa* (A History of Economic Aggression under Japanese Imperialism). Seoul: Minjung Sŏgwan, 1971.

Kim Ok-kŭn, *Chosŏn hugi kyŏngje-sa yŏn-gu* (A Study of Economic History of the Latter Half of the Yi Dynasty). Seoul: Sŏmundang, 1977.

Kim Sang-gi, *Koryŏ shidae-sa* (A History of the Koryŏ Period). Seoul: Tongguk Munhwasa, 1961.

_____, *Tonghak kwa Tonghangnan* (The *Tonghak* Sect and the *Tonghak* Uprising). Seoul: Taesŏng Ch'ulp'ansa, 1947.

Kim To-t'ae, *Sŏ Chae-p'il paksa chasŏjŏn* (Autobiography of Dr. Sŏ Chae-p'il). Seoul: Susŏnsa, 1948.

Kim Yŏl-guk, *Han-guk shinhwa wa musok yŏn-gu* (Korean Mythology and a Study of Shamanism). Seoul: Ilchogak, 1979.

Kim Yŏng-gŭn, *Chosŏn kaehwa pidam* (Hidden History of Korean Modernization). Seoul: Chŏng-ŭmsa, 1947.

Kuksa P'yŏnch'an Wiwŏnhoe, ed., *Han-guk tongnip undong-sa* (A History of Korean Independence Movement). Seoul, 1965.

Min T'ae-wŏn, *Kapshin chŏngbyŏn kwa Kim Ok-kyun* (The Kapshin Political Incident and Kim Ok-kyun). Seoul: Kukche Munhwa Hyŏp'oe, 1947.

_____, *Kim Ok-kyun chŏn-gi* (A Biography of Kim Ok-kyun). Seoul: Ŭlyu Munhwasa, 1969.

Mun Chŏng-ch'ang, *Kŭnse Ilbon ŭi Chosŏn ch'imt'al-sa* (A History of Modern Japanese Aggression in Korea). Seoul: Tajakkyo Ch'ulp'ansa, 1964.

O Ch'ŏn-sŏk, *Han-guk shinkyoyuk-sa* (A History of New Education in Korea). Seoul: Hyŏndae Kyoyuk Ch'ongsŏ Ch'ulp'ansa, 1964.

Paek Ch'ŏl, *Chosŏn shin munhak sajo-sa* (A History of New Korean Literary Thoughts). Seoul: Susŏnsa, 1948.

Paek Nam-un, *Chōsen shakai keizai-shi* (A Study of Korean Social and Economic History). Tokyo: Kaizōsha, 1937.

Shidehara Dan, *Chōsen siwa* (Historical Episodes of Korea). Tokyo: Fusanbō, 1925.

Shin Kuk-chu, *Kindai Chōsen gaikō-shi kenkyū* (A Study of Diplomatic History of Recent Korea). Tokyo: Yūshindo, 1965.

Son Chong-ho, *Han-guk nongjŏng ŭi paltal-sa* (A History of the Development of Agricultural Management in Korea). Seoul: Insŏng Ch'ulp'ansa, 1980.

Tabohashi Kiyoshi, *Kindai Nissen kankei no kenkyū* (A Study of Recent Japanese-Korean Relations). Keijō (Seoul): Chūsui-in, 1940.

Tsuboe Senji, *Chōsen minzoku tokuritsu undō hishi* (A Secret History of Independence Movement of the Korean People). Revised. Tokyo: Gannandō, 1959.

Watanabe Manabu, et al., tr. and ed., *Kin Kyoku-kin no kenkyū* (Studies of Kim Ok-kyun). Tokyo: Nihon Chosen Kenkyujo, 1968.

Yamabe Kentarō, *Nihon no Kankoku heigō* (Japanese Annexation of Korea). Tokyo: Taihei Shuppansha, 1966.

_____, *Nikkan heigō shōshi* (A Short History of Japanese Annexation of Korea). Tokyo: Iwanami Shoten, 1966.

Yang Chu-dong, *Hang-il haksaeng-sa* (A History of anti-Japanese Student

Movement). Seoul: Ch'ōngp'a Ch'ulp'ansa, 1956.

Yi Chong-hang, *Han-guk chōngch'i-sa* (A Political History of Korea). Seoul: Pagyōngsa, 1974.

Yi Hyōn-hūi, *Han-guk kūndae yōsōng kaehwa-sa* (A History of Modernization of Women in Recent Korea). Seoul: Iu Ch'ulp'ansa, 1978.

Yi Ki-baek, *Han-guk-sa shillon* (A New History of Korea). Seoul: Ilchogak, 1961.

Yi Ki-ha, *Han-guk chōngdang paltal-sa* (A History of the Development of Korean Political Parties). Seoul: Ūihoe Chongch'isa, 1961.

Yi Kwang-rin, *Han-guk kaehwa-sa yōn-gu* (A Study of the History of Korean Modernization). Seoul: Ilchogak, 1969.

_____, *Han-guk kaehwa sasang yōn-gu* (A Study of Reform Thoughts of Korea). Seoul: Ilchogak, 1979.

_____, *Kaehwadang yōn-gu* (A Study of the Progressive Party). Seoul: Ilchogak, 1973.

Yi Nūng-hwa, *Chosōn kidokkyo kūp oegyo-sa* (A History of Korean Christian Churches and Diplomacy). Seoul: Chosōn Kidokkyo Ch'angmunsa, 1925.

Yi Pyōng-do, *Han-guk kuksa taegwan* (An Overview of Korean History). Seoul: Pomungak, 1960.

_____, *Koryō shidae yōn-gu* (A Study of the Koryō Period). Seoul: Ūlyu Munhwasa, 1949.

_____, ed., with commentaries, *Samguk yusa* (The Anecdotes of the Three Kingdoms). Seoul: Tongguk Munhwasa, 1956.

Yi Pyōng-hōn, *3.1 undong pisa* (A Secret History of the March First Movement). Seoul: Shisa Shibosa, 1959.

Yi Son-gūn, *Chosōn ch'oegūn chōngch'i-sa* (A Political History of Recent Korea). Seoul: Chōng-ūmsa, 1950.

_____, *Han-guk-sa* (A History of Korea), Seoul: Ūlyu Munhwasa, 1961.

_____, *Han-guk tongnip undong-sa* (A History of Independence Movement of Korea). Seoul: Sangmunwōn, 1956.

Yōksa Hak'oe, ed., *Shirhak yōn-gu immun* (Introduction to the Study of *Shirhak*). Seoul: Ilchogak, 1973.

Index

CHRONOLOGICAL CHART OF EAST ASIAN HISTORY I

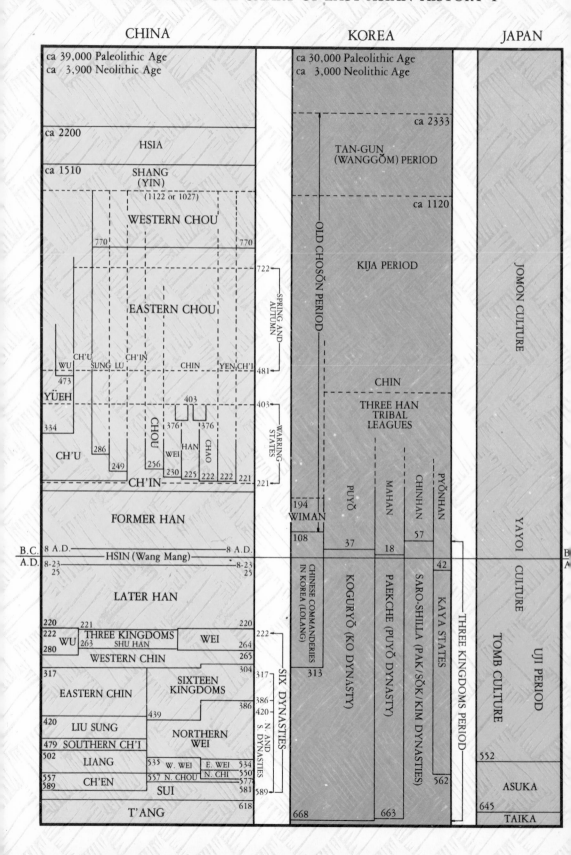